PAUL

Life-Study
of
Matthew

Witness Lee

Living Stream Ministry
Anaheim, California

First Edition, 5,000 copies. April 1986

Library of Congress Catalog
Card Number: 85-50854

ISBN 0-87083-162-3

Published by
Living Stream Ministry
1853 W. Ball Road, P. O. Box 2121
Anaheim, CA 92804 U.S.A.
Printed in the United States of America

CONTENTS

iii

David the King Begetting Solomon — Rehoboam — Joram Begetting Uzziah — Josiah Begetting Jeconiah — The Captives to Babylon — Jeconiah — Jeconiah Begetting Salathiel, and Salathiel Begetting Zerubbabel — Zerubbabel — Jacob Begetting Joseph — Joseph the Husband of Mary, of Whom Jesus Was Born — Mary — The One Who Is Called Christ — Abraham, David, and Mary — To David and from David — Until the Carrying Away and from the Carrying Away — Three Groups of Fourteen Generations — "To the Christ"

The King Traveling through All the Cities and Villages, Teaching, Preaching, and Healing — The King Being Moved with Compassion Concerning the People as Sheep without a Shepherd — The Harvest Being Vast But the Workers Being Few — Beseeching the Lord of the Harvest to Thrust Out Workers into His Harvest

Giving Them Authority to Cast Out Demons and to Heal Diseases — Pairing Them Two by Two

The King Sending the Twelve Apostles Only to the House of Israel — Preaching that the Kingdom of the Heavens Has Drawn Near — Exercising the Authority of the Kingdom — The Worker Being Worthy of His Food — Bringing Peace to the House Where They Stay — The Judgment upon the Rejecting People

The Apostles Sent as Sheep into the Midst of Wolves — Delivered to the Sanhedrin and Scourged in the Synagogues — Brought before Governors and Kings as a Testimony for the Heavenly King's Sake — Hated by the Relatives — Fleeing from City to City — Not Above Their Teacher — Not Fearing the Persecutors but Preaching the Heavenly King's Message on the Housetop

The Heavenly King Coming Not to Bring Peace, but a Sword on the Earth — The Way to Follow the Heavenly King

Receiving the Heavenly King's Apostles Being the Receiving of Him — The Reward of Receiving a Prophet or a Righteous Man — The Reward for Giving a Cup of Cold Water to a Little Disciple

The Imprisoned Forerunner Sending His Disciples to Provoke the King — The Heavenly King's Answer

xv

Jerusalem Killing the Prophets — The Lord as a Hen Desiring to Gather Her Children Together under Her Wings — The House—the Temple—Left Desolate — Not Seeing the Lord until His Coming Back

FOREWORD

The church has been on the earth for almost twenty centuries. During such an extended period of time, many saints have authored studies on various books of the New Testament, and numerous commentaries and expositions have been written. However, most of them touch only the objective and doctrinal side of the divine revelation and have failed to stress the side of life. Because of this, Brother Witness Lee became burdened by the Lord to prepare this Life-study of the New Testament. From 1974 to 1986 he gave twenty-five trainings plus additional conferences, in which he had a thorough life-study of the entire New Testament. The messages given during these trainings and conferences constitute the contents of this twenty-volume set.

In the Lord's recovery during the past five hundred years the church's knowledge of the Lord and His truth has been continually progressing. This monumental and classical work by our brother builds upon and is a further development of all that the Lord has revealed to His church in the past centuries. It is filled with the revelation concerning the processed Triune God, the living Christ, the life-giving Spirit, the experience of life, and the definition and practice of the church.

In this set Brother Lee has kept three basic principles that should rule and govern every believer in their interpretation, development, and expounding of the truths contained in the Scriptures. The first principle is that of the Triune God dispensing Himself into His chosen and redeemed people; the second principle is that we should interpret, develop, and expound the truths contained in the Bible with Christ for the church; and the third governing principle is Christ, the Spirit, life, and the church. No other study or exposition of the New Testament conveys the life nourishment or ushers the reader into the divine revelation of God's holy Word according to His New Testament economy as this one does.

The purpose of this Life-study as expressed by Brother Lee is to present the truths contained in the New Testament, to minister the life supply, to solve the common and hard problems found in the New Testament, and to open up every book of the New Testament by giving a thorough interpretation of it. We believe that these volumes, containing the very essence of the New Testament ministry which is for the carrying out of God's divine economy, will serve as an entrance into a deeper and extensive understanding of the divine truths and will also render much life supply and nourishment to the church of God today and in the coming generations. May the Lord use the ministry of His word in these volumes to sanctify the church until she is fully prepared to be His bride, His counterpart, for His satisfaction (Eph. 5:26-27).

April, 1986   Benson Phillips
Irving, Texas

LIFE-STUDY OF MATTHEW

MESSAGE ONE

THE KING'S ANTECEDENTS
AND STATUS

(1)

A WORD OF INTRODUCTION

The Bible is God's speaking. It has two sections. In the first section, the Old Testament, God spoke by the prophets, and in the second section, the New Testament, He spoke in the Son (in the Person of the Son, Heb. 1:1-2). This section is composed of the four Gospels, the book of Acts, the Epistles, and the book of Revelation. While He was in the flesh, the Son began to speak in the four Gospels. After His resurrection, He continued to speak as the Spirit through the Apostles (see John 16:12-14). Thus, the New Testament is just the Son's speaking to us, His ministering Himself as life and everything that we may become His Body, His expression, the church.

The Bible is a book of life. This life is nothing less than the living Person of Christ. In the Old Testament Christ is portrayed as the coming One. In the New Testament, the One whose coming was predicted has come. Thus, the New Testament is the fulfillment of the Old. St. Augustine once said that the New Testament is contained in the Old, and the Old Testament is expressed in the New. These two testaments are actually one, revealing one Person who is our life.

THE OPENING WORD
OF THE NEW TESTAMENT

Nearly all Christians are bothered by the first page of the New Testament. It has many names that are difficult

to pronounce. But this page is the first part of the New
Testament. In any kind of writing, both the opening word
and the closing word are important. When many
Christians come to the New Testament, they skip over the
first part of chapter one of Matthew and start reading at
verse 18. It seems that in their New Testament there is no
such paragraph as Matthew 1:1-17. But thank God for this
rich portion of the Word! This genealogy of Christ is an
abstract of the whole Old Testament. It includes
everything except the first ten and a half chapters of
Genesis. If we would know the meaning of this genealogy,
we need to know the entire Old Testament.

A LIVING PICTURE OF CHRIST

We need to say a word concerning the New Testament.
The New Testament is simply a living picture of a Person.
This Person is too wonderful. He is both God and man. He
is the mingling of God with man, for in Him the divine
nature and the human nature are mingled together. He is
the King, and He is a bondslave. He is wonderful!

No human being has ever spoken words like He spoke,
words so profound, yet so clear. For example, Jesus said, "I
am the bread of life" (John 6:35), and, "I am the light of
the world" (John 8:12). Plato and Confucius were two great
philosophers, and people appreciated the things they said,
but neither of them could say, "I am the light of the
world." No one else could say, "I am the life," or, "I am the
way," or, "I am the reality" (John 14:6). These are simple
words and short sentences — "I am," "I am what I am,"
and "I am that I am" — but they are great and profound.
Can any of us say that we are the light of the world or that
we are the life? If we did, we would surely be sent to a mental hospital. But Jesus could say these things. How great
He is!

FOUR BIOGRAPHIES OF ONE PERSON

Jesus is all-inclusive. With Him there are many
aspects. No one can exhaust in language who and what He

is. Who else in history has four unique biographies written of him? Although the New Testament is a short book, it begins with four biographies of one Person, four books telling us of the life of Christ.

Each of us has four sides: the front and the back, the right and the left. If you look at me from the front, you can see seven holes on my face. But if I turn my back to you, all the holes disappear. On my right side you can see a little hole, and on my left side, another little hole. If you would make an accurate copy of my image, you need to take a picture of every side. This is exactly what has been done in the New Testament.

Why do we have four Gospels? Because Christ has at least four main aspects. Christ is great! Because He is all-inclusive and unsearchably rich, He needs several biographies. Matthew, Mark, Luke, and John present different aspects of Christ because each writer was a different kind of person. Matthew, for instance, was a tax collector. Among the Jewish people in ancient times, a tax collector was a despised person. Nevertheless, Matthew wrote the first biography of Christ. Mark was an ordinary man, and Luke was a physician and a Gentile. At first, John was a common fisherman, but eventually he became the very aged, experienced apostle. Each wrote a different biography about the same Christ. This living Person needs many biographies.

THE EXPANSION OF CHRIST

The book of Acts is the expansion of this wonderful Person. It is the branching out of the all-inclusive Christ. This Christ has expanded from one Person to thousands and thousands of persons. He was once the individual Christ, but in Acts He has become a corporate Christ. Following the Acts, we have all the Epistles, which give a full definition of this wonderful, universal, great Man. Christ is the Head, and the church is the Body: this is the universal Man, Christ and the church. Finally, we have the book of Revelation as the consummation of the New Testament.

This book gives us a full picture of the Body-Christ, the individual Christ incorporated with all His members to become the New Jerusalem.

THE ORDER OF THE FOUR GOSPELS

Let us return to the four Gospels. If I were to arrange the four Gospels, I would put the Gospel of John first. When reading the Bible, many Christians start with John and then proceed to read Luke, Mark, and Matthew. The human concept is the exact opposite of the divine. The divine concept starts with Matthew and proceeds through John; the human thought starts with John and goes back to Matthew. Many of us would begin reading the New Testament with John because John is so wonderful. It is a book of life. After John, we would read Luke because Luke is a book of the Savior, telling us of many cases of salvation. Then, of course, we would come to Mark because Mark is short and simple. People read Matthew last because Matthew is too difficult, too mysterious. Not only is chapter one difficult to understand; the parables in chapter thirteen and the prophecies in chapters twenty-four and twenty-five are also difficult. Chapters five, six, and seven, the Sermon on the Mount, are especially difficult. No one can practice it! You strike me on the right cheek, and I turn to you the left. You force me to walk one mile, and I walk two miles. You take my outer garment, and I give you my inner garment. This is too much! Only Jesus can do it! Thus, many place Matthew last. John is dear and precious. In John, Jesus is everything, and we do not need to do anything. Hence, we like John, but not Matthew. We may not say this in plain words, but we have such a feeling in our heart. Nevertheless, the divine order is best. God put Matthew first.

THE GENERAL SKETCH

With every book of the Bible we need a general sketch. The general sketch of Matthew is:

Christ is Jehovah God incarnated to be the King-Savior who came to establish the kingdom of the heavens (the heavenly rule) by saving His people from sin (of rebellion) through His death and resurrection.

THE CENTRAL THOUGHT

With every book of the Bible we also need to find the central thought. The central thought of Matthew is:

Christ, as Jesus (Jehovah the Savior) and Emmanuel (God with us), is the King, the Baptizer, the light, the Teacher, the Healer, the Forgiver, the Bridegroom, the Shepherd, the Friend, the wisdom, the rest, the greater temple, the real David, the Lord of the Sabbath, the greater Jonah, the greater Solomon, the Sower, the seed, the Feeder, the bread, the crumbs under the table, the Christ, the Son of the living God, the rock for the church, the Builder of the church, the Founder of the kingdom, the present Moses, the present Elijah, the Head of the corner, the Lord, the resurrected One, the One with authority, and the One ever-present to His people in resurrection.

How rich Christ is in the book of Matthew, even richer than in John. As Jesus and Emmanuel He is another thirty-three items to us. We must enjoy Him and partake of Him. We need to experience Him in all these aspects in resurrection, not in the natural state. He is the ever-present One. Matthew begins with "God with us" and ends with "Lo, I am with you all the days, even unto the completion of the age." How wonderful this is!

THE KING'S ANTECEDENTS
AND STATUS

I. HIS GENEALOGY

Among the four Gospels only two, Matthew and Luke, have genealogies. Matthew tells us that Jesus is the proper descendant of the royal family, that He is the legal heir of the royal throne. Such a person surely needs a genealogy telling of His origin and descent. Luke presents Jesus as a proper, normal man. To show Jesus as a proper man also requires a genealogy. In Mark, Jesus is pictured as a

bondslave, as one sold into slavery. A bondslave has no
need of a genealogy; hence, Mark does not include one.
John tells us that Jesus is God. "In the beginning was the
Word . . . and the Word was God." With Him there was no
beginning, no descent. He is eternal, with no beginning of
life nor end of life (Heb. 7:3). In the beginning was God!
For John to talk about His genealogy would be ridiculous.

With anybody else, no matter who he is or how many
biographies people write about him, the genealogy will be
exactly the same. But Jesus has two genealogies. Later on
we shall see how these genealogies eventually become one.
Once again we see that He is wonderful. In every aspect,
He is too wonderful.

A. The Generation of Christ

Now we come to the genealogy of Jesus in the Gospel of
Matthew. We need to realize who Jesus is. Who is Jesus?
We may answer by saying that He is the Son of God, but
this genealogy does not have such a term. Rather, it calls
Him the son of David and the son of Abraham. Because
Jesus is so wonderful, it is difficult to say who He is.

Jesus is the mingling of God with man, the mingling of
divinity with humanity. This is the generation of Jesus.
The generation of Jesus means that He is the mingling, the
wonderful mingling. In this generation we have the mingling of the divine Being with so many human beings, with
all kinds of people. We should no longer think that
Matthew 1:1-17 is just a list of names.

The generation of Christ is composed of:

1. The Fathers

These are the forefathers, the great persons. All
together they make up fourteen generations (1:2-6a).

2. The Kings

These are the kings, the royalty, who also make up
fourteen generations (1:6b-10).

3. The Civilians (the Captured Ones and the Recovered Ones)

The generation of Christ not only includes the high-ranking people, but also the civilians, the insignificant ones, like Mary and Joseph. The poor people, the little people, are also included in the generation of Christ. Christ was ranked not only with the patriarchs and with the kings, but also with a group of civilians. He was not only of the great ones, of the royal ones, but also of the little ones. From this picture of the generation of Christ, we can see that it includes all kinds of people.

This generation includes both the called ones, like Abraham, and the ones carried away to captivity. In this brief record we have the words "carrying away" (v. 17). Abraham was called out of Babel, the origin of Babylon. The generation of Christ includes not only the called ones, but also the backsliders. Perhaps five years ago you were a called one, but today you are a backslider. Do not be disappointed. The generation of Christ includes you. This generation includes Jeconiah, a king who was dethroned and carried away to Babylon as a captive. Have you ever been dethroned? Do not think you have not. In your Christian life you sometimes have been dethroned. Once you were a king, but you lost your kingship and became a backslider. Our forefather Abraham came from Babylon; yet you went back, not willingly, but were carried back. Praise the Lord that the generation of Christ includes even the fallen ones!

After captivity there was the recovery. Hence, we have another name, Zerubbabel, the name of recovery. Many captives returned with Zerubbabel. The generation of Christ includes all kinds of people: good ones, bad ones, called ones, fallen ones, and recovered ones. If I were to ask you which kind you are, you may say that firstly you were a called one, then a fallen one, and finally a recovered one. You were an Abraham, you became a Jeconiah, but today you are a Zerubbabel. We are all Zerubbabels. We are the called ones, the fallen ones, and the recovered ones.

4. The Four Remarried Women

According to Jewish custom, a writer of a genealogy would never include a female name; he would include only the names of males. But in this brief genealogy five women are mentioned. These five women are like the fingers of my hand: four form one group and the other one stands alone. Four of these five women were remarried, and one of the four was a harlot. It seems that the divine record here would not mention the good ones, such as Sarah or Rebekah, but the bad ones. Listen to the divine record: "David begot Solomon of the wife of Uriah" (1:6). The record does not even give her name; it gives only her history in order to remind us of what kind of person she was.

Do you know the history of Tamar? She was the daughter-in-law of Judah. Judah begot twins of his daughter-in-law (Gen. 38:24-30). How terrible! The second woman named is Rahab, the harlot of Jericho, and the third, Ruth, a Moabitess. The Moabites were not allowed to enter the congregation of the Lord even to their tenth generation (Deut. 23:3). The Moabites are descendants of Moab, who was born of Lot with his daughter. The fourth woman was Bathsheba, the wife of a Canaanite named Uriah whom David murdered. David took her to be his wife, and with her he begot Solomon.

Why does this brief record mention all these women? It is because they are our representatives. Do not think you are so pure, that you are more pure than these women. Trace your own origin. If you do, you will find out by what way and of whom your grandfather was born, by what way and of whom your father was born, and by what way and of whom you were born. We are worse. But the worst ones are included in the generation of Christ! Praise the Lord! He is truly the Savior of sinners.

The number four signifies all the creatures, including the entire human race. Humanity is dirty; no one is clean. But, thank the Lord, we are all associated with Christ. We are part of the generation of Christ.

If we were to write a biography of Christ and there were no biographies of Him in the Bible, we would not dare to write it this way. We would hide all these impure grand-mothers and give the names of the good grandmothers, such as Sarah and Rebekah. But the Holy Spirit did not mention Sarah, Rebekah, and all the good ones; however, He purposely included these impure ones. If this divine record had listed the names of the good women without the names of the impure ones, I would be in doubt about the present situation of the church. I would say, "Look at today's situation in the church. Not many are very pure." Do not think that you are so pure, so clean. We are not pure. Nevertheless, the generation of Christ includes both good ones and bad ones. In fact, it includes more bad ones than good ones.

5. *The One Virgin*

Besides the four remarried women, a virgin stands out: Mary, the mother of Jesus. Mary was good, pure, and clean. This indicates that everyone mentioned in this book of generation is a sinner except Jesus. With the exception of Jesus, all are unclean.

B. The Son of David

Christ is the son of David (Matt. 22:42, 45; Rev. 22:16). Solomon, the son of David, was a type of Christ in three main aspects. First, he was a type of Christ inheriting the kingdom (2 Sam. 7:12b, 13; Jer. 23:5; Luke 1:32-33). Second, Solomon had wisdom and spoke the word of wisdom. In Matthew 12 we see that Christ also had wisdom and spoke the word of wisdom. In this chapter Christ referred to Himself as the greater Solomon (v. 42). A greater than Solomon was there, and He spoke words of wisdom. No human words are as wise as the words of Christ. Third, Solomon built the temple of God (2 Sam. 7:13). As the son of David, Christ builds up God's temple, the church.

C. The Son of Abraham

Christ is also the son of Abraham. This book of generation says only that Christ is the son of David and the son of Abraham, not the son of any one else. In the Old Testament there was a clear prophecy that Christ would be the son of Abraham. Isaac was a type of Christ. With Isaac as a type of Christ there were also three main aspects. First, Isaac brought the blessing to all nations, both Jews and Gentiles (Gen. 22:18a; Gal. 3:16, 14). Second, he was offered to God unto death and was resurrected (Gen. 22:1-12; Heb. 11:17, 19). Third, he received the bride (Gen. 24:67). This is a type of Christ as the promised One who brought the blessing to all nations, who was also offered to death, who was resurrected, and who, after His resurrection, will receive His Bride (John 3:29; Rev. 19:7). One day the Holy Spirit, typified by Abraham's servant, will bring the spiritual, divine, heavenly Rebekah to her heavenly Isaac.

The son of Abraham received the bride, and the son of David built up the temple. With Christ, the Bride is the temple, and the temple is the Bride. This is why it says that Christ is the son of Abraham and the son of David. He offered Himself unto death and was resurrected, now He is building God's temple, and in the future He will receive the Bride. Christ also spoke wisdom and brought God's blessing to all nations. He is the One to fulfill all of these things. In the four Gospels we can find each of these six aspects. The Gospels reveal that Christ came to inherit the kingdom, that He offered Himself unto death and He was resurrected, that He spoke the word of wisdom, that He brought blessing to all people, that He is building up God's house, and that He will come to receive the Bride. Christ is surely the real Isaac and the real Solomon.

As the son of David, Jesus was a great blessing to the Jews. But as the son of Abraham, He brings blessing to all the Gentiles. As the son of David, He is for the Jews; as the son of Abraham, He is for us all. If Jesus were only the son of David, He would have nothing to do with me. Praise the

Lord that He is also the son of Abraham! All nations are
blessed in Abraham's seed, which is Christ. This blessing is
the participation in the Triune God. The blessing which
God promised to Abraham was the Spirit (Gal. 3:14), and
the Spirit is the ultimate realization of the Triune God. By
Christ as the son of Abraham, we have the Spirit, and we
share in the Triune God. Hallelujah!

LIFE-STUDY OF MATTHEW

THE KING'S ANTECEDENTS
AND STATUS

(2)

D. Abraham

The genealogy in Matthew begins with Abraham, but the genealogy in Luke goes back to Adam. Matthew does not cover Adam and his descendants, but Luke does. What is the meaning of this difference? Luke is a book of God's salvation, whereas Matthew is a book of the kingdom. God's salvation is for the created and fallen race represented by Adam, but the kingdom of the heavens is only for God's chosen people, the called race represented by Abraham. Therefore, Matthew starts from Abraham, but Luke traces the genealogy back to Adam.

1. Called

In the first ten and a half chapters of Genesis God tried to work with the created race, but He did not get through. The created race failed Him. Man fell to such an extent that all mankind rebelled against God to the uttermost, and built the tower and city of Babel to express their rebellion (Gen. 11:1-9). So God gave up the created and fallen race, and He called one, Abraham, out of that race to be the father of another race. Out of a place filled with rebellion and idolatry, a place where everyone was one with Satan, God called a man named Abraham (Gen. 12:1-2; Heb. 11:8). From the time God called him out of Babel (later Babylon) into Canaan, God gave up the Adamic race and invested all His interest in this new race, with Abraham as its head. This is the called race, the transformed race. It is not a race according to nature, but a race according to faith.

God's kingdom is for this race. It could never be with the fallen race. Thus, Matthew, dealing with the kingdom of the heavens, begins with Abraham. Because the book of Luke concerns God's salvation (and surely salvation must be for the fallen race), his genealogy goes back to Adam. After being saved in Luke, we are spontaneously trans- ferred from the fallen race to the called race. We used to be descendants of Adam; now we are descendants of Abraham. Galatians 3:7 and 29 tell us that whoever believes in Jesus Christ is a son of Abraham. Whose son are you? Are you the son of Adam or the son of Abraham? We are the real Jews (Rom. 2:29). Our grandfather is Abraham. We are in the same category he is. If we were not descendants of Abraham, then we would have no share in the book of Matthew. We would not even have a share in the short book of Galatians, because Galatians was written to the descendants of Abraham. Only if we are descendants of Abraham do we have a share in Galatians. Praise the Lord that we are the sons of Abraham! "If you are Christ's, then you are Abraham's seed, heirs according to promise" (Gal. 3:29).

Abraham was called out by God. The Greek word for church, *ecclesia*, means "the called out ones." Thus, we in the church are also the called out ones. Abraham was called out of Babel, the place of rebellion and idolatry, into the good land, which typifies Christ. We also were in Babel. We were fallen, we were rebellious, and we worshipped idols. Today the whole human race is in Babel. We used to be there, but one day God called us out and put us into Christ, the high land. We were called by God into "the fellowship [the participation] of His Son, Jesus Christ our Lord" (1 Cor. 1:9). "To those who are called,...Christ, [is] God's power and God's wisdom" (1 Cor. 1:24).

2. Justified by Faith

Abraham, as a called one, was justified by faith (Gen.

15:6; Rom. 4:2-3). The fallen ones depend on their work, but the called ones believe in God's work, not in their own work. No fallen person can be justified by works in the sight of God (Rom 3:20). Therefore, the called ones, having been called by God out of the fallen race, put no trust in their own effort; they trust in God's work of grace. Abraham and all other believers are like this. "They who are of faith are blessed with believing Abraham" (Gal. 3:9). The blessing of God's promise, "the promise of the Spirit" (Gal. 3:14), is for the believing ones. By faith we received the Spirit, which is the reality and realization of Christ (Gal. 3:2). Thus, both Abraham and we are associated with Christ and joined to Him by faith. It is by faith in God's work of grace that God's called people are justified by Him and participate in Christ, their eternal portion.

3. Living by Faith

Hebrews 11:8 says that Abraham was called, and that he answered this call by faith. Then, verse 9 says that he also lived in the good land by faith. As the called one of God, not only was Abraham justified by faith, but he also lived by faith. As one called by God, he should no longer live and walk by himself, but live and walk by faith. For Abraham to live and walk by faith meant that he had to reject himself, to forget himself, to set himself aside, and to live by Someone else. Whatever he had by nature had to be set aside.

If we compare Genesis 11:31 and 12:1 with Acts 7:2-3, we see that when God called Abraham in Ur of the Chaldees, he was very weak. Abraham did not take the initiative to leave Babel; his father, Terah, did. This forced God to take away Abraham's father. In Genesis 12:1 God called him again, telling him to leave not only his country and his kindred, but also his father's house, which meant not to bring anyone with him. But once again Abraham, like us, was weak and he took Lot, his nephew (Gen. 12:5).

What is an Abraham? An Abraham is a person who has

been called out, who no longer lives and walks by himself, and who forsakes and forgets everything he has by nature. This is exactly the message of the book of Galatians. Galatians 3 says that we are the sons of Abraham and that we should live by faith, not by our works. Galatians 2:20 says that to live by faith means "no longer I who live, but Christ." I, the natural I who came out of the fallen race, have been crucified and buried. Thus, it is no longer I, but Christ who lives in me. This is Abraham. If we are true Jews, the real descendants of Abraham, we must leave everything and live by faith. We must forget about all that we can do and repudiate all that we are and have by nature. This is not easy.

Christians appreciate Abraham very much. However, we should not esteem Abraham too highly. He was not that outstanding. He was called, but he did not dare to leave Babel; his father took him out. This forced God to remove his father. Then Abraham relied on his nephew, Lot. After this, he put his trust in his servant, Eliezer (Gen. 15:2-4). It seemed that God was saying, "Abraham, I don't like to see your father with you, I don't like to see your nephew with you, and I don't like to see Eliezer with you. I want you to have no one to rely upon. You must rely on Me. Don't depend upon anything else or anything you have by nature." This is believing in God, walking in Him, and living by Him. It is no longer I, but Christ who lives in me.

If we are real Jews, then we are real Abrahams. In order to be an Abraham, we must believe in the Lord. To believe in the Lord is to become associated with Him. Abraham was called out of the fallen race, and he became associated with the Lord. All the sons of Abraham must likewise be associated with Christ. "If ye be Christ's, then are ye Abraham's seed." In other words, if we are the seed of Abraham, we belong to Christ and we are associated with Christ. If we would be associated with Christ, we must repudiate ourselves and take Christ as everything. This is believing in Christ, and this believing is righteousness in the eyes of God. Do not try to do anything. Simply believe in Christ.

The fallen race always likes to do something, to work and to exert some effort. But God says, "Come out of that. You are the called race. Don't try, don't do, and don't work any more! Forget your past. Forget what you are, what you can do, and what you have. Forget everything, and put your full trust in Me. I am your good land. Live in Me, and live by Me." These are the real Abrahams, the real Galatians. As the sons of God, they trust in God and forget about themselves. These are the ones who make up the generation of Christ. We all must be Abrahams, those who forget their past, give up what they are and have, and put their trust in Christ, their good land. Today our walk and our living must be by faith in Christ. If so, then, as heirs of God's promise, as those who inherit the promise of the Spirit, we shall participate in Christ as God's blessing.

At a certain time the Lord asked Abraham to offer Isaac, the one God had given according to His promise, for a burnt offering (Gen. 22:1-2). The Lord had given Isaac to Abraham; now Abraham had to give Isaac back to the Lord. The Lord had already charged him to cast out Ishmael (Gen. 21:10, 12); now He charged him to kill his son Isaac.

Are you able to do this? What a difficult lesson this is! Nevertheless, this is the way to experience Christ. Last month or last week you may have experienced Christ in a certain way, but today the Lord says, "Consecrate that experience. That was a real experience of Christ, but don't keep it." Again, the lesson is to never trust in what we have, not even in what God has given us. If God has given you something, it must be given back to Him. This is the daily walk by faith. To walk in the presence of the Lord by faith means that we do not hold on to anything, not even to the things given by God. The best gifts, given by the Lord Himself, must be given back to Him. Do not keep anything as something to rely on; rely only and always on the Lord.

Abraham did this. Eventually he lived and walked in the presence of God purely by faith.

E. Isaac

Matthew 1:2 says, "Abraham begot Isaac." What is the outstanding point here concerning Isaac? It is that Isaac was born by promise (Gal. 4:22-26, 28-31; Rom. 9:7-9). He was the only heir (Gen. 21:10, 12; 22:2a, 12b, 16-18), and he inherited the promise of Christ (Gen. 26:3-4).

God had promised Abraham a son. Sarah, wanting to help God fulfill his promise, made a proposal to Abraham. Sarah seemed to say, "Look, Abraham, God promised to give you a seed, an heir to inherit this good land. But look at yourself — you are nearly ninety years of age! And look at me — I'm too old! It is impossible for me to bring forth a child. We must do something to help God fulfill His purpose. I have a maid named Hagar. She is quite good. Surely you could have a son by her" (Gen. 16:1-2). This is the natural concept, and it is quite tempting. Many times our natural concept has some proposal to get us out of the spirit. Often our natural concept says, "Here is a good source. Do it this way." But such a proposal will surely keep us from God's promise!

Abraham took Sarah's proposal (Gen. 16:2-4), and the result was Ishmael (Gen. 16:15). This terrible Ishmael is still here today! Acting on Sarah's proposal did not help God; rather, it frustrated Abraham from fulfilling God's purpose. This is not a small matter.

The lesson we derive from this is that, as the called race, whatever we do on our own results in an Ishmael. Whatever we do on our own in the church life, even in the preaching of the gospel, will only produce an Ishmael. Do not produce Ishmaels! Terminate yourself! Did you not cross over that great river, the Euphrates? When you were called out of Babel, you crossed that great river and you were buried there. You were terminated there. Do not live by yourself or do anything by yourself. Instead, you should say, "Lord, I am nothing. Without You, I can do nothing. Lord, if You don't do anything, then I won't do anything. If You rest, I rest. Lord, I put my trust in You." This is easy to say, but difficult to practice in our daily life.

Remember what an Abraham is: an Abraham is a called one who does nothing by himself. God had to wait until Abraham and Sarah were through (Gen. 17:17; see Rom. 4:19). He waited until their natural energy had died out, until they had come to realize it was impossible for them to bring forth a child.

Abraham wanted to keep Ishmael and rely on him, but God rejected Ishmael (Gen. 17:18-19). We also like to keep our own work and rely on it, but God does not accept it. Eventually, God asked Abraham to cast out Ishmael and his mother (Gen. 21:10-12). This was difficult for Abraham to do. But he had to learn the lesson of not living by himself, the lesson of giving up his own effort and not doing anything by himself. He had a son, but he had to give him up. This is the lesson of Abraham and the lesson in the book of Galatians.

Participating in Christ requires that we never rely on our own effort nor on anything we are able to do. Just as Ishmael was a frustration to Isaac's inheriting of God's promise, so our own effort or work will always frustrate our participation in Christ. We must forsake all that we are and all that we have in order to trust God's promise. We must renounce everything of our natural life; otherwise we cannot enjoy Christ. After our natural strength has been exhausted, the promise of God comes. After Ishmael was cast out, Isaac had the full position to participate in the blessing of God's promise. The termination of our natural effort, the forsaking of what we can do or have done, is "Isaac," the inheriting of God's promised blessing, which is Christ. We have been baptized into Christ (Gal. 3:27, Gk.). Having been terminated in Christ, we are now His, and we have Him as our portion. Thus, we are Abraham's seed, God's called race, and heirs according to God's promise (Gal. 3:29).

What is Isaac? Isaac is the issue of the life and walk by

faith. This is Christ. Isaac was a full type of Christ inheriting all the riches of the Father. We all must experience Christ in such a way; not by our doing, striving, or endeavoring, but simply by trusting in Him. Our trust in Him will issue in Isaac. Only Isaac is the real element of the generation of Christ. Not all the children of Abraham of the flesh are the children of God; only in Isaac will God have His children (Rom. 9:7-8). Therefore, God considered Isaac as Abraham's only son (Gen. 21:10, 12; 22:2a, 12b, 16-18), the only one to inherit the promise concerning Christ (Gen. 26:3-4).

Although we are the race of Abraham today, are we walking in the way of Ishmael, or are we living in the way of Isaac? The way of Ishmael is to fulfill God's purpose by our own energy and work. The way of Isaac is to put ourselves into God, trusting Him to do everything to fulfill His purpose for us. What a great difference between these two ways! Ishmael has nothing to do with Christ. Whatever we do, whatever we try to accomplish, has nothing to do with Christ. We must have Isaac. If we would have Isaac, we must cast out Ishmael, stop our work, and place ourselves into the very working of God. If we let Him fulfill His promise for us, then we shall have Isaac.

F. Jacob

Verse 2 also says, "Isaac begot Jacob." Isaac and Ishmael were brothers by the same father, but by different mothers. Jacob and Esau were more intimate; they were twins. Jacob means a superseder. He supersedes others, puts them under him, and climbs above them. When he and his older brother Esau were coming out of the womb, Jacob held Esau's heel. Jacob seemed to be saying, "Esau, don't go yet! Wait for me. Let me go first!" Jacob was a real heel-holder. The meaning of the name Jacob is the heel-holder, the supplanter. Beat others down. Put them under your feet by any deceitful means. That is Jacob.

Because God had already chosen Jacob, all his

endeavors were in vain. Jacob needed a vision. He did not
need to supplant others, because God had chosen him to be
number one. Even before the twins were born, God had
told the mother that the younger would be the first, and
the elder would be second. It is written, "Jacob I loved, but
Esau I hated" (Mal. 1:2-3; Rom. 9:13).

Unfortunately, Jacob did not realize this. If he had, he
never would have tried to do anything. Rather, he would
have said to Esau, "If you want to go out first, just go out.
No matter how much you try to be first, I will still be first.
You can never beat me because God elected me." Jacob,
however, did not know this. Even when he had grown up,
he still did not realize it. Therefore, he was constantly
supplanting. Wherever he went, he supplanted. He
supplanted his brother (Gen. 25:29-33; 27:18-38), and he
supplanted his uncle (Gen. 30:37—31:1). He schemed and
he stole from his uncle, Laban. Yet, all his labor was in
vain. God could say, "Stupid Jacob. You don't need to do
that. I will give you more than what you have gained." But
Jacob kept striving. Although he was a descendant of
Abraham, according to his striving and his nature, he was
altogether a descendant of the Devil. Do you see this?
Positionally speaking, Jacob was a descendant of
Abraham, but dispositionally speaking, he was a child of
the Devil.

What did Jacob need? He needed God's dealing.
Hence, God raised up his brother, Esau, and then his
uncle, Laban, to deal with him. God even raised up four
wives plus twelve male helpers and a female helper. There
was a great deal of suffering in the life of Jacob, but this
suffering came from his striving, not from God's election.
The more Jacob strove, the more he suffered. We may laugh
at Jacob, but we are exactly the same as he. The more we try
to do something, the more problems we have.

In Christ, we need, firstly, the life of Abraham. We need
to forget what we are, live by Christ, and trust in Him.
Secondly, in Christ we have no need of Ishmael, our doing;
we need Isaac, His doing. Thirdly, we do not need Jacob,

but Israel. We do not need the natural Jacob, but the transformed Israel, the prince of God.

Do you realize that it is absolutely not up to you? When you hear this, you may say, "If it is not up to me, but completely up to God, then I'll stop my seeking." Good. If you can stop your seeking, I encourage you to do it. Tell the whole universe that you have heard that it is up to Him, and that you have stopped your seeking. If you can stop it, it should be stopped. But, I assure you, the more you stop, the better. The more you stop, the more He will stand up. Try it. Tell the Lord, "Lord, I stop my seeking!" The Lord would say, "That's wonderful! Your stopping opens the door for Me to do something. I will burn you. You may stop your seeking, but I will burn you!"

We all have been elected. In a sense, we are caught. What can we do? We can never get away. This is absolutely due to the Lord's mercy. We did not choose this way. I certainly did not choose it, but here I am. What can I do? What can I say? Because God has chosen us, we can never get away.

If we read Romans 9, we shall discover that it is up to Him, not us. He was and still is the source. Praise Him that His mercy has come to us! No one can reject His mercy. We may reject His doing, but we can never reject His mercy (Exo. 33:19; Rom. 9:15). What a mercy that we have been selected to be associated with Christ and to participate in Him as God's eternal blessing! In one sense we are Abraham, in another sense we are Isaac, and in still another sense, we are Jacob. Later, in a fourth sense, we shall be Israel. Thus, we have Abraham, Isaac, and Jacob.

The genealogy of Christ is a matter of the birthright, and the birthright is mainly the association with Christ and the participation in Christ. Jacob's supplanting was not justified, but his seeking after the birthright surely was honored by God. Esau despised the birthright and sold it cheaply (Gen. 25:29-34). Thus, he lost it and was not able to get it back, even when he regretted and wept for it (Gen. 27:34-38; Heb. 12:16-17). He had lost the blessing of participating in Christ. This should be a warning to us. Jacob respected and sought the birthright, and he obtained it. He inherited God's promised blessing, the blessing of Christ (Gen. 28:4, 14).

G. Judah

Verse 2 also says, "Jacob begot Judah and his brothers." Jacob's first son was Reuben. Reuben should have had the first son's portion, which was the birthright. The birthright included three elements: the double portion of the land, the priesthood, and the kingship. Although Reuben was the first son, he lost his birthright because of his defilement (Gen. 49:3-4; 1 Chron. 5:1-2). Then the double portion of the land went to Joseph. This must have been due to his purity (Gen. 39:7-20). He was the son closest to his father and the one most after his father's heart (Gen. 37:2-3, 12-17). Each of Joseph's two sons, Manasseh and Ephraim, received a portion of the land (Joshua 16 and 17). Thus through his two sons he inherited two portions of the good land.

The priesthood portion of the birthright went to Levi (Deut. 33:8-10). Levi was very much after God's heart. In order to fulfill God's desire, Levi forgot his parents, his brothers, and his children and only took care of God's desire. Thus, he received the priesthood portion of the birthright.

The kingship, another portion of the birthright, was given to Judah (Gen. 49:10; 1 Chron. 5:2). If we read Genesis, we find the reason for this. When Joseph was suffering under the conspiracy of his brothers, Judah took care of him (Gen. 37:26). He also took care of Benjamin in time of suffering (Gen. 43:8-9; 44:14-34). Because of this, I believe, the kingship went to Judah.

Today we are the "church of the firstborn" (Heb. 12:23). Our birthright is also composed of these three elements: the double portion of Christ, the priesthood, and the kingship. We are in Christ, and we can enjoy Him in double portion. We are also priests and kings of God.

However, many Christians have lost their birthright. They have been saved and can never be lost, but they have lost their extra portion of Christ. If we would enjoy the extra portion of Christ, we must keep our birthright.

All Christians have been reborn as priests (Rev. 1:6). But today many have lost their priesthood. Because they have lost their praying position, it is hard for them to pray. If we would keep our priesthood, we must be like the Levites, and forget our father, our brothers, and our children and take care of God's interest. God's desire, not our families, must be first. If God's desire has first place in our hearts, then we shall be close to Him and keep the priesthood.

All Christians are also reborn as kings (Rev. 5:10), but many have lost their kingship. When the Lord Jesus returns, the overcoming saints will be with Him to be priests of God and co-kings of Christ (Rev. 20:4-6). At the same time, they will enjoy the inheritance of this earth (Rev. 2:26).

Hebrews 12:16-17 warns us not to lose our birthright as Esau did. "For one meal" Esau "gave up his birthright." Later, he regretted that he had sold it so cheaply, but he was not able to get it back. We all need to be on the alert. We have the position to possess the birthright and we have it already, but maintaining it depends on whether or not we keep ourselves from being profane or becoming defiled. We have seen that Esau lost his birthright because he was profane and that Reuben lost his birthright because of his defilement. But Joseph inherited the double portion of land because of his purity; Levi obtained the priesthood because of his absolute separation unto the Lord; and Judah received the kingship because of his care for his suffering brothers. We need to keep ourselves pure for the extra portion of the enjoyment of Christ; we need to separate ourselves absolutely to the Lord with a heart caring for the Lord's desire above all things; we need to care lovingly for our suffering brothers. If we are like this, we shall surely keep our birthright. The extra portion of the enjoyment of Christ, the priesthood, and the kingship will be ours. Even today we can enjoy Christ in a double measure. We can pray, we can rule, and we can reign. Then, when the Lord Jesus returns, we shall be with Him enjoying the inheritance of this earth. We shall be priests contacting God continually and kings reigning over the people.

Because Judah gained the kingship portion of the birthright, he brought forth the kingly Christ (Gen. 49:10), Christ the Victor (Rev. 5:5; Gen. 49:8-9). "It is clearly evident that our Lord has risen out of Judah" (Heb. 7:14).

Abraham, Isaac, Jacob, and Judah are all associates of Christ. If we have the life of these four generations — Abraham's faith, Isaac's inheritance, Jacob's dealings, and Judah's care of love — then we are the associates of Christ in His generation.

H. His Brethren

When this genealogy mentions Isaac and Jacob, it does not say "and his brother"; only when it mentions Judah does it say "and his brothers." Both Isaac's brother Ishmael and Jacob's brother Esau were rejected by God. But all eleven brothers of Judah were chosen; not one of them was rejected by God. Judah and his eleven brothers became the fathers of the twelve tribes which formed the nation of Israel as God's chosen people for Christ. Hence, all Judah's brothers were related to Christ. For this reason, the genealogy of Christ also includes them.

LIFE-STUDY OF MATTHEW

THE KING'S ANTECEDENTS
AND STATUS

(3)

Whatever is recorded in the Old Testament is related to Christ. The whole Old Testament is a record of Christ, either directly or indirectly. If we want to understand the genealogy of Christ, we must go back to the Old Testament and read it carefully. If we do this, we shall realize that the Old Testament is a record of Christ. This proves that the entire Bible is a revelation of Christ.

We have seen from the genealogy of Christ that His generation includes all kinds of people: low, high, good, bad, fathers, kings, civilians, captives, recovered ones, and even women with a poor reputation. Nevertheless, we must realize that there are some governing principles here. From the lives of all these persons, we can discover certain principles which govern our association with Christ. The generation of Christ includes all kinds of persons, but not in a loose way. No matter what we are or where we came from, we can be included in the generation of Christ if we fulfill the principles. Although we have seen this already, we have not seen it adequately, for there are many more persons to cover.

I. Tamar

The first one we shall consider is Tamar. Tamar conceived through committing incest with her father-in-law (Gen. 38:6-27). Morally speaking, this was deplorable and ethically speaking, it was awful. Nobody would justify this. Although I have been studying Genesis for many years, my heart still aches whenever I read chapter thirty-eight. In a sense, what Tamar did was not good at all.

Nevertheless, she was righteous. The fault was not on her side, but on the side of her father-in-law, Judah, who admitted that she was more righteous than he (Gen. 38:26). You may say that there was no excuse for Tamar's deed and that incest always involves both sides. Although Tamar may be held responsible to a certain extent, she was righteous, and she had a heart for the birthright.

Because we come from a different background and have little understanding of the birthright and of its meaning to the people in those days, I need to say a word about it. In Tamar's time, the birthright meant a great deal (Gen. 38:6-8). As I pointed out in the last message, the birthright included a double portion of the land, the priesthood, and the kingship. The double portion of the land refers to the double enjoyment of Christ. The land is Christ, and the double portion of the land is not the ordinary, common enjoyment of Christ, but something special, something extraordinary in the enjoyment of Christ. Both the priesthood and the kingship are also related to Christ. For the generation after Abraham, the birthright was altogether a matter of inheriting Christ. In Ephesians 2:12, we are told that when we were unbelievers, we were without Christ. But by believing in the Lord Jesus, we have been brought into the birthright. We have been put into Christ, Christ has become our portion, and He will even be our double portion. Through Him, in Him, and with Him we have the priesthood and the kingship. Christ Himself is our good land, our priesthood, and our kingship.

Now we can understand why Tamar was anxious to have the birthright. She knew that if she were cut off, she would be through with God's promise. And God's promise was simply the promise of Himself to be the portion of His chosen people in Christ. Tamar was not willing to miss this blessing.

Tamar was the wife of the first son of Judah. This son should have inherited the birthright. But Tamar's husband was wicked in the eyes of the Lord, and the Lord took his life (Gen. 38:7). The Lord also slew Judah's second son (Gen. 38:8-10). According to the ancient regulations, Judah should have arranged for his next son to marry Tamar in order that a son might be brought forth to inherit the birthright. Judah, however, did not fulfill his responsibility. In a sense, Judah cheated Tamar (Gen. 38:11-14). But Tamar did not give up; rather, she even used an unseemly means to obtain the birthright. Whether the means was unseemly or not, Tamar did her best to get that birthright.

To have the birthright is simply to gain Christ. In order to gain Christ, we must be ready to take a way that does not seem to be the best way. Let me tell you a story that illustrates this, but try to understand me; do not misunderstand me. In the past, some young people in China were inspired by my preaching, believed in the Lord Jesus, and desired to be baptized. However, their parents, who were Buddhists, were very much opposed to this. When they learned that their children were planning to be baptized, they gave them no opportunity to leave home. The young people prayed about this. Eventually, they told their parents that they had to be in school for a certain half-day period. That was surely a lie, for they did not go to school; they went to the church to be baptized. Although they told a lie, it was a pure lie. Their intention in telling that lie was very pleasing to God. If you want to gain Christ, you should not care for the way. Do not be religious; do not keep the rules and regulations. Gain Christ! You need to gain Christ. By any means, get the birthright.

It was through an unseemly means that Tamar acquired the birthright. But in the divine record in the Bible, the name of Tamar is not a bad name. Ruth 4:12 indicates that this name is sacred. In this verse the elders said, "And let thy house be like the house of Pharez, whom Tamar bare unto Judah." The name of Tamar is sacred because she did not care for anything sinful; she cared only for the birthright. The significance of this for us today is that if we care for Christ and are seeking Him, any way we can truly gain Him is the right way.

J. Pharez and Zarah

From Tamar we go on to her son, Pharez (v. 3). Tamar

conceived twins (Gen. 38:27-30). At the time of delivery, one boy, Zarah, tried to come out first, but he did not succeed. He put out his hand, and the midwife marked it with a scarlet thread, indicating that he would be the first-born. However, Pharez preceded him to be the firstborn. Thus, the first became the last, and the last became the first. The midwife was surprised. This is a good illustration of how to gain the birthright. Pharez inherited the birthright. Man did not choose him, but God sent him. This proves that it is not up to man's endeavoring; it is up to God's choice. The mother's story tells us one side: that we should be anxious for the birthright, trying our best to obtain it; the son's story tells us the other side: that although we may strive to obtain the birthright, it is actually a matter of God's choice, not our efforts (see Rom. 9:11).

I remember a story concerning D.L. Moody. One day a student at his Bible institute said to him, "Mr. Moody, by reading the New Testament I have learned that all the saved ones are the chosen ones, predestinated by God before the foundation of the world. Now I have a problem. If I preach the gospel and convince people to believe, I may do something wrong and persuade someone whom God has not chosen. What shall I do?" Moody replied, "My son, just go ahead to do your best. As people enter the door, they will see written on the outside, 'Whosoever will may come.' But once they have entered the door, they will look back and see written on the inside, 'Chosen before the foundation of the world.'" Tamar's story means, "Whosoever will may come." Tamar willed and Tamar came. But her son's story means, "Chosen before the foundation of the world." Perhaps you are today's Tamar, striving and laboring to obtain the birthright. But once you gain it, you will look back and see that you were chosen before the foundation of the world. The birthright does not depend on us; it depends on His choice.

K. Rahab

We proceed to Rahab (v. 5). Rahab was a harlot in

Jericho (Josh. 2:1), a place cursed by God for eternity. Although she was a harlot in such a place, she became a grandmother of Christ. How could a harlot become a grandmother of Christ? In order to answer this question, we need to find the principles. The entire population of Jericho was destroyed except Rahab, her family, and her possessions. She was saved because she turned to God and God's people (Josh. 6:22-23, 25; Heb. 11:31). After she turned to God and His people, she married Salmon, a leader in the army of the leading tribe of Judah and one of the men sent by Joshua to spy out Jericho. At that time, Salmon became acquainted with Rahab and, in a sense, saved her. Eventually, Rahab married him, and they brought forth a godly man named Boaz.

Now we must pay our full attention to the principles governing our association with Christ. The first principle is that, no matter what our background is, we must turn to God and to God's people. Second, we must marry the proper person, not in a physical sense, but in a spiritual sense. After we have turned to God and to God's people, we must be joined, built up, and involved with the proper person. Third, we must bring forth the proper fruit. Then we will be fully in the portion of the birthright of Christ.

It seems that many Christians today have lost their birthright. They do not have Salmon and Boaz. If you would have a Salmon and a Boaz, you must become involved with the proper believers, with the proper leading ones in the leading tribes. Then you need to bring forth the proper fruit, Boaz, who will be a forefather of David. We must turn to the Lord, and we must turn to the Lord's people; we must also take care of how we become involved with others. If we become involved with the proper persons, surely we shall bring forth the proper fruit. This will keep us in the full enjoyment of the birthright of Christ.

L. Boaz

If we are to know the story of Boaz, we must read the book of Ruth. It is a good story. Boaz is a type of Christ, and Ruth is a type of the church. The book of Ruth tells us that Boaz redeemed Ruth; he also redeemed the birth-right for her. This means that Christ, as our real Boaz, has redeemed both us and the birthright.

Boaz redeemed his kinsman's inheritance and married the man's widow (Ruth 4:1-17); hence, he became a notable forefather of Christ, a great associate of Christ. As a brother and a Boaz, you should take care of others' birthright of Christ, not only your own birthright. In other words, you should not only take care of your own en-joyment of Christ, but also others' enjoyment of Christ.

Ruth was the daughter-in-law of Naomi. As we read this story, we see that Ruth and Naomi had lost the en-joyment, the birthright, but according to God's regulation there was a way to restore the birthright, to redeem it. But it had to be redeemed by someone else. The principle is the same in the church life today. If I lose the birthright, the brothers have a way to redeem it for me. Quite often, some dear ones lose their enjoyment of Christ. In a sense, they become Naomi or Ruth. If so, you need to be a Boaz, able to redeem the lost birthright and marry the redeemed one.

Suppose I am a real Ruth who has lost her husband. To lose the husband means to lose the enjoyment of the birthright. I have the birthright, but I have lost the en-joyment of the birthright. Thus, I need you, as my brother, to redeem my birthright. But you need to be somewhat richer in Christ. You need to have some riches with which to redeem my birthright. Then you pay the price to regain my birthright, and you also marry me. This means that you become involved with me. This kind of spiritual in-volvement will produce Obed, the grandfather of David. Boaz became one of the great forefathers of Christ. In a spiritual sense, he was the one who enjoyed the largest and richest portion of Christ. If a brother becomes a Boaz to me, he will be the one with the greatest enjoyment of Christ. Because he redeemed my birthright and became so involved with me, our involvement in the Lord will even-tually bring forth the full enjoyment of Christ.

In the church life today we need to have a number of Boazes. The book of Ruth tells us that there was another kinsman who was even closer to Ruth than Boaz was. But that man was selfish; he only took care of his own birthright. He was afraid that taking care of another's might mar his own. This is exactly today's situation. Some brothers should take care of me, the poor Ruth, but they are selfish in the spiritual enjoyment of Christ. Even in the spiritual enjoyment of Christ it is quite possible to be selfish. However, a Boaz will be generous and pay the price to redeem my birthright. All this indicates that we should take care of not only our own birthright, but also others' birthright. Day by day we should take care of others' enjoyment of Christ. The more we do this, the better.

M. Ruth

We come now to Ruth (1:5). We may say that Ruth was certainly a good woman, but she had a great shortage. Although she herself was not involved in incest, her origin was a matter of incest. Ruth belonged to the tribe of Moab (Ruth 1:4). Moab was the son of Lot, the fruit of Lot's incestuous union with his daughter (Gen. 19:30-38). According to Deuteronomy 23:3, the Moabites were forbidden to enter the congregation of the Lord, even to the tenth generation. Thus, Ruth was an excluded one. However, not only was she accepted by the Lord, but she became a wonderful person who partook of the enjoyment of Christ.

Although, as a Moabitess, Ruth was not allowed to enter the congregation of the Lord, she was seeking God and God's people (Ruth 1:15-17; 2:11-12). This reveals a most prevailing principle: no matter who we are or what our background is, as long as we have a heart which seeks after God and God's people, we are in a position to be accepted into the birthright of Christ. Ruth married Boaz, a godly man among God's people, and brought forth Obed, the grandfather of David the king.

Boaz's mother was Rahab, a Canaanitess, and his wife Ruth was a Moabitess. Both were Gentiles. Nevertheless, they were associated with Christ. This is a strong proof that Christ is joined not only to the Jews, but also to the Gentiles, even the Gentiles of a low and mean class.

You may have been born of a poor origin and have a pitiful background, but do not be bothered or frustrated by that. Forget it! Nothing can be worse than a person born of Moab. But as long as you have a heart to seek after God and God's people and as long as you become involved with the proper person, such as Boaz, you will enter into the double portion of the enjoyment of Christ.

N. Jesse

We continue with Jesse (vv.5-6). Although the Bible does not have much to say about Jesse, what it does say about him is important. Isaiah chapter eleven speaks twice regarding Jesse. Isaiah 11:1 says that Christ will be the shoot ("rod" should be "shoot," Heb.) out of the stem of Jesse and a branch out of the root of Jesse. Christ came out of him. Isaiah 11:10 says that Christ is the root of Jesse, indicating that Jesse came out of Christ. Jesse is a man altogether out of Christ; he is also a person who brings forth Christ. Christ comes out of him, and he comes out of Christ. Christ was his branch, and Christ was also his root. We need light from the Lord to understand these things.

What is a Jesse? A Jesse is a person who brings forth Christ, who branches out Christ by being rooted in Christ. When you branch out Christ, do not forget that Christ is not only your branch, but also your root. Christ branches out of you, and you come out of Christ. Christ is our source, and Christ is also our issue. This means that we are one with Christ and very closely associated with Him. We are in Him, and He is in us. He issues out of us, and we are rooted in Him. This is the kind of person who enjoys the birthright of Christ.

We all must be a Boaz, a Ruth, a Jesse, and a Tamar. We need to be this person and then that person. Eventually we shall say, "Praise the Lord for everybody! Everybody's condition is the same as mine. Tamar's condition is also my condition. The good conditions and the bad conditions are all the same as mine. I am Tamar, I am Pharez, I am Rahab, I am Boaz, I am Ruth, and I am Jesse. Hallelujah!" After Jesse, eventually we are David.

O. David

David was the eighth son of his father, the youngest one. This is meaningful. In the Bible the number eight signifies resurrection, a new start. The eighth day is the first day of the second week; hence, it signifies something new, something of resurrection. When Samuel came to anoint the king of God's people, Jesse presented his seven sons to him. Samuel looked at them and said, "The Lord hath not chosen these." When Samuel learned that there was an eighth one, David, he sent for him and anointed him (1 Sam. 16:10-13). This means that we who are chosen and saved are not people of the first week; we are those of the first day of the second week. We are the eighth child.

David was the last of the generations of the fathers, which were fourteen generations. David was the conclusion of the fathers' section in the genealogy of Christ.

David was also the first of the generations of the kings. In this genealogy, only of David does it say "the king," because it was through him that the kingdom with the kingship was brought in. He was the conclusion of one section and the beginning of the next section. He was the landmark of two ages. He was the ending of one and the beginning of the other because he was very much in the enjoyment of Christ. If we would have the rich enjoyment of Christ, we shall often need to be the end of one situation and the beginning of another situation. However, many of the dear ones can neither be the ending nor the beginning. Eventually, they are just nothing. In the church life, we need some Davids, some stronger ones to conclude certain situations and open up other situations. We need someone to close the fathers' generation and to open up the kings' generation. We must be strong; we must be the eighth son; we must be David.

David was a man after the heart of God (1 Sam. 13:14). God Himself told Saul that He would replace him, for He had found a man after His heart. In his whole life, David did nothing wrong, except one great thing: he murdered a man and took his wife. In one act David committed two great sins, murder and adultery. God Himself condemned this. The Bible says that David did right in the eyes of the Lord all the days of his life, except for this one thing (1 Kings 15:5).

P. The Wife of Uriah (Bathsheba)

David murdered Uriah and took his wife, Bathsheba. She was the wife of a Hittite, a heathen (2 Sam. 11:3). She was remarried as a result of adultery (2 Sam. 11:26-27).

Q. Solomon

After David committed murder and adultery, he was rebuked by the prophet Nathan, whom God sent purposely to condemn him (2 Sam. 12:1-12). After he was condemned, David repented. Psalm 51 is David's psalm of repentance. David repented and God forgave (2 Sam. 12:13). There was repentance and there was forgiveness. Altogether we have three items here: transgression, repentance, and forgiveness. If we put all three together, the result is Solomon. First there were transgression and repentance plus forgiveness. After that, there was Solomon (2 Sam. 12:24), the one who built God's temple. Solomon is the result not only of transgression and repentance, but of transgression, repentance, and God's forgiveness. Here we see two marriages. The first was a marriage between David and Bathsheba. The second was a spiritual marriage, the marriage of David's transgression and repentance with God's forgiveness. God's forgiveness married David's transgression and repentance. This marriage brought forth the man named Solomon who built the temple of God. The church is always built up by this kind of person, Solomon, the issue of man's transgression and repentance plus God's forgiveness.

After David received God's forgiveness and the joy of his salvation was restored, he prayed for Zion, for the building of the walls of Jerusalem, for the strengthening of his kingdom (Psa. 51:18). Eventually, as the result of God's forgiveness of his sin, God gave him a son to build the temple of God for God's presence as the center of the city of Jerusalem.

I hope the Lord will show you what human words cannot say. If you have been and still are a typically good person who has never murdered others, who has never transgressed, and who has never needed to repent, then God does not need to forgive you. If this is the case, then there will never be a Solomon, and the temple of God will never be built up. As we have seen, the building up of God's temple comes from man's transgression and repentance plus God's forgiveness.

One day I said to the Lord, "Lord, my transgression and repentance need Your forgiveness. But, Lord, You know better than I that Your forgiveness also needs my transgression. My transgression needs Your forgiveness, and Your forgiveness needs my transgression. If I have no transgressions, then You don't have a place to spend Your forgiveness." When I said this to the Lord, it seemed that He said, "Yes. Because of your transgression and repentance, I do have an opportunity to spend My forgiveness. I am happy about this." But you should never say, "Let us do evil that good may come." You must do your best. But no matter how hard you may try to do everything right in the eyes of the Lord, sooner or later something will happen. Suddenly, you will murder, take over others, transgress. However, after you transgress, there will be a way for you to repent. If you repent, God will be ready to forgive you. Then you will beget a son and name him Solomon. The name Solomon means "peaceful" (2 Sam. 12:24; 1 Chron. 22:9). But Solomon also has another name, "Jedidiah" (2 Sam. 12:25), which means "beloved of the Lord." To you, Solomon means "peaceful," but to the Lord, he means "beloved of the Lord." This son will be the one who will build up the house of God, today's church.

You need to be right in the eyes of God all the time. But be assured that your being right is not good for building up the church. However, you should not say, "Let me do wrong!" I tell you, even if you try to be wrong, you will discover that you are not able to do wrong. I do not know what kind of sovereignty this is. But one day you will do something awful. All the brothers will shake their heads, unable to believe that you could have done such a thing. Nevertheless, you have done it! Then you need to read Psalm 51, make it your psalm, and go to the Lord, saying, "Lord, I repent. Against Thee and only Thee have I done this evil thing. Forgive me." After this repentance, you will have another marriage, the marriage of your transgression and repentance with God's forgiveness. This will bring forth a Solomon, one who is peaceful to you and beloved of the Lord. This person will build up the church, God's temple. At that time you will be very useful in the building up of the church.

You may say, "What about today? What shall we do — wait for that kind of person to come?" No, do not wait. Your waiting does not avail. We should just walk in the presence of the Lord and let the Lord do it. As Charles Wesley said in one of his hymns, " 'Tis mercy all!" Yes, it is altogether a matter of God's mercy. Forget about your background, your situation, or what may happen in the future. You simply need to trust in the Lord's sovereign mercy. If you have a heart for Him and for His people, He will work everything out. He will give you the full enjoyment of the birthright of Christ.

These verses in the genealogy of Christ are very difficult. They are not milk or meat; they are bones. If we spend an hour or two praying over these verses and over the points covered in this message, we shall see something more. We shall see that we need to be a person with a real seeking heart, a heart seeking God and God's people. Then we shall be today's Boaz, Ruth, Obed, Jesse, David, and eventually today's Solomon, building up the house of God.

LIFE-STUDY OF MATTHEW

THE KING'S ANTECEDENTS
AND STATUS

(4)

We come now to the last part of the genealogy of Christ according to Matthew. In the previous message I said that this part of the Word is not milk or meat, but bones. All the points in this message will help us penetrate the bone and see what is inside it.

R. David the King Begetting Solomon

Matthew 1:6 says, "David begot Solomon." Compare this statement with the record that says, "Nathan, the son of David" (Luke 3:31). Nathan also was the son of David. The genealogy in Matthew says that the son of David was Solomon, and the genealogy in Luke says that the son of David was Nathan. If we read 1 Chronicles 3:1 and 5, we see that these are two different persons. Luke's record is the genealogy of David's son Nathan, who was Mary's forefather, whereas Matthew's record is the genealogy of David's son Solomon, who was Joseph's forefather. One genealogy is the line of Mary, the wife's line; the other genealogy is the line of Joseph, the husband's line. Both Mary and Joseph were descendants of David, but they were from two families descended from the same grandfather. One family is the family of Solomon; the other is the family of Nathan. Under God's sovereignty Mary and Joseph, descendants of these two families, were betrothed and brought forth Christ. Christ may be counted as the descendant of David through both Solomon and Nathan. This is the reason He has two genealogies.

Solomon's relationship with Christ was not direct.

Strictly speaking, Solomon was not a direct forefather of Christ. His relationship with Christ was indirect through his descendant Joseph's marriage to Mary, of whom Christ was born (Matt. 1:16).

The Old Testament did not say that Christ would be Solomon's descendant, but it prophesied repeatedly that Christ would be the descendant of David (2 Sam. 7:13-14, 16; Jer. 23:5). Although Christ was not a direct descendant of Solomon, the Old Testament prophecies concerning Christ were nevertheless fulfilled.

S. Rehoboam

We proceed to Rehoboam, the son of Solomon (v. 7). With Rehoboam, the kingdom of David was divided (1 Kings 11:9-12; 12:1-17). Of the twelve tribes, one tribe was kept for David's sake (1 Kings 11:13), that is, for Christ. Christ needed the kingdom that belonged to the house of David because Christ had to be born as the heir of David's throne. If the whole kingdom had been dissolved, nothing would have remained to allow Christ to be born as David's royal heir. Thus, God preserved one of the tribes for David. Apparently it was preserved for David; actually it was preserved for Christ.

After this division, the kingdom of David was in two parts: the northern part, called the kingdom of Israel, and the southern part, called the kingdom of Judah. The northern part was called the kingdom of Israel, a universal name, because it was made up of the ten tribes of Israel; the southern part was called the kingdom of Judah, a local name, because it was composed of the two tribes of Judah and Benjamin. As far as you are concerned, which title has the better meaning — the kingdom of Israel or the kingdom of Judah? I would surely favor the kingdom of Israel, for that is something universal, something for the majority. I would never favor Judah, because Judah is too local, too narrow. However, although the kingdom of Israel was more universal than that of Judah, in the genealogy of Christ, not one name of the kings of Israel is included.

They were universal, but they were excluded from the generation of Christ. They were excluded because they were not associated with Christ.

This picture, like all other items in the Old Testament, was written for our learning, and it is a type of the occurrences in the New Testament age. We see the same thing today. In principle, at the beginning the church was one. But after a certain time, the church was divided, not into two parts, but perhaps into more than two thousand parts. Some may say, "Were not those in the kingdom of Israel still the people of God?" Certainly they were. They were the people of God, but they were outside of the line of Christ. What does this mean? To be outside of the line of Christ means that, although you are God's people, you are not for Christ. You are for something other than Christ. Consider the situation today. We are all real Christians, and we are all God's people. But are we solely, purely, fully, and ultimately for Christ or are we for something else? If you are for something other than Christ, then you are outside of the line of Christ. For this reason, none of the kings of the northern kingdom, the larger and more universal kingdom, is included in the genealogy of Christ.

T. Joram Begetting Uzziah

Verse 8 says, "Joram begot Uzziah." Compare this record with 1 Chronicles 3:11 and 12, which say, "Joram his son, Ahaziah his son, Joash his son, Amaziah his son, Azariah" (who is Ozias or Uzziah — 2 Kings 15:1, 13). Matthew omitted three generations which are found in 1 Chronicles — Ahaziah, Joash, and Amaziah.

This must have been due to the evil marriage of Joram to the daughter of Ahab and Jezebel, which corrupted his descendants (2 Chron. 21:5-6; 22:1-4). Ahab was the king of the northern kingdom, and his wife Jezebel was a wicked woman who was fully related to idols. Because she was one with the Devil, she corrupted her husband. They brought forth a daughter, and Joram, one of the kings of Judah, married her. This woman taught Joram to worship idols, to be one with the idols. Thus their family was corrupted. According to Exodus 20:5, three generations of Joram's descendants were cut off from the generation of Christ. Exodus 20:5 says that anyone who forsakes God and worships idols corrupts himself and will suffer God's curse for three or four generations. Therefore, three generations of King Joram were cut off from the genealogy of Christ. Here we must learn a lesson. If we would be associated with Christ, we should never be involved with anything related to idols. God is a jealous God and He will never tolerate idolatry.

U. Josiah Begetting Jeconiah

Verse 11 says, "Josiah begot Jeconiah." Compare this record with "the sons of Josiah . . . the second Jehoiakim . . . and the sons of Jehoiakim; Jeconiah his son" (1 Chron. 3:15-16). One generation — Jehoiakim — was omitted from the genealogy of Christ. This must have been because he was made king by Pharaoh of Egypt and collected tax for Pharaoh (2 Kings 23:34-35). Because he was so closely related to Egypt, he was excluded from the genealogy of Christ. Egypt represents the world. From these two records we see that anyone who is related to idols or associated with the world will be excluded from the generation of Christ.

V. The Captives to Babylon

Those who were carried away to Babylon as captives (vv. 11-12) were indirectly related to Christ through their descendant Joseph's marriage with Mary. Even these captives are included in this sacred record of Christ's genealogy because they had an indirect relationship through Mary, the mother of Jesus.

W. Jeconiah

Jeconiah was not reckoned as a king in this genealogy because he was born during the captivity and was carried away as a captive (2 Chron. 36:9-10, Jehoiachin is Jeconiah). According to the prophecy of Jeremiah 22:28-30, none of Jeconiah's descendants would inherit the throne of David. All of his descendants were cut off from David's throne. If Christ had been a direct descendant of Jeconiah, He would not have been entitled to the throne of David. Although Jeremiah 22:28-30 says that all the descendants of Jeconiah are excluded from the throne of David, the next chapter, verse 5, says that God will raise up a branch to David, a King who will reign and prosper. This Branch is Christ. This prophecy confirms that Christ will be the descendant of David, although not a direct descendant of Jeconiah, and will inherit the throne of David.

X. Jeconiah Begetting Salathiel, and Salathiel Begetting Zerubbabel

Verse 12 says, "Jeconiah begot Salathiel; and Salathiel begot Zerubbabel." Compare this record with that in 1 Chronicles 3:17-19, "the sons of Jeconiah . . . Salathiel . . . and Pedaiah . . . and the sons of Pedaiah were Zerubbabel . . . ," showing that Zerubbabel was the son of Pedaiah, Salathiel's brother. Zerubbabel was not Salathiel's son, but his nephew, who became his heir. Perhaps this was a case in accordance with Deuteronomy 25:5 and 6, which say that if a man dies without a son as his heir, his brother must marry his wife in order to produce a son to be his heir. Without this case, we cannot understand why there is such a regulation in Deuteronomy 25. Even that word in Deuteronomy is related to the genealogy of Christ.

Y. Zerubbabel

Ezra 5:1 and 2 say that Zerubbabel was one of the leaders who returned to Jerusalem from the captivity at Babylon. This means that he was a leader in the Lord's recovery. This is a great thing. He was also a leader in the rebuilding of God's temple (Zech. 4:7-10).

Without this return from captivity, it would have been

impossible for Christ to be born at Bethlehem. The Old Testament definitely predicted that Christ, as the descendant of David, would be born in Bethlehem (Matt. 2:4-6; Micah 5:2). Suppose none of the people of Israel had returned to Judah, and the time came for Christ to be born at Bethlehem. No one would have been there. Now we can understand why God commanded the captives to return. God's commandment that the captives return was not only for the rebuilding of the temple but also the preparation for Christ to be born in Bethlehem.

It is exactly the same today. Some may ask, "What is the difference between remaining at Babylon and returning to Jerusalem? Isn't it the same, as long as we worship God and walk in the spirit?" It may be all right with you, but it is not all right with Christ. Christ needs some people to bring Him to Bethlehem. You may worship God and you may walk in the spirit in Babylon, but be assured that Christ could never be born into humanity through you. This requires a specific place. You must return from Babylon to Judah. When the time came for the Lord Jesus to be born, some Israelites, descendants of the returned captives, were waiting in Judah. At that time, Joseph and Mary were not in Babylon; they were in Judah. For Christ to come to earth, some of His captured people had to return. For His second coming, Christ also needs some of His captured people to return from their captivity to the proper church life.

Z. Jacob Begetting Joseph

The genealogy here says, "Jacob begot Joseph" (v. 16), but Luke 3:23 says, "Joseph, the son of Heli." Whose son was Joseph? Luke's record says "as was supposed." A literal translation would be "as to the law." This indicates that Joseph was not actually the son of Heli, but was reckoned as his son according to the law. Joseph was the son-in-law of Heli, Mary's father. This might have been a case according to Numbers 27:1-8 and 36:1-12, in which a regulation was made by God that if any parents had only daughters as heirs, their inheritance should go to the daughters; the daughters then must marry a man of their own tribe in order to keep their inheritance within that tribe. If we did not have Matthew chapter one we may wonder why such a record exists. Now we see that this is not merely the record of a certain regulation; it is a matter related to Christ, because the virgin daughter who brought forth Christ was such a case. We believe that Mary's parents had no sons and that she inherited her parent's heritage and married Joseph, a man of the same tribe, the tribe of Judah. Even the regulation in Numbers 27 and 36 is related to the genealogy of Christ. Either directly or indirectly the whole Bible is a record of Christ.

AA. Joseph the Husband of Mary, of Whom Jesus Was Born

At this point, the record of this genealogy does not say "Joseph begot Jesus," as mentioned of all the foregoing persons; it says, "Joseph, the husband of Mary, of whom was born Jesus" (v. 16). Jesus was born of Mary, not of Joseph, since it was prophesied that Christ would be the seed of a woman and born of a virgin (Gen. 3:15; Isa. 7:14). Christ could not have been born of Joseph, because Joseph was a man and a descendant of Jeconiah, of whose descendants none could inherit the throne of David (Jer. 22:28-30). If Christ had been born of Joseph, he would have been excluded from the throne of David. However, Mary was a virgin (Luke 1:27) and a descendant of David (Luke 1:31-32), the right person of whom Christ should be born. The marriage of Joseph with Mary brought him into relationship with Christ and united into one the two lines of Christ's genealogy for the bringing forth of Christ.

Now we need to examine the chart (p. 52) which shows that the generation of Christ begins from God and continues until it reaches Jesus. The first name is God, and the last name is Jesus. It proceeds from God to Adam, from Adam to Abraham, from Abraham through Isaac and Jacob and on to David. After David, it is divided into two lines, the first running from Nathan to Mary and the second from Solomon to Joseph. Eventually, in God's sovereignty, these two lines are brought together by the marriage of Mary to Joseph to bring forth Christ. If we spend time to consider this chart, we shall realize how wonderful is God's sovereignty.

All marriages are under God's sovereignty, especially marriages related to Christ. From God to David the genealogy was one line, and from David to Jesus it was two lines; yet these two lines were united through the marriage of Joseph and Mary. The Jesus who was brought forth by Mary fulfills the prophecies: the prophecy concerning the seed of woman (Gen. 3:15); the prophecy of a virgin bringing forth a son (Isa. 7:14); the prophecy of Abraham having a seed who would bring blessing to all the nations (Gen. 22:18); the prophecy to Isaac and Jacob, which was the same as the prophecy made to Abraham (Gen. 26:4; 28:14); the prophecy made to Judah that Judah would be the royal tribe (Gen. 49:10); and the prophecy made to David (2 Sam. 7:12-13). Although the birth of Jesus fulfilled many prophecies in the Old Testament, He was not the descendant of Jeconiah. Seemingly, the descendants of Jeconiah were still in the royal line. But according to God's sovereignty, Mary, the mother of Jesus, married Joseph, a descendant of Jeconiah, who seemed to be in the line of the royal family. Apparently, Jesus was the descendant of Jeconiah; actually, He was not. He was the descendant of David. Only God can arrange such a thing. Praise Him!

If you consider your history, the history of your salvation, you will see that the principle is the same. Do not think that the marriage of Joseph and Mary was an accident. It was no accident; rather it was planned by the sovereign hand of God. Likewise, your association with Christ — your salvation — was not an accident; it also was planned by the divine hand. Sometimes I have thanked the Lord and said to Him, "I am so happy that You did not put me on earth in 20 B.C., but in the twentieth century. You put me on this earth in a place where the missionaries came with the Bible. One day I was born of a Christian mother. Later, I was given the opportunity to hear the gospel, and I was saved. Hallelujah!" This was no accident. Neither was your association with Christ an accident. God carefully planned it all. God has arranged all this for little people like us. This is not an insignificant matter. When we enter eternity, we may be very surprised. We may shout, "Praise the Lord!"

BB. Mary

We come now to Mary, the virgin (1:16). Being a virgin, she was different from the other four women mentioned in this genealogy. Mary was pure and unique. She conceived of the Holy Spirit, not of man, to bring forth Christ (Luke 1:34-35; Matt. 1:18b, 20b). This account of the four re-married women and the one virgin proves that all the persons recorded in this genealogy were born of sin, except Christ, who was born in holiness.

CC. The One Who Is Called Christ

Matthew uses the phrase, "Who is called Christ" (v. 16). In Luke's genealogy, the title Christ is not mentioned. Luke mentions the name Jesus because Luke proves that the Lord came to be a man, not to be the Anointed One, the King, the Messiah. Matthew, on the contrary, proves that Jesus is the King, the Messiah prophesied in the Old Testament. Hence, he added the word, "Who is called Christ."

DD. Abraham, David, and Mary

Abraham, David, and Mary are three pleasant names in the Bible, names sweet to the ears of God (vv. 2, 6, 16). Abraham represents a life by faith, David represents a life under the dealing of the cross, and Mary represents a life of absolute surrender to the Lord. It was through these three kinds of lives that Christ was brought forth into humanity.

The principle is the same today. Consider the matter of

preaching the gospel. The purpose of preaching the gospel is to bring Christ into humanity. This requires a great deal of faith, a life under the dealing of the cross, and a life of absolute surrender to the Lord. If we have these kinds of lives, we shall surely bring Christ into humanity.

EE. To David and from David

David is the end of the generations of the fathers and the beginning of the generations of the kings (v. 17). He was the one person used by God as a landmark both to conclude the section of the fathers and to begin the section of the kings.

FF. Until the Carrying Away and from the Carrying Away

At the time of degradation, there was no person as a landmark to divide the generations as did Abraham and David. So, the carrying away itself became a landmark, a landmark of shame. At that time, the landmark was not a person; it was the carrying away to Babylon. The Bible is careful to show us that no person prevailed as the landmark for that generation. This was a shame.

GG. Three Groups of Fourteen Generations

Verse 17 mentions three groups of fourteen generations. The number fourteen is composed of ten plus four. Four signifies the creatures. In Revelation 4:6 we have the four living creatures, and in Revelation 7:1 we have "the four corners of the earth" and "the four winds." The number ten signifies fullness. We often speak of one tenth, meaning the tenth part of fullness (see Gen. 14:20). Therefore, in Matthew 25:1 we have ten virgins. Look at your two hands and your feet: you have ten fingers and ten toes. Thus, the number ten denotes fullness, and the number fourteen signifies the creatures in full.

Three times of fourteen generations indicates that the Triune God mingles Himself with the creatures in full. This is very meaningful. The Persons of the Triune God are

the Father, the Son, and the Spirit. This genealogy is of
three sections: the section of the fathers, the section of the
kings, and the section of the civilians, including the captured ones and the recovered ones. God the Father fits into
the section of the fathers, God the Son fits into the section
of the kings, and God the Spirit fits into the section of the
civilians. This is wonderful! Therefore, three times fourteen means the mingling of the Triune God with His
creatures. This record of the generation of Christ indicates
the mingling of the Triune God with these human
creatures.

The Triune God has been traveling through Abraham
and Isaac, Jacob and Judah, Boaz and Obed, Jesse and
David, and then through many other generations to Mary
and Joseph. Finally, Jesus came. Who is Jesus? Jesus is
the Triune God traveling through all the generations and
coming forth as the mingling of divinity with humanity.

Three times fourteen is forty-two. Forty is the number
of trials, temptations, and sufferings (Heb. 3:9; Matt. 4:2;
1 Kings 19:8). Christ is the forty-second generation. Forty-
two signifies rest and satisfaction after trials. Numbers
33:5-48 shows us that the children of Israel traveled
through forty-two stations before they came into Canaan.
According to the record of the Old Testament, the Israelites suffered all the way through these forty-two stations.
They were tried, they were tempted, and they were tested.
They had no rest. However, after passing through these
forty-two stations, they entered into rest. This not only
happened in the past, but will happen again in the future.
In Revelation 13, we see that there will be forty-two
months, three and one-half years. These forty-two months
will be the concluding part of the final seven years, the last
week mentioned in Daniel 9:24-27. There are seventy
weeks: the first seven weeks, then sixty-two weeks, and
then the last week, each week representing seven years. The
second half of these last seven years, a period of forty-two
months, will be the great tribulation, and it will be awful.
There will be many trials, testings, temptations, and

sufferings. But, when these forty-two months have been
completed, the kingdom will come and there will be rest.
From Abraham through Mary was a time of sufferings,
tests, and temptations. After all the generations of trials,
temptations, and sufferings, Christ came as the forty-
second generation to be our rest and satisfaction. With Him
we have complete rest and full satisfaction.

If we read the history in Chronicles, we shall discover that
the generations from Abraham to Christ were actually forty-
five generations. Why then does Matthew have only forty-
two? By deducting from the forty-five generations the three
cursed generations and the one improper generation, and
by making David two generations (one of the fathers and
one of the kings), the generations become forty-two, which
are divided into three ages of fourteen generations each.

Remember: this is not only a life-study, but also a Bible
study. Hence, we need some knowledge. We need to see
that the record of Matthew is not a record according to
history, but a record according to doctrine. The record of
John, on the contrary, is according to history, for John
wrote his Gospel according to the events of history. According to history, it was forty-five generations, but according
to Matthew's doctrinal purpose, it was forty-two generations. Matthew must have had a doctrinal purpose in saying that from Abraham to David was fourteen generations, from David to the carrying away was another fourteen generations, and from the carrying away to Christ was
still another fourteen generations. It was not inaccurate for
Matthew to say this. Three generations were omitted
because they were not qualified, and a fourth generation
was disqualified and cut off. But there was a wonderful
person, David the king, who was doubly qualified. He
became two generations, closing one section and opening
another. He brought in the kingship, for through him the
kingdom was established. Therefore, by David's being
counted as two generations, this genealogy of Christ can
consist of forty-two generations in three sections, each with
fourteen generations.

HH. "To the Christ"

Let us now consider the words "to the Christ" (v. 17). Luke's record begins with Jesus and traces back to God, a total of seventy-seven generations. Matthew's record proceeds from Abraham to Christ. Luke goes back and up to God; Matthew comes forward and down to Christ. All the generations were directed toward Christ and brought forth Christ. Without Christ, there are just forty-one generations; there is no goal, no consummation, and no conclusion. Forty-one is not a good number; we must have the number forty-two. Christ is the goal, the consummation, the conclusion, the completion, and the perfection of all the generations, fulfilling their prophecies, solving their problems, and meeting their needs. Christ came to fulfill all the prophecies, the prophecies of Abraham, Isaac, Jacob, Judah, and David. Without the coming of Christ, all these prophecies would have been in vain. When Christ comes, light, life, salvation, satisfaction, healing, freedom, rest, comfort, peace, and joy all come with Him. From this point on, the whole New Testament is the full expounding of this wonderful Christ. The twenty-seven books of the New Testament — the Gospels, the Acts, the Epistles, and Revelation — tell us how this Christ fulfills all the prophecies, solves all our problems, and meets all our needs and how He is everything to us. Hallelujah, Christ has come!

The Generation of Jesus Christ

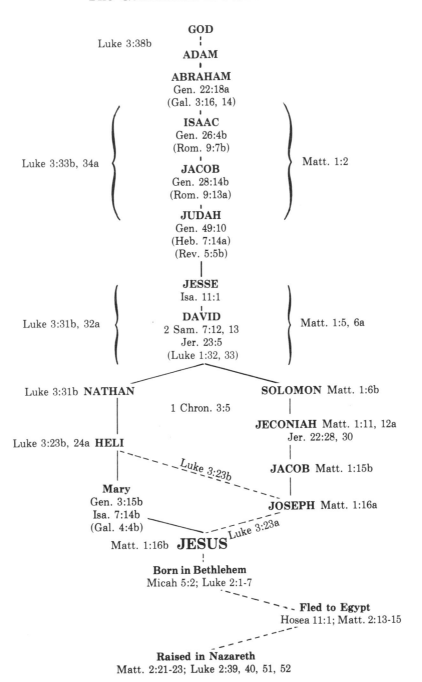

Luke 3:38b

GOD
⋮
ADAM
|
ABRAHAM
Gen. 22:18a
(Gal. 3:16, 14)
|
ISAAC
Gen. 26:4b
(Rom. 9:7b)
|
JACOB
Gen. 28:14b
(Rom. 9:13a)
|
JUDAH
Gen. 49:10
(Heb. 7:14a)
(Rev. 5:5b)

Luke 3:33b, 34a

Matt. 1:2

JESSE
Isa. 11:1
|
DAVID
2 Sam. 7:12, 13
Jer. 23:5
(Luke 1:32, 33)

Luke 3:31b, 32a

Matt. 1:5, 6a

Luke 3:31b NATHAN

1 Chron. 3:5

SOLOMON Matt. 1:6b

JECONIAH Matt. 1:11, 12a
Jer. 22:28, 30

Luke 3:23b, 24a HELI

Luke 3:23b

JACOB Matt. 1:15b

Mary
Gen. 3:15b
Isa. 7:14b
(Gal. 4:4b)

JOSEPH Matt. 1:16a

Luke 3:23a

Matt. 1:16b JESUS
⋮
Born in Bethlehem
Micah 5:2; Luke 2:1-7

Fled to Egypt
Hosea 11:1; Matt. 2:13-15

Raised in Nazareth
Matt. 2:21-23; Luke 2:39, 40, 51, 52

LIFE-STUDY OF MATTHEW

THE KING'S ANTECEDENTS AND STATUS

(5)

II. HIS BIRTH

In this message we come to the birth of Christ. Because the birth of Christ is altogether a mystery, it is difficult to talk about it. First, we need to consider some matters related to the preparation for Christ's birth.

A. By God's Sovereignty

The birth of Christ was prepared and carried out by God's sovereignty (1:18; Luke 1:26-27). By His sovereignty, God brought Joseph and Mary together in marriage to bring forth Christ to be the legal heir to the throne of David. Marriage is a mystery. It is not easy to bring two persons together, especially when it concerns the birth of Christ. It was not a simple matter to bring Joseph and Mary together. Look into the history here. According to the genealogy of Christ in Matthew, Joseph was a descendant of Zerubbabel, a returned captive. Zerubbabel, a leader of the tribe of Judah and a descendant of the royal family, led the captives from Babylon to Jerusalem (Ezra 2:2). Eventually, he also took the lead in rebuilding the temple (Ezra 3:8; 5:2). Joseph was his descendant. If there had been no return of the captives, where would Joseph have been born? He would have been born in Babylon. The same would have been true for Mary, also a descendant of the returned captives. If the forefathers of Joseph and Mary had remained in Babylon and if both Mary and Joseph themselves had been born there, how could Jesus have sovereignty in bringing back the forefathers of Joseph and Mary.

By His sovereignty, God placed both Joseph and Mary in the same city, Nazareth (Luke 1:26; 2:4). If they had lived far away from each other, it would have been difficult for them to come together in marriage. Joseph and Mary not only were descendants of the returned captives, but also lived in the same little town. This allowed them to come together in marriage.

Furthermore, when we examine the genealogies in Matthew and Luke, we discover that Joseph was a descendant of the royal line, the line of Solomon (v. 6-7), and Mary was a descendant of the common line, the line of Nathan (Luke 3:31). Although Joseph and Mary came together in marriage, Jesus was born of Mary, not of Joseph. Apparently, He was born of Joseph; actually, He was born of Mary (1:16). This was absolutely a matter of God's sovereignty.

As we have seen in a previous message, the curse recorded in Jeremiah disqualified any descendant of Jeconiah from inheriting the throne of David (Jer. 22:28-30). If, in actuality, Jesus had been born of Joseph, He would have been disqualified from the throne of David. Because Joseph was still in the royal line, he was a royal descendant according to man's eyes. By the marriage of Mary, Jesus' mother, with Joseph, Jesus was apparently associated with this royal line. Again, we see God's sovereignty. God found a young woman, also the descendant of David, to bring forth Christ. Jesus was born of her and was actually the seed of David qualified to inherit the throne of David.

By this sovereign arrangement, Jesus was both an ordinary person and the heir of the royal throne. This is the reason He has two genealogies, one in Luke, telling us of His common status, and another in Matthew, telling us of His royal status. His common status came from Mary, and His royal status came from Joseph. Thus Jesus was born by God's sovereignty. None of us was born under this kind of

God's sovereignty. None of us was born under this kind of sovereignty. Only Jesus was qualified to enjoy such a sovereign arrangement.

B. Through Mary's Surrender

According to Luke 1:26-38, the birth of Christ was carried out through Mary's surrender. Here I would say a word to the young people. It was not easy for a young virgin like Mary to accept the commission to conceive a child. If I had been she, I would have said, "Lord, if You would ask me to do anything other than this, I would do it. But You ask me to conceive a child! This is not humanly possible; it is neither moral nor ethical. I can't do it!" For us to read this record is easy. However, suppose a young sister among us were to receive such a commission tonight. Could she accept it? This is not an insignificant matter. Mary might have said, "Gabriel, don't you know that I am espoused to a man already? How can I conceive a child?" Who among us would accept such a commission? If an angel spoke such a word to you, could you accept it?

After listening to the word of the angel, Mary said, "Behold the slave of the Lord; may it be to me according to your word" (Luke 1:38). This may appear simple, but the price was extremely high. To bring forth Christ Mary paid a very high price — the cost of her whole being. It is not easy to bring forth Christ; it is not cheap. If we would bring forth Christ, we must pay a price. Mary did.

Joseph reacted immediately, planning that he would put Mary away secretly (v. 19). Thus, Mary was in trouble. I assure you, whenever you accept the commission to bring forth Christ, you will find yourself in trouble. All the angels will understand you, but not one human being will understand. Do not expect anyone to be like the angel Gabriel. Everyone will misunderstand you. In fact, the person closest to you may misunderstand you the most. Nevertheless, in large measure, the birth of Christ was accomplished through Mary's surrender.

C. Of the Holy Spirit's Power

However, Mary's surrender was not directly related to the conceiving of Jesus. The conceiving of Jesus was directly related to the Holy Spirit (vv. 18, 20; Luke 1:35). Without the Holy Spirit, Mary's surrender would have meant nothing. No matter how much we may surrender, without the power of the Holy Spirit our surrender means nothing. Do not estimate your surrender too highly. Our surrender means little; it simply affords the opportunity for the Holy Spirit's power to come into us and accomplish something.

D. With Joseph's Obedience and Coordination

Although there was the sovereignty of God, the surrender of Mary, and the power of the Holy Spirit, there was the need of Joseph's obedience and coordination (vv. 19-21, 24-25). What would have happened if Joseph had insisted on a divorce? He was planning this. However, he was the person selected by God for the birth of Christ. Therefore, he was not so rough and quick; rather, he was considerate and thoughtful. Because at that time Joseph was a young man, I would take this opportunity to say a word to the young people: Do not make decisions too fast or act too quickly. Be a little slow and give the Lord a chance to come in. At least, give the matter another night. During that night, the angel may come and speak to you. This happened to Joseph. While he thought on these things, the angel of the Lord appeared to him in a dream (v. 20). Joseph obeyed the word of the angel.

Suppose you were engaged to a young girl and discovered that she was with child. Would you still take her? To take such a woman would surely be a shame. Therefore, not only Mary paid a price, but Joseph also paid a price. The bringing forth of Christ cost him a great deal, for it caused him to suffer shame.

The points we have covered thus far in this message are merely some minor points. We come now to the major points.

E. Fulfilling the Prophecies

The birth of Christ was a great fulfillment of prophecies in the Old Testament. The first prophecy in the Old Testament is Genesis 3:15. There are no prophecies in chapters one and two of Genesis, but in chapter three, after the fall of man, after the serpent had worked himself into man through the woman, God gave a promise. In giving this promise, God seemed to say, "Serpent, you came in through the woman. Now I shall deal with you by the seed of this woman." Thus, the promise concerning the seed of the woman was the first prophecy in the Bible.

In 1:22 and 23 this promise is fulfilled by a virgin conceiving a child. This child came to be the seed of the woman. In Galatians 4:4 Paul says that Christ was born under the law and also was born of the woman. Christ came not only to fulfill the law, but also to fulfill the promise that the seed of the woman would bruise the head of the serpent.

From Genesis we proceed to Isaiah 7:14, where there is another prophecy concerning Christ. "Behold, a virgin shall conceive, and bear a son." The fulfillment of this promise brought God into man. Hallelujah, God became man!

F. God Becoming Flesh

However, it is difficult to find a verse which says that God became man. What the Bible says is this: "The Word was God . . . and the Word became flesh" (John 1:1, 14). Man is a good term, but flesh is not. If I tell you that you are a man, you will be happy. But if I say that you are flesh, you will not be happy because the word flesh is not a positive term. In 1 Timothy 3:16 Paul says, "Great is the mystery . . . Who was manifested in the flesh." Although flesh is not a good term, the Bible says that God was manifest in the flesh.

It is not easy to understand what the Bible means by the flesh. In the Bible the flesh has at least three meanings. First, in a good sense, it means the meat of our body

(John 6:55). Our body has meat and bone, blood and skin. This is physical. Second, flesh means our fallen body. God did not create fallen flesh; He created a body. When man fell, the poison of Satan was injected into his body, and the body was corrupted and became the flesh. Therefore, Romans 7:18 says, "For I know that in me, that is, in my flesh, nothing good dwells." This indicates that the fallen body, the body of sin (Rom. 6:6), is called the flesh. All human lusts come from this flesh. Hence, the New Testament has the term "the lusts of our flesh" (Eph. 2:3). Third, the flesh, especially in the New Testament, means the fallen man. Romans 3:20 says, "By the works of the law no flesh shall be justified before Him." In this verse flesh is the fallen man.

Nevertheless John 1:14 says, "The Word [which was God] became flesh." As we have seen, flesh means the fallen man. How, then, shall we interpret John 1:14? The Word was God, and the Word became flesh. Great is the mystery that God was manifest in the flesh. The Bible says that God became flesh and that flesh is not the created man, but the fallen man. Can we say that God became a fallen man? This surely is a difficult matter.

However, there are two verses that can help us. The first verse is Romans 8:3, which says that God sent "His own Son in the likeness of the flesh of sin." This verse does not say "the flesh of sin"; it says "the likeness of the flesh of sin." The other verse is John 3:14: "As Moses lifted up the serpent in the wilderness, even so must the Son of Man be lifted up." The serpent lifted up on a pole in the wilderness was not actually a serpent with poison; it was a brass serpent made in the likeness of a real serpent (Num. 21:9). John 3:14 is the word of the Lord Jesus to Nicodemus. The Lord told him that as Moses lifted up the serpent in the wilderness, even so must He Himself be lifted up on the cross. When Jesus was on the cross, in the eyes of God He was in the form, the likeness, of a serpent. But as was the case with the brass serpent in the wilderness, there was no poison in Him because He was not born of a fallen man. He was born of a virgin.

Now we must clearly differentiate two points: Christ was conceived of the Holy Spirit and He was born of a virgin. His source was the Holy Spirit, and His element was divine. Through the virgin Mary as a means, He put on flesh and blood, the human nature, taking "the likeness of the flesh," "the likeness of men" (Phil. 2:7). However, He did not have the sinful nature of the fallen flesh. He knew no sin (2 Cor. 5:21), and He had no sin (Heb. 4:15). He had flesh, but it was the "likeness of the flesh of sin." In appearance He was made in the form of a fallen man, but in actuality there was no fallen nature within Him. His birth was exactly the same in principle. Apparently, He was the son of Joseph; actually, He was the son of Mary.

Why was the Lord Jesus viewed by God as being in the form of a serpent when He was on the cross? Because, since the day man fell (Gen. 3:1), the serpent had been in man, and he made every man a serpent. According to Matthew 3:7 and 23:33, both John the Baptist and the Lord Jesus called people the "generation of vipers," that is, serpents, indicating that all fallen ones are descendants of the serpent. We all are little serpents. Do not think that you are good. Before you were saved, you were a serpent. This is the reason the Lord Jesus died on the cross to suffer God's judgment. When Jesus was on the cross, He was not only a man, but was also in the form of a serpent. In the eyes of God, for all of us serpentine people, He took on the form of a serpent and died on the cross. Perhaps you have never heard that Jesus took the form of a serpent, the likeness of the flesh of sin. You have heard that Jesus is God and that He took the form of a man, but not that He also took the form of a serpent. How wonderful He is!

We are fallen flesh, and Jesus came into this flesh that He might bring God into humanity. In Him, the divine Person of God was mingled with humanity. The birth of Christ was not simply to produce a Savior, but also to bring God into man. Although humanity was fallen, God did not take on any part of this fallen nature. God took only the likeness of the fallen flesh, and through this He mingled

Himself with humanity. We should not think of Jesus in the way many others think of Him. We must realize that Jesus is nothing less than God Himself mingled with fallen humanity, taking the form of humanity, but without man's sinful nature. This was the birth of Christ.

G. Jehovah to Be Jesus

The wonderful One who was born in this wonderful way is Jehovah. And He is not only Jehovah — He is Jehovah with something else. The name Jesus means "Jehovah the Savior" or "the salvation of Jehovah" (Matt. 1:21). This wonderful Person is the very salvation which Jehovah renders people. He Himself is salvation. Because Jehovah Himself becomes salvation, He is the Savior.

Do not think that when we call Jesus we are just calling the name of a man. Jesus is not simply a man; He is Jehovah our salvation, Jehovah our Savior. This is simple, yet profound. When you call on Jesus, the whole universe realizes that you are calling on Jehovah as your Savior, Jehovah as your salvation.

The Jews believe in Jehovah, but not in Jesus. In a sense, they have Jehovah, but they do not have salvation or the Savior. We have more than the Jews have, for we have Jehovah the Savior, Jehovah our salvation. This is why we have such a wonderful feeling when we call on Jesus. Even if you were to say that you hate Jesus, there would still be a feeling within you. If you were to say, "I hate Abraham Lincoln," there would be no feeling. If you say, "I hate Jesus," some feeling is there. Abraham Lincoln has nothing to do with you, but Jesus does. Many have said, "I hate Jesus," and later were caught by Jesus. Whoever calls on the name of Jesus will be saved. If you touch the name of Jesus, you will be touched by Him. When we preach the gospel, it is good to help people call on Jesus. As long as they call on Jesus, something will happen.

Jesus is a wonderful name because Jesus is Jehovah. In Genesis 1 we do not find the name Jehovah. We find only the name God: "In the beginning God created . . . ." Elohim

— God — is the term for the God of creation. The name Jehovah, which is not used until Genesis 2, is used especially when God relates to man. The name Jesus is something added to Jehovah — that is, Jehovah our salvation, Jehovah our Savior.

Jesus is the real Joshua (Num. 13:16; Heb. 4:8). Joshua is the Hebrew equivalent of Jesus, and Jesus is the Greek translation of Joshua. Moses brought God's people out of Egypt, but Joshua brought them into rest. As our real Joshua, Jesus brings us into rest. Matthew 11:28 and 29 tell us that Jesus is the rest and that He brings us into Himself as rest. Hebrews 4:8, 9, and 11 also speak of Jesus as our real Joshua. The Joshua in the Old Testament text becomes Jesus in the Greek text of Hebrews. The Jesus mentioned in Hebrews 4 is our Joshua.

It is difficult to separate Jesus from Joshua because Jesus is Joshua, and Joshua is Jesus. Today, Jesus is our real Joshua who brings us into rest, the rest of the good land. He is not only our Savior saving us from sin, but also our Joshua bringing us into rest, the good land. Whenever we call on His name, He saves us from sin and brings us into rest, into the enjoyment of Himself. A line in a hymn speaks about saying the name Jesus a thousand times a day. The more you say, "Jesus," the better. We must learn to speak the name of Jesus all the time. Jesus is our salvation. Jesus is also our rest. Whoever calls on the name of the Lord Jesus shall be saved and enter into the rest.

H. God to Be Emmanuel

In 1:23 we have another wonderful name — Emmanuel. Jesus was the name given by God, and Emmanuel was the name called by man. Emmanuel means "God with us." Jesus the Savior is God with us. Without Him we cannot meet God, for God is He, and He is God. Without Him we cannot find God, for He is God Himself incarnated to dwell among us (John 1:14).

Jesus is not only God; He is God with us. The "us" refers to the saved people. We are the "us." Day by day, we have Emmanuel. In Matthew 18:20 Jesus said that whenever two or three are gathered together in His name, He will be with them. This is Emmanuel. Whenever we Christians gather together, He is in our midst. In Matthew 28:20, the last verse of this Gospel, Jesus told His disciples, "Lo, I am with you all the days, even until the completion of the age." Jesus as Emmanuel is here today. According to Matthew, Jesus came, but He never went away. He was buried in the tomb for three days, but He came in resurrection and never left. He is with us as Emmanuel.

When we call on Jesus, we have the sense that God is with us. We call on Jesus, but we have God. Sometimes, we Christians are rather stupid. We call on Jesus and we find God; yet we wonder whether or not Jesus is God. Jesus is God! He is not only God — He is God with us. When we call on Jesus, we have Jehovah, we have the Savior, we have salvation, and we have God with us. We have God in the very place where we are.

I. Jehovah God Born in the Flesh
to Be the King

This Jesus, who is Jehovah God, was born in the flesh to be the King to inherit the throne of David (1:20; Luke 1:27, 32-33). Matthew is a book on the kingdom with Christ as the King, the Messiah. When you call on Jesus, you have Jehovah, the Savior, salvation, God, and eventually, the King. The King rules. When we call on Jesus, immediately we have One ruling over us. If you have some unseemly pictures or photos on your walls and you call on Jesus, He will be your King and say, "Get rid of that!"

Jesus, the King, intends to establish His kingdom within you and to set up the throne of David in your heart. The more you call on Jesus, the more the ruling power will be there. If you do not believe me, I ask you to try it. Call on the name of Jesus for ten minutes and see what happens. The King will rule over you and bother you. The first night He may say that your attitude toward others has never been very good, especially toward your husband or your wife and that you must be ruled. Call on His name and you will be ruled by Him.

Jesus is a wonderful Person. He is Jehovah, God, the Savior, and the King. The King has been born and is here today. Every day, morning and evening, we appreciate Christ as our Savior, as our King, and as the King of kings.

When no one can rule over you, this King of kings will be able to rule you. When no one else can control you — neither your parents, your husband, your wife, or your children — the King of kings will do something. Simply call on the name of Jesus. If you do, you will enjoy Jehovah, the Savior, salvation, the presence of God, and also the kingship of Jesus. Jesus the King will be born in you, and He will establish His kingdom within you. This is the very Jesus Christ we find in Matthew.

The Christ in Matthew is the Savior-King and the King-Savior who sets up the kingdom of the heavens within us and over us. Matthew 1 not only gives us the origin of this King; it also gives us the presence of this King. This King's name is Jesus. Whenever we call on His name, we have the sense that He is ruling within us by saving us. He is setting up the kingdom of the heavens within us. Hallelujah, this is our Christ!

LIFE-STUDY OF MATTHEW

THE KING'S ANTECEDENTS
AND STATUS

(6)

Matthew 1 is a chapter of names. We have spent considerable time on the names of Abraham, Isaac, Jacob, and even on the names of Tamar and Rahab. The last two names, however, Jesus and Emmanuel, are more than wonderful. Although the last part of Matthew 1 seems to deal with the birth of Christ, it actually deals with the names of Jesus and Emmanuel. In this message I am burdened to give you a hint concerning how to dwell on these names.

J. Jesus, the Name Given by God

Jesus was the name given by God, whereas Emmanuel was the name called by man. The angel Gabriel told Mary that the child she would conceive was to be called Jesus (Luke 1:31). Later, the angel of the Lord appeared to Joseph and also told him to call the child Jesus (Matt. 1:21, 25). Hence, Jesus was a God-given name.

1. Three Elements in the Name of Jesus

a. Jehovah — "I Am That I Am"

The name Jesus includes the name Jehovah. In Hebrew, the name God means the mighty One, God the Almighty; and the name Jehovah means I Am — I Am That I Am (Exo. 3:14). The verb "to be" in Hebrew not only refers to the present, but also includes both the past and the future. Hence, the correct meaning of Jehovah is I Am That I Am, the One who is now in the present, who was in the past, and who will be in the future and in eternity forever. This is the name of Jehovah. Only God is the eternal One. From eternity past to eternity future, He is the I Am. Therefore, the Lord Jesus could say of Himself, "Before Abraham came into being, I am" (John 8:58). He also said to the Jews, "Unless you believe that I am, you shall die in your sins," and, "When you lift up the Son of Man, then you will know that I am" (John 8:24, 28). We must realize that Jesus is the great I Am and believe in Him as the great I Am.

Because the name of the Lord is the I Am, we may say, "Lord, You told me that Your name is I Am. Then, what are You?" His answer will be, "I am whatever you need." The Lord is whatever we need. If we need salvation, He Himself will be salvation to us. We have a signed check with the space for the amount left blank, and we may fill in whatever we need. If we need one dollar, we may insert one dollar. But if we need one million dollars, we may insert one million dollars. If we feel that we need one billion, we simply fill in this amount. The check covers whatever we need. Whatever you need, Jesus is. Do you need light, life, power, wisdom, holiness, or righteousness? Jesus Himself is light, life, power, wisdom, holiness, and righteousness. Everything we need is found in the name of Jesus. How high and how rich is this wonderful name!

b. Savior

The first element included in the name of Jesus is Jehovah. The second is the Savior. Jesus is Jehovah-Savior, the One who saves us from all negative things: from our sins, from hell, from God's judgment, and from eternal condemnation. He is the Savior. He saves us from everything God condemns and from everything we hate. If we hate our temper, He will save us from it. He saves us from the evil power of Satan, from all our besetting sins in our daily life, and from every bondage and addiction. Hallelujah, He is the Savior!

c. Salvation

Jesus is not only the Savior, He Himself is also our salvation. Do not ask Him to give you salvation. Instead, you should say, "Lord Jesus, come to me and be my salvation." Jesus will never give you salvation. He will come to you as salvation. We believers do not realize how much we need to be saved. Every day, every hour, and even every moment we have something from which we need to be saved.

In the messages on Genesis 1 we spoke about the need to grow in life. But what does it mean to grow in life? On the positive side, to grow in life is to enter into the riches of what Christ is. On the negative side, it is to be delivered from certain things, or to forsake certain things. Although we are small men, we have accumulated many negative things. Probably you do not realize how many negative things you have accumulated. Wherever we go, we collect things. We pick up a great many negative things, and we acquire a number of habits from which we need to be saved. As you are reading this, you may not sense that you need salvation from anything. Suppose, however, you were suddenly raptured to the heavens. If you were taken to the heavens right now, you would immediately sense that you need a great deal of saving. To grow in life is simply to be saved from all unnecessary things, from all that is not needed for our living. If you have the light, the exposure of the fourth-day lights, you will say, "Lord, save me!" At such times we realize that Jesus is truly Jehovah as our Savior and our salvation.

2. The Name of Jesus
Being above Every Name

The name of Jesus is above every name (Phil. 2:9-10). No name is as high and as exalted as the name of Jesus. Whether you hate Jesus or love Him, whether you are for Him or against Him, you realize that the name of Jesus is a special name. History tells us that during the past two thousand years, everyone has recognized that His name is the highest name, that it is an extraordinary name. My burden in this message is to point out to you that this exalted name of Jesus is for us to do many things.

a. To Believe In

Firstly, the name of Jesus is for us to believe in (John 1:12). We all must believe in the name of Jesus. This is not an insignificant matter. We should not only say that we believe in the Lord Jesus, but also declare that we believe in the name of Jesus. When we preach the gospel, we should help people not only to pray, but also to make a declaration to the whole universe that they believe in the name of Jesus. Whenever a sinner comes to believe in the Lord Jesus, he should declare, "Today I believe in the name of Jesus!" This makes a great difference.

b. To Be Baptized Into

The name of Jesus is for us to be baptized into (Acts 8:16; 19:5). Among some Christians there is a controversy regarding the name in which they baptize people. Some argue strongly that we must baptize people only in the name of Jesus. Others insist on the name of the Father, the Son, and the Holy Spirit. These two groups argue, debate, and fight. Actually, it is not a matter of *in* the name, but of *into* the name. We baptize people into the name of Jesus. The name needs the person, and the name is the person. Without the person, the name means nothing. To be baptized into the name of Jesus means to be baptized into His Person. Suppose a certain young man has just believed in the name of Jesus. What should we do? We should baptize him into the name of Jesus, that is, put him into Jesus. This is not a ritual nor a ceremony of accepting a religious member. It is an act of faith in which we take one who believes in the name of Jesus and put him into this name, baptizing him into the Person of Jesus. Romans 6:3 says that many of us have been baptized into Christ Jesus, and Galatians 3:27 says, "As many as were baptized into Christ." This is the reality of being baptized into the name of Jesus.

c. To Be Saved

The name of Jesus is also for us to be saved. Acts 4:12 says, "Neither is there another name under heaven given among men in which we must be saved." The name of Jesus has been given to us purposely that we may be saved. The name of Jesus is a saving name.

d. To Be Healed

To the lame man whom he met at the gate of the temple Peter said, "Silver and gold I do not possess, but what I have, this I give to you: In the name of Jesus Christ the Nazarene—walk! (Acts 3:6). Immediately the man was healed. Then Peter said to the people, "In the name of Jesus Christ the Nazarene...this man stands before you well" (Acts 4:10). This testifies that the name of Jesus is also a healing name. We may call on the name of Jesus for healing from any kind of sickness.

e. To Be Washed, Sanctified, and Justified

The name of Jesus has been given to us so that we may be washed, sanctified, and justified (1 Cor. 6:11). As defiled persons, we were washed, sanctified, and justified in the name of Jesus and by the Spirit of God. I read 1 Corinthians 6:11 for years without seeing a crucial point: in the name and by the Spirit. The name is closely related to the Person and to the Spirit. If the name of Jesus were an empty name, how could it wash us? How could it sanctify and justify us? This would be impossible. However, this name is linked to the Spirit. The Spirit is the Person of the name and the reality of the name. Therefore the name can wash us, sanctify us, and justify us. The Spirit is one with the name. Jesus is the name of the Lord, and the Spirit is the Person of the Lord. When we call on the name of a real person, that person comes. The name of Jesus is linked with the Person who washes us, sanctifies us, and justifies us. This is not merely doctrine or theory — it is reality. When we believe in the name of Jesus and are put into the name of Jesus, we are placed into a living Person, that is, in the Holy Spirit. This Holy Spirit washes us, sanctifies us, and justifies us.

f. To Call Upon

The name of Jesus is for us to call upon (Rom. 10:13; 1 Cor. 1:2). I was a Christian for at least thirty-five years before I found the secret of calling on the name of Jesus. I thought that calling on the name of Jesus was the same as praying. Eventually, from the record of the Bible, I discovered that praying is one thing and calling is another. Fifteen years ago, I did a great deal of praying, mostly on my knees. I did not know the secret of calling upon the name of Jesus, nor did I know that calling is different from praying.

Many of us have experienced praying, but with little inspiration. However, when we call on Jesus for five minutes, we are inspired. Try it! Many of us can testify that when we prayed in the old way, we sometimes prayed ourselves to sleep. But calling on the Lord never puts us to sleep. On the contrary, it stirs us up.

Acts 9:14 says that Paul, when he was Saul of Tarsus, tried to damage all the saints. He intended to go from Jerusalem to Damascus to bind all those who called on the name of Jesus. This verse does not say that he was about to bind all those who prayed to Jesus, but all those who called on Jesus. By this one verse we can see that the early Christians were those who called on Jesus. Whenever they prayed, they called. They called upon the name of Jesus, and that became a mark of recognition.

The Bible does not say that whoever prays shall be saved. It says that whosoever *calls* upon the name of the Lord shall be saved (Rom. 10:13). Suppose that I am a sinner and I believe in the Lord Jesus. You help me to pray, and I say, "Lord Jesus, I am a sinner. You are my Savior. You love me. You died on the cross for me. Thank you." Although it is good to pray this way, praying like this makes it very difficult for the Spirit to get into us. However, if you would help me to call, "O Lord Jesus," louder and louder, it would make a big difference. When you preach the gospel, do not try so hard to change people's thinking. Instead, help them to open up their being, their heart and their spirit, from deep within and to use their mouths to call upon the name of Jesus. If you help new believers to call on the name of Jesus in this way, the door will be open wide for the Spirit to enter in. There is no need to pray with vain words. After calling on the name of Jesus ten times, you will be in the heavens. Your sins will be forgiven, your burden will be lifted, and you will have life eternal. You will have everything.

Even for a believer of many years, the best way to touch the Lord Jesus, to enjoy the Lord Jesus, to share something of the Lord Jesus, is not to say very much, but to go to the Lord and call, "Jesus! Jesus! Lord Jesus!" Call on the name of Jesus and you will taste something. "The same Lord of all is rich to all who call upon Him" (Rom. 10:12). Many times, our words are too vain. It is better just to call, "Jesus." If you call on His name, you will taste Him and enjoy Him. The name of Jesus is a wonderful name. We all need to call on Him.

g. To Pray

We may also pray in the name of Jesus (John 14:13-14; 15:16; 16:24). This does not mean that we pray a long prayer and conclude it with the words "in the name of Jesus." That is too formal. However, I do not oppose this, for I have done this many times. Rather, I would say that in our prayer it is good to call on the name of Jesus and say, "O Jesus! Jesus! I come to pray!" In the name of Jesus, you will have a real burden to pray, and it will be very easy to have the assurance that your prayer has been heard and answered. If we call on the name of Jesus, we shall have the assurance that we shall receive what we have asked.

After the Lord Jesus told us to pray in His name, He proceeded to say that the Spirit will come to dwell in us (John 14:13-17). This indicates that the indwelling Spirit has very much to do with our prayer in the name of the Lord Jesus. In order to pray in the name of Jesus, we need the Spirit. When we are in the Spirit, we are in the reality of the name of Jesus in which we are praying.

h. To Be Gathered Into

The name of Jesus is also for us to be gathered into (18:20, Greek, into). Whenever we come together to meet, we should be gathered together into the name of Jesus. Although we may meet for the purpose of having the life-study, we do not gather into the life-study, but into the name of Jesus. Whenever you come to a Christian meeting, you must realize that you are being gathered once again into the name. We have been put into the name of Jesus, but we are not yet very deep into Him. Hence, we need to come back again and again to be gathered into His name. We can all testify that after every meeting we have had the sense deep within that we have entered further into the Lord. The Christian gatherings will bring us more deeply into the appreciation of the name of Jesus.

i. To Cast Out Demons

The name of Jesus is also good for casting out demons (Acts 16:18). To know the power of the name of Jesus, use it to cast out demons. Demons know the power of the name of Jesus better than we do. Demons are subtle. From our experience in China, where there were many cases of demon possession, we have learned that when we cast out demons, we must tell them that this Jesus is not the ordinary, common Jesus, but that He is the designated Jesus. We must say, "Demon, I come in the very name of Jesus, the Son of God, who was incarnated to be a man, who was born of a virgin in Bethlehem, who was raised in Nazareth, who died on the cross for my sins and for the sins of this person that is possessed, who was resurrected from the dead, and who has ascended to the heavens. I come in the name of this Jesus, and I command you to leave!" Immediately, the demon will depart. However, if you say, "I cast you out in the name of Jesus," the demon will not listen. Demons know the power of the name of Jesus. When you cast out a demon, there is no need to pray that much. Simply say, "I come in the name of the designated Jesus, and you must go!" When Jesus comes, demons must flee.

j. To Preach

The name of Jesus is for us to preach (Acts 9:27). When we preach, we must preach in the name of Jesus. Preaching in the Lord's name must be done in the Spirit, for the Spirit is the Person of the Lord and the reality of His name. When we preach in His name, we need the Spirit to make it real.

Through all the things that can be done in the name of Jesus, we see that whatever we do and whatever we are must be in the name of Jesus. Never forget the name of Jesus. His name is a sweet name, a rich name, a powerful name, a saving name, a healing name, a comforting name, and an available name. This is the name that is exalted, honored, and respected. And it is the name feared by the enemy.

3. Satan's Hatred of the Name of Jesus

a. Attacking This Name

Satan hates the name of Jesus. In 1935 the church in my home town was revived, and we were all burdened to preach the gospel. Every night we went to the streets to preach. One night, as we were preaching on a street corner, a man about thirty years of age was very bold to scoff at the name of Jesus. A brother went up to him in a very nice way and asked if they could have a little talk. When he agreed, the brother asked, "Have you ever met Jesus?" He said, "No." Then the brother asked, "Have you ever heard of Jesus?" Again, he said, "No." After that, the brother said, "Has Jesus done something bad to you?" He said, "Never." Then the brother inquired, "You have never met Jesus, and He has never done anything bad to you. Why then do you hate Him?" He replied, "Although I've never met Him and although I've never been damaged by Him, I still hate Him." Then the brother asked, "Why don't you hate me?" The man answered, "I don't hate you; I hate Jesus." "Why?" inquired the brother. "I don't know," said the man. Then the brother asked, "Sir, may I relate a fact to you?" The man consented and the brother said, "Let me tell you, you do not hate Jesus. It is someone else who hates Jesus. Why? Because you have never met Jesus. It is not you!" When the man asked the brother who it was who hated Jesus, the brother answered, "It is the Devil within you who hates Jesus." By all this we see that Satan utilizes people to attack the name of Jesus (Acts 26:9).

As a believer, you probably have had the following experience. When you are about to talk to others about Plato or Abraham Lincoln, you do not feel ashamed; but whenever you talk to people about Jesus, a strange feeling comes over you. When the Chinese speak about Confucius, they feel glorious. We should also feel glorious whenever we speak to others about Jesus, but often we do not have a glorious feeling. Instead, we have a rather strange feeling. This is devilish! In this universe and on this earth there is a devilish element that is against Jesus. You have no problem as long as you are talking about the world situation, the economy, science, and so many things; but whenever you talk about the name of Jesus, you have a strange sense. This comes from the Devil. Because Satan and all his demons hate the name of Jesus, we must proclaim it all the more. We must be bold with this name and say, "Satan, Jesus is my Lord! Satan, stay away!" We need to shout the name of Jesus.

b. Preventing Speaking in This Name

If you read the book of Acts, you will see that in the early days the religionists attacked the name of Jesus, forbidding the believers to preach or teach in that name (Acts 4:17-18; 5:40). The Pharisees warned Peter and John not to preach in the name of Jesus, not to do anything or say anything in His name. It was all right to preach the Bible, but not to preach in the name of Jesus. Satan hates the name of Jesus because he knows that God's salvation is in this name. The more we preach in the name of Jesus and the more we pray to Jesus, the more people will get saved. This is the reason Satan hates this name.

c. Having to Suffer for This Name

When the Apostles were persecuted, they rejoiced that they were worthy to suffer for the name of Jesus (Acts 5:41). Is this not wonderful? They even hazarded their lives for this name (Acts 15:26). Because Satan attacks the name of Jesus with all his evil power, we must learn to suffer for this name.

d. Not Denying This Name

In Revelation 3:8 the Lord Jesus praised the church in Philadelphia because they did not deny His name. We should never deny the name of Jesus. We should deny every other name, but keep the name of Jesus. We must testify that we do not belong to any person or to any sect, but that we simply belong to Jesus. The name of Jesus is the only name we own.

K. Emmanuel, the Name Called by People

1. Jesus as Emmanuel Experienced by Us

Now we come to the second name, Emmanuel (1:23). The angels did not speak to Joseph or Mary of this name. Rather, Emmanuel is the name called by people who have had a certain amount of experience. Whenever you have some experience of Jesus, you will be able to say that He is

God with you. Jesus is nothing less than God with us. This is our experience. God told us that His name is Jesus. But as we receive Him and experience Him, we say that Jesus is God with us. This is wonderful.

Often we turn to our mind and ask the question, "Is this Jesus the very God?" We may be confident that He is the Son of God, but we may not yet be assured that He is actually God Himself. When I was young, I was taught by some fundamental Christian teachers to be careful of saying directly that Jesus was God. I was taught that the Son of God was different from God Himself. Therefore, I was told not to say directly that Jesus was God. I was told that I must pray through Jesus to God. I received a teaching that suited the human concept. However, after much practice, the more I prayed, the more I realized that this Jesus was simply God with me. To argue by theory is one thing; to experience the fact is another thing. Quite often, Christians do not agree with their experience; instead, they agree with their concepts.

I believe that all Christians have this experience. Deep within, do you not have the sense that, according to your experience, Jesus is God? You do, but you dare not say this in doctrine. However, you should not consider Jesus as someone other than God. Jesus is nothing less than God Himself. He is not only the Son of God, but also God Himself. Some good writers have said that apart from Jesus we can never find God. God is with Jesus, and God is Jesus. In the beginning was the Word, and the Word was not only with God, but the Word was God (John 1:1). This Word became flesh and was called Jesus.

When we experience Jesus, He is Emmanuel, God with us. We have heard that Jesus is our comfort, our rest, our peace, and our life. Jesus is so much to us. If we would experience Him, we would immediately say, "This is God! This is not God far away from me, or God in the heavens, but God with me." Whenever we experience Jesus in a certain way, we realize that Jesus is God with us. Jesus is our salvation. After we experience this salvation, we say,

"This is God with us to be our salvation." Jesus is our patience. But when we experience Him as our patience, we say, "This patience is God with me." Jesus is the way and the truth, but when we experience Him as the way and the truth we say, "This way and this truth are just God with me." Hallelujah, Jesus is God with us! In our experience, He is Emmanuel.

2. With Us in Our Gatherings

Whenever we are gathered together into the name of Jesus, He is with us (18:20). Once again, this is Emmanuel, God with us. The presence of Jesus in our meetings is actually God with us.

3. With Us All the Days

Jesus is with us all the days, even until the completion of the age (28:20, Gk.). "All the days" includes today. Do not forget about today. Many Christians think that Jesus is present all the days, except today. But Jesus is with us now, today!

4. With Us in Our Spirit

Jesus is not only among us; He is in our spirit. Second Timothy 4:22 says, "The Lord be with your spirit." This Jesus who is with our spirit is Emmanuel, God with us.

5. His Presence Being the Spirit

We can never separate the Spirit from the presence of Jesus. The Spirit is simply the reality of Jesus' presence (John 14:16-20). This presence is Emmanuel, God with us.

6. Receiving the Spirit by Calling on the Name of Jesus

When we call on the name of Jesus, we receive the Spirit, who is the Person, the reality, and the realization of Jesus. First Corinthians 12:3 says, "No one can say, Lord Jesus, except in the Holy Spirit." Whenever we say

"Lord Jesus," we are in the Spirit and we receive the Spirit. We have all been under the influence of tradition, thinking that we must fast and pray before we can receive the Spirit. However, it is simple to receive the Spirit — just call on the name of Jesus.

7. The Enemy Trying to Take Over the Land of Emmanuel

According to Isaiah 8:7-8, the enemy may try to take over the land of Emmanuel. Do not think this word is only for the children of Israel. Today our spirit is the land of Emmanuel. Thus, we ourselves are the land of Emmanuel. The enemy, Satan, with all his army will do everything He can to take over this land of Emmanuel, that is, to take over our spirit and our being.

8. The Enemy Unable to Take Us Over

Isaiah 8:10 tells us that because God is with us, the enemy can never take over the land of Emmanuel. Although Satan has tried his best to take you over, you are still here. Perhaps during the past week Satan tried twenty-one times to take you over, but he failed every time. You are still here because of Emmanuel, because of God with us. This Emmanuel is Jesus. Today we may enjoy Jesus and experience Him in such a real way as our Emmanuel.

LIFE-STUDY OF MATTHEW

THE KING'S ANTECEDENTS
AND STATUS

(7)

We come now to chapter two of Matthew. In the previous messages we have covered the genealogy of Christ and the birth of Christ. In this message we shall consider the youth of Christ.

III. HIS YOUTH

A. The Record of Christ's Youth
in Matthew and Luke

If we pay attention to the four Gospels, we shall see that John and Mark contain no record of Christ's youth. John tells us that Christ is God. With God there is neither youth nor old age. God is ancient, yet unchanging. Thus, there is no problem of youth with God. In Mark, Christ is revealed as a slave. No one cares about the youth of a slave. On the contrary, both Luke and Matthew record the youth of Christ. However, as was the case with the genealogies, there is a difference between these two records of Christ's youth.

1. Luke's Record
Proving the Humanity of Christ

The Gospel of Luke proves that Christ was a perfect man. Hence, Luke's record testifies and demonstrates the humanity of Jesus (Luke 2:21-52). The items of Christ's youth recorded by Luke show that Jesus was a proper, normal man. Jesus was circumcised on the eighth day accord-

ing to Jewish law (Luke 2:21). Also, according to Jewish
custom, He was named Jesus on the eighth day, not on the
first day. He was offered to God with the sacrifice of a pair
of turtledoves, or two young pigeons (Luke 2:22-24). The
fact that Mary and Joseph could only afford a small
sacrifice shows that they were poor. They nevertheless fulfilled the requirement of the law. Furthermore, Jesus was
brought to Jerusalem every year at the time of the feast of
the Passover (Luke 2:41). This was also according to the
law requiring that all Israelite males attend the feasts three
times a year. Luke specifically notes that Jesus was
brought to the feast when He was twelve years old (Luke
2:42). Luke also records that Jesus grew physically, that
He became strong in His spirit, and that He found favor
with God and man (Luke 2:40, 52). All these items
recorded by Luke demonstrate that Jesus was a typical
man.

2. Matthew's Record
Proving the Kingship of Christ

Matthew's record demonstrates that the young Jesus
was the King of God's people (2:1-23). Luke did not include
this point, but Matthew, ignoring all the points covered by
Luke, dwells on it. By this we see that the Bible has an
intention: in Luke it is to prove that Jesus was a man; in
Matthew it is to show that Jesus was a kingly child. We
shall now consider Matthew's record to see how Jesus was
such a kingly child.

We should not try to understand the Bible by the black
and white letters alone. We must enter into it and find
something of life in it. Matthew 1 tells us that the Old
Testament contained prophecies concerning Christ and
that the people of God were waiting for His coming. In
Matthew 1 Jesus came. Christ has been brought into
humanity; He has appeared on the earth. Chapter two continues by showing the way to find Christ. His coming was
prophesied, He has come, and He is here. However, there is
the problem of how to find Him.

a. Found in Bethlehem by Pagan Men

Matthew 1 reveals that Jesus, the Messiah, has come. If you had been an Israelite at that time, you would have said, "You tell me Jesus has come, but how can I find Him?" Thank the Lord that the matter of finding Jesus was not initiated by us: it was initiated by God.

Consider the background. At the time of Jesus' birth, there was a religion called Judaism. It was a fundamental, sound, scriptural religion that was formed, organized, and constituted according to the thirty-nine books of the Old Testament. Through the record of Matthew 2, we see that Judaism was very much for the Bible. However, hardly anyone in that religion knew that Christ had come. We find no record in the New Testament that some of those religious people went to find Christ. On the contrary, there is a record that some pagan men, magi, came to find Him (2:1-12). Of course, this was initiated by God, not by them.

(1) LED BY THE STAR, THE HEAVENLY VISION

God gave the magi a shining star to guide them (2:2). This star did not appear in the Holy Land. It appeared to men far away — far away from the Holy Land; far away from the holy city; far away from the holy temple and the holy religion; far away from the holy Bible, the holy people, and the holy priests. Far away from all these holy things, the shining star appeared to some pagan men in a pagan land. The shining of that star stirred up these pagan wise men regarding the King of the Jews. I do not know how these wise men were stirred up regarding the King of the Jews, and I do not want to guess. There have already been too many imaginations concerning these wise men. At any rate, they came from the East, the Orient, and realized that the star indicated the King of the Jews.

The wise men had the living vision, the heavenly star, and the Jewish religionists had the Bible. Which do you prefer to have — the Bible or the star? It is best to have both. I like to have the Bible in my hand, and I like to see the star in the heavens. It is best to be both a pagan and a Jew as well. As to the Bible, I am a Jew; as to the star, I am a pagan wise man.

(2) DISTRACTED BY THEIR HUMAN CONCEPT

After the wise men experienced the vision of the heavenly star, they got into trouble. This trouble came from their natural concept. Although we may have the Bible and the star, we must recognize that trouble may come from our natural concept. The wise men saw the vision and, realizing that it indicated the King of the Jews, they assumed that they should go to Jerusalem, the capital of the Jewish nation, where the King of the Jews was presumed to be (vv. 1-2). Their decision to go to Jerusalem did not come from the light of the star. They went to Jerusalem because they were distracted from the right track by their natural concept. Jerusalem was the wrong place. It was the capital and the city where the temple was located, but it was not the place where Jesus was born. Because the wise men were misled, they caused a serious problem and nearly caused the young child Jesus to be killed. If it had not been for the sovereignty of God, the young Jesus would have been killed as a result of their mistake. Their error cost the lives of many young ones (vv. 16-18). Be careful: you may have the Bible and the star, but do not follow your natural concept.

(3) CORRECTED BY THE SCRIPTURES

Many times you have the vision, but when you consider the matter in your mind, you are distracted and misled by your natural concept. Your human concept distracts you from the right track. Whenever you are distracted like this, you need the Bible. After you have arrived at the wrong place, you need the right book. After the magi had gone to Jerusalem, the wrong place, they were corrected through the Scriptures. From the Scriptures they learned that the right place was Bethlehem, not Jerusalem (vv. 4-6). If they had not been misled by their natural concept, the star certainly would have led them directly to the place where Jesus was in Bethlehem. But they were distracted and went astray. Thus, they needed to be corrected by the knowledge of the Bible. When the magi had been corrected by the Scriptures, had departed from Jerusalem, and had been restored to the right track, the star appeared again (v. 9). Living vision always goes along with the Scriptures.

However, none of the religious people in Jerusalem went with the magi to Bethlehem. This is quite strange. If you had been a priest among those priests, would you not have gone with the wise men to see if Jesus had actually been born in Bethlehem? If I had been there, I certainly would have gone to find out for myself whether or not Christ had actually been born. But none of them went. They had knowledge and they could tell people that the Messiah would be born in Bethlehem; yet, none of them went for themselves. Although they were for the knowledge of the Bible, they were not for the living Person of the Messiah.

How about today's situation? Many are very scriptural, but they care only for the Scriptures, not for the living Christ. If the Jewish religionists had cared for Christ, they would have gone to Bethlehem, which was not far from Jerusalem even by the ancient method of travel. Although Bethlehem was not far, none of the scribes, elders, or priests bothered to go. This proves that you can have the knowledge of the Bible without having a heart for the living Christ. To have the vision is one thing, to have the knowledge of the Bible is another thing, and to have a heart for the living Christ is still another thing. We all need to pray, "Lord, give me a heart for You. I want to see the vision and I want to know the Bible. But even more, I want to have a heart that seeks You."

(4) LED AGAIN BY THE STAR
TO FIND AND WORSHIP CHRIST

After the magi saw the star again, the star led them to the place where Christ was (vv. 9-10). The star led them not only to the city of Bethlehem, but to the exact spot where Jesus was.

Christians often say that to know the Lord it is sufficient to have only the Bible. In a sense, I agree with this. However, in another sense — I say this carefully — I do not agree fully. Although we have the Bible, we still need a living vision. The Bible does say that Christ will be born in Bethlehem, but it does not say where, on what street, or in which house. The living star led the wise men to the city of Bethlehem and also to the exact street and the house where the child was. At that place, the star stopped (v. 9). The magi did not need to knock on any doors; they knew where Jesus was. This proves that we all need a clear, up-to-date vision that leads us directly to the place where Jesus is.

The magi not only found Christ; they also worshipped Him (v. 11). Among the Israelites, no one was allowed to receive worship from others. That was considered an insult to God, a blasphemy against Him. According to them, only God was worthy of people's worship. But the wise men worshipped a child, and that child was God. Isaiah 9:6 says, "Unto us a child is born . . . and his name shall be called . . . The mighty God." The child found by the magi was called the mighty God. The wise men worshipped Him and they offered to Him gold, frankincense, and myrrh (v. 11).

We need to know the meaning of the gold, the frankincense, and the myrrh. In the typology of the Bible, gold signifies the divine nature. This indicates that the child Jesus had the divine nature. He was divine. Frankincense signifies the fragrance of resurrection. According to our naturally religious mentality, the resurrection of Jesus came only after His death. However, before He died, Jesus told Mary and Martha that He was the resurrection and the life (John 11:25). Thus, even before He died, He was the resurrection. The life Christ lived on this earth was a life of resurrection. Luke 2:52 tells us that even in His childhood He found favor with God and man. That was not something natural; it was the life of resurrection. The record in Luke 2 reveals that the child was an extraordinary child. He was a unique child because He was a child in resurrection. In His entire human life and living there was the fragrance, the sweetness of resurrection. Death could not hold Him or even touch Him. Not only was He the life — He was resurrection.

Myrrh signifies death and also the fragrance of death. Among the human race, death has no fragrance; however, with Jesus there was the fragrance of death.

When the wise men presented the gold, the frankincense, and the myrrh, I do not believe they knew the meaning of the gifts they offered. They surely offered their gifts under the inspiration of the Holy Spirit. They presented gold, frankincense, and myrrh, signifying that the child Jesus had the divine nature; that His life would be a life of resurrection, full of the fragrance of frankincense; and that His life would be full of the fragrance of death.

When Jesus was twelve years old, He went to Jerusalem with His parents (Luke 2:42). Because He was burdened to see what people were doing in His Father's house, the temple, He stayed in Jerusalem after the feast (Luke 2:43). Mary and Joseph did not understand Him. They looked for Him and eventually found Him in the temple (vv. 44-48). In a sense, Mary rebuked Him. If I had been Jesus, I would have rebuked her. I would have fought back and said, "Don't you know what I'm doing here? Why do you come to bother Me?" If we read Luke's account, we shall see that Jesus did say something to them. He said, "Did you not know that I must be in the things of My Father?" (v. 49). After He said this, He went along with them and returned with them to Nazareth. That was a real killing to Him. His intention was killed, and in that killing we can smell myrrh. That was not the fragrance of frankincense; it was the sweet aroma of myrrh.

If we read the four Gospels, the biographies of Jesus, we shall see that in the life of Jesus the gold, the frankincense, and the myrrh were very prevalent. He was always living the resurrection life, and He was constantly under the killing of the cross. He did not wait until thirty-three and a half years had passed before He went to the cross to be crucified. Throughout His whole life He was continually being crucified on the cross. Thus, He had not only the fragrance of resurrection, but also the sweet myrrh of the cross.

The wise men found the kingly child Jesus in Bethlehem, which Micah 5:2 tells us is "little among the thousands of Judah." He was born in such a humble town in such lowly circumstances. However, due to the vision that came through the star, the wise men paid their full respect to the kingly child, not caring about the place. Therefore, they offered to Him the three precious items. Each of these items signifies some precious element of the Lord Jesus' nature and life. In nearly every page of the four Gospels, we see the preciousness of the Lord's humanity, the fragrance of His resurrection life, and the sweet aroma of His sacrificial death. Even in the early days, soon after the Lord's birth, the wise men did such an appropriate thing. It exactly suited the Lord's nature and life. Their offering was certainly presented under the inspiration of the Holy Spirit.

It may be that these precious treasures offered by the magi provided for the Lord's trip from Judea to Egypt and from Egypt to Nazareth. The worship and offering of the wise men truly accomplished something.

(5) WARNED BY GOD TO RETURN ANOTHER WAY

After the wise men had found Christ, had worshipped Him, and had offered Him these precious treasures, they were warned by God to return another way (v. 12). This other way, not the original way, was the right way. Whenever we find Christ and meet Him, we are always told not to return to the original way. Finding Christ and meeting Him always turns us to another way.

The situation today is exactly the same. We have the Bible, and Christ is coming, but how shall we find Him? The basic principle is not with the Bible. Although the

Bible helps, the basic principle is with the living star, the heavenly vision.

Now we must see how we can have this star, how we can have this heavenly vision. The Bible tells us that the living star is Christ. It was prophesied that Christ would be the star (Num. 24:17), He came as the star (Matt. 2), and He remains as the star (Rev. 22:16). He is shining. How can we have Christ as the star? According to 2 Peter 1:19, the star is associated with the Bible. Peter tells us to take heed to the "prophetic word made more firm." If we take heed to this sure word, something within us will dawn, and the daystar will arise in our hearts. To take heed to the sure word is to pay attention to the living Word. It is not just to read the Word; it is to enter into the Word until something arises within us. We may call this the dawn or the daystar. In 2 Peter 1:19 the daystar is actually the morning star. The word in Greek is *phosphoros*, a light-bearing substance. A piece of phosphorus can shine in darkness. Christ is the real phosphorus shining in today's darkness. However, the Word cannot shine over you unless you take heed to it. You must take heed until something begins to shine within you. That shining will become the phosphorus in your heart. Then you will have the daystar. You will be like the wise men, and something from the heavens will shine over you.

Christ is the star. The Bible says that the followers of Christ are stars also. Revelation 1:20 tells us that all the leading ones in the proper church life are stars. They are stars because they are the shining ones. Daniel 12:3 says that the righteous will shine like stars. Those who turn others to righteousness, who turn them from the wrong way to the right way, will shine like stars.

Today there are only two ways to have the star shining over you. According to the first way, you must come to the sure Word and open up your whole being to the Word — your mouth, your eyes, your mind, your spirit, and your heart — until something rises up in you and shines over you. That is Christ. The second way is to come to the shining saints, the followers of Christ. If you come to them, you will receive light. You also will receive some leading, for they will lead you to the place where Christ is.

Both ways of having the star are linked to the Spirit and the church. Immediately after Revelation 22:16, which says that the Lord Jesus is the morning star, the following verse says, "And the Spirit and the bride say . . . ." This proves that, as the morning star, the Lord Jesus is linked to the Spirit and to the church, which is the Bride. Revelation 3:1 says that the Lord Jesus has the seven Spirits and the seven stars, and Revelation 1:20 says that the seven stars are the angels of the churches. These verses show that the stars are linked not only to the Spirit, but also to the churches. If we would have the living star or the living stars, we need the Spirit and the church. By the Spirit and through the church, it will be easy to have the heavenly vision so that we may find Christ and render our appreciation to Him.

b. Fleeing to Egypt

Christ was found in Bethlehem. This discovery of Christ created trouble. God used this trouble to bring the young child out of Bethlehem to Egypt (Matt. 2:13-18). Hosea 11:1 prophesied that Jesus would be called out of Egypt. Without the trouble that occurred after Jesus was found in Bethlehem, there would have been no occasion for Him to flee to Egypt.

This is very meaningful. The wise men made a great mistake, but their mistake offered God the opportunity to fulfill His prophecy. But do not make mistakes purposely. That will not work. Try your best to do things right. Nevertheless, no matter how hard you try to be right, eventually you will make as big a mistake as the wise men did. Never say, "Let us do evil, that good may come." If you do evil, good will not come. However, if you try to be right but still make a mistake, that mistake will offer God a chance to fulfill His purpose.

Because Joseph fled with Mary and Jesus into Egypt, the young child Jesus escaped the first martyrdom, the martyrdom caused by the mistake of the wise men. Satan is always busy, waiting for an opportunity to cause martyrdom. However, God is sovereign over all, even over Satan, to preserve His dear ones from the enemy's wiles. By God's sovereignty the young Jesus was preserved.

c. Raised in Nazareth

At this point I need to present a little history. Although you know the story, you may still need more light. Mary conceived a child in Nazareth (Luke 1:26-27, 31). According to the prophecy in Micah 5:2, however, Christ had to be born in Bethlehem. Under God's sovereign arrangement, Caesar Augustus ordered the first census of the Roman Empire (Luke 2:1-7). This forced all the people to return to their native places. Mary and Joseph were forced to return to Bethlehem, their home town. Immediately after they arrived in Bethlehem, the child Jesus was born. The mistake of the magi aroused the hatred and jealousy of King Herod, who was angered that a kingly child had been born. Then Joseph received guidance in a dream to take the child to Egypt (Matt. 2:13-15). This enabled God to fulfill the prophecy of Hosea 11:1. After Herod had died, Joseph received word in another dream to return to the Holy Land (vv. 19-20). When Joseph had returned and had learned that Archelaus, the son of Herod, was in power, he was afraid to remain in the territory around Bethlehem. Therefore, he went to Nazareth, where Jesus was raised (vv. 21-23). For this reason Jesus was called Jesus of Nazareth.

What does all this mean? It means that when Jesus was born into the human race, He appeared in a way that was somewhat hidden, in a way that was not open or evident. Sometimes I have even used the word "sneaky" to describe it. Everyone called Him Jesus of Nazareth, for He was a Nazarene. But the Bible said that Christ would be born in Bethlehem. The hidden way of Christ's birth bothered all the religious people. When Philip met Jesus, he realized that Jesus was the Messiah. Then Philip went to Nathanael and told him that he had met the Messiah and that He was the son of Joseph, a man of Nazareth. Immediately Nathanael said, "Can anything good come out of Nazareth?" (John 1:45-46). Did Philip give Nathanael the wrong information? It is difficult to say. Philip only knew that Jesus was the son of Joseph and that He was a Nazarene. Although Jesus was from Nazareth and was a Nazarene, He had not been born in Nazareth, but in Bethlehem. Nathanael was troubled. However, Philip did not argue with him; he simply said, "Come and see" (John 1:46).

On another occasion, Nicodemus, who had come to know Jesus, tried to argue with the Pharisees concerning Him. The Pharisees asked him, "Are you also from Galilee?" (John 7:52). Galilee was a Gentile region, and the Bible says "Galilee of the nations" (Matt. 4:15). The Pharisees seemed to say to Nicodemus, "Are you from Galilee? We know that Jesus came out of Galilee. But out of Galilee there comes no prophet." Apparently, Jesus was from Galilee, from Nazareth; actually, He was born in Bethlehem. That was His somewhat hidden and secret way of appearing to people.

The principle is the same today. I refer you to the type of the tabernacle. The tabernacle was covered with rough, tough badgers' skin; outside, it did not appear to be very attractive. Inside, however, was fine linen, gold, and precious stones. The spiritual principle of the church is the same. Do not look at the church from the outside. You need to come inside the church. I am sure that if the Apostle Paul would come to visit you, you would be surprised. You would ask, "Are you Brother Paul? I thought that the Apostle Paul would be like a shining angel. But what are you? You are just a small man without a comely appearance."

We should never make a display of ourselves; neither should we ever know others according to the outward appearance. We must know them according to the inward spirit. In appearance, Jesus was a Nazarene, but within Him there was gold, frankincense, and myrrh. Within Him there was the glory of God. Second Corinthians 5:16 says that we should not know Christ or any man after the outward appearance. Rather, we must discern the inward reality of Christ.

We must keep this principle today. In order to find Christ, we must have the shining star. We must not go according to the outward appearance, but according to what is within. If you would know the church or the saints, do not be bothered by the outward appearance. Do not give any value to outward things, such as huge cathedrals, large church buildings, or pipe organs. Forget all that. Jesus had nothing outstanding outwardly. He was a little Nazarene, One who grew up in a province that was called "Galilee of the nations" and who was raised in a city despised by people — "Can anything good come out of Nazareth?" But if you "come and see" and get into Him, you will appreciate Him and be caught by Him. Likewise, you need to come into the church and stay with the church for some time. If you do, you will find something precious. The same is true with the seeking saints. The more they seek the Lord, the more they hide their experiences of spiritual things. You need to go to them and stay with them. Then you will get into them and find the riches that are within them. You will see the frankincense, the myrrh, and many other precious treasures. Then you will be attracted and caught. This is the way to find Christ and to appreciate all He is and all His precious items, the gold, the frankincense, and the myrrh.

Matthew 2:23 says, "He shall be called a Nazarene." Some have guessed this word Nazarene refers to "Nazarite" in Numbers 6:2. Others have guessed that it refers to the Hebrew word for branch, *netzer,* in Isaiah 11:1. But I do not think that we have to guess that much. We know that in appearance Jesus was a Nazarene. This was spoken by the prophets.

LIFE-STUDY OF MATTHEW

MESSAGE EIGHT

THE KING'S ANOINTING

(1)

Matthew 3:1—4:11 is concerned with the King's anointing. This section of the Gospel of Matthew is in three parts: the King recommended (3:1-12), the King anointed (3:13-17), and the King tested (4:1-11). In this message and in the message following we shall deal with the recommendation of the King.

I. RECOMMENDED

A. The Recommender

Matthew chapter three covers the recommendation and the anointing of the King. In this chapter firstly the recommender of the King, John the Baptist, is himself recommended. Matthew 3:1 says, "Now in those days John the Baptist came."

1. Born a Priest

John the Baptist was born a priest (Luke 1:5, 13). In the life-study of Genesis we saw that the birthright included three items: the double portion of the land, the priesthood, and the kingship. Reuben, Jacob's firstborn, should have received all three items of the birthright. However, due to his defilement, he lost the birthright. As a result, the double portion of the land went to Joseph, the priesthood, to Levi, and the kingship, to Judah. The main function of the priesthood is to bring the people to God, and the main function of the kingship is to bring God to the people. According to the Bible, the priests brought others

to God so that they might obtain God's blessing. This is the
priestly service. The kings were those who represented God
and brought God to others. Thus, the kingship is the ministry that brings God to others so that they may gain Him.
Through this traffic of coming and going, man and God,
God and man, have real fellowship, true communication.
Eventually, man and God become one. This is the ministry
of the priesthood and the kingship.

The first ministry in the Old Testament was the
priesthood. Following the priesthood there was the kingship. All the books prior to 1 Samuel were on the priesthood. But beginning with 1 Samuel the second section of
the Old Testament is on the kingship. In the book of
1 Samuel, Samuel represents the priesthood and David
represents the kingship. Samuel, the priest, introduced
David, the king. The priesthood introduces the kingship. It
is the same in the church life today. If we are genuine
priests, then we shall also become kings, for the priesthood always introduces the kingship. First we are priests
bringing others into the presence of God. Then we become
kings bringing God to them.

Every true evangelist is a king. If you are not a king,
you are not qualified to preach the gospel. In 28:18 and 19
the Lord Jesus, the King of the kingdom, said, "All
authority has been given unto me in heaven and on earth.
Go therefore and disciple all the nations." Here the Lord
told the disciples to go with His authority. Those who go
with this authority are kings in the kingdom of heaven.
Without doubt He shares this authority with us. Therefore, we must go and disciple the nations, that is, preach
the gospel to subdue the rebellious ones. As we go to preach
the gospel, we must be kings.

Many Christians do not know God's secret in His
economy. When you are burdened to preach the gospel,
you must first carry out the function of the priesthood. In
order to preach the gospel you must first go to God as a
priest and bring others to Him. Through the priesthood
you will be authorized and anointed, and then you will

come out of God's presence to be a king. The proper preaching of the gospel is the issuing of a kingly edict. It is the utterance of a kingly command. Consider Peter's preaching on the day of Pentecost. Although he was a young Galilean fisherman, he nonetheless was a king. Every proper evangelist must be a king.

We have seen that the priest introduces the king. The first occurrence of this was Samuel's introduction of King David. In Matthew chapter three we see another Samuel, John the Baptist, who was born a priest of the tribe of Levi. Matthew 3 testifies to the consistency of the Bible, for here we see one from the priestly tribe, the tribe of Levi, recommending One from the kingly tribe, the tribe of Judah. In Matthew 3 John appeared as Samuel and Jesus appeared as David. There in the wilderness John was bringing people to God. Hence, he was a genuine priest. As he was bringing others to God, the King came, and John introduced Him. This King brought God to man. John brought others to God, and Jesus brought God to them.

As sinners we came to God through John's ministry. By repentance we came into God's presence. That was the ministry of the priesthood, the ministry of John the Baptist. We all have come into the presence of God through John. It was John who brought us back to God. Then the new King David, Jesus Christ, brought God to us. Through John's ministry of repentance and Jesus' ministry of imparting life, we have all been made priests and kings. Today we are the continuation both of the priest, John the Baptist, and of the King, Jesus Christ. If you are a proper Christian, then you are firstly today's John and secondly today's Jesus. Young people, as you go to the campuses, you must be real priests. You need to say, "Lord, have mercy on these people. O Lord, remember all these young people. I bring them to You." This is the priesthood, the ministry of John the Baptist. After you bring others to God, immediately, in a sense, you will become Christ bringing God to them so that they may gain God. This is today's priesthood and kingship.

2. Forsaking the Outward Position of the Priest

Although John the Baptist was born a priest, he forsook the outward position of the priest. By the outward position of his birth he was not a real priest, but a priest in figure, a priest in shadow. In 3:1 John came preaching in the wilderness as the true priest. John the Baptist's preaching was the initiation of God's New Testament economy. He did his preaching not in the holy temple within the holy city, where the religious and cultured people worshipped God according to their scriptural ordinances, but in the wilderness, in a "wild" way, not keeping any old regulations. This indicates that the old way of the worship of God according to the Old Testament was repudiated and that a new way was about to be brought in. The wilderness here indicates that the new way of God's New Testament economy is contrary to religion and culture. It also indicates that nothing old was left and that something new was about to be built up.

The dispensation of law was terminated by the coming of John the Baptist (11:13; Luke 16:16). Following the baptism of John, the preaching of the gospel of peace began (Acts 10:36-37). The preaching of John was the beginning of the gospel (Mark 1:1-5). Hence, the dispensation of grace began with John.

Neither John, the new priest, nor Jesus, the new King, was in the old way. According to the old way, the priests stayed in the holy temple in the holy city, wore the priestly garments, ate the priestly food, and observed the priestly rituals. But with the coming of John the Baptist, all that was terminated. That was not the reality; it was a shadow. Now with John the Baptist, the genuine priest, reality came. As the real priest, John came to bring the people back to God. That was his ministry.

3. Living in a Way Contrary to Religion and Culture

John fulfilled his ministry by living in a way that was absolutely contrary to religion and culture and outside both of them. Verse 4 says, "Now John himself had his garment of camel's hair and a leather girdle about his loins; and his food was locusts and wild honey." According to the regulations of the law, John, who was born a priest, should have worn the priestly garment, which was made mainly of fine linen (Exo. 28:4, 40-41; Lev. 6:10; Ezek. 44:17-18); and he should have eaten the priestly food, which was composed mainly of fine flour and the meat of the sacrifices offered to God by His people (Lev. 2:1-3; 6:6-18, 25-26; 7:31-34). However, John did altogether otherwise. He wore a garment of camel's hair and a leather girdle, and he ate locusts and wild honey. All these things are uncivilized, uncultured, and not according to the religious regulations. For a priestly person to wear camel's hair was an especially drastic blow to the religious mind, for the camel was considered unclean under the Levitical regulations (Lev. 11:4). In addition, John did not live in a civilized place, but in the wilderness (Luke 3:2). All this indicates that he had altogether abandoned the Old Testament dispensation, which had fallen into a kind of religion mixed with human culture. His intention was to introduce God's New Testament economy, which is constituted solely of Christ and the Spirit of Life.

We have seen that during John's time being a priest was a matter of religion, of wearing priestly robes, eating priestly food, and dwelling in a priestly building. When anyone conducted himself as a priest, everyone thought of him as a religious person, a person in religion. But here in Matthew 3 we see a real priest. Instead of staying in the priestly building, he went out to the wilderness, to a wild place where there was neither religion nor culture. There in the wilderness he lived in a "wild" way, eating locusts and wild honey. His honey was not the cultured honey processed and sold in stores today. It was wild honey. John was a real priest living in such a "wild" way. However, if you try to copy him, you will be false.

John was truly outside religion and culture. He not only ate wild things, but he also wore camel's hair. Notice that the Bible does not say that he wore camel's fur, which would have been somewhat orderly, but camel's hair, which certainly must have been messy. Furthermore, his leather girdle was probably not very refined. John was truly "wild." Nevertheless this real priest was the recommender of the King.

From the time of John the Baptist until today, a great many people have been brought back to God through the ministry of John. Whenever we tell others to repent, we should remember John the Baptist.

The ministry of John the Baptist was outside both religion and culture. When John was born, in Jerusalem there were two main things — Hebrew religion and Greco-Roman culture. John, however, did not stay in Jerusalem where his parents undoubtedly lived. He left Jerusalem and went out to the wilderness where there was neither religion nor culture, but where everything was natural. John ministered there in the wilderness bringing others to God and introducing the King, the One who represents God, to them. This was a strong indication that, during John's time, the age was changed from the old dispensation to the new dispensation, from the dispensation of shadows and figures to the dispensation of reality. Those priests who wore the priestly robes, ate the priestly food, and stayed in the priestly building burning the incense and carrying out the priestly functions never brought anyone to God. But this "wild," unreligious, uncultured John brought hundreds to Him. And he also introduced the King to them. This King was the One who brought God to repentant people.

When this King was introduced to people and they were truly brought back to God, the kingdom was present immediately. The King with the people is the kingdom. The kingdom was there because both the King and the people were there. The New Testament begins with the genuine priesthood introducing the genuine kingship. The real priest introduced the real King. This introduction ushers in the kingdom.

John's message was, "Repent, for the kingdom of the heavens has drawn near" (v. 2). People had to repent because the kingdom was coming and because the King was there. We also need to repent that the King may gain us and that we may be His people. After we repent, the King gains us, and we gain Him. Through the King's gaining us and our gaining Him, we and the King become the kingdom. The kingdom immediately follows the King. If you receive the King and if He takes you as His people, the kingdom is immediately present. Why has the kingdom not yet come? Because you have not received the King, and the King has not yet gained you. Because you are still far away from Him, the King has not been able to gain you. Thus, the kingdom is not yet here. Rather, it is off somewhere waiting for your repentance. If you repent, the King will gain you, you will gain the King, and the kingdom will be here.

Many Christians who are preaching the gospel today do not know the divine principles in God's economy. If we would be real evangelists, real preachers of the gospel, we must firstly be John the Baptist. This means that we must be priests, not formal priests, priests in shadow, but geniune priests, priests in reality. After we become such priests, we must also be Jesus Christ. This means that we must be the King who brings God to others. When we go to God praying for others, we are priests bringing them to God. But when we come out of God's presence and go to the people, we are kings bringing God to them. If we do this, they will repent to the King, the King will gain them, and the kingdom will be present.

The proper church life today is the kingdom. We all have repented, the King has gained us, and we have received Him. Now we are one with the King, and the kingdom is here with us. Hallelujah, the kingdom is here right now! All this depends upon the recommender.

My burden in this message is to emphasize the matter of the recommender. Are you today's recommender of Christ? If you are, then you must be clear whether or not

you are still in religion and culture. We must all be in the
wilderness, in an environment that is "wild," not in an
environment that is religious or cultured. The proper
environment is outside religion and culture, but it is full of
the presence of God.

When John was there in the wilderness, he was a great
magnet drawing large numbers to himself. For this reason,
verse 5 says, "Then Jerusalem, and all Judea, and all the
district of the Jordan went out to him." Because of his
drawing power, many came to John the Baptist. I hope the
young people who go to the campuses will stand there as
magnets. If you are such a magnet, others will flock to you.
First you will be the priests appointed by God to bring
others into His presence. Then you will be able to introduce the heavenly King to them. At that time, you will not
only introduce the King to others; you will actually be the
King. Thus, you will give a command to others, and many
will turn to Christ. In this way Christ will gain the people,
and they will gain Him. Then, immediately, the kingdom
will appear on the campuses. This is the proper way to
carry out the preaching of the gospel.

B. The Place of Recommendation

We have seen that the place of recommendation was
neither in the holy city nor in the holy temple, but in the
wilderness. Verse 1 says that John the Baptist came
preaching in the wilderness, and verse 3 says, "For this is
he who was spoken of through Isaiah the prophet, saying, A
voice of one crying in the wilderness." It was according to
prophecy that John the Baptist began his ministry in the
wilderness. This indicates that the introduction of God's
New Testament economy by John was not accidental, but
planned and foretold by God through Isaiah the prophet.
This implies that God intended His New Testament
economy to begin in an absolutely new way.

If you trace the history of the past few centuries, you
will see that every prevailing revival took place in some
kind of "wilderness." When John Wesley and George

Whitefield were raised up as evangelists two centuries ago, they mainly did their preaching on the street corners. According to his biography, George Whitefield often preached on the foothills in the wilderness. However, at that time, the Church of England had regulations forbidding the expounding of the Holy Word outside the "sanctuary." According to these regulations, anyone who preached or taught from the Bible had to do so in the "sanctuary." Nevertheless, God raised up George Whitefield and John Wesley to conduct their preaching outside the "sanctuary." The principle must be the same today. But this does not mean that we should copy John the Baptist in an outward way. It means that we should not take either the religious way or the cultural way. Rather, we must take the way that is full of the presence of God. We should not be in the holy city or in the holy temple, but in a place outside religion and culture, yet in a place full of the presence of God. I hope the young people will bring this matter to the Lord and pray, "Lord, make us today's John the Baptist. Lord, take us into the wilderness and show us how to be genuine priests to bring others to You and how to introduce You to them as their King."

The Gospel of Matthew is absolutely different from the Gospel of John. The Gospel of John is a book of life, whereas the Gospel of Matthew is a book of the kingdom. In John Jesus is life, but in Matthew He is the King. According to the book of Matthew, the Jesus we are to receive is the King. As we consider the Gospel of Matthew, we must be thoroughly and deeply impressed that we are now in the kingdom. Everything written in this book is related to the kingdom. Therefore, we must look into this book from the angle of the kingdom, viewing every chapter and even every verse from the perspective of the kingdom.

The repentance called for in chapter three is for the kingdom. You must repent because you are not in the kingdom, because you are not under God's authority. You must repent because you have not yet submitted to the authority of Christ or come under His kingship. Although you may not feel that you are sinful, as long as you are not in the kingdom, you are a rebellious one. As long as you have nothing to do with the kingship of Christ, you are in rebellion and must repent. Repent of not being in the kingdom! The genuine Christians of today are saved, yet many of them still are not in the kingdom. Thus, even these Christians must repent. As long as you are not under the kingship of Christ, you must repent. If you are not actually in the kingdom of the heavens, not under the heavenly ruling, you must repent. It does not matter how spiritual, holy, or good you are. The only thing that matters is whether or not you are under the heavenly ruling. If you are not, it means that you are not in the kingdom and that you must repent. If you are not in the kingdom, you are in rebellion. You consider yourself scriptural, fundamental, and holy, but in actuality you are rebellious. Even your spirituality is a form of rebellion against the kingship of Christ. You care for your spirituality, not for the kingship of Christ. This indicates that you are in rebellion, that you are not in the kingdom. Repent of your rebellion! Repent of not being in the kingdom and of not being under the kingship and authority of Christ! This is the basic thought of the Gospel of Matthew.

Do not think that Matthew is only for unbelievers, outsiders, or Gentiles. Many of us have never heard the Gospel of Matthew. I do not know what kind of gospel you have heard, but I do know that you need to hear the Gospel of Matthew, the Gospel of the kingdom that requires you to repent of not being under the kingship of Christ. We all must repent to the Lord and say, "Lord, forgive me. Even today I am still in rebellion. I am not under Your Lordship, Your authority, Your heavenly ruling. Lord, I confess that I have been ruled only by myself. Lord, grant me a true repentance for my rebellion, for my not being under Your authority." We all need to repent. Praise the Lord that John the Baptist and this ministry of the priesthood are still with us! On the one hand, this priesthood brings us to God; on the other hand, it recommends the heavenly King who brings God to us. When we receive this King, He gains us, and the kingdom is here. This is the Gospel of Matthew.

LIFE-STUDY OF MATTHEW

MESSAGE NINE

THE KING'S ANOINTING

(2)

In both the Old Testament and the New Testament there are two basic ministries that constitute the kingdom of God: the priesthood and the kingship. In the Bible there is also a third type of ministry, the ministry of the prophet. However, the prophetic ministry is not a basic ministry; rather, it is a supplement to the priesthood and the kingship. When either the priesthood or the kingship is weak, the prophets come in to strengthen it. According to the Old Testament, the priesthood was with the tribe of Levi. Eventually, the Old Testament priesthood consummated in John the Baptist, a descendant of this tribe. In like manner, Jesus was the consummation of the Old Testament kingship, which was with the tribe of Judah. Jesus came as a descendant of Judah to be the consummation of the kingship. On the one hand, John the Baptist and Jesus Christ terminated the Old Testament priesthood and kingship; on the other hand, they germinated the New Testament priesthood and kingship. In other words, they terminated the Old Testament dispensation and began the New Testament dispensation.

When the priesthood brings people to God and the kingship brings God to the people, there is the heavenly reign, the heavenly rule. This heavenly reign is the kingdom, which today is the proper church life. Today's church life is the kingdom with the priesthood and the kingship. This church life will continue until the millennium. In the millennial kingdom there will still be the priesthood and the kingship. On the one hand, we, the overcomers, shall be priests and, on the other hand, we shall be kings. Thus, in the millennial kingdom, the priesthood and the kingship will be even stronger than they are today. They will maintain God's kingdom on earth so that the King may gain the people and that the people may gain the King. After the millennium there will be no further need of the priesthood. In eternity there will be only the kingship because in the new heaven and new earth with the New Jerusalem everyone will be in the presence of God. At that time God will be with man. Thus, there will no longer be the need for the priesthood to bring the people to God. In eternity God's presence will eliminate the priesthood. Nevertheless, the kingship will remain so that those in the New Jerusalem may reign over the nations surrounding the city. This is a summary of the Bible in the light of the priesthood and the kingship.

In the previous message we considered the recommender, John the Baptist. In this message we shall consider John's message of recommendation.

C. The Message of Recommendation

1. Repentance for the Kingdom of the Heavens

John's message of recommendation is short, but it is crucial and all-inclusive. Matthew 3:2 says, "Repent, for the kingdom of the heavens has drawn near." The first significant word in this verse is the word "repent." John began his ministry with this word. To repent is to have a change of mind issuing in regret, to have a turn in purpose. In Greek the word translated repent means to have a change of mind. To repent is to have a change in our thinking, our philosophy, our logic. The life of fallen man is absolutely according to his thinking. Everything he is and does is according to his mind. When you were a fallen one, you were directed by your mind. Your mentality, logic, and philosophy governed your way of life. Before we were saved, we all were under the direction of our fallen mentality. We were far away from God, and our life was in direct opposition to His will. Under the influence of our fallen mentality, we went farther and farther astray from God. But one day we heard the preaching of the gospel telling us to repent, to have a turn in our thinking, philosophy, and logic.

This was just my experience when I was saved. I was like a young horse running in my own direction. Actually I was not taking my direction, but the Devil's direction, for the Devil was directing me through my fallen mentality, driving me far away from God. But one day I heard the call to repent — to have a change in my philosophy, to have a change in my logic and thought. Praise the Lord, I underwent a great change! I was moving in one direction, but when I heard the call to repent, I made an about-face. I believe we all have made this kind of turn, which is called conversion. When we were converted, we turned our back upon our past and turned our face to God. This is what it means to repent, to experience a change of our mind.

Every ism is a philosophy that directs one's life. Nearly every political party has an ism, and that ism is virtually a god. But we do not have an ism — we have the Lord. We have God. Formerly, we were under the direction of a certain ism, but now we are under the direction of God. Our mind has been radically changed. We used to be heading in a certain direction, but now we are heading in the opposite direction. We have had a turn in our thought, in our concept.

The second crucial word in verse 2 is kingdom. In the preaching of John the Baptist, repentance, as the opening of God's New Testament economy, was to have a turn for the kingdom of the heavens. This indicates that God's New Testament economy is focused on His kingdom. For this we should repent, change our mind, have a turn in our pursuit of life. The goal of our pursuit has been toward other things; now our pursuit must turn toward God and His kingdom, which is specifically and purposely called in Matthew the kingdom of the heavens (cf. Mark 1:15). The kingdom of the heavens, according to the context of the entire Gospel of Matthew, is different from the Messianic kingdom. The Messianic kingdom will be the restored kingdom of David (the rebuilt tabernacle of David — Acts 15:16), made up of the children of Israel, earthly and physical in nature; whereas the kingdom of the heavens is constituted of regenerated believers and is heavenly and spiritual.

In his message, John the Baptist told people to repent for the kingdom. He did not say to repent that we might go to heaven or even to obtain salvation. He said that we must repent for the kingdom. The kingdom denotes a kind of reign, rule. Before we were saved, we were not under any rule. If there had been no police force, government, or law courts to tell us what to do, we would have done whatever we liked. However, when we heard the preaching of the gospel, we turned from a condition of no rule to a condition full of rule. Thus, we are now in the kingdom. Before we were saved, we did not have a king. But after we turned to the Lord, He became our King. Now we are all under the rule of this King. With the King there is the kingship, and this kingship is the kingdom. Today we are in the kingdom of this King.

The third crucial word in verse 2 is heavens. John said to repent for the kingdom of the heavens. The term "the heavens," a Hebrew idiom, does not refer to anything plural in nature; rather, it refers to the highest heaven, which according to the Bible is the third heaven, the heaven above the heaven. This third heaven is called the heavens. The kingdom of the heavens does not denote a kingdom in the air, but a kingdom above the air, a kingdom in the heaven above the heaven, where God's throne is. In this kingdom there is the ruling, the reigning, of God Himself. Therefore, the kingdom of the heavens is the kingdom of God in the third heaven where He exercises His authority over everything created by Him. This kingdom of the heavens must come down to earth. This heavenly reign must descend to earth to be the authority over the earth.

According to John's word in verse 2, "The kingdom of the heavens has drawn near." This clearly indicates that before the coming of John the Baptist, the kingdom of the heavens was not there. Even after his appearance, during his preaching, the kingdom of the heavens was still not there; it had only drawn near. At the time the Lord started His ministry and even at the time He sent His disciples to preach, the kingdom of the heavens had still not come (4:17; 10:7). Hence, in the first parable in chapter thirteen (vv. 3-9), the parable of the seed, which indicates the Lord's preaching, the Lord did not say, "The kingdom of the heavens is like. . . . " Not until the second parable, the parable of the tares (v. 24), which indicates the establishment of the church at the day of Pentecost, did the Lord say this. The fact that Matthew 16:18 and 19 use the terms the "church" and the "kingdom of the heavens" interchangeably proves that the kingdom of the heavens came when the church was established.

When John the Baptist came, the kingdom of the heavens had only drawn near. It was approaching, arriving, but it had not yet come. This proves that in the Old Testament there was no kingdom of the heavens. Even at the time of Moses and David the kingdom of the heavens was not there. John said that the kingdom of the heavens was on its way; he did not say that it had arrived. When the Lord Jesus began His ministry, He also said, "Repent, for the kingdom of the heavens has drawn near" (4:17). This indicates that even when the Lord Jesus began His ministry, the kingdom of the heavens had still not arrived. In his message, John the Baptist told the people to repent for the kingdom of the heavens, which, at that time, was on the way. The kingdom of the heavens arrived in Jerusalem on the day of Pentecost. This means that it arrived at the very time the church came into existence. Today anyone who has a change in his philosophy and comes back to God will immediately be in the kingdom of the heavens. Hallelujah, we are in the kingdom of the heavens! We have a King and we are under His rule.

Many times the ruling of the King within us makes it unnecessary for us to be ruled by the policemen or by the law court. This inward King can put the attorneys out of a job. However, those who have not repented and come back to God are not under the King. Instead, they constantly violate the law. For this reason, a great many are summoned to the law court. But we, the kingdom people, are under the King of the kingdom of the heavens. This King has come into our being. At this very moment He is dwelling in our spirit. When He speaks to us, He mainly says one word — "no." According to my experience, His favorite word is "no." We have a ruling "no" within us. Thank the Lord for this little word, for it saves us from a great deal of trouble. The speaking of the inward "no" is the ruling of the King within. Perhaps today you have heard the King's "no" a number of times. If the kingdom people do not care for this "no," they will become backsliders. Because we are in the kingdom of the heavens, the King rules us mostly by speaking the word "no."

Now let us consider how John the Baptist was able to bring others into the kingdom. John's ministry was to bring others to God (Luke 1:16-17). John the Baptist, a genuine priest, was "filled with the Holy Spirit, even from his mother's womb" (Luke 1:15). There is no doubt that as he grew from infancy to adulthood, to the age of thirty, he was continually immersed in the Holy Spirit. Because he was flooded and saturated with the Holy Spirit, he could be bold. It is a serious matter to stand against the current of the age. To do this requires a great deal of boldness. How could John the Baptist be so bold as to stand against the Judaistic religion and the Greco-Roman culture? He was bold because for thirty years he was being immersed in the Holy Spirit. He was a person thoroughly soaked with the Spirit. Therefore, when he came out to minister, he came out in the Spirit and with power. Yes, he wore camel's hair as a sign of his repudiation of the old dispensation. But that was merely an outward sign. There was also reality within him, and that reality was the Spirit and the power. The reality in John was not just the presence of God, but also the Spirit of God.

John was immersed, saturated, and soaked with the Holy Spirit. Spontaneously this caused him to be a great magnet. He could be a magnet because he himself had been fully charged. Year after year and day after day, he was charged with the Spirit. Therefore, in his ministry, he was a powerful magnet. With John there was the Spirit and the attracting power. Therefore, as Luke 1:16 says, he turned many of the children of Israel to the Lord their God. (The Lord here is the equivalent of Jehovah.) The fact that John turned many of the Israelites to the Lord indicates that the nation of Israel had turned away from God. If they had not turned away from Him, they would not have needed John the Baptist to turn them back. Even those priests who served God in the temple by lighting the lamps and burning the incense had turned from God and were far away from Him. Elsewhere in the New Testament we are told that many priests turned to God (Acts 6:7). Thus, even the priests, the ones who served God, needed a turn to God. Therefore, John the Baptist was used to turn many to the Lord.

2. The Need for the Nature to Be Changed

John's word to the Pharisees and Sadducees who came to him reveals our need to have our nature changed. Verse 7 says, "But seeing many of the Pharisees and Sadducees coming to his baptism, he said to them, Brood of vipers, who warned you to flee from the coming wrath?" The Pharisees were the strictest religious sect of the Jews (Acts 26:5), formed about 200 B.C. They were proud of their superior sanctity of life, devotion to God, and knowledge of the Scriptures. Actually, they were degraded into pretentious conduct and hypocrisy (Matt. 23:2-33). The Sadducees were another sect in Judaism (Acts 5:17). They did not believe in the resurrection, nor in angels, nor in spirits (Matt. 22:23; Acts 23:8). Both the Pharisees and the Sadducees were denounced by John the Baptist and the Lord Jesus as a brood of vipers (3:7; 12:34; 23:33). The

Pharisees were supposed to be the orthodox ones, and the Sadducees were the ancient modernists.

In verses 8 and 9 John said, "Produce then fruit worthy of repentance. And do not presume to say within yourselves, We have Abraham for our father; for I say to you that God is able out of these stones to raise up children to Abraham." Due to the impenitence of the Jews, both this word and the word in verse 10 have been fulfilled. God has cut them off and raised up the believing Gentiles to be children unto Abraham in faith (Rom. 11:15, 19-20, 22; Gal. 3:7, 28-29). John's word in this verse clearly indicates that the kingdom of the heavens preached by him is not constituted of the children of Abraham by birth, but of the children of Abraham by faith. Thus, it is a heavenly kingdom, not the earthly kingdom of the Messiah.

The Pharisees and Sadducees were the leaders of the children of Israel. When they came to John the Baptist, with a rebuking tone he called them a brood of vipers. Vipers are poisonous snakes. John spoke this word to the Jews, to the chosen race. The children of Israel were not heathen swine. They considered the Gentiles as swine and themselves as the holy people. But when the leaders of this holy people came to John, he did not say, "Welcome. How good it is of you to come to my ministry. What an honor it is to me for you, the leaders of the children of Israel, to pay me a visit." John did not speak like the pastors in today's Christianity. He neither thanked the Pharisees and Sadducees for their visitation, nor did he address them as leaders; instead, he called them a brood of vipers. Can you believe that the children of Israel, the descendants of Abraham, the called one, could have become so evil?

John also told them not to presume to say that they had Abraham for their father, for God was able of the stones to raise up children to Abraham. John seemed to be saying, "Don't presume anything. Don't presume that you are the children of Israel with Abraham as your father. God is able to raise up children out of these stones." John's word was a strong indication and actually a prophecy of the fact that the age had changed. Because the age had changed, it was no longer a matter of the natural birth, but of the second birth, the spiritual birth. Although you might have been born a lifeless stone, God is able to make you His living child. Hallelujah, this is just what He has done to us! We need to recall our condition before we were saved. As far as life was concerned, we were lifeless stones. But as far as sin was concerned, we were filled with sin and active in sin. Praise the Lord that on the day of our repentance we believed in the Lord Jesus, and God made us His living children.

Through John's word here we see that God was prepared to forsake this brood of vipers, His chosen people of old, and to pursue another people. He was ready to forsake the children of Israel and to turn to the stones, which mainly were the Gentiles. Although the Gentiles were lifeless stones, they were destined to become the living children of God. This proves that God is truly able to make every lifeless stone a child of God.

In verse 10 John said to the Pharisees and Sadducees, "And already the axe is laid at the root of the trees; every tree therefore that does not produce good fruit is cut down and cast into the fire." John seemed to be saying, "Brood of vipers, the cutting axe is now at the root of the tree. If you are a good tree producing good fruit, you will be all right. If not, you will be cut down and cast into the fire." As we shall see, the fire spoken of in this verse is the fire in the lake of fire.

3. Christ the Baptizer

Verse 11 says, "I indeed baptize you in water unto repentance; but He Who is coming after me is mightier than I, Whose sandals I am not worthy to bear; He shall baptize you in the Holy Spirit and fire." In this verse John seemed to be saying, "I have come to baptize you with water, to terminate you, to bury you. But the One who comes after me is mightier than I. He will baptize you with the Spirit and fire. Whether He will baptize you with the

Spirit or with fire depends on whether or not you repent. If you repent, He will put you into the Spirit. But if you continue to be a brood of vipers, He will certainly baptize you in the lake of fire. This means that He will put you into the fire of hell."

According to the context, fire here is not the fire in Acts 2:3, which is related to the Holy Spirit, but the same fire as in verses 10 and 12, the fire in the lake of fire (Rev. 20:15), where the unbelievers will suffer eternal perdition. The word of John spoken here to the Pharisees and Sadducees means that if the Pharisees and Sadducees would truly repent and believe in the Lord, the Lord would baptize them in the Holy Spirit that they might have eternal life; otherwise, the Lord will baptize them in fire, putting them into the lake of fire for eternal punishment. John's baptism was only for repentance, to usher people to faith in the Lord. The Lord's baptism is either for eternal life in the Holy Spirit or for eternal perdition in fire. The Lord's baptism in the Holy Spirit began the kingdom of the heavens, bringing His believers into the kingdom of the heavens, whereas His baptism in fire will terminate the kingdom of the heavens, putting the unbelievers into the lake of fire. Hence, the Lord's baptism in the Holy Spirit, based upon His redemption, is the beginning of the kingdom of the heavens, whereas His baptism in fire, based upon His judgment, is its ending. Thus, in this verse there are three kinds of baptisms: the baptism in water, the baptism in the Holy Spirit, and the baptism in fire. The baptism in water by John introduced people to the kingdom of the heavens. The baptism in the Holy Spirit by the Lord Jesus began and established the kingdom of the heavens on the day of Pentecost and will carry it on to its consummation at the end of this age. The baptism in fire by the Lord, according to the judgment at the great white throne (Rev. 20:11-15), will conclude the kingdom of the heavens.

Some Christians, thinking that the fire in verse 11 refers to the tongues of fire on the day of Pentecost, say that the Lord will baptize believers with both the Holy Spirit and with fire. But we must take care of the context of verse 11. Notice that the word fire is found in verses 10, 11, and 12. In verse 10 the trees that do not produce good fruit are cut down and cast into the fire. Certainly this fire is the lake of fire. The fire in verse 11 must also denote the lake of fire, for it is a further explanation of the fire spoken of in the preceding verse. According to verse 12, the Lord will burn the chaff with unquenchable fire. The wheat that is gathered into the Lord's barn is those who are put into the Spirit. However, the chaff is burned with fire. Certainly this fire is also the lake of fire. Therefore, the fire that is spoken of in verses 10 through 12 refers in every case to the same fire, the fire of the lake of fire. John seemed to be saying to the Jewish leaders, "You Pharisees and Sadducees may be able to deceive me, but you cannot deceive Him. If you are truly repentant, He will put you into the Spirit. But if you remain in your evil, He will put you into fire." This is the correct understanding of these verses.

Verse 12 says, "Whose winnowing fork is in His hand, and He will thoroughly cleanse His threshing floor and will gather His wheat into His barn, but He will burn the chaff with unquenchable fire." Those typified by the wheat have life within. The Lord will baptize them in the Holy Spirit and gather them into His barn in heaven by rapture. Those typified by the chaff, like the tares in 13:24-30, are without life. The Lord will baptize them in fire, putting them into the lake of fire. Chaff here refers to the unrepentant Jews, whereas the tares in chapter thirteen refer to the nominal Christians. The eternal destiny of both will be the same — perdition in the lake of fire (13:40-42).

Jesus the King exercises two kinds of baptism: the baptism in the Spirit and the baptism in fire. The baptism in the Spirit began the kingdom of the heavens, and the baptism in fire will end it. The beginning of the kingdom of the heavens was on the day of Pentecost. On that day Jesus the King baptized the believers into the Holy Spirit. By that baptism in the Spirit, the kingdom of the heavens began. The kingdom of the heavens will end with the judgment at the great white throne. At that time the unbelievers will be judged and cast into the lake of fire. That will be the baptism in fire. This fire baptism will terminate the kingdom of the heavens.

The baptism in water practiced by John was preliminary to the kingdom of the heavens. It was a preparation for the coming of the kingdom of the heavens. Many nominal Christians have been baptized in water. But whether they participate in the baptism in the Spirit or suffer the baptism in fire depends on whether or not they repent. If they truly repent, the Lord Jesus will put them into the Spirit. If not, the Lord Jesus as the Judge on the great white throne will cast them into the lake of fire. Therefore, in the Bible there are three kinds of baptisms: the water baptism, the Spirit baptism, and the fire baptism. The water baptism of John was a preparation for the kingdom to come, the Spirit baptism was the beginning of the kingdom, and the fire baptism will be the termination of the kingdom. We should not continue to be a brood of vipers. Neither should we be the chaff in chapter three nor the tares in chapter thirteen. Rather, we must become wheat, the living children of God. In order to become the children of God, you must be baptized through water into the Spirit. John 3:5 says that you must be born of water and of the Spirit. Firstly, we are baptized through water; then we are baptized in the Spirit. In this way we are regenerated. Therefore, we have the two kinds of positive baptism, the baptism in water and the baptism in the Spirit. But we want nothing to do with the baptism in fire.

D. The Way of Recommendation

We have covered the recommender and the message of recommendation. Now we must consider the way of recommendation.

1. To Baptize People in Water

The first aspect of John's way of recommendation was to baptize people in water. Verses 5 and 6 reveal that many were baptized by him in the Jordan River, confessing their sins. To baptize people is to immerse them, to bury them in water, signifying death. John the Baptist did this to indicate that anyone who repents is good for nothing but burial. This also signifies the termination of the old person, that a new beginning may be realized in resurrection, to be brought in by Christ as the life-giver. Hence, following John's ministry, Christ came. John's baptism not only terminated those who repented, but also ushered them to Christ for life. Baptism in the Bible implies death and resurrection. To be baptized into the water is to be put into death and buried. To be raised up from the water means to be resurrected from death.

It was in the Jordan River that twelve stones representing the twelve tribes of Israel were buried and from it that another twelve stones representing the twelve tribes of Israel were resurrected and brought up (Josh. 4:1-18). Hence, to baptize people in the Jordan River implied the burial of their old being and the resurrection of the new. Just as crossing the Jordan River ushered the children of Israel into the good land, so to be baptized brings people into Christ, the reality of the good land.

Whenever anyone repented in the presence of John the Baptist, John put him into the water. According to the New Testament, to immerse someone in water firstly meant to bury him, and secondly it meant to raise him up. Thus, on the negative side, baptism signifies death and burial; on the positive side it signifies resurrection. In his message of recommendation, John indicated that God would raise up living children out of dead stones. By baptizing the repentant ones, John indicated that they and all their past had to be terminated and buried. Burial, however, was not the end, because burial always brings in resurrection. Thus, on the one hand, burial is termination, but on the other hand, it is also germination. Those whom John terminated in baptism were to be resurrected, not in him, but in the One who was to come after him. John's baptism was an indicator that One was coming to raise up the dead.

Baptism means that our natural being and all of our past must be terminated. Our being and our past are only good for burial. Therefore, as John, the genuine priest, was bringing others to God and introducing the King to them, he terminated and buried everyone who came to him in repentance, indicating thereby that those who were buried by him would be raised up by the resurrected One. This is the way of recommendation, the true way to bring the repentant ones to the King who would raise them up.

In the New Testament there are two ministries: the ministry of John and the ministry of the Lord Jesus. John's ministry is to bring others to God by terminating and burying them. These terminated and buried ones need the resurrection that only Christ can afford. Hence, Christ came after John to minister life to the dead and buried ones. This is the reason we need to be reborn, to be baptized in water and in the Spirit. To be baptized in water is to have our natural life and our past terminated. To be baptized in the Spirit is to have a new start by being germinated with the divine life. This germination is only possible through Christ as the life-giving Spirit.

Anyone who is brought to God must be terminated in the presence of God. In a sense, it is wonderful to be brought into the presence of God. But in another sense it means that you must be terminated. If you are not terminated, you will be killed. Hence, to be brought into the presence of God is both wonderful and serious, for it means that we shall either be terminated or killed. The two sons of Aaron, Nadab and Abihu, came into the presence of God, but they were killed by fire (Lev. 10:1-2). If we are willing to be terminated in the presence of God, it means that we are ready to be germinated, to be resurrected, to have a new beginning. This termination is the genuine way of recommendation. It is the way of preparation to bring us into the presence of the King so that the King may be brought to us to give us a new start in resurrection. In Matthew chapter three we have both a strong termination and a prevailing germination. Through this termination and germination, the King gains a people, and the people receive the King.

2. To Prepare People to Receive Christ

Verse 3 says, "For this is he who was spoken of through Isaiah the prophet, saying, A voice of one crying in the wilderness, Prepare the way of the Lord, make His paths straight." This verse reveals that John the Baptist was one who prepared the way of the Lord and made His paths straight. To prepare the way of the Lord and to make His paths straight is to change people's minds, to turn their minds toward the Lord and make their hearts right, to cause every part and avenue of their heart to be straightened by the Lord through repentance for the kingdom of the heavens (Luke 1:16-17). John the Baptist prepared the way and straightened the paths. This indicates that the way was rough, full of hills and valleys. In some places it was very low, and in others it was very high. But John came and paved the way, leveling the hills, filling the gaps, and making the way smooth and flat. John also straightened the paths, which were full of curves. The fact that John paved the way and straightened the paths means that His ministry dealt with the mind and the heart.

Consider your past before you were saved. Did you not have a rough way within you? Certainly the way in your mind was filled with many hills and valleys. Before I was saved, my mind was filled with ups and downs. Nothing was flat. Moreover, in the lanes of your thought, emotion, will, and desire, there were many curves. One day you said your wife was an angel; the next day you said she was a devil. This indicates that your emotion was full of curves. Before you repented, all the paths within you were curved; nothing was straight.

When John the Baptist came, he commanded the people to repent. Genuine repentance prepares the way and straightens the paths. Before I repented, my mentality was rough. But, through the Lord's mercy, on the day of my repentance, my whole inward being became smooth. From

the time of my repentance, every avenue, lane, and path in
my being has been made straight. This is to prepare us to
receive the Lord, to prepare the way for the Lord, and to
make His paths straight. The way to prepare others to
receive the Lord is to help them to repent. John the Baptist
seemed to be saying, "You children of Israel are far away
from the Lord. Your mind is a rough way, and your emotion,
will, desire, and intention are curved paths. You need to
repent and straighten out every avenue within your being so
that the Lord may come in." When many heard John's
word, they repented, and their way was paved and their
paths were straightened. Therefore, the King was able to
come in. This is true repentance. Genuine repentance prepares the way for the Lord as the King to enter in. I can testify that along this paved way and in these straightened
paths, I continually enjoy the Lord. My way is paved, the
Lord Jesus is walking within me, and along my straightened paths I always have the Lord Jesus with me. This is
the way to prepare ourselves to receive Christ the King.

LIFE-STUDY OF MATTHEW

MESSAGE TEN

THE KING'S ANOINTING

(3)

In this message we come to the actual anointing of the King (3:13-17).

II. ANOINTED

A. Through Baptism

Verse 13 says, "Then came Jesus from Galilee to the Jordan unto John to be baptized by him." Two of the crucial words in this verse are Galilee and Jordan. This verse does not say that Jesus came from Bethlehem to Jerusalem to be sanctified. It says He came from Galilee to the Jordan to be baptized. We need to consider the significance of the phrase "from Galilee to the Jordan." It is not easy to see why Jesus came not from Bethlehem but from Galilee and not to Jerusalem but to the Jordan. We also need to see why He came to John, who was a "wild" person, not to the high priest, who would have been a cultured and religious person. Moreover, we need to know why He came to be baptized, not to be sanctified.

1. Coming from Galilee

In the New Testament, Galilee, a despised region, signifies rejection. Jesus did not come from Bethlehem because at that time Bethlehem was a place of honor and welcome. If you came out of Bethlehem, everyone would honor you and give you a warm welcome. But if you came from Galilee, everyone would despise you and reject you. Jesus came from such a despised and rejected place. This place was not rejected by God, but it was rejected by

religion and culture. All those who come to the Lord's
recovery do not come from Bethlehem; rather, they come
from Galilee. Do not try to come from a place of honor and
warm welcome, but come from a place that is despised and
rejected by religion and culture. Even if the president of a
nation took the way of the church, he would also have to be
one coming from Galilee to the Jordan. Throughout my
years of watching and observing, I have seen that those of a
high rank who turned to the way of the church were
despised and rejected by today's religion and culture. I am
quite certain that if you are still honored and welcomed by
today's religion and culture, you are not on the way from
Galilee to the Jordan. The way from Galilee to the Jordan
is the correct way for the church. The way of today's
church life is not from Bethlehem to Jerusalem; it is from
Galilee to the Jordan.

The way of the church is a narrow way. Even if there
were no opposition to the Lord's recovery but rather a high
appraisal from every Christian organization, the number of
those who would turn to the way of the church would still
be about the same as it is today, simply because the way of
the church is a narrow way. When some consider the
church, they may say, "This is the kingdom of the heavens.
Certainly this way must be very high." Although this way
is high, it is not high according to your concept. Instead, it
is a highway from Galilee to the Jordan.

2. Coming to Jordan

As we have pointed out, Jordan was a place of burial
and resurrection. Thus, Jordan signifies termination and
germination. The children of Israel traveled through the
wilderness for about forty years, and eventually they were
all buried in the Jordan River. Hence, the Jordan
terminated them, ended their history of wandering in the
wilderness, and terminated the age of wandering. But
the Jordan also gave them a new beginning, for it
germinated them and ushered them into a new age. It was
the Jordan that brought the children of Israel out of the

wilderness and into the good land, which is Christ. This is the significance of the Jordan.

In the church life our way today is the way from Galilee to the Jordan, the way from rejection to termination and resurrection. We all need to say to those who despise and reject us, "Farewell. I shall not seek to be welcomed by you. I am going to the place where I can be terminated and germinated." In the church life there is no honor; instead, there is termination. Day by day we are terminated. In the church we have a mutual termination. We terminate one another every day, even every hour. But it is a good thing to be terminated. Termination is not the end; it is the beginning, because termination always leads to germination. Therefore, we can testify that every termination becomes a germination.

Sometimes the sisters say, "Brother Lee, the church life is wonderful, but it is often difficult for us sisters. We know that the brothers are the head and that we sisters must submit to them. The brothers are good, but they are too strong. We just cannot take it. Many times they have nearly killed us." Whenever I hear this, I say, "Isn't that good? How good it is to be terminated. Isn't it good for the sisters to be killed by the brothers?"

A few years ago I was invited to a certain church. The brothers there told me that the sisters were so emotional and opinionated that they found it very difficult to have fellowship with them. They simply did not know how to handle the situation. Several days later some of the very sisters in question invited me to lunch. Their purpose in doing so was to have an opportunity to express their opinion. They told me their patience was exhausted because the brothers were so strong. They wanted me to give them the way to go on. Several days earlier I had been pressed by the brothers, but now I was being pressed by the sisters. I saw what a serious and terrible termination that was for both the brothers and the sisters. Both the brothers and the sisters were being terminated. But that mutual termination is very positive. Do you not love to be ter-

minated? If you have never been terminated in the church
life, get yourself prepared. I can assure you that in the
church life we all shall be terminated, because we are on
the way from Galilee to the Jordan.

When new ones come into the church life, they may say,
"Hallelujah! I have seen the church life! How wonderful!"
Whenever I hear this, I say within, "Yes, it is wonderful,
but wait awhile. Sooner or later, this wonderful church life
will terminate you." In the church life I have been
terminated dozens of times. I have experienced at least ten
major terminations. I was terminated in Chefoo, Shanghai, Taipei, Manila, Los Angeles, and Anaheim. The
marvelous church life is surely a terminating life. The
wonderful church life terminates us all. Be prepared to be
terminated. Those who have been in the church life for just
a short time are probably still on their church honeymoon.
The honeymoon is fine. But as every married couple
knows, the honeymoon eventually turns into termination.
Nearly every husband has terminated his wife, and every
wife has terminated her husband. But this termination is
very positive because it brings in germination. Hallelujah,
termination issues in resurrection!

The church life truly is wonderful, but not wonderful
according to our concept. The wonderful church life sooner
or later will terminate us all. It will both terminate you and
germinate you. I assure you that whatever you are, whatever you have, and whatever you can do will all be terminated. It may take a history of ten years in the church to
accomplish this. Those who have been in the church for ten
years can testify that every part of their being has been terminated. The longer we stay in the church, the more we are
terminated. At first, the experience of termination is
bitter. But later it becomes sweet. For me today it is sweet
to be terminated. After a number of years of being
terminated in the church life, you will be happy to be terminated. At first when you are terminated in the church
life, you feel ashamed. Gradually, however, it becomes a
sweet experience for you. We are on the way from Galilee to

the Jordan, from the place of rejection to the place of termination.

It is in this place of termination that we meet the King. Here, in the church life, is where we meet Him. From the time I came into the church life, I have been brought to the Lord again and again. Day after day, the church life brings me to Christ, and it brings Christ the King to me. Eventually, the kingdom is here. This is the reason the church life is the kingdom.

I was taught by the Brethren that the kingdom had been suspended until a future time. I was also taught that the church today was not the kingdom. But in my experience I gradually realized that every time I was terminated I was brought to the King and the King was brought to me. In my experience this was the reality of the kingdom. It was through experience that I first came to know that the church life is the kingdom. My experience told me that the teaching I received from the Brethren regarding the kingdom was not accurate. According to my experience, I knew I was in the kingdom. Every time I was terminated, I met my King, and the kingdom was present. This is not a matter of doctrine; it is a matter of experience. Later, through further study of the New Testament, I received light on the matter of the kingdom, and my experience was confirmed. Now I can boldly say that according to the New Testament the kingdom is here today. Because they have not been terminated, some Christian teachers say that the kingdom has been suspended until some future time. They have not been brought to the King, and the King has not been brought to them. Thus, in their daily experience they do not have the kingdom. However, after you have been terminated on the way from Galilee to the Jordan, both the King and the kingdom will be present.

3. Baptized by John

The Lord Jesus came from Galilee to the Jordan to be baptized by John. As a man, the Lord Jesus came to be baptized by John the Baptist according to God's New Testament way. Of the four Gospels only John's does not give a record of the Lord being baptized, because he testifies that the Lord is God. Verse 13 does not say that Jesus came to John to be sanctified; it says that He came to be baptized. Although every Christian likes to be sanctified, no one likes to be baptized in the sense of being terminated and buried. To be baptized is to be terminated. If I told you that the church will not sanctify you, but rather terminate you, you would turn away from the church and say, "I don't want to stay here. I want to be sanctified. I want the church to make me more holy." But the church will not firstly make you more holy; it will terminate you again and again. The church is not firstly a sanctifying church, but a baptizing church. Consider the case of the Lord Jesus. He was the true Shepherd. A shepherd always takes the lead. As the Shepherd-King, the Lord Jesus took the lead to walk from Galilee to the Jordan to be baptized. He did not come to the Jordan to be enthroned, but to be put to death, to be buried.

4. To Fulfill All Righteousness

Verses 14 and 15 say, "But John would have prevented Him, saying, I have need to be baptized by You, and You are coming to me? But Jesus answering said to him, Permit it now, for in this way it is fitting for us to fulfill all righteousness. Then he permitted Him." John did not understand very well, He wondered how Jesus could be baptized by him, and he thought that he should have been baptized by Jesus. This indicates that John was still somewhat in his natural life. Although he had been soaked in the Holy Spirit for more than thirty years, some natural element still remained. His word in verse 14 was uttered according to his natural concept. Thus, in answering him the Lord seemed to say, "You must permit Me to be baptized. Don't frustrate Me by your natural concept. Do not think that because I am mightier than you I don't need to be baptized by you. Permit Me to be baptized so that we may fulfill all righteousness."

Righteousness is to be right by living, walking, and doing things in the way God has ordained. In the Old Testament, to keep the law that God had given was righteousness. Now God had sent John the Baptist to ordain baptism. To be baptized is also to fulfill righteousness before God, that is, to fulfill the requirement of God. The Lord Jesus came to John, not as God, but as a typical man, a real Israelite. Hence, He must be baptized to keep this dispensational practice of God; otherwise, He would not be right with God.

Righteousness is a matter of being right with God. Suppose God opens a door in the ceiling of a room and says that this is the proper way to enter the room. Anyone who does not enter the room through that door is not right with God. Perhaps you would say, "I don't agree with entering the room through that door. According to my concept, this door is not right. The front door or the side door is the right door." Your way may be right in your eyes, but not in God's eyes. Righteousness is not a matter of your opinion; it is a matter of God's ordination.

At the time of John the Baptist, God ordained baptism as the way. Anyone who wanted to enter the kingdom of the heavens had to pass through the gateway of John's baptism. Not even Jesus Christ could be an exception. Even He had to pass through this gateway. Otherwise, He would have lacked the righteousness of passing through this doorway. After the Lord answered him in such a way, John understood and baptized Him.

To be baptized is to be righteous in the eyes of God. The termination and germination of our being is righteousness before God. One who has been baptized, who has been terminated and germinated, is right with God. God's economy is to terminate our natural man and germinate us with a new life. If we would be right with God, we must be terminated in our natural life and germinated with His divine life. Termination and germination is the highest righteousness. The Lord Jesus, as the King of the heavenly kingdom, took the lead to be terminated. In this way He fulfilled righteousness in the eyes of God. Thus, He was the right person to establish the kingdom of the heavens.

The Lord was baptized not only to fulfill righteousness according to God's ordination, but also to allow Himself to be put into death and resurrection that He might minister, not in a natural way, but in the way of resurrection. By being baptized He lived and ministered in resurrection even before His actual death and resurrection three and a half years later. According to our understanding, the Lord Jesus was put to death on the cross and resurrected on the third day. But in the eyes of God and according to the Lord's realization, He was put to death three and a half years before His crucifixion. Before He began His ministry, He was already put to death and resurrected. Thus, He did not minister in a natural way. His ministry was absolutely in His resurrection life. Thus, He entered into the gateway of righteousness and walked along the pathway of righteousness. Whatever He did on this pathway was righteous.

When the Lord Jesus comes back, many will say to Him, "Lord, Lord, did we not prophesy in Your name, and in Your name cast out demons, and in Your name do many works of power?" (7:22). The Lord will say to them, "I never knew you; depart from Me, workers of lawlessness" (7:23). The Lord will seem to say, "You are a lawless person. I never approved of you nor agreed with what you did, because you did not do things in resurrection. All the good things you did were done in your natural way and in your natural life. You are not righteous; you are lawless." Through baptism the Lord Jesus entered into the gateway of righteousness, and then He walked continually along the pathway of righteousness. Therefore, He was the just One, the righteous One (Acts 3:14; 7:52; 22:14).

B. With the Holy Spirit

Verse 16 says, "And having been baptized, Jesus went up immediately from the water, and behold, the heavens were opened to Him, and He saw the Spirit of God descending as a dove and coming upon Him." Not only was

Jesus anointed through baptism, but He was also anointed with the Holy Spirit.

1. Rising Up from the Water

In His baptism the Lord rose up from the water. This signifies that after His death and burial, He was raised from the dead.

2. The Heavens Being Opened to Him

The Lord's baptism to fulfill God's righteousness and to be put into death and resurrection brought Him three things: the open heaven, the descending of the Spirit of God, and the speaking of the Father. It should be the same today with us.

Because the Lord Jesus was baptized, fulfilling God's righteousness, the heavens were opened to Him, the Holy Spirit descended upon Him, and the Father spoke concerning Him. His being baptized to fulfill God's righteousness pleased God. Thus, His baptism opened the heavens, brought down the Holy Spirit, and opened the mouth of the Father. The way we can have an open heaven, the descending Spirit, and the speaking of the Father is to be terminated. Many of us can testify that whenever we have been terminated, the heavens have been opened. On the contrary, whenever we were welcomed and honored, the heavens were closed. Whenever we are terminated in the church life, the heavens are opened. Moreover, every termination brings down the Holy Spirit and opens the mouth of our heavenly Father. At that time the Father will say, "My beloved." I can testify that my sweetest times of hearing God's speaking have been times of termination. Perhaps I was terminated to the point of tears, but my termination opened the mouth of the Father, who spoke a sweet word to me. He only said, "My beloved child." This simple word is sufficient. It is full of mercy and grace. What a comfort and a strength it is for Him to say, "My beloved child"! In the church life we have many experiences like this. However, seldom are such things experienced outside the church. In the church life, when we are terminated, the heavens are opened, the Spirit comes, and the Father speaks. We have an open heaven, the anointing Spirit, and the speaking Father.

3. The Spirit of God Descending upon Him

Verse 16 says, "He saw the Spirit of God descending as a dove and coming upon Him." Before the Spirit of God descended and came upon Him, the Lord Jesus was born of the Spirit (Luke 1:35), which proved that He already had the Spirit of God within Him. That was for His birth. Now, for His ministry, the Spirit of God descended upon Him. This was for the fulfillment of Isaiah 61:1; 42:1; and Psalm 45:7 to anoint the new King and introduce Him to His people.

A dove is gentle, and its eyes can see only one thing at a time. Hence, it signifies gentleness and singleness in sight and purpose. By the Spirit of God descending upon Him as the dove, the Lord Jesus ministered in gentleness and singleness, focusing solely on the will of God.

The Lord Jesus was conceived of the Holy Spirit (1:18, 20). He was born of the Holy Spirit and constituted with the Holy Spirit. The Holy Spirit was His constituent. Nevertheless, He still needed the baptism of the Holy Spirit, the outpouring of the Holy Spirit. When He was in the womb of the virgin Mary, He was constituted with the Holy Spirit. This means that He was a constitution of the Holy Spirit. That was something inward. Outwardly, He still needed the Holy Spirit to come down upon Him.

Since the Spirit was in Jesus before He was baptized, why did the Spirit come down upon Him? Are these two Spirits? Was not the Spirit of God in Jesus? Certainly He was. Then why did the Spirit still descend upon Him? Was the Spirit within Him different from the Spirit who came down upon Him? Is the Spirit who descended upon Him another Spirit in addition to the Spirit who was already within Him? If you say that these two were one Spirit, I would ask how these two Spirits could be one. The same

Spirit who already indwelt the Lord Jesus came down upon Him. Did Jesus have the Spirit or not? Yes, He did. Why then did the Spirit still descend upon Him? I am here with you. Since I am here, how could I still come to you? Although it is not possible for me to be here and yet still be coming, it is not impossible with the divine Person. The Lord is wonderful. At the same time, He can be both here and also coming. Is Christ in you or is He in the heavens? He is both in us and in the heavens. Thus, the Lord is both here and coming.

4. The Father Speaking to Him

Verse 17 says, "And behold, a voice out of the heavens, saying, This is My beloved Son, in Whom I delight." While the descending of the Spirit was the anointing of Christ, the speaking of the Father was a testimony to Him as the beloved Son. Here is a picture of the divine Trinity: the Son went up from the water, the Spirit descended upon the Son, and the Father spoke concerning the Son. This proves that the Father, the Son, and the Spirit exist simultaneously. This is for the accomplishment of God's economy.

LIFE-STUDY OF MATTHEW

MESSAGE ELEVEN

THE KING'S ANOINTING

(4)

III. TESTED

In this message we come to the testing of the newly appointed King (4:1-11). After His anointing, the Lord was tested. In God's administration the sequence is always selection, anointing, and testing. There is an illustration of this in married life. Prior to getting married, you certainly made a selection. Among the many you could have married, you selected a certain one. After the selection came the appointment, and after the appointment came the test. Nearly every married couple has failed the marriage test. Although we were successful in the appointment, we were not successful in the test.

After the heavenly King was anointed and appointed, He was led by the Holy Spirit into the wilderness to be tested. He did not go to the wilderness on His own; He was led there by the very Holy Spirit who had descended upon Him. In married life God will also lead us into the test. A number of young brothers and sisters have complained to God, saying, "Lord, before I was married, I prayed a great deal. Eventually You told me that it was Your will that I marry this one, that this was the one whom You had prepared for me. Lord, You know I was not interested at first, but in Your sovereignty You arranged for us to come together. But look at the situation today. Look at the one You have given me. Is this Your mistake or mine?" Neither the Lord nor you made a mistake. This is the Lord's test.

I believe that all marriages are sovereign, even those that seem to be the most mistaken. Nothing happens to God's children without His sovereign permission. We know that all things work together for our good (Rom. 8:28), including even a seemingly mistaken marriage. Who knows what is the right marriage? I have many years' experience in married life. Forty-five years ago, I could tell others definitely, clearly, and emphatically what was the right marriage. But if you ask this question today, I would say, "I cannot know this until we enter eternity. After so many years' experience in married life, I truly don't know what is the right marriage." But I have learned that every marriage under God's sovereignty is right. Therefore, you all have the right marriage. Brothers, your wife is the right one for you. Sisters, your husband is the right one for you. Whether you believe this or not, you cannot escape from your situation. After the young people and the middle-aged ones have been married for a number of years, they may conclude that they have made a mistake and that if they could do it again they would do it differently. I can assure you that even if you could do it over many times, you would still come to feel that you had made a mistake. Almost all those who are about to be married think they have made the right choice, but after some years there may be times that they feel that they were mistaken. The reason for this is that God puts us to the test in married life.

The Lord tests us not only in married life, but also in the church life. When we first came into the church life, we experienced a church life honeymoon. We were enjoying the glorious church life, and everything was wonderful. However, sooner or later we shall be put to the test. Every brother who is put into the eldership is tested, and the test usually comes from the other elders. Perhaps at the beginning in your locality you were the only elder. You were looking for some others to help you, and later two were added. After several months, all three of you were tested by one another. The Lord allows this. In God's economy, after we have been appointed to something, we shall always be tested. If the Lord Jesus needed a test, then how about us?

For many years I was not able to thoroughly understand this portion of the Word. Although I heard a number of messages on this portion, none of them truly touched the heart of it. For a thorough understanding we need to see that in God's economy we shall always be tested after we have been anointed and appointed to something. Not even the Lord Jesus was an exception. As we shall see, in principle all the tests are the same.

A. Being Led by the Spirit

Verse 1 says, "Then Jesus was led up by the Spirit into the wilderness to be tempted by the Devil." After being baptized in water and anointed with the Spirit of God, Jesus, as a man, moved according to the leading of the Spirit. This indicates that His kingly ministry in His humanity was according to the Spirit.

First of all, the Spirit led the anointed King to be tempted by the Devil. This temptation was a test to prove that He was qualified to be the King for the kingdom of the heavens. The Greek word translated Devil is *diabolos*, meaning accuser, slanderer (Rev. 12:9-10). The Devil, who is Satan, accuses us before God and slanders us before man.

B. Having Fasted
Forty Days and Forty Nights

Verse 2 says the Lord fasted forty days and forty nights. These forty days and forty nights were a time of testing and suffering (Deut. 9:9, 18; 1 Kings 19:8). The newly anointed King was led by the Spirit to fast such a period of time that He might enter into His kingly ministry.

C. The Tempter's Temptations
1. To Change Stones into Loaves of Bread

The first test was in the matter of human living, in the matter of making a living. Our relatives and in-laws, especially those of the older generation, are always concerned about how we shall make our living. They may say, "It is all right to love the Lord, but do not love Him in a foolish way. You must consider your need to make a good living." When in 1933 I was burdened by the Lord and led of Him to leave my job, my in-laws said, "You have a good job. You are making excellent money to take care of your family and to help others. You can speak on Sunday and hold meetings at night during the week. Why must you quit your job? Many are looking eagerly for such a job, but have no opportunity to get it. But you are leaving. We wonder how you will be able to make a living. We don't know how you will take care of your wife and children." I did not listen to their advice, and they could not discourage me from leaving my job to serve the Lord full time. A number of times my in-laws even sent their little daughter to sneak into our kitchen to see if we had food to eat. They were worried that we might be starving. The matter of our living touches us deeply, and even the Lord Jesus was tested regarding it.

The Lord was led to fast for forty days and forty nights. After these forty days and forty nights, He was physically hungry, and the tempter came to Him and said, "If You are the Son of God, speak, that these stones may become loaves of bread" (v. 3). To this proposal the Lord replied, "Man shall not live on bread alone, but on every word that proceeds out through the mouth of God" (v. 4). Many Christians think that because the Lord was fasting during this time He did not eat anything. However, this word reveals that while the Lord Jesus was fasting, He was eating. Physically He was fasting, but spiritually He was eating.

Here we see an important principle. In the Lord's ministry and economy, if we do not know how to lower our physical demands and take care of the spiritual demand, we are not qualified for His ministry. In order to be qualified in the Lord's ministry, we must be tested. We must lay down our physical requirements. A good living, good food, good clothing, and proper housing are all secondary. Eating spiritual food is primary. Immediately after His baptism, the Lord Jesus was led into a situation where He could declare to the whole universe that He was not for the physical need, but that He would take care of the spiritual need only. For forty days and forty nights, He for-

sook all physical food, forgetting the physical requirements. However, He took care of the spiritual need.
Although He did not eat to nourish His physical body, He
ate a great deal for the nourishment of His spirit. Satan
was absolutely wrong in thinking that the Lord Jesus was
not eating during those days in the wilderness. While He
was fasting from physical food, He was partaking of
spiritual food. This is the test in the matter of our living.

Many wives have not been able to withstand this test.
Every wife is very concerned about her security. The wives
desire to have good food, clothing, and housing. In other
words, they desire a good living. This has posed a
problem to many brothers. Although these brothers had a
heart to take the way of the church, their wives were not
willing to follow them because there was no guarantee of a
good living. Many of us can testify that, when we first
began to take the way of the church, our wives said, "What
about our future? What about our living? What about our
food, clothing, and housing?" This is a test we must face if
we would take the way of the church and go the way of
God's economy.

The first test we must pass is the test regarding our living. We must care for the spiritual food more than for the
physical food. Whether we live or die is secondary. We only
care that our spirit is fed, that our spirit feasts on the Word
of God, on God Himself.

Some pastors, missionaries, and Bible teachers saw the
way of the church and had a thorough talk with me about
it. However, realizing that this way is narrow, they were
concerned about what would happen to their living if they
went this way. The wives of many of these dear ones simply did not agree that their husbands should take this
narrow way. They knew their standard of living would be
lowered if their husbands went the way of the church.

Forty-five years ago in China, this way was truly
narrow, and we were daily on the test concerning our living. Time after time just one dollar kept some of us from
having nothing to eat. In order to take this narrow way, we
had to live by faith in God. Although it was very difficult,

we lived by faith for many years. I can testify that we feasted on God and His Word during those testing days when our standard of living was greatly lowered. Our experience was the same as that of the Lord Jesus in the wilderness. He neither chose to go to the wilderness nor did He go there by His own preference. He was led there by the Holy Spirit. Likewise, we were led by God into the wilderness of the church life. Fifty years ago, the church was truly in the wilderness. Nearly every day we were tested concerning what we would eat that night. But that was the time we enjoyed feasting on the Word of God. On the one hand, we did not have very much physical food to eat, but on the other hand, we did feast on the rich Word.

The principle is the same today in the church life. In taking the way of the church, the first test we shall encounter is that of lowering our standard of living. This is the test in the realm of our physical living. Everyone who takes the way of the church will be tested in this matter of his daily living. We shall be tested to show to the whole universe that our concern is not for physical food, but for spiritual food. During those days in the wilderness, Jesus was not concerned for His physical food, but for His spiritual food. He was fasting physically, yet He was eating the Word of God. In the wilderness He did not live by bread alone; He lived on the Word of God.

a. Tempted to Give Up
the Standing of Man
by Assuming to be the Son of God

Now we come to the main point of the first test. At the time of Christ's baptism, the Father opened the heavens and declared, "This is My beloved Son" (3:17). A voice from heaven declared that a little man from Nazareth was God the Father's beloved Son. Immediately after this declaration was made, the Holy Spirit led this man into the wilderness to be tested to see whether He would care for His physical life or for His spiritual life. Then, based upon the declaration of God the Father, the tempter came to tempt this man by saying, "If You are the Son of God,

speak, that these stones may become loaves of bread"
(v. 3). Satan seemed to be saying, "We heard the
declaration made forty days ago by God the Father that
You are the beloved Son. Now if You are truly the Son of
God, do something to prove it. Simply say, 'Stones, I want
you to become loaves of bread.' If You are the Son of God,
You must prove it to Yourself and to me and to everyone in
the whole universe by doing something which no one else
can do."

The newly anointed King fasted in His humanity,
standing on the ground of a man. However, He was also the
Son of God, as God the Father had declared at His baptism. For Him to accomplish His ministry for the kingdom
of the heavens, He had to defeat God's enemy, the Devil,
Satan. This He must do as a man. Hence, He stood as a
man to confront the enemy of God. The Devil, knowing
this, tempted Him to leave the standing of man and
assume His position as the Son of God. Forty days before,
God the Father declared from the heavens that He was the
beloved Son of the Father. The subtle tempter took that
declaration of God the Father as the ground to tempt Him.
If He assumed His position as the Son of God before the
enemy, He would have lost the standing to defeat him.

To make the stones become loaves of bread would certainly be a miracle. This was proposed by the Devil as a
temptation. Many times the thought of having a miracle
performed in certain situations is a temptation from the
Devil. The Devil's temptation of the first man, Adam,
concerned the matter of eating (Gen. 3:1-6). Now his temptation of the second man, Christ, also concerned the matter
of eating. Eating is always a trap used by the Devil to snare
man.

b. Defeating the Tempter
by Standing in the Position of a Man

Verse 4 says, "But He answered and said, It is written,
Man shall not live on bread alone, but on every word that
proceeds out through the mouth of God." The tempter
tempted the new King to take His position as the Son of
God. But He answered with the Word of the Scriptures,

"Man," indicating that He stood in the position of man to deal with the enemy. The demons addressed Jesus as the Son of God (8:29), but the evil spirits did not confess that Jesus came in the flesh (1 John 4:3), because by confessing Jesus as a man, they would be defeated. Although the demons confess Jesus as the Son of God, the Devil does not want people to believe that He is the Son of God, because in so doing they will be saved (John 20:31).

The word "man" spoken by the Lord Jesus to the tempter was a killing word. The Lord seemed to be saying, "Satan, don't tempt me to assume My position as the Son of God. I am here as a man. If I were only the Son of God, I could never be here, and I could never be tempted by you. But because I am a man, I am being tempted. Satan, I know that you are not afraid of the Son of God, but you are afraid of man. The first man, the man whom God created to defeat you and to fulfill His purpose, was defeated by you. Thus, God sent Me as the second man to defeat you. Now you are tempting Me to leave My position as a man to assume My position as the Son of God. But I tell you, Satan, I am standing here as a man."

Although the demons shouted, "Son of God," the evil spirits do not confess that Jesus came as a man. They will admit that He is the Son of God, but they will not recognize that He is a man. The reason the evil spirits do not want anyone to believe that Christ is the Son of God is that anyone who does so will be saved. But they do not dare recognize Jesus as a man; for if they did, they would be defeated. In dealing with the demons, Jesus is the Son of man. In saving us sinners, He is the Son of God. When we believe in Him as the Son of God, we are saved. But if the demons recognize Him as the Son of man, they will be defeated. Therefore, the Lord Jesus took a strong standing as a man to defeat Satan. In this first test Satan was defeated because Jesus took the position of a man.

The newly anointed King confronted the enemy's temptation not by His own word, but by the word of the Scriptures, quoting Deuteronomy 8:3. This word indicates that the Lord Jesus took the word of God in the Scriptures as His bread and lived on it. The Greek word translated "word" in verse 4 is *rhema*. *Rhema*, the instant word, differs from *logos*, the constant word. In this temptation, all the words quoted from Deuteronomy by the Lord were *logos*, the constant word in the Scriptures. But when He quoted them, they became *rhema*, the instant word applied to His situation.

All Scripture is God-breathed (2 Tim. 3:16). Hence, the words in the Scriptures are the words that proceed out of the mouth of God.

2. To Cast Himself Down
from the Wing of the Temple

a. Tempted to Make a Show
That God Would Protect Him

Verse 5 says, "Then the Devil took Him into the holy city and set Him on the wing of the temple." The Devil's first temptation of the new King was in the matter of human living. Defeated in this, he turned his second temptation to religion, tempting the new King to demonstrate that He is the Son of God from the wing of the temple. In verse 6 the Devil said to Him, "If You are the Son of God, cast Yourself down; for it is written, He shall give charge to His angels concerning You, and on their hands they shall bear You up, lest You strike Your foot against a stone." There was no need for the Lord Jesus to do this. It was simply a temptation to show that as the Son of God He was able to do things in a miraculous way. Any thought of doing things miraculously in religion is a temptation of the Devil.

The second test is a matter of religion. The most exciting thing in religion is miracles. According to the human concept, any religion that does not have miracles is powerless; the most powerful religion is a religion of miracles. Therefore, Satan brought the new King to the wing of the temple and tempted Him to leap down from it by saying that the angels would protect Him. Do not think that you have never had the thought of doing this kind of thing. In my early days I often thought of doing things to show people that I was a supernatural person and that I had supernatural powers. Have you not had this kind of concept in your Christian life? Sometimes we are tested when there is a need to do something, and at other times we are tested when there is no need. In this instance, there was no need for Jesus to leap down from the wing of the temple.

Sometimes there does seem to be a need for a miracle. Once my youngest brother-in-law became seriously ill. At that time I was tempted to make a show of myself by praying for his healing. I thought, "Now is the time for me to prove to my in-laws and relatives that I am a wonderful person. I shall pray just one prayer, and my brother-in-law will be healed. Doesn't the Bible say that Jesus heals, that He is the same yesterday, today, and forever, and that we must pray for others? If I do this miracle for my brother-in-law, my mother-in-law will be convinced that I am a supernatural person. In her eyes I am too religious, daily talking about God, Christ, and faith. Imagine what would happen if I went to my brother-in-law and said, 'Lord Jesus, heal him,' and he immediately rose up! Not only would he be healed, but I would be manifested. What a wonderful person I would be in the eyes of my mother-in-law!" Was that the Lord's anointing, the Lord's leading and guidance, or was it a temptation? Surely it was a temptation. Have you not had such a temptation in the past?

Many young Christians have peculiar concepts regarding the performing of miracles. Some may say, "Since I am one following the Lord and I am in the Lord's presence as my Emmanuel, I must do something to show others that God is with me." I know of one dear brother who had such a thought. Convinced that the Lord was with him, he asked the Lord to give him two hundred thousand dollars within a certain number of days. He said, "Lord, You must show the people that You are one with me. You must show them that whatever I ask in Your name, You give me. Lord, I am asking You for two hundred thousand dollars. Within a certain number of days, You must give it to me." This brother stopped eating and sleeping and began to pray for this amount of money. What kind of prayer was that? It was leaping from the wing of the temple to make a show of himself. In principle we have all done this many times. Every Christian has been tempted in this way.

If the Devil does not tempt us in the matter of our living, he will tempt us in the matter of religion. You may desire to be a great one in religion, to be recognized as a powerful person. Everyone else must walk down from the wing of the temple, but you, a supernatural person, one who is more powerful than others, can leap down. By doing this you become great in Christianity. All the religious "big shots" are those who have yielded to this temptation. If you have become famous in Christianity, if you have succeeded in becoming recognized as a supernatural person, then you have already yielded to this temptation. You have already been defeated by the enemy. However, if you desire to defeat the enemy in this test, you must not leap from the temple. Rather, you must walk down from it as slowly as possible. Let others think that you are weak and incompetent. But you must tell yourself, "I am not walking in power. I am walking in life. I do not care for power — I care for life." It is easy to say this, but it is difficult to do it. When the opportunity presents itself, although you may not leap from the wing of the temple, you will run down, at least showing that you are a good runner, able to run faster than others. Nevertheless, if we would defeat the enemy, we must be a nobody. Never do anything to prove that you are somebody or something. Let others think that you are nothing. Actually, I am nothing, and my Christ is everything. If you take the standing of being a nobody, you will kill the enemy. You will slay the tempter.

b. Defeating the Tempter
by Not Tempting God

When the Devil tempted Jesus to cast Himself down from the wing of the temple, Jesus said to him, "Again it is written, You shall not tempt the Lord your God" (v. 7). Because the Lord Jesus defeated him the first time by quoting the Scriptures, the tempter imitated His way and in his second temptation tempted Him by also quoting the Scriptures, however in a subtle way. To quote the Scriptures concerning something in one aspect requires us to take care of the other aspect as well, in order to be safeguarded from the deception of the tempter. This was what the new King did here to counter the tempter's second temptation. Many times we need to tell the tempter, "*Again* it is written."

The Lord Jesus defeated Satan in the first temptation by quoting the Scriptures. Thus, in the second temptation, the tempter himself quoted them. He seemed to be saying, "Jesus, You quoted the Bible. I know the Bible also. Let me quote a verse to You." But the Lord Jesus said, "Again it is written." The word "again" is very strong. Do not think that you can quote the Bible and that the enemy cannot. Satan knows more of the Bible than you do. Therefore, the best safeguard is to have a word again as either a balance or a confirmation. Then, in the second temptation, the enemy will also be defeated.

The Lord Jesus said to Satan, "You shall not tempt the Lord your God" (v. 7). Do not tempt God. Do not go to the wing of the temple and cast yourself down. If you find yourself there by accident, you must find a way to come down. But you must never go there purposely. If you are there by mistake, ask the Lord to forgive you and to help you walk down step by step. But do not cast yourself down to make a show. You are nobody. The Lord Jesus overcame the tempter by not taking his proposal to tempt God.

3. To Worship the Devil
a. Tempted to Gain the Kingdoms
of the World and Their Glory

Verses 8 and 9 say, "Again, the Devil took Him to a very high mountain and showed Him all the kingdoms of the world and their glory; and he said to Him, All these will I give You if You will fall down and worship me." Defeated in his temptation in the religious sphere, the Devil presented his third temptation to the new King, this time in the realm of the glory of this world. He showed Him all the

kingdoms of the world and their glory. The temptations of
the subtle one always come in this way: firstly, in human
living; secondly, in religion; and thirdly, in worldly glory.
In any temptation, all three of these items will be present.
The third temptation is a matter of worldly glory,
promotion, ambition, position, and a promising future. All
this is the glory of the world.

Luke 4:6 says that the kingdoms of the world and their
glory were delivered unto the Devil; hence, to whomever he
wills he gives them. Before his fall, Satan as the archangel
was appointed by God to be the ruler of the world (Ezek.
28:13-14). Thus, he is called the ruler of this world (John
12:31), holding all the kingdoms of this world and their
glory in his hand. He presented all these to the newly
anointed King as a temptation in order to secure worship.
The heavenly King overcame this temptation, but the
coming Antichrist will not (Rev. 13:2, 4).

This temptation involves the matter of ambition and
promotion. Even among the saints, there is the desire to be
a leader. This is the desire for worldly glory. Your eagerness
to be a leader is your ambition. This is the glory of the
world. Whenever you are tempted in this manner, you
must realize that behind this temptation is the tempter
seeking to gain your worship. Satan told the Lord Jesus
that if He would worship him, he would give Him all the
kingdoms of the world and their glory. Behind every ambition there is a hidden idol. If you are ambitious to have a
position, a promotion, or a name, there is an idol behind
that ambition. If you do not worship any idol, you will
never fulfill your ambition. In order to have any part of the
glory of the world, you must worship some idol. Without
worshipping idols it is impossible to have a position.
Whenever you are seeking a certain position, deep within
you know that you are worshipping an idol. For this reason,
the Apostle said that covetousness is idolatry (Col. 3:5).

Suppose some brothers who came into the church life
four years later than you become leaders and you feel that
you have been passed by. If you complain about this, asking why they have been made leaders and you have not,

this is a proof that you are seeking worldly glory. Perhaps among a group of ten sisters three are appointed to take the lead in a particular service. If the other seven have no feeling about this, they have gained the victory. But if they question why those three were appointed, this indicates that they are seeking vain glory, the glory of this age. In this matter, we all are weak. If this desire for ambition and position can wedge even into the church life, then how much we need to be on guard in other things!

b. Defeating the Tempter
by Worshipping God and Serving Him Only

In verse 10 the Lord Jesus said, "Go, Satan! For it is written, You shall worship the Lord your God, and Him only shall you serve." Satan in Greek means adversary. He is not only God's enemy outside God's kingdom, but also the adversary within God's kingdom, rebelling against God. The new King rebuked the Devil's presentation and defeated him by standing on the ground of man to worship and serve God only. To worship or to serve anything other than God for gain is always the Devil's temptation to secure worship. The Lord seemed to be saying to Satan, "Satan, as a man, I, Jesus, worship God and serve Him only. You are God's enemy, and I will never worship you. I don't care for the glory of the world or for the kingdoms of the world. Satan, get away from Me!"

If we consider our experience, we shall see that all temptations are included in these three aspects: the temptation in the matter of our living, the temptation of religious miracles, and the temptation in the realm of worldly glory. All day long we are tempted in the aspects of our living, religion, and worldly position. But the Lord Jesus overcame every aspect of the enemy's temptation. He could say, "My living is secondary. I don't care for religious power. And worldly glory has nothing to do with Me. I know only God's word and God Himself. I care only to serve God." Therefore, as the One who passed the test, the Lord Jesus was qualified to be the King of the kingdom of the heavens.

D. The Result

Verse 11 says, "Then the Devil leaves Him; and behold, angels came and ministered to Him." The Devil's temptation of the first man, Adam, was a success; his temptation of the second man, Christ, was an absolute failure. This indicates that he will have no place in the new King's kingdom of the heavens. After the Lord Jesus defeated Satan, angels came and ministered to the tempted King as a suffering man (cf. Luke 22:43).

Not only the King but also all the kingdom people must overcome the matters of their daily living, religious power, and worldly glory. If we cannot overcome these three temptations, we are outside the kingdom. If we would be the kingdom people, these three things must be under our feet. If we kill these three temptations, saying, "I don't care for my living, for religious power, or for worldly position," Satan will not be able to do anything to us.

We should not be concerned about our daily living. Consider the example of the Apostle Paul. Paul said, "I know both how to be abased, and I know how to abound; in everything and in all things I have learned the secret both to be filled and to hunger, both to abound and to be in want" (Phil. 4:12). Paul seemed to be saying, "It does not matter to me whether I have poverty or abundance. I can live in either scarcity or plenty. The matter of my daily living does not worry me."

Furthermore, instead of caring for religious power, we should be weak, just as Jesus Christ was weak when He was arrested and crucified. If He had not been weak, who could have arrested Him and put Him on the cross? When He was arrested, tried, and crucified, He made no display of His power. He refused to exhibit any religious power. Instead, He was weak to the uttermost. Paul said that Christ "was crucified out of weakness"; he also said, "We are weak in Him" (2 Cor. 13:4). Many devilish people challenged Paul, saying, "If you are the true apostle of Christ, you must do something to prove it." But when Paul was in prison, the Lord did not do anything miraculous for him.

Paul's situation was the same as that of John the Baptist, who also had been imprisoned. After a certain period of imprisonment, John sent his disciples to challenge the Lord, saying, "Are You the coming One, or should we expect someone else?" (11:3). John seemed to be saying, "If You are the coming One, why don't You do something for me? Don't You know that I, Your forerunner and recommender, am in prison? Are you not powerful? Are You not Christ the almighty? If so, do something for me." In His answer, the Lord said, "Blessed is he who shall not be stumbled in Me" (11:6). The Lord seemed to be saying, "Yes, I can do anything, but I don't want to do anything for you. Although you are My recommender, My forerunner, I don't care to do anything for you. I would rather that you would be beheaded. John, will you be stumbled by Me?" Brother Nee's experience is an up-to-date illustration of this. He was in prison from 1952 until he died in 1972. During those twenty years, the Lord did not do anything for him in a miraculous way.

How we need to overcome these three kinds of temptation: the temptation of our living, the temptation of so-called religious power, and the temptation of vain glory. If we conquer these things, we are truly the kingdom people following our heavenly King. Hallelujah, our heavenly King overcame the tempter and defeated him in these three temptations!

LIFE-STUDY OF MATTHEW

MESSAGE TWELVE

THE BEGINNING OF THE KING'S MINISTRY

We come now to a very important section of the Gospel of Matthew, the section of the King's ministry (4:12—11:30). In this message we shall consider the beginning of the ministry (4:12-25). After the Lord was anointed, He was tested to prove that He was qualified, and then He began to minister.

I. BEGINNING OF THE MINISTRY

A. After John the Baptist Was Imprisoned

Verse 12 says, "Now having heard that John was delivered up, He withdrew into Galilee." Although John the Baptist ministered in the wilderness, not in the holy temple in the holy city, he was still in Judea, not far from the so-called "holy" things. Due to the people's rejection of John, the Lord Jesus withdrew into Galilee to begin His ministry, far away from the holy temple and holy city. This occurred sovereignly to fulfill the prophecy of Isaiah 9:1 and 2.

According to the human concept, Jesus should have begun to minister from the holy temple in the holy city, Jerusalem. But the report came to Him that His forerunner, John the Baptist, had been imprisoned. This was an indication to this new King that Jerusalem had become a place of rejection; therefore, He should not begin His kingly ministry there.

In His economy God intended to have a thorough change, a change from the old economy to the new. The old economy had resulted in an outward religion, an outward temple, an outward city, and an outward system of worship. Everything in the old economy was systematized in an outward way. In God's new economy, He gave all that up and had a new beginning. The environment under God's sovereignty matched this change in God's economy. Because Jerusalem had rejected the recommender of the new King, the Lord Jesus knew that He should not begin His ministry there. There was no welcome for Him in Jerusalem.

Although the new King was the Son of God, and although He had been anointed with the Spirit of God, we are not told here that He prayed concerning where He should go to minister. We are not told that He had the deep sense that He was being led to the north, away from Jerusalem. Rather, the Lord considered the environment and received from it the clear indication where He should go. Do not think that we can be so spiritual that we need no indications from our environment. Even the King of the heavenly kingdom, the Son of God anointed with the Holy Spirit, moved according to the environmental indicators. The Lord's concept was neither natural nor religious. Furthermore, it was not according to past history. According to history, as the anointed King, He should have gone to the capital, Jerusalem, for Jerusalem is the proper place for the King. However, because His forerunner, His recommender, had been cast into prison, He went to Galilee. According to the human expectation, it was ridiculous for the newly anointed King to leave the capital and go to a despised region to begin His kingly ministry. He did not even go south to Hebron, the place where David was enthroned, nor to Beersheba, the place where Abraham lived. He went to Galilee.

By considering the Lord's move after the imprisonment of John the Baptist, we must learn not to try to be supernaturally spiritual. Jesus was not spiritual in that way. We must also learn not to go according to past history or to human understanding. According to history and the human concept, the King of the Jews should be in Jerusalem sitting on the throne. However, Jesus did not move purely according to the spiritual leading, nor did He move according to past history or the natural concept.

Rather, He moved according to the environment which corresponded to God's economy. By so doing, He spontaneously fulfilled the prophecy of Isaiah 9:1 and 2. Although the Lord moved apparently according to the environment instead of following the Spirit, His move was a fulfillment of the prophecy in the Scriptures.

In moving with the Lord we must avoid two extremes. The first extreme is the supernatural extreme. Some claim that there is no need to consider their environment because they have the Spirit. The other extreme is to pay too much attention to history and to the natural inclination and natural understanding. But in Matthew 4 the new King did not move merely according to the so-called spiritual leading nor according to history or the natural inclination. Rather, He moved along with God's economy according to the indicators in the environment. He went to Galilee, to the region of Zebulun and Naphtali, to shine as a great light upon those sitting in darkness and in the region and shadow of death (4:15-16).

Nothing that happened either to John the Baptist or to the Lord Jesus was accidental. When John came out to minister at the age of thirty, he was very bold. It was not very long before he was imprisoned. You may find it difficult to believe that John the Baptist could be imprisoned. There seemed to be no reason for this. Once again, his imprisonment was due to the environment. John was imprisoned by Herod the king, not by the Jewish leaders. However, both the religious power and the political power, the Jewish religion and the Roman government, collaborated for the accomplishment of God's purpose. It was sovereign according to God's economy that John the Baptist was imprisoned at that time. The reason for this is that there comes a time when every recommending ministry must cease. If John the Baptist had not been imprisoned, it would have been difficult for him to stop his ministry. Because John was the recommender, his ministry should not have continued. In John chapter three we see that the disciples of John the Baptist were in competition with the ministry of the new King (v. 26). The ministry of the recommender was competing with that of the King. Therefore, the ministry of the recommender had to be stopped, and the best way to stop it was to put John himself into prison and even to let him be beheaded.

You may say that God could not be so cruel as to allow this. But God sometimes allows things like this. No doubt, God brought you forth, prepared you, constituted you, qualified you, and then used you very much. But after He has used you, He may say, "Go to prison and wait there to be executed." Are you able to take this? You may say, "This is altogether unfair. God shouldn't allow this." But in the past God has allowed this very thing many times, and I believe He will allow it again. If He allows this to happen to you, you should simply say, "Amen." Do not send some of your disciples to challenge Christ, saying, "Are You the Christ, the almighty Lord whom I serve? If You are, why don't You do something to rescue me from prison?" The King would say, "I shall not save you from this. You must die. You must be terminated. Let the new King be on the throne." John the Baptist and his ministry were terminated because the new King was there. When the new King is here, there should not be any competition.

B. Starting from Galilee

The new King began His ministry in Galilee, even at the Sea of Galilee, not in the holy city or in the holy temple. His forerunner ministered by the riverside, in the wilderness, but He began His ministry by the Sea of Galilee. Galilee was a place of mixed population with both Jews and Gentiles. Hence, it was called "Galilee of the nations" (Gentiles) and was despised by orthodox Jews (John 7:41, 52). The newly appointed King began His kingly ministry for the kingdom of the heavens in such a despised place, far from the capital of the country, dignified Jerusalem, with its sacred temple, the center of the orthodox religion. This implied that the ministry of the newly anointed King was for a heavenly kingdom, different from the earthly kingdom of David (the Messianic kingdom). John the Baptist ministered by the riverside because he was prepared to bury everyone who came to him in repentance. The new King ministered around the Sea of Galilee. In the Bible the Jordan River signifies burial and resurrection, termination and germination. But the Sea of Galilee signifies the world corrupted by Satan. Thus, Jordan was a place of burial, and the Sea of Galilee was the corrupted world.

In this portion of the Word there are four disciples who were called by Jesus: Peter, Andrew, James, and John. Do you know where and when these four were saved? The answer to this question is in John chapter one. As John the Baptist was ministering, Andrew was brought to the Lord Jesus (John 1:35-37, 40). Andrew then found Peter, his brother, and led him to the Lord (John 1:40-42). When the Lord met Peter, He changed his name from Simon to Cephas, which means a stone (John 1:42). Therefore, in John chapter one both Peter and Andrew met the Lord Jesus. I believe they were saved at that time at the riverside of Jordan. The same thing happened to James and John. Of the two disciples of John the Baptist mentioned in John 1:35, one was the Apostle John. This John also brought his brother James to the Lord. Therefore, the four disciples mentioned in Matthew 4 had been terminated, germinated, and saved by the riverside of Jordan in John chapter one. However, they probably did not clearly understand what had happened to them.

I believe all this took place before the Lord's temptation, while John was still ministering by the Jordan. After that, they returned to Galilee to continue their work of fishing. Probably they forgot what had happened to them by the riverside. They simply returned to their old occupation around the sea. But the Lord Jesus did not forget them. After His temptation, He began His ministry and came after them. It was the same with many of us. The first time we came to the Lord, He did many things to us, but we had no realization of their significance. Perhaps your riverside was in Canada or China. After meeting the Lord by the riverside, you came to a Sea of Galilee to make a living, to do your job of fishing, forgetting what the Lord had done to

you by the riverside. Many of us simply forgot what the
Lord had done to us in the past by the riverside of Jordan
and did our best to make money working around our Sea of
Galilee, in the evil, devilish, Satan-corrupted world. But
one day, much to our surprise, the One who had saved us
by the riverside came to our Sea of Galilee as the newly
appointed King purposely to find us.

C. As a Great Light Shining in Darkness

When the Lord came to us by our Sea of Galilee, there
was something different about Him. In John chapter one,
Christ's recommender declared, "Behold, the Lamb of
God!" When John declared that Christ was the Lamb of
God, two of his disciples, Andrew and the Apostle John,
followed the Lord Jesus. Eventually, as we have seen, both
Andrew's brother, Peter, and John's brother, James, were
also brought to the Lord and saved. Although it was
wonderful to be saved, they later forgot their experience.
Many of us did the same thing. Perhaps you said, "What
happened there by the riverside of the Jordan? That was
silly! We were put into the water and we met a Nazarene
who was called the Lamb of God. But now we need to make
a living. Let's go back to our job. We have plenty of fishing
and mending of nets to do." Nevertheless, the King has His
goal, and He needs you, just as He needed Peter, Andrew,
James, and John. Thus, suddenly, the Lamb of God
appeared at the very place where these four men were
working to make a living. But this time He did not come as
the Lamb — He came as a great light.

Verse 16 says, "The people sitting in darkness saw a
great light, and to those sitting in a region and shadow of
death, to them light sprang up." John the Baptist was a
burning and shining lamp (John 5:35). But this new King
was the light. In fact, He was not only the light, but a great
light. Peter, Andrew, James, and John did not realize that
they were in darkness as they were working there by the
Sea of Galilee to make a living. They were in the shadow of
death. This is a picture of today's situation. Many
Christians met the Lord Jesus at some riverside and were

saved. But later they did not care for that experience; rather, they cared for making a living. Therefore, they went to the Sea of Galilee to earn a living. Without knowing it, by going to the Sea of Galilee to earn a living, they entered into darkness and into the shadow of death. All those striving to earn a living in the large cities like Los Angeles, New York, and Chicago are in darkness and in the region and shadow of death. Praise the Lord, the new King did not remain in Jerusalem! He came to the Sea of Galilee, and He is still coming to the Sea of Galilee today, walking about the seashore seeking to catch us. This time He comes not as a little Lamb, but as a great light. As Peter and Andrew were casting their nets into the sea, this great light shined upon them. As He stood there shining upon them, He might have said, "Peter and Andrew, what are you doing here? Don't you remember that I met you by the riverside of Jordan? Peter, don't you recall how I changed your name?" That day by the Sea of Galilee a great light was shining upon them.

Our experience was the same as theirs. We were saved at the riverside of Jordan. But we later forgot what had happened to us and went to the Sea of Galilee to make a living. As we were working there for our living, the One whom we had met as the Lamb of God by the riverside of Jordan came as a great light to shine upon us. As He was shining upon us, He inquired, "What are you doing there?" I can testify that this happened to me one day. As I was working by the Sea of Galilee earning a good living, suddenly a light shined upon me, and the Lord said, "What are you doing here? Don't you remember what happened to you by the riverside? You may not remember it, but I do." Then the call came, "Follow Me," and I followed Him. I believe that, in principle, a great many of us have had this kind of experience. You were saved at the riverside by the Lamb of God, but you were called by the Sea of Galilee by the shining of a great light. Although it may be easy to forget about what happened by the riverside, you cannot forget the time the great light shined upon you by the Sea of Galilee.

Although the record is very simple, the actual history is not that simple. It was not a simple matter for the Lord to call you. Firstly, He had to meet you by some riverside. Later, He had to come to you by some seashore. One day as you were working, the room where you were sitting was enlightened, a great light shined upon you, and the Lord asked you, "What are you doing here day after day?" When this happened to certain brothers, they threw down their pen and said, "What am I doing here?" Then the Lord asked, "Don't you remember what I did to you by the riverside? Now you must follow Me." Do not read the record of Matthew 4 merely in an objective way. We must read this chapter and even the whole Bible in a subjective way, applying it to ourselves. Praise the Lord that so many of us have had the experiences at two places — by the riverside and by the seashore!

The new King's ministry for the kingdom of the heavens began not with earthly power, but with heavenly light, which was the King Himself as the light of life, shining in the shadow of death. When the Lord began His ministry as light, He made no display of power and authority. He walked upon the seashore as a common person. But as He came to those four disciples by the Sea of Galilee, He shined upon them like a great light, shining in the darkness and in the region of the shadow of death. At that juncture, Peter, Andrew, James, and John were enlightened and attracted. We have pointed out that John the Baptist was a great magnet. But the Lord Jesus is the greatest magnet of all. As He shined upon those four disciples, they were attracted and captured. They immediately forsook their jobs and followed this little Nazarene.

In Matthew 4 there is no record, as in Luke 5, of any miracle being done by the Lord when Peter was called. However, in Matthew 4, there was the great light that attracted the first four disciples. This attraction came not from what the Lord Jesus did; it came from what He was. He was a great light, a great magnet, with the power to attract people and to capture them. In this way He attracted and captured the first four disciples. No one who follows the Lord because of what He does can be trustworthy or faithful. The trustworthy ones are those who are caught by what the Lord is. Peter, Andrew, James, and John were attracted and captured at the seashore, not by seeing what the Lord did, but by realizing what the Lord was. Because they had been attracted and captured, they became faithful followers of the Lord Jesus unto the end. Eventually, they were all martyred because they followed the King of the heavenly kingdom.

Moreover, when the Lord Jesus called these four disciples, He did not start a movement or a revolution. Rather, He attracted the disciples to Himself for the establishment of the kingdom of the heavens.

D. Preaching Repentance for the Kingdom of the Heavens

Verse 17 says, "From that time Jesus began to preach and to say, Repent, for the kingdom of the heavens has drawn near." The new King continued the preaching of His forerunner, John the Baptist, that is, the preaching of repentance for the kingdom of the heavens as the preliminary to the gospel of the kingdom.

E. Calling Four Disciples

1. Peter and Andrew

Verse 18 says, "And walking beside the sea of Galilee, He saw two brothers, Simon who was called Peter and Andrew his brother, casting a net into the sea, for they were fishermen." The new King's ministry was not in the capital, but beside the sea. His forerunner's ministry began by the riverside and consisted of burying the religious ones and terminating their religion. The new King's ministry began by the seashore and consisted of catching men who were not so religious, who lived around the sea instead of in the holy place, and making them fishers of men for the establishment of the kingdom of the heavens.

Verses 19 and 20 say, "And He said to them, Come,

follow Me, and I will make you fishers of men. And immediately, leaving the nets, they followed Him." When I read this portion of the Word as a young man, I could not understand why these fishermen suddenly followed a Nazarene who said, "Follow Me." I thought that they must have been beside themselves. However, after a number of years of reading the Word and considering my experience, I began to understand. Andrew, one of the two disciples of John the Baptist, had brought Peter to the Lord, in the place where John preached, prior to this (John 1:35-36, 40-42). That was the first time they met the Lord. Here the Lord met them the second time, this time at the Sea of Galilee. They were attracted by the Lord as the great light in the darkness of death and followed Him for the establishment of the kingdom of the heavens in the light of life.

When Peter and Andrew were called by the Lord, they were casting a net into the sea. The Lord called them to follow Him and promised to make them fishers of men. They left the net and followed the King of the kingdom of the heavens to be the fishers of men. Eventually, Peter became the first great fisher for the establishment of the kingdom of the heavens on the day of Pentecost (Acts 2:37-42; 4:4).

2. James and John

The same thing happened to James and John (Matt. 4:21-22). When they were called by the Lord, they were mending their nets in the boat. When the Lord called them, they left the boat and their father and followed Him. John and his brother, like Peter and Andrew, were attracted by the Lord and followed Him. Eventually, John became a real mender, mending the breakages in the church by his ministry of life. (See his three Epistles and Revelation chapters two and three.)

The calling of the four disciples was the beginning of the kingly ministry of the newly anointed King. It was the very foundation for the establishment of the kingdom of the heavens. These four disciples became the first four of the twelve Apostles. Peter and Andrew were the first pair, and James and John were the second. Thus, the first four disciples caught by the Lord Jesus became the first four foundation stones of the kingdom of God, which are four of the twelve foundations of the New Jerusalem (Rev. 21:14).

F. Attracting Great Crowds

1. By Traveling through the Whole of Galilee

Verse 23 says, "And Jesus went around the whole of Galilee, teaching in their synagogues, and preaching the gospel of the kingdom, and healing every disease and every sickness among the people." Jesus spread His ministry by traveling throughout the whole of Galilee.

2. By Teaching in the Synagogues

Verse 23 says that Jesus taught in the synagogues of Galilee. A synagogue is a place for the Jews to read and learn the Scriptures (Luke 4:16-17; Acts 13:14-15). The heavenly King took the opportunity to teach there.

3. By Preaching the Gospel of the Kingdom

From the beginning of His ministry, the heavenly King preached the gospel of the kingdom. The gospel in this book is called the gospel of the kingdom. It includes not only forgiveness of sins (cf. Luke 24:47) and the imparting of life (cf. John 20:31), but also the kingdom of the heavens (Matt. 24:14) with the power of the coming age (Heb. 6:5) to cast out demons and heal diseases (Isa. 35:5-6; Matt. 10:1). Both forgiveness of sins and imparting of life are for the kingdom.

4. By Healing Every Disease
and Those Possessed by Demons

As the Lord traveled throughout Galilee, He healed every disease and sickness among the people. The Lord Jesus spread His ministry by doing four things: traveling, teaching, preaching, and healing. In the work of the gospel today, we also must travel, teach, preach, and heal. We need all four items; we should neither ignore the matter of healing nor look down upon it. We should not follow the practice of either fundamental Christianity, which has very little healing, or Pentecostal Christianity, which places too much emphasis upon it, even having false healings that are mere performances. Instead of following these two extremes, we should walk in the footsteps of the Lord Jesus who traveled, taught, preached, and healed. Do not think that we do not believe in miracles. We definitely believe in them. We follow the Lord's leading to travel, preach, and heal.

Through shining as a great light, the Lord captured four young fishermen to be His disciples. These four disciples traveled with the King throughout Galilee as He taught, preached, and healed. The result was that "great crowds followed Him" (v. 25) for the kingdom of the heavens. This was the beginning of the founding of the kingdom of the heavens. It was absolutely different from the way of the world. The Lord did not start a political movement or form a political party. He did not carry on any kind of movement. In evangelism we must not follow the way of politics or the way of religion. We must follow the way of the Lord Jesus to shine upon others and to attract them by what we are. Then we must travel, teach, preach, and heal. This will attract a crowd.

LIFE-STUDY OF MATTHEW

THE DECREE
OF THE KINGDOM'S CONSTITUTION

(1)

In this message we come to the decree of the kingdom's constitution recorded in chapters five, six, and seven. Throughout the years, these three chapters have been either misunderstood or misused by many Christians. In the messages on these chapters we hope that we shall all see the real meaning of this section of the Word.

One of the most difficult things for believers to understand is the kingdom of the heavens. The kingdom of the heavens does not correspond to any natural or religious concept. As we shall see, it refers to something very specific. To understand the kingdom of the heavens, we all must be unloaded of the traditional concepts we received from our background in Christianity. None of the teachings regarding the kingdom of the heavens received in our background was according to the pure Word. We have studied this matter of the kingdom of the heavens again and again for more than fifty years. The first book I published on this subject was put out in 1936. In all the years since then, we have been on this subject. Thus, we have the full assurance that what we have seen in the Bible concerning the kingdom of the heavens is accurate. Nevertheless, it is somewhat different from the traditional concepts concerning the kingdom. Therefore, we must spend considerable time on these chapters to see this matter very clearly.

Matthew 5, 6, and 7 may be called the constitution of the kingdom of the heavens. Every nation has a constitution. Certainly the Gospel of Matthew, the book on the kingdom of the heavens, also must have a constitution. In these three chapters, the words spoken by the new King as the constitution of the kingdom of the heavens, we see a revelation of the spiritual living and heavenly principles of the kingdom of the heavens. The nature is singular, but the principles are plural. The constitution of the kingdom of the heavens is composed of seven sections: the nature of the kingdom people (5:1-12); the influence of the kingdom people upon the world (5:13-16); the law of the kingdom people (5:17-48); the righteous deeds of the kingdom people (6:1-18); the dealing of the kingdom people with riches (6:19-34); the principles of the kingdom people in dealing with others (7:1-12); and the ground of the kingdom people's living and work (7:13-29). The first section, 5:3-12, depicts the nature of the kingdom of the heavens under nine blessings. It unfolds the kind of people who live in the kingdom of the heavens. The kingdom people must also exert an influence upon the world. The nature of the kingdom people, the very nature of the kingdom, exercises an influence upon the world. The kingdom people also have a law. This law is not the old law, the law of Moses, the ten commandments; it is the new law of the kingdom of the heavens. The kingdom people are those who perform righteous deeds and who have the proper attitude concerning material riches. Because the kingdom people are still on earth in human society, the constitution of the kingdom of the heavens reveals principles by which they deal with others. Finally, in the last section of this constitution we see the ground, the base, of the daily life and work of the kingdom people. All these aspects of the kingdom people are covered in the seven sections of the constitution of the kingdom of the heavens.

I. THE PLACE AND THE AUDIENCE

A. On the Mountain

Matthew 5:1 says, "And seeing the crowds, He went up into the mountain; and when He sat down His disciples came to Him." The new King called His followers by the

seashore, but He went up into the mountain to give them
the constitution of the kingdom of the heavens. This indicates that we need to go higher with Him for the realization of the kingdom of the heavens.

It is very meaningful that the constitution of the
kingdom of the heavens was decreed upon a mountain. The
sea signifies the Satan-corrupted world. When we were
caught by the Lord, we were in the Satan-corrupted world
endeavoring to make a living. But after the Lord caught us,
He led us up to a high mountain signifying the kingdom of
the heavens. This indicates that the kingdom of the
heavens was not established on the seashore, but on the
mountain. In the Bible a mountain sometimes signifies the
kingdom. For example, according to Daniel 2:34-35, the
stone cut without hands broke the image into pieces and
became a great mountain that filled the whole earth. This
mountain signifies the millennial kingdom. Hence, in the
Bible a mountain signifies the kingdom, especially the
kingdom of the heavens.

Furthermore, being brought up to the mountain
signifies that if we would listen to the decree of the constitution of the kingdom of the heavens, we must not stay on
a low plain, but climb up a high mountain. We must be on
a high level to hear this constitution. On the seashore, the
Lord simply said, "Follow me." But for the decree of the
constitution of the kingdom of the heavens, He brought
them to the top of a mountain. Following the Lord may be
rather easy, but listening to the constitution for the establishment of the kingdom of the heavens requires that we
climb up to the top of a high mountain.

B. To His Disciples

Verse 1 says, "And when He sat down His disciples
came to Him." When the new King sat down on the mountain, His disciples, not the crowds, came to Him to be His
audience. Eventually, not only the believing Jews became
His disciples, but also the discipled nations (Gentiles,
28:19). Later the disciples were called Christians (Acts

11:26). Hence, the word the new King spoke on the mountain in chapters five, six, and seven concerning the constitution of the kingdom of the heavens was spoken to the believers of the New Testament, not to the Jews of the Old Testament.

In verses 1 and 2 we see that the Lord taught the disciples, not the crowds. The crowds that gathered around Him were the outer circle, but His disciples were the inner circle. Although you may be on the mountain, you must also be in the inner circle, for the constitution is not for those in the outer circle; it is for those in the inner circle.

Throughout history, there has been a great debate concerning to whom this decree was given, to the Jews, the Gentiles, or the believers. According to our study, we have come to see that it was given neither to the Jews nor to the Gentiles but to the New Testament believers. There is no doubt that the disciples were the Jewish believers at the time the decree of the constitution was given. However, when they were there on the mountain listening to the decree of the kingdom's constitution, they were the representatives not of the Jewish people, but of the New Testament believers. In 28:19 the Lord told His disciples to go and disciple the nations, that is, the Gentiles. This means that the nations would be converted into disciples. Therefore, both the Jewish and Gentile believers were disciples. The audience on the mountain, composed mainly of Jews, represented all the disciples.

II. CONCERNING THE NATURE
OF THE KINGDOM PEOPLE

Now we come to the first section of the constitution, the section concerning the nature of the kingdom people. Probably not many Christians have seen that 5:1-12 reveals the nature of the kingdom people. All Christians should be kingdom people. However, the situation today is not normal. Many believers are not on the high level of the kingdom people. The kingdom people are the overcomers. In God's economy, every believer should be an overcomer.

To be an overcomer is not to be something special; it is to be normal. Thus, every believer should be a part of the kingdom people.

These verses describe nine aspects of the nature of the kingdom people. They are poor in spirit, mourning for the present situation, meek in suffering opposition, hungry and thirsty for righteousness, merciful toward others, pure in heart, making peace with all men, suffering persecution for righteousness, and suffering being reproached and evil spoken of. Every aspect begins with the word, "Blessed." For instance, verse 3 says, "Blessed are the poor in spirit, for theirs is the kingdom of the heavens." The English word "blessed" does not adequately translate the Greek word here, for the Greek word conveys the meanings of both blessed and happy. A number of versions use the word happy instead of blessed. However, we should not use the word happy in a loose way. The blessedness and the happiness here is not a light thing; it is something that is rather weighty. When you hear the words, "Happy are the poor in spirit," you should not shout or jump up and down. To be happy in these verses is something deep.

A. Poor in Spirit to Receive
the Kingdom of the Heavens

In verse 3 the new King said, "Blessed are the poor in spirit, for theirs is the kingdom of the heavens." Although many have spoken about the blessings in these verses, I have not heard anyone speak about the spirit in verse 3. The translation of verse 3 in the Chinese version is very poor. It says, "Blessed are the humble in heart." Although the scholars who worked on the Chinese version generally did a very good job, they did not see the difference between the heart and the spirit. Another verse in this chapter, verse 8, speaks about being pure in heart. Hence, the Chinese translation speaks of the humble in heart and the pure in heart. Before we came into the church, many of us did not see the difference between the heart and the spirit. The kingdom of the heavens is firstly related to our spirit.

The spirit in verse 3 refers not to the Spirit of God, but to our human spirit, the deepest part of our being, the organ for us to contact God and realize spiritual things. To be poor in spirit does not mean to have a poor spirit. Our spirit should never be poor. To have a poor spirit would be pitiful. But if we are poor in our spirit, we are blessed. To be poor in spirit is not only to be humble, but also to be emptied in our spirit, in the depth of our being, not holding on to the old things of the old dispensation, but unloaded to receive the new things, the things of the kingdom of the heavens. We need to be poor, emptied, unloaded, in this part of our being so that we may realize and possess the kingdom of the heavens. This implies that the kingdom of the heavens is a spiritual matter, not a material one.

We need to empty our spirit of all the old things that have filled it. Those who are the most filled in their spirit are the Moslems. There is absolutely no empty space in their spirit. For this reason, it is very difficult to talk with them about the gospel. The Devil has utterly filled their spirit. Because their spirit is so filled, it is difficult for any Moslem to believe in the Lord Jesus. The Jews also are filled in their spirit. Their spirit is fully loaded with the things of their religion. The Greeks are filled in their spirit with their philosophy. I once worked with a Greek who boasted about the Greek language and philosophy. Although the mind and spirit of the Greeks are loaded, according to my experience with them, it is rather easy for the Greeks to be unloaded. They are not nearly as stubborn as the Moslems. Today a great many Christians are also loaded in their spirit. If you talk to those in the denominations, you will find that their spirit is loaded. Nearly every kind of Christian today is filled in his spirit with something other than God.

When the Lord Jesus came preaching, "Repent, for the kingdom of the heavens has drawn near" (4:17), not many

could receive His word because their spirit was filled with
other things. The best drink was being offered, but their
vessel was already filled. Thus, they were not thirsty.
When our spirit is filled, we have no capacity in our vessel
for even the best drink. Therefore, when the Lord spoke to
the disciples on the mountain, the opening word of His decree was that we must be poor in spirit, that our spirit must
be emptied of everything.

Many years ago I visited some Brethren assemblies in
this country. As I looked at the people, my heart was ach-
ing and my spirit was broken. What deadness there was!
Everyone was dry. In the first place I was invited, I gave a
word telling them that they did not need the teachings. I
told them that they had enough teachings and that what
they needed was life and the spirit. My word offended
them. They did not hear my word about life and the spirit;
they only heard what I had said about doctrine.
Immediately after the message, the leader came to me and,
rebuking me to my face, said, "Brother Lee, your teaching
is certainly wrong. You have just told us that we don't need
doctrine. Certainly we need doctrine! Isn't the Bible a book
of doctrine?" I did not say a word, but I thought, "Poor
people, if you like doctrine, go to doctrine and die there."
Later I was invited to speak to another Brethren assembly.
Both the situation and the reaction were the same. There
was such a reaction because those in these Brethren
assemblies were not poor in spirit. Rather, their spirit was
filled with all their so-called Brethren doctrines. All these
doctrines were like dead wood that was only good for
deadening them.

We all need to heed the Lord's word about being poor in
our spirit and say, "Lord, unload me. Empty my spirit. I
don't want to store anything in my spirit. Lord, I want the
full capacity in my spirit to be available to You."

Verse 3 says that those who are poor in spirit are blessed
because theirs is the kingdom of the heavens. Many
Christians are anxious to go to heaven, but hardly any
desire to be in the kingdom of the heavens. It is a mistake

to be anxious about heaven. God's heart is not on the heavens; it is on the kingdom of the heavens. Those who are poor in spirit are blessed because the kingdom of the heavens is theirs.

The kingdom of the heavens is a specific term used by Matthew, indicating that the kingdom of the heavens differs from the kingdom of God, the term used in the other three Gospels. The kingdom of God refers to God's reign in a general way, from eternity past to eternity future. It comprises eternity without beginning before the foundation of the world, the paradise of Adam, the chosen patriarchs, the nation of Israel in the Old Testament, the church in the New Testament, the coming millennial kingdom with its heavenly rule (the manifestation of the kingdom of the heavens), and the new heaven and the new earth with the New Jerusalem without end for eternity. The kingdom of the heavens is a special section within the kingdom of God, composed only of the church today and the heavenly part of the coming millennial kingdom. Hence, the kingdom of the heavens, a section of the kingdom of God, is also called the kingdom of God in the New Testament, especially in the other three Gospels. While the kingdom of God already existed with the nation of Israel in a general way in the Old Testament (21:43), the kingdom of the heavens had still not come in a specific way, but only drew near when John the Baptist came (3:1-2; 11:11-12).

According to Matthew, there are three aspects concerning the kingdom of the heavens: the reality, the appearance, and the manifestation. The reality of the kingdom of the heavens is the inward contents of the kingdom of the heavens in its heavenly and spiritual nature, as revealed by the new King on the mountain in chapters five, six, and seven. The appearance of the kingdom of the heavens is the outward state of the kingdom of the heavens in name, as revealed by the King on the seashore in chapter thirteen. The manifestation of the kingdom of the heavens is the practical coming of the kingdom of the heavens in power, as unveiled by the King on the Mount of

Olives in chapters twenty-four and twenty-five. Both the reality and the appearance of the kingdom of the heavens are with the church today. The reality of the kingdom of the heavens is the proper church life (Rom. 14:17), which is within the appearance of the kingdom of the heavens, known as Christendom. The manifestation of the kingdom of the heavens will be the heavenly part of the coming millennial kingdom, which is called the kingdom of the Father in 13:43. The earthly part of the millennial kingdom will be the Messianic kingdom, which is called the kingdom of the Son of Man in 13:41 and which will be the restored tabernacle of David, the kingdom of David (Acts 15:16). In the heavenly part of the millennial kingdom, which will be the kingdom of the heavens manifested in power, the overcoming believers will reign with Christ a thousand years (Rev. 20:4, 6). In the earthly part of the millennial kingdom, which will be the kingdom of the Messiah on earth, the saved remnant of Israel will be the priests, teaching the nations to worship God (Zech. 8:20-23).

If we are poor in spirit, the kingdom of the heavens is ours: we are in its reality now in the church age, and we shall share in its manifestation in the kingdom age.

According to the teaching of the four Gospels, there is a crucial difference between the kingdom of the heavens and the kingdom of God. If you would understand Matthew, you must differentiate the kingdom of the heavens from the kingdom of God. The kingdom of God is simply the divine ruling. It is God's ruling from eternity past to eternity future. Thus, the kingdom of God refers to the divine government, the rule of God. Between eternity past and eternity future we have the paradise of Adam, the patriarchs, the nation of Israel, the church, and the millennium. The millennium is divided into the upper part and the lower part. The upper part is called the kingdom of the Father, and the lower part is called the kingdom of the Son of Man and the kingdom of the Messiah, which is the restored kingdom of David. Everything from the paradise of

Adam to the New Jerusalem is included in the kingdom of God which extends from eternity to eternity.

The kingdom of the heavens is a part of the kingdom of God, just as California is a part of the United States. Because the kingdom of the heavens is part of the kingdom of God, it is sometimes called the kingdom of God. For example, California, part of the United States, is sometimes called the United States. When someone from abroad comes to California, he may say that he has come to the United States. Although California may be called the United States, the United States cannot be called California. Likewise, although the kingdom of the heavens may be called the kingdom of God, the kingdom of God cannot be called the kingdom of the heavens.

Matthew 21:43 indicates that the kingdom of God would be taken away from Israel. For the kingdom of God to be taken away from Israel indicates that it already was with Israel. If it had not been with Israel, how could it have been taken away? Although the kingdom of God was there already, John the Baptist said, "Repent, for the kingdom of the heavens has drawn near" (3:2). On the one hand, the kingdom of God was there; on the other hand, the kingdom of the heavens was not yet there. Even when the Lord spoke to the Jews in chapter twenty-one regarding the kingdom of God being taken away from Israel, the kingdom of the heavens had still only drawn near. It was not until the day of Pentecost that the kingdom of the heavens came. Therefore, in the first parable in chapter thirteen, the parable of the sower, the Lord Jesus did not say, "The kingdom of the heavens is likened to a sower," because He was already the sower before the day of Pentecost. Pentecost was the fulfillment of the second parable, the parable of the tares. Thus, in introducing that parable the Lord Jesus said, "The kingdom of the heavens was likened to . . . ." By all this we see that the kingdom of God was already present before the kingdom of the heavens came.

The kingdom of the heavens is composed of two sections. The first section is the church, and the second section is the upper part of the millennium. All genuine Christians are in the church today. But only the overcoming Christians will be in the upper part, the heavenly part, of the millennium. What we have in the church today is the reality of the kingdom of the heavens, not the manifestation. The manifestation of the kingdom will not take place until the millennium. The manifestation of the kingdom of the heavens will be seen in the upper part of the millennium.

Those who are poor in spirit are blessed, for theirs is the kingdom of the heavens. (Notice that the Lord did not say, "For theirs is the kingdom of God.") When we become poor in our spirit, we are ready to receive the heavenly King. When He comes in, He brings the kingdom of the heavens with Him. Immediately after receiving the heavenly King, we are in the church, where the reality of the kingdom of the heavens is. If we are overcomers, at His coming back the Lord will bring us into the manifestation of the kingdom of the heavens. To have the kingdom of the heavens is firstly to participate in the proper, normal church life and secondly to inherit the manifestation of the kingdom of the heavens in the upper part of the millennium. This is the meaning of the words, "For theirs is the kingdom of the heavens." Those Christians who backslide will lose the reality of the kingdom of the heavens in this age and will miss the manifestation of the kingdom of the heavens in the coming age. What a blessing it is to be poor in spirit! If we are poor in spirit, ours is the kingdom of the heavens. Hallelujah for the first blessing and for the kingdom of the heavens! How good it is to be poor in our spirit!

LIFE-STUDY OF MATTHEW

THE DECREE
OF THE KINGDOM'S CONSTITUTION

(2)

The kingdom of the heavens is absolutely related to our spirit. The first blessing in chapter five is a blessing in our spirit: "Blessed are the poor in spirit" (5:3). Thus, the first aspect of the kingdom of the heavens covered in this chapter is related to our human spirit.

There are some very poor translations of verse 3, such as, "Happy are the humble minded," and "Blessed are the humble in heart." Most Christians do not understand what the Lord Jesus was talking about when He spoke of being poor in spirit. Furthermore, they do not know that the kingdom of the heavens is altogether a matter in our spirit. If we do not know our spirit, we are through with the kingdom of the heavens because the kingdom of the heavens is related to our spirit.

As the Lord Jesus was speaking there on the mountain, He knew the actual situation of His audience, an audience composed of Galileans. Those Galileans were filled with the traditional concepts of religion. Even the immoral Samaritan woman in John chapter four had a number of religious concepts. Her conversation with the Lord Jesus exposed this fact. If even such a woman of low class was filled with religious concepts, certainly the Galilean fishermen were filled also. Three times a year they went up to Jerusalem for the feasts and stayed each time for at least a week. This one fact shows you that the Galilean fishermen were not empty vessels. During the time the Lord Jesus was on earth, all the people, whether they were

Jews or Romans or Greeks, were filled up. The Jews were filled with their traditional religious concepts, with their scriptural knowledge, and with the teachings of the law. They knew all about the holy city, the holy temple, and the sacred system of priestly service. They knew about the altar, the sacrifices, the festivals, the ordinances, and the regulations, all of which they considered outward blessings. There is no need to mention the Greeks and the Romans, for even the Jews that stood in front of the Lord Jesus were filled with their traditional concepts.

The Lord Jesus came as the new King to start a new dispensation. With the coming of the new King, God began a new economy. God's new dispensation is involved with a wonderful Person. Speaking figuratively, this new economy is simply this Person. Do not consider the kingdom of the heavens as something apart from Christ. No, it is Christ Himself. Without the King, we could not have the kingdom. We cannot have the kingdom of the heavens without Christ. When the Pharisees asked the Lord Jesus when the kingdom of God would come, He replied, "Behold, the kingdom of God is among you" (Luke 17:21). The Lord's word to the Pharisees indicated that He Himself was the kingdom. Where Jesus is, there the kingdom is also. The kingdom is simply the Person of the the King. Therefore, when we have the King, we also have the kingdom.

When Peter, Andrew, James, and John went up to Jerusalem to attend the feasts, John the Baptist was ministering in the wilderness outside Jerusalem. No doubt these four were attracted to him. Eventually, they met the Lord Jesus and were saved there by the riverside of the Jordan. The Lord Jesus was baptized in the Jordan, as were these four disciples, and He was anointed there. Following the anointing of the Lord Jesus, there was a period of forty days when He was tested. Those forty days were also a test to these four newly saved disciples. The Lord Jesus passed the test, but the disciples failed it, forgetting their experience of salvation by the riverside of Jordan and return-

ing to the Sea of Galilee to make a living. Two carried on
the work of fishing, and two the work of mending the nets.
The fact that they returned to the Sea of Galilee to fish and
to mend the nets proves that they had been defeated. Although they had been saved, they returned to their old
situation. Hence, they were failures.

The new King was led into the wilderness where He
gained the victory over the enemy. After winning the battle
against Satan, the new King came to the Sea of Galilee,
much to the surprise of Peter, Andrew, James, and John.
There by the Sea of Galilee the Lord Jesus contacted them
the second time. As we saw in message twelve, the first
time these four disciples were brought to the Lord, they
saw Him as the Lamb of God. But the second time, the
Lord paid them a gracious visitation as the great light. The
Bible is very economical in its description of the calling of
these four disciples. Peter and Andrew were fishing, and
James and John were mending their nets. Suddenly, the
One whom they had met more than forty days before
appeared as a great light shining upon them. They realized
that this was the Lamb of God, and they were attracted to
Him. However, this time the Lamb of God was the great
light shining upon them. After shining upon them, the new
King said, "Follow Me," and these four disciples followed
Him. Eventually, these four influenced others to follow the
Lord Jesus, and crowds were drawn to Him.

When the Lord Jesus went up to the top of the mountain, His disciples came to Him to be the inner circle, the
direct audience, for the decree of the new King. The first
thing He said was, "Blessed are the poor in spirit." This
word was the continuation of the Lord's preaching in 4:17,
where He had said, "Repent, for the kingdom of the
heavens has drawn near." In His preaching the Lord dealt
with the mind, the thoughts. He seemed to be saying, "You
must repent. You must have a change in your thinking, in
your mentality. Your mind needs to be turned." Undoubtedly Peter, Andrew, James, and John all had a genuine
turn in their understanding. By the time they were in the

inner circle to be the direct audience for the decree of the new King, there was no problem concerning their mind. Their thinking had already undergone a change.

Turning our mind provides a gateway for us to enter into the kingdom and for the kingdom to enter into us. The mind is neither the receiver nor the inner chamber; it is the gateway. The receiver, the inner chamber, is our spirit. Thus, our mind is the gateway, and our spirit is the inner chamber. We must put the Lord's word in 4:17, "Repent, for the kingdom of the heavens has drawn near," with His word in 5:3, "Blessed are the poor in spirit, for theirs is the kingdom of the heavens." The mind that has turned is the gateway through which the kingdom of the heavens comes into us. When the kingdom comes in, it is implanted in our spirit. It enters through the gateway of our mind and it arrives at our spirit. It is our spirit, not our mind, that receives the kingdom and retains it. Therefore, our spirit is the receiver and container of the kingdom of the heavens.

In their preaching, those evangelists who know the secret of the gospel firstly deal with people's mind. Then they proceed to deal with their spirit. The preaching of the gospel must deal with people's mind, with their way of thinking. This is to cause them to repent, to have a turn in their thinking and way of life. As soon as someone has repented, the proper preacher of the gospel will ask him to pray and to call on the name of the Lord. This is not the dealing with the mind, but the dealing with the spirit. After a person exercises his spirit to pray and to call on the name of the Lord, the Lord will immediately come into his spirit, passing through the gateway of the mind and arriving at his spirit.

The very Lord Jesus, who has entered our spirit through our mind, is the king. The kingdom is with Him. When the King enters someone's spirit, this means that the kingdom also enters into his spirit. From that time onward, both the King and the kingdom remain in his spirit. In the teaching of today's degraded Christianity, very few point out that the Christ who enters into our spirit is the very

King with the kingdom. When He comes into your spirit, the kingdom arrives with Him. Now in our spirit not only do we have the Savior; we also have the King with the kingdom.

Throughout the years, we have emphasized the importance of 2 Timothy 4:22: "The Lord be with your spirit." We have always applied this to the matter of life. However, now we must also see that whenever we say that the Lord Jesus is with our spirit, it means that the kingdom is with our spirit. This Lord Jesus is not only the Savior and the life, but also the King with the kingdom. Today we may declare, "In my spirit I have the Savior, the life, the King, and the kingdom!" When we repented and believed in the Lord Jesus as the Savior, the life, and the King with the kingdom, He entered our spirit and was implanted there. Therefore, in our spirit we now have the Savior, the life, and the King with the kingdom. We received such a One into us by being repentant in our mind and poor in spirit.

When I was walking in my fallen condition far away from God, I was filled with philosophy and religion. Not only was I walking in the wrong direction, but I was also filled with worthless concepts and thoughts. When I heard the preaching of the gospel, I had a turn in my mind; my mind was changed. Nevertheless, I was still full of many philosophical and religious concepts. Thus, I not only needed to have a turn in my mind, but also to become poor in spirit. To be poor in our spirit is to empty our spirit. It is to open up from the depths of our being and to be unloaded of all other things so that the Lord Jesus may be able to enter our spirit. When He came into me, He came as the King with the kingdom. Therefore, if you are poor in spirit, yours is the kingdom of the heavens. Although you may have made an about-face in your life and you may now be standing face to face with the Lord, what about your spirit? Is your spirit open to Him, or is it filled with other things? Are you still filled with philosophical and religious concepts? The Greeks may be filled with the philosophy of

Plato, the Chinese with the teachings of Confucius, and the Jews with the teachings of Moses. For the King with the kingdom to come into you, you must be poor in your spirit. This means that you must open up from the depths of your being and cast out all the concepts, opinions, and thoughts that have been filling you. When you have emptied your spirit, the King with the kingdom will come into you. Then yours is the kingdom of the heavens.

Please pay careful attention to the tense of the predicate in verse 3. It is not future tense, but present tense. This verse does not say, "Theirs will be the kingdom of the heavens"; it says, "Theirs is the kingdom of the heavens." When you open from the depths of your being, that is, from your spirit, and unload yourself and empty your spirit, the King as the life-giving Spirit will enter in through the gateway of your repentant mind and come into your spirit to be your King with the kingdom. From then on, the kingdom is within you, and the kingdom of the heavens is yours. This is salvation according to the New Testament.

However, today's degraded Christianity has missed this. When you received the Lord Jesus, did you realize that a kind of ruling had come into you? This ruling is the reigning of the kingdom. We have not only the Savior and the life, but also the King. This King exercises His authority from within our spirit. Even if you were just saved today, you already have this kingdom within you. Although I was saved more than fifty years ago, I do not have anything more than someone who has just been saved. The One within us is our Savior, our life, and our King with the kingdom. How rich and how high He is! Because we have received Him into our spirit, ours is the kingdom of the heavens. The kingdom is ours, and the kingdom is in our spirit.

Now we should understand the meaning of verse 3: "Blessed are the poor in spirit, for theirs is the kingdom of the heavens." We need to change the pronoun and say, "Blessed are the poor in spirit, for ours is the kingdom of the heavens." Once we understand the meaning of this verse, we see what a mistake it is to teach that the kingdom has been suspended until the millennium. The word, "is" in this verse proves that the kingdom of the heavens is ours right now. How blessed we are! How blessed it is to be poor in spirit! If we are poor in spirit, ours is the kingdom of the heavens. If you take this word into you, you will never be the same. This one verse is better than a hundred messages. Hallelujah, ours is the kingdom of the heavens! We are truly blessed and happy. Blessed and happy are the poor in spirit, for ours is the kingdom of the heavens.

B. Those Mourning to Be Comforted

Although we should be very happy to hear that we are in the kingdom of the heavens today, in the very next verse the Lord Jesus told us to mourn. Verse 4 says, "Blessed are those who mourn, for they shall be comforted." It does not seem logical to say that those who mourn are blessed and happy. However, if we pray for a certain period of time, with a spirit filled with the King and the kingdom, we shall begin to mourn over the negative situation of today. The entire situation of the world is negative in relation to God's economy. Satan, sin, self, darkness, and worldliness predominate among all people on earth. God's glory is insulted, Christ is rejected, the Holy Spirit is frustrated, the church is desolated, self is corrupted, and the whole world is evil. Hence, God wants us to mourn over such a situation. Because the kingdom is in us, we are subdued, controlled, and ruled by the indwelling King. If, while we are under this rule, we look at the environment and the situation of today's world, we shall sigh and mourn.

This mourning, however, is a blessing, for the Lord said that those who mourn "shall be comforted." If we mourn according to God and His economy, we shall be comforted by being rewarded with the kingdom of the heavens. We shall see God's heavenly ruling over all the negative situation. Many times I have had the experience of mourn-

ing and being comforted. Do not be disappointed. We must
mourn, yet we are filled with hope. The King is coming, the
enemy will be defeated, and the earth will be regained by
Christ. Sooner or later, we shall be comforted. Is it not a
comfort to see so many in the Lord's recovery seeking the
Lord and His kingdom? What a comfort this is to me! If
you have never experienced mourning in your spirit, then
you cannot realize how sweet and comforting it is to see so
many who care only for the Lord's kingdom. For this
reason, we love all the dear saints in the Lord's recovery.
All the churches with all the seeking saints are a real comfort to every mourning spirit.

C. The Meek to Inherit the Earth

The sequence in these verses is very significant. Firstly
we are poor in spirit to receive the King with the kingdom
and to contain Him. Then we mourn over the pitiful
situation and are comforted. Following this, we have a
word about the meek. Verse 5 says, "Blessed are the meek,
for they shall inherit the earth." Some translators have
said that the Greek word rendered "earth" should be
"land." But whether we translate this as earth or land, it
refers to the coming subdued world. Today the earth is a
worldly kingdom under the rule of Satan. But the day is
coming when the Lord, the King, will regain this world.
Revelation 11:15 says, "The kingdom of the world has
become the kingdom of our Lord and of His Christ, and He
shall reign forever and ever." The world spoken of in
Revelation 11:15 is the earth in verse 5.

In Matthew 5:5 the Lord says that the meek will inherit
the earth. Those who are poor in spirit in verse 3 and who
mourn in verse 4 are now the meek in verse 5. Many
Christians do not understand what it means to be meek. It
does not mean simply to be gentle, humble, and submissive. To be meek means not to resist the world's opposition, but to suffer it willingly. To be meek means not to
fight or to resist. If we are meek, willing to suffer the

world's opposition in this age, we shall inherit the earth in the coming age, as revealed in Hebrews 2:5-8 and Luke 19:17, 19.

Today, those who fight are those who gain the land. If you do not fight, you will not receive any territory. This is the reason there are so many wars. Nations wage war with one another to gain more territory for themselves. The human way is to obtain the land by fighting for it, but the way of the kingdom of the heavens is to gain it by being meek. There is no need to fight, but there is the need to be meek. Some of the young people have been shouting slogans about taking the earth. The way to take the earth is not by slogans, shouting, or fighting. The way is through meekness. Blessed are the meek, for they shall inherit the earth. Are you a fighting one or a meek one? If you would inherit the earth, you must be meek. When the Lord Jesus comes back, He will regain the earth. However, when He was arrested, tried, and crucified at Golgotha, He was meek. As He was nailed to the cross, He did not resist. In every way He was meek, meek to the very end. Eventually, the earth will be gained not by the fighting ones, but by the meek ones. Several weeks ago an opposer told one of our brothers, "We are going to stop you!" Time will tell who will be stopped. The fighting ones will be stopped, but the meek ones will not be stopped. Rather, they will inherit the earth. Satan is always fighting, but the Lord Jesus never fights. Instead, He is meek. In this we see that the economy of God is opposite to the economy of man. If you want to gain the earth, you should be meek. If you have not received any territory, this may indicate that you are not yet meek enough. Young people, you must be meek on the campuses. I realize that this is a heavenly language. But the Lord Jesus did not say, "Blessed are those who fight, for they shall gain the earth. The fighters shall take the earth!" Do not say, "Let's take the earth by fighting for it." No, you must say instead, "Let's take the earth by being meek." You may think that meekness is related to material things. However, if you consider the matter carefully, you will see that meekness is not related to outward material things. Rather, it is related to something inward, to what we are in our very being.

D. Those Hungry and Thirsty
for Righteousness to Be Satisfied

In verse 6 the Lord said, "Blessed are those who hunger and thirst for righteousness, for they shall be satisfied." Righteousness here is to be right in our behavior. This righteousness is related to what we are inwardly. This is indicated by the fact that we are told to hunger and thirst for righteousness so that we might be satisfied.

In order to understand verse 6 we must also consider verse 20. Verse 20 says, "For I say to you, that unless your righteousness surpass that of the scribes and Pharisees, you shall by no means enter into the kingdom of the heavens." In verses 3 and 20 we see two aspects of the kingdom of the heavens. In verse 3 the verb is present tense, and in verse 20 it is future tense. On the one hand, the kingdom of the heavens is ours; on the other hand, we shall enter into the kingdom of the heavens. If we are poor in our spirit, the reality of the kingdom of the heavens is ours today. But we still need to enter into the manifestation of the kingdom of the heavens. Remember the two aspects of the kingdom of the heavens: the reality in the church today and the manifestation in the upper part of the millennium in the future. If we are truly poor in our spirit, seeking after Christ, the reality of the kingdom of the heavens is ours. Then at the time of the millennium we shall enter into the manifestation of the kingdom of the heavens. However, in order to enter into the manifestation of the kingdom of the heavens we need the surpassing righteousness, the righteousness that surpasses that of the scribes and the Pharisees. We need to hunger and thirst for this righteousness, to seek after such righteousness, that we may enter into the kingdom of the heavens (vv. 6, 10, 20). If we hunger and thirst for righteousness, God will grant us to be satisfied with the very righteousness we seek. If we seek this surpassing righteousness, it will be given to us.

Righteousness is to be right not only with God, but also with man. The righteousness of the scribes and the Pharisees was rather low because it was the righteousness according to the law. Our righteousness must not be according to the old law, but according to the new law. As we shall see, the new law is much higher than the old. The old law says, "You shall not murder." But the new law says, "Everyone who is angry with his brother shall be liable to the judgment" (v. 22). By this one example we see that our righteousness must be on a higher level than the righteousness of the Pharisees. We must take care not only of not murdering, but even of not being angry with our brother. This righteousness is on the highest plane.

Our natural life is not able to attain this righteousness. This inward subjective righteousness must be Christ. Only Christ can fulfill the requirements of the new law. When I read Matthew 5 as a young man, I was disappointed and said, "I simply can't make it. I'll just have to quit." But the more I have grown, the more I have come to realize that I can make it because I have a life within me that can do it. The King with His kingdom within me can make it. However, this King needs our cooperation. We cooperate by being hungry and thirsty. We cooperate by saying, "O Lord Jesus, I hunger and thirst after You. Lord, I want to be filled with You." If you hunger and thirst in this way, you will be satisfied.

The righteousness in verse 6 is simply Christ. It is the surpassing righteousness, the righteousness on the highest plane, that can only be attained by Christ. Because He is the One who produces this highest righteousness, we must seek after Him. We need to pray, "Lord, make me hungry. Grant me an appetite for Yourself. Grant me the appetite to seek the surpassing righteousness." If you seek righteousness in this way, you will be satisfied. You will receive what you have been seeking.

E. The Merciful to Receive Mercy

Verse 7 says, "Blessed are the merciful, for they shall receive mercy." To be righteous is to give one what he deserves, whereas to be merciful is to give someone better than he deserves. For the kingdom of the heavens, we need to be not only righteous, but also merciful. To receive mercy is to get better than we deserve. If we are merciful to others, the Lord will grant us mercy (2 Tim. 1:16, 18), especially at His judgment seat (James 2:12-13).

To be righteous is to deal with yourself in a strict way. We must be righteous in dealing with ourselves. We should not give ourselves any excuse. Toward others, however, we must be merciful. If we are diligent to seek the surpassing righteousness, we shall eventually become merciful toward others. In our seeking we shall find that our natural man is weak and that we are prone to failure. If you do not realize the pitiful condition of your natural man, you will never have mercy on others. Instead of showing mercy to them, you will condemn them when they fail or fall. The reason you condemn them is that you do not know yourself. If you know yourself, whenever someone fails, you will say, "Lord, have mercy on me and on my brother. We all are weak vessels and cannot fulfill Your requirements. Lord, even though my brother has offended me, I would still be merciful toward him." If you have never failed, you will never be merciful. If you are always successful in your pursuit of holiness and perfection, you will have no sympathy toward others when they fail. You will always condemn them. But if you know how weak you are and how many mistakes you have made, you will be merciful to others.

There is a promise for us in verse 7. The promise is that those who are merciful will receive mercy. If you judge your brother without mercy today, you will not receive any mercy at the judgment seat of Christ. Because you judge others unmercifully, Christ will judge you unmercifully. But if you have mercy on your brother, the Lord will have mercy on you at His judgment seat. Thus, the kingdom people are strict in dealing with themselves, but very merciful in dealing with others. Once again, this is not an outward matter, but a matter related to our inward being.

F. The Pure in Heart to See God

Verse 8 says, "Blessed are the pure in heart, for they shall see God." To be righteous is to deal with ourselves, to be merciful is to deal with others, and to be pure in heart is to deal with God. Toward ourselves, we must be strict and allow no excuses. Toward others, we should be merciful, giving them more than they deserve. But toward God we must be pure in heart, seeking nothing besides Him. The reward for being pure in heart is to see God. God is our reward. No reward is greater than God Himself. We gain this reward by being strict, righteous, with ourselves, by being merciful toward others, and by being pure in heart toward God.

To be pure in heart is to be single in purpose, to have the single goal of accomplishing God's will for God's glory (1 Cor. 10:31). This is for the kingdom of the heavens. Our spirit is the organ to receive Christ (John 1:12; 3:6), whereas our heart is the ground where Christ as the seed of life grows (13:19). For the kingdom of the heavens we need to be poor in spirit, empty in our spirit, that we may receive Christ. We also need to be pure in heart, single in our heart, that Christ may grow in us without frustration. If we are pure in heart in seeking God, we shall see God. Seeing God is a reward to the pure in heart. This blessing is both for today and for the coming age.

G. Those Making Peace
to Be Called the Sons of God

Verse 9 says, "Blessed are the peacemakers, for they shall be called sons of God." Satan, the rebellious one, is the instigator of all rebellion. For the kingdom of the heavens, under its heavenly ruling, we must be peacemakers with all men (Heb. 12:14).

In all of the first seven blessings we see that we should not be fighters or troublemakers; rather, we must be peacemakers, always making peace with others. If we are peacemakers, we shall be called the sons of God. The sons of the Devil make trouble, but the sons of God make peace. As the Son of God, the Lord Jesus made peace with God and man. Now, as the sons of God, we must follow Him to make peace. Then we shall be called the sons of God.

Our Father is the God of peace (Rom. 15:33; 16:20), who has a peaceful life with a peaceful nature. As those born of Him, if we would be the peacemakers, we must behave in His divine life, according to His divine nature. Thus, we shall express His life and nature, and we shall be called sons of God.

H. Those Persecuted for Righteousness to Participate in the Kingdom of the Heavens

Verse 10 says, "Blessed are those who have been persecuted for the sake of righteousness, for theirs is the kingdom of the heavens." The whole world lies in the evil one (1 John 5:19) and is filled with unrighteousness. Every aspect of the world is unrighteous. If we hunger and thirst for righteousness, we shall be persecuted for the sake of righteousness. We need to pay a price for the righteousness we seek for the kingdom of the heavens. If we are righteous, we shall be condemned, opposed, and persecuted. Hence, we shall suffer persecution. Many saints who have done their best to be righteous have suffered persecution as a result. In their environment, business, or employment there were many unrighteous things. Because they desired to be righteous in that situation, they suffered persecution from others.

This verse says that those who are persecuted for righteousness are blessed, "for theirs is the kingdom of the heavens." If we seek righteousness at a cost, the kingdom of the heavens becomes ours: we are in its reality now, and we shall be rewarded with its manifestation in the coming age. We have pointed out that, according to verse 20, in order to be in the kingdom of the heavens, we need the surpassing righteousness, the righteousness on the highest plane. To enter the manifestation of the kingdom of the heavens we need this kind of righteousness. Therefore, we need to hunger and thirst after it and to suffer persecution for it.

I. Those Reproached, Persecuted, and Evil Spoken Of for His Sake to Receive Great Reward in the Heavens

In verse 11 the new King said, "Blessed are you when they reproach and persecute you, and say every evil thing against you, lying, for My sake." The persecution in verse 10 is for the sake of righteousness, because of our seeking for righteousness; whereas the persecution in verse 11 is directly for the sake of Christ, the new King, because of our following Him.

When we live a life for the kingdom of the heavens in its spiritual nature and according to its heavenly principles, we are reproached, persecuted, and evil spoken of, mostly by the religious people who hold onto their traditional religious concepts. The Jewish religionists did all these things to the Apostles in the early days of the kingdom of the heavens (Acts 5:41; 13:45, 50; 2 Cor. 6:8; Romans 3:8). This is also true today. If you are truly seeking Christ, many in the denominations will rise up against you. This is what we are suffering now. We are suffering reproach, persecution, and evil rumors circulated about us. Recently a reputable publishing firm published a book associating us with Hinduism. What an evil rumor! This reproach and persecution comes to us because we do not care for tradition, but for Christ and the pure word of the Bible.

In verse 12 the Lord Jesus speaks an encouraging word to those who are persecuted for His sake: "Rejoice and be glad, for your reward is great in the heavens; for thus they persecuted the prophets before you." This reward of the ninth blessing indicates that all the results of the foregoing eight blessings are also rewards. This reward is great and is in the heavens, a heavenly reward, not an earthly one.

LIFE STUDY OF MATTHEW

MESSAGE FIFTEEN

THE DECREE
OF THE KINGDOM'S CONSTITUTION

(3)

In order to have a good nation or kingdom, there must be good people. A proper country needs proper people. Thus, in the constitution of the heavenly kingdom, the Lord Jesus firstly reveals the kind of people who live in the kingdom of the heavens.

THE INWARD BEING
OF THE KINGDOM PEOPLE

The nine blessings in 5:3-12 are all related to the nature of the kingdom people. The kind of people we are depends upon our nature. Every aspect of these nine blessings deals mainly with our inward being, not with outward material things. Along with our inward being, these verses also deal somewhat with the outward expression. Take the example of righteousness. If you read these verses carefully, you will see that righteousness here is not merely a matter of outward behavior. Rather, it is the outflow of our inner being, the expression of what we are within. Thus, the first section of the constitution (5:1-12) deals with the inward being of the kingdom people.

NINE CRUCIAL WORDS

In considering the nature of the kingdom people as revealed in these verses, we need to remember nine crucial words, one for each of the nine blessings: poor in spirit, mourning, meek, hungry and thirsty for righteousness, merciful, pure, peaceful, persecuted, and reproached. These words reveal what kind of people the kingdom people should be. They should always be poor in spirit, mournful over the present situation, meek in facing opposition, righteous toward themselves, merciful toward others, pure toward God, peaceful toward all men, persecuted for righteousness, and reproached for the sake of Christ. The totality of these nine words is the nature of the kingdom people.

POOR IN SPIRIT AND MOURNING

The sequence of these verses is very significant. Firstly we must be poor in spirit, and then we can mourn. If we are not poor in our spirit, we do not have the capacity for the King to come in to establish His kingdom within our being. If we do not have the heavenly kingdom established within us, we cannot realize how negative and pitiful the whole world is. However, when the Lord Jesus is able to set up His kingdom within us and when the full capacity of our whole being, even the depths of our being, our spirit, is available to Him, we shall realize that the earth is dark, corrupt, and filled with sin. Spontaneously we shall mourn for this sad situation. For this reason, the Lord Jesus did not speak first of mourning and then of being poor in spirit. He put the matter of being poor in our spirit first. Only when we are poor in spirit can we mourn.

MOURNING AND MEEKNESS

If we are poor in spirit and mourn for the pitiful situation of others, spontaneously we shall be meek. Even if your mother-in-law is in a pitiful condition, do not tell her so. Even the condition of your dear wife may not be very positive in the eyes of the Lord. If her heart and her interests are not for the Lord, and she does not care for the Lord's kingdom, her situation is pitiful. You have the Lord Jesus with the heavenly kingdom in your spirit, but what about your wife? You may be in the highest heaven, but she may be in the lowest hell. Furthermore, consider your children. You may love the Lord to the uttermost, but they may not love Him at all. Therefore, you must mourn for your mother-in-law, your wife, and your children. You must also mourn for your relatives, your colleagues, and your neighbors. Where is one who is truly for the Lord? Look at the deplorable condition of the world today, including that of Christianity. The merchants care only for money, the students care only for their education, and the working people care only for promotions and positions. When we are poor in spirit, we shall surely mourn for the whole situation. We shall mourn for our environment and for the people around us.

Because we mourn for others, we would never fight against them. Instead of fighting them, spontaneously we shall be meek toward them. If you are not yet meek with your wife, it reveals that you have not been possessed by the kingdom of the heavens. This indicates that other things are still occupying you. If you have been fully occupied within by the heavenly kingdom, you will mourn for your wife and be meek with her. You will be meek toward every pitiful person. If you are a student, you will be meek toward your teachers and classmates. You will be meek toward others because you have a deep feeling within about their pitiful situation. Because you have been praying for them in the way of mourning, whenever you contact them, you will be meek.

A WORD ABOUT MEEKNESS

Let me say a further word about meekness. The New Testament tells us that we do not fight against flesh and blood, but against the Devil, against the enemy of God. We must fight against the Devil, God's enemy, day and night. However, we are not to fight against people, not even against those who oppose us. Toward all men, including the adversaries and opposers, we must be meek. Although we fight Satan and the principalities in the air, we do not fight people. Instead, we love them all. Young people, do not go to the campuses to fight with the students. Never say, "We shall defeat the students and take the earth!" Do not go to the campuses to fight — go there to be meek. We need to be so meek that, even if a persecutor hits us on the right cheek, we would turn to him the left cheek. To be meek means not to resist or to fight back. However, as we turn our left cheek to the persecutor, we should pray, "Lord, bind the powers of darkness!" While we are being meek toward other people, we must fight against the powers of darkness. The enemy is not the people; it is Satan and his angels, the evil powers in the air.

HUNGERING AND THIRSTING
FOR RIGHTEOUSNESS

As we are being meek toward others, we must hunger and thirst for righteousness. We ourselves must be right with everyone. We must be right with our parents, our husband or wife, our children, our in-laws, our relatives, and our neighbors. The people of the heavenly kingdom are righteous in this way. Do not think that, if we are mournful and meek, we can afford to be loose. No, we must hunger and thirst for the highest righteousness.

RIGHTEOUS WITH OURSELVES,
MERCIFUL TOWARD OTHERS

Although we must be strict with ourselves in righteousness, we must learn to be merciful to others and not to place demands on them. It is wrong for any Christian to place demands on others. If you are truly strict with yourself, then you will know how to be merciful to others. But do not try to be merciful to others without first being righteous with yourself. Every sloppy person is merciful to others because he has already been merciful to himself. If he sleeps late every morning, he will be very merciful to others who sleep late. This kind of mercy is not mercy at all; it is absolutely wrong. No one who is sloppy knows how to be merciful to others. Only a strict person, a righteous person, knows how to be merciful. If you would be merciful to others according to the fifth blessing, you must first be righteous toward yourself according to the fourth blessing.

We must be righteous and strict with ourselves, never making excuses for ourselves. But when others offend us, thereby exposing their shortage, we must be merciful toward them. All those who are self-righteous condemn others and never let them go. The word spoken by the Lord on the mount is completely different from this. To ourselves, we must be righteous and strict, serious and sober. But toward others we must be merciful. In Himself God is righteous. However, if He were righteous to the uttermost in dealing with us, we would all be killed. Although God is righteous in relation to Himself, He is full of mercy in dealing with us. As fallen sinners, we surely need God's mercy. We also must learn to be righteous with ourselves, and merciful toward others. This matter of being righteous toward ourselves and merciful toward others is not firstly a matter of outward behavior; it is firstly a matter of our inward attitude, of our inward being.

As a brother taking the lead, either as an elder in the church or as a brother in the brothers' house, you may find it difficult to be strict with yourself and yet be merciful toward others. Suppose everyone is supposed to be home by a certain time. To come home later than that time is not righteous. Likewise, it is not right to inconvenience others. However, when some young people come home, they like to throw their shoes anywhere they please. I knew of one co-worker, a preacher and teacher of the Bible, who used to throw his socks without any concern for where they landed around the room. One time this brother and I were guests in a certain home. The hostess, quite concerned, spoke to me about this brother's sloppiness. What a shame that was to me! Some of the brothers living in the brothers' houses may act the same way.

Other brothers may be unhappy about being required to wash dishes; therefore, they may not clean them thoroughly. This is not righteous. It is never righteous to take advantage of others, to invade their rights. Not doing an adequate job in washing dishes is taking advantage of others. If you are such a one, you are not a righteous per-

son. If you are a leader in the brothers' house, you must be
strict with yourself about the time, about excessive talking, about noise, about washing dishes, and about many
other things. Do not say this is too much. It may seem too
much to you, but it is not too much to Christ who lives
within you. In everything you do, you must be strict with
yourself.

However, as one taking the lead in the brothers' house
or in any aspect of the church life, you must also be merciful. Sometimes a leader may warn a sloppy one about his
dishwashing, saying, "This is your first warning about the
way you wash the dishes. After two more warnings, you will
have to move out." Remember the word of the Lord Jesus
about how many times you must forgive your brother
(18:21-22). Even if a certain brother does not clean the
dishes thoroughly after you have spoken to him a number
of times, you must still be merciful to him. Do not drive
away even such a sloppy and pitiful brother. Instead, be
merciful to him. This does not mean that you go to the opposite extreme and say, "I have learned that I must be
merciful toward this brother. Therefore, from now on, I will
never talk to him about the way he does the dishes. Let
him do the dishes any way he wants. We'll just have to
tolerate it in order to keep him." This attitude is not right
either. You need to take care of such a sloppy brother day
after day. Let him have a turn at washing the dishes. But
each time he does so, you must be patient and merciful
toward him.

It is easy for us to be either strict or sloppy. But we
must learn to be strict on the one hand and merciful on the
other. If we give others a strict dealing, we must immediately be merciful toward them. This is an important
lesson for elders to learn. The kingdom people are both
righteous and merciful. When you are righteous, you must
be absolutely righteous; and when you are merciful, you
must be very merciful. Although righteousness and mercy
are two opposite poles, they must meet in your experience.
Your righteousness must come together with your mercy.

PURE IN HEART AND SEEING GOD

According to the sequence of the blessings in Matthew 5, being pure in heart comes after the showing of mercy to others. This also corresponds to our experience. If you are not righteous with yourself and merciful to others, you will find it difficult to be pure in heart toward God. In order to be pure in heart toward God, you must be strict in dealing with yourself and merciful in dealing with others. As far as logic is concerned, there seems to be no reason for this. But our practical experience proves that it is so. If you are not right with yourself and merciful with others, you will never be pure with God. I believe that at least some of those among us in the churches have the experience of what I am speaking about here. Throughout the years, we have learned the lesson of being strict with ourselves and of not making excuses for ourselves. But we have also learned to be merciful to others, especially to those who are weaker. As a result, our heart is pure in seeking God. When we are righteous with ourselves and merciful with others, we see God. But when we are loose with ourselves and condemn others, our eyes are absolutely blind, and we cannot see God. If you excuse yourself, yet make demands of others, your heart is not pure. A pure heart toward God comes only from strict dealings with yourself and merciful dealings with others.

Even in the churches, a number of saints always excuse themselves and place demands on others. For example, they may excuse their sleeping late in the morning by saying that last night they received a long distance call. But if they hear that a certain brother did not come to morning watch, they would say, "Why didn't he come? As a leader in the brothers' house, he should rise up early in the morning." The eyes of such a person are blind, indicating that his heart is not pure. We must be strict toward ourselves and merciful toward others. If others are loose, idle, or sloppy, we may have to warn them in a proper way. Nevertheless, we must still be merciful toward them. No matter how strict we may need to be at times in dealing with others, mercy must still be shown to them. If we are strict with ourselves and merciful to others, we shall have a pure heart, a heart single toward God. The reward of having a pure heart is seeing God. I can assure you that if you will practice being strict with yourself and merciful with others, you will see God.

PEACEMAKERS

You will also be a peaceful person. Those who are strict with themselves, merciful to others, and pure toward God are peacemakers. They do not like to offend, hurt, or damage anyone. Rather, they like to make peace with everyone. To be a peacemaker does not mean to be political. To be political is falsehood and hypocrisy. We must be righteously square, not politically round. Remember, the New Jerusalem is square, not round. We Christians must be like this. Although we are righteously square, we are still merciful toward others. This enables us to be pure toward God and to see Him. If we are such a person, spontaneously we shall be peacemakers. Instead of fighting with others and hurting them, we shall always maintain peace with those with whom we are involved. This is what it means to be a peacemaker.

SONS OF GOD

Those who are peacemakers will be called sons of God. This means that those around us will say, "These people are not only the sons of men, but the sons of God. All the sons of men fight against one another, but the sons of God, like their heavenly Father, are peaceful and always make peace with others. Romans 12:18 says, "If possible, as far as it depends on you, living in peace with all men." However, this keeping of peace should not be merely an outward behavior. That is politics. Our peace must issue out of our nature. We have a nature that makes us strict with ourselves, merciful with others, and pure with God. Because we have this nature, we spontaneously keep the peace with others. This is not political peacemaking; it is the spontaneous issue of our nature. This will cause others to say, "These are truly the sons of God."

SUFFERING PERSECUTION
FOR RIGHTEOUSNESS

If we have a nature corresponding to what is revealed in these verses, some in society will persecute us. This persecution will be for two reasons: for righteousness and for the sake of Christ. The eighth blessing concerns the persecution for righteousness (v. 10), and the ninth, the persecution for Christ (vv. 11-12). Why would others persecute us for righteousness and for Christ? Simply because we are poor in spirit, concerned for the negative situation of today's world and mourning about it, meek toward attackers and opposers, righteous with ourselves, merciful toward others, pure with God, and making peace with all. Therefore, the evil society will not agree with us. Because we desire to be righteous, they will persecute us for the sake of righteousness. Because we want to be truthfully and honestly right, they will persecute us.

If we suffer persecution for the sake of righteousness, ours is the kingdom of the heavens. Suffering for the sake of righteousness is a condition for participation in the kingdom of the heavens. If we do not remain in righteousness, we are outside the kingdom. But if we stay in righteousness, we are in the kingdom because the kingdom is absolutely a matter of righteousness. In the kingdom there is nothing wrong, unjust, or dark; everything is righteous and light. This is the nature of the kingdom. When we are poor in spirit, the kingdom of the heavens comes into us. But when we stay in righteousness, the kingdom of the heavens remains in us. In both cases, ours is the kingdom of the heavens. If we would receive the kingdom of the heavens, we must be poor in our spirit, and if we would have the kingdom of the heavens remain in us, we must stay in righteousness. But if you would stay in righteousness, be prepared to confront persecution. You will be persecuted for the sake of righteousness.

REPROACHED FOR THE SAKE OF CHRIST

The entire world, whether it is the political, religious, educational, commercial, or industrial world, is against Christ. Therefore, if you live by Christ, for Christ, and with Christ, you will surely be reproached and evil spoken of. People will circulate many rumors about you. You may work in the educational sphere, but sometimes you may refuse to cooperate with certain things that take place there, preferring to follow the way of Christ. Some may be in the economic field or in the commercial realm. But while they work in these realms, they live by Christ and for Christ and move with Christ. The others in your field will rise up and persecute you, speaking lies and falsehoods concerning you. Nevertheless, you must suffer this for the sake of Christ.

CHRIST WITH THE KINGDOM

Each of the nine blessings has a reward. The reward of the first is the kingdom of the heavens; of the second, comfort; of the third, the earth; of the fourth, satisfaction; of the fifth, mercy; of the sixth, seeing God; of the seventh, being called the sons of God; of the eighth, the kingdom of the heavens; and of the ninth, Christ. If we have Christ, we have the kingdom of the heavens. But if we do not have Him, we do not have the kingdom of the heavens. Thus, the real blessing is Christ with His kingdom. In order to share this blessing, we need to be poor in spirit, mournful over the negative situation, meek in facing opposition, righteous with ourselves, merciful to others, pure in heart toward God, making peace with all, suffering persecution for righteousness, and suffering reproach for Christ. This is the nature of the kingdom people. Eventually, the kingdom people are the very reality of the kingdom. This is the kingdom, which is the church life today. The church today is the reality of the kingdom.

LIFE-STUDY OF MATTHEW

MESSAGE SIXTEEN

THE DECREE
OF THE KINGDOM'S CONSTITUTION

(4)

In this message we come to the second section of the decree of the kingdom's constitution (5:13-16), which concerns the influence of the people of the kingdom of the heavens upon the world. The kingdom people are salt to the corrupted earth and light to the darkened world.

III. CONCERNING THE INFLUENCE
OF THE KINGDOM PEOPLE UPON THE WORLD

After revealing the nature of the kingdom people, this decree goes on to cover their influence. The sequence here is significant. If the kingdom people did not have the nature described in 5:3-12, they could not have any influence on the world. The influence of the kingdom people comes out of their nature, out of what they are. If we, the kingdom people, the church people, are poor in our spirit, the kingdom of the heavens will have room within the depths of our being. Then we shall mourn, be meek, hunger and thirst for righteousness, be merciful, be pure in heart, be peacemakers, suffer persecution, and be reproached for Christ. If we are such people, we shall certainly exercise a great influence upon the worldly people around us. We shall spontaneously influence the corrupted earth and the darkened world.

Because the influence of the proper church life is lacking, the whole world is corrupt and in darkness. If you travel throughout the world, studying and observing the situation in various countries, you will see that two of the worst places are France and Sweden, countries without the influence of the proper church life. Moreover, due to the predominance of Catholicism, in Central America and South America there is nothing but darkness. Wherever Catholicism prevails, there is darkness and corruption. Today, as a preparation for the Lord's coming back, there is the urgent need for all these dark and corrupted countries to be brought under the influence of the proper church life.

In verse 13 the Lord said, "You are the salt of the earth," and in verse 14 He said, "You are the light of the world." According to the Greek text, the pronoun here is plural. The "you" in these two verses does not refer to an individual, but to a corporate people. Most readers apply these verses to individuals. Those who have the nine blessings spoken of in verses 3 through 12 are a corporate people, not individuals. Therefore, the Lord's word about salt and light does not concern individuals. Individually, none of us can be proper salt or proper light. In verse 14 the Lord likens us to a city, not to individual stones. This clearly reveals that the Lord's word here is not intended for individuals, but for a corporate people built together on a high level. The Lord did not say, "You are the lights of the world." He said, "You are the light of the world." The plural "you" is just one light.

Do not consider the influence of the kingdom people upon the world an individual matter. If you try to be individually spiritual, you will not succeed. Even if you attain some individual spirituality, it will be a cancer. All individualistic spirituality is a cancer that absorbs into itself the nourishment intended for the whole Body. Cancer is not caused by germs; it is caused by cells in the body that separate from the body and care only for themselves. If you attempt to be individualistically spiritual, you will become a cancer. We all need to hear this word of warning.

During the past twenty-five years, I have come to see that spirituality is not an individualistic matter; it is absolutely a corporate matter. Take the example of physical

health. The health of our body is not a matter of the
individual members; it is a corporate matter. We do not
say that our ears are healthy, but that our body is healthy.
If your ears are not healthy, then your body must not be
healthy either. Thus, health is a matter of the whole body.

When I was young, I took the Lord's word in these
verses about salt and light in an individualistic way, thinking that I personally was to be the salt and the light. But
now I see that being salt is a corporate matter. We need to
be impressed with the fact it is as a corporate entity that
the kingdom people are salt and light. If we separate
ourselves from the church life, we can no longer be salt or
light.

Both the salt and the light refer to the corporate people
of the kingdom. Today the church people are the kingdom
people. Concerning discipline and exercise, we are the
kingdom people. But concerning life and grace, we are the
church people. In these verses it is a matter of exercise and
discipline; hence it concerns the kingdom people. The
kingdom people as a whole, as a corporate body, are salt
and light.

In verse 13 the Lord speaks of the earth, and in verse 14
He speaks of the world. There is a difference between the
earth and the world; the terms are not synonymous. What
was created by God is the earth, and what came in through
the corruption of Satan is the world. To the God-created
earth, the kingdom people are salt. But to the Satan-
corrupted world, they are light. We are the salt of the earth
and the light of the world.

A. Being the Salt of the Earth

1. To Kill and Eliminate the Germs of Corruption from the Earth

When we say that we are salt, it means that we exercise
our influence over the earth created by God to keep it in its
original condition. The earth, which was created by God,
has become fallen. In a sense, it has become rotten and corrupted. Salt kills the germs and eliminates this rottenness.

Any medical doctor can tell you that salt kills germs, eliminates rottenness, and preserves things in their original condition. By nature, salt is an element that kills the germs of corruption and eliminates them. Thus, through its killing and preserving function, salt brings the earth back to its original condition or keeps it in its original condition. Hence, the function of salt is to preserve what God has created. The entire earth is becoming more and more rotten. Therefore, we must exercise our influence over this corrupted earth. To the corrupted earth, the people of the kingdom of the heavens are the element that keeps the earth from being fully corrupted.

2. The Possibility of Becoming Tasteless

In verse 13 the Lord said, "But if the salt has become tasteless, with what shall it be salted? It is no longer good for anything but to be cast out and trampled under foot by men." For the kingdom people to become tasteless means that they have lost their salting function. They have become the same as the earthly people, with nothing to distinguish them from unbelievers. To become tasteless is to lose the distinction between us and the worldly people. It is to become the same as the worldly ones. Being the same as the worldly people is the opposite of the nature revealed in verses 3 through 12. It means that we are no longer poor in spirit, mourning for the negative situation, meek, hungry and thirsty for righteousness, merciful, pure in seeking God, making peace, willing to be persecuted for the sake of righteousness, and willing to be reproached for Christ. It means that we live, walk, and behave like the worldly people. If such is our case, we become tasteless, and the salt has lost its function.

Lot's wife is an illustration of this (Gen. 19:26). She became a pillar of salt, which indicates salt that has lost its function. When salt becomes a pillar, it cannot function, mainly because it has lost its taste. The fact that Lot's wife became a pillar of salt is a strong warning to us not to lose the distinction between us and the world. We should never lose our taste, but maintain the salting function of killing germs, of eliminating rottenness, and of keeping things in their original condition or of bringing them back to their God-created condition.

Wherever the kingdom people are, they should exercise a salting influence over those around them. In our neighborhoods we must exercise our function of killing germs. But if we become the same as the worldly people, we lose our function and our taste. Because we have lost our taste, we no longer have the salting ability and we cannot fulfill our salting function. If we have the nature of the kingdom people revealed in the nine blessings, we shall be truly salty. We shall be salt to our relatives and in-laws. If we are poor in spirit, mourning, meek, righteous, merciful, and pure in seeking God, we shall have a salting function. There will be no need to rebuke others or to point out their mistakes and wrongdoings. They will be salted simply by our presence. Sometimes certain evil ones will stay away from us because we are so salty. This is what it means to kill the germs of this rotten earth.

The Lord's intention is to bring this earth back to its original condition. Although we cannot see this in the present age, we shall see it in the next age. When the millennial kingdom comes, the whole earth will be salted. All the germs on this earth will be utterly killed, and the whole earth will be not only regained by Christ, but also brought back to its God-created condition. This work will be done by the kingdom people.

In verse 13 the King said that salt which has lost its taste will be cast out and trampled under foot by men. To be cast out is to be put away from the kingdom of the heavens (Luke 14:35). To be trampled under foot by men is to be treated as useless dust.

B. Being the Light of the World

1. As a City upon a Mountain

Verse 14 says, "You are the light of the world." Light is the shining of the lamp to enlighten those in darkness. To

the darkened world, the people of the kingdom of the
heavens are such a light effacing its darkness. In nature
they are the healing salt, and in behavior they are the shining light.

As the shining light, the kingdom people are like a city
situated upon a mountain. Such a city cannot be hidden.
This is ultimately consummated in the holy city of the
New Jerusalem (Rev. 21:10-11, 23-24). For many years I
was troubled by the Lord's illustration of a city situated
upon a mountain. Until I came into the church life, I could
not understand how light could be illustrated by a builded
city. After I was in the practical building of the church, I
saw that only by being built together can the kingdom
people be a city situated on a mountain. This city becomes a
shining light. In Anaheim the saints are grouping together
in their neighborhoods. If this practice becomes prevailing
and the saints in these groups are built together, every
group will be part of the shining city situated on a mountaintop.

In these three chapters the Lord Jesus did not use the
term "church." However, the term "kingdom," used many
times in these chapters, actually refers to the church. The
kingdom mentioned in Matthew 5, 6, and 7 is that aspect
of the church concerned with discipline and exercise. The
church is the aspect of grace and life for the kingdom, and
the kingdom is the aspect of discipline and exercise for the
church. Therefore, the Lord's word in these chapters
regarding the kingdom actually refers to the exercise and
discipline in the church.

As we have seen, many Christians understand these
chapters in an individualistic way. Most have not seen that
this constitution is not for individuals, but for a corporate
people. We know that this decree is for a corporate people,
because the light is not an individual person, but a builded
city. This indicates that the kingdom people need the
building. If the saints in the church in your locality are not
built up, but are scattered, divided, and separated, there is
no city there. And as long as there is no city, there is no

light, because the light is the city; the light is not an individual believer. The light is a corporate city built up as one entity to shine over the people surrounding it. It is impossible to find such a thing in today's Christianity. But every local church in the Lord's recovery must be a builded city.

In the book of Revelation the churches are golden lampstands (Rev. 1:20). The principle of the city and the lampstand is the same: neither is individual. Both are corporate. The lampstand, like the city, is not an individual believer, but the church. If you are outside the church, you are not a part of the lampstand. In order to be part of the lampstand, you must be built into the local church. The local church, which is the lampstand, is likened by the Lord to a builded city set on the top of a mountain. If we are built up in our locality, we shall be on the mountaintop. But if we are scattered, separated, and divided, we shall be in a low valley. In every locality there must be just one lampstand, one city situated on a mountain. For this, we must keep the unity and remain one entity, a corporate Body. Then we shall be able to shine. But if we are divided, we are finished with the shining. There is no shining in Christianity today because it is so divided. There are many divisions in Christianity. In the Lord's recovery, however, we must come back to the unique unity, which is the corporate Body. When we have truly been built together, we shall be the city on a mountaintop shining upon those around us.

2. As a Lamp on the Lampstand

Verse 15 says, "Neither do men light a lamp and place it under the bushel, but on the lampstand, and it shines to all who are in the house." The shining of the light has two aspects. In the first aspect, the light is likened to a city shining upon the outsiders. In the second aspect, the light is likened to a lamp on a lampstand shining to those who are in the house. We have seen that the city is the builded church, but what is the house? You may think that the house here also refers to the church. However, there is no need to interpret the house in this manner. According to the context, the main point is that the shining of the light has two aspects: the outward aspect and the inward aspect. The light as a city on a mountain shines over the outsiders, whereas the lighted lamp on the lampstand shines over those who are in the house. As the city, the light shines upon people, but as the lamp in the house, the light shines into people. This indicates that our influence over others should not be just outward, but also inward.

In order to shine upon others outwardly, we need to be built up. But to shine upon others inwardly, we need to be without any covering. As the light on the mountain, the light cannot be hidden; and as the lamp on the lamp-stand, the light should not be hidden.

In verse 15 the Lord speaks about placing the lamp under the bushel. A lighted lamp placed under the bushel cannot shine out its light. The kingdom people as the lighted lamp should not be covered by the bushel, an item pertaining to eating, a matter which causes anxiety (6:25). We should never be covered by the bushel; rather, we must be on the lampstand.

The Lord wisely spoke about not being covered by a bushel. In ancient times a bushel, as a measure for grain, was something related to eating and therefore related to the matter of making a living. Thus, hiding the lamp under the bushel indicates anxiety concerning our living. If we Christians are anxious about our living and concerned about how much money we are making, this anxiety will become a bushel covering our light.

The kingdom people firstly exercise an influence upon people outwardly, from the outside. However, we still need to influence them from within. When the church as a whole lives together as a city on the mountaintop, those surrounding it will be under the shining of such a builded church. But this is merely the shining from the outside. The church also needs to exert another kind of influence, the influence of the inner shining that gets into people.

Thus, the city on the mount signifies the shining from outside, and the lamp in the house signifies the shining from inside. Our shining must not be only outside the people, but also inside them. In order to shine upon others outwardly, we must be builded as a city on the mountaintop. But in order to shine upon them inwardly, we need to come out from under our covering. This indicates that the kingdom people live without anxiety and the care for their existence. They care only for Christ and the church. Day after day they are the happy people, the praising people, the hallelujah people. When our neighbors, relatives, and classmates contact us, they can sense that we have no anxiety. We are not worried about our living, about what we shall eat or what we shall put on. Day after day, morning and night, the kingdom people care only for Christ and the church.

We know from experience that our lack of anxiety touches others. If every time someone contacts you, you are happy and enjoying the Lord, he will be deeply touched. Filled with anxiety and occupied with all kinds of worries, the worldly people talk about the fear of losing their job or the difficulties they are having with their boss. But the kingdom people, the hallelujah people, those not covered by the bushel, care only to talk about Christ and the church. By being such a people, we touch the hearts of others and shine upon them from within. This shining penetrates them.

The outward shining of the kingdom people is general, and all of society can see it. Society can see a group of people who are built up, situated upon the top of a mountain, and shining. The inward shining, on the contrary, is particular. One of your cousins may be touched by your lack of anxiety and your shining face. Whenever he contacts you, he never hears you talking about how to make a living. Instead, he always hears you praising the Lord and telling how wonderful the church life is. This will be a light penetrating into his being and shining within him. Through the shining of this light, he will be convinced. This is not the general shining from outside; it is the particular shining

from within. If we are the proper kingdom people, we shall
have this twofold shining. We shall be a city on a mountaintop shining out upon all those surrounding us, and
among them we shall be the hallelujah people, those with
no anxicty or care about this life, shining into them. This
inward shining penetrates the inward being of others and
convinces them.

3. Glorifying the Father in the Heavens

Eventually, both aspects of our shining will give glory
to the Father. Verse 16 says, "Thus let your light shine
before men, so that they may see your good works, and
glorify your Father Who is in the heavens." The title Father
proves that the disciples, who were the new King's
audience, were regenerated children of God (John 1:12;
Gal. 4:6). The good works here are the behavior of the kingdom people through which men may see God and be
brought to Him. Our shining will glorify the Father
because it expresses what God is. To glorify God the Father
is to give Him the glory. Glory is God expressed. When the
kingdom people express God in their behavior and good
works, men see God and give the glory to God. God hidden
is God Himself. But when God is expressed, that is the
glory of God. If as the kingdom people we have such a shining light, God will be expressed in this shining, and all
those around us will see the glory, God expressed. When
others see God in our shining, that is a glory to God.

We, the kingdom people, are the light of the world. As
light we are like a city on a mountaintop and like a lamp
shining in a house. From without and within, we shine to
express God, to let God have the glory in the eyes of others.
May we exercise such an influence upon those around us.

LIFE-STUDY OF MATTHEW

MESSAGE SEVENTEEN

THE DECREE
OF THE KINGDOM'S CONSTITUTION

(5)

The teaching and preaching concerning the kingdom of the heavens began with repentance (3:2; 4:17). Repentance means a change of mind. Hence, the kingdom begins with our mind. From our mind, it proceeds to our spirit (5:3). We need to repent in our mind and to be poor in our spirit. Following this, we must be pure in heart in order to see God (5:8). The mind, the spirit, and the heart are the three major aspects of our inner being. If we put 4:17 together with 5:3-12, we see a number of items related to the kingdom of the heavens. The first three, as we have seen, are the mind, the spirit, and the heart. Next we need to have a normal, proper, uplifted emotion. This is seen in the matter of mourning (5:4), which comes from our adjusted emotion. We also need to be meek, which requires a strong, normal, proper will. The hunger and thirst for right-eousness spoken of in 5:6 is a matter of a pure and proper desire. We must desire this righteousness for the kingdom. Being merciful to others involves our attitude (5:7). Our at-titude toward others must be one of mercy. If we have a proper emotion, will, desire, and attitude, we shall be able to make peace with others. Thus, our whole being — our mind, spirit, heart, emotion, will, desire, and attitude — needs to be exercised for the kingdom life. When we have all these virtues, we are qualified to be persecuted. If you do not have these, you will not be able to withstand persecution. Eventually, those who are qualified by hav-ing all these virtues will be not only persecuted for righteousness, but reproached for Christ. This is the nature of the kingdom people.

Each of the nine blessings in 5:3-12 has a reward. For example, if you are poor in spirit, the kingdom of the heavens is yours. This is a reward. If you mourn, you will be comforted, and if you are meek, you will inherit the earth. Thus, comfort and the earth are also rewards. According to verse 12, the reward is great for those who are persecuted and reproached for the sake of Christ. It is difficult to give a name to this reward. If we are reproached, persecuted, evil-spoken of, for the sake of Christ, our reward in the heavens is great, so great that it is beyond our understanding. Hebrews 13:13 and 1 Peter 4:14 both speak of being reproached for the sake of Christ. Hebrews 13:13 says, "Let us therefore go forth unto Him outside the camp, bearing His reproach." First Peter 4:14 says, "If you are reproached in the name of Christ, you are blessed." This matter of reproach is also spoken of in Romans 15:3. There is a great reward awaiting those who are reproached for the sake of Christ. We need to be the kingdom people with the nature revealed in these verses. Then we shall be able to bear the reproach for Christ.

IV. CONCERNING THE LAW
OF THE KINGDOM PEOPLE

In this message we come to the third section of the King's word on the mountain, 5:17-48, which concerns the law of the people of the kingdom of the heavens. The constitution of the heavenly kingdom must certainly cover the matter of law. Prior to the time of the Lord Jesus, the children of Israel had the law of Moses. They also had the prophets. Prophecy is always a help to the law. When the people are weak in fulfilling the law, there is the need for the prophets to come in to strengthen them to keep the law. Thus, the fulfillment of the law needs the strengthening through the prophets. Therefore, in the Old Testament there were the law and the prophets. This is the reason the Lord spoke of the law and the prophets in verse 17.

A. Not to Abolish the Law or the Prophets, but to Fulfill Them

Verse 17 says, "Do not think that I came to abolish the law or the prophets; I did not come to abolish, but to fulfill." To fulfill the law here means three things: that Christ has kept the law on the positive side; that through His substitutionary death on the cross Christ has fulfilled the requirement of the law on the negative side; and that Christ complements the old law by His new law in this section, as continually expressed by the word, "But I say to you" (vv. 22, 28, 32, 34, 39, 44).

Concerning the law, there are two aspects: the commandments of the law and the principle of the law. The commandments of the law are fulfilled and complemented by the Lord's coming, whereas the principle of the law is replaced by the principle of faith according to God's New Testament economy.

Before Christ came, there was the law with the strengthening through the prophets. Why then was there still the need for the law of the kingdom of the heavens? The reason is that the demands of the old law were not high enough. The requirements of the old law were not complete. Take the example of murder. The old law commanded us not to murder (Exo. 20:13), but it did not say a word about anger. If you killed someone, you would be condemned by the law of Moses. But no matter how angry you were with someone, as long as you did not murder, you would not be condemned by Moses' law. Here we see the shortage, the incompleteness, of the old law. However the requirement of the law of the kingdom of the heavens is much higher than that of the law of Moses. According to the law of the kingdom of the heavens, we are forbidden to be angry with our brothers. In verses 21 and 22 the Lord said, "You have heard that it was said to the ancients, You shall not murder, and whoever murders shall be liable to the judgment. But I say to you that everyone who is angry with his brother shall be liable to the judgment." Hence, the law of the kingdom of the heavens is higher than the law of the old dispensation.

Another illustration of this is the law concerning adultery. The old law forbade the committing of adultery, but the new law forbids looking at a woman to lust after her (vv. 27-28). Thus, the basic principle of the law of the kingdom of the heavens is that it is higher than the old law. We do not annul the old law; we complement it to make it higher. For this reason, the Lord Jesus said that He did not come to abolish the law, but to fulfill it.

Many Christians do not adequately understand the meaning of the word "fulfill" in verse 17. Through many years of study, observation, and experience, we have come to see that the word "fulfill" in this verse means three things.

1. Keeping the Law on the Positive Side

Firstly, it means that Christ came to keep the law on the positive side. When He lived on earth, He kept every aspect of the old law. No one else has ever kept the ten commandments; the Lord Jesus kept them completely. He kept the law of the old dispensation in a very positive way.

2. Fulfilling the Requirement of the Law on the Negative Side through the Substitutionary Death on the Cross

Because Christ kept the law, He became the perfect One. His perfection qualified Him to die on the cross for us. This is the keeping of the law in a negative sense. This is the second way Christ has fulfilled the law. All of us have broken, transgressed, the law. But our transgressions have been dealt with through the Lord's substitutionary death. On the cross He was our substitute, dying for us to fulfill the law's requirement on the negative side.

3. Complementing the Old Law with the New

To fulfill the law also means that Christ complements the old law by His new law. This is expressed by the word, "But I say to you" (vv. 22, 28, 32, 34, 39, 44). Christ's keeping of the law qualified Him to fulfill the requirement of the law through His substitutionary death on the cross. Christ's fulfilling the requirement of the law through His substitutionary death on the cross brought in the resurrection life to complement the law, to fill the law to the full. The old law, the lower law, with its keeping-demand and punishing-requirement, is over. The kingdom people, as the children of the Father, only need now to fulfill the new law, the higher law, by the resurrection life, which is the eternal life of the Father.

Christ's substitutionary death brought in the resurrection life. When this resurrection life comes into us, it is able to do the wonderful job of completing the law. It enables us to fulfill the higher law. By the resurrection life within us, we are able to be kept not only from murdering others, but even from being angry with them or hating them. This resurrection life is much higher than the natural life, for it is actually the divine life, the eternal life, the life on the highest plane. This highest life within us can fulfill the requirements of the highest law.

In the New Testament, Matthew, the book of the kingdom, comes first with the requirements. Then John, the book of life, comes with the life to fulfill these requirements. By our natural life, we are not able to fulfill the requirements given in Matthew 5. But in the Gospel of John we have the highest life that enables us to meet the highest requirements. All Christians love John, but not many love Matthew. I doubt if I have ever heard a Christian say that he loves Matthew. Some of you may say that the Gospel of Matthew is too troublesome and that John is very simple. It says that in the beginning was the Word and the Word was God, and that the Word became flesh, full of grace and reality (John 1:1, 14). The Gospel of John has many golden verses, such as John 3:16. In this Gospel there are very few requirements and demands, but there is the rich life supply. However, in the New Testament, Matthew comes first, not John. We cannot afford to bypass Matthew. Nevertheless, many Christians have been instructed to do this. Thirty-five years ago I was taught that new believers should not read Matthew. I myself charged new believers not to read Matthew first. I said that if they read Matthew chapter one first, they would be frustrated in their reading of the Bible and think that it was too difficult to read. Hence, I told the new believers to begin their reading with the fourth book, the Gospel of John. Then I would tell them to read Romans or some other book, but not Matthew. But we need to come back to Matthew. Matthew needs John, and John is for Matthew. Matthew gives us the highest requirements of the kingdom, requirements that can be fulfilled only by the divine life revealed in John. In order to fulfill the requirements of the kingdom of the heavens unfolded in Matthew, we must receive the supply of life found in the Gospel of John.

Jesus, the new King, did not come to abolish the law of Moses. Rather, He came to uplift the standard of the old law. Now that the requirement has been so greatly uplifted, it is no longer the old law, but the new law of the kingdom of the heavens. Christ uplifted the standard of the old law in two ways: by complementing the old law and by changing it. In verses 17 through 30 we see the complementing of the old law. The change of the law begins with verse 31. In this message we can cover only the complementing of the old law.

Verse 18 says, "For truly I say to you, Until the heaven and the earth pass away, one iota or one tittle shall by no means pass away from the law until all come to pass." After the millennial kingdom, the old heaven and old earth will pass away and the new heaven and new earth come in (Rev. 21:1; Heb. 1:11-12; 2 Pet. 3:10-13). What the law covers extends only to the end of the millennial kingdom, whereas what the prophets cover extends to the new heaven and new earth (Isa. 65:17; 66:22). This is why both the law and the prophets are referred to in verse 17, but only the law, not the prophets, is mentioned in verse 18.

The fulfillment of the law will last until the end of the millennium, at which time the heavens and the earth will pass away. Before that takes place, not one iota or tittle of the old law will be annulled. However, what is covered by the prophets goes farther than the millennium, reaching into the new heaven and the new earth.

Christ fulfilled the law in three ways. He Himself kept the law. However, because we did not keep it, He died on the cross for our transgressions of the law. His substitutionary death brought in the resurrection life, which has been imparted into our being. By His resurrection life we are able to fulfill the requirements of the new, higher law. By these three steps Christ has more than fulfilled the old law. He kept it, He died for us, and His death brought into us the resurrection life to strengthen us for fulfilling the requirements of the new law. Today we are not trying to keep the lower law; rather, we are keeping the uplifted, higher law through the highest life that is in us. Now we are able to keep the highest law.

B. Keeping Even the Least of the Commandments of the Law Being the Condition to Be Great in the Kingdom

Verse 19 says, "Whoever therefore shall annul one of the least of these commandments, and shall teach men so, shall be called least in the kingdom of the heavens; but whoever practices and teaches them, he shall be called great in the kingdom of the heavens." The commandments here refer to the law in verse 18. The kingdom people not only fulfill the law, but complement the law. Actually, they do not annul any commandments of the law, not even one of the least. Whether we shall be great or small in the kingdom of the heavens depends upon whether or not we keep even the least of the commandments of the law. In this verse Christ stressed the fact that if we do not keep all of the least of the commandments of the law, but annul them and teach others to annul them, we shall become the least in the kingdom of the heavens. In other words, Christ seemed to be saying, "If you would be great in the kingdom of the heavens, you must have the highest standard of morality. If your standard of morality does not reach the standard of the new law, you will be the least in the kingdom of the heavens." The morality of no other people is as high as that of the kingdom people. Never think that we care only for life and not for morality. Life must have its expression, and the highest life has the highest expression. Morality is simply the expression of life. Thus, if you have the highest life, you will certainly have the highest morality as the expression of this life. We need to pray, "Lord, grant me the highest expression of life. Grant me to have the highest level of morality. Lord, we are not only moral people, but kingdom people."

Because the standard of the kingdom is higher than the standard of morality, we must do more than keep the standard of the old law. According to the standard of morality, we should not commit murder or adultery. If we abstain from murder and adultery, we are moral people. But such a standard is much lower than that of the kingdom. According to the standard of the kingdom of the heavens, we should not be angry with our brother or look at a woman to lust after her. This is not the standard of morality; it is the standard of the kingdom, which is much higher than that of morality. The standard of morality says, "Eye for eye, tooth for a tooth" (Exo. 21:24; Lev. 24:20; Deut. 19:21). But the standard of the kingdom tells us to love our enemies, to pray for those who persecute us, and not to resist one who is evil (vv. 44, 39). If someone strikes us on our right cheek, we should turn to him the other also (v. 39). How much higher is this standard than the standard of morality!

The crucial point that Christ is stressing in these verses is that the kingdom people must have the highest standard of morality. If we see this matter, then we are able to understand 5:17-48. We have the highest law, the highest life, the highest standard. By the highest life we fulfill the highest law and have the highest standard.

C. The Surpassing Righteousness
Being the Condition to Enter
into the Kingdom

In verse 20 the King said, "For I say to you, that unless your righteousness surpass that of the scribes and Pharisees, you shall by no means enter into the kingdom of the heavens." The surpassing righteousness is the condition of entering into the manifestation of the kingdom of the heavens in the millennium. By keeping the highest law to the highest standard we fulfill the condition for entering into the coming manifestation of the kingdom of the heavens.

Righteousness in verse 20 does not refer to the objective righteousness, which is the Christ we receive when we believe in Him that we may be justified before God (Phil. 3:9; 1 Cor. 1:30; Rom. 3:26). It refers to the subjective righteousness, which is the indwelling Christ lived out of us as our righteousness that we may live in the reality of the kingdom today and enter into its manifestation in the future. This subjective righteousness is not obtained merely by fulfilling the old law, but by completing the old law through the fulfillment of the new law of the kingdom of the heavens, the law given by the new King here in this section of the Word. This righteousness of the kingdom people, according to the new law of the kingdom, surpasses that of the scribes and Pharisees according to the old law. It is impossible for our natural life to gain this surpassing righteousness; it can be produced only by a higher life, the resurrection life of Christ. This righteousness, which is likened to the wedding garment (22:11-12), qualifies us to participate in the wedding of the Lamb (Rev. 19:7-8) and inherit the kingdom of the heavens in its manifestation, that is, to enter into the kingdom of the heavens in the future.

To enter into the kingdom of God requires regeneration as a new beginning of our life (John 3:3, 5), but to enter into the kingdom of the heavens demands surpassing righteousness in our living after regeneration. To enter into the kingdom of the heavens means to live in its reality today and to participate in its manifestation in the future.

D. Regarding Murder

1. The Old Law — Not to Murder

Verse 21 says, "You have heard that it was said to the ancients, You shall not murder, and whoever murders shall be liable to the judgment." The old law was the command not to murder. What "you have heard" in verses 21, 27, 33, 38, and 43 is the law of the old dispensation; whereas what "I say to you" in verses 22, 28, 32, 34, 39, and 44 is the new law of the kingdom, complementing the law of the old dispensation.

2. The New Complementing Law —
Not to Be Angry with the Brother,
Not to Contemn the Brother,
and Not to Condemn the Brother

In verse 22 the King said, "But I say to you that everyone who is angry with his brother shall be liable to the judgment; and whoever shall say to his brother, Raca, shall be liable to the Sanhedrin; and whoever shall say, Moreh, shall be liable to the Gehenna of fire." The law of the old dispensation deals with the act of murder, but the new law of the kingdom deals with anger, the motive of murder. Hence, the demand of the new law of the kingdom is deeper than the requirement of the law of the old dispensation. The word "brother" in verse 22 proves that the King's word here is spoken to believers.

The most difficult thing for us to do is to control our anger. Some were supposed to be very gentle, but their anger was like a wild horse when they lost their temper. When our anger is released, no one can bridle us or control us. For a number of years I could not get through this chapter because of the problem of my anger.

It is also very difficult for us not to contemn or condemn others. In verse 22 the Lord speaks about saying to our brother, "Raca," or "Moreh." The word Raca is an expression of contempt meaning stupid, good-for-nothing. Moreh, that is, fool, is a Hebrew expression of condemnation indicating a rebel (Num. 20:10). This expression is more serious than the expression of contempt, Raca. How difficult it is neither to condemn a brother nor to hold him in contempt! Perhaps you cannot go for even a week without condemning or contemning someone. It seems that nearly every day we either contemn or condemn. Husbands and wives contemn and condemn one another. I do not believe there is one exception. Every wife has contemned and condemned her husband, and every husband has done the same to his wife. This is a real problem. When you read this, can you still say that you are the overcomers, the kingdom people? Do not be disappointed. Rather, be encouraged. Remember, we have an overcoming life. Do you not have the King within you? We are the kingdom people, and we have the King within us. This King is the kingly, overcoming life. Do not look at yourself. If you do, you will be fully discouraged. Forget yourself and look at the kingly life within you. It is this life that makes us the kingdom people. Forget your natural life and follow this kingly life.

In verse 22 there are three kinds of judgment. The first is the judgment at the gate of the city, which is the district judgment. The second is the judgment by the Sanhedrin, which is the higher judgment. The Sanhedrin is a council composed of the chief priests, the elders, the lawyers, and the scribes. It is the highest court of the Jews (Luke 22:66; Acts 4:5-6, 15; 5:27, 34, 41). The third is the judgment by God through the Gehenna of fire, which is the highest judgment. These three kinds of judgment were mentioned by the new King, using figures of the Jewish background, because all His audience was Jewish. However, concerning the kingdom people, the believers of the New Testament, all these judgments refer to the judgment of the Lord at the judgment seat of Christ, as revealed in 2 Corinthians 5:10; Romans 14:10, 12; 1 Corinthians 4:4-5; 3:13-15; Matthew 16:27; Revelation 22:12; and Hebrews 10:27, 30. This clearly reveals that the New Testament believers, although forgiven by God forever, are still liable to the Lord's judgment, not for perdition, but for discipline, if they sin against the law of the kingdom as given here. However, when we sin against the new law of the kingdom, if we repent and confess our sins, we shall be forgiven and cleansed by the blood of the Lord Jesus (1 John 1:7, 9).

In verse 22 the new King speaks of the Gehenna of fire.

The word Gehenna is the Greek equivalent of the Hebrew *Ge Hinnom*, valley of Hinnom. It was a deep and narrow valley near Jerusalem, the refuse-place of the city, where the bodies of criminals and all kinds of filth were cast. It was also called Tophet, or Topheth (2 Kings 23:10; Isa. 30:33; Jer. 19:13). Because of its continual fire, it became the symbol of the place of eternal punishment, the lake of fire (Rev. 20:15). This word is also used in Matthew 5:29, 30; 10:28; 18:9; 23:15, 33; Mark 9:43, 45, 47; Luke 12:5; and James 3:6.

a. Before Offering a Gift to God, Reconciling Yourself to Your Brother

Verses 23 and 24 say, "Therefore, if you are offering your gift at the altar and there remember that your brother has anything against you, leave your gift there before the altar and go away; first be reconciled to your brother, and then come and offer your gift." Sacrifice, as the sacrifice for sin, is for dealing with sin; whereas a gift is for fellowship with God. The altar spoken of in verse 23 was a piece of furniture (Exo. 27:1-8) in the outer court of the temple (1 Kings 8:64), on which all sacrifices and gifts were offered (Lev. 1:9, 12, 17). The King, in decreeing the new law of the kingdom, referred here to the gift and the altar of the old dispensation because, during the transitory period of His ministry on earth, the ritual law of the old dispensation had not yet ceased. In the four Gospels, before His death and resurrection, in things regarding circumstances, the Lord treated His disciples as Jews according to the old law; whereas in things concerning spirit and life, He considered them as believers who constitute the church according to the New Testament economy.

The words "anything against you" in verse 23 must refer to the anger or scolding in verse 22. According to verse 24, we must first be reconciled to our brother that our remembrance of offense may be removed and that our conscience may be void of offense. Then we may come and offer our gift to the Lord to fellowship with Him with a pure conscience. The King of the kingdom will never tolerate two brothers not reconciled one to another either sharing the kingdom in its reality or reigning in its manifestation. If, as you come to contact the Lord, you have the sense that a brother or sister has a complaint against you, you must stop your fellowship with the Lord and go to this one and be reconciled. Then you may come back to continue your fellowship with the Lord. Although this is a small thing, it is not easy to do. Nevertheless, we must do it.

b. Before You Die, Your Opponent Dies, or the Lord Comes Back

Verses 25 and 26 say, "Be well disposed quickly with your opponent, while you are with him in the way, lest the opponent deliver you to the judge, and the judge to the officer, and you be thrown into prison. Truly I say to you, You shall by no means come out from there until you have paid the last quadrans." We need to be disposed quickly with our opponent lest we die, our opponent dies, or the Lord comes back, and thus there be no opportunity for us to be reconciled to our opponent. The words "in the way" signify that we are still living in this life. The matter of being delivered to the judge, to the officer, and thrown into prison will transpire at the judgment seat of Christ when He comes back (2 Cor. 5:10; Rom. 14:10). The judge will be the Lord, the officer will be the angel, and the prison will be the place of discipline. To come out from there, that is, to come out from prison, is to be forgiven in the coming age, the millennium.

The Roman quadrans spoken of in verse 26 is a small brass coin equal to a quarter of an assarion, which is equal to one cent. The meaning here is that even with the smallest thing we need to make a thorough clearance. This shows the strictness of the new law.

We need to be reconciled to our opponent before we die, before he dies, or before the Lord comes back. If we do not take care of any matter now, we shall have to deal with it in the coming age. Do not wait for the next age, for the dealing then will be more troublesome. Take care of every problem now, before you die or before your opponent dies.

While both of you are still living, you still have the opportunity to be reconciled to him. Furthermore, if you wait, the Lord may come back before you are reconciled. On the one hand, the Lord's coming back will be marvelous. On the other hand, it will be rather serious, for it will close the opportunity to deal with the problems in this age and compel us to deal with them in the next age. Therefore, it is much better to solve every problem before the coming age. This means that we must take care of every problem before we die, before the other party dies, or before the Lord comes back.

E. Regarding Adultery

1. The Old Law — Not to Commit Adultery

Verse 27 says, "You have heard that it was said, You shall not commit adultery." This is the old law, the commandment not to commit adultery (Exo. 20:14; Deut. 5:18).

2. The New Complementing Law — Not to Look at for Lusting

The new complementing law regarding adultery is found in verse 28: "But I say to you, that every one who looks at a woman to lust for her has already committed adultery with her in his heart." The law of the old dispensation deals with the outward act of adultery, whereas the new law of the kingdom deals with the inward motive of the heart.

a. Considering the Seriousness of Such a Sin in Relation to the Kingdom

We must consider the seriousness of such a sin in relation to the kingdom. The seriousness of this sin is indicated by the Lord's word in verses 29 and 30 about plucking out our eye and casting it from us and cutting off our hand and casting it from us. In both of these verses the Lord said, "It is better for you that one of your members perish and not your whole body be cast into Gehenna."

This, however, should not be observed literally; it can only be carried out spiritually, as revealed in Romans 8:13 and Colossians 3:5. I know the cases of some who applied this word in a literal way. One of these cases was a gambler who literally cut off his hand after reading this portion of the Word. Eventually he discovered that, although his hand had been cut off, there was still within him an inner hand desiring to gamble. He learned that cutting off his physical hand did not work, for the problem was with the inner hand. Although this word is not to be taken literally, it reveals the seriousness of such a sin.

According to the Lord's word in verses 29 and 30, it is possible for saved persons to be cast into Gehenna. This means that even the saved ones may be hurt by the second death. In Revelation 2:11 the Lord Jesus said, "He who overcomes shall by no means be hurt of the second death." As we have pointed out, Gehenna is a symbol of the lake of fire, which is the second death (Rev. 20:15). The Lord's word in Revelation 2:11 indicates that it is possible for believers to be hurt by the second death. The Lord's word in Revelation 2:11 corresponds to His word in Matthew 5:29 and 30. As a saved one, if you are not serious in dealing with this kind of sin, you will some day be hurt by the second death. As the Lord Jesus says here, you will be cast into Gehenna. This does not mean that you will perish; it means that you will be disciplined. Furthermore, the Gehenna of fire does not refer to the purgatory of Catholicism. But this word on Gehenna warns you that if you are not serious in dealing with this sin today, when the Lord Jesus comes back, He will exercise His judgment over you. (For a further word on the matter of being hurt by the second death, see Life-Study of Revelation, message eleven, pp. 136-138).

As we have seen, the three kinds of judgment spoken of in verse 22 all refer to the judgment of Christ at His judgment seat. This judgment has nothing to do with the unsaved, who will be judged at the great white throne after the millennium (Rev. 20:12, 15). No unsaved person will be qualified to stand before the judgment seat of Christ at His

coming back. All those who appear before this judgment
seat will be saved ones. The believers will be judged there,
not for the matter of salvation or perdition, but for reward
or punishment.

The word spoken by the Lord concerning judgment and
being cast into the Gehenna of fire is a serious word. Such a
word should make us sober and cause us not to be loose in
dealing with this kind of sin. Never consider this sin as an
insignificant matter. The situation today regarding fornication is deplorable. We must never be loose about this.
The Lord's own word shows us how serious it is. We must
be sober and deal with this in a very serious manner.
However, we do not deal with our members in a literal way.
Rather, we must mortify our sinful members by the cross of
Christ. As Romans 8:13 reveals, by the Spirit we must "put
to death the practices of the body," and, as Colossians 3:5
says, we must mortify our "members which are on the
earth." This is the proper way to deal with our sinful
members.

b. Putting Away the Motive of
Such a Sin at Any Cost

Verses 29 and 30 also indicate that we must put away
the motive of such a sin at any cost. The Lord's intention
here is to make us sober so that we would put away not only
the action, but also the motive of this kind of sin. If we fail
to do this, He will put us into the Gehenna of fire when He
comes. This is a very sobering word.

LIFE-STUDY OF MATTHEW

THE DECREE
OF THE KINGDOM'S CONSTITUTION

(6)

In this message I am burdened to give a further word on the law. There has been much debate among Christian teachers over this matter of the law. These debates have been mainly due to the shortage of light from the Bible regarding the law. According to the Old Testament economy, God's dealings with His people were based upon the law. This was the principle of the law. But in the New Testament economy, God deals with His people today, not according to the law, but according to faith. Thus, the law was the principle of God's dealing with His people in the Old Testament, but faith is the principle of His dealing with us in the New Testament. According to the Old Testament economy, it was necessary to keep the law in order to be acceptable to God. But today being acceptable to God is a matter of faith.

The principle of the law has been abolished, but the commandments of the law have not been abolished. Just because the principle of the law has been abolished, never think that the commandments of the law have also been abolished and that there is no need to honor our parents or to refrain from stealing. No, instead of being abolished, the commandments of the law have been uplifted. Although our contact with God is not based upon the principle of the law, we must still observe the uplifted commandments of the law.

NO NEED TO KEEP THE SABBATH

At this point the Seventh Day Adventists might say, "Yes, we must keep all the commandments of the law. One of these commandments is to keep the Sabbath. Based upon what you have said about not abolishing the commandments of the law, we tell you that you must keep the Sabbath." Although the commandments of God have not been abolished, one of these commandments, the law about keeping the Sabbath, is not related to morality. Rather, it is a ritual law. A ritual is a form, a shadow, that we need no longer observe today. For example, we do not need to offer animal sacrifices, do we? Likewise, we no longer need to keep the Sabbath. In the Old Testament, the age of shadows, there was the need for the sacrifices, the feasts, and the keeping of the Sabbath. But today is an age of reality. Our sacrifice is not a lamb or a goat; it is Christ, the reality of all the Old Testament sacrifices. In like manner, our rest is not a particular day; it also is Christ. Because Christ, the reality, is here, all the shadows are over. Because the commandment to keep the Sabbath is a ritual commandment, not a moral commandment, we are not obligated to keep it today. This commandment is not related to morality, but to the shadow, the form, which is now over.

THE PRINCIPLE OF THE LAW

We need to be impressed concerning the principle of the law. God's dealing with His people always depends upon a principle. For example, God's dealings with Abraham were based upon God's promise. God did not give Abraham the commandments of the law; He gave him only the promise. Thus, God dealt with him according to His promise. The promise given by God to Abraham became the principle according to which God dealt with him. Later, God gave the law to the children of Israel through Moses. The law given on Mount Sinai thus became the principle according to which God dealt with the children of Israel. In this way the law became the principle for God's dealings with His people in the Old Testament. Now in the New Testament God deals with the believers according to faith, no longer according to the law. This is fully developed in the books of

Romans and Galatians. If you read these books, you will
see that God deals with the believers in Christ not according to the law, but according to faith. In Old
Testament times God accepted people according to the law.
If anyone wanted to be accepted by God, he had to meet
the standard of the law. But today God accepts us, not according to the law, but according to whether or not we
believe in Christ. Thus, God's acceptance of us today is
based on faith.

THE COMMANDMENTS OF THE LAW
NOT ABOLISHED, BUT UPLIFTED

The fact that God no longer deals with us, the believers,
according to the principle of the law does not mean that
the commandments of the old law have been abolished.
For instance, the first two commandments of the old law
were concerned with not having other gods and with not
making images. To say that the principle of the law has
been abolished does not mean that these commandments
have been abolished. Rather, according to the New
Testament, these commandments are emphasized,
strengthened, and uplifted. In the Old Testament we were
told not to make a physical image, but in the New
Testament we are told that even our covetousness is a form
of idolatry (Col. 3:5). Greediness is an idol. By this we see
the uplifting of the commandment regarding idolatry. Yes,
the principle of the law has been abolished, but not the
commandments of the law. The commandment about
honoring our parents has never been abolished. In the New
Testament this commandment is also repeated, strengthened, and uplifted. We must honor our parents much more
today than the children of Israel did in the past.

We have seen that the Lord Jesus also uplifted the
commandments regarding murder and adultery. Because
the Old Testament commandments regarding murder and
adultery were not adequate, the Lord complemented
them. The old commandment concerning murder did not
cover the matters of hatred or anger. Thus, the Lord

complemented the old law concerning murder by saying that anyone who was angry with his brother would be liable to judgment. He also complemented the commandment concerning adultery by saying that anyone who looks at a woman to lust for her has committed adultery with her in his heart. By these examples we see that the moral laws have never been abolished; rather, they have been uplifted. All of the ten commandments have been repeated and uplifted in the New Testament except the fourth commandment, the commandment to keep the Sabbath. This commandment is over because it is not related to morality. Instead, it is a ritual commandment.

A HIGHER STANDARD OF MORALITY

Now we come to my real burden in this message. Yes, in the New Testament salvation is based upon the principle of faith; it has nothing to do with the law. We all have been saved through faith, not through the keeping of the law. But after we are saved, we must live a life that has a standard of morality higher than that of the old law. Never think that we are free to be loose, sloppy, or even immoral just because we are not saved through the keeping of the law. Do not think that, just because God does not deal with us according to the principle of the law, but according to the principle of faith, we should not care for the commandments of the law. Anyone who thinks this has been drugged by the teachings found in part of today's Christianity. We must be sober. Again I say, after we have been saved, we need to live a life with a standard far higher than that of the old law. Our standard must be higher than that of the requirements of the law. The law requires that we should not murder anyone. But we should not even be angry with others. Even if we say to our brother, "Raca," an expression of contempt, or, "Moreh," a word of condemnation indicating a rebel, we shall be in danger of the judgment. Although we may not kill our brother, if we even call him a fool or a rebel, we shall find ourselves in serious trouble.

THE PROBLEMS OF TEMPER AND LUST

In Matthew 5 the Lord Jesus spoke about murder and adultery. Murder refers to our temper, and adultery, to our lust. Our temper and our lust constantly damage and trouble us. If we were stone, we would not be bothered by these two things. No matter how much you irritate, insult, or offend a stone, it will never react, because it does not have any temper. Furthermore, a stone has no lust. Thus, it can never be tempted by lust. But daily we are either troubled by our temper or tempted by our lust. How easy it is for us to be irritated and offended! Some of us may be offended at least ten times a day. You may be offended by your husband or wife, by your children, by your neighbors, or by your in-laws. You may even be offended by your shoes, the stove, or the tea kettle. I know some sisters who have been offended by their kitchens. It seems that their anger could never be exhausted. Others are troubled with lust. For this reason, I pointed out in one of the life-study messages on Genesis that you should never be alone with a member of the opposite sex for any length of time. If you are, you will be tempted by your ferocious lusts.

In order to live up to a moral standard higher than that of the old law, you must overcome your temper and your lusts. You may say that this is not easy to do. Right, it is not easy. This is why you need Christ. This is why you need another life. How we need to stay with Christ! We must contact Him not only day by day, but even hour by hour. Because of the temper and lust within us, we need to remain in constant fellowship with Him. You must recognize that you are neither wood nor stone. If you were wood or stone, you would not be concerned about the matter of anger and lust. But because you are a living being, you have these two things within you. Do you not have both temper and lust within? At any time we may be stumbled by our temper or tempted by our lust. Be on the alert! Be watchful and pray regarding these two "demons," our temper and our lust. After we have been saved according to the principle of faith, we need to live a higher life, a life with the highest standard. This life with the highest standard is a life that overcomes our temper and our lust.

A WARNING REGARDING
THE JUDGMENT OF THE BELIEVERS

Week after week many are drugged by the teachings of Christianity. These teachings neither warn the Christians nor tell them the truth. So many are not warned that they will be caused much trouble by being angry and contemning or condemning others or by giving in to their lusts. By showing even a little contempt for our brother we shall be liable to the judgment (5:22). This does not mean that we shall perish. No, a saved person will never perish, and no one who is lost will be qualified to appear before the judgment seat of Christ. Only those who have been saved according to the principle of faith will be qualified to be there. But do not think that it is impossible for you to have a problem at the judgment seat of Christ. You may tell the Lord, "I never robbed a bank or murdered anyone. The only thing I did was to lose my temper." But the mere act of losing your temper may bring you into judgment.

In 5:22 the judgment of the believers at the judgment seat of Christ is described by three kinds of judgment according to the background of the Jewish people: the judgment at the gate of the city, the judgment before the Sanhedrin, and the judgment of the Gehenna of fire. These three levels of judgment all refer to the one judgment at the judgment seat of Christ. We Christians, saved according to the principle of faith, will not be judged at the white throne spoken of in Revelation 20. Rather, we shall be judged at the judgment seat of Christ a thousand years before the judgment at the white throne. The judgment at the great white throne will be for unbelievers concerning their eternal perdition. But the judgment at the judgment seat of Christ will be for believers concerning whether they will be rewarded or punished.

Although many of you were in Christianity for years, you probably never heard such a sobering message. Did you ever hear a sermon telling you that, although you are saved by faith through grace, you must still live a life that is of a higher moral standard than that required by the old law? Were you ever told that you must live a life that never loses its temper or that does not look at a woman to lust? The higher law, the law of the kingdom of the heavens, not only touches the outward acts, but also the inward motives. How high is the standard of this law! The Lord's warning concerning the standard of this law is serious. It even speaks of being put into the Gehenna of fire. I say again, this does not mean that the believers will perish. Pitiful Christianity merely tells people that they will go to either heaven or hell. But the Bible says clearly that after we have been saved according to the principle of faith, we must fulfill all the requirements of the new law. The law is no longer the principle according to which we are saved, but it is a standard of morality that we are required to keep. The principle of the law has been abolished, but the morality required by the commandments of the law remains and has been uplifted. Do not think that there is no need to take care of morality because we are not under the law for salvation. This is absolutely a wrong concept. The crucial point of the Lord's decree concerning the law is that we do not need to keep the law in order to be saved, but that we must have a standard of morality much higher than the standard of the old law after we have been saved by faith.

FORCED TO STAY WITH CHRIST

After hearing this, you may say that you cannot fulfill it. It is good to say that we cannot make it, because then it is necessary for Christ to come into us. The very One who fully kept the law and who died in our stead has come into us in resurrection to be our life. The Lord's warning in Matthew 5 must force us to stay with Christ. We must have a daily life full of fear and trembling. We need to say, "I must stay close to the resurrected Christ. I must be one with Him. I must trust Him and rely on Him. Because the standard of morality of the kingdom of the heavens is too high for me to fulfill, I must remain with the Lord. If I even lose my temper with my brother, I may be burned in the fire. How serious this is!"

When some Christian teachers hear this, they may say, "It is heresy to teach that saved ones will be burned in the fire." Read Matthew 5 again. This chapter is not a word spoken to unbelievers; it is a word given to the disciples, the saved ones, the sons of God. If they do not bridle their anger, they will be cast into the Gehenna of fire. Some may say, "This is the Gehenna of fire, not the lake of fire." Do not argue about what fire it is, for even a small fire can cause us much suffering. Sunday after Sunday, so many Christians are being filled with sugar-coated teachings. They have never heard a sobering word from Matthew 5. We thank the Lord for His mercy and grace and for the faith He has given us through which we have been saved. How wonderful it is to be saved by faith! But as those who are saved, we must listen to a serious word of warning! Even losing our temper with our brother may cause us to be burned in the Gehenna of fire.

This thought of being burned by fire is found in both 1 Corinthians 3 and Hebrews 6. First Corinthians 3:15 says, "If anyone's work shall be consumed, he shall suffer loss; but he shall be saved, yet so as through fire." Although such a one will be saved, he will be saved through fire. Hebrews 6:7 and 8 say, "For the earth which drinks the rain which often comes upon it and brings forth vegetation suitable to those for whose sake also it is tilled, partakes of blessing from God; But bringing forth thorns and thistles, it is disapproved and near a curse, whose end is to be burned." Here the believers are likened to earth which may grow vegetation approved by God or produce thorns and thistles that will be burned. How awful it would be to pass through such a burning! Moreover, in Revelation 2:11

the Lord said, "He who overcomes shall by no means be hurt of the second death." This word implies that the defeated Christians will be hurt by the second death, the lake of fire (Rev. 20:15). To be hurt by the second death is to be touched by the lake of fire. Certainly none of us wants to be touched by this fire.

DISPENSATIONAL PUNISHMENT

This matter of the judgment of the believers and of their being hurt by the fire is neither Calvinism nor Arminianism. According to Calvinism, once we are saved, we are saved forever, and there can be no further problem. In a sense, Calvinism is correct, for once we are saved, we are saved for eternity. However, we should not say that there can be no problems. There is the possibility of being burned in the fire. According to Arminianism, some may be saved in the morning and lose their salvation that night. Their salvation goes up and down like an elevator. Neither Calvinism nor Arminianism is according to the pure word of the Bible. The Bible reveals that we are saved for eternity, but that after we are saved, we need to overcome every sinful thing. If not, we shall be disciplined, punished. If you do not repent and confess your sin, but stay in adultery, in the next age you will be put into the fire and burned, not for eternal perdition, but as a dispensational punishment.

FLEEING OUR TEMPER AND LUST

Our age is an age of fornication and adultery. Every country is filled with immorality. Concerning this matter, so many have been drugged by "garlic" and have lost their sense concerning this sin. May this word sober us! We must stay away from today's trend. Nothing insults God more than fornication, which damages the man created by God in His image. We all must flee our temper and our lust. Flee your temper! Flee your lust! It is not an insignificant thing to lose our temper or to give in to our lust. Indulging in these things may cause us to be burned. Thus, we need to heed this sober word, a word that will force us to stay close to Christ. We need to pray, "Lord, I have temper and lust within me. But, Lord, I thank You that I have You in my spirit. Lord, I don't want to stay with my physical lust or my psychological temper. I want to stay in my spirit with You, dear Lord Jesus." Here is our salvation, our rescue, our holiness. Day and night we must stay with the Lord Jesus in our spirit, looking to Him, contacting Him, and trusting in Him.

Temper, a problem to every Christian, is like a gopher: it is hidden, subtle, and prevailing. We all must be on guard concerning it. Lust is also a great problem. I am sorry to say that even among saints there have been a number of cases of fornication. What a shame! Nothing is more shameful than fornication or adultery among the saints. This damages the people created by God, the church life, and the testimony of the church. Again and again the Apostle Paul warned us that no fornicator would share in God's kingdom (1 Cor. 6:9-10; Gal. 5:19-21; Eph. 5:5). Those believers who commit adultery or fornication are through with the kingdom of the heavens. The kingdom people must have the highest standard of righteousness. Do not lose your temper or look at a woman to lust after her. Be careful! You need to consider these matters seriously and deal with the motive at the very root. This word is not a threat; it is a warning that forces us to stay close to Christ.

Thank the Lord that we have both the Gospel of Matthew and the Gospel of John. We need to trust in the life revealed in the Gospel of John. Hallelujah, we have such a life! This life is the resurrection life, the overcoming life. Christ has already overcome and now in resurrection He is living in us. This is the life by which we fulfill the highest requirements of the kingdom of the heavens.

WALKING ACCORDING TO THE SPIRIT

We must be very clear about the fact that actually we are not keeping the law. Rather, we are walking according to the spirit. Romans 8:4 says that when we walk according to the spirit, we spontaneously fulfill all the righteous requirements of the law. We are not trying to keep the law, for the more we try to keep it, the more we break it. This is fully revealed and recorded in Romans 7. Today we are neither under the law nor obliged to keep the law. We are free from the law, and now we are walking according to the spirit. Within the spirit, there is the King, Christ, who is our resurrection life. As we walk according to the spirit, we fulfill even the requirements of the highest law.

I believe that now we are clear about the law. We can tell others that the principle of the law is over, but that the commandments of the law remain and have been uplifted. Although we are not able to meet the standard of these higher requirements, we have the resurrection life in our spirit. Therefore, we need not keep the law in the sense of striving in ourselves, but we must walk according to the spirit. When we walk according to the spirit, we spontaneously fulfill all the requirements of the law and have the highest standard of morality. This is the testimony of Jesus, the testimony of the church. This is the proper church life, the reality of the kingdom of the heavens.

LIFE-STUDY OF MATTHEW

THE DECREE
OF THE KINGDOM'S CONSTITUTION

(7)

In this message we come to 5:31-48, which covers four laws. In verses 21 through 30 the Lord covered two laws that were complemented, the law regarding murder and the law regarding adultery. But the four laws in this section, the laws regarding divorce, swearing, resisting evil, and loving our enemies, have all been changed. What the King decreed in verses 21 through 30 as the new law of the kingdom complements the law of the old dispensation, whereas what the King proclaimed in verses 31 through 48 as the new law of the kingdom changes the law of the old dispensation.

F. Regarding Divorce

1. The Old Law — to Divorce with a Writing

Let us firstly consider the changing of the law regarding divorce. Verse 31 says, "And it was said: Whoever shall put away his wife, let him give her a divorce." According to the old law, a man could divorce his wife simply by giving her a writing of divorcement. The law of the old dispensation concerning divorce was ordained because of the people's hardness of heart; it was not according to God's design in the beginning (19:7-8). The King's new decree recovers marriage back to the beginning designed by God (19:4-6).

2. The New Law — Not to Divorce
except in a Case of Fornication

Verse 32 says, "But I say to you that every one who puts away his wife, except in a case of fornication, makes her commit adultery, and whoever marries one that has been put away commits adultery." The marriage tie can be broken only by death (Rom. 7:3) or fornication. Hence, to have a divorce for any other reason is to commit adultery.

According to the word of the Lord Jesus, the only cause for divorce is fornication. Only two things can break the marriage tie: either the death of one of the parties or fornication, adultery. If either party commits adultery, the marriage tie is broken. This is the principle. Therefore, the Lord Jesus said that there must be no divorce except in the case of fornication. But you should not take advantage of this as an excuse to remarry simply because an act of fornication has been committed. This also is a matter of motive. If possible, the offending one should be forgiven. However, it is different if the guilty party refuses to repent and lives in that kind of sin or marries someone else. In such a case as this, the marriage tie is broken, and the other party is free.

In His original design for marriage, God ordained one wife for one husband. But due to the weakness and hardness of heart of the children of Israel, when the law was given, Moses gave a man permission to divorce his wife with a writing of divorce. But now, with the coming of the kingdom of the heavens, this law regarding divorce is changed, and the matter of marriage is recovered to God's intention at the beginning. At the beginning God did not create two or three Eves for Adam so he could have one or more divorces. No, there was only one husband and one wife. Hence, the Lord Jesus as the King of the heavenly kingdom brings the matter of marriage back to the beginning.

Here I would say a word to the young people. In this country there are a great number of divorces every year. Some have even been married several times. How deplorable! No child of God should ever have a divorce. This is serious. To divorce and remarry means to commit adultery. In the previous message we saw how serious adultery is. For this reason, I would speak a warning word to the young people who are not yet married: do not leap into marriage in a light way. You must pray to the Lord and wait on Him for His clear leading. Never be directed by your lusts or desires. If you do this, you will regret it later, for the lusts and desires will not last. Before you are married, both your eyes should be open to consider the matter carefully. But after you are married, your eyes must be closed. There is a proverb which says that love blinds you, but that marriage opens your eyes. We, however, need to change this proverb. Our eyes should be opened before marriage and closed after marriage. Young people, before you get married, ask the Lord to give you eyes to see every aspect of the situation. But after you are married, you must close your eyes and be blind. Be a blind wife or a blind husband, always considering your husband or wife so dear. If you do this, there will be no divorce.

I am surprised whenever I hear of a brother and sister who get married after knowing each other for just a short time. Do not get married in a hasty way or in a quick way. No hasty marriage is of the Lord's leading. If there is any matter that requires prayer, it is marriage. And if there is anything for which you need to present yourself to the Lord, it is your marriage. Present yourself and the other party to the Lord, offering yourself on the altar as a burnt offering to the Lord for your coming marriage. After you present yourself to the Lord, seek His leading and wait on Him for a period of time. I would encourage you to wait for at least another month. Do not be in a hurry. As an old man with much experience, I advise you to take your time in this matter. Even if you get married a year later, it will not make much difference. If marrying a certain one is of the Lord, the Lord will keep that one for you. You do not need to be in a rush. Furthermore, do not make your own choice, your own selection. Be content with the Lord's will and with the Lord's timing. This will save you from the possibility of divorce.

Again, I say, once you are married, you must be blind. Blessed are the blind husbands and wives. The wife who tries to be clear-sighted concerning her husband will suffer, but the one who does not try to be clear-sighted will enjoy life. To her, the sky is blue, the sun is shining, and the air is fresh. She does not seek to find all her husband's faults. She can simply praise the Lord for her husband.

G. Regarding Swearing

1. The Old Law — Not to Perjure Yourself But to Keep Your Oath to the Lord

Verse 33 says, "Again, you have heard that it was said to the ancients: You shall not perjure yourself, but you shall render to the Lord what you have sworn." This is the old law regarding swearing.

2. The New Law — Not to Swear at All

In verses 34 through 36 we see the Lord's new law regarding swearing: it is not to swear at all. The new law of the kingdom forbids the kingdom people to swear in any manner, by the heaven, by the earth, by Jerusalem, or by their head, because the heaven, the earth, Jerusalem, and their head are not under their control, but under God's. We should not swear by either the heaven or the earth, for they are not ours. Likewise, we should not swear by Jerusalem because, as the city of the great King, it is not our territory. We should not even swear by our head because we "cannot make one hair white or black." All these things — heaven, earth, Jerusalem, and even the hairs of our head — are not under our control. We are nobody and we control nothing.

In verse 37 the Lord says, "But let your word be, Yes, yes; No, no; for whatever is more than this is of the evil one." The kingdom people's word needs to be simple and true: "Yes, yes; No, no," not convincing others with many words. Our words should be brief and clear. Those who are honest do not talk very much. But beware of talkative people: they may be liars. Liars are very talkative, always giving many reasons and excuses for things. But an honest person is usually brief. Furthermore, we must realize that much talk in the presence of God does not make the Lord

happy. When we go to the Lord, we must go to Him in
honesty, saying things to Him in a brief way.

In verse 37 the Lord says that whatever is more than a
straight yes or no is of the evil one. Here we come to a
crucial point: in our talking the evil one may be present.
When we speak more words than are necessary, those
words are not of us, but of the Devil, the evil one. This indicates that in our talking the evil one is with us. This is
especially true in married life. Although we may not talk
that much with others, it is easy for there to be excess talk
between a husband and wife. If you want to avoid a poor
marriage, let there be no loose talk between you and your
husband or wife. Be on the alert! While you are talking, the
evil one may be with you. This is not my word; it is the
word of the Lord. The Lord's word in this verse is a strong
indication the evil one is seeking the opportunity to express
himself through our excessive talking. Do not say too
much. Simply say as much as is needed. Do not go any further. If you go further than is necessary, the evil one will be
expressed. If you follow this advice, you will be a very
happy husband or wife. However, if you talk too much, you
will have difficulty. This will open the shaft of the bottom-
less pit and allow the demons to come out. We should learn
to speak only what is necessary. Never try to convince
others by many words. Such convincing words are not
reliable; rather, they are falsehoods that come from the evil
one.

H. Regarding the Resistance of Evil

1. The Old Law — Eye for Eye,
Tooth for Tooth

Now we come to the third law changed by the Lord, the
law regarding the resistance of evil. Verse 38 says, "You
have heard that it was said, An eye for an eye, and a tooth
for a tooth." This is the old law.

2. The New Law — Do Not Resist

In verse 39 the Lord says, "But I say to you, Do not
resist one who is evil; but whoever strikes you on your right

cheek, turn to him the other also." The new law is not to resist one who is evil. In this verse the Lord said that when someone strikes our right cheek, we should turn to him the other also. To do this indicates that there is no resistance. Verse 40 says, "And to him who would sue you and take your tunic, let him have your cloak also." If someone claims your tunic, a shirt-like undergarment, give him your cloak also. This will prove that you have no resistance. In verse 41 the Lord says, "And whoever shall compel you to go one mile, go with him two." To turn the other cheek to the striker, to let the one who sues have the cloak, and to go with the compeller the second mile prove that the kingdom people have the power to suffer and to be meek instead of resisting and to walk not in the flesh, nor in the soul for their own interest, but in the spirit for the kingdom.

Suppose someone comes to you and wants your shirt, and you give him your jacket also. Perhaps you can afford to give him ten jackets. The issue here is not whether your financial status allows you to give him your jacket; it is whether your temper allows you to do it. If someone demands your shirt, your anger may be aroused. Thus, it is not a matter of a shirt or a jacket, but of your temper. It is the same in principle with being struck on the right cheek or compelled to walk a mile.

To resist by claiming an eye for an eye means that you are releasing your temper. Here the Lord is saying that we cannot satisfy our temper. Instead of releasing the "gopher" of our temper, we must kill it. Do not deal with the one making a claim upon you; deal with your temper. The problem is not your opponent; it is your temper. The Lord allows someone to claim your tunic as a test to expose where you are, to prove that the "gopher" of your temper is still lurking within you. We are a spiritual people, even the kingdom people, but our temper is still hidden within us and needs to be exposed. Those who make claims of you expose this little "gopher." If someone demands your tunic, you may say, "I don't owe you anything! Why do you come to me?" Do not blame the one making a claim — the

Lord has sent him — but kill the "gopher" of your temper. Instead of displaying anger, say to him, "Since you want my undershirt, I will give you my jacket also." This proves that your temper has been killed. All the kingdom people should be able to say, "No matter how many unjust claims you place on me, my anger is not stirred up. I still love you and I am willing to share with you all I have. If you want my shirt, I shall gladly give you my jacket also." The attitude of the kingdom people should always be like this.

I say again, the issue here is not one of money, but of our temper. All the matters mentioned in verses 39 through 41 touch our temper. Millionaires can afford to give thousands of dollars away. But they often display their temper with a taxi driver over a mere twenty-five cents. The money does not mean anything; it is a matter of the temper. We, the kingdom people, must be above our temper.

In verse 42 the Lord says, "To him who asks of you, give; and from him who wants to borrow from you, do not turn away." To give and not turn away from the borrower proves that the kingdom people do not care for material riches and are not possessed by them. However, the real issue is not material wealth. Giving to those who ask or who want to borrow touches our being. The Lord is not saying that we should lack discernment and behave in a foolish way regarding material possessions. He is telling us that we must be above both material things and our temper. We should never be stirred in our temper by this kind of thing nor touched by the material things. This is the overcoming attitude of the kingdom people. This does not mean that we are overly generous or careless in managing money. Although you may be very careful in the way you spend money, you will be above material possessions and above your temper when such a time comes as described in verse 42. No claim will stir up your anger. The old law did not touch people's anger or their heart. But the new law, the changed law, touches both our temper and our heart.

I. Regarding Enemies

1. The Old Law — Love Your Neighbor and Hate Your Enemy

Now we come to the last law changed by the Lord, the law regarding the enemy. Verse 43 says, "You have heard that it was said, You shall love your neighbor and hate your enemy." Legally speaking, the old law is fair and righteous; for a good neighbor deserves our love and an enemy deserves our hatred. Thus, to love a neighbor and to hate an enemy is right and fair.

2. The New Law — Love Your Enemies and Pray for Your Persecutors

Verse 44 says, "But I say to you, Love your enemies, and pray for those who persecute you." Once again, this is a matter that touches our being. The reason you love your neighbors is that they are good according to your feeling. Although your neighbors correspond to your feeling, an enemy does not. Instead, he stirs up your temper. Hence, the matter of loving our enemies is a test. If you read chapters five, six, and seven of Matthew, you will see that this heavenly constitution does not allow even an inch to our natural being. Rather, it kills every germ in us. You hate your enemy because he does not agree with your natural choice, and you love your good neighbor because he does suit your natural choice. If the Lord arranged for you to have only good neighbors, you would behave like an angel and say, "Lord, thank You for giving me such lovely neighbors." But the Lord would never arrange for you to have only nice neighbors. At least some of them will be troublesome, and the Lord will use them to expose what is within you. He may ask you if you love these difficult neighbors. Perhaps you would say that you find it very difficult. The reason it is difficult is that they are against your being and your natural feeling. This is a test to prove whether you live by yourself or by Christ. Sometimes Christ may love your enemies more than your neighbors, and you must follow Him. However, this is not merely an outward act.

All these laws touch our being and put us on the cross. The one commandment regarding divorce is enough to crucify all the husbands and wives. Furthermore, the word about saying yes and no also nails us to the cross. The same is true about not resisting the one who is evil and especially about not hating our enemies. All these laws kill our natural man, our natural taste, and our temper.

a. To Behave as the Sons of the Heavenly Father

Verse 45 says, "That you may become sons of your Father Who is in the heavens." The title "sons of your Father" is a strong proof that the kingdom people, who are the audience here for the new King's decree on the mountain, are the regenerated believers of the New Testament. As sons of our Father, we should deal with the evil and the unjust as with the good and the just (v. 45), love not only those who love us but those who do not love us (v. 46), and greet not only brothers but also others (v. 47).

Verse 45 also says of the Father, "He makes His sun to rise on the evil and the good, and sends rain on the just and the unjust." Sending rain on the just and the unjust is in the age of grace, but in the coming age, the age of the kingdom, no rain will come upon the unjust (Zech. 14:17-18).

In verse 46 the Lord asks a question: "For if you love those who love you, what reward have you? Do not also the tax-collectors do the same?" The kingdom people who observe the new law of the kingdom in its reality will be given a reward in the manifestation of the kingdom. The reward differs from salvation. Some may be saved, but may not be qualified to receive a reward.

b. To Be Perfect as the Heavenly Father

Verse 48 says, "You, therefore, shall be perfect as your heavenly Father is perfect." For the kingdom people to be perfect as their heavenly Father is perfect is to be perfect in His love. They are the Father's children, having the Father's divine life and divine nature. Hence, they can be perfect as the Father. The demand of the new law of the kingdom is much higher than the requirement of the law of the old dispensation. This higher demand can be met only by the Father's divine life, not by their natural life. The kingdom of the heavens is the highest demand, and the divine life of the Father is the highest supply to meet that demand. The Gospels firstly present the highest demand of the kingdom of the heavens in the Gospel of Matthew and lastly afford us the highest supply of the divine life of the heavenly Father in the Gospel of John so that we may live the life of the kingdom of the heavens. The demand of the new law of the kingdom in Matthew 5 through 7 is actually the regenerated kingdom people's expression from within their new life — the divine life. This demand, by opening up the inner being of the regenerated people, is to show them that they are able to attain to such a high degree.

All the requirements of these changed laws reveal how much the divine life within us can do for us. These laws are not merely a requirement; they are a revelation, showing us that the divine life can even make us perfect as our heavenly Father is perfect. We have this perfecting life within us. We have a life with such a divine nature that it can make us as perfect as our heavenly Father.

We have seen that according to verse 45 the Father makes His sun to rise on the evil and the good and that He sends rain on the just and the unjust. First the Father makes His sun to rise on the evil, then on the good. If you were the Father, would you make your sun to rise first on the evil or on the good? Certainly you would first make it rise on the good. This verse also says that the Father sends His rain on the just and on the unjust. Notice that the order in this part of the verse is changed. This indicates that in the eyes of the heavenly Father there is no difference in sending the sunshine first on the evil and then on the good and sending the rain first on the just and then on the unjust.

Let us apply this to the matter of dealing with our children. Even in dealing with your own children, you have your choice. This indicates how natural you are. Suppose you have three children. One of your three children may be lovable, one may be naughty, and one may be neutral. Day after day these three children expose you, revealing how much you dislike the naughty one and blame him. Although you do not like him, the heavenly Father loves him more than the lovable one. He has sent him to expose your natural taste.

We also have our natural taste in the church life. We like the brothers who are gentle and the sisters who are nice. We want all the brothers and sisters to be like this. But this is just a dream, for there will always be some who bother us. Consider the problem of the shortage among the elders. Many brothers are nice and gentle, but they are not capable of being elders. However, the capable ones may be rather sharp. God uses this to expose your natural choice.

Now we understand the implication and significance of the Lord's word in verses 31 through 48. It is not simply a matter of outwardly loving our enemy. No, it is a matter of having our natural being exposed. After we have been exposed, we shall say, "Lord, have mercy on me. How I need Your deliverance! I want to stay near to You and trust in You. Then I will be perfect as my Father."

Do not take the Lord's word as a teaching concerning how you should behave. This way will not work. The Lord's word was intended to touch our being, our natural choice, and to expose what we are and where we are. When we have been exposed and subdued, we shall give the full opportunity to the divine life to live in us. This will make us perfect even as our heavenly Father is perfect. We cannot imitate the Father. When I was young, I was taught by those in Christianity that our heavenly Father loves those who are bad and that we should love our enemies just as our Father does. Although this sounds good, it actually is like trying to teach a monkey to behave like a person. You may teach a monkey to behave like a kind gentleman. The monkeys, however, will fail to do this because they are not the sons of that man. We are the sons of our heavenly Father. Thus, the Father's life and nature are within us. All the outward enemies, compellers, and opponents expose what we are. Because they expose our natural being, we learn not to trust ourselves any longer, but to look to our

Father and to realize that we have His life and nature within us. Through this exposure we come to see that we must stay close to Him and live by His life and nature. In this way we shall be perfect as our heavenly Father. This is the kingdom life, the kingdom living.

Misunderstanding these verses, many Christians have taken them as instructions concerning their outward behavior. This is the reason so many have been disappointed and have said, "This is too much for us. We are far away from it, and we are unable to fulfill it." This is not a common word given by the Lord Jesus; it is the constitution of the heavenly kingdom. Because we are His kingdom people, we can certainly fulfill these requirements. We have the kingdom life within us, and we can fulfill these laws, not in ourselves, but by the Father's life and nature. Therefore, we must thank Him for sending so many contrary things into our environment in order to touch our being and to expose what we are so that we may be fully subdued, turn to Him, stay near to Him, trust in Him, and live by Him. Then we shall be the genuine kingdom people with the kingdom life for a proper kingdom living. This is God's kingdom on earth today, and this is the proper church life.

LIFE-STUDY OF MATTHEW

THE DECREE
OF THE KINGDOM'S CONSTITUTION

(8)

For centuries, Christians have not had a clear understanding of the law. On the one hand, in Romans and Galatians we are told that the law is over. For example, Romans
10:4 says, "Christ is the end of the law unto righteousness
to every one who believes." Based upon this, many Christians think that they can forget the law. On the other hand,
in Matthew 5:17 the Lord Jesus said, "Do not think that I
came to abolish the law or the prophets; I did not come to
abolish, but to fulfill." This word has troubled a great
many Christians. We praise the Lord that He has given us
the clear light on this matter.

THREE ASPECTS OF THE LAW

In order to understand this matter of the law, we must
know the three aspects of the law: the principle of the law,
the commandments of the law, and the rituals of the law. If
you do not differentiate between these three things, you
will never have a proper understanding of the law. As we
have seen, the principle of the law is over. Today, in the
dispensation of grace, God does not deal with us according
to the principle of the law; rather, He deals with us according to the principle of faith. Whether or not we shall be
justified, saved, and accepted by God depends on the principle of faith, not the principle of the law. As long as we
have faith in Christ, we are justified by God, accepted by
Him, and saved. This is what it means for the principle of

the law to be abolished in Christ under the dispensation of grace.

Although the principle of the law has been abolished, the commandments of the law have not been annulled. Instead, the standard of these commandments has been uplifted. Thus, the commandments, related to the moral standards, have not been abolished; they will remain for eternity. Even for eternity we should not worship an idol, murder, steal, or lie. In His heavenly kingdom the King has uplifted the standard of the law in two ways: by complementing the lower laws and by changing the lower laws into higher laws. In this way the morality in the commandments of the law has been uplifted to a higher standard.

The kingly Savior Himself kept all the commandments of the law when He was on earth. Then He went to the cross to die for us. Through His substitutionary death, He fulfilled the law on the negative side. Furthermore, through His substitutionary death, He released His resurrection life into us, and we now have this resurrection life in our spirit. Because we are able to live by this resurrection life, we have the strength, ability, and capacity to have the highest standard of morality. As we walk according to the spirit (Rom. 8:4), we fulfill the righteous requirements of the law, fulfilling even more than the law requires. Therefore, we do not abolish the law; rather, we fulfill it in the highest way.

The third aspect of the law is the rituals of the law. For example, offering sacrifices and keeping the Sabbath are outward rituals of the law. These rituals were also terminated because they were part of the old dispensation of shadows, figures, and types, all of which have been fulfilled by Christ as the reality. We are no longer obligated to observe the rituals of the law. Therefore, the principle of the law and the rituals of the law have been terminated, but the commandments of the law, which require a high moral standard, have not been terminated. Rather, these commandments have been uplifted. By means of Christ as the resurrection life in our spirit, we can fulfill the standard of morality required by the higher law of the kingdom of the heavens. This word should make us clear concerning the law according to its three aspects: the principle of the law, the commandments of the law, and the rituals of the law.

LIVING BY THE FATHER'S LIFE AND NATURE

At the end of Matthew 5 the Lord Jesus said, "You, therefore, shall be perfect as your heavenly Father is perfect" (v. 48). This word concludes this section of the constitution, a section which is exceedingly high. After reading all these requirements, we all would say that we cannot possibly fulfill them. Then we come to verse 48 which tells us that we must be perfect as our heavenly Father is perfect. This verse is an indicator that we have the Father's life and nature within us. We have been born of Him and we are His children. Because we are His children possessing His life and nature, there is no need for us to imitate Him or copy Him. As long as we grow in His life, we shall be the same as He is. Thus, all the requirements of the law of the kingdom of the heavens reveal how much this divine life and nature can do for us. Our only need is to be exposed so that we may give up all hope in ourselves. When we are exposed, we shall realize that our natural life is hopeless. Then we shall renounce our natural life, turn to the life of our Father, and stay with the divine nature. Spontaneously, this life will grow in us and fulfill the requirements of this highest law. Our need today is to turn to our spirit and walk in our spirit. Whenever we do this, we live by our Father's life and nature; then spontaneously we fulfill the righteous requirements of the law. It is crucial that we understand this matter, for it is altogether different from our natural concept.

From my experience I can testify that today I am not under the principle of the law. Hallelujah, I am under the principle of faith, and I have the life of my heavenly Father within me! This life is nothing other than the Father's dear Son. I am now living by this life in my spirit and walking

according to the spirit. By this life in my spirit I spontaneously fulfill the highest requirements of the law of the
kingdom of the heavens. This is not my boast; it is my
humble testimony to give glory to the Lord. This does not
mean that I am able to do anything. It means that He is
able, for He is in me as my life. He is able to do the same in
you and for you. In order for this to be your experience, you
need to have a vision of the hopelessness of your natural
life. After your natural life has been thoroughly dug out
and exposed, you will realize that it is a hopeless case, that
you should have no trust in it, and that you must turn to
the Father's divine life and nature within you. Turn to the
Father's life, stay with the Father's life, and live by the
Father's life. You can easily turn to the Father's life
because at this very moment it is in your spirit. Simply
walk according to your spirit, and all the righteous requirements of the law will be fulfilled in you.

FULFILLING THE RIGHTEOUS REQUIREMENT
OF THE LAW
BY WALKING ACCORDING TO THE SPIRIT

At this point we need to consider some verses in
Romans 8. Romans 8:3 says, "For what is impossible to the
law, in that it was weak through the flesh, God sending His
own Son in the likeness of the flesh of sin and concerning
sin, condemned sin in the flesh." Due to the weakness of
our flesh, it is impossible for us to fulfill the law. We can do
nothing. As far as the law is concerned, our case is impossible. Therefore, God, sending His own Son in the likeness
of the flesh of sin and concerning sin, condemned sin in the
flesh, so that "the righteous requirement of the law might
be fulfilled in us, who do not walk according to flesh, but
according to spirit" (v. 4). Because it was impossible, due
to the weakness of our flesh, for the law to be fulfilled, God
sent His Son to keep the law on the positive side, and to die
for our weakness on the negative side. His purpose in doing
so was that the righteous requirement of the law might be
fulfilled in us. The "us" in verse 4 refers to those who do

not walk according to the flesh, but according to the spirit. God sent His Son to keep the law and to die for us that we may walk in the spirit to fulfill the righteous requirement of the law.

HOW OUR SPIRIT IS FORMED

Romans 8:16 reveals how our spirit is formed: "The Spirit Himself witnesses with our spirit that we are the children of God." This verse reveals that our spirit in which we walk to fulfill the righteous requirement of the law is formed through the witnessing of the Holy Spirit with our spirit. This indicates that the Holy Spirit of God has come into our spirit. This took place at the time of our regeneration. The Spirit of God came into our spirit to regenerate us. From that time onward, the Holy Spirit has been witnessing with our spirit that we are the children of God. Thus, verse 14 says, "For as many as are led by the Spirit of God, these are sons of God."

NOT ONLY GOD'S CREATURES,
BUT ALSO HIS REGENERATED CHILDREN

With these verses before us, we can understand why the Lord concluded His word in Matthew 5 by saying, "You, therefore, shall be perfect as your heavenly Father is perfect." We are not only God's creatures; we are also His regenerated children, possessing His life and nature. Thus, we are not God's creatures trying to copy and imitate Him; we are the Father's children living the Father's life. How did we become the children of God? It was by the coming of the Spirit of God into our spirit to regenerate us and to make our spirit the very habitation of God Himself (Eph. 2:22, Gk.). Here, in our spirit, we have become God's children having God's life and nature. If we walk according to this regenerated spirit, we are the children of God living by God's life. When we live and walk in the spirit, spontaneously we shall be perfect as our heavenly Father is perfect.

Consider a brother who has four children. The more these little ones grow, the more they live like their father. These children are not four monkeys trying to imitate a human being. No, they are children of their father who are growing into the image of their father. The more they grow, the more they live their father's life. Likewise, we are not monkeys — we are children of God. Although some of us may be rather babyish or childish, we are growing nonetheless. These young ones may be naughty, but they are growing. Wait for a certain number of years, and you will see that all these naughty little ones will be perfect as their heavenly Father is perfect. I am so happy that all the saints in the churches are not monkeys, but dear children. Let these children be naughty for a while. Eventually they will grow. We are not trying to imitate God. Rather we are the Father's children growing in the Father's life. This is the reason the Lord Jesus said that we should be perfect as our heavenly Father is perfect.

Now we can understand why in Matthew chapter five the Lord refers to us as the children of God or the sons of God. He was not giving a word to unbelievers, to those who were merely God's creatures; He was giving a word to the sons of God. God is no longer merely our Creator; He is also our heavenly Father. Because He is our Father, we have His life and nature. Eventually, through our growth in life, we shall be the same as He is. Wait for another period of time, and you will see that many of us will have become perfect as the Father is perfect.

NO TIME ELEMENT WITH GOD

Some may wonder how the disciples on the mountain could have been regenerated. Since the life-giving Spirit had not yet entered into them, how can we say that those disciples were regenerated? Remember, there is no time element with God. Instead, there is the principle. When the Lord Jesus was speaking with the disciples on the mountain, giving them the decree of the constitution of the kingdom, He spoke according to the principle, not according to the time element. God has no time element; He does things once for all. In our mind there is such a thing as before and after, but not in God's mind. Yes, one day Christ accomplished the work of redemption on the cross, and one day the life-giving Spirit was formed. But in God's eyes it is difficult to determine when these things took place, for in God's economy they are eternal. Both the cross and life-giving Spirit are eternal. Because those disciples on the mountain had believed in the Lord Jesus and had decided to follow Him, in principle they had been regenerated, and the Lord regarded them as regenerated people.

LIFE-STUDY OF MATTHEW

THE DECREE
OF THE KINGDOM'S CONSTITUTION

(9)

In this message we come to the fourth section of the King's decree on the mountain, 6:1-18, concerning the righteous deeds of the kingdom people.

V. CONCERNING THE RIGHTEOUS DEEDS
OF THE KINGDOM PEOPLE

A. The Principle —
Not to Do Your Righteousness before Men

In 5:17-48 we saw the complementing and the changing of the law. In these verses, all the new laws of the kingdom of the heavens dig out and expose our temper, lust, and natural being. Thus, in these verses it is not a matter of dealing with our outward behavior, but with our anger, our lust, and our natural being all hidden deeply within us.

Matthew 6:1 says, "But take heed not to do your righteousness before men to be gazed at by them; otherwise, you surely have no reward with your Father Who is in the heavens." Righteousness here denotes righteous deeds, such as giving alms, mentioned in verses 2 through 4; praying, in verses 5 through 15; and fasting, in verses 16 through 18. No doubt these verses speak about the righteous deeds of the kingdom people. Actually, however, they expose the self and the flesh. We have something within us that is worse than anger and lust. Everybody knows how ugly lust is, but even many Christians do not know how ugly the self and the flesh are. Of course, the words "self" and "flesh" are not used in these verses. Nevertheless, both the self and the flesh are exposed here. In these eighteen verses the Lord uses three illustrations — the giving of alms, praying, and fasting — to reveal how we are filled with the self and the flesh.

Man's flesh, seeking to glorify itself, always wants to do good deeds before men to be praised by them. But the kingdom people, who live in an emptied and humbled spirit and walk in a pure and single heart under the heavenly ruling of the kingdom, are not allowed to do anything in the flesh for the praise of men, but must do all things in the spirit for the pleasing of their heavenly Father.

To the kingdom people, God is not only their God, but also their Father. They are not only created by God, but also regenerated by the Father. They have not only the created natural human life, but also the uncreated spiritual divine life. Hence, the new law of the kingdom, decreed by the King on the mountain, is given to them with the intention that they should keep it not by their fallen human life, but by the Father's eternal divine life, not to gain man's glory, but to receive the Father's reward.

Regarding each of the three illustrations, the Lord uses the word "secret" (vv. 4, 6, 18). We must do our righteous deeds in secret, for our Father is in secret. In verse 4 the Lord says that our Father sees in secret. The kingdom people as children of the heavenly Father must live in the presence of the Father and care for the Father's presence. Whatever they do in secret for the Father's kingdom, the Father sees in secret. The heavenly Father's seeing in secret must be an incentive to doing their righteous deeds in secret. In this verse the Lord also said that the Father will repay us. This may transpire in this age (2 Cor. 9:10-11) or in the coming age as a reward (Luke 14:14).

The effect of doing our righteous deeds in secret is that the self and the flesh are killed. If people in society today are not allowed to make a show of their good deeds, they will not do them. As long as people have an opportunity to make a public display of their righteous deeds, they are glad to perform them. This is the deplorable practice of today's degraded Christianity, especially in the matter of fund raising, which provides an excellent opportunity for the donors to make a display. The greater the public show, the more money people are willing to give. Certainly such making of a show is of the flesh. Giving alms to the poor in order to show how generous you are is not a matter of anger, lust, or the natural being; it is a matter of the self, the flesh. Making a show in such a way is simply boasting for yourself. Thus, for us as kingdom people, a basic principle concerning righteous deeds is never to make a show of ourselves. As much as possible, hide yourself, keep yourself covered, and do things in secret. We should be so hidden that, as the Lord Jesus says, our left hand does not know what our right hand is doing (v. 3). This means that we should not let others know what we are doing. For example, if you fast for three days, do not disfigure your face or show a sad countenance. Rather, give the impression to others that you are not fasting so that your fasting may be in secret. Do not fast in the presence of men, but in the secret presence of your heavenly Father. To do this is to slay the self and the flesh.

We encourage the saints to function in the church meetings. However, there is the danger of functioning in order to make a show of ourselves. There is the danger of doing things in the presence of man. If you consider your own experience, you will realize that perhaps nine times out of ten your functioning has been before men. This is to glorify the self and the flesh. But the constitution of the heavenly kingdom does not yield an inch to our anger, lust, or natural being; neither does it yield any ground to our self and flesh. By the Lord's mercy and grace, we must do as much as possible in a hidden way. Always try to do those things that are pleasing to God and righteous with man in a secret way. Try not to let others know of them. Simply do your righteous deeds in the presence of God.

Our Father sees in secret. As you are praying alone in your room, no one else can see you, but your heavenly Father sees. Do not pray on the street corner or in the synagogues to be seen by men. Pray in secret to be seen by your Father who sees in secret. Then you will also receive an answer from Him in secret. I am concerned that many of us have experiences only in the open and that we do not have any experiences in secret. Not only does the Father see our experiences; everyone else sees them as well. This indicates that we are not rejecting the self or repudiating the flesh. We must always do things in such a way as to constantly reject the self and repudiate the flesh. If possible, do everything in secret, not giving any opportunity to your self or yielding any ground to your flesh.

Although the Lord speaks about the matter of reward (vv. 1, 5), the important thing here is not the reward, but the growth in life. The saints who grow openly do not grow in a healthy way. We all need some secret growth in life, some secret experiences of Christ. We need to pray to the Lord, worship the Lord, contact the Lord, and fellowship with the Lord in a secret way. Perhaps not even the one closest to us will know or understand what we are doing. We need these secret experiences of the Lord because such experiences kill our self and our flesh. Although anger and lust are ugly, the thing that most frustrates us from growing in life is the self. The self is most visible in the fact that it enjoys doing things in a public way, in the presence of man. The self likes to do righteous deeds before man. We all must admit that, without exception, we have such a self. Those who always want to do things in such a way as to make a public show are full of self, full of the flesh. The self loves to be glorified, and the flesh loves to be gazed upon. Probably you have never heard a message on these verses that dealt with the self and the flesh. Whenever we come to this portion of the Word, we must realize that it exposes our self and our flesh.

To repeat, the crucial matter here is not the reward, but the growth in life. Those saints who know only to make a

show of the self and a display of the flesh will not grow in
life. The genuine growth in life is to cut off the self. Those
whose self has been cut off and whose flesh has been dealt
with may sometimes speak concerning their deeds. However, I am quite cautious in saying even this. It is not
healthy to expose our righteous deeds. Rather, we should
pray much, yet not let others know how much we pray.
This is healthy. If you pray every day without telling others
or letting them know about it, it means that you are
healthy and that you are growing. However, suppose you
always tell others how much you pray. If you do this, you
will not only lose your reward, but you will not grow in life
or be healthy. We all must admit that we have the subtle
self, the subtle flesh, within us. We all have such a weak
point. When we pray alone in our room, we often wish that
others could hear us. Likewise, we do our righteous deeds
with the intention that others could see them. Such desires
and intentions are not healthy; they indicate that we are
not growing in life. Making a public display before men
will never help us grow in life. If you want to grow and be
healthy in the spiritual life, you must slay the self in the
doing of righteous deeds. No matter what kind of righteous deeds we do — giving material things to the saints,
praying, fasting, doing something to please God — we
must try our best to do them in secret. If your righteous
deeds are in secret, you may be assured that you are growing in life and are healthy. But any time you exhibit yourself in your righteous deeds, you are not healthy. Such an
exhibition greatly frustrates your growth in life.

The universe indicates that God is hidden, that God is
secret. Although He has done a great many things, people
are not aware that He has done them. We may have seen
the things done by God, but none of us has ever seen Him,
for He is always hidden, always secret. God's life is of such
a secret and hidden nature. If we love others by our own
life, this life will seek to make a display of itself before
men. But if we love others by the love of God, this love will
always remain hidden. Our human life loves to make a dis-

play, a public show, but God's life is always hidden. A
hypocrite is one who has an outward manifestation without
having anything within. Everything he has is merely an
outward show; there is no reality inwardly. This is absolutely contrary to God's nature and to His hidden life.
Although God has so much within Him, only a little is
manifested. If we live by this divine life, we may pray
much, but others will not know how much we have prayed.
We may give a great deal to help others, but no one will
know how much we give. We may fast often, but this also
will not be known by others. We may have a great deal
within us, but very little will be manifested. This is the
nature of the kingdom people in the doing of their righteous deeds.

This is vastly different from the nature of the worldly
people. When the worldly ones donate a hundred dollars,
they advertise it, making it appear that they have given a
much greater amount. But when we Christians give a hundred dollars, it is better that we only let others know that
we have given a dime. We do more than what is visible to
others. We can never practice this kind of giving in our
natural life. It is possible only in the divine life, the life
that does not enjoy making a show. This is the crucial
point in this portion of the Word.

If we are serious about being the kingdom people, we
must learn to live by the hidden life of our Father. We must
not live by our natural life, which is always making a display of itself. If we live by our Father's hidden life, we shall
do many things without making any public show of them.
Rather, all that we do will be in secret, hidden from the
eyes of others. The biographies of many saints reveal that
they did certain things in secret, things that often were not
made known until after they had died. This is the right
way. I have known a number of dear saints who have done
things for the Lord, for the church, and for the saints in
secret. They never desired to make a display or to let others
know that those things were done by them. These deeds are

done according to our Father's nature and according to His secret and hidden life.

B. Regarding Alms

1. *Not Sounding a Trumpet*

Verse 2 says, "When therefore you give alms, do not sound a trumpet before you as the hypocrites do in the synagogues and in the streets that they may be glorified by men. Truly I say to you, They have their reward." Surely the heaven-ruled spirit of the kingdom people restricts them from such fleshly boasting.

When I was in a certain denomination, the offering plate was passed during every Sunday morning service. At that time, copper coins or silver dollars were used instead of paper currency. Some people used to place their donations in the offering plate in such a way as to draw attention to themselves. That was a display of the self. Of course, they did not say anything. Rather, they dropped the coins in the plate in a noisy way. By doing this, they were sounding a trumpet before them. When the time came for public notice regarding contributions to be posted in the lobby, the one who gave the most was listed first, and the one who gave the least was listed last. If the one who had given the most had been listed last, he probably would not have given as much in the future.

For this reason, we in the churches do not keep records of the giving of the saints. The cash is put in the offering box, and there is no opportunity for the self or the flesh to be glorified. The use of checks, however, poses somewhat of a problem. In our practice of the church life in China many years ago, we did not use checks very often. But the use of checks is not a legal matter. Everything depends on our motive and our attitude. I am not saying that the saints should not use checks. The principle is that we do not give with the intention of making a show or receiving glory from man. Instead, we do everything in secret in the presence of our heavenly Father. In this matter, you know what your motive and attitude are.

2. Not Letting the Left Hand Know
the Doing of the Right

Verse 3 says, "But you, when you give alms, let not your left hand know what your right hand is doing." This word indicates that the kingdom people's righteous deeds should be kept secret as much as possible. What they do in their spirit under the heavenly rule to please their Father alone must not be interfered with by their flesh lusting for man's glory.

3. Giving Alms in Secret

In verse 4 the King said, "So that your alms may be in secret; and your Father Who sees in secret shall repay you." The kingdom people's living is by the Father's divine life according to their spirit. Thus they are required to do good things in secret, not in public. Any public exhibition does not correspond to the mysterious hidden nature of the divine life.

C. Regarding Prayer

1. Not to Make a Public Show

In praying, as in giving alms, the kingdom people are not to make a public show. Verse 5 says, "And when you pray, you shall not be as the hypocrites; for they love to pray standing in the synagogues and on the street corners that they may appear to men. Truly I say to you, They have their reward." Prayer to seek man's praise may gain a reward from men, but it does not receive an answer from the Father. Thus, it is vain prayer.

2. To Pray in Secret

Our prayer should be in secret. In verse 6 the King decreed, "But you, when you pray, enter into your private room, and having shut your door, pray to your Father Who is in secret, and your Father Who sees in secret shall repay you." The kingdom people must have some experience of prayer in their private room, contacting their heavenly

Father in secret, experiencing some secret enjoyment of the Father, and receiving some secret answer from Him.

3. Not to Repeat Empty Words

As we pray, we are not to repeat empty words. Verse 7 says, "And in praying do not repeat empty words as the nations do; for they suppose that they will be heard through their much speaking." This does not mean, however, that we should not repeat our prayer. The Lord repeated His prayer in Gethsemane (26:44), the Apostle Paul prayed the same prayer three times (2 Cor. 12:8), and the great multitude in heaven praised God with hallelujahs repeatedly (Rev. 19:1-6). It means that we should not repeat with empty words, words in vain.

Verse 8 says, "Therefore do not be like them, for God your Father knows what things you have need of before you ask Him." Although God our Father knows our need, we still need to ask Him, because he who asks receives (7:8).

4. The Pattern of Prayer

In verses 9 through 13 we find the pattern of prayer. However, it is not the pattern for all prayers. The prayer presented here in Matthew 6 is absolutely different from the prayer taught in John. In Matthew 6 we are not told to pray in the Lord's name, but in John chapters fourteen through seventeen the Lord Jesus tells us repeatedly to pray in His name. The reason for this difference is that the prayer here in Matthew is not related to life; it is related to the kingdom. In this short pattern of prayer the kingdom is mentioned at least twice. Verse 10 says, "Let Your kingdom come," and verse 13 says, "For Yours is the kingdom." The prayer in John, on the contrary, is related to life. Praying in the Lord's name is not a matter of the kingdom, but a matter of life. To pray in the Lord's name means that we are one with the Lord. In praying to the Father, we are one with the Lord. Hence, we are praying in His name. To pray in the Lord's name is actually to pray in the Person of the Lord. We are praying with Him in one name and in one life. Therefore, we are one with Him in life, praying to God the Father. But as we have seen, the prayer in Matthew 6 is absolutely different, for it is a prayer of the kingdom.

If you would have some prayer in life, you must go to John. You must abide in the Lord and be one with Him. You must remain in your spirit and pray in oneness with Him. This is what it means to pray in His name. But the prayer in Matthew 6 concerns the kingdom. In other words, it is a fighting prayer, a prayer of warfare against God's enemy for God's kingdom.

Verse 9 begins with the words, "Pray, then, like this." The words "like this" do not mean to recite. In the Acts and the Epistles there is no example of such reciting. However, in certain Christian denominations today this prayer is recited during every Sunday morning service. I recited this prayer very often as a youth in a denomination. This is not to say that those who recite this prayer are not sincere in doing so. No doubt there have been a good number who were very sincere in their repeating of this prayer.

a. Praying that God's Name May Be Sanctified

In the example of prayer patterned by the Lord, the first three petitions imply the Trinity of the Godhead. "Let Your name be sanctified" is mainly related to the Father, "let Your kingdom come" to the Son, and "let Your will be done" to the Spirit. This is being fulfilled in this age, and it will be fulfilled in the coming kingdom age, when the name of God will be excellent in all the earth (Psa. 8:1), the kingdom of the world will become the kingdom of Christ (Rev. 11:15), and the will of God will be accomplished.

Verse 9 says, "Our Father Who is in the heavens, let Your name be sanctified." Today God's name is not sanctified; rather, it is profaned and made common. Unbelievers may ask, "What is God? Who is God?" People speak about Jesus Christ in the same way that they speak about Plato or Hitler. They make the name of the Lord

Jesus common. But we know that the day will come, in the millennium, when the name of God will be sanctified. But, prior to that time, our Father's name is wholly sanctified in the church life today. We do not call upon the Father or speak the name of the Lord in a common way. Rather, when we say "Father" or "Lord," we sanctify these holy names. Thus, we need to pray, "O Father, let Your name be sanctified."

b. Praying that God's Kingdom May Come

Verse 10 says, "Let Your kingdom come." Although the kingdom is here in the church life today, the manifestation of the kingdom is yet to come. Thus, we must pray for the coming of the kingdom. This matter of the kingdom is clearly related to God the Son.

c. Praying that God's Will
May Be Done on Earth

Verse 10 also says, "Let Your will be done, as in heaven, so on earth." Following the rebellion of Satan (Ezek. 28:17; Isa. 14:13-15), the earth fell into the usurping hand of Satan. Thus, the will of God could not be done on earth as in heaven. Hence, God created man with the intention of recovering the earth for Himself (Gen. 1:26-28). After the fall of man, Christ came to bring the heavenly rule to earth so that the earth might be recovered for God's right, that the will of God might be done on earth as in heaven. This is the purpose of the new King establishing the kingdom of the heavens with His followers. The kingdom people must pray for this until the earth is fully recovered for God's will in the coming kingdom age.

When the Father's name is sanctified, the Son's kingdom has come, and the Spirit's will is done on earth as in heaven, that will be the time of the manifestation of the kingdom. But we who are in the reality of the kingdom today must pray for these things.

d. Praying that God May Give Us
Our Daily Food

Verse 11 says, "Give us today our daily bread." This prayer is all-inclusive. The patterned prayer firstly cares for God's name, God's kingdom, and God's will; then secondly, for our need. This reveals that in this fighting prayer the Lord will still take care of our needs. According to verse 11 we are to ask "today" for our "daily bread." The King does not want His people to worry about tomorrow (v. 34); He only wants them to pray for their needs today. The term "daily bread" indicates living by faith. The kingdom people should not live on what they have stored; rather, by faith they should live on the Father's daily supply.

e. Praying that God May Forgive Us Our Sins

Verse 12 says, "And forgive us our debts, as we also forgive our debtors." Thirdly, the patterned prayer cares for the kingdom people's failures before God and their relationship with others. They should ask the Father to forgive their debts, their failures, and their trespasses, as they forgive their debtors to maintain peace. Verse 12 indicates that in this fighting prayer we must admit and confess that we have shortcomings, mistakes, and wrongdoings. We are in debt to others. Hence, we must ask the Father to forgive us as we forgive others for the Father's sake.

f. Praying that God May Keep Us from Trial
and Deliver Us from the Evil One

Verse 13 says, "And do not bring us into trial, but deliver us from the evil one." Fourthly, the patterned prayer cares for the kingdom people in dealing with the evil one. They should ask the Father not to bring them into trial, but to deliver them from the evil one, Satan, the Devil. Remember, the King was led into temptation. The word "trial" in verse 13 actually means temptation. Sometimes the Father brings us into a situation where we are tried and tempted. Thus, as we pray to the Father, we must recognize our weakness and say, "Father, I am very weak. Do not bring me into trial." This implies that you admit that you are weak. If you do not recognize your weakness, you will probably not pray in this manner. Rather, you may feel that you are strong. That will be the very time the Father will bring you into trial to show you that you are not strong at all. Thus, it is better for our prayer to indicate to the Father that we know our weakness. We should say, "Father, I fully realize that I am weak. Please do not bring me into trial. There is no need for You to do that, Father, for I recognize my weakness." Never say to yourself, "Whatever happens, I am confident I can stand." If that is your attitude, be prepared to be led into the wilderness to confront temptation. Instead of having such an attitude, pray that the Father would not bring you into trial, but that He would deliver you from the evil one.

g. Recognizing God's Kingdom, Power, and Glory

According to this pattern of prayer, the kingdom people must recognize God's kingdom, power, and glory. Verse 13 also says, "For Yours is the kingdom, and the power, and the glory forever. Amen." The kingdom is the realm for God to exercise His power that He may express His glory.

5. The Condition of Prayer — to Forgive Others Their Offenses

Verses 14 and 15 reveal that the condition of prayer is to forgive others their offenses. These verses say, "For if you forgive men their offenses, your heavenly Father will also forgive you; but if you do not forgive men their offenses, neither will your Father forgive your offenses." "For" indicates that the word in verses 14 and 15 is an explanation of why the kingdom people must forgive their debtors (v. 12). If they do not forgive man's offenses, neither will their heavenly Father forgive their offenses; hence, their prayer will be frustrated.

D. Regarding Fasting

In verses 16 through 18 the King speaks regarding fasting. Instead of appearing to men to fast, we should fast in secret. Verse 16 says, "And whenever you fast, do not be as the hypocrites of a sad countenance; for they disguise their faces so that they may appear to men to be fasting. Truly I say to you, They have their reward." To fast is not to refrain from eating; it is being unable to eat because of being desperately burdened to pray for certain things. It is also an expression of self-humbling in seeking mercy of God. To give alms is to give what we have the right to possess, whereas to fast is to give up what we have the right to enjoy.

Verses 17 and 18 say, "But you, when you fast, anoint your head and wash your face, so that you may not appear to men to be fasting, but to your Father Who is in secret; and your Father Who sees in secret shall repay you." This indicates that our fasting, like our giving of alms and praying, must be done in secret, not before men. The Father sees in secret, and He will repay us.

LIFE-STUDY OF MATTHEW

THE DECREE
OF THE KINGDOM'S CONSTITUTION

(10)

In this message we come to the fifth section of the King's decree, 6:19-34, which concerns the dealing of the kingdom people with riches.

VI. CONCERNING THE DEALING
OF THE KINGDOM PEOPLE WITH RICHES

A. Laying Up Treasures
Not on Earth but in Heaven

In verses 19 and 20 the King decrees that the kingdom people should not lay up for themselves treasures on earth, but treasures in heaven. To lay up treasures in heaven is to give material things to the poor (19:21) and to care for the needy saints (Acts 2:45; 4:34-35; 11:29; Rom. 15:26) and for the Lord's servants (Phil. 4:16-17).

1. The Heart Being Where the Treasure Is

Verse 21 says, "For where your treasure is, there will your heart be also." The kingdom people must send their treasure to heaven so that their heart can also be in heaven. Before they go there, their treasure and their heart must go there first.

2. The Eye Being Single
and the Whole Body Being Illuminated

Verse 22 says, "The lamp of the body is the eye. If therefore your eye is single, your whole body will be illuminated." Our eyes can focus on only one thing at a time. If we endeavor to see two things at once, our sight will be blurred. If we focus our eyes on one thing, our sight will be single, and our whole body will be illuminated. If we lay up our treasure both in heaven and on earth, our sight will be blurred. If we would have single sight, we must lay up our treasure in one place.

3. The Eye Being Evil and the Whole Body Being Dark

Verse 23 says, "But if your eye is evil, your whole body will be dark. If then the light that is in you is darkness, how great the darkness!" To see two objects at one time is to make our eye evil. Thus, our whole body will be dark. If our heart is fixed on treasure laid up on earth, the light that is in us will become darkness, and great will be the darkness.

B. Being Unable to Serve Two Masters

Verse 24 says, "No one can serve two masters, for either he will hate the one and love the other, or he will hold to one and despise the other. You cannot serve God and mammon." The word mammon is an Aramaic word signifying wealth, riches. Here mammon, standing in opposition to God, indicates that wealth or riches is the opponent of God, robbing God's people of their service to Him.

C. Not Being Anxious about Our Living

1. The Life Being More than Food and the Body More than Clothing

Verse 25 says, "Therefore I say to you, Do not be anxious about your life, what you should eat and what you should drink; nor for your body, what you should put on. Is not the life more than food, and the body than clothing?" In this verse the Lord tells us not to be anxious about our life. The Greek word translated "life" here is soul, in which is the desire, the appetite, for food and clothing (Isa. 29:8). Our life is more than food, and our body is more than clothing. Both our life and our body came into existence by God, not by our anxiety. Since God has created us with a life and a body, surely He will care for their needs. The kingdom people do not need to be anxious about these things.

2. Not Being Anxious about Eating, Drinking, and Clothing

Verse 31 says, "Therefore do not be anxious, saying, What shall we eat? or, What shall we drink? or, With what shall we be clothed?" Here we come to the crucial matter in verses 19 through 34. Apparently, in this section of the constitution, the Lord is speaking about the dealing of the kingdom people with material riches. Actually, He is dealing with the matter of anxiety. The Lord is wise. After touching our temper, lust, natural being, self, and flesh, He goes on to touch our anxiety. In these verses the word "anxious" is used six times (vv. 25, 27, 28, 31, 34). It may also seem that the Lord is touching our heart, for where our treasure is, there our heart is also. However, our heart is related not only to riches, but to many other things.

The constitution of the kingdom of the heavens is composed with the Father's life and nature. Although these chapters do not actually use the words "life" and "nature," from the context we can see that apart from the Father's divine life and nature, these chapters are in vain. No one would be able to fulfill the requirements of the kingdom of the heavens without having the Father's life and nature. Every constitution is based upon a certain kind of life. Suppose you intend to make a constitution for dogs. Undoubtedly such a constitution would be based upon the dog life. It would be unreasonable for this constitution to decree that, every morning, dogs should observe morning watch by flying in the air. Because dogs cannot fly, they could not fulfill such a requirement. But if the constitution told the dogs to keep morning watch by barking, there would be no problem. In like manner, the constitution given by the Lord Jesus on the mount was for the sons of God, and it was based upon the life and nature of the Father. Two verses in chapter five indicate this fact. Verse 9 says, "Blessed are the peacemakers, for they shall be called sons of God," and verse 48 says, "You, therefore, shall be perfect as your heavenly Father is perfect."

Many Christians do not understand this section of the Word because they have not seen that it is based upon the divine life and divine nature. Even many unbelievers have quoted verses from these chapters in their writings, thinking that these chapters are words spoken to all human beings. No, just as the dog life cannot fly, so the human life cannot fulfill the requirements of the constitution of the kingdom of the heavens. This is a constitution based upon the divine life and the divine nature.

There is no anxiety in the divine life and the divine nature. Anxiety is not of the divine life, but of the human life, just as barking is of the dog life, not of the bird life. Our human life is a life of anxiety, whereas God's life is a life of enjoyment, rest, comfort, and satisfaction. To God, anxiety is a strange term. With Him, there is no such thing as anxiety. Do you think that God has ever been anxious? Has He ever been afflicted with anxiety? Although God has many desires, He has no anxiety. Our human life, on the contrary, is virtually composed of anxiety; it is constituted with it. Take anxiety away from a human being and the result will be death. A dead man has no anxiety. A figure in a wax museum or a statue in front of a Catholic cathedral has no anxiety, but as long as you are a living person, you cannot escape from anxiety.

If we consider the style of the Lord's speaking in the New Testament, we shall see that it is absolutely different from the speaking of the Apostles. The Apostles, especially Paul, wrote many spiritual books. Although Paul spoke of many divine, spiritual, and heavenly things, his style is nonetheless human. It is the same with the writings of Peter and John. No matter how much the New Testament writers spoke of spiritual and divine things, their style remained human. But the style of the Lord's speaking in the New Testament is unique. It is utterly impossible to describe it. If you read Matthew 5, 6, 7, 13, 24, and 25 and John 14 through 17, you will see that the style of the Lord's speaking is extraordinary. It is not human or common; it is profound, yet brief, simple, and to the point. This is the divine speaking with the divine style. When I was young, I read a statement written by a certain great French philosopher who said that if the four Gospels were falsehoods, then the person who wrote them was qualified to be Christ. I agree with this word.

In His speaking in chapter six of Matthew, the Lord apparently is dealing with the matter of riches. In reality, however, He is touching the matter of anxiety, the basic problem of our human living. As we have seen, in 6:1-18 He apparently dealt with the righteous deeds of the kingdom people, but actually He was touching the self and the flesh. I came to know this not by reading books, but from my experience in the church life. Through my experience I have learned that making a display of righteous deeds is certainly of the self and of the flesh. If we remain on the cross, we would never make such a display. In the same principle, 6:19-34 seemingly touches our wealth, our riches; actually, the Lord's intention here is to touch anxiety, the source of the problem of our daily living. The whole world is involved with anxiety. Anxiety is the gear that makes the world move. It is the incentive for all human culture. If there were no anxiety regarding our living, no one would do anything. Rather, everyone would be idle. Thus, by touching our anxiety, the Lord touches the gear of human life.

When the young people hear this word, they may say, "Hallelujah! Because the Lord Jesus has touched anxiety, the gear of human life, we don't need to study or work hard. If we are hungry, we can simply eat some leftovers." This concept is wrong. In 6:26 the Lord Jesus says, "Look at the birds of the heaven, that they do not sow, nor reap, nor gather into barns, and your heavenly Father nourishes them." If the Lord Jesus were here, I would ask Him, "Lord, You liken us to birds. The birds neither sow nor harvest; they just fly in the air and do nothing. Lord, does this mean that we should not do anything? The birds feed on human labor. Lord Jesus, do You mean that we should take advantage of others? Should we forget about working and simply be birds in the air, enjoying life and taking advantage of the labor of others?" I would also ask the Lord, "Lord, You also liken us to lilies. Lilies don't do anything, but are clothed in more glory than Solomon (vv. 28-30). Are You saying that we should not do anything, that we should simply enjoy the air, the sunshine, the soil, and the water?" This is the concept held by many young people who quote these words of the Lord Jesus. They say, "Let's be birds in the air and lilies in the valley." There is a difficulty in understanding the Lord's word here. Again I say, if the Lord were here, I would ask Him, "Do You mean that we should just be like birds soaring in the air, taking advantage of the labor of others? They sow and grow the crops, and we simply come to enjoy them. Is this legal? Is it fair? It seems that all birds are thieves. I have only a small yard, but the birds come and take advantage of what I am growing in my yard. Are You saying that we should do the same thing?" I ask these questions because I know the psychology of the young people. After spending so many years in school, they may be tired of studying. As they go from junior high to high school, from high school to college, and from undergraduate school to graduate school, the work becomes more difficult. Instead of studying so hard, many of the young people would rather be like birds flying in the air. If the young people are honest, they will admit that they have such a concept.

Let us now consider the Lord's intention in verses 19 through 34. Does the Lord intend that the young people finish school, or drop out and be like birds in the air? It is wrong to have anxiety, for anxiety does not belong to the divine life. There is no anxiety in the life of God. However, the Lord does not mean that we should not do our duty. When the Lord brought the children of Israel into the good land, they all had to work on the land. That was their duty. Whether or not the good land produced a rich harvest depended on a number of things: the weather, the sunshine, the proper amount of rain, and the right temperature. None of these things was under the control of the children of Israel. Their responsibility was just to labor on the land. They labored not only for themselves, but also for the birds. If they did not do the work of farming, it would have been difficult for the birds to live. To do their duty was right and necessary, but to have anxiety was wrong. Likewise, we must do our duty today, but do it without being anxious about our living. The reason you are so reluctant to give to others is your anxiety. Because of anxiety, you love the material things. If you had no anxiety, you would not care for the material things. Rather, you would let others have them. It is anxiety that causes us trouble.

In God's economy we all must labor. We are not like the children of Israel, for we cannot literally work on the good land. Instead, the young people today must study and acquire a good education. Studying is equal to tilling the ground, and graduating from college is equal to reaping a harvest. Young people, studying is your duty, and you must do it. In ancient times, the children of Israel had to labor by tilling the ground, sowing the seed, watering, and harvesting. This was their duty. But whether or not they received the harvest depended upon God. Their responsibility was to labor without having any anxiety. If they were anxious, that would have been an offense to God. There was no need for them to be anxious. They simply had to do whatever God asked them to do. For example, according to Deuteronomy, God required them to set aside one tenth for Himself, another tenth for the Levites, and still another tenth for a different purpose. They were not permitted to keep all the produce for their enjoyment. They were not to have any anxiety. If they had no anxiety, they could be generous, willing to give to others and put their material things into the hand of the Lord.

We need to read 6:19-34 in such a light. Under God's sovereignty, the children of Israel had to labor on the land. Under God's sovereignty, the young people today must study and finish school. If we are to have the proper church life, all our young people must finish college. Failing to finish college is like sowing without having a harvest. The requirement for making a living today is much different from what it was hundreds of years ago. Today the young people must till the ground, sow the seed, and water the crop by studying diligently and graduating from high school and college. But they must not do this because of anxiety. We must differentiate anxiety from duty. Your duty is to finish your work of farming, that is, to graduate from high school and college. Otherwise, it will be difficult to live. To live on this earth for God, you must finish your education. But as you are studying and completing your education, you must be different from the worldly people. The worldly ones study for the sake of their anxiety; you should not study for anxiety, but to fulfill your duty. If you do not see this point, this portion of the Word will simply be a legal matter to you.

Boaz, a forefather of David, is an example of one who did his duty without anxiety. Boaz was a rich farmer; he was very productive. However, this man was not productive for the sake of anxiety, but for the sake of fulfilling his duty. When the time came, the Lord told him to give a certain amount away, and he did it. Certainly Boaz treasured the things in heaven. Through the overcoming of anxiety, he laid up treasures in heaven.

After a number of years, many of our young people will have college degrees. I believe that under the Lord's sovereign blessing, many riches will come in. At that time you will need to remember that you have gone to school not for anxiety, but to do your duty. Therefore, the riches that you bring in should not be used for your anxiety, but for your duty. Your duty is to give, to lay up treasures in heaven. Do not aspire to be a millionaire. Do not endeavor to have a savings account of a million dollars. Rather, learn to give and lay up treasures in heaven. Transfer your treasures from the earth to the heavens. In this way you will not be a millionaire on earth, but a millionaire in the heavens. Your duty is to earn your degree and then to make riches. But do not seek to become a millionaire. Instead, be a good giver according to the life and nature of your heavenly Father. This is the meaning of this portion of the Word.

My burden in this message is to dig out this basic point. We all have our duty to do. As we are fulfilling our duty, we should not do anything for the sake of our anxiety, because we have a divine life that knows no anxiety. And we have an almighty and all-inclusive heavenly Father who takes care of us in every way. Today's world is filled with anxiety, but the kingdom people should not be anxious about anything. We are not able to add one cubit to our stature by our anxiety (v. 27). Concerning morality, we have the life and nature of our Father within us to enable us to fulfill the highest moral requirements. Concerning our living, we have the heavenly Father Himself to take care of us. However, this does not mean that there is no need for us to do our duty. Although we must fulfill our duty, we should have no anxiety. Like the children of Israel who had enough to live on and who gave certain portions away for various purposes, we also should have a harvest and be willing to give a certain amount away for various purposes. Eventually, all we give will be laid up in the heavenly bank, and all our riches will be there.

This also is related to our daily growth in life. Both sloppiness and anxiety will delay your growth in life. No one who is idle, who does not fulfill his duty, will ever grow in life. Everyone who grows in life is diligent and industrious. Of course, this diligence and industriousness will yield a reward, and some material riches will come to you. All these riches must be used, not for your anxiety, but for your giving. Anxiety must go. Do not allow anxiety to occupy your daily living. Because the life of the Father within you knows no anxiety, you should not have any anxiety. Any surplus you have should not be used for the sake of your anxiety. Use it to build up savings in the heavenly bank. I assure you that if you do this, you will grow in life. The only kind of person who grows in life is one who is diligent, yet who does not use his surplus for his anxiety. You need to study diligently, make good grades, and acquire the highest degree. However, the riches that come to you should not be used for your anxiety. We labor and fulfill our duty, but we have no anxiety. This is the proper way to grow in the Father's life.

3. The Heavenly Father Knowing All These Needs

In verse 32 the Lord says, "For all these things the nations are seeking; for your heavenly Father knows that you need all these things." The kingdom people have the divine life of their heavenly Father as their strength to keep the new law of the kingdom. They also have their heavenly Father to care for their material needs, so that they need not be anxious about them. Their heavenly Father is the source of their strength and supply. Hence, they need not be weak or lacking in anything.

4. Seeking First the Father's Kingdom and His Righteousness

Verse 33 says, "But seek first His kingdom and His righteousness, and all these things shall be added to you." The Father's kingdom is the reality of the kingdom of the heavens today and the manifestation of the kingdom of the heavens in the coming age. The Father's righteousness is the righteousness by keeping the new law of the kingdom, as mentioned in 5:20 and 6:1. Since the kingdom people seek first the kingdom and righteousness of their heavenly Father, not only will His kingdom and His righteousness be given to them, but also all their necessities will be added.

5. Not Being Anxious for Tomorrow

Finally, verse 34 says, "Therefore do not be anxious for tomorrow, for tomorrow will be anxious for itself. Sufficient for the day is its own evil." The kingdom people should never live in tomorrow, but always in today. The word "evil" here denotes trouble and affliction. This indi-

cates that the King of the kingdom has made it clear to the
kingdom people that their days on earth for the kingdom
will be days of trouble and affliction, not of ease and comfort.

LIFE-STUDY OF MATTHEW

MESSAGE TWENTY-THREE

THE DECREE
OF THE KINGDOM'S CONSTITUTION

(11)

We come now to the sixth section of the new King's decree on the mountain, 7:1-12.

VII. CONCERNING THE PRINCIPLES
OF THE KINGDOM PEOPLE
IN DEALING WITH OTHERS

Apparently, the Lord's intention in 7:1-12 is to cover the principles according to which the kingdom people deal with others. Actually, His intention here is to encourage us to forget ourselves and to take care of others. In the two previous chapters, the Lord has dug out our temper, our lusts, our inner being, the self, the flesh, and our anxiety. Now He brings us to the point where we must learn to take care of others. When you judge others, you must judge them according to how you want them to judge you. To consider the matter in this way is to take care of others.

The heavenly ruling over the kingdom people requires that they take care of others. Although a number of negative points were touched in chapters five and six, the matter of taking care of others is not covered until chapter seven. In whatever we do, we must think about others. We have a real lack in this area, because in our natural life we do not consider others. From beginning to end, we only consider ourselves. Our thinking and our consideration are wrapped up with ourselves. Therefore, we are always centered around ourselves and never consider others. I would ask you to recall the way you lived in the past. Was it your practice to consider others? If we consider others when we are about to criticize or judge them, we shall neither criticize nor judge. The reason we judge others and criticize them is that we do not care for them. If we cared for others, we would sympathize with them.

A. Not Judging Lest You Be Judged with What You Judge

In 7:1 the Lord said, "Do not judge, lest you be judged." The kingdom people, living in a humble spirit under the heavenly ruling of the kingdom, always judge themselves, not others. The Lord's word about not judging lest we be judged does not seem to be a word about taking care of others. However, when we probe into this word, we see that it actually means to take care of others. When you are about to judge others, instead you must take care of them.

Let us seek to find out the secret of this word about not judging. How can we tell that the real meaning here is to take care of others? Are you afraid of being judged? If you are, then you should realize that others are also afraid of being judged. Do you feel bad about being judged by others? If you do, then you should know that others also feel bad about being judged by you. No one likes to be judged. If you do not like to be judged, then what about others? You need to take care of them. If you do not like to be judged by others, why do you judge other people? If you are afraid of being judged, then you must consider others, who also are afraid of being judged. Always take care of others.

Verse 2 says, "For with what judgment you judge, you shall be judged; and with what measure you mete, it shall be measured to you." Under the heavenly ruling of the kingdom, the kingdom people will be judged with what they judge. If they judge others with righteousness, they will be judged by the Lord with righteousness. If they judge others with mercy, they will be judged by the Lord with mercy. Mercy boasts against judgment (James 2:13, Gk.). Do not judge others so much, for you will be judged in the same degree that you judge others. If you take care of others, you will not be judged by them.

Verse 2 says that with what measure we mete, it shall be measured to us. The principle here is the same as with judgment. Apparently, in these verses the Lord does not charge us to take care of others; actually, however, these verses mean that we must take care of others. Are you afraid of being measured by others? If so, then you must take care of others, for they also are afraid of being measured by you. If you take care of others, you will not judge them, criticize them, or measure them.

In the past I knew a certain group of Christians who talked a great deal about spirituality. In a sense, their talk was genuine. However, this group had one weak point: it was the practice of measuring others. It seemed that everyone in this group had a little scale in his pocket. Whenever they invited you to tea, they measured you with their invisible scale. Later they would come together to talk about you. Some would ask, "Have you found out where he is?" This means, "Have you measured him?" I also learned that this group did not care at all for the feelings of others; they cared only for their practice of measuring others. Their measuring was actually their criticizing and their judging. I would take this opportunity to encourage you not to measure others. Do not try to determine how spiritual others are, how much growth they have, or what is their condition in life. If you refrain from measuring others, you will be kept from criticizing them and judging them. This is based on the principle of taking care of others.

Those in the group to which I just referred had a difficult time helping others. The reason they could not help others was that the others were under their measurement, judgment, and criticism. In helping others, we must be blind. If you want to help others in the church life, you need to be blind. If you would be a good husband or wife, be blind in taking care of your spouse. Do not measure, judge, or criticize. Do not have any measurement of others. This is a way of showing mercy toward them. If you show mercy toward others, you will receive mercy. But if you measure others without mercy, then you will also be measured without mercy. With what measurement you mete, it will be measured to you.

Mercy does not do any measuring. This means that mercy imposes no requirements. Anything that requires a measurement is not mercy. Mercy does not know mathematics; it does not know how to add or subtract. Mercy is absolutely blind. Why do you treat me so well when I am so pitiful? It is because you are merciful toward me.

Sometimes, by the Lord's mercy, I have been merciful toward others. Afterwards some of my children, whose eyes were so clear about the situation, said to me, "Daddy, don't you know how poor this person is? Why were you so good to him?" I was good to him because I was blind. My children, however, were very clear-sighted. But those who are so clear-sighted cannot be merciful. If you would be merciful, you must be like Isaac, who blessed Jacob in a blind way. Likewise, we, the kingdom people, must be blind in dealing with others. If so, we shall be merciful to them and always take care of them. Whenever my children asked me why I was kind to those who did not deserve kindness, I answered, "You don't know what I am doing. Your eyes are too big and clear. Why did I treat him that way? It was because I was considerate of him." This is the principle of the kingdom people in dealing with others. For us to deal with others, we must consider them, sympathize with them, and be merciful toward them. The kingdom people must take care of others in their dealings with them.

If you read these verses again and again, you will see that the basic principle hidden here is that we must forget ourselves and take care of others. Do you know why you criticize others and judge them? It is because you think of yourself too much. You neglect the feelings of others and do not care for them. You care only for your feeling. Hence, you judge and criticize others. Therefore, if we would be kept from judging others, we must take care of them. This requires that we forget ourselves and consider others. If we center around ourselves and ignore the feelings of others, we shall criticize them. But if we take care of others, we shall not judge them.

1. Considering the Log in Your Own Eye When You Look at the Splinter in Your Brother's Eye

In verse 3 the Lord says, "And why do you look at the splinter in your brother's eye, but do not consider the log in your own eye?" As the kingdom people, living in a humble spirit under the heavenly ruling of the kingdom, we must consider the log in our own eye whenever we look at the splinter in our brother's eye. The splinter in our brother's eye must remind us that we have a log in our own eye.

2. Removing the Log from Your Eye First

Verse 4 continues, "Or how can you say to your brother, Let me remove the splinter from your eye, and behold, the log is in your eye?" The Lord's word in verses 3 and 4 is very deep. His intention here is not to charge us to take care of ourselves; it is to charge us to take care of others.

Verse 5 says, "Hypocrite, first remove the log from your eye, and then you will see clearly to remove the splinter from your brother's eye." As long as the log remains in our eye, our sight is blurred, and we cannot see clearly. In pointing out a brother's fault, we must realize that we have a greater fault. Our brother's fault is likened to a splinter, and ours is likened to a log. Thus, once again, the Lord's intention is that we take care of others. Whenever you try to point out someone else's fault, you may care for the fault, but not for the person. When you make someone else's fault to be as large as a log, it shows you care only for his fault, not for him. If you care for the brother, you will not care only for his fault. Rather, you would say, "His fault is merely a splinter when compared to mine, which is a huge log. Therefore, I am happy to overlook his fault."

The Lord's intention in 7:1-12 is that we take care of

others. The principle for the kingdom people in dealing with others is that we must take care of others. We should observe this principle in all our dealings with people. Do not simply act according to your feeling, but take care of the other person. This is the basic principle.

B. Not Giving the Holy Things to the Dogs nor Casting Pearls before the Hogs

Verse 6 says, "Do not give that which is holy to the dogs, neither cast your pearls before the hogs, lest they trample them with their feet, and turn and tear you." "That which is holy" must refer to the objective truth that belongs to God, and "your pearls" must refer to the subjective experiences which are ours. Dogs do not have hoofs nor do they chew the cud, and hogs divide the hoofs, but do not chew the cud. Thus, both are unclean (Lev. 11:4, 7). According to what is revealed in 2 Peter 2:12, 19-22, and Philippians 3:2, the dogs and the hogs here refer to people who are religious, but not clean.

Matthew 7:6 is also related to the matter of taking care of others. Many times when you have seen a certain truth, doctrine, or light, you tell others about it with no regard to whether they are "dogs," "lambs," or "wolves." You care only for your feeling of excitement. You may say, "Oh, I have seen the light concerning the church life! The church is glorious and wonderful!" In your excitement, you may share this with the wrong person. This is giving what is holy to the dogs. When you are about to give something holy to others, you must consider those you are speaking to. You should not give the holy things to dogs, nor cast your pearls before hogs. When you talk to others about the holy things, or the truths, and the pearls, or the experiences, you must observe the basic principle of taking care of others. You must determine whether or not people can receive what you intend to share. You must also perceive how much they can receive. In other words, when you talk to others about spiritual things, do not speak according to your feelings or desires; rather, speak to them according to their capacity to receive what you have to say.

Many times the young people have gone out to tell others about the church or about certain spiritual things they have experienced. They cared only for their feeling, not for the feelings of the others. Unfortunately, a number of times the others were dogs or hogs, unable to receive anything that was said. Instead, they turned upon the ones sharing, trampled upon the pearls, and tried to bite the brothers. Thus, when we have seen the light concerning certain truths or have experienced certain precious things of the Lord and desire to share them with others, we must take care of those with whom we are sharing. We must ask ourselves, "Can these people receive my testimony? Can they take what I intend to share with them?" If you take care of others, you will not share everything with everybody, and there are some to whom you will not give your testimony. This is the principle of the kingdom people in dealing with others.

Often, we talk to others according to our feelings without taking care of their feelings. Perhaps on a certain day you may be very zealous regarding the church life and the Lord's recovery. But in your zeal you may offend some "dogs." At other times, because of some fresh experience of Christ, you may say, "Oh, Christ is wonderful! Christ is the brass, the iron, and the weapons to defeat the enemy." You are so excited about your experience that you tell everyone about it. But some may turn to attack you, saying, "What! We never heard that Christ is weapons. Where did you learn this? And how can you say that Christ is brass and iron? This is blasphemy!" However, if you take care of others, you may not say a word about your fresh experience of Christ. Rather, you will be wise in dealing with them, considering what the "dogs" can take or what the "hogs" can understand. But if you are excited and care only for yourself and not for others, you will get into trouble or even cause trouble. In the past some of our young people have gone to other meetings, and, caring only for their zeal, they spoke out unwisely. They were on fire, but because they did not care for others, they only caused trouble.

The kingdom people must be the wisest of people. Whenever we contact others, we should know what their temperature is, and we should care for their situation. We should do things in a proper way and not provoke the dogs to bite us or the hogs to attack us. They may turn and tear us.

C. Asking, Seeking, and Knocking

Verses 7 through 11 present a difficulty because it seems that these verses should not be here. For some years, I skipped over these verses, going from verse 6 to verse 12, because verse 12 matches verses 1 through 6. Verse 12 says, "All things therefore whatever you wish that men would do to you, so also you do to them; for this is the law and the prophets." This verse is the continuation and conclusion of the first six verses. However, between verse 6 and 12, we have verses 7 through 11 as an apparent insertion. What is the significance of this? As we have pointed out, 7:1-12 is concerned with the principles of the kingdom people in dealing with others. We have seen that the kingdom people must mainly observe the principle of taking care of others. In judging others or in speaking about holy things, we must take care of others. Let us now consider how verses 7 through 11 fit in with this matter.

Verses 7 and 8 say, "Ask and it shall be given to you; seek and you shall find; knock and it shall be opened to you. For every one who asks receives, and he who seeks finds, and to him who knocks it shall be opened." It takes experience to understand these verses. By reading these verses again and again in the light of our experience, we can realize that they mean that we must look to the heavenly Father as we are dealing with others. We must ask Him, seek Him, and knock for Him. Many times we have failed to do this. But these verses indicate that at the very time we are contacting people and dealing with them, we must look to the Lord and say, "Lord, tell me how to contact these people. Lord, show me how to deal with them." Sometimes simply asking will not be adequate. We must seek and even knock. This indicates that contacting people is a serious matter. Never think that it is an insignificant thing. We, the kingdom people, must approach it seriously, never doing it in a light or loose way or merely according to our feeling. Rather, we must do so by taking care of others. We must ask for a way, seek after a way, and even knock at the heavenly door for a way. Thus, we must ask, seek, and knock; then we shall have the proper way to contact people.

In Matthew, the proper way to contact people is according to the principle of the kingdom. In verse 11, after using the examples of a son asking for a loaf and a fish in verses 9 and 10, the Lord says, "If you then being evil know how to give good gifts to your children, how much more shall your Father Who is in the heavens give good things to those who ask Him?" Because Matthew is a book on the kingdom, no doubt the "good things" in verse 11 are the things of the kingdom. However, Luke 11:13, the sister verse of Matthew 7:11, says, "If you then, being evil, know how to give good gifts to your children, how much more shall the Father who is from heaven give the Holy Spirit to those who ask Him?" In Luke 11:13 the "good things" are changed to "the Holy Spirit." If we put these two verses together, we see that the best way for the kingdom people to contact others is according to the kingdom and according to the Holy Spirit. Both the kingdom and the Holy Spirit are the way to contact others. The wisdom we need in properly contacting others is of the kingdom and of the Spirit. As we deal with others, we must ask, seek, and knock. Eventually, we shall receive the guidance to deal with people according to the kingdom and according to the Spirit. Thus, the controlling principle for our contact with others is the kingdom and the Spirit. If our contact with others is based upon this principle, we shall not make mistakes.

If we consider the past, we shall have to admit that we

have made mistakes in contacting people. Some of those contacts were not profitable to anyone. But now we are being trained by the kingdom. We are not loose believers, but serious and strict kingdom people. Our contact with others is according to the principle of the kingdom and the principle of the Holy Spirit. We receive the guidance we need in contacting others by asking, seeking, and knocking. If we ask, we shall receive; if we seek, we shall find; and if we knock, the door will be opened.

According to our human thought, we first take the way and then arrive at the door. But the divine concept in the Bible is exactly the opposite. First we pass through the door, and then we walk along the way. The Lord said, "Knock and it shall be opened to you." This means that the door will be opened to us and then we shall be on the way. If we ask, seek, and knock, the door will be opened to us, and the way will be set before us. Then we shall know how to contact others. In order to contact people, we need an open door and a straight way as our guidance. We can have this open door and straight way only by asking, seeking, and knocking. How much we all need to find a proper and profitable way to contact others, whether unbelievers, saints, or the churches.

We all must learn to take care of others and to pray, "Lord, show me the way." First you need to ask. If the way does not open up, then you must seek. If the way still does not open up, then you must knock. To knock means to come close to the One whom you are seeking. When you ask, there may still be a distance, but when you knock, there is no distance. Rather, you are directly in front of the One you are seeking. Thus, you need to spend time to seek the Lord. In contacting others, we need the asking, the seeking, and the knocking. Then the door will be opened, a straight way will be given to contact people, our contact will be profitable, and we shall be saved from making mistakes. We shall also know to beware of the dogs and the hogs. This is the significance of the insertion of verses 7 through 11 between verses 6 and 12.

Before we consider verse 12, we need to add a further word about asking, seeking, and knocking. To ask is to pray in a common way, to seek is to supplicate in a specific way, and to knock is to reach the door in the closest way. The matter of asking and receiving in verse 8 is good for the kingdom people's prayer concerning their keeping of the new law of the kingdom. They ask for it and they will receive it. The matter of seeking and finding is good for 6:33. The kingdom people seek the Father's kingdom and His righteousness and will find them. The matter of knocking and having the door opened is good for 7:14. The narrow gate will open to the kingdom people by their knocking.

Verse 11 contains a great promise. This promise affirms that the kingdom people are under the care and supply of the Father who is in the heavens. Thus, they are well able to fulfill the new law of the kingdom and live in its reality that they may enter into its manifestation.

In verses 9 and 10, the loaf and fish which are requested indicate the need of the one asking. When we ask, seek, and knock, we always have a need. Our heavenly Father knows our need and will give us what we need. No human father would give his children a stone for a loaf or a serpent for a fish, but would always give them good gifts. How much more will our heavenly Father give us things which He considers good. Even in our seeking for a way to contact others, He will give us the best way, the way that we need.

D. Doing to People What You Wish Them to Do to You

Now we come to verse 12, the conclusion to the section on the principles of the kingdom people in dealing with others. This verse says, "All things therefore whatever you wish that men would do to you, so also you do to them; for this is the law and the prophets." The new law of the kingdom does not contradict the law and the prophets; rather, it fulfills them and even complements them.

LIFE-STUDY OF MATTHEW

MESSAGE TWENTY-FOUR

THE DECREE
OF THE KINGDOM'S CONSTITUTION

(12)

In this message we come to the last section of the King's decree, 7:13-29.

VIII. CONCERNING THE GROUND
OF THE KINGDOM PEOPLE'S LIVING AND WORK

Before we consider 7:13-29, let us review what has already been covered in this constitution. We must be deeply impressed with the fact that the constitution of the kingdom of the heavens is based upon the divine life and nature of the kingdom people. We need to keep in mind that the constitution of any people is always according to the life and nature of that people. No one can fulfill the requirements of this constitution unless he has been regenerated and possesses the life and nature of the heavenly Father. Those unbelieving philosophers and teachers who have quoted certain verses from Matthew 5 through 7 have not understood the words they were quoting. This constitution is not given to unbelievers. Because it is based upon the spiritual, heavenly, and divine life and nature of the kingdom people, only the kingdom people can live according to it. Moreover, not even the kingdom people can fulfill the requirements of this constitution if they do not live according to the divine nature and the divine life within them. This constitution is not given according to the natural life or to the human nature of the kingdom people. To repeat, it is formed according to the divine life and divine nature.

This constitution firstly reveals the nature of the kingdom people, as unfolded in the nine blessings in 5:3-12.
Those items of the constitution that describe what the
kingdom people should do and how they should act all correspond to the nature of the kingdom people. Whatever the
kingdom people do is an expression of their nature. Their
actions, behavior, speech, and outward deeds are the
expression of their divine life and nature. What is within
them is manifested in their outward behavior. The first
section of the constitution, the section concerning the
nature of the kingdom people, is therefore very basic. The
second section covers the influence of the kingdom people
upon the world, and the third deals with the law of the
kingdom of the heavens. As we have seen, all the complemented and changed laws expose our anger and lust.
Beginning in chapter six, the constitution of the heavenly
kingdom proceeds to deal with the way the kingdom people
perform their righteous deeds. This portion of the constitution digs out the self and the flesh. Following this, the
next section tells us that the kingdom people should live on
earth without any anxiety. We are not here for anxiety,
but for the fulfillment of our duty under the care of our
heavenly Father. He will feed us, clothe us, and supply all
our needs. Nevertheless, we must fulfill our responsibility
for the accomplishment of God's purpose, yet without anxiety. In 7:1-12 the constitution reveals the attitude we
should have toward others, how we should deal with them,
and how we should take care of them. By the time we reach
7:12, nearly every aspect of our living and behavior has
been covered. It seems that the constitution is now complete, perfect, and all-inclusive.

However, one thing remains to be covered: the fact that
the kingdom people are on earth doing the will of God our
Father. Hence, in the last section there is no dealing with
anger, lust, the natural being, the self, the flesh, anxiety, or
our attitude toward others. Instead, in this section we read
of entering the narrow gate and walking the constricted
way (7:13-14). We also see that we must build a house and

do the will of the heavenly Father (vv. 24-27, 21). Therefore, the conclusion of the constitution of the heavenly kingdom ushers us through the narrow gate and to the constricted way; thus we may do the will of the heavenly Father and we may build a house.

As we consider the constitution of the kingdom of the heavens as a whole, we see that it fully reveals what the kingdom people are, what they should be, and what they should do. It also reveals where they are and where they are going. It reveals that on the constricted way, we must do the will of the heavenly Father and we must build a house according to the word of the heavenly King. In the last section of the constitution there is no anger, lust, self, flesh, anxiety, nor any word about our attitude toward others. Instead, there are four crucial words: gate, way, will, and house. Here we have the narrow gate, the constricted way, the will of the heavenly Father, and the house built upon the rock, which is the wise word of the heavenly King. If we are not the people described in the nine blessings and if we are not those fulfilling the complemented and changed laws, we cannot enter through the narrow gate, walk on the constricted way, do the will of the heavenly Father, or build a house on the rock. Thus, this last section is the consummation of the constitution.

A. Entering the Narrow Gate and Taking the Constricted Way

Verses 13 and 14 say, "Enter in through the narrow gate; for the gate is wide and the way is broad that leads to destruction, and many are those who enter through it. For the gate is narrow and the way is constricted which leads to life, and few are those who find it." Who can enter through the narrow gate spoken of in verse 13? Only the kingdom people with the nature described in the nine blessings in chapter five. Those who enter the narrow gate must be poor in spirit, mourning, meek, hungry and thirsty for righteousness, merciful, pure in heart, making peace with all men, willing to be persecuted for the sake of righteousness, and willing to be reproached for Christ. Only those with such a nature can enter through the narrow gate. Furthermore, those who enter through this narrow gate must be under the higher laws of the kingdom, the complemented and changed laws, and they should not have any anxiety concerning their living. Rather, they must have the confidence that their heavenly Father is taking care of them. Moreover, they should not be lazy or idle, but diligent and industrious. These are the people who enter through the narrow gate and walk on the constricted way.

This way is constricted, limited, on every side. The gate is narrow and the way is constricted because the new law of the kingdom is stricter and the demand of the kingdom is higher than that of the old covenant. It deals not only with outward conduct, but also with inward motive. The old man, the self, the flesh, the human concept, and the world with its glory are all excluded. Only that which corresponds to God's will can enter in. The kingdom people need firstly to enter such a narrow gate and then to walk on such a constricted way. It is not walking the way first and then entering the gate. To enter the gate is simply to begin walking on the way, a way which is lifelong.

We all are happy to be in the Lord's recovery and appreciate the recovery very much. But let me ask you this question: As one in the Lord's recovery, are you walking on the constricted way? We all must be able to say that we are not taking the way of Christianity, but the way of constriction. We are constricted on every side. Those in Christianity can use rock music or other worldly methods in their services, but we cannot, because our way is constricted. All young people desire to be free, that is, to put off all restriction. When the young people graduate from high school, they are like caged birds wanting to be free. However, many are so free that they have no constriction, no restriction. We in the Lord's recovery, on the contrary, are taking a constricted way. We must even have some restriction in the practice of pray-reading. In our pray-reading we should not be like worldly people at a ball game who have no restrictions. We in the Lord's recovery must walk in our spirit. Living in spirit and walking in spirit restrict us. Even when we are loving, rejoicing, and happy, we must be under restriction. We must not be like those who throw off all restraint in their excitement. Rather, we must be excited within the limit of the spirit. This must even be true in the meetings. Although we may fully release our spirit, we should be restricted as far as physical activity is concerned. In everything, we need to take the constricted way, not the broad way.

We must take the constricted way in our fellowship with the brothers. Do you intend to praise a brother? You must praise him in a constricted way. Are you about to rebuke a brother? You must rebuke him in a constricted way. Are you having fellowship with some brothers? This is excellent, but you must fellowship with them in a constricted way. Sometimes when you are having fellowship, you forget all limitation. You go on hour after hour without taking care of the need for food or rest. Furthermore, in your fellowship you talk about everything from the archangel Michael, to Martin Luther, to all the brothers and sisters in the church. You fellowship about everyone without any restriction. Praise the Lord that we are truly free. Nevertheless, we still have the limitations, restrictions, and constrictions.

Consider the example of the Lord Jesus in John chapter seven. When His brothers proposed that He go into Judea and make Himself known to the public, the Lord said, "My time has not yet come, but your time is always ready" (John 7:6). The Lord's word indicates that He was limited, that He was walking a constricted way. As the kingdom people, we also must walk on a constricted way. Our way is full of limitations, restrictions, and constrictions. But do not consider any limitation a frustration. Rather, the limitations will speed us on our way. If we refuse to be constricted, our progress will be slowed down. However, if we are willing to be limited and constricted, our speed will increase. After having passed through all the preceding six sections of the constitution, in the last section we are ushered through the narrow gate, and we are on the constricted way.

1. The Wide Gate and the Broad Way Leading to Destruction and Many Entering It

In verse 13 the Lord said, "For the gate is wide and the way is broad that leads to destruction, and many are those who enter through it." Destruction here does not refer to the perdition of the person, but to the destruction of his deeds and works (1 Cor. 3:15). There is no doubt that today's Christianity leads people to destruction. Time will prove that this is true. By the Lord's mercy, I will never take the way of Christianity, because deep in me I have the conviction that it is a broad way leading to destruction. But the narrow gate and the constricted way lead to life. If you take the way of Christianity, the broad way, your spirit will become deadened immediately. Eventually, everything you do will be destroyed, for that broad way leads to destruction. This is not my opinion; it is the word of the Apostle Paul in 1 Corinthians 3.

In 1 Corinthians 3:10 Paul says that he has laid the foundation, which is Christ, and that others are building upon it. Paul then says, "Let each one take heed how he builds upon it," for we may build upon this foundation with gold, silver, precious stones, or with wood, hay, and stubble. In verses 13 through 15 Paul says, "The fire itself will test each one's work, of what sort it is. If anyone's work which he has built upon it shall remain, he shall receive a reward. If anyone's work shall be consumed, he shall suffer loss, but he shall be saved, yet so as through fire." In these verses Paul seems to be saying, "Take heed how you are building. If you build with gold, silver, and precious stones, you will be rewarded." This is the work on the constricted way which leads to a living reward in life. However, Paul also seems to be saying, "If your work is of wood, hay, and stubble, it will be burned by fire, and you will not receive a reward." In other words, such a work will result in destruction. You may claim to be a Christian worker, but what kind of material are you building with? From these verses in 1 Corinthians 3 we see that not only those who build theaters and gambling casinos will be led to destruction, but also those who build Christian cathedrals and chapels. The fire will try the nature of your work. If your work is of wood, hay, and stubble, it is certainly on the broad way leading to destruction.

Because we are not on the broad way, but on the constricted way, there are many things that we cannot do. I would rather have an ounce of gold than many pounds of wood. I do not want to have a huge pile of wood, hay, and stubble, for that will only result in a larger fire. I would rather have a small amount of gold, silver, and precious stones. Although we want to see the increase in all the churches, we do not want the increase on the broad way. Rather, we want the increase on the constricted way, the increase of gold, silver, and precious stones. If we have this kind of increase, the Lord will have a testimony on the constricted way.

2. The Narrow Gate and the Constricted Way Leading to Life and Few Finding It

Verse 14 says, "For the gate is narrow and the way is constricted which leads to life, and few are those who find it." Life here refers to the ever blessed condition of the kingdom, which is filled with the eternal life of God. This life is in the reality of the kingdom today and will be in the manifestation of the kingdom in the coming age (19:29; Luke 18:30). In the Lord's recovery today we are taking the constricted way which leads to life.

B. Discerning the False Prophets by Their Fruit

Verse 15 says, "Beware of false prophets, who come to you in sheep's clothing, but within are ravenous wolves."

As we are taking the constricted way, we must discern who the false prophets are. This means that on the constricted way we must be alert for any kind of falsehood. The Lord said regarding the false prophets, "By their fruits you shall know them" (v. 16). We know a prophet not by his talk, preaching, or work, but by his fruit. All Christians today are accustomed to being influenced by people's talk. An eloquent speaker with enticing words is able to seduce many. Do not listen to eloquent speech or to enticing words. Rather, wait and see what kind of fruit is produced. This is the way to discern whether a prophet is true or false.

The church is going on, and the Lord's testimony is spreading throughout the world. Because the doors are wide open, some self-appointed prophets may try to come in, claiming that they know certain things and can do certain works. Let them say whatever they will, for we shall look to the Lord to prove them by their fruit. We need to apply this principle to every such case. Do not listen to eloquent speech, but consider the fruit. Every good tree produces goodly fruit, but the corrupt tree produces evil fruit. Every tree that does not produce goodly fruit will be cut down and cast into the fire (7:17-19).

C. The Condition of Entering into the Kingdom of the Heavens

1. Not Merely Calling on the Lord, but Doing the Will of the Heavenly Father

Verse 21 says, "Not every one who says to Me, Lord, Lord, shall enter into the kingdom of the heavens, but he who does the will of My Father Who is in the heavens." This does not refer to the reality of the kingdom of the heavens today, but to the coming manifestation of the kingdom in the future. To enter into the kingdom of the heavens we need to do two things: call on the Lord and do the will of the heavenly Father. To call on the Lord suffices for us to be saved (Rom. 10:13), but to enter into the kingdom of the heavens we also need to do the will of the heavenly Father. Hence, "Not everyone who says . . . Lord, Lord, shall enter into the kingdom of the heavens," but those who call on the Lord and do the will of the heavenly Father.

Since entering into the kingdom of the heavens also requires doing the will of the heavenly Father, it is clearly different from entering into the kingdom of God by being regenerated (John 3:3, 5). This latter is by the birth of the divine life; the former is by the living of that life.

In verse 21 the Lord does not say "your Father," but "My Father." Here the Lord seems to be saying, "I, the Son of Man and the Son of God, have been doing the will of My Father. You also are sons of God and My brothers. Therefore, you must be My companions and take the same way that I take. Now you are not to do the will of your Father, but the will of My Father. You are My brothers, My companions, and My partners. You and I are walking the same way and doing the same will. You are living with Me according to the will of My Father." In this last section of the constitution, it is no longer a negative matter of dealing with our temper, lust, self, flesh, and anxiety. It is absolutely a positive matter of doing the will of the Father who is in heaven. The kingdom people are not for anything other than doing the will of the Father. We are not here merely to overcome our temper, our lusts, our self, and our flesh, and to be kind and sympathetic to others. We are here for the accomplishment of the will of the heavenly Father. In order to do the will of the Father, we need to walk in the constricted way. In the teachings of the worldly philosophers, there is neither the divine life and divine nature nor the divine way. But here the ultimate issue of the constitution of the kingdom of the heavens is the will of the heavenly Father. This means that we have a heavenly Father and that we are the Father's sons. However, in the last section of the constitution it is not only a matter of life, but also a matter of the will of the Father. Our Father has a will to accomplish, but we can accomplish it only by His life. We need to live in the life of the heavenly Father and also by that life. This kind of living is for the doing of the Father's will.

In the constitution of the kingdom of the heavens we cannot see what the will of the Father actually is. However, it is clearly revealed in chapter sixteen. The Father's will is to build the church upon the Son as the rock. This is fully developed in the Acts, the Epistles, and the book of Revelation. The New Testament reveals that God's divine, eternal will is to build up the church.

2. Many Prophesying, Casting Out Demons, and Doing Many Works of Power in the Lord's Name, but Not According to the Heavenly Father's Will

Verse 22 says, "Many will say to Me in that day, Lord, Lord, did we not prophesy in Your name, and in Your name cast out demons, and in Your name do many works of power?" The words "that day" refer to the day of the judgment seat of Christ (1 Cor. 3:13, 4:5; 2 Cor. 5:10). On the day of judgment, when all the believers will stand before the judgment seat of Christ, many will say to the Lord that they prophesied, cast out demons, and did works of power in His name, but they will be rejected by the Lord.

3. The Lord Not Approving Them, but Considering Them as Workers of Lawlessness

Verse 23 says, "And then I will declare to them, I never knew you; depart from Me, workers of lawlessness." Here the word "knew" means "approved." The same Greek word in Romans 7:15 is translated "allowed" by the King James Version. In this verse Paul says, "For that which I do, I allow not." The Lord never approved those who prophesied, cast out demons, and did many works of power in His name, but not according to the will of the heavenly Father (v. 21). The Lord did not deny that they did those things, but He considered those things as lawlessness because they were not done according to the will of the heavenly Father. They were not done in the line of the divine will. The Lord seemed to be saying, "You prophesied in My name, you cast out demons in My name, and you did many works of power in My name, but I never allowed you to do them. I never approved you because you did all those things in a lawless way. You did them in yourself, in your own desire, and according to your own intention, not according to the will of My Father." Thus, those who do such things, even in the Lord's name, will not enter into the kingdom of the heavens, but will depart from the Lord; that is, they will be rejected from the manifestation of the kingdom in the coming age.

We see from the Lord's word here that certain works may be done in the Lord's name, and yet not be done according to the will of God. Are you doing this kind of work, or are you doing God's will? We have talked a great deal about going to the campuses, but are we going there to do a certain work, or to do the will of our heavenly Father? Young brothers and sisters, how would you answer this question? Are you going to the campuses to do the will of the heavenly Father? We must have the assurance in whatever we do, that we are doing the will of the heavenly Father. Otherwise, the Lord Jesus will say to us, "Workers of lawlessness." Even prophesying in the Lord's name, but not according to the will of the Father, is a type of lawlessness. Moreover, casting out demons in the Lord's name and doing works of power in the name of the Lord, but not according to the will of God, are also considered in the eyes of the heavenly King as lawlessness.

The runners in any race must run in the proper lanes. Although you may run faster than others, your running will not be recognized if you run outside the lines of your lane. Rather, that type of running will be considered lawlessness. You must run the race between the lines, that is, you must run in a constricted way. Today the work of many Christian workers is not restricted by the heavenly lines. In their own eyes, they have done a great deal in the Lord's

name and for the Lord. In the eyes of the Lord, however,
their work is a kind of transgression, a violation of the
heavenly lines. Hence, their work is lawlessness. The
Lord's word in 7:21-23 is a strong word of warning to us all
that we should not care only for prophesying, for casting
out demons, or for works of power. We must take care of
the heavenly lines. If you transgress the lines as a runner in
the heavenly race, you will be disqualified. There are constricting lines in the Lord's recovery, and we must be constricted in our running. If we run between the lines, not
outside of them, we shall be approved by the Lord.

Again I say that the consummation of the constitution
of the kingdom of the heavens is to usher us through the
narrow gate and into the constricted way. Now we are
running on this constricted way. We should not care for
prophesying, for casting out demons, or for works of power.
Instead, we should care only for doing the will of our
heavenly Father. You may wonder how we can know the
Father's will. We can know it by the Father's life and
nature within us. The Father's nature will always tell us
"yes" or "no." If you are running according to the divine
nature and within the constricted lines, the divine nature
will indicate, "Yes, you are right; go on." But if you are not
running according to the divine nature or if you step outside the lines, the divine nature will say, "Don't go this
way." There is no need for anyone to tell you what to do,
for the regulating, constricting, divine nature is within you.
This nature tells you where you are. Because a runner in a
race can see the lines, he needs no one to tell him whether
or not he is inside the boundaries. Likewise, we have the
constricting lines within us, the lines of the divine life and
the divine nature, and we can tell where we are. According
to the divine nature within us, we cannot use rock music in
our meetings. Although you may try various worldly
methods, the divine nature would disagree with them all
and indicate that you are transgressing the lines. All those
who are the kingdom people, all those who have been
regenerated by the Father, have His life and nature within

them. The Father's life and nature indicate whether or not we are in the constricted way. Let us all run the race according to the Father's nature.

D. Two Kinds of Building
upon Two Kinds of Foundation

1. The Building on the Rock
According to the Lord's Words

In verse 24 the King said, "Every one therefore who hears these words of Mine and does them shall be likened to a prudent man, who built his house on the rock." The rock here does not refer to Christ, but to His wise word, the word that reveals the will of His Father who is in the heavens. The kingdom people's living and work must be founded on the word of the new King for the accomplishment of the will of the heavenly Father. This is to enter the narrow gate and walk the constricted way which leads to life.

Verse 25 says, "And the rain descended, and the rivers came, and the winds blew and fell on that house; and it did not fall, for it had been founded on the rock." The rain is of God, descending from the heavens; the rivers are of man, coming from the earth; and the winds are of Satan, blowing from the air. All these will test the living and work of the kingdom people. Although the rain may descend, the rivers may come, and the winds may blow, the house built upon the rock will not fall because it is built according to the constricted way, the way of doing the will of the Father. The house built on the rock which does not fall is like the building work of gold, silver, and precious stones, which can stand the testing fire (1 Cor. 3:12-13).

2. The Building on the Sand
Not According to the Lord's Words

Verse 26 says, "And every one who hears these words of Mine and does not do them shall be likened to a foolish man, who built his house on the sand." Sand here refers to human concepts and natural ways. If we live and work according to our human concepts and natural ways, our living and work will be founded on sinking sand. This is to enter the wide gate and walk on the broad way that leads to destruction. Verse 27 says, "And the rain descended, and the rivers came, and the winds blew and beat against that house; and it fell, and the fall of it was great." The house built on the sand which falls is like the building work of wood, hay, and stubble, which will be burned by the testing fire. However, the builder himself will be saved (1 Cor. 3:12-15). To build our house upon our opinion and concept is to build the house upon sinking sand. When the rain, the rivers, and the winds test the house built upon the sand, the house, not having a solid foundation, will fall. This is the Lord's conclusion of the constitution of the kingdom of the heavens.

The basic concept of the constitution of the kingdom of the heavens is that the kingdom people should be righteously strict with themselves, mercifully kind toward others, and secretly pure toward God.

I cannot tell you how much this constitution has controlled me throughout the years. I can testify that my living, my walk, and my work are under this constitution. I hope that all of us will be ushered into this constricted way to build a house upon the solid rock according to the will of our heavenly Father.

IX. AUTHORITY IN SPEAKING

Verses 28 and 29 say, "And it came to pass, when Jesus finished these words, the crowds were astounded at His teaching, for He was teaching them as One having authority, and not as their scribes." Christ, as the new King of the kingdom of the heavens, spoke with authority in decreeing the new law of the kingdom.

LIFE-STUDY OF MATTHEW

THE CONTINUATION OF THE KING'S MINISTRY

(1)

In the constitution of the kingdom of the heavens there are four verses that tell us how we can enter into the kingdom of the heavens. The first is Matthew 5:3, which says, "Blessed are the poor in spirit, for theirs is the kingdom of the heavens." The second says, "Blessed are those who have been persecuted for the sake of righteousness, for theirs is the kingdom of the heavens" (5:10). Both of these verses refer to the present. If we would be in the reality of the kingdom today, we need to be poor in our spirit and to be persecuted for the sake of righteousness. The reality of the kingdom today depends mainly upon righteousness. We are ushered into the reality of the kingdom by being poor in spirit. After we have had a change in our mind, we turn to the Lord and become empty in our spirit. In this way the Lord enters our spirit with His heavenly kingdom. From that moment, we begin to live in the reality of the kingdom. By being righteous, we are kept in this reality. However, if we are unrighteous, we are outside the reality of the kingdom. As long as we maintain righteousness, we are preserved in the reality of the kingdom. Examine your daily life. If you are loose, too free, and careless about righteousness, you are immediately separated from the reality of the kingdom. If we would be in the reality of the kingdom today, we must be poor in our spirit, and we must keep ourselves in righteousness, willing even to suffer for the sake of righteousness.

The other two verses that tell us how to enter the kingdom both refer to entering into the manifestation of the kingdom of the heavens in the future. Matthew 5:20 says,

"For I say to you, that unless your righteousness surpass that of the scribes and Pharisees, you shall by no means enter into the kingdom of the heavens." This refers to participating in the manifestation of the kingdom. If we would enter into the manifestation of the kingdom of the heavens, we need the surpassing righteousness. Hence, righteousness not only keeps us in the reality of the kingdom, but also brings us into the manifestation of the kingdom.

The last verse is 7:21, which says, "Not every one who says to Me, Lord, Lord, shall enter into the kingdom of the heavens, but he who does the will of My Father Who is in the heavens." This verse reveals that in order to enter into the kingdom of the heavens, we must do the will of the Father. Therefore, it is righteousness and the doing of the Father's will that will usher us into the manifestation of the kingdom. Righteousness refers mainly to our living, and doing the will of the Father refers mainly to our work. Both our living and our work must be according to the constitution of the kingdom of the heavens. If our living is according to this constitution, it will be righteous. And if our work is according to the constitution, it will be the doing of the will of God. This kind of living and work qualifies us to enter into the manifestation of the kingdom. Therefore, by being poor in our spirit, we are ushered into the reality of the kingdom, and through righteousness we are kept in this reality. By the surpassing righteousness and the doing the will of the Father, we shall enter into the manifestation of the kingdom of the heavens.

After delivering the constitution of the kingdom of the heavens on the mountain, the Lord Jesus came down from the mountain to continue His ministry. In this message we shall consider the continuation of the King's ministry (8:1—9:34).

I. SIGNS WITH DISPENSATIONAL SIGNIFICANCE

After the new King came down from the mountain to carry on His kingly ministry, the first thing He did was to cleanse the unclean, heal the sick, and cast the demons out of the possessed that they might all become people of the kingdom of the heavens (8:2-17).

The miracles, or signs, recorded in verses 2 through 17 have a dispensational significance. The order of the four instances recorded in Matthew 8:2-16 differs from that in Mark 1:29—2:1 and Luke 4:38-41; 5:12-14; and 7:1-10. The order of Mark's record, showing that Jesus is the Servant of God, is according to history. The order of Matthew's record, proving that Christ is the King of the kingdom of the heavens, is according to doctrine. In his Gospel, Matthew put certain instances together to present a doctrine. The order of Luke's record, revealing that Jesus is the proper man to be man's Savior, is according to morality. The order of John's record, testifying that Christ is the Son of God and even God Himself, is also somewhat according to history. Therefore, in the four Gospels there are three kinds of sequences: historical, doctrinal, and moral. In Matthew 8:1-17 three miracles — the cleansing of the leper, the healing of the paralyzed Gentile servant boy, and the healing of Peter's mother-in-law — and the healing of many are grouped together to present a meaningful doctrine, that is, they have a dispensational significance. Let us first consider the healing of the leper (vv. 1-4).

A. Healing of the Leper
1. The King Coming Down from the Mountain

Verse 1 says, "Now when He had come down from the mountain, great crowds followed Him." The coming down of the King from the mountain signifies that the heavenly King has come down from the heavens to the earth. He comes firstly to reach the Jews, for undoubtedly the leper here represents the Jewish people. The heavenly King came down from the heavens to bring salvation firstly to the leprous Jews. According to Romans chapter one, salvation is for the Jews first and then for the Gentiles (v. 16).

2. A Leper Approaching Him for Cleansing and Worshipping Him

Verse 2 says, "And behold, a leper approached and worshipped Him, saying, Lord, if You are willing, You can cleanse me." The leper worshipped the new King and called Him Lord, recognizing that He is the Lord God. In reality the new King is Jehovah God (1:21, 23).

The diseases healed in the cases recorded in Matthew 8 are significant, for every disease signifies a specific spiritual sickness. The first class of people saved by the kingly Savior to be the people of the kingdom is represented by a leper. According to the scriptural examples, leprosy comes from rebellion and disobedience. Miriam became leprous because of her rebellion against Moses, God's deputy authority (Num. 12:1-10). Naaman's leprosy was cleansed because of his obedience (2 Kings 5:1, 9-14). All fallen human beings became leprous in the eyes of God because of their rebellion. Leprosy is the expression of rebellion. Rebellion is inward, and leprosy is the outward manifestation. Now the kingly Savior comes to save men from their rebellion and cleanse them from their leprosy that they may become His kingdom people.

Leprosy is a filthy disease. In the Old Testament a leper had to be excluded from the camp of the children of Israel until he was cleansed. This indicates that anyone among the people of God who is rebellious and thereby becomes leprous will be cut off from the fellowship of God's people until he is healed. The leper here represents the Jews. The Jews have become rebellious against God. Thus, in God's eyes they are lepers. Nevertheless, the heavenly King came first to them, not to judge them, but to heal them. As the Lord indicated in 9:12, He came as a Physician to heal the sick. He came first to reach the Jews to heal them and to bring them salvation.

3. The King Stretching Out His Hand and Touching Him to Cleanse Him

Verse 3 says, "And stretching out His hand, He touched him, saying, I am willing; be cleansed. And immediately his leprosy was cleansed." According to the law, a leper should be excluded from the people because of his uncleanness. No one could touch him (Lev. 13:45-46). But the new King, as a man and as the kingly Savior, touched him.

What mercy and sympathy! By His one touch, immediately his leprosy was cleansed. What wonderful cleansing!

4. The Cleansed Leper Being Charged by the King to Offer the Gift for a Testimony

Verse 4 says, "And Jesus says to him, See that you tell no one, but go, show yourself to the priest, and offer the gift which Moses prescribed for a testimony to them." The new King told the cleansed leper still to do things according to the regulations of the old law for his cleansing, because the transitory period still remained, when the old law was not yet fulfilled by His redeeming death.

B. Healing of the Centurion's Servant Boy

1. A Centurion Approaching and Beseeching Him for the Healing of His Servant Boy

After the Lord had entered into Capernaum, "A centurion approached Him, beseeching Him and saying, Lord, My servant boy is lying in the house paralyzed, terribly tormented" (vv. 5-6). A centurion was an officer over one hundred soldiers in the Roman army. The leper in verses 2 through 4 represents the Jews, whereas the centurion in verses 5 through 13 represents the Gentiles. Before God, the Jews became leprous, unclean, because of their rebellion and disobedience; whereas the Gentiles became paralyzed, dead in function, because of their sinfulness. The kingly Savior came firstly to the Jews and then to the Gentiles (Acts 3:26; 13:46; Rom. 1:16; 11:11). The believing Jews are saved by His direct touch (v. 3), whereas the believing Gentiles are saved through faith in His word (vv. 8, 10, 13).

2. The Centurion, Knowing Authority, Asking Only for a Word

When the Lord told the centurion that He would come and heal his servant, "The centurion answered and said, Lord, I am not fit that You should enter under my roof; but

only speak a word, and my servant boy shall be healed."
The Gentile centurion recognized the authority of the
kingly Savior and realized healing authority was in His
word. Thus he believed not only in the kingly Savior, but
also in His word, asking Him not to go personally but only
to send His word. This is stronger faith, and it was
marveled at by the Savior (v. 10).

3. The King Marveling
at the Gentile Centurion's Faith
and Indicating
that Many Gentiles Will Participate
in the Enjoyment of the Kingdom

Verse 10 reveals that the Lord Jesus marveled at the
centurion's faith and said, "Truly I say to you, With no one
in Israel have I found so much faith." Therefore, in verses
11 and 12 the Lord said that many would come from the
east and west to recline with Abraham and Isaac and Jacob
in the kingdom of the heavens, but that the sons of the
kingdom would be cast into outer darkness. This indicates
that the Gentiles will participate in the gospel of the kingdom (Eph. 3:6, 8; Gal. 2:8-9; Rom. 1:13-16). The reference
to the kingdom of the heavens in verse 11 refers to the
manifestation of the kingdom of the heavens. It will be in
the manifestation of the kingdom that the overcoming
Gentile believers will feast with Abraham, Isaac, and
Jacob.

The sons of the kingdom in verse 12 refer to the saved
Jews who are the good seed (13:38), but who do not have
strong faith enabling them to enter the narrow gate and
walk the constricted way (7:13-14). They will miss the feast
in the manifestation of the kingdom (Luke 13:24-30). The
outer darkness will be the darkness outside the bright glory
in the manifestation of the kingdom of the heavens (25:30;
16:28). To be cast out into the outer darkness in the coming
kingdom age differs from being cast into the lake of fire
after the millennium and for eternity (Rev. 20:15).

4. The Centurion's Servant Boy Being Healed According to the Centurion's Faith

Verse 13 says, "And Jesus said to the centurion, Go; as you have believed let it be done to you. And the servant boy was healed in that hour." The Jewish leper was healed by the King's direct touch. The King stretched out His hand and touched him, and the leper was healed. But the centurion's servant was not healed by the King's direct touch. Rather, he was healed by the King's word. The Gentile centurion believed in this word, and his servant was healed. The Jews are always saved through the King's direct touch, but we Gentiles are saved, not by His direct touch, but by the sending out of His saving word. We believe in this word and we are healed. None of us Gentiles has had a direct touch from the Lord. We have been saved through believing the enlivening, regenerating word of the gospel. Hence, the centurion's servant represents all the Gentile believers. The Lord did not commend the faith of the leper, because faith was not the outstanding characteristic there. The significant thing was the King's touch. But with the healing of the centurion's servant, faith is very outstanding. Hence, the Lord praised the centurion's faith. Consequently, the servant boy was healed.

The boy had been paralyzed. To be paralyzed means that the body is out of function. Before we Gentiles were saved, we were totally out of function. The Jews were leprous, but we were paralyzed, out of function, because of our sinfulness. We need the heavenly King's healing salvation. He has sent us a word, and we have believed it. Therefore, we have been healed, our function has been recovered, and now we may begin to serve our Master. We are just like the servant boy who was healed and was able to serve again.

C. Healing of Peter's Mother-in-law

Verses 14 and 15 say, "And when Jesus had come into Peter's house, He saw his mother-in-law laid aside and in a fever; and He touched her hand, and the fever left her; and she arose and ministered to Him." Peter's mother-in-law represents the Jews at the end of this age who will be saved by receiving the kingly Savior. At that time, during the great tribulation, in the eyes of God the Jews will be in a fever (v. 14), hot in things other than God. The kingly Savior, after the fullness of the salvation of the Gentiles, will come back to this remnant of Jews that they might be saved (Rom. 11:25-26; Zech. 12:10). Peter's mother-in-law was healed in Peter's house, which represents the house of Israel. At the end of this age all the remnant of the Jews will be saved in the house of Israel. They will also be saved by the kingly Savior's direct touch (v. 15), as the Jewish leper was (v. 3).

At the end of this age salvation will come back from the Gentiles to the Jews. However, it will not come back to the scattered Jews, but to the Jews in the house of Israel. At that time the Jews will be sick of a fever. This is even true of the Jews today. So many of them are fervent in science, in finance, in education, and in all manner of worldly pursuits. But in the eyes of God all this is a fever. The temperature of the Jews today is very high in their fervency for politics, industry, agriculture, and warfare. They are represented by the feverish mother-in-law of Peter. But in their heat and fervency they neither trust in God nor care for morality. Just as the Lord healed Peter's mother-in-law, so will He come back again at the end of this age to heal the Jews who will be fervent, burning, and sick of a fever. He will not heal them through their faith, but through His direct touch. At the Lord's second coming, the Jews will be directly touched by His arrival and be saved.

Immediately after Peter's mother-in-law was healed, she arose and ministered to the Lord (v. 15). This signifies that at the Lord's coming back, the remnant of the Jews, after being saved, will arise and minister to Him in the millennium.

D. Healing of Many — Restoration to All on Earth in the Millennium

1. Evening Having Come

Verse 16 says, "And when evening had come, they

brought to Him many who were demon-possessed, and He cast out the spirits with a word and healed all those who were ill." The words "many" and "all those" represent all the people on earth in the millennium. The millennium will be the last dispensation of the old heaven and old earth; thus it is considered the evening of the old heaven and old earth. After this "evening," there will be a new day, that is, the new heaven and new earth with the New Jerusalem.

2. Many Demon-Possessed and All the Sick Being Healed — a Foretaste of the Power of the Coming Age

In the millennium, there will be to the uttermost the power to cast out demons and heal illnesses. Hence, all the demon-possessed and all the sick will be healed. The prophecies of Isaiah testify of this (Isa. 35:5-6). That will be a real restoration. The casting out of demons and the healing of the sick in this age are just a foretaste of the extensive power of the coming age. In verse 16, after the Lord had healed Peter's mother-in-law, when evening had come, He healed many who were demon-possessed and all who were ill. This indicates that after Christ comes back and the Jews are saved, the millennium will begin. During that period of time, all sicknesses will be healed. Hence, the signs recorded in verses 2 through 17 have a dispensational significance.

3. The Fulfillment of the Word of the Prophet

Verse 17 says, "In order that what was spoken through Isaiah the prophet might be fulfilled, saying, He Himself took our infirmities and bore our diseases." All healings accomplished on fallen people are due to the Lord's redemption. He took our infirmities and bore our diseases on His cross and accomplished full healing for us there. However, the application of healing by divine power can only be a foretaste in this age; the full taste will be accomplished in the coming age.

II. THE WAY TO FOLLOW THE KING

A. The King Giving Orders to Depart from the Great Crowds

Verse 18 says, "Now when Jesus saw great crowds around Him, He gave orders to depart to the other side." In His ministry, as recorded in the four Gospels, the Lord always withdrew from the crowds. He did not want the curious ones to be with Him. He did not care for great crowds, but only for the sincere seekers after Himself.

B. A Scribe Coming to Follow the King

In verses 18 through 22 we see the way to follow the heavenly King. The way is revealed through the cases of two who came to the King. The first, a scribe, said to Him, "Teacher, I will follow You wherever You go." In saying this, he did not consider the cost. Hence, the King answered in verse 20 in a way to cause him to consider the cost.

C. The King Unveiling to the Scribe that He Has Nowhere to Rest

In verse 20 the Lord said to the scribe who wanted to follow Him, "The foxes have holes, and the birds of the heaven have roosts, but the Son of Man has nowhere that He may lay His head." Here the Lord referred to Himself as the Son of Man. The new King in His kingly ministry continually took the standing of the Son of Man until 16:13-17. The King of the kingdom did not even have a resting place, as the foxes and birds do. This proves that the kingdom which He was establishing was not material in the earthly nature, but spiritual in the heavenly nature. The Lord seemed to be saying to the scribe, "Do you intend to follow Me? You have underestimated the price. You, a scribe, a learned one with a high rank in society, must realize that I am nothing and that I have nothing. I have even less than the birds and the foxes, for I have nowhere to lay My head." I believe that the scribe was disappointed and that he did not follow Him. The principle of following the Lord is the same today. We must consider the price. In following this King, there is no material enjoyment.

D. Another Disciple Asking Permission to Bury His Father First

Verse 21 says, "And another of the disciples said to Him, Lord, permit me first to go away and bury my father." In saying this, this disciple, who was not a scribe, overly considered the cost of following the King of the heavenly kingdom. This disciple, apparently warned by the first case, overestimated the cost. He seemed to be saying to the Lord, "I will follow You, but I have a dead father. Let me first go back to bury him, and then I will come back to follow You."

E. The King Telling the Disciple to Follow Him and Leave the Dead to the Dead

Because this disciple overestimated the cost of following the King, He answered him in the way of encouraging him to follow Him and drop his consideration of the cost, leaving the burial of his father to others. The Lord said, "Follow Me and leave the dead to bury their own dead." How wonderful the Lord Jesus is! He purposely disappointed the first and deliberately encouraged the second. The Lord was very wise in dealing with people. If I had been the Lord Jesus, I would have been excited to hear that a scribe wanted to follow me, and I would have encouraged him to do so. The Lord, however, was cool toward him and did not encourage him at all. Rather, He seemed to say, "Will you follow Me? You have a nice bed, a comfortable place to lay your head. But if you come to follow Me, you will not have a place to lay your head. I have even less than the birds and the foxes do." Thus, He discouraged this person of high rank. But to the disciple who had been warned by this case not to follow the Lord in a light or loose way, the Lord gave a word of encouragement. The Lord's word encouraged him to forget about all the preparations he was making, to leave the dead to bury the dead, and to follow Him.

By these two cases we see that it is not easy to contact people. How would you deal with these two if they came to you today? Probably you would accept both of them. However, the Lord differentiated between them, discouraging the one and encouraging the other.

In these two cases we see the way to follow the heavenly King. First, as we follow Him, we should not expect to have any material enjoyment. Second, in order to follow Him, we must ignore the requirements of the dead. The Lord told the disciple to "leave the dead to bury their own dead." The first dead refers to the people who are spiritually dead, as mentioned in Ephesians 2:1, 5; the second refers to the physically dead father of the disciple. Eventually, the spiritually dead will fulfill the duty of burying the physically dead. Through experience we have learned that we should not go back to fulfill the duty for the dead. Let the dead perform these duties on behalf of the dead. We are the living ones and we must go on to follow the King. But do not expect any material enjoyment, for you may have no nest, no roost, no place to lay your head. If you do not expect any material enjoyment and if you will leave the dead duties to the dead, you can go on to follow Him.

LIFE-STUDY OF MATTHEW

THE CONTINUATION OF THE KING'S MINISTRY

(2)

III. THE AUTHORITY OF THE KING

In 8:23—9:8 we see the authority of the King. The sequence of Matthew is wonderful. After the King spoke in a way to indicate that He had nothing, not even a home or a place to rest, and after not allowing His followers to perform the dead duties, the record of Matthew reveals the authority of this King. Although He had nothing, He had authority. In 8:23—9:8 this authority is of three aspects: the authority over the winds and the sea (8:23-27); the authority over the demons (8:28-34); and the authority to forgive sins (9:1-8).

A. Over the Winds and the Sea

The Lord's authority was manifested over the winds and the sea. This is not an ordinary authority; rather, it must be counted as an extraordinary authority. The Lord and His disciples were in a boat, and "a great tempest arose in the sea, so that the boat was covered by the waves" (v. 24). When the disciples, fearing that they would perish, roused the Lord from sleep (v. 25), He said, "Why are you fearful, you of little faith?" (v. 26). Faith comes from the word of the Lord and depends upon that word (Rom. 10:17). The Lord gave them the word in verse 18 "to depart to the other side." If they had believed that word, they would not have needed to pray as they did in verse 25. Their realization of the Lord's word was not a full realization; thus, they were those of little faith.

Verse 26 says, "Then He arose and rebuked the winds and the sea, and there was a great calm." As the Lord and the disciples were sailing across the sea, on their way to cast out the demons, something in the air and under the sea began to cause them difficulty. In the air there were the fallen angels, and in the water there were the demons. Thus the Lord's command was not actually spoken to the winds or to the sea, but to the fallen angels in the air and to the demons underneath the water. A rebuke is not given to things without life, but to things with personality. The King rebuked the winds and the sea because in the wind are the fallen angels of Satan (Eph. 6:12), and in the sea are the demons (Matt. 8:32). The fallen angels in the air and the demons in the water collaborated to frustrate the King from going to the other side of the sea, because they knew He would cast out the demons there (vv. 28-32). As soon as the King commanded the fallen angels and evil demons to stop, they immediately obeyed, and there was a great calm. The calm being great was in contrast to the measure of their faith, which was little (v. 26).

Verse 27 says, "And the men marveled, saying, What kind of man is this that even the winds and the sea obey Him?" Actually, it was not the winds and the sea, but the fallen angels above the winds and the demons under the sea that obey the King's authority. Hence, in verses 23 through 27 we see a manifestation of the King's supernatural authority. He had no hole, no roost, no place to lay His head; however, He had supernatural authority over the natural environment. He is fully qualified to be the heavenly King of the heavenly Kingdom. Apart from Him, there has never been on earth a King with such extraordinary authority.

B. Over the Demons

When the Lord Jesus had come to the country of the Gadarenes, He was met by two who were possessed by demons. When the two possessed by demons met the Lord Jesus, the demons cried out, saying, "What have we to do with You, Son of God? Have You come here to torment us before the time?" (v. 29). The King called Himself the Son of Man (v. 20), but the demons called Him the Son of God, tempting Him to deviate from His standing as the Son of Man. The demons asked Him if He had come to torment them before the time. The words "before the time" imply that God has appointed a time for the demons to be tormented and that the demons knew that time. It will be after the millennium and for eternity. (See note on Revelation 20:13 in Recovery Version of Revelation.)

The demons, not wanting to be tormented before the time, entreated the Lord Jesus, saying, "If You cast us out, send us into the herd of hogs" (v. 31). The fact that the demons entreated Him indicates that they were under the power and authority of the King. Verse 32 says, "And He said to them, Go! And they came out and went into the hogs; and behold, the whole herd rushed down the precipice into the sea and died in the waters." The word "Go!" was the King's authoritative order, and the demons obeyed it. The King answered the demons' entreaty to enter into the hogs because hogs are unclean in the eyes of God (Lev. 11:7). Unable to tolerate being possessed by the demons, the hogs rushed into the sea. The demons agreed to this, because the water is their lodging place (12:43-44).

The Lord's intention in permitting the demons to go into the hogs was not to damage the occupation of those who fed them. Because hogs are dirty in the eyes of God, the Lord Jesus destroyed their unclean occupation with the expectation that those employed in it might be saved and turn to Him. The hogs, unclean and condemned by God, should not have been present.

When the report concerning the hogs came to those who owned them, the owners were offended. Verse 34 says, "And behold, the whole city came out to meet Jesus, and when they saw Him, they entreated Him that He might depart from their districts." They begged the Lord Jesus to leave, and He did depart (9:1). The city people, having lost their hogs, rejected the King. They wanted their unclean hogs, but not the King of the heavenly kingdom. They were probably Gentiles. (Gadara was on the shore of the Sea of Galilee, opposite to Galilee of the Gentiles — 4:15.) They rejected the heavenly King because of their unclean way of making a living.

The King's coming to this district set everything in order. Not only were the demons cast out of the two men, but the hogs were drowned. Hence, the whole region was cleared, and the demons returned to their dwelling place. This was an exhibition of the Lord's authority.

C. To Forgive Sins

In 9:1-8 we see the King's authority to forgive sins. After the Lord had come to His own city, Capernaum, where He now dwelt (4:13), a paralytic was brought to Him. Verse 2 says, "And Jesus, seeing their faith, said to the paralytic, Have courage, child, your sins are forgiven." The men who had brought the paralytic to the Lord Jesus had uncovered the roof where the Lord was and had broken it up (Mark 2:4). By this the Lord saw their faith. The mention of sins in verse 2 indicates that the paralytic was sick because of his sins.

Verse 3 says, "And behold, some of the scribes said within themselves, This man blasphemes." The scribes, assuming that they knew the Scriptures, thought that only God had authority to forgive sins, and that Jesus, who in their eyes was only a man, blasphemed God when He said, "Your sins are forgiven." This indicates that they did not realize that the Lord was God. By uttering such a word, they rejected the King of the heavenly kingdom. This was the first rejection by the leaders of the Jewish religion. According to the scribes, the Lord Jesus was assuming to be God and was blaspheming Him. But the Lord Jesus, of course, did not blaspheme at all, for He is God. As God, He not only has authority over the natural environment and over demons; He also has the full authority to forgive people of their sins.

The Lord perceived in His spirit (Mark 2:8) the reasoning of the scribes. Verses 4 and 5 say, "And Jesus, knowing their inward reasonings, said, Why are you thinking evil things in your hearts? For which is easier, to say, Your sins are forgiven; or to say, Rise and walk?" The Greek word rendered "inward reasonings" also means cogitations, thoughts, evil surmisings with strong feeling or passion. The scribes did not have to give utterance to their reasonings because the Lord Jesus through the perception of His spirit was able to discern the reasonings within their hearts, and He asked them concerning them. The Lord's perceiving of the reasonings of the scribes indicates that He is truly God. If He were not God, how could He have known these things? Notice that the Lord did not say, "Which is more difficult?" because to Him nothing is difficult. For Him to say, "Your sins are forgiven," was easier than to say, "Rise and walk," because no one knows whether or not one's sins are forgiven. Hence, it is easy to say this. But everyone can tell if a person rises and walks.

The Lord's salvation not only forgives our sins, but also causes us to rise and walk. It is not to rise and walk first and then be forgiven of our sins; that would be by works. Rather, it is to be forgiven of our sins first and then to rise and walk; this is by grace.

Verse 6 says, "But that you may know that the Son of Man has authority on earth to forgive sins — then He says to the paralytic, Rise, pick up your bed and go to your house." To forgive sins is a matter of authority on earth. Only this kingly Savior, who had been authorized by God and who would die to redeem sinners, had such authority (Acts 5:31; 10:43; 13:38). This authority was for the establishment of the kingdom of the heavens (Matt. 16:19).

The Lord enabled the paralytic not only to walk, but also to pick up his bed and walk. Formerly the bed bore him; now he bears it. This is the power of the Lord's salvation. This paralytic was brought to the Lord by others, but he went home by himself. This indicates that it is not that the sinner can go *to* the Lord, but that the sinner can go *from* the Lord by the Lord's salvation.

Verse 7 says, "And he rose and went away to his house." The paralytic's rising and going proved that he was healed, and his being healed proved that his sins were forgiven. This was a strong proof that the Lord Jesus had the authority to forgive people's sins.

What these cases reveal to us is not the power of Christ, but the authority of the heavenly King. The authority, of course, is backed by the power. However, authority is higher than power. Some may have power, but without authority. For Jesus, the Lord, to be vindicated as the heavenly King, there is the need for Him to show His followers His authority. This authority is to deal with the negative things, the opposing environment instigated by the evil spirits, the demons and the corrupting sins. Christ as the heavenly King has the full authority to deal with all of these, and all of these are subdued under His authority. This brings in the establishment of His heavenly kingdom on earth.

If we put together all the cases recorded in 8:1—9:8, we see a clear picture of who this heavenly King is. He is the Savior of the Jews and also of the Gentiles. He will be the Savior of the repentant Jews, and He will also be the One who will restore the entire earth in the millennium. He has authority over the wind, the sea, and the demons. He also has authority to forgive people of their sins, and to cause these people to rise and walk. If we would follow this heavenly King, we must not expect any material enjoyment, and we also need to ignore the dead obligations and duties. This bird's-eye view of this portion of the Word affords us a vivid portrait of who the heavenly King is.

LIFE-STUDY OF MATTHEW

MESSAGE TWENTY-SEVEN

THE CONTINUATION OF THE KING'S MINISTRY

(3)

IV. FEASTING WITH THE SINNERS

In 9:9-17 we come to a very fine, sweet, and intimate portion of the Gospel of Matthew. After the King decreed the constitution of the kingdom of the heavens and after He manifested His authority as the King in many situations, in 9:9-13 we see Him feasting with sinners.

A. The Calling of Matthew

In 9:9 we have the calling of Matthew. This verse says, "And as Jesus passed on from there, He saw a man called Matthew, sitting in the customs office, and says to him, Follow Me. And he rose and followed Him." Matthew was also called Levi (Mark 2:14; Luke 5:27). He was a tax collector who became an apostle by God's grace (Matt. 10:2-3; Acts 1:13, 26). He was the writer of this Gospel.

The calling of Matthew is somewhat different from the calling of Peter, Andrew, James, and John. When Peter and Andrew were called, they were casting a net into the sea; and when James and John were called, they were mending their nets. The Lord called them, they left their work, and they followed the Lord Jesus. As the Lord Jesus was passing by the customs office, where the tax collectors were, He saw Matthew and called him, and Matthew followed Him. According to the record in 9:9 it seems that this was the first time the Lord met Matthew. There must have been some attracting power with the Lord, either in

His word or appearance, that caused Matthew to follow Him.

To follow the Lord includes believing in Him. No one follows Him unless he believes in Him. To believe in the Lord is to be saved (Acts 16:31), and to follow Him is to enter the narrow gate and walk the constricted way to participate in the kingdom of the heavens (Matt. 7:13-14).

B. A Feast Prepared for the King

Verse 10 says, "And it came to pass as He was reclining at the table in the house, that behold, many tax collectors and sinners came and reclined at the table together with Jesus and His disciples." The house spoken of in this verse was Matthew's house (Luke 5:29; Mark 2:15). As the writer of this Gospel, Matthew purposely did not say that it was his house and that it was he who had made a great feast for the Lord. This was his humility. But Luke 5:29 says clearly that Levi, that is, Matthew, "made a great reception for Him in his house." Thus, Matthew opened his house and prepared a great feast for the Lord and His disciples.

C. Many Tax Collectors and Sinners Participating in the Feast with the King and His Disciples

Verse 10 says that "many tax collectors and sinners came and reclined at the table together with Jesus and His disciples." This reveals the kind of person Matthew was. He was a sinful, despised tax collector who had many sinners as his friends. If he had not been such a low person, why were only tax collectors and sinners and not those of a higher rank feasting in Matthew's house with the Lord Jesus? Although Matthew was such a low person, he was made not only a disciple, but one of the twelve apostles.

A tax collector was a despised person. Nearly all tax collectors abused their office by demanding more than they should by false accusation (Luke 3:12-13; 19:2, 8). To pay taxes to the Romans was very bitter to the Jews. Those engaged in collecting them were despised by the people and counted unworthy of any respect (Luke 18:9-10). Hence, they were classed with sinners (Matt. 9:10-11). How we must worship the Lord that even a person of such a low rank as Matthew, under God's mercy and by His grace, could become an apostle! After being saved, Matthew was so grateful to the Lord that he opened his house and prepared a feast for Him and His disciples. Thus, this section of the Word opens in such a sweet, intimate way.

D. The Pharisees Condemning the King for Eating with Tax Collectors and Sinners

Verse 11 says, "And when the Pharisees saw it, they said to His disciples, Why does your teacher eat with the tax collectors and sinners?" The Pharisees, the strictest religious sect of the Jews, were proud of their superior sanctity of life, devotion to God, and knowledge of the Scriptures. While the Lord Jesus was enjoying the feast with all the tax collectors and sinners, the Pharisees criticized and condemned Him, and they asked the disciples why their teacher ate with such people. This question indicates that the self-righteous Pharisees did not know the grace of God. They assumed that God deals with man only according to righteousness. By asking this, they were exposed as dissenters to the heavenly King, thus rejecting Him. This is a continuation of the rejection of the heavenly King begun in verse 3 by the leaders of the Jewish religion.

E. The Lord Revealed as the Physician and as the One Who Came to Call Sinners

The Lord took the opportunity given Him by the Pharisees' question to give a very sweet revelation of Himself as the Physician. In verse 12 we see the Lord's reply to the Pharisees' question: "Those who are strong have no need of a physician, but those who are ill." The Lord was telling the Pharisees that these tax collectors and sinners were patients, sick ones, and that to them the Lord was not a judge, but a physician, a healer. In calling people to follow Him for the kingdom, the King of the heavenly kingdom ministered as a physician, not as a judge. The judgment of the judge is according to righteousness, whereas the healing of the physician is according to mercy and grace. Those whom He made people of His heavenly kingdom were lepers (8:2-4), paralytics (8:5-13; 9:2-8), the fever-ridden (8:14-15), the demon-possessed (8:16, 28-32), those sick of all kinds of illnesses (8:16), the despised tax collectors, and sinners (9:9-11). Had He visited these pitiful people as a judge, all would have been condemned and rejected, and none would have been qualified, selected, and called to be the people of His heavenly kingdom. Rather, He came to minister as a physician, to heal, recover, enliven, and save them, so that they might be reconstituted to be His new and heavenly citizens, with whom He could establish His heavenly kingdom on this corrupted earth. The Lord's word here implies that the self-righteous Pharisees did not recognize their need of Him as a physician. They considered themselves strong; hence, blinded by their own self-righteousness, they did not know that they were ill.

The self-righteous Pharisees criticized the Lord Jesus and condemned all those unclean people. But the Lord seemed to say, "These people are not unclean; they are sick. I have not come as a judge to condemn them, but as a physician, as their dear, lovely, intimate healer." As the Lord Jesus was speaking these words, He was surely indicating that the Pharisees, who thought they were righteous, were actually just as sick as the others were.

The Lord Jesus gave the Pharisees a further word in verse 13: "Now go and learn what this means, I desire mercy and not sacrifice, for I did not come to call the righteous, but sinners." The self-righteous Pharisees assumed they knew all things concerning God. In order to humble them, the Lord told them to learn more.

Mercy is a part of grace for man to receive from God. But self-righteous men do not like to receive mercy or grace from God; they prefer to offer sacrifice to God, to give something to God. This contradicts God's way in His economy. Just as God desires to show mercy to pitiful sinners, so He wants us also to show mercy to others in love (Micah 6:6-8; Mark 12:33).

The Lord says here that He did not come to call the righteous, but sinners. Actually, there is none righteous, not even one (Rom. 3:10). All the righteous are self-righteous like the Pharisees (Luke 18:9). The kingly Savior did not come to call them, but to call sinners. The Pharisees were proud of their knowledge of the Scriptures, and they thought that they knew the Bible very well. But here the Lord Jesus told them to go and learn something, to learn the meaning of the word, "I desire mercy and not sacrifice." The Lord seemed to be telling the Pharisees, "You Pharisees are self-righteous, and you condemn these people without mercy. But God desires mercy. Now is the time for Me to exercise God's mercy upon these pitiful people by being a physician to them. I am not here as a judge. I am here as a lovely physician taking care of their problems, and now I am healing them."

Are you righteous? If you say, "No, I am not righteous," you are blessed. Blessed are those who do not think that they are righteous, but who recognize that they are sinful. The reason for this is that the Lord did not come to call the righteous; He came to call the sinners. The Lord could say to the self-righteous ones, "If you consider yourselves righteous, you are not suitable for My coming, because My coming is for the sinners. Do not consider yourselves to be righteous. Rather, you must realize how sinful you are. If you consider yourselves as sinners, then you are ready for My coming."

Without the environment portrayed in these verses, the Lord Jesus would not have had the opportunity to reveal Himself as the Physician. The Lord did not simply tell His disciples, "You must know that I have not come as a judge, but as a physician." This would have been merely a doctrine. As the Lord was feasting with all those sick ones, He revealed Himself as the Physician. Those tax collectors

and sinners were not physically sick; they were spiritually
sick. While the Lord Jesus was feasting with them, He was
healing them. The Lord was telling the Pharisees, "Pharisees, you are the judges, but I am the Physician. As a
Physician, I can heal only the sick ones. If you feel that you
are not ill, then I have nothing to do with you, and I cannot
heal you. I have come here to call the sinners, the sick ones,
not the righteous, the whole ones. On which side do you
stand — the side of the righteous or the side of the sinners?
If you take the side of the sinners, then I am here to be your
Physician."

Matthew reveals more than thirty-three aspects of
Christ, one of which is Christ as the Physician. He is not
only our King, our Savior, and our life; He is also our
Physician. If we have this vision, we shall have faith in
Him and trust Him whenever we are sick physically, spiritually, or mentally. We need to trust Him as our Physician.

The Gospel of Matthew is a book of the kingdom, yet it
is also a book full of the riches of the heavenly King. This
heavenly King is our Physician with healing authority. His
healing is not simply a matter of power; it is a matter of
authority. To heal us there is no need for Him to touch us
directly. He needs only to speak a word, and His authority
will come with His word. Remember the case of the healing of the centurion's servant. The centurion said to the
Lord, "Only speak a word, and my servant boy shall be
healed" (8:8). Furthermore, the centurion could say, "I am
also a man under authority, and many others are under
me. I simply speak a word, and they obey it, because with
my word there is authority. Lord, You don't need to come
to my home. Simply give a word, and Your authority will
go with Your word." The Lord's word heals us not with
power, but with authority. Often Christians think that the
Lord heals because He is able to heal. This is a natural concept. The Lord's healing is not a matter of His ability to
heal; His healing is a matter of authority. He simply needs
to say, "Illness, go away." This is authority. With this

same authority He is also fully able to command mental illnesses to flee. Thus, He heals us with authority.

Because the Pharisees were religious and self-righteous, the Lord dealt with them. The Pharisees thought that the tax collectors and sinners were rejected. This was their religious concept. The Lord took advantage of the Pharisees' expression of their religious concept to reveal Himself as the Physician. He seemed to say, "You Pharisees, you religious people, are wrong. I am not here as a judge condemning the people. I am here as a Physician healing them. And I would heal you also, if you were willing to be healed." How sweet and intimate is this portion of the Word!

V. FASTING WITHOUT THE BRIDEGROOM

A. The Disciples of John and the Pharisees

As a book of doctrine, Matthew presents us another case in 9:14-17: the case of fasting without the Bridegroom. Verse 14 says, "Then the disciples of John came to Him, saying, Why do we and the Pharisees fast much, but Your disciples do not fast?" Verses 10 through 13 record the Lord's dealing with the question of the Pharisees, who were in the old religion. Now in verses 14 through 17 the Lord deals with the problem of John's disciples who were in the new religion. John the Baptist dropped the old religion and began his ministry in the wilderness outside of religion. However, after a short time, his disciples formed a new religion to frustrate men from enjoying Christ, just as the Pharisees in the old religion did. John the Baptist's ministry was to introduce men to Christ that Christ might become their Redeemer, their life, and their all. However, some of his disciples drifted away from his goal, Christ, to some of John's practices and turned those practices into a religion. To be religious means to do something for God without Christ. To do anything without the presence of Christ, even though it is scriptural and fundamental, is religious. Both the disciples of John, the new-timers of religion, and the Pharisees, the old-timers of religion, fasted much, yet without Christ. They did not own Christ as the Bridegroom, but made fasting a matter of religion. Meanwhile, they condemned the disciples of Christ who did not fast, but had Christ with them and lived in His presence.

John the Baptist was born a priest, but later he fully abandoned everything religious. Nevertheless, less than three years after he had been put into prison, his disciples formed a new religion. To have a religion is to worship God, to serve God, and to do certain things to please God, yet without Christ. A religion is anything you do for God without the Spirit, without Christ. The Pharisees did a great many things for God, but Christ was not in them. They did many things to serve God, but they did them without the Spirit. Now the disciples of John the Baptist were fasting without Christ, without the Spirit. Nevertheless, this fasting was for God. Hence, they formed another religion. Therefore, in verse 14 we have the old religion, the religion of the Pharisees, and the new religion, the religion of the disciples of John.

How easy it is to have a religion! Do not think that you can be free from religion by simply dropping an old way and picking up another way. No matter whether the way is old or new, it is a religion as long as it does not have Christ and the Spirit in it. Your new way may simply be your new religion. Remember what religion is: it is doing things to please God apart from Christ and the Spirit.

The self-righteous Pharisees, the old-timers of religion, were bothered by the fact that Christ made Himself a companion of tax collectors and sinners, who were condemned by them (v. 11). They condemned Him for feasting with the sinners. The fasting disciples of John, the new-timers of religion, were troubled by the feasting of Christ and His disciples (v. 10) and condemned them for not fasting. The situation is similar today. On every hand the religionists condemn us. What then should we do? We should stay with the Physician.

B. Not Fasting with the Bridegroom

In the case of the new religion, the Lord is not only the Physician, but also the Bridegroom. In verse 15 the Lord Jesus said to them, "Can the sons of the bridechamber mourn as long as the bridegroom is with them? But the days will come when the bridegroom is taken away from them, and then they will fast." Both the Physician and the Bridegroom are pleasant. I appreciate the Lord's wisdom. In the case concerning the Pharisees, He likened Himself to a Physician. Now in the case with the disciples of John, He likens Himself to a bridegroom at a wedding. The Lord asked if the sons of the bridechamber can mourn as long as the bridegroom is with them. It is a joyful time with the Bridegroom. But when the Bridegroom is taken away, they may fast.

The phrase "sons of the bridechamber" refers to the disciples of the Lord. In the transitory period of the Lord's ministry on earth, His disciples were sons of the bridechamber. Later they will become the Bride (John 3:29; Rev. 19:7). The Bridegroom was taken away from the sons of the bridechamber when the kingly Savior was taken up from the disciples into heaven (Acts 1:11). After that, they fasted (Acts 13:2-3; 14:23).

In dealing with the self-righteous and dissenting Pharisees of the old religion, the kingly Savior indicated that He was a Physician to heal the sick (v. 12). In dealing with the fasting and dissenting disciples of John who had formed the new religion, He revealed Himself as a Bridegroom to take the Bride. John the Baptist told his disciples that Christ was the Bridegroom to take the Bride (John 3:25-29). Now Christ, the kingly Savior, reminded some of them of this. The kingly Savior firstly healed His followers, then made them the sons of the bridechamber. Eventually He will make them His Bride. They should appropriate Him not only as their Physician for the recovery of their life, but also as their Bridegroom for a living of enjoyment in His presence. They were at a joyful wedding with Him, not at a sorrowful funeral without Him. How then could they fast and not feast before Him? This dissenting question indicates that some of John's disciples had fallen into a new religion and also had rejected the kingly Savior.

The question of John's disciples seemed to be one of doctrine. But the Lord did not answer with a doctrine, but with a Person, the most pleasant Person, the Bridegroom. The religious people always care for their doctrine with their doctrinal reasonings. But Christ cares only for Himself. The living and walk of His followers should be regulated and directed only by His Person and His presence, not by any doctrine.

It would be ridiculous for someone to fast at a wedding. Moreover, to fast while others are enjoying the wedding feast would be an insult to the bridegroom. Here we see the Lord's wisdom. He did not argue with them, but He certainly condemned the religious ones. The Lord seemed to be saying, "You religious people have missed the mark. Don't you realize that I am the Bridegroom and that all My disciples around Me are the sons of the bridechamber? They shouldn't be fasting. They must feast with Me." Without these two cases, the Lord Jesus could never have been revealed as the Physician and as the Bridegroom. We should thank the Lord for the Pharisees and for the disciples of John. We should even thank the Lord for all the religions, for without the occasions afforded by religion the Lord could not be revealed in so many different aspects. It is the same today.

LIFE-STUDY OF MATTHEW

THE CONTINUATION OF THE KING'S MINISTRY

(4)

This message is the continuation of the previous message on 9:9-17.

C. Not Putting a Patch of Unshrunk Cloth on an Old Garment

In 9:16 the Lord continues with something even finer, sweeter, and more intimate. He says, "Now no one puts a patch of unshrunk cloth on an old garment, for that which fills it up pulls away from the garment, and a worse tear is made." The Greek word translated "unshrunk" is *agnaphos,* formed with *a,* which means not, and *gnapto,* which means to card or comb wool; hence, to dress or full the cloth. Thus, the word means uncarded, unfulled, unfinished, unshrunk, untreated. The unshrunk cloth signifies Christ from His incarnation to His crucifixion as a piece of new cloth, untreated, unfinished; whereas the new garment in Luke 5:36 signifies Christ, after being treated in His crucifixion, as a new robe. (The Greek word for "new" in Luke 5:36 is *kainos,* the same as the word for "fresh" in Matthew 9:17.) Christ was firstly the unshrunk cloth for making a new garment, and then through His death and resurrection He was made a new garment to cover us as our righteousness before God that we might be justified by God and acceptable to Him (Luke 15:22; Gal. 3:27; 1 Cor. 1:30; Phil. 3:9). A patch of unshrunk cloth put on an old garment pulls away from the garment by its shrinking strength, thus making the tear worse. To do this means to imitate what Christ did in His human life on earth. This is what today's modernists are attempting. They only imitate Jesus' human deeds to improve their behavior; they do not believe in the crucified Jesus as their Redeemer or the resurrected Christ as their new garment to cover them as their righteousness before God.

The old garment in verse 16 signifies man's good behavior, good deeds, and religious practices by his old natural life. The Lord Jesus was very wise. In verse 16 He did not say, "You disciples of John must realize that your garments are torn and full of holes. By fasting you are actually cutting a piece of unshrunk cloth and using it to patch the holes in your garments." Instead of saying this directly, the Lord Jesus indicated to the disciples of John that they did not have a perfect garment. He indicated that their garments had holes and that by fasting they were trying to patch the holes. No human being could utter such a word as that spoken by the Lord Jesus in verse 16. His wise word is full of meaning, rebuke, revelation, and instruction. The Lord was saying to the disciples of John, "Why do you ask Me about fasting? Your fasting is a way of patching your torn garment. By your fasting, you show that you realize that you have holes in your garments that need to be mended. Your teacher, John, introduced you all to Me. Now you are utilizing Me to patch your holes. This means that you are cutting a piece from My unshrunk cloth to mend the holes in your garments. But My cloth is full of shrinking power. Don't put any part of it on your old torn garments. If you do, the hole will become larger."

The account in Luke 5:36 is somewhat different from that in Matthew 9:16. Luke 5:36 says, "No man tears a patch from a new garment and puts it on an old." Notice that Matthew says "cloth" and that Luke says "garment." The Lord Jesus likened Himself to a piece of unshrunk cloth. This points to what He was between His incarnation and His crucifixion. During this period of time He was unshrunk cloth, new cloth that had never been fulled or dealt with. Through His death and resurrection this new cloth was dealt with and was made a new garment. The Lord's intention was to give Himself to us not as a piece of unshrunk cloth, but as a complete, finished garment that we

might put on as our righteousness to be justified before
God. After His death and resurrection, He was made the
finished garment for us to put on so that we may attend
His wedding. Thus, He is not only the Bridegroom, but also
our wedding garment that qualifies us to attend His wedding feast.

Why did the Lord Jesus, after telling us that He is the
Bridegroom, go on to speak of the new cloth, the new garment? We must look deeper to discern His meaning. The
Lord tells us that the Bridegroom is with us. But look at
yourself — do you deserve His presence? Do you think that
your real condition in the eyes of God is worthy of the presence of the Bridegroom? We must all answer, "No." All we
have and all we are does not deserve the Lord's presence.
To enjoy the Lord's presence we need certain qualifi-
cations; we need to be in a certain condition, in a certain
situation. What we are by birth, what we are naturally,
whatever we can do, and whatever we have, do not qualify
us to be in the presence of the Bridegroom. The Bridegroom is Christ, and Christ is God Himself. Suppose God
appeared to you today. Could you just sit there? He is the
holy God, the righteous God, and such a One is the Bridegroom. Recall the story of the prodigal son in Luke 15. The
prodigal son came home. The father undoubtedly loved
him deeply, but the son's condition was utterly unfit for
the presence of the father. Therefore, the father immediately told his servant to take the best robe and to put it on
him, thus making him fit for his presence. Our Bridegroom is God Himself. How may we, poor sinners, enjoy
the presence of the heavenly King? We must remember the
context of these verses in Matthew 9: the Lord Jesus was
eating with tax collectors and sinners. We are "tax collectors" and sinners. We are not qualified; we need something to cover us that we may sit in the presence of the
Lord. This is why, after the Lord spoke of Himself as the
Bridegroom, He told us that we need to be clothed in a new
garment. When we put on the new garment, we are worthy
of His presence. When the prodigal son was clothed with
the best robe, he could immediately stand in the presence

of his honored father. The best robe qualified him to enjoy the father's presence. We as sinners and "tax collectors" need to be clothed in a new garment that we may be worthy of the Bridegroom's presence.

I do not like to present mere teachings and doctrines — I prefer the practice, the experience. Let me check with you: Since Christ became the new garment after His resurrection, how then may we put Him on? Galatians 3:27 says, "As many as were baptized into Christ have put on Christ." We must put on Christ, and the way to put Him on is to be baptized into Him. Now we must see how we may be baptized into Christ. We have seen that after His resurrection Christ became a new garment, but the Bible also tells us that after His resurrection He was made a life-giving Spirit (1 Cor. 15:45). If Christ were not the Spirit, how could we be baptized into Him? By being crucified, buried, and resurrected, Christ was made a life-giving *pneuma,* a life-giving breath, the living air. As the breath, it is so easy for Him to get into us, and as the air, it is so easy for us to get into Him. Christ in resurrection was made a Spirit. This life-giving Spirit is the all-inclusive One. In this Spirit is all that Christ is and all He has accomplished. This all-inclusive Spirit is the all-inclusive Christ Himself, and this Christ as the Spirit is the new garment for us to wear. Hence, even the garment is the Spirit. We were baptized into Christ as the Spirit — it is thus that we put on Christ. Christ is the *pneuma,* the all-inclusive Spirit. When we are baptized into Him, we put Him on. Immediately He as the Spirit becomes our clothing, our covering, and we are qualified. Therefore, the new garment which we must put on is Christ Himself as the all-inclusive Spirit.

This is the meaning of the Lord's word in 28:19, "Go therefore, and disciple all nations, baptizing them into the name of the Father, and of the Son, and of the Holy Spirit." The reality of the name is in the Spirit. To baptize people into the name means to baptize them into the Spirit, who is Christ as the all-inclusive *pneuma.* Christ became incarnated, He lived on earth, He was crucified and accomplished redemption, and He was resurrected. After everything was finished, He became the all-inclusive *pneuma* in His resurrection. Incarnation is included in this *pneuma*; crucifixion and redemption are included in this *pneuma*; resurrection, the power of His resurrection, and the life of the resurrection are all included in this *pneuma*. When we were baptized into Him, we were baptized into this *pneuma*. When we were baptized into Him, we put Him on. We must put on Christ as the new garment, and this new garment is the all-inclusive Spirit. Christ is no longer the untreated cloth; He is now the finished garment. In this finished garment we have redemption, resurrection power, and all the elements of the divine Person. This new garment is not just a piece of clothing, but the divine *pneuma*, the all-inclusive Spirit, including Christ's incarnation, His crucifixion, His redemptive work, His resurrection, and His resurrection power. Now He is the finished garment for us to put on. Hallelujah, we can put on such a Christ!

D. Not Putting New Wine into Old Wineskins

Verse 17 says, "Neither do they put new wine into old wineskins; otherwise, the wineskins burst, and the wine pours out, and the wineskins are destroyed; but they put new wine into fresh wineskins, and both are preserved." The Greek word translated "new" in this verse is *neos*, which means new in time, recent, young. The new wine here signifies Christ as the new life, full of vigor, stirring people to excitement. The new wine is Christ's cheering life. The divine life is likened to wine that has cheering strength. When we receive His life, it works within us all day long to stir us up and to excite us. This new wine strengthens us, energizes us, and makes us very happy. The kingly Savior is not only the Bridegroom to the kingdom people for their enjoyment, but also their new garment to equip and qualify them outwardly for attending the wedding. Furthermore, He is also their new life to excite them inwardly for the enjoyment of Him as their Bridegroom. He, as their heavenly King, is the Bridegroom for the kingdom people's enjoyment, and His heavenly kingdom is the wedding feast (22:2) that they may enjoy Him. To enjoy Him as the Bridegroom in the kingdom feast, they need Him as their new garment outwardly and their new wine inwardly.

Consider again the example of the prodigal son. After putting on the best robe the prodigal son could still say, "O father, the best robe satisfies you, but it doesn't satisfy me. I am still hungry and need to be satisfied." Immediately the father told the servant to kill the fatted calf and said, "Let us eat, and be merry." Thus, the father's provision is not just for something outward, but also for something within. Therefore, after the Lord spoke about the new garment, He directly proceeded to speak of the new wine. The new wine is not a provision for the outward need, but for the inward need. We need something to cover us, and we also need something to fill us. We are so poor outwardly, and we are so empty inwardly. We need the robe upon us for the Father's sake, and we need the new wine within us for our own sakes. We need both the new garment and the new wine. The Lord is the new garment to us, and He is also the new wine. He is our covering and also our content. He not only qualifies us, but He satisfies us as well. Hence, He is our qualification and our satisfaction, the provision for our outward need and the provision for all our inward hunger and thirst.

In verse 17 the Lord said that we should not put new wine into old wineskins. Old wineskins signify religious practices, such as the fasting held by the Pharisees in the old religion and the disciples of John in the new religion. All religions are old wineskins. New wine put into old wineskins bursts the wineskins by its fermenting power. To put new wine into old wineskins is to put Christ as the exciting life into any kind of religion. This is what the so-called fundamentalists and Pentecostals are practicing today. They attempt to squeeze Christ into their different modes of religious ritual and formality. The kingdom people should never do this. They must put the new wine into fresh wineskins.

The new wine needs a wineskin, a container. Because the new wine is filled with fermenting power, if you put it into an old wineskin, the fermenting power of the new wine will burst the old wineskin. Any religious practice is an old wineskin. In this verse Christ seemed to be saying to the Pharisees and the disciples of John, "Fasting is an old wineskin. Do not try to put the new wine of My life into the wineskin of your old religious practices. The wine will burst your religious practices. The new wine of My life requires a new wineskin."

Some indeed have received the new wine, but they have attempted to take the new wine back and pour it into an old wineskin. I have been observing this kind of folly for more than forty years. Many people have come to the local church and tasted the new wine. They have said, "This is really wonderful. This is just what 'my church' needs." Then they tried to bring this new wine back to that old wineskin. Do you know what happened? The old wineskins burst, and the new wine was spilled. However, if you put the new wine into a new wineskin, both will be preserved.

We have seen that the new wine belongs in the new wineskins. But today the so-called charismatic movement has been brought into the old Catholic wineskin. Even some Catholic churches have charismatic masses. The charismatic things are being mixed with the mass and with the worship of Mary. What confusion! This is the leaven mixed with the fine flour (13:33). In other words, it is the new wine put into the old wineskin. I am concerned that this wine is no longer the new wine, for it seems to have no fermenting power. If it did, the old wineskin would burst. If the charismatic movement were the genuine new wine filled with the fermenting power, it would burst that old Catholic wineskin.

E. Putting New Wine into Fresh Wineskins

In verse 17 the Lord also said, "They put new wine into fresh wineskins, and both are preserved." The Greek word for "fresh" is *kainos*, which means new in nature, quality, or form; unaccustomed, unused; hence, fresh. The fresh wineskins signify the church life in the local churches as the container of the new wine, which is Christ Himself as the exciting life. The kingdom people are built into the church (16:18), and the church is expressed through the local churches in which they live (18:15-20). They are regenerated persons constituting the Body of Christ to be the church (Rom. 12:5; Eph. 1:22-23). This Body of Christ as His fullness is also called "the Christ" (1 Cor. 12:12, Gk.), the corporate Christ. The individual Christ is the new wine, the exciting life inwardly, and the corporate Christ is the fresh wineskin, the container to hold the new wine outwardly. With the kingdom people, it is not a matter of fasting or of any other religious practice, but a matter of the church life with Christ as their content. Christ came not to establish an earthly religion of rituals, but a heavenly kingdom of life, not with any dead religious practices, but with Himself, the living Person, as the Physician, the Bridegroom, the unshrunk cloth, and the new wine to His followers as their full enjoyment that they might be the fresh wineskin to contain Him and become the constituents of His kingdom.

We see then that the new wineskin is the church life. The church is actually the enlargement of Christ. The individual Christ is our wine within us. When this individual Christ is enlarged into a corporate Christ, that is the church. This corporate Christ is the wineskin, the container, to contain the individual Christ as our wine. Never consider the church a religion; the church is a corporate entity full of Christ, because the church is Christ enlarged.

Christ is not only our new garment and new wine, but, being increased, He is also our new wineskin to contain the wine. He is our outward qualification, He is our inward satisfaction, and He is in a corporate way the church, the Body (1 Cor. 12:12), capable of holding the wine. Christ is everything. He is the Bridegroom, the new garment, the new wine, and also the corporate vessel to contain what we enjoy of Him. The meaning here is very profound.

We need to see something more concerning Christ as the new wineskin. First Corinthians 12:12 says, "For even as the body is one and has many members, but all the members of the body being many are one body, so also is Christ." We read in this verse not only that the members composed together are the one Body, but that this Body is Christ. We have always considered Christ as the Head; we have considered little, if at all, that Christ is also also the Body. How, speaking in a practical way, is Christ the Body? He is the Body because the Body is composed of so many members who are filled with Christ. Christ is in you, Christ is in me, and Christ is in every one of us. We all have Christ within. In 1 Corinthians 1 Paul said that Christ is not divided. The Christ in you is one with the Christ in me, and the Christ in us is one with the Christ in all other Christians. Therefore, Christ is the Body composed of so many members who are filled with Him. This is the new wineskin, which is the church life to contain Christ as the new wine.

Without the wineskin, how could we keep the wine? Do not consider that you yourself as an individual are the vessel. No, you are just a part of the vessel. How can a glass contain water if it is cut into pieces? How can the pieces contain the water? It is impossible. Do not consider that you are somebody. You are nobody. You are just a member of the Body, a minute part of the Body. It is true that some amount of blood is in my little finger, but this little finger is just a part of my body. If you sever it from the body, the flow of blood in the finger immediately ceases. Instead of containing the blood, the finger will lose the blood. From the day you leave the church life, you begin to lose Christ; the new wine starts to run out. Nothing but the church life can contain the very Christ we enjoy. Never consider the church as an insignificant matter.

We must also realize that the wineskin is not only the container of the wine, but also the means for us to drink the wine. Many of us can testify that whenever we come into a church meeting, we discover that it is truly the place where we can drink Christ. It is here that we drink the Lord as never before. The church life is not merely a container, but a vessel from which we may drink. We need Christ as the new garment, we need Christ as the new wine, and we also need Christ in a corporate way as the new wineskin. We need the church life. We do not care for religion, forms, or rituals. We care only for Christ in you and Christ in me. This is the new wineskin.

At this point, I would like to say a word to the young people. The young people may say, "As long as we stay with the older ones, we will be in religion. But if we get away from them, we will not be religious." This concept is wrong. Everything depends on whether or not the church is the enlargement of Christ. It is not a matter of age. Even if all the babes came together, they could still be in religion because they do not have Christ as their content. If the older ones are filled with Christ and saturated with Him, they are the church, no matter how old they may be. Remember that religion is something for God without Christ. But the church is Christ enlarged; it is the enlargement of Christ. And the new wineskin is Christ enlarged into a corporate expression. This is the church. The church is not something for God without Christ and without the Spirit. The church is an entity which is the enlargement of Christ and which is full of Christ. The church is filled with Christ and constituted with Christ. No matter what our age may be, we must be filled with Christ. Then when we come together, we shall be the local expression of the church. This is the wineskin. No matter how much fermenting power there is in the divine life of Christ, it can never burst the church.

Today there are four kinds of Christians. The first are called Christians, but they are not truly Christians. They are the modernists, the so-called modernistic Christians. They only take Christ as the new cloth. They say, "Look how Jesus lived: He was so full of love and self-sacrifice. We must imitate Him and follow Him." But to do this is just to cut out a piece of new cloth with which to patch an old garment. The modernists are trying to take the unshrunk cloth of the Lord's human living and use it to patch the holes in their behavior. But this unshrunk cloth pulls back and makes their holes larger. The modernists do not believe that Christ died for their sins on the cross, they do not believe that Christ is God, and they do not believe in His resurrection. They simply believe that they should imitate the human living of Jesus.

The fundamentalists are the second kind of Christians. They believe that Christ is God, that Christ is their Redeemer, that Christ died on the cross for their sins, and that He was resurrected. The fundamentalists receive and accept the resurrected Christ as their righteousness. They take Christ, not as a piece of new cloth, but as the new, finished garment. However, they know little of the inner life, of the inner wine. They put on Christ as the outer garment, but they do not drink Him as the wine within.

The third kind of Christian may be called the inner life Christians. They not only put on Christ as their new garment, but they also know Him as their inner life. In fact, they place great emphasis on the inner life. The inner life Christians are an improvement over the previous two groups. However, as good as they are, they lack one thing: they lack the wineskin, the church life.

The fourth are the church people. The church people are not modernists. Moreover, they are neither merely fundamentals nor only the inner life people. They are churching, because they have the new wineskin.

In the last days the Lord is recovering not only the new garment — this He recovered through Martin Luther in the matter of justification by faith. Neither is the Lord only recovering the inner life — this He recovered through ones such as Madame Guyon, William Law, Andrew Murray, and Jessie Penn-Lewis. We thank the Lord for all these items that have been recovered. However, at the end of this age the Lord is recovering the last and ultimate item, the church life. Those who enjoy the church life are the church people. Among the church people the new garment, the new wine, and the new wineskin have all been recovered. We have Christ in a corporate way as our church life. The Lord did not stop with either the new garment or the new wine. He went on from the Bridegroom to the new cloth, from the new cloth to the new garment, from the new garment to the new wine, and from the new wine to the new wineskin. After the wineskin, the church, there is nothing more. The church is God's ultimate goal. When we arrive at the church, we are in the ultimate consummation of God's purpose. Thus, after the wineskin, the Lord mentioned nothing else.

Praise the Lord that He is our Physician! After He heals us, He becomes our Bridegroom. He is also our garment to qualify us and our new wine to stir us up. As I see the faces of the brothers and sisters in the meetings, I can tell that they have been stirred up by the new wine. How we praise the Lord that this new wine is in His enlargement, the new wineskin. Christ is everything to us! We need to know our Lord to such an extent. He is not only our King, our Savior, and our life. He is also our Physician, and this dear Physician is our lovely Bridegroom. And this Bridegroom becomes our garment, our new wine, and eventually the wineskin. We are now in the wineskin, in the church life, enjoying Him to such a high degree. Hallelujah for Christ and the church!

LIFE-STUDY OF MATTHEW

MESSAGE TWENTY-NINE

THE CONTINUATION OF THE KING'S MINISTRY
(5)
AND
THE ENLARGEMENT OF THE KING'S MINISTRY
(1)

THE CONTINUATION OF THE KING'S MINISTRY
(5)

In Matthew 9 Christ is revealed as the Physician, the Bridegroom, and even as the unshrunk cloth, the new wine, and the new wineskin. Following this, a further revelation of Christ is needed. This revelation requires a certain environment that will enable Christ to be revealed in another aspect. Having Christ revealed to us is not a matter of doctrine. In order for Christ to be revealed, there is always the need of a particular environment. In chapter nine Christ is revealed in so many sweet, lovely, pleasant aspects. The environment required for the revelation of Christ in chapter nine was produced by His ministry. In order for Christ to be revealed to us, there must be a certain environment, and that environment always comes out of Christ's ministry. Christ began to minister in chapter four. After calling the first four disciples and attracting great crowds, He went up to the mountain where He issued the decree of the constitution of the kingdom of the heavens. After He descended from the mountain, He continued His ministry. His ministry before giving the constitution on the mountain was good for the constitution, but it was not sufficient for the further revelation of who He is and of what He is. In order for Him to be revealed as the lovely items found in chapter nine, there

was the need for the continuation of His ministry. This
further ministry created the environment for Him to be
revealed not only as the King, but also as the Physician, the
Bridegroom, the new cloth, the new wine, and the new wineskin. If you do not see this ministry in such a way, if you cannot see the environment created by this ministry for the
revelation of Christ, and if you cannot see all the items of
what Christ is, you may read the Gospel of Matthew a hundred times without receiving anything from it. It may seem
to you to be either a book of stories or doctrines. But you will
never receive any life from this book. If you would see light
in the Gospel of Matthew, you must first see the heavenly
King. After He was anointed and tested, He began His
ministry. His ministry is crucial, for it is absolutely
necessary for His revelation. Christ would not just tell us
that He is the Physician, the Bridegroom, the new cloth, the
new wine, and the new wineskin. That would be like the
teaching given in a seminary. How poor it would be simply
to gather a group of people together and merely tell them
what Christ is. To repeat, in order to receive the revelation
of Christ, there is the need of the environment created by
His ministry.

In the continuation of His ministry the King did many
signs. He healed the leper, He healed the servant boy of a
Roman centurion, and He healed the mother-in-law of
Peter. Following this, He healed a great many other people.
This was His ministry. The continuation of the King's
ministry was different from the beginning of His ministry,
for in the beginning there were no dispensational signs.
Rather, He contacted people, attracted them, and captured them. Because a great crowd followed Him, He was
able to deliver the decree of the constitution of the kingdom
of the heavens.

Although Matthew is a book on the kingdom, it is also a
revelation of Christ. One day Christ led His disciples to
Caesarea Philippi and asked them, "Who do men say that
the Son of Man is?" (16:13). After they gave some answers,
He asked them, "But you, who do you say that I am?" (v.

15). This indicates that the book of the kingdom reveals who Christ is. What a blessing it is to see the revelations of Christ in this book! The genealogy of Christ in chapter one is a revelation of Christ. It reveals that Christ is the Son of David, the Son of Abraham, and the issue of a marriage that unites the two lines of David's descendants. According to Matthew chapter one, Jesus is not that simple. He is Jehovah the Savior and Emmanuel, God with us. Christ is the Son of David, the Son of Abraham, the seed of the woman, Jehovah the Savior, and Emmanuel, God with us. In chapter two He is visited as a king. Thus, chapter two reveals that He is the King. In chapter three this King is recommended and anointed, and in chapter four He is tested, qualified, and approved. Then, after His testing, this King came into His ministry. By means of His ministry, He attracted crowds. After giving the constitution of the kingdom of the heavens, He continued His ministry, doing some signs with a dispensational significance. These miracles signify that He came with salvation firstly to the Jews and then turned from the Jews to the Gentiles. These signs also signify that after the fullness of the salvation of the Gentiles, Christ will bring His salvation back to the Jews. Then will take place the restoration of the whole earth during the time of the millennium. At that time all diseases will be healed. Through this continuation of the King's ministry, an environment — a feast — was prepared. This feast came out of Christ's ministry. Through His ministry, the Lord gained a sinner, a tax collector named Matthew, who prepared a great feast for the Lord and His disciples. To this feast Matthew also invited a great many of his friends, who also were sinners and tax collectors. There is a proverb which says that we know what kind of person you are by looking at your friends. Matthew, a tax collector, had friends who were tax collectors and sinners. The feast prepared by Matthew was the right environment for the Lord to reveal Himself as the Physician, the Bridegroom, the new cloth to cover us, the new wine to fill us, and the new wineskin to preserve the wine we have received. Christ in all these aspects was revealed through the environment brought forth by His ministry.

The situation is the same today. Without the ministry, nothing of Christ and nothing concerning the church could be revealed. I cannot simply gather some people together and deliver them a lecture. In that kind of environment I simply have nothing to say. But in the proper environment I can tell you about one item of Christ after another. What a Christ we have! We need to thank the Lord for His ministry and for the environment He creates through His ministry. Even the Pharisees of the old religion and the disciples of John of the new religion were used by the Lord. The old religion gave the Lord Jesus the opportunity to reveal Himself as the Physician, and the new religion gave Him the opportunity to reveal Himself as the Bridegroom, the new cloth, the new wine, and the new wineskin. We need to say, "Thank you, Pharisees, and thank you, disciples of John. Without you, we could not have such a vision of Christ. We would never know that our heavenly King is the Physician, the Bridegroom, the new cloth, the new wine, and the new wineskin."

When I was young, I read through Matthew chapters eight and nine without seeing anything. I read about the new cloth, the new wine, and the new wineskin, but none of these things made any impression on me. Later, in the proper environment, my eyes were opened to see how sweet and pleasant the Lord Jesus is. Oh, He is our Bridegroom! How pleasant! He is the new cloth, our covering, and the new wine to fill us up. And He is also the new wineskin, the container. I also came to see the four kinds of Christians indicated by these items: the modernists, the fundamentalists, the inner life people, and the church people. I am glad to be among the church people. I enjoy being in the new wineskin. I am covered by the new garment, I am drinking the new wine, and I am in the new wineskin enjoying the presence of the Bridegroom. How wonderful this is! This is our Christ! Today, we do know what the church is. We are churching Christ! In the Lord's recovery Christ is our Bridegroom, our new garment, our new wine, and our new wine-skin. Therefore we may coin a new phrase: we are "churching Christ."

VI. SIGNS WITH DISPENSATIONAL SIGNIFICANCE REPEATED

In 9:18-34 we have the repetition of signs with dispensational significance. These verses give a brief picture of this age and the coming age. Hence, this record is also with dispensational significance, as that in 8:1-17. The daughter of the ruler of the synagogue represents the Jews, and the woman with the hemorrhage represents the Gentiles. When the daughter died, the woman was healed. After the woman was healed, the daughter was revived. Following this, two blind men and one dumb man were healed. This is a type, showing that when the Jews are cut off, the Gentiles are saved and that after the fullness of the salvation of the Gentiles, the Jews will be saved (Rom. 11:15, 17, 19, 23-26). Following this, the millennium will begin, and at that time all the blind and the dumb will be healed (Isa. 35:5-6).

A. The Daughter of the Ruler of the Synagogue Having Died

Verse 18 says, "As He was speaking these things to them, behold, a ruler came and worshipped Him saying, My daughter has just died, but come and lay Your hand on her, and she will live." The ruler here was a ruler of the synagogue (Mark 5:22; Luke 8:41) named Jairus, which means "he will enlighten," or "enlightened," signifying that the Lord will enlighten the Gentiles, and they will be enlightened (Acts 13:46-48). According to the record in Mark and Luke, this ruler's daughter was twelve years of age. This ruler was interested in the heavenly King, but he did not have as much faith as the centurion. The centurion had told the Lord Jesus that He did not need to come to his home. It was sufficient for Him to speak a word. If this ruler of the synagogue had had this kind of faith, his daughter would have been healed. However, he asked the

Lord to come to his home and to lay His hand upon his daughter. His faith could reach this far, no farther. Sympathizing with him, the Lord Jesus arose and followed him.

B. The Healing of a Woman with a Hemorrhage

As the Lord was on the way to the ruler's house, a woman who had been sick of a hemorrhage for twelve years "approached from behind and touched the fringe of His garment." This woman suffered from a bloody flux, a flow or issue of blood (Lev. 15:25). The life of the flesh is in the blood (Lev. 17:11). Hence, this disease signifies the life that cannot be retained. The woman was sick for twelve years, the age of the daughter of the ruler (Luke 8:42). This woman approached the Lord from behind and touched the fringe of His garment, saying within herself, "If only I may touch His garment, I shall be healed." The woman here and the centurion in 8:5-10, both representing the Gentiles, came to contact the Lord in the same way, with faith. She was healed while the Lord was on the way to the ruler's house. This signifies that the Gentiles are saved while Christ is on the way to the house of Israel.

The Lord's garment signifies Christ's righteous deeds, and the fringe signifies the heavenly ruling. According to Numbers 15:38-40, Israelite males had to wear a blue fringe on their garments, a ribbon in the color of blue. This meant that their lives, their walk, were restricted by a heavenly limitation. When the Lord Jesus was on earth, He probably dressed in this way. Garments signify virtue in human behavior. In the human virtue of the Lord Jesus there was healing power. Therefore, when the sick woman touched the fringe of His garment, the power of His virtue went to her, and she was healed. Out of Christ's heavenly-ruled deeds comes the virtue that becomes the healing power (Matt. 14:36).

The healing of the woman with the hemorrhage indicates that the Lord was met and caught by the Gentiles as He was journeying to the Jews. According to history, the Gentiles are sick, and the Jews are growing in order to die. In other words, the Gentiles are sick, and the Jews are dying. The Jewish girl was twelve years of age, and the woman had been sick for twelve years. For twelve years the woman suffered from the issue of blood, and for twelve years the girl was growing in order to die. This signifies that while the Gentiles are sick of sinful things, the Jews are growing in order to die. After the woman was healed, the Lord Jesus arrived at the home of the Jewish ruler, signifying that when the salvation of the Gentiles is in full, Christ will reach the house of Israel.

C. The Healing of the Daughter of the Ruler of the Synagogue

In verses 23 through 26 we have the healing of the synagogue ruler's daughter. The daughter here and Peter's mother-in-law in 8:14-15, both representing the Jews at the end of this age, were healed in a house by the Lord's coming and direct touch. This indicates that at the end of this age all the remnant of the Jews will be saved in the house of Israel by the Lord's coming and His direct touch (Rom. 11:25-26; Zech. 12:10).

When Jesus came into the ruler's house and saw the flute players and the crowd making a tumult, He said, "Depart, for the girl has not died, but sleeps. And they ridiculed Him" (vv. 23-24). In His ministry, the Lord never cared for any crowd. Verse 25 says, "But when the crowd was put out, He entered and took hold of her hand, and the girl was raised up." By this we see that the Lord Jesus intended to raise the Jews, but that they did not have the faith. This gave an excellent chance to the Gentiles to contact the Lord to receive salvation. After the fullness of the salvation of the Gentiles, the Lord Jesus will reach the house of Israel, and all the dead Jews will be healed.

D. The Healing of the Blind and Dumb

Immediately after the raising of the ruler's daughter, two blind men and a dumb man are brought to the Lord (vv. 27-33).

1. Healing of the Two Blind Men

In verses 27 through 31 we have the healing of the two blind men. As the Lord Jesus passed by, "Two blind men followed Him, crying out and saying, Have mercy on us, Son of David." Blindness signifies lack of sight in seeing God and the things related to Him (2 Cor. 4:4; Rev. 3:18). These two blind men called the Lord the Son of David. In the millennial kingdom, which will be the restored tabernacle of David (Acts 15:16), the Messianic kingdom, the Jews will recognize Christ as the Son of David, and their blindness will be healed. This is typified by the two blind men recognizing Christ in this way. The two blind men were healed in the house by the Lord's direct touch (v. 29), as were both the daughter of the ruler (v. 25) and Peter's mother-in-law (8:14-15). The opening of the blind men's eyes signifies the recovery of inward sight to see God and spiritual things (Acts 9:17-18; 26:18; Eph. 1:18; Rev. 3:18).

2. The Healing of a Demon-Possessed Dumb Man

In verses 32 and 33 we see the healing of the demon-possessed dumb man. Dumbness by demon possession signifies the inability to speak for God (Isa. 56:10) and praise God (Isa. 35:6) due to the worship of dumb idols (1 Cor. 12:2). The speaking of a dumb man signifies the recovery of the speaking and praising ability by being filled with the Lord in the spirit (Eph. 5:18-19).

3. A Shadow of the Millennium

The healing of the blind and the dumb signifies the restoration to the people on earth during the millennium. Thus, these healings are a shadow of the millennium. In the millennium all the blind will see, and the mouths of the dumb will be opened. Isaiah 35:5 and 6 say, "Then the eyes of the blind shall be opened, and the ears of the deaf shall be unstopped. Then shall the lame man leap as a hart, and the tongue of the dumb sing." The blind will see God's glory, and the dumb will speak of God's glory. They will praise

Him continually. The millennium therefore will be a time of restoration, a time of revival. Whenever there is a revival among Christians today, the blind eyes are opened, and the dumb mouths are opened. Before such a revival, so many Christians are blind, unable to see God or the things of God, and dumb, unable to speak a word for God. If those in the denominations today are asked to give a prayer, many are unable to do so and they will reply, "This is not my job, my profession. Ask the pastor to pray." This indicates that they are possessed by a dumb demon. First Corinthians 12 reveals that we are not serving dumb idols. Thus, we must be speaking, bubbling. Our eyes are opened to see the things of God, and our mouths are opened to praise Him and to testify of Him. We all must be this kind of person. This healing is a shadow, a miniature, of the coming millennium.

4. The Pharisees' Rejection of the King

Verse 34 says, "But the Pharisees said, He casts out the demons by the ruler of the demons." The ruler of the demons is the Devil, who is called Beelzebub (12:24). This blaspheming word by the Pharisees is a stronger continuation of the rejection of the heavenly King by the leaders of Judaism.

THE ENLARGEMENT OF THE KING'S MINISTRY
(1)

Now we come to the enlargement of the King's ministry (9:35—10:15).

I. THE NEED FOR SHEPHERDING AND REAPING

The continuation of the King's ministry in chapter nine brought forth another situation that enabled Him to reveal Himself. After the healing of the woman with the flow of blood, the raising of the young girl, and the healing of the two blind men and the dumb man, the Lord is revealed as the Shepherd and as the Lord of the harvest.

A. The King Traveling
through All the Cities and Villages,
Teaching, Preaching, and Healing

Verse 35 says, "And Jesus went about all the cities and the villages, teaching in their synagogues and preaching the gospel of the kingdom and healing every disease and every sickness." Every disease and every sickness in this verse signify spiritual illness.

B. The King Being Moved with Compassion
Concerning the People
as Sheep without a Shepherd

Verse 36 says, "And seeing the crowds, He was moved with compassion concerning them, because they were harassed and cast away as sheep not having a shepherd." This indicates that the heavenly King considered the Israelites as sheep and Himself as the Shepherd. When Christ came to the Jews the first time, they were like lepers, paralytics, demon-possessed, and all manner of pitiful persons, because they had no shepherd to care for them. Now in His kingly ministry for the establishing of His heavenly kingdom, He ministered to them not only as a Physician, but also as a Shepherd, as prophesied in Isaiah 53:6 and 40:11.

In the midst of the situation portrayed in verse 36 the Lord revealed Himself as the Shepherd. This is a further revelation. He is not only the Physician and the Bridegroom, but also the Shepherd. Without the further continuation of His ministry, this environment would not have been produced. Therefore, we see once again that in order to have Christ revealed to us, we must have the ministry to bring forth a certain environment. The great feast attended by tax collectors and sinners was an excellent opportunity for the Lord to reveal Himself as the Physician. Furthermore, the environment when so many were rejoicing and feasting together gave the Lord the opportunity to reveal Himself as the Bridegroom, the new cloth, the new wine, and the new wineskin. Then in verse 36 when the Lord was moved with compassion because of having seen the people harassed and cast away as sheep not having a shepherd, He could reveal Himself as the Shepherd.

C. The Harvest Being Vast But the Workers Being Few

In verse 37 the Lord said to His disciples, "The harvest indeed is vast, but the workers are few." The heavenly King considered the people not only as sheep, but also as the harvest. The sheep needed shepherding, and the harvest needed reaping. Although the leaders of the nation of Israel rejected the heavenly King, there was still a good number among the people that needed reaping.

D. Beseeching the Lord of the Harvest to Thrust Out Workers into His Harvest

The King of the heavenly kingdom considered Himself not only the Shepherd of the sheep, but also the Lord of the harvest. His kingdom is established with things of life that can grow and multiply. He is the Lord who owns this crop. We are both the flock and the crop. The flock is made up of living animals and the crop of living vegetation. Under the hand of the Lord Jesus, nothing is lifeless. He does not care for lifeless things, but for things that are living. Everything under the care of this heavenly King is living.

We all need to see a vision of the Lord Jesus as the Lord of the harvest. In verse 38 the Lord told us to beseech the Lord of the harvest that He may thrust out workers into His harvest. Firstly, in His economy, God has a plan to accomplish. Then His economy requires His people to beseech, to pray, for it. In answering their prayer, He will accomplish what they have prayed concerning His plan. Many times when we sense the need for workers, we sound out the call for help. But from now on, whenever you sense the need for workers, you must firstly pray to the Lord of the harvest, saying, "Lord, here is Your harvest. You are the Lord of the harvest. We call on You to thrust out some reapers. Lord, send more reapers into Your harvest." Praying like this will make a difference. To pray like this means that we have seen a vision that our Christ, the kingly One, the Shepherd, is the Lord of the harvest. Whenever you pray that the Lord would send reapers into His harvest, you honor Him very much. How different this is from inviting people to help you in your work! When you do that, you do not honor Christ as the Lord of the harvest. Rather, it is a matter of your work, not of His harvest. You become the master of that work, and He is not considered as the Lord of the harvest. Therefore, we need to call on Him and say, "Lord, You are the Lord of the harvest. The work in this field is Yours, and this harvest is Your crop. We call on You for Your crop. Lord, send Your reapers."

Recently, a brother told me that the church life in his locality was wonderful and that I should come there for a visit. Although this brother's talk was nice, it was rather natural. It had no vision whatever. Instead of inviting me, this brother should have prayed, "Lord, the church in my locality is the harvest of the heavenly King. Lord of the harvest, I call on You to send reapers." Is the church in your locality your harvest or His harvest? Since it is the Lord's harvest, you have no right to invite others to go there to labor. To do this is to infringe upon the Lord's honor. In doing this you fail to recognize that you are not the Lord. He is the Lord of the harvest. The only thing you can do is to ask Him to thrust out reapers. We need further revelation regarding this aspect of the Lord.

I believe that the twelve disciples prayed according to the Lord's word. Although the Bible does not tell us this, I believe that they did pray. It is a principle in the Bible that, whenever you pray to the Lord for something, the Lord will send you to accomplish that for which you have prayed. The twelve disciples prayed for the Lord of the harvest to send out reapers, and the Lord answered their prayer by sending them out. Whoever prays will be the one sent. For example, you may pray to the Lord regarding the shortage of elders. (However, do not pray according to your ambition, lest the Lord not answer your prayer.) You may simply pray, "Lord, there is the need of elders." After a certain period of time, the Lord may say, "How about you?" This is the principle. The twelve prayed, and eventually the twelve were sent out.

II. THE APPOINTMENT OF THE TWELVE APOSTLES

In 10:1-4 we have the appointment of the twelve apostles. Prior to chapter ten the Lord carried out His kingly ministry alone. But beginning in this chapter the twelve apostles were added for the enlarging, the spread, of the ministry.

A. Giving Them Authority to Cast Out Demons and to Heal Diseases

Verse 1 says, "And calling His twelve disciples to Him, He gave them authority over unclean spirits, so that they should cast them out and heal every disease and every sickness." The authority here to cast out unclean spirits and heal diseases is a foretaste of the power of the coming age (Heb. 6:5), that is, of the millennium, in which all demons will be cast out and all diseases healed (Isa. 35:5-6).

B. Pairing Them Two by Two

In verses 2 through 4 the names of the twelve apostles are given. An apostle is a sent one. Now the twelve disciples (v. 1) were to be sent, thus becoming the twelve apostles. In sending out the twelve apostles, the Lord arranged them in pairs: Simon Peter and Andrew, James and John, Philip and Bartholomew, Thomas and Matthew, James the son of Alphaeus and Thaddaeus, and Simon the Cananaean and Judas Iscariot. We need to be impressed with this principle. We all must be paired. None of us, especially the young people, should go anywhere by ourselves. We need another one to match us. Look at your eyes, ears, nostrils, lips, shoulders, arms, hands, legs, and feet: your body is arranged in pairs. Whenever you are burdened by the Lord to go to a certain place, do not go by yourself. Rather, go in pairs. If you do not have another one to match you, you will miss the blessing. In order to receive the blessing, you must be paired. This is not my opinion; it is the Lord's economy.

Hence, we all must learn the lesson to be paired, to be matched with others.

Mark and Luke list Matthew before Thomas (Mark 3:18; Luke 6:15), but Matthew, the writer of this book, lists himself after Thomas. This shows his humility. In verse 3 Matthew specifically designates himself as the tax collector, remembering his salvation, perhaps with gratitude. Even a despised and sinful tax collector could become an apostle of the King of the heavenly kingdom. What a salvation!

Simon the Cananaean was paired with Judas Iscariot, the one who betrayed the Lord. "Cananaean" comes from the Hebrew *kanna,* zealous, referring to a Galilean sect known as the Zealots, not to the land of Canaan (see Luke 6:15; Acts 1:13). Iscariot is a Greek word, probably from the Hebrew, which means a man of Kerioth. Kerioth is in Judah (Josh. 15:25). Thus, Judas was the only apostle from Judea; all the rest were Galileans.

III. THE WAY TO SPREAD THE GOSPEL OF THE KINGDOM
TO THE HOUSE OF ISRAEL

A. The King Sending the Twelve Apostles
Only to the House of Israel

In 10:5-15 we have the way to spread the gospel of the kingdom to the house of Israel. In verses 5 and 6 we see that the Lord Jesus charged the twelve apostles not to go into the way of the nations or into a city of the Samaritans, but only to "the lost sheep of the house of Israel." The nations were the Gentiles, and the Samaritans were a mixture of Gentiles with Jews (2 Kings 17:24; Ezra 4:10; John 4:9).

The twelve apostles were sent to the house of Israel and were charged not to go to the nations nor to the Samaritans. Those who are sent by the Lord have the authority of the Lord. When the Lord sent out the twelve, He gave them authority. Whenever we are sent, we must believe that the Lord's authority is with us.

B. Preaching that the Kingdom of the Heavens Has Drawn Near

Verse 7 says, "And as you go, preach, saying, The kingdom of the heavens has drawn near." Even by this time the kingdom of the heavens had not come, but had only drawn near.

C. Exercising the Authority of the Kingdom

As they were sent out to preach the kingdom of the heavens, the apostles were authorized to heal the sick, raise the dead, cleanse the lepers, and cast out demons (v. 8). They should exercise such an authority in their commission.

D. The Worker Being Worthy of His Food

In verses 9 and 10 the Lord said, "Do not acquire gold, nor even silver, nor even copper in your belts, nor a bag for the way, nor even two tunics, nor even sandals, nor even a staff; for the worker is worthy of his food." The twelve apostles (sent to the house of Israel, not to the Gentiles), as workers worthy of their food, did not need to bring their living necessities with them. (However, the Lord's workers sent to the Gentiles should take nothing from the Gentiles — 3 John 7.) This principle was changed when the Lord was fully rejected by the house of Israel (Luke 22:35-38).

E. Bringing Peace to the House Where They Stay

Verses 12 and 13 say, "And as you enter into the house, greet it; and if the house indeed be worthy, let your peace come upon it; but if it is not worthy, let your peace return to you." When the Lord sends us, we have the presence, the peace. Wherever we are sent, the authority, the presence of the Lord, and the peace follow us. This is the reason the Lord told the apostles to look for one worthy of their peace. He seemed to be saying, "Look to see who is worthy of your peace. If they don't receive you, your peace will go with you when you go." This means a great deal. To receive the

Lord's sent ones, the apostles, means to receive the presence of the Lord and the peace. To reject them means to reject the presence of the Lord and the peace. It is not an insignificant matter to be sent by the Lord, for as sent ones, we become the Lord's representatives. We have His authority, His presence, and His peace. Wherever we go, we bring these things with us. Whoever receives us will have the Lord's presence and the Lord's blessing. It is in this way that the ministry of the King is spread.

F. The Judgment upon the Rejecting People

In verses 14 and 15 the Lord said, "And whoever does not receive you nor hear your words, as you go out of that house or city, shake off the dust of your feet. Truly I say to you, It will be more tolerable for the land of Sodom and Gomorrah in the day of judgment than for that city." This indicates that the punishment of God's judgment is in varying degrees. To reject the Lord's apostles and their words will cause more punishment than the sin of Sodom and Gomorrah.

This is the way the ministry of the King is enlarged. It has spread from the traveling of One to the traveling of the twelve. This spread of the ministry will produce another environment for a further revelation of the heavenly King. We shall see this environment and this revelation in chapters ten and twelve. We thank the Lord for His ministry, for the continuation of His ministry, and especially for the spread of His ministry. It is through the ministry that the environment is brought forth for the revelation of the kingly Christ.

LIFE-STUDY OF MATTHEW

THE ENLARGEMENT OF THE KING'S MINISTRY

(2)

The Lord's word in Matthew 10 is a word spoken to the sent ones. In 10:16—11:1 many things are brought to the surface. By seeing these things, we shall be able to understand the situation in which we find ourselves today.

IV. PERSECUTION AND THE WAY TO MEET IT

In verses 16 and 17 the Lord predicted the persecution that would come from Judaism upon His apostles. The heavenly King's prediction here concerning the persecution of His apostles by Judaism indicated that the kingdom He was establishing through His apostles' preaching would be rejected by Judaism. This also proves that His kingdom is not earthly but heavenly.

A. The Apostles Sent as Sheep into the Midst of Wolves

Verse 16 says, "Behold, I send you forth as sheep in the midst of wolves; become therefore prudent as serpents and guileless as doves." The Lord's apostles, as sheep, not as serpents, in the midst of wolves, need to be prudent as serpents to escape the hurt of the wolves, but guileless as doves not to hurt others.

B. Delivered to the Sanhedrin and Scourged in the Synagogues

The Lord's word reveals that the whole world is under the usurping hand of the enemy and thus opposes God's economy. The entire world, whether the Jewish world or the Gentile world, opposes God's kingdom. Verse 17 says,

"But beware of men; for they will deliver you up to Sanhedrins, and in their synagogues they will scourge you." This verse indicates that even the Jewish nation had been fully taken over by God's enemy. When the Lord Jesus was on earth, this nation belonged to God in name, but not in actuality. Therefore, in verse 17 the Lord spoke of persecution coming from the Sanhedrin and the synagogues. The Sanhedrin was the highest council among the children of Israel. The Sanhedrin's function was to see that the Jews followed the law of the Old Testament. The synagogue was a place where the Word of God was taught to the children of Israel. It is very significant that the Lord exposed the Sanhedrin and the synagogues as being opposed to God's economy. He said that His apostles, His sent ones, would be delivered up to Sanhedrins and scourged in the synagogues. A synagogue is obviously not a theater, a casino, or an idol temple. In a sense, it was a holy place, a place where the holy Word of God was taught to God's people. Nevertheless, the Lord said that the apostles of the King of the heavens would be scourged even in the synagogues. By this we see what an evil thing the synagogue had become. Although the Jews went there to learn the Word of God, those in the synagogues persecuted the apostles of the heavenly King. Furthermore, the Sanhedrin, organized with the intention of overseeing the children of Israel in the matter of keeping the Scriptures, was a place that would also oppose the apostles of the heavenly King.

The situation is the same today. If the ancient Sanhedrin and synagogues opposed the King's sent ones, then how about the system of today's religion? If we are truly the ones sent by the heavenly King, we shall be opposed by today's religious organizations just as the apostles were opposed by Judaism. In ancient times the apostles were persecuted not primarily by the Gentiles, but by the so-called holy people in the Sanhedrin and in the synagogues. In our experience throughout the years, nearly all the persecution, rumors, opposition, and attack have come from the religious organizations, not from the Gentiles.

According to verse 16, the Lord Jesus likened those in the Sanhedrin and in the synagogues to wolves, saying that He was sending out His apostles "as sheep in the midst of wolves." Can you believe that those in the Sanhedrin and in the synagogues, the ones who expounded and taught the holy Word of God and exhorted others to obey it, were wolves? If the Lord Jesus had not said this Himself, I certainly would not believe it. Rather, I would say, "Those in the Sanhedrin and in the synagogues may have made some mistakes, but they are certainly God's people, for daily they talk about the Scriptures and teach people to fear God, to worship God, to honor God, and to glorify God. They're not that bad. How can you say that they are wolves?" But the Lord Jesus called them wolves. At that time, the wolves spoken of in verse 16 were those in the Sanhedrins and in the synagogues mentioned in verse 17.

Saul of Tarsus studied at the feet of Gamaliel, a great Bible teacher, "a teacher of the law, honored by all the people" (Acts 22:3; 5:34). Gamaliel was one of the leaders in the Sanhedrin. Was Gamaliel for God? Yes, he was. He feared God and he was for God, but he was in an environment that was absolutely against God's economy. He was part of a system, the Sanhedrin, that opposed God. It has been the same down through the centuries until today. No matter how much certain ones are for God, they are in a system, an organization, which is against God's economy. In Revelation 2:9 and 3:9 the Lord Jesus spoke of "the synagogue of Satan." In Matthew 10 the Lord indicated that there were wolves in the synagogues, and in Revelation He spoke of the synagogue of Satan. This indicated that the synagogues had become satanic.

The Lord Jesus did not come firstly to the Gentile world. He came to a nation that was supposed to be the holy people of God. This nation had the holy Scriptures, the holy city, the holy temple, the holy priesthood, and the holy sacrifices. He came to this nation with the purpose of establishing the kingdom of the heavens. It seems that there should have been no difficulty whatever. But when this heavenly King was sending out His apostles for the spread of His ministry, He warned them that He was sending them out as sheep in the midst of wolves. The Lord seemed to be saying, "Those in the Sanhedrin, the ones who care for the holy Scriptures, will persecute you, and those in the synagogue, the ones who teach the Word of God, will scourge you. Be careful! They are not the holy people of God—they are wolves. They are not for God; they are against Him." Suppose you were among those Jews sent out by the heavenly King and you heard that those in the Sanhedrin and in the synagogues were wolves. Would you not be shocked? Nevertheless, this is exactly what the Lord was saying here. The Lord did not say that the soldiers in the Roman army were wolves, but that those in the Sanhedrin and in the synagogues, those handling the Word of God and teaching it to God's people, were wolves. Throughout the centuries, the situation has been the same in principle.

In 9:36 the Lord likened the people to sheep. Among the children of Israel, there were both sheep and wolves. These wolves were in the Sanhedrin and in the synagogues. They were cultured wolves, civilized wolves, religious wolves. Those wolves knew the Bible rather well. Although they could quote verses and worship God according to the Scriptures, the Lord Jesus did not consider them as sheep, but as wolves. Therefore, at the time of Matthew 10, there was a complicated situation among the children of Israel, for the sheep and the wolves were mixed together. There was no problem as long as the sheep went along with the wolves. However, the Shepherd came and sent out the undershepherds to collect the sheep. If we read these chapters carefully, we shall see that the gathering of the sheep is the reaping of the harvest. All the sheep, the harvest, were scattered among the wolves and mixed in with the wolves. When the sheep desired to go with the undershepherds sent by the Shepherd, the wolves would rise up and say, "What! You are proselytizing. You are stirring up the sheep!" In this way the wolf nature is exposed, and the wolves attack the undershepherds. Hence, the Lord said that, as sheep in the midst of wolves, His sent ones must be prudent as serpents and guileless as doves. When the wolves attack, the sent ones must be prudent as serpents to escape. At the same time, they should also be as harmless as doves.

C. Brought before Governors and Kings as a Testimony for the Heavenly King's Sake

Verse 18 says, "And you shall be brought before governors and kings for My sake, for a testimony to them and to the nations." No doubt this refers to the Gentiles. Thus, the Lord indicated that God's kingdom would be opposed not only by the Jewish religious world but also by the Gentile secular world. Eventually, the apostles were brought before the Roman governors and kings. They were persecuted, and they became a testimony. This reveals that both the religious world and the political world are the same in opposing the kingdom of the heavens, for both are under the usurping hand of God's enemy. The intention of the heavenly King is to establish His kingdom on earth within the territory of religion and politics. This will certainly arouse opposition and persecution.

In verses 19 and 20 the Lord said, "But when they deliver you up, do not be anxious about how or what you shall speak; for it shall be given to you in that hour what you shall speak; for you are not the ones speaking, but the Spirit of your Father is the One speaking in you." The apostles have not only the authority of the heavenly King (v. 1), but also the Spirit of their heavenly Father. The King's authority deals with the unclean spirits and diseases; the Father's Spirit deals with the opposers' persecution. The Lord was charging His sent ones not to speak from themselves whenever they met persecution. He seemed to be saying, "Don't be anxious, and don't talk from yourselves. The Spirit of your Father is with you." As long as we have the Spirit of the Lord, we have the presence of the Lord. The presence of the Lord here is the Spirit for speaking. We should learn to face persecution not in ourselves, but learn to turn to our spirit and trust the indwelling Spirit. We must believe that the Father's Spirit is with us and that He will deal with the opposers and persecutors. This is not an easy thing to learn. We must face opposition and confront attack, not in ourselves, but by turning to our spirit where the Spirit of God dwells. We must trust in Him, let Him lead us, and let Him do the speaking.

D. Hated by the Relatives

The Lord also told His sent ones that they would be hated by their relatives. Verse 21 says, "And brother will deliver up brother to death, and father his child, and children will rise up against parents and put them to death." To be the heavenly King's apostles for the preaching of the gospel of the kingdom, the sent ones must suffer the breaking of the closest human ties.

In verse 22 the Lord continued, "And you will be hated by all because of My name; but he who endures to the end, he shall be saved." To be saved here does not mean to be saved from hell. It may include being saved from those who hate, but eventually it means to be saved into the manifestation of the kingdom of the heavens, a reward to the overcoming believers. It is to be saved from dispensational punishment during the millennium. This differs from eternal salvation as revealed in Ephesians 2:8.

E. Fleeing from City to City

Verse 23 says, "And when they persecute you in this city, flee into another; for truly I say to you, you shall by no means complete the cities of Israel until the Son of Man comes." This word was not fulfilled by the twelve apostles' preaching before Christ's crucifixion. It will not be fulfilled until the great tribulation (24:21). What is predicted in verses 17 through 23 is very similar to 24:9-13. Here the heavenly King sent the apostles to preach the gospel of the kingdom to the Jews. After His resurrection, He sent His apostles to preach the gospel to the Gentiles. After the fullness of the salvation of the Gentiles, He will send His apostles to preach the gospel of the kingdom to the Jews again. At that time this word will be fulfilled, and He will come.

F. Not Above Their Teacher

In verse 24 the King said to His sent ones, "A disciple is not above his teacher, nor a slave above his lord." According to the context, the word here means that in suffering persecution His apostles cannot be above Him, because His persecution was to the uttermost.

Verse 25 says, "It is sufficient that he become as his teacher, and the slave as his lord. If they have called the master of the house Beelzebub, how much more those of his household!" Beelzebub means "the lord of the flies," the name of the god of the Ekronites (2 Kings 1:2). It was changed in contempt by the Jews to Baalzebel, which means lord of the dunghill, and used for the ruler of the demons (12:24, 27; Mark 3:22; Luke 11:15, 18-19). The Pharisees, the leading ones of the Jewish religion, reviled the heavenly King by saying that He cast out demons by the ruler of demons (9:34). This most blasphemous name expressed their strongest contempt and rejection.

G. Not Fearing the Persecutors but Preaching the Heavenly King's Message on the Housetop

In verses 26 and 27 the King told His sent ones not to fear the persecutors, but rather to speak in the light and to preach on the housetops. In verse 28 He said, "And do not fear those who kill the body, but are not able to kill the soul; but fear rather Him Who is able to destroy both soul and body in Gehenna." God is the only One who is able to destroy both soul and body in Gehenna. This word implies that if the apostles sent by the Lord fail in the suffering of persecution, they will be disciplined by God. This will transpire in the coming age, after the judgment at the judgment seat of Christ, when believers will receive reward or punishment (2 Cor. 5:10; Rev. 22:12).

In verses 32 and 33 the Lord said, "Everyone therefore who shall confess Me before men, I also will confess him before My Father Who is in the heavens; but whoever shall deny Me before men, I also will deny him before My Father Who is in the heavens." This word was spoken by the heavenly King to His apostles who were sent by Him to preach the gospel of the kingdom. He foretold that they would be persecuted (vv. 17, 21-23). If anyone under persecution denies Him, He will deny him. This will transpire at His coming back (16:27). To be denied or confessed by Him at that time determines whether or not His apostles are worthy to enter the kingdom of the heavens in the coming age as a reward. Here the King seemed to be saying, "If you are afraid of this persecution and do not confess My name before the persecutors, I will not confess your name before the Father when I come back and the millennium begins." This means that such a person will be put into the outer darkness (25:30) and will not participate in the manifestation of the kingdom.

V. THE KING'S DISTURBANCE
AND THE WAY OF THE CROSS TO FOLLOW HIM
A. The Heavenly King Coming
Not to Bring Peace, but a Sword on the Earth

In verse 34 the Lord Jesus said, "Do not suppose that I came to bring peace on the earth; I did not come to bring peace, but a sword." The whole earth is under Satan's usurpation (1 John 5:19). The heavenly King came to call some out from his usurpation. This certainly aroused Satan's opposition. Satan instigated the people under his usurpation to fight against the heavenly King's called ones. Thus, the King's coming did not bring peace, but a sword. In order for the kingdom of the heavens to be established, there must be a confrontation between the kingdom of the heavens and the kingdom of the world. These two kingdoms cannot co-exist. Because the heavenly King is establishing His kingdom on earth, warfare between these two kingdoms is inevitable.

In verses 35 and 36 the Lord said, "For I came to set a man against his father and a daughter against her mother and a daughter-in-law against her mother-in-law; and a man's enemies shall be those of his household." The fighting instigated by the usurping Satan against the heavenly King's called ones is waged even in their household. The heavenly called ones are attacked in their homes by their kindred who remain under the evil one's usurping hand. When some are attracted and caught by the heavenly King and decide to follow Him, some in their family may be instigated by Satan to fight against them, even to kill them.

Let me tell you about a brother who was persecuted by his unbelieving wife. This man had an excellent job with the customs office of the government, and he was quite wealthy. After he was brought to the Lord, his wife began to persecute him. One night, this brother invited several of us to his home for dinner. Whenever her husband invited his colleagues from work to dinner, the wife was very happy and prepared the best food. But now as a believer her husband had invited some of the church people to their home. On the night he invited us, she purposely did not cook. Rather, she set cold leftovers on the table. The brother looked at us with tears in his eyes. We looked at him and said, "Praise the Lord! This dinner is delicious. Let us all eat." Then we proceeded to eat all those leftovers. This was an example of his wife's persecution.

Those sent by the Lord must realize that persecution awaits them. The Lord Jesus does not leave us in darkness. Rather, he makes the whole situation very clear. The Jewish nation is full of opposers, and even the relatives of the sent ones will rise up in opposition; they will even kill the followers of the heavenly King.

B. The Way to Follow the Heavenly King

1. Not Loving Relatives above Him

In verses 37 through 39 we have the way to follow the heavenly King. In verse 37 the Lord said, "He who loves father or mother above Me is not worthy of Me; and he who loves son or daughter above Me is not worthy of Me." Our love must be absolute for the Lord. In our love nothing should be above Him. He is the One absolutely worthy of our love, and we must be worthy of Him.

2. Taking the Cross and Following after Him

Verse 38 continues, "And he who does not take his cross and follow after Me is not worthy of Me." Christ was crucified by taking the Father's will (26:39, 42). When He was baptized, He was counted as crucified, and from that time He bore His cross to do the will of God. His called ones were identified with Him. He asked them to take their cross and follow after Him, that is, to take the will of God by putting themselves aside. This demanded that they, at any cost, give their love first to Him that they might be worthy of Him.

3. Losing the Soul-life for His Sake

Verse 39 says, "He who finds his soul-life shall lose it, and he who loses his soul-life for My sake shall find it." To find the soul-life is to allow the soul to have its enjoyment and not to suffer. To lose the soul-life is to cause the soul to suffer the loss of its enjoyment. If the heavenly King's followers allow their soul to have its enjoyment in this age, they will cause their soul to suffer the loss of its enjoyment in the coming kingdom age. If they allow their soul to suffer the loss of its enjoyment in this age for the King's sake, they will cause their soul to have its enjoyment in the coming kingdom age, that is, to share the King's joy in ruling over the earth (25:21, 23).

VI. IDENTIFICATION WITH THE KING

A. Receiving the Heavenly King's Apostles Being the Receiving of Him

In 10:40—11:1 we have the matter of identification with the heavenly King. Verse 40 says, "He who receives you receives Me, and he who receives Me receives Him Who sent Me." The apostles sent by the heavenly King, having been entrusted with His authority (v. 1) and peace (v. 13) and having been indwelt by the Spirit of the Father (v. 20) and identified with the King in His suffering (vv. 22, 24-25) and death (vv. 21, 34-39), were one with Him. Thus, he who receives them receives Him. To participate in such an identification with the heavenly King requires us to love Him above all, at any cost, and to follow Him by taking the narrow way of the cross, as revealed in verses 37 through 39. Not only do the sent ones have the King's authority and peace and the Spirit of the Father, but they are also one with the King and are identified with Him. To receive the King's sent ones means to receive the King Himself, because the sent ones are identified with the King. This is an encouragement to those who are sent. In the Lord's recovery we have the authority, the peace, the Spirit, and the identification with our King. We are one with Him. Whoever receives us receives the King, and whoever rejects us rejects the King. This is not an insignificant matter. It is very serious. We all need to have the assurance that we have the authority, the peace, the Spirit, and the identification. All this is for the spreading of the King's ministry. The King is still spreading His ministry today, and we are His sent ones with the authority, the peace, the Spirit, and the identification.

B. The Reward of Receiving a Prophet or a Righteous Man

Verse 41 says, "He who receives a prophet in the name of a prophet shall receive a prophet's reward, and he who receives a righteous man in the name of a righteous man shall receive a righteous man's reward." A prophet is one who speaks for God and speaks forth God. A righteous man is one who seeks after righteousness, who does righteousness, and who is persecuted for righteousness for the kingdom (5:6, 10, 20; 6:1). The heavenly King was such a Prophet sent by God (Deut. 18:15) and such a righteous man (Acts 3:14). His apostles sent by Him, having been identified with Him, were also such prophets and righteous men. Hence, whoever receives them shall receive a reward. One who receives a prophet is joined to the prophet's word, and one who receives a righteous man is joined to the righteousness of the righteous man. Thus, such a one shall receive a reward as the prophet and as the righteous man.

The King's sent ones go out as prophets and as righteous men. The prophet always comes with the word of God, and the righteous man always comes with righteousness. If you receive the prophet, you will receive the word of God; and if you receive the righteous man, you will receive his righteousness. How good it is to have the word of God and righteousness! This will help us to be ushered into both the reality of the kingdom today and also the manifestation of the kingdom in the future.

C. The Reward for Giving a Cup of Cold Water to a Little Disciple

Verse 42 says, "And whoever gives to one of these little ones only a cup of cold water to drink in the name of a disciple, truly I say to you, he shall by no means lose his reward." This reward will be given in the coming age (Luke 14:14).

VII. THE HEAVENLY KING GOING TO TEACH AND PREACH IN THE CITIES

Matthew 11:1 says, "And it came to pass when Jesus had finished instructing His twelve disciples, He departed from there to teach and to preach in their cities." After the Lord appointed the twelve and sent them to spread the preaching of the kingdom, He Himself went on in His ministry to teach and preach in the cities.

LIFE-STUDY OF MATTHEW

THE RESULT OF THE KING'S MINISTRY

In Matthew 11 we see the result of the King's ministry. The record of chapter ten indicates that both the King's ministry and the enlargement of His ministry by the twelve apostles were rejected. In chapter ten the Lord told the apostles that they would be persecuted and hated, even by the so-called holy people in the Sanhedrin and in the synagogues. He warned them that they would be persecuted even by their relatives. In chapter eleven we see that three ministries are rejected: the ministry of John the Baptist, the ministry of the King, and the ministry of the King's sent ones, the twelve apostles. John was rejected, the Lord Jesus was rejected, and according to His charge to the twelve apostles, their ministry also was to be rejected. In chapter eleven we see how the King deals with this rejection. The main point in this chapter is how we should face rejection.

I. STRENGTHENING HIS IMPRISONED FORERUNNER

A. The Imprisoned Forerunner
Sending His Disciples
to Provoke the King

In verses 2 and 3 we see that the patience of John the Baptist, the King's rejected forerunner, was exhausted. Thus, John "sent by his disciples and said to Him, Are You the coming One, or should we expect someone else?" John the Baptist's word here does not mean that he was in doubt concerning Christ. He questioned Christ in this way in order to provoke Him to deliver him. He knew that Christ was the coming One, and he had strongly recommended

Him to the people (John 1:26-36). After that, he was put into prison (Matt. 4:12) and waited, expecting that Christ would do something to deliver him. However, although Christ did much to help others, He did nothing for him. For this reason, John was in danger of being stumbled (v. 6). Hence, he sent his disciples to Christ with such a stirring question. There was no doubt in John's mind that Christ was the Messiah. He did not send his disciples to ask the Lord whether or not He was the Messiah. He was trying to provoke Christ to rescue him from prison. But it is very difficult to stir up the Lord Jesus. The more you try to provoke Him, the colder He becomes to you. You can never stir Him up by provoking Him. If you try to do this, He will become less willing to do something for you.

B. The Heavenly King's Answer

In verses 4 through 6 we have the Lord's answer to John. Verses 4 and 5 say, "Go, report to John what you hear and see: the blind receive sight, and the lame walk, the lepers are cleansed, and the deaf hear, and the dead are raised, and the poor have the gospel preached to them." The Lord mentioned the blind receiving sight first, because there was no such miracle in the Old Testament. By this, He gave clear evidence to John that no other could have done such a miracle but the Messiah (Isa. 35:5). In spiritual significance, the blind receiving sight is also first. In the Lord's salvation, He firstly opens our eyes (Acts 26:18); then we can receive Him and walk to follow Him. The lame signify those who cannot walk in God's way. After being saved, they can walk by new life (9:5-6; John 5:8-9). The cleansed lepers signify those who have been saved from their rebellion (leprosy) to become the kingdom people. The deaf signify those who cannot hear God. After being saved, they can hear the Lord's voice (John 10:27). The dead signify those who are dead in sins (Eph. 2:1, 5), unable to contact God. After being regenerated, with their regenerated spirit they can fellowship with God. The poor signify all the ones without Christ, without God, who have no hope in the world (Eph. 2:12). Upon receiving the gospel, they are made rich in Christ (2 Cor. 8:9; Eph. 3:8). Verse 6 says, "And blessed is he who shall not be stumbled in Me." This word implies that John the Baptist was in danger of being stumbled in the Lord, because the Lord did not act on his behalf according to his way. Here the Lord encouraged him to take the way the Lord had ordained for him that he might be blessed. This blessing has much to do with the participation in the kingdom of the heavens.

In these verses the Lord seemed to be saying to John, "There is no doubt that I am the Messiah. My being the Messiah does not depend on whether or not I do something for you. I have healed the blind, the deaf, and the sick. I have even raised the dead. But I don't choose to do anything for you. Do not expect anything from Me. I will leave you in prison until you are beheaded. Blessed is the one who is not stumbled in Me." In the Lord's recovery we need to learn this lesson. Whenever the Lord does something positive for us, we are excited. But many times the Lord will not do anything for us. The reason He did nothing to rescue John from prison was that if John had been released from prison his ministry would have been in competition with the Lord's ministry. John's imprisonment was arranged sovereignly of the Lord to terminate his ministry, which was the ministry of recommendation. After the recommending work had been done, his ministry should be terminated. Therefore, God sovereignly terminated John's ministry by imprisoning him.

II. APPRAISING HIS FORERUNNER

The questions John's disciples asked the Lord might have given the Lord's apostles a negative impression of John. Thus, in verses 7 through 15 the Lord publicly appraised His forerunner. Concealed within the Lord's reply to John was an indication of John's weakness. However, His words to the crowds concerning John testified publicly for John. Remember that the first four disciples were brought in through John's ministry of recommendation. John had declared, "Behold the Lamb of God," and John and Andrew followed the Lord Jesus. Eventually they brought James and Peter to the Lord as well. Thus, the first four disciples were brought to Christ through the ministry of John the Baptist.

A. Not a Reed in the Wilderness Shaken by the Wind or a Man Dressed in Soft Clothing

In His public appraisal of John the Baptist, the Lord Jesus vindicated him. In verse 7 the Lord said, "What did you go out into the wilderness to see? A reed shaken by the wind?" A reed signifies a weak and fragile person (12:20; 1 Kings 14:15). When John the Baptist was testifying for Christ in the wilderness, he was not like a reed, a weak person. However, now in prison he was somewhat like a reed shaken by the wind. The Lord Jesus is wise, kind, and merciful. If we had been the Lord, we would have been offended by John. Because the Lord knew that John was somewhat weakened, He encouraged him. He seemed to be saying, "John, be careful. It seems that you are at least somewhat weakened concerning Me." This was the meaning of the Lord's word to John. But when He spoke to the crowds and to the other disciples, He vindicated John, indicating that he was not a weak, timid person, but a strong witness. In verse 8 the Lord asked, "But what did you go out to see? A man dressed in soft clothing? Behold, those who wear soft clothing are in the houses of kings." After testifying boldly for Christ in the wilderness, John the Baptist became weak when he had been imprisoned for a time. Some might think that he would desire to wear soft clothing in the houses of kings. But the Lord testified that he was neither a reed shaken by the wind nor a man dressed in soft clothing.

B. Much More Than a Prophet

Verse 9 says, "But why did you go out? To see a prophet? Yes, I say to you, and much more than a prophet." The Lord testified that John was much more than a prophet. He was a great prophet, greater than all the prophets who had gone before him.

C. Being a Messenger
before the Heavenly King's Face,
Preparing the Way for Him

John was sent by God as a messenger before Christ to prepare the way for Him (11:10) that the people might be turned to God and receive the heavenly King and the heavenly kingdom. His ministry was to pave the way for the kingdom.

D. Greater Than All Who Were Born before
the Kingdom of the Heavens,
but Smaller Than He Who Is
in the Kingdom of the Heavens

In verse 11 the Lord says, "Truly I say to you, Among those born of women, there has not arisen a greater than John the Baptist; yet he who is smaller in the kingdom of the heavens is greater than he." Although John was greater than all the prophets, he was not in the kingdom of the heavens. Compared to the Old Testament prophets, John was greater; but compared to the New Testament people, he was smaller. John was in a transitory period, greater than those who preceded him, but smaller than those who were to come after him. All the prophets prior to John prophesied only that Christ was coming, but John testified that Christ had come. The prophets were looking forward to Christ, but John saw Christ. Hence, John was greater than all the prophets. Although John saw the incarnated Christ and introduced Him to people, he did not have the resurrected Christ indwelling him. But the kingdom people do. John could only say, "Here is Christ," but the kingdom people can say, "For to me to live is Christ" (Phil. 1:21). Hence, the least in the kingdom of the heavens is greater than he. Whether anyone is greater or lesser depends upon his relationship to Christ. Christ is the deciding factor. The closer anyone is to Christ, the greater he is.

The prophets prophesied concerning the coming of Christ, and John recommended the Christ who had come. The prophets said that Christ was coming, and John said that Christ was there. Although John the Baptist was close to Christ, he was not as close to Him as we are, for we have Christ within us. Christ is in us, and we are in Him. Because Christ is mingled with us, our relationship with Christ is most intimate. We are in Christ, Christ is in us, and we are mingled with Him, even joined to Him. First Corinthians 6:17 says, "He who is joined to the Lord is one spirit." What could be closer than this? This close relationship to Christ makes us greater than all those who preceded us. What a great blessing this is!

We need to realize in what age we are living. Peter, John, and even Paul were in the beginning of the kingdom age, but we are in the closing of this age. Where would you rather be — in the beginning, in the middle, or in the conclusion? Martin Luther was in the middle, but we are neither in the beginning nor in the middle, but at the end. Great men like Martin Luther stood on the shoulders of the early apostles, but now we are on the shoulders of Martin Luther and other great ones. Hence, we are higher than all of them. Even the smallest among us is able to give a strong testimony on being justified by faith both objectively and subjectively. Do not regard this day as an insignificant day.

When I was seeking the Lord fifty years ago, the situation was quite poor. We spent much money on books, and we traveled to see certain people. There is no comparison with the situation of today. Today you are all buried with riches. My only concern is that you do not have the adequate appetite. We are feasting every day. We are not in the transitory period, neither are we in the beginning nor in the middle of the New Testament age; we are in the conclusion of this age. At the conclusion everything is better, higher, and richer. Praise the Lord that we are so close to Christ! Many of the messages you have heard concerning Christ have not been heard by others in the past. Many of you were in Christianity for years. Were you ever told about the all-inclusive Christ? Did you ever hear about eating Jesus? But now we are eating Him and enjoying Him. Thus, we are greater. Do you dare to say that you are greater? According to the principle in the Bible, the later is always the greater. The last will be the first. Because we are the last, we are the greatest.

E. Being Elijah

Verse 14 says, "And if you are willing to receive it, he is Elijah, who is about to come." Malachi 4:5 prophesied that Elijah would come. When John the Baptist was conceived, it was said that he would go before the Lord in the spirit and power of Elijah (Luke 1:17). Hence, in a sense, John may be considered Elijah who was about to come (Matt. 17:10-13). However, the prophecy of Malachi 4:5 will actually be fully fulfilled in the great tribulation, when the real Elijah, one of the two witnesses, will come to strengthen God's people (Rev. 11:3-12).

F. The Prophets and the Law Having Prophesied until John

Verse 13 says, "For all the prophets and the law prophesied until John." This proves that the Old Testament dispensation was terminated by the coming of John.

G. From John until Now, the Kingdom of the Heavens Being Taken by Violence

Verse 12 says, "And from the days of John the Baptist until now, the kingdom of the heavens is taken by violence, and violent men seize it." From the days of John the Baptist until now, the Pharisees had been violently frustrating people from entering the kingdom of the heavens. Hence, those who desired to enter must do so by violence.

H. Ears Needed to Hear This

The word of Christ concerning His forerunner John the Baptist was deeply related to Himself and the heavenly kingdom. It was different from any of the old, traditional teachings. Hence, there was the need for ears to hear it (11:15).

III. REPROACHING THE STUBBORN GENERATION

After the Lord appraised John, He turned to the rejecting generation and reproached them. His appraisal reminded them that John had been rejected. No matter how great John was, he was nonetheless in prison due to the rejection of that generation.

A. The Generation Not Having Responded to the Preaching of the Forerunner or of the Heavenly King

In verses 16 and 17 the Lord said, "But to what shall I liken this generation? It is like children sitting in the market places, who call to the others and say, We have played the flute to you, and you did not dance; we have sung a dirge, and you did not beat the breast." Christ and John the Baptist "played the flute" to preach the gospel of the kingdom, but the Judaizers "did not dance" for the joy of salvation. John and Christ sang "a dirge" to preach repentance, but the Judaizers "did not beat the breast" for the grief of sin. The righteousness of God required them to repent, but they would not obey. The grace of God afforded them salvation, but they would not receive it.

Verses 18 and 19 say, "For John came neither eating nor drinking, and they say, He has a demon. The Son of Man came eating and drinking, and they say, Behold, a gluttonous man and a wine drinker, a friend of tax collectors and sinners. And wisdom was justified by her works." John, coming to bring men to repentance (Mark 1:4) and to cause them to grieve for sin, had no taste for eating and drinking (Luke 1:15-17); whereas Christ, coming to bring salvation to sinners and to cause them to rejoice in it, had the joy of eating and drinking with them (Matt. 9:10-11). The kingdom people, under no regulation, follow the divine wisdom, concentrating their attention upon the indwelling Christ who is their wisdom (1 Cor. 1:30), not upon their outward manner of life.

Because John the Baptist lived in a strange and peculiar way, not eating and drinking in the regular way, the opposers said, "He has a demon"— he is demon-possessed. But they called Christ a gluttonous man and a wine drinker, a friend of tax collectors and sinners. Christ is not only the Savior, but also the friend of sinners, sympathizing with their problems and sensing their griefs.

In verse 19 the Lord said, "And wisdom was justified by her works." Wisdom is Christ (1 Cor. 1:24, 30). Whatever Christ did was done by the wisdom of God, which is Himself. This wisdom was justified, vindicated, by His wise works, His wise deeds. In this verse some authorities read "children" instead of "works." The kingdom people are the children of wisdom, who justify Christ and His deeds and follow Him as their wisdom. Christ is justified by the kingdom people, who know when to eat and when not to eat and who recognize the playing of the flute and the singing of the dirge, knowing when to rejoice and when to repent. We, the kingdom people, the children of wisdom, have the wisdom to discern when to repent and when to rejoice. But the rejecting generation is absolutely foolish. If you play them a song, they do not respond. If you sing them a dirge for repentance, they do not respond to that either. They are stubborn and foolish, and they lack wisdom.

B. The Cities Not Having Repented

Verse 20 says, "Then He began to reproach the cities in which most of His works of power took place, because they did not repent." The Lord proceeded, Woe to you, Chorazin, Bethsaida, and Capernaum, because, in a general way, they had all rejected Him. Of Capernaum He said, "You shall be brought down to Hades." Hades, like Sheol in the Old Testament (Gen. 37:35; Psa. 6:5), is the place where the souls and spirits of the dead are kept (Luke 16:22-23; Acts 2:27). He also said of Capernaum, "It shall be more tolerable for the land of Sodom in the day of judgment than for you" (v. 24). This indicates that Capernaum was worse than Sodom.

IV. ACKNOWLEDGING THE FATHER'S WILL
WITH PRAISE

A. Answering the Father
in His Fellowship with Him
at the Time He Was Reproaching
the Stubborn Generation

Verse 25 opens with the words, "At that time." This refers to the time the Lord was rebuking the cities. Verse 25 says, "At that time Jesus answered and said, I praise You, Father, Lord of the heaven and of the earth." When the Lord was rebuking those leading cities, He answered and said, "I praise You, Father." The word "answered" is very meaningful. Whom did the Lord answer? He answered the Father. While the Lord was rebuking the cities, He fellowshipped with the Father. At that time, answering the Father, He spoke praise to Him.

As the Lord was rebuking the cities, a third party was present. The Lord was the first party, the cities were the second party, and the Father, who was with Him, was the third party. As the Lord was rebuking Chorazin, Bethsaida, and Capernaum, the Father might have asked Him, "Are you happy about this?" Then the Lord answered and said, "I praise You, Father." The Father might have said to the Son, "You are rebuking these cities because they have rejected You. Do You feel good about this?" The Lord immediately answered and praised the Father, the Lord of heaven and earth.

Sometimes a third party is present when you are talking to your wife. You are the first party, your wife is the second party, and the Lord is the third party. Perhaps you say to your wife, "Yesterday, you did not treat me very well; your behavior was poor." As you are saying these words, the third party standing by may ask, "How about it? Do you like it? Yes, your wife was not so good yesterday." At such a time could you say, "I praise You, Father"? This is not an easy thing for us to do. But the Lord Jesus could do it, saying, "I praise You, Father, Lord of heaven and earth. I recognize Your authority. If this were not of You, none of these cities would reject Me. Even their rejection is of You. Father, I take sides with You. This situation is quite good. I tell You that I feel good about it, and I can praise You for it."

B. Acknowledging the Father's Will
with Praise

The Greek word rendered "praise" in verse 25 means to make acknowledgement with praise. The Lord acknowledged the Father's way in carrying out His economy with praise. Although people, instead of responding to His ministry, slandered Him (vv. 16-19), and the leading cities rejected Him (vv. 20-24), He praised the Father, acknowledging the Father's will. He did not seek prosperity in His work, but He sought the Father's will. He would be satisfied and rest, not in man's understanding and welcome, but in the Father's knowing (vv. 26-27). Christ believed that the cities' rejection of Him was of the Father. What about our situation today? When we are rejected, opposed, criticized, attacked, and condemned, could we praise the Father? Have you ever said, "Father, I praise You for the rejection and opposition of my parents and friends"? We need to recognize that such rejection is sovereignly of the Lord and praise Him for it.

In the Lord's address of praise, Father refers to the Father's relationship with Him, the Son; whereas the Lord of the heaven and of the earth refers to God's relationship with the universe. When God's people were defeated by His enemy, He was called the God of heaven (Ezra 5:11-12; Dan. 2:18, 37). But when there was a man standing for God on the earth, He was called the Possessor of heaven and earth (Gen. 14:19, 22). Now, the Lord, as the Son of Man, also called the Father the "Lord of the heaven and of the earth," indicating that He was standing on the earth for God's interest.

1. The Father Having Hidden the Knowledge of the Son and of the Father from the Wise and the Intelligent

Verse 25 also says that the Father has "hidden these things from the wise and intelligent." "These things" refer to the things regarding the knowledge of the Son and of the Father (v. 27). The "wise and intelligent" refer to the people of the three cities condemned in verses 20 through 24, who were wise and intelligent in their own eyes. The Father's will was to hide the knowledge of the Son and the Father from such people.

2. The Father Having Revealed These Things to Babes

The Lord praised the Father for having revealed these things to babes. The word "babes" refers to the disciples, who were the children of wisdom. The Father was pleased to reveal both the Son and the Father to them. To know the Son and the Father is altogether a matter of the Father's sovereignty. In 16:17, after Peter had received the revelation that Jesus was the Christ, the Son of the living God, Jesus said to him, "You are blessed, Simon Bar-jona, because flesh and blood did not reveal this to you, but My Father Who is in the heavens." Thus, knowing the Son is a matter of the Father's revelation.

3. Well Pleasing in the Father's Sight

Verse 26 says, "Yes, Father, for thus it was well pleasing in Your sight." It was well pleasing in the Father's sight that the Son was rejected. The Father was glad to see the Son's rejection. It is very difficult for us to believe this. If your parents and relatives would be one with you regarding the Lord's recovery, you would be excited and praise the Lord. But you must praise the Lord as you are experiencing rejection, saying, "I praise You, Father, because You are the Lord of the heavens and of the earth. All things are of You, and I praise You for this situation."

4. All the Remnant Having Been Delivered to the Son by the Father

Verse 27 says, "All was delivered to Me by My Father." "All" refers to all the remnant whom the Father has given the Son (John 3:27; 6:37, 44, 65; 18:9). This word implies that the wise and intelligent rejected the Son because the Father was not pleased to give them to the Son. However, all the remnant has been delivered to the Son by the Father. Peter, John, James, and Andrew were some of those given to the Son by the Father. The Lord Jesus said, "All that the Father gives Me shall come to Me, and him that comes to Me I will by no means cast out" (John 6:37). It is absolutely of the Father's sovereign mercy that we are in the Lord's recovery today. We need to worship the Father for this. Among the many Christians in the world, we are in the recovery. I have the deep sense within that through the years the Lord's recovery has been in this country, He has been reaping a harvest. He has been gathering a remnant among the Christians. During the years we were in Elden hall in Los Angeles, the Lord was gathering His remnant. Month after month, the Lord brought His remnant from various cities, states, and countries. That was a real gathering of the remnant. All those who were gathered together can testify that we were delivered by the Father. The Lord's recovery is not a com-

mon Christian work; it is the gathering of the Lord's remnant to recover God's kingdom in the church life. The Lord
is still doing the work of gathering His remnant today.

5. No One Knowing the Son
except the Father,
and No One Knowing the Father
except the Son
and He Who Receives the Son's Revelation

In verse 27 the Lord says, "No one knows the Son except the Father, neither does anyone know the Father except the Son and he to whom the Son wills to reveal Him."
The Greek word translated "knows" in this verse means
full knowledge, not mere objective acquaintance. Concerning the Son, only the Father has such knowledge; and
concerning the Father, only the Son has such knowledge.
Hence, to know the Son requires the Father's revelation
(16:17), and to know the Father requires the Son's revelation (John 17:6, 26). The Greek word translated "wills"
means to deliberately exercise the will through counsel.
"These things" mentioned in verse 25 are difficult for the
natural man to understand. The Lord's recovery is absolutely against the enemy's kingdom of darkness. No doubt
the evil one is not willing to let people know the things of
the Father, the Son, and the Lord's recovery. Thus, there is
the need of the Father's sovereign mercy. It is sovereign of
the Lord that we have seen certain things and have been
brought into them. Although others condemn them, we rejoice over them because we have seen them. Our seeing is
not due to our intelligence; it is due to the mercy of the
Father. The Father has shown us all these things.

V. CALLING THE BURDENED TO REST
AND THE WAY TO REST

A. The Call

In verse 28 the Lord sounded out a call: "Come to Me,
all who labor and are burdened, and I will give you rest."

The Lord seemed to be saying, "All you who labor and are burdened, come to Me and rest. All you religious people and all you worldly people who are laboring and are burdened, come to Me and I will give you rest." What a gracious word! The labor mentioned in verse 28 refers not only to the labor of striving to keep the commandments of the law and religious regulations, but also to the labor of struggling to be successful in any work. Whoever labors thus is always heavily burdened. After the Lord had praised the Father, acknowledging the Father's way and declaring the divine economy, He called this kind of people to come to Him for rest. Rest refers not only to being set free from labor and burden under the law and religion or under any work and responsibility, but also to perfect peace and full satisfaction.

B. The Way

1. Taking the Heavenly King's Yoke

In verses 29 and 30 we have the way to rest: "Take My yoke on you and learn from Me; for I am meek and lowly in heart, and you shall find rest to your souls; for My yoke is pleasant and My burden is light." The Lord's yoke is to take the will of the Father. It is not to be regulated or controlled by any obligations of the law or religion, nor to be enslaved by any work, but to be constrained by the will of the Father. The Lord lived such a life, caring for nothing but the will of His Father (John 4:34; 5:30; 6:38). He submitted Himself fully to the Father's will (26:39, 42). Hence, He asks us to learn from Him. God's will is our yoke. Thus, we are not free to do as we please; rather, we are yoked. Young people, do not think that you are so free or liberated. In the Lord's recovery we all have been yoked. How good it is to be yoked! The Lord's yoke is pleasant and His burden is light. The Lord's yoke is the Father's will, and His burden is the work to carry out the Father's will. Such a yoke is pleasant, not bitter, and such a burden is light, not heavy. The Greek word rendered "pleasant" signifies fit for use; hence, good, kindly, mild, gentle, easy, pleasant, in contrast to what is hard, harsh, sharp, and bitter.

2. Learning from Him

In verse 29 the Lord tells us to learn from Him. He is meek and lowly in heart. To be meek means not to resist any opposition, and to be lowly means not to esteem oneself highly. In all the opposition the Lord was meek, and in all the rejection He was lowly in heart. He submitted Himself fully to the will of His Father, not wanting to do anything for Himself nor expecting to gain something for Himself. Hence, regardless of the situation, He had rest in His heart. He was fully satisfied with His Father's will.

The Lord said that if we take His yoke upon us and learn from Him, we shall find rest to our souls. The rest we find by taking the Lord's yoke and learning from Him is for our souls. It is an inward rest; it is not anything merely outward in nature.

If we are opposed as we minister, and we resist, we shall not have peace. But if instead of resisting we submit to the will of the Father, testifying that the opposition is of the Father, we shall have rest in our souls. John the Baptist did not regard his imprisonment as of the Father; therefore, he was not at rest. If he had realized that his imprisonment was due to the Father's will, he would have been at rest, even in prison. Christ, the heavenly King, always submitted to the Father's will, taking God's will as His portion and not resisting anything. Hence, He was always at rest. We must learn of Him and also take this view. If we do, we shall have rest in our souls.

LIFE-STUDY OF MATTHEW

MESSAGE THIRTY-TWO

THE ESTABLISHMENT
OF THE KING'S REJECTION

(1)

In this message we come to the establishment of the King's rejection (12:1-50).

I. THE REASON FOR REJECTION —
THE BREAKING OF THE SABBATH

The reason for the rejection of the Lord was the breaking of the Sabbath (12:1-14).

A. Picking and Eating the Ears
in the Grain Fields on the Sabbath

1. The Heavenly King and His Disciples
Going through the Grain Fields on the Sabbath
and the Disciples Picking the Ears to Eat

Matthew 12:1 says, "At that time Jesus went on the Sabbath through the grain fields; and His disciples were hungry and began to pick the ears and to eat." "At that time" joins chapter twelve to chapter eleven. At the time the Lord called people to rest from striving to keep the law and religious regulations, He went on the Sabbath through the grain fields, and His disciples began to pick the ears and to eat, seemingly breaking the Sabbath. Remember, in his record Matthew puts certain facts together to present a doctrine. The record in the other gospels is not exactly the same as the record here. The phrase "at that time" is very important. It refers to the time of calling people into His rest. At that time, all His disciples were hungry. Whenever we are hungry, we do not have rest. Rest in-

cludes satisfaction. When you are satisfied, you are at rest.
But if you do not have satisfaction, you do not have rest.

When the Lord called people into rest, His disciples
were hungry. For this reason, He brought them to the grain
fields, fields growing wheat. No doubt He knew that these
fields were rather ripe, full of ears good for eating. The
Lord Jesus purposely did this. Realizing that His disciples
were hungry, He took them to the grain fields for rest. This
is a sign. The call to come to Him for rest given in chapter
eleven was sounded on the Sabbath day. This is proved by
the words "at that time" which begin chapter twelve. The
Sabbath was a day of rest. On the day of rest the Lord
called people into rest. He seemed to be saying, "You
people are keeping the Sabbath, yet you are still laboring
and striving to keep the law. You are heavily burdened with
all the laws, rituals, forms, and regulations. Although you
are keeping the Sabbath outwardly, actually you do not
have any rest. You need to come to Me. You labor and are
burdened with the matter of law keeping. Come to Me, and
you will find rest." Peter and John might have said, "We are
hungry and cannot rest. We need something to eat." But
that day was the Sabbath, and virtually all activity had
ceased. Hence, it was difficult for the disciples to find anything to eat. Knowing this, the Lord Jesus took them into
the grain fields.

Years ago I could not understand why the Lord Jesus
did this. Now I understand that He did it because He had
called people into His rest on the Sabbath. He knew that
His disciples were hungry and that, because it was the
Sabbath, it was difficult to find something to eat. They
could not buy anything, do anything, or go anywhere. The
disciples could have said, "Lord Jesus, what shall we do?
You have called us to come to You for rest; but we are
hungry, and there seems to be no way for us to get anything to eat. How can we rest when we have such hunger?"
The disciples were under the burden of keeping the Sabbath regulations. These regulations had become a heavy
burden to the hungry disciples. Thus, the Lord Jesus took

the lead not to keep these regulations by bringing His disciples out of a regulation-keeping situation into the grain fields. The Lord's intention in doing this was to free the disciples from the Sabbath-keeping regulations. When they came into the grain fields, everyone was freed from this burden and was satisfied. Everyone entered into rest. This is the background of the Lord's rejection in chapter twelve. Should the disciples suffer hunger and keep the Sabbath, or should they forget the Sabbath and find something to eat to satisfy their hunger? The Lord took the lead to bring His hungry disciples into the grain fields where they all found something to eat.

2. The Pharisees Seeing and Condemning

Verse 2 says, "But the Pharisees seeing it said to Him, Behold, your disciples are doing what is not lawful to do on the Sabbath." The Pharisees, the "Sabbath Patrol," caught the Lord Jesus and His disciples. They must have been watching the Lord. Otherwise, why would they have been in the grain fields on the Sabbath day? The Pharisees must have been deliberately following Him and spying on Him.

The Pharisees condemned what the Lord's disciples were doing, saying it was not lawful on the Sabbath. The Sabbath was for the Jews to remember the completion of God's creation (Gen. 2:2), to keep the sign of God's covenant with them (Ezek. 20:12), and to remember God's redemption for them (Deut. 5:15). Hence, to profane the Sabbath was a serious matter in the eyes of the religious Pharisees. To them it was not lawful, not scriptural. But they did not have adequate knowledge of the Scripture. According to their meager knowledge, they cared for the ritual of keeping the Sabbath, not for the hunger of the people. What folly to observe a vain ritual!

3. The King's Defense

This environment afforded the Lord Jesus the opportunity to reveal more of Himself. To the Pharisees, Jesus

had been caught. But to the Lord Jesus this was an oppor-
tunity to reveal both to them and to His disciples who He
was. Thus far, He had been revealed as the Physician, the
Bridegroom, the Shepherd, and the Lord of the harvest.
After being caught by the Pharisees, the Lord revealed
Himself in at least five other major aspects.

a. David and His Men Having Entered
into the House of God
and Having Eaten the Showbread

According to verses 3 and 4, the Lord asked the Pharisees,
"Have you not read what David did when he was hungry
and those who were with him; how he entered into the
house of God, and they ate the showbread, which was not
lawful for him to eat, nor for those who were with him, but
for the priests only?" The Pharisees said that it was not
lawful for the Lord's disciples to pick the ears in the grain
fields and to eat, condemning them for acting contrary to
the Scriptures. But the Lord answered, "Have you not
read," pointing out to them another aspect in the Scriptures that justified Him and His disciples. This condemned the Pharisees for lacking adequate knowledge of
the Scriptures. The Lord Jesus seemed to be saying, "You
come here to catch Me according to the Scriptures. Do not
think that you know the Bible so well. You only know it in
part, in a very superficial way. You have never touched the
depths of the Scriptures. You might have read it, but you
do not understand it. Read about what David did when he
and those with him were hungry. They ate something, the
showbread in the temple, which according to the Levitical
regulations they should not have eaten. You Pharisees
think that I have done something illegal. But have you not
read that David and his followers did the same thing?" We
must admire the Lord's knowledge of the Bible.

The Lord's word here implies that He was the real
David. In ancient times, David and his followers, when rejected, entered into the house of God and ate the show-

bread, seemingly breaking the Levitical law. Now the real David and His followers were also rejected and took action to eat, seemingly against the sabbatical regulation. Just as David and his followers were not held guilty, neither should Christ and His disciples be condemned. Both cases were related to eating. King David was a prefigure of Christ, the real David. David had followers, and Christ, the real David, also had disciples as His followers. King David and his followers were rejected by the people, and the real David and His followers were rejected also. Just as David and his followers were hungry, so Christ and His disciples were also hungry. Furthermore, neither David and his followers nor Christ and His followers had anything to eat, but there was the place where there was something to eat. For David it was the house of God, and for Christ it was the grain fields. All this implies that David and his followers were a type, a shadow, of Christ and His disciples.

Furthermore, the Lord's word here also implies the dispensational change from the priesthood to the kingship. In ancient times, the coming of David changed the dispensation from the age of the priests to the age of the kings, in which the kings were above the priests. In the age of the priests, the leader of the people should listen to the priest (Num. 27:21-22). But in the age of the kings, the priest should submit to the king (1 Sam. 2:35-36). Hence, what King David did with his followers was not illegal. Now by the coming of Christ, the dispensation was also changed, this time from the age of the law to the age of grace, in which Christ was above all. Whatever He did was right. The matter of keeping the Sabbath belonged to the old dispensation of the law. But in the age of grace Christ has the final word. It is not a matter of the law, but of Christ. Therefore, the Lord seemed to be saying to the Pharisees, "You shouldn't condemn Me or My disciples. It is no longer the law that gives the final word, but I, the Christ, I give you the final word. I am the real King, the real David. I am also the Christ who has brought in the dispensation of grace. Thus, whatever I say or do is the final decision." Supposedly the Pharisees knew the Bible, but here they clearly lost the case. How strong was the Lord's defense!

b. The Priests Profaning the Sabbath
on the Sabbath in the Temple

In verse 5 the Lord asked the Pharisees, "Or have you not read in the law that on the Sabbaths the priests in the temple profane the Sabbath and are guiltless?" The Lord brought to the attention of the Pharisees another case in the Scriptures to prove to them how little they really knew the Bible. He pointed out that whatever the priests did in the temple on the Sabbath, they were guiltless.

c. The Heavenly King Being Greater
than the Temple

Then in verse 6 the Lord declared, "Now I say to you that a greater than the temple is here." What boldness the Lord had! He was a Nazarene, but as He stood before the Pharisees He seemed to be saying, "Look at Me. I am greater than the temple." The Pharisees must have been shocked to such an extent that they could not say anything.

The Lord's revealing to the Pharisees that He was greater than the temple was another change, a type-fulfilling change from the temple to a Person. In the case of David, it was a change from one age to another. In this case, a case concerning the priests, it was a change from the temple to a Person who is greater than the temple. Since the priests were guiltless in doing things on the Sabbath in the temple, how could the Lord's disciples be guilty in doing things on the Sabbath in Him who is greater than the temple? In the first case, it was the king breaking the Levitical regulation; in the second case, it was the priests breaking the sabbatical regulation. In the Scripture, neither was guilty. Hence, what the Lord did here was scripturally right.

Apparently the priests were profaning the Sabbath, but actually they were not profaning the Sabbath, because they were in the temple. In that sphere every day and everything were holy. Outside the temple everything was common. But once something was brought into the temple, it was sanctified by the temple. Likewise, every day was sanctified by the temple. Outside the temple, there were common days and holy days, but within the temple there was no such distinction. Everything, every day, every matter, and everyone in the temple were holy. The temple, however, was a shadow, not the reality. The reality is Christ, the greater temple. The Lord seemed to be saying, "I am the greater temple, the real temple. In Me, Peter, John, and all the Galilean fishermen are sanctified, holy. In Me every day is a holy day. If the priests were free to move and engage in various activities on the Sabbath in the temple, then how much more can these dear ones freely do things within Me? The temple protected the priests, and I, the greater temple, protect all My disciples. Pharisees, don't bother Me. Let My disciples be free, for they are all in the greater temple." This was a change from the type to the reality. The Lord's defense was too deep for the Pharisees to argue with. They had nothing with which to counter the Lord's defense. Thus, they were silent.

d. God Desiring to Have Mercy
Rather than Sacrifice

Following this, the Lord said, "But if you had known what this is: I will have mercy and not sacrifice, you would not have condemned the guiltless" (v. 7). By this, the Lord pointed out that what the Pharisees did was not according to God's heart. They were strict in the regulations, but neglected God's mercy. But God desires to have mercy rather than sacrifice.

e. The Son of Man
Being the Lord of the Sabbath

Finally, in verse 8 the Lord said, "For the Son of Man is Lord of the Sabbath." How bold the Lord Jesus was! He won the case, and the Pharisees, who were shocked and frightened, were silenced. They had nothing to say. The Lord's telling the Pharisees that He was Lord of the Sabbath was like someone today telling a highway patrolman that he is lord of the highway. Suppose you are stopped by a highway patrolman. Then you tell him, "Don't bother me. I am the lord of the highway, and the highway belongs to me. You are simply a highway patrolman hired by me. As the lord of the highway, I can change all the regulations. Yes, I gave you some instructions concerning the highway, but now I am changing them. Because I am the lord of the highway, I don't need to notify you about it."

In verse 8 the Lord indicated a third change, a right-asserting change from the Sabbath to the Lord of the Sabbath. As the Lord of the Sabbath, He had the right to change the regulations concerning the Sabbath. Thus, the Lord gave the condemning Pharisees a threefold verdict. He was the real David, the greater temple, and the Lord of the Sabbath. Therefore, He could do whatever He liked on the Sabbath, and whatever He did was justified by Himself. He was above all rituals and regulations. Because He was there, no attention should be paid to any rituals and regulations.

B. Healing a Withered Hand in the Synagogue on the Sabbath

1. The Heavenly King Coming into a Synagogue

Verse 9 says, "And departing from there, He came into their synagogue." After winning the case with the Pharisees, the Lord Jesus came into their synagogue. This took place on another Sabbath day (Luke 6:6). The Lord Jesus certainly was a troublemaker. After causing trouble in the grain fields, defeating the "Sabbath Patrol," according to Matthew's record He went with His disciples to the synagogue to cause even more trouble.

2. A Man Having a Withered Hand

In the synagogue was a man with a withered hand. When the Pharisees inquired of the Lord whether it was lawful to heal on the Sabbath, He said to them, "What man shall there be of you who shall have one sheep, and if it fall into a pit on the Sabbaths, will he not lay hold of it and lift it out? Of how much more value then is a man than a sheep! Wherefore it is lawful to do good on the Sabbaths" (vv. 11-12). Here we see the Lord's wisdom. This time He did not quote a verse, but He referred to their practice. In other words, in the first case the Lord quoted from the Bible, and in the second He appealed to history. Once again their mouths were shut.

3. The Withered Hand Being Restored

Verse 13 says, "Then He says to the man, Stretch out your hand. And he stretched it out, and it was restored sound as the other." The Lord gave the man the word, "Stretch out your hand." In the Lord's word was the enlivening life. By stretching out his hand, the man took the Lord's life-giving word, and his withered hand was restored by the life in this word.

Leading the disciples into the grain fields indicates that the Lord cares for Himself as the Head of the Body. As the Head, He is everything — the real David, the greater temple, and the Lord of the Sabbath. Restoring the withered hand signifies that He cares for His members. He healed a man's withered hand, likening this man to a sheep. The hand is a member of the body, and the sheep is a member of the flock. The Lord would do anything for the healing of His members, for the rescue of His fallen sheep. Sabbath or no Sabbath, the Lord is interested in healing the dead members of His Body. Regulations do not matter, but the rescue of His fallen sheep means everything to Him.

Instead of reading Matthew as a book of stories or merely as a book of doctrine, we must get into the depths of this book. By putting these two cases together, we see that in the first case Christ took care of Himself as the Head and in the second He took care of the members of His Body. The hand is a member of the body, and the sheep is part of a flock, which also refers to the Body. In the first case the Lord Jesus took care of His lordship, of His headship. In the second case He took care of one of His weak, sickly members. He does not care for the Sabbath. He cares only for His headship and for the members of His Body. Therefore, we must conclude that the Lord cares only for Christ and the church. The Lord could say, "The Sabbath means nothing. I don't care for that. I care for My headship and for the members of My Body. Because I am the Head, the Lord, whatever I say is right. I care for My headship. And I also care for My members. I want to make My members living. I want to rescue them, uplift them, and heal them. I don't care for all these doctrinal, religious practices. I care only that My members are strong and living." On the heart of this heavenly King was not the Sabbath, not any kind of doctrine, and not any regulation. Rather, on His heart was His lordship. We must see that He is Lord and that He is above the Sabbath. The Sabbath is merely an instrument used by Him, but He Himself is the Lord of the Sabbath. The Lord also cares for His members, including any member of His Body who is sick, weak, or in a difficult situation. He will do something for that member to rescue him, to heal him, and to make him living. I look to the Lord that we all would see this.

The principle is the same today. As long as we are for Christ and for the church with all the members, everything is all right. There is no burden or regulation. On the Sabbath the twelve apostles were satisfied and at rest, and on the Sabbath the man with the withered hand was also at rest. Thus, these were genuine Sabbaths to the disciples and to the man with the withered hand because they received either the nourishment from Christ or the healing from Christ. Whatever they needed they received from Him. It is the same today.

4. The Pharisees Taking Counsel to Destroy the Heavenly King

Verse 14 says, "And going out, the Pharisees took counsel against Him, how they might destroy Him." In the eyes of the religious Pharisees, for the Lord to break the Sabbath was to destroy the covenant of God with the nation of Israel, that is, to destroy the relationship between God and Israel. Hence, they took counsel against Him, how they might destroy Him. The breaking of the Sabbath caused the Jewish religionists to reject the heavenly King. The Pharisees, the scriptural ones, plotted to kill Jesus for God! This is difficult to believe. But they were blinded by their religion. They could see neither Christ nor the church, neither the Head nor the members. They were absolutely blinded, veiled, covered, by their religion. According to their understanding, the Lord Jesus had to be destroyed, and they took counsel together for this very purpose. Eventually, they did put Christ on the cross; however, they did it according to the sovereignty of God.

At this point, 12:14, the rejection of Christ by religion reaches its peak. Religion has fully rejected the heavenly King and has plotted to destroy Him.

II. REJECTION CAUSING THE TURN TO THE GENTILES

A. The King Departing From the Rejecting Ones

This rejection caused the King with His kingly salvation to turn from the Jews to the Gentiles (12:15-21). Verse 15 says, "But Jesus, knowing it, departed from there."

B. The King Healing All the Sick

Verse 15 also says that many followed Him and that He healed them all. According to verse 16, He "warned them that they should not make Him known." He warned them regarding this because the Pharisees were plotting to destroy Him. Therefore, from that time onward, the Lord Jesus did His best to conceal Himself.

C. The Prophecy of Isaiah
Regarding the King's Turn to the Nations

Verses 17 and 18 say, "That what was spoken through Isaiah the prophet might be fulfilled, saying, Behold, My Servant Whom I have chosen, My Beloved in Whom My soul delights; I will put My Spirit upon Him, and He shall announce judgment to the nations." This indicates clearly that due to the Jews' rejection, the heavenly King with His heavenly kingdom will turn to the nations, the Gentiles, and that the Gentiles will receive Him and trust in Him (v. 21).

1. Not Striving nor Crying Out

Verse 19, also a quotation from Isaiah, says, "He shall not strive nor cry out, nor shall anyone hear His voice in the streets." This indicates that He was no longer free to minister openly. Instead, He had to hide Himself. The reason for the rejection and the cause for the Lord's needing to hide was the breaking of the religious regulations. This was due to caring for His headship and for the members of His Body. Because of this, the rejection reached the ultimate. It is the same in principle today. The less we care for religious regulations and the more we care for Christ and His Body, the more intense the opposition will be.

2. Not Breaking a Bruised Reed
and Not Quenching a Smoking Flax

Verse 20, a further quotation from Isaiah, says, "A bruised reed He shall not break, and smoking flax He shall not quench, until He brings forth judgment unto victory." As the One anointed with the Spirit, Christ not only will make no noise in the streets, but He will not break a bruised reed or quench smoking flax. This indicates that while He was being rejected and opposed, He was still full of mercy. The Jews who were opposing Him were like bruised reeds and smoking flax. The Jews used to make flutes or reeds. When a reed was bruised, they broke it. They also made torches with flax to burn oil. When the oil ran out, the flax smoked, and they quenched it. Some of the Lord's people are like the bruised reed that cannot give a musical sound; others are like the smoking flax that cannot give a shining light. Yet the Lord will not break the bruised ones or quench the smoking ones. Although the Lord was rejected, He was still merciful. Even those who had become bruised reeds He would not break, and those who had become smoking flax He would not quench. Rather, He would still keep open the door of mercy and grace to them all. Among His followers and believers today, many have become bruised reeds that can no longer give a musical song. As a rule, these bruised reeds should be broken and thrown away. But Christ will not do this. Moreover, many of His believers no longer burn as a bright light. As a rule, He should quench them all and cast them away. But He will not do this either. Instead, He is merciful. No matter how much opposition, persecution, and attack, this heavenly King is always merciful. He is a merciful, kingly Savior. You may reject Him today, but He will still be merciful to you. Tomorrow if you say, "Lord Jesus, I repent," He will deal with you lovingly. What a merciful Savior He is! He will never break a bruised reed or quench smoking flax. Rather, He would wait for you to receive His mercy and grace.

D. The Nations (the Gentiles)
Hoping in His Name

Verse 21 says, "And in His name the nations shall hope." Due to the rejection by the Jewish religionists, the heavenly King with His salvation turned to the nations. Now the nations put their hope in His name, believing in Him and receiving Him as their kingly Savior.

This portion of the Word reveals that, on the one hand, the Lord is bold and that, on the other hand, He is merciful. On the one hand, He is strong; on the other hand, He is merciful and meek. This is the King who established the kingdom of the heavens, and this is the way for Him to establish His kingdom. Do not think that in chapter twelve the Lord was defeated. That is a mistaken concept. He was not defeated; He was establishing His kingdom. It is the same with us today. Do not say, "There is so much attack and opposition. Many rumors are being spread against us. How difficult it is for the Lord's recovery. The recovery will be defeated." This is wrong. Although we are so small in number, it seems that all of Christianity is rising up against us. But actually we are not wrong. Who loves the Bible and knows it more than we do? Do we not live in the presence of God and love the Lord Jesus? Do we not take Him as our life day by day? Then why do so many dear Christians oppose us and not others? It is the same today with us as it was with the Lord Jesus when He was on earth. Although He was a little man, the enemy of God knew that He was the One who would defeat him and establish the kingdom of the heavens. The principle is the same today. The enemy knows that this is the Lord's recovery and that the recovery will defeat him and establish the kingdom of the heavens. Never consider the Lord's recovery as an ordinary Christian work. The more opposition, persecution, criticism, and attacks there are, the more we are confirmed. Do not expect the opposition to decline. If no one opposed us, that would be a sign that we are wrong, that we have lost the testimony. But as long as we are being opposed and attacked, this is an indication that we are right. Instead of losing by being attacked, we are gaining. This is the way the kingdom of the heavens is built. It is built through being attacked, persecuted, and criticized. In Matthew chapter twelve the Lord Jesus was not losing the battle — He was gaining. It is the same today. Praise the Lord that we do not fight the battle in a human way, but in the way of the Lord Jesus. While He was being attacked, He was gaining the victory. Likewise, the more the recovery is attacked, the more the kingdom of the heavens will be established. Without doubt, it is being established among us in the Lord's recovery. Praise Him!

LIFE-STUDY OF MATTHEW

MESSAGE THIRTY-THREE

THE ESTABLISHMENT
OF THE KING'S REJECTION

(2)

We have seen that Matthew is a book concerned with the doctrine of the kingdom. In his Gospel Matthew does not give us a record of history; he takes the facts of history and puts them together to reveal the doctrine of the kingdom. Thus far, we have seen that Christ was born, was anointed, was tested, began His ministry, drew a crowd, decreed the heavenly constitution, and continued His ministry. His ministry produced the environment that enabled Him to reveal Himself in many aspects. Furthermore, His ministry caused Him to be fully rejected by that evil generation. We have also seen that the Lord called the laboring and burdened ones to come to Him for rest. He showed them that the way to rest is to break the regulations of religion and to care for the Head and for the members of the Body. It is through all this that the kingdom of the heavens is established on earth among men. We all need to be impressed with such a clear view.

Now we must see that in order for the kingdom of the heavens to be established, there is the need of a spiritual battle, of spiritual fighting. This fighting is implied in 12:22-37. In the establishment of the kingdom a fight is raging on. Although we have covered many things, we have not yet seen that the establishment of the kingdom requires spiritual fighting. As Christ, the heavenly King, was establishing the heavenly kingdom among men on earth, He was fighting. People, however, did not see this warfare. They saw what He did outwardly, but they did not realize what was taking place inwardly. Thus, Matthew selected another historical fact to point out the fighting that was going on as the King was establishing the heavenly kingdom.

III. CLIMAX OF REJECTION

At the time of 12:22-37 the Lord's ministry was no longer so public. Instead of carrying out His ministry publicly, He did so in a rather cautious, calm way. Nevertheless, what the Lord did in verse 22 in healing a man possessed by a demon was a fact of history and could not be concealed.

A. A Person Possessed by a Demon Brought to the Heavenly King and the King Healing Him

Verse 22 says, "Then there was brought to Him one possessed by a demon, blind and dumb; and He healed him, so that the dumb man spoke and saw." A blind and dumb man signifies one who has no sight to see God and spiritual things; thus he is unable to praise God and speak for God. This is the real condition of all fallen people. Such a man was brought to the King, the King cast out the demon, and the man was able to see and to speak. He uttered what he saw. This undoubtedly was a miracle and a sign. In the Old Testament there is no record of a blind man miraculously receiving his sight. For a blind man to receive his sight is a great sign.

B. All the Crowds Being Amazed and Wondering that the King is the Son of David

Verse 23 says, "And all the crowds were amazed and said, Is this not the Son of David?" The miracle performed in healing the blind and dumb person amazed the crowds, and they said, "Is this not the Son of David?" This was the recognizing of Christ as their Messiah, their King.

C. The Pharisees Saying that the King
Casts Out the Demons by Beelzebub,
the Ruler of the Demons

Although the crowds were amazed, the Pharisees were offended, unable to tolerate the fact that through an extraordinary miracle the Lord Jesus had gained all the crowds. Hence, these Pharisees had to say something to deal with the situation. According to verse 24, they said, "This man does not cast out the demons except by Beelzebub, ruler of the demons." This was the greatest blasphemy heaped upon the heavenly King by the opposing Pharisees. Beelzebub means the lord of the flies. It was changed in contempt by the Jews to Baalzebel, which means the lord of the dunghill, and was used for the ruler of the demons (Mark 3:22; Luke 11:15, 18-19). The king of the dunghill, the most dirty place, full of flies, was Satan. Therefore, in the eyes of the ancient Jews, Beelzebub referred to Satan as the king of the demons and as the king of the dirty flies on the dunghill. To say that Christ cast out demons by Beelzebub meant that He cast them out by Satan. What blasphemy to accuse the heavenly King of this!

D. The Heavenly King's Answer

The Pharisees' accusation afforded Christ an opportunity to reveal something further. Once again His ministry produced a situation that enabled Him to reveal something that we would otherwise be unable to see. Apparently the Lord had cast out a demon. Actually, that was not only the casting out of a demon; it was a fighting.

1. Satan's Kingdom Unable to Stand
if Satan Casts Out Satan

Verses 25 and 26 say, "But knowing their thoughts, He said to them, Every kingdom divided against itself is brought to desolation, and every city or house divided against itself shall not stand. And if Satan casts out Satan, he is divided against himself. How then will his kingdom stand?" The Lord seemed to be saying to the Pharisees, "How could I cast out a demon by Satan? If I did this, then Satan would be fighting against Satan, and his kingdom could not stand." Verse 26 is unique in the whole Bible in that no other verse opens the secret that Satan has his kingdom. Satan is the ruler of this world (John 12:31) and the ruler of the power of the air (Eph. 2:2). He has his authority (Acts 26:18) and his angels (Matt. 25:41), who are his subordinates as principalities, powers, and rulers of the darkness of this world (Eph. 6:12). Hence, he has his kingdom, the authority of darkness (Col. 1:13, Gk.). Satan's kingdom is built on earth and among men. But the heavenly King has come to establish a heavenly kingdom also among men on earth. Therefore, these two kingdoms are in conflict. Satan's kingdom is the old kingdom, but the heavenly King is about to establish a new kingdom, the kingdom of the heavens. By this we see that a battle is raging.

2. The Sons of the Pharisees
Casting Out Demons by Beelzebub

In verse 27 the Lord told the Pharisees, "And if I by Beelzebub cast out the demons, by whom do your sons cast them out? Therefore they shall be your judges." Actually, it was not the Lord Jesus but the sons of the Pharisees who cast out demons by Beelzebub. This word of the Lord indicates that the Pharisees were one with Satan, the ruler of the demons.

3. The King Casting Out Demons
by the Spirit of God
that the Kingdom of God May Come

Verse 28 says, "But if I by the Spirit of God cast out demons, then the kingdom of God is come upon you." The Spirit of God is the power of the kingdom of God. Where the Spirit of God is in power, there the kingdom of God is, and there the demons have no ground. By the Lord's word here we see that the battle fought for the kingdom is not fought by just a man himself, but by a man with the Spirit of God. In verse 28 the Lord said that He cast out demons by the Spirit of God and that this is the coming of the kingdom of God. Wherever the Spirit of God exercises His authority over the opposing situation, that is the kingdom of God.

The Lord is always careful with His words. In verse 28 He speaks of the kingdom of God, not of the kingdom of the heavens. Even at that time, the kingdom of the heavens had still not come. The kingdom of God, however, was there already.

4. Binding the Strong Man,
Entering into His House,
and Plundering His Vessels

Verse 29 reveals that before the Lord cast out the demon, He firstly fought against Satan. This verse says, "Or how can anyone enter into the house of the strong man and plunder his vessels unless he first bind the strong man? And then he will plunder his house." The "house" here signifies the kingdom of Satan, and "the strong man" is Satan, the evil one. The Greek word translated "vessels" also means instruments, apparatus; hence, goods, stuff. The fallen people under Satan are his vessels, his instruments for his use. They are his goods kept in his house, his kingdom. The word about binding the strong man indicates that when the Lord cast out demons, He first bound Satan. The people saw only the casting out of the demon. They did not see the binding of Satan, the strong man. Thus, the Lord used the opportunity afforded Him by the accusation of the Pharisees to reveal the secret of spiritual fighting. Apparently, the Lord was only casting out the demon; actually, He was fighting, binding the strong man. This shows us that if we would build the kingdom today, we must first bind the strong man.

The way to bind the strong man is to pray. When we

come to chapter seventeen, we shall see that the disciples came to the Lord and asked Him why He could cast out the demon and they could not. In 17:21 the Lord told His disciples, "This kind does not go out except by prayer and fasting." If you do not pray and fast, you simply cannot cast out this kind of demon. The Lord's word to His disciples indicates that before He cast out a demon, He surely fasted and prayed. In order to bind the strong man, we must fast and pray. The Lord fasted and prayed secretly. The disciples did not see this. We must learn of the Lord to fast in secret and to pray in secret. I believe that when the Lord Jesus was on earth, He often fasted and prayed to fight the battle and to bind the strong man. We all must be in the same spirit today. Every day our spirit must be a fasting spirit and a praying spirit so that we may daily bind the strong man, who is Satan, the king of the kingdom of darkness.

Satan has a kingdom of darkness on earth, and the whole earth is under his usurpation. It is difficult to take one out of Satan's hand. Every fallen person is a vessel in Satan's house. Satan's house is his kingdom, and in his house are many vessels, the many fallen persons. In order to take a fallen person out of Satan's house, we must bind the strong man by prayer and fasting. This is the fighting of the spiritual battle for the establishment of the kingdom of the heavens.

Chapter twelve of Matthew occupies a special place in the New Testament because it reveals that Satan has a kingdom, that Satan is the strong man usurping all the God-created people, and that in order to take people out of his usurping hand, there is the need to bind him. The way to bind the strong man is by fasting and praying. The battle unveiled in chapter twelve is not seen in the foregoing eleven chapters. In those chapters we see the rest and the breaking of the regulations for the Head and for the members of the Body. But we do not see the kingdom of darkness. There are two kingdoms on earth: one is the kingdom of darkness, and the other is the kingdom of the heavens in the light. These two kingdoms are now confronting each other on earth. Therefore, there is the need to fight the battle. We all must fast and pray to bind the strong man. Then we shall be able to plunder his house.

This is a real revelation. Not many Christians have read Matthew twelve in this way because they do not see the kingdom. To them, the kingdom is either simply a doctrinal term or something suspended for a future time. But we realize that all that the Lord is doing with us today is for the establishment of the heavenly kingdom. We are the kingdom people. Today a battle is raging between two kingdoms. The continuation of the Lord's ministry produced the opportunity for this further revelation.

5. The One Not with the King
Being against the King and the One Not
Gathering with the King Scattering

In verse 30 the Lord says, "He who is not with Me is against Me, and he who is not gathering with Me is scattering." At that time the Pharisees were not one with the heavenly King, so they were against Him. They were not gathering with Him, but were scattering away from Him. Hence, they were absolutely separated from Him and joined to His enemy, Satan.

6. The Blasphemy of the Spirit
Not Being Forgiven

In verse 31 the Lord said to the Pharisees, "Every sin and blasphemy shall be forgiven men, but the blasphemy of the Spirit shall not be forgiven." The blasphemy of the Spirit differs from insulting the Spirit (Heb. 10:29). To insult the Spirit is to disobey Him willfully. Many believers do this. If they confess this sin, they will be forgiven and cleansed by the Lord's blood (1 John 1:7, 9). But to blaspheme the Spirit is to slander Him, as the Pharisees did in verse 24. It was by the Spirit that the Lord cast out a demon. But the Pharisees, seeing it, said that the Lord cast out demons by Beelzebub, ruler of the demons. This was blasphemy against the Spirit. By such blasphemy, the Pharisees' rejection of the heavenly King reached its climax.

The Lord seemed to be saying to the Pharisees, "Your blasphemy is not forgivable. I cast out the demon by the Spirit of God, but you say that I cast it out by Satan, the king of the demons. You go too far in saying this. You have uttered a blasphemy that is unforgivable. You have not merely insulted the Spirit or disobeyed the Spirit, but you have blasphemed the Spirit. He is the Spirit of God, even God Himself. I cast out the demon by God Himself as the Spirit; yet you say that this God is Satan, the king of the demons and the king of the dirty flies of the dunghill. In saying this you have committed an unforgivable sin."

7. Speaking against the Holy Spirit Not Forgiven in This Age or in the Coming Age

In verse 32 the Lord continued, "And whoever speaks a word against the Son of Man, it shall be forgiven him; but whoever speaks against the Holy Spirit, it shall not be forgiven him, neither in this age nor in the coming one." In the economy of the Triune God, the Father conceived the plan of redemption (Eph. 1:5, 9), the Son accomplished redemption according to the Father's plan (1 Pet. 2:24; Gal. 1:4), and the Spirit reaches sinners to apply the redemption accomplished by the Son (1 Cor. 6:11; 1 Pet. 1:2). If the sinner blasphemes the Son as Saul of Tarsus did, the Spirit still has the ground to work upon him and cause him to repent and believe in the Son that he may be forgiven (see 1 Tim. 1:13-16). But if the sinner blasphemes the Spirit, the Spirit will have no ground to work upon him, and there will be none left to cause him to repent and believe. Hence, it is impossible for such a person to be forgiven. This is not only logical, according to reason, but governmental according to God's administrative principle, as revealed here by the Lord's word.

In God's governmental administration, His forgiveness

is dispensational. For His administration, He has planned different ages. The period from the first coming of Christ to eternity is divided dispensationally into three ages: this age, the present one, from Christ's first coming to His second coming; the coming age, the millennium, the one thousand years for restoration and heavenly reigning, from Christ's second coming to the end of the old heaven and old earth; and eternity, the eternal age of the new heaven and new earth. God's forgiveness in this age is for sinners' eternal salvation. This forgiveness is given both to sinners and believers. God's forgiveness in the coming age is related to the believers' dispensational reward. If a believer, after being saved, commits any sin, but will not make a clearance through confession and the cleansing of the Lord's blood (1 John 1:7, 9) before he dies or the Lord comes back, this sin will not be forgiven in this age, but will remain to be judged at the judgment seat of Christ (2 Cor. 5:10). He will not be rewarded with the kingdom to participate in the glory and joy with Christ in the manifestation of the kingdom of the heavens, but will be disciplined to make a clearance of this sin and will be forgiven in the coming age (Matt. 18:23-35). This kind of forgiveness will maintain his eternal salvation, but it will not qualify him to participate in the glory and joy of the coming kingdom.

8. The Tree Known by the Fruit

In verse 33 the Lord said, "Either make the tree good and its fruit good, or make the tree corrupt and its fruit corrupt; for by the fruit the tree is known." A tree is known by its fruit. That the Pharisees were evil was exposed by their evil deeds.

9. The Mouth Speaking Evil out of the Abundance of the Heart

Verses 34 and 35 say, "Brood of vipers, how can you, being evil, speak good things? For out of the abundance of the heart the mouth speaks. The good man out of the good treasure brings forth good things, and the evil man out of the evil treasure brings forth evil things." The Pharisees were filled in their hearts with the abundance of evil. Hence, their mouth uttered the evil out of their heart.

10. Every Idle Word to Be Accounted For in the Day of Judgment

Verse 36 says, "And I say to you that every idle word which men shall speak, they shall render account concerning it in the day of judgment." The Greek word rendered "idle" is *argos*, composed of two words: *a* meaning not, and *ergon* meaning work. An idle word is a non-working word, an inoperative word, having no positive function, useless, unprofitable, unfruitful, and barren. In the day of judgment, those who speak such words will render account concerning every one of them. Since this is the case, how much more must man account for every wicked word!

The Lord seemed to be telling the opposers, "Be careful with your speaking. Every idle word, every unimportant word, will be judged. There will be a day of judgment, and whatever you say will be judged at that time." This is a very serious matter.

11. By Words People Being either Justified or Convicted

In verse 37 the Lord concludes, "For by your words you shall be justified, and by your words you shall be convicted." What a warning this is! We must learn to control and restrict our speaking.

The opposing Pharisees were not only defeated, but also subdued. They did not have a case. Whenever the Lord Jesus gives an answer, there is no more argument.

LIFE-STUDY OF MATTHEW

MESSAGE THIRTY-FOUR

THE ESTABLISHMENT
OF THE KING'S REJECTION

(3)

In this message we shall consider 12:38-50.

IV. THE SIGN TO THE REJECTING GENERATION

A. The Rejecting Generation
Wanting to See a Sign

Because the Pharisees could not argue with the Lord
Jesus, they changed the subject seemingly from the negative side to the positive side. Verse 38 says, "Then some of
the scribes and Pharisees answered Him, saying, Teacher,
we want to see a sign from you." Because they could not
defeat the Lord Jesus by arguing, to save face they changed
the subject from one thing to another; they asked the Lord
for a sign. This was a subtle proposal. A sign is a miracle
with some spiritual significance. The Jews always seek for
signs (1 Cor. 1:22). Once again this gave the Lord the
opportunity to reveal to the whole universe something further concerning Himself.

B. No Sign Given to Them except the Sign
of the King's Death

Verse 39 says, "But He answered and said to them, An
evil and adulterous generation seeks a sign, and no sign
shall be given to it except the sign of Jonah the prophet." If
you had been one of those Pharisees, would you not have
been bothered by the Lord's reply? The Pharisees seemed
to be saying, "We want you to show us a sign, and you call
us an evil and adulterous generation. Before this, you

called us a brood of vipers. We recognize that you are a good teacher. Teacher, show us a sign. Show us a miracle with some significance." The Lord Jesus seemed to say, "Yes, you will see a sign. Although you are not an honest generation nor a pure generation, but an evil and adulterous generation, there is a sign for you — the sign of Jonah."

The Lord Jesus proceeded to tell them the significance of the sign of Jonah. In verse 40 He said, "For as Jonah was in the belly of the sea monster three days and three nights, so shall the Son of Man be in the heart of the earth three days and three nights." This was to be a very meaningful sign to them. "The heart of the earth" is called the lower parts of the earth (Eph. 4:9) and Hades (Acts 2:27), where the Lord went after His death. Hades, equal to Sheol in the Old Testament, has two sections: the section of torment and the section of comfort (Luke 16:23-26). The section of comfort is paradise, where the Lord went with the saved thief after they died (Luke 23:43). Hence, the heart of the earth, the lower parts of the earth, Hades, and paradise are synonymous terms, referring to the one place where the Lord stayed for three days and three nights after His death and before His resurrection.

In verse 41 the Lord continued, "Men, Ninevites, will stand up in the judgment with this generation and will condemn it, because they repented at the preaching of Jonah, and behold, a greater than Jonah is here." The Greek word rendered "greater" in verses 41 and 42 is *pleion,* meaning more in quantity and quality; hence, greater. It differs from *meizon,* the word for greater in verse 6, which means greater in external size or measure. Christ, as the Prophet sent by God to His people (Deut. 18:15, 18), is greater than Jonah the prophet. Jonah was the prophet who turned from Israel to the Gentiles and was put into the belly of the great fish. After He had remained there for three days, he came out to become a sign to that generation for repentance (Jonah 1:2, 17; 3:2-10). This was a type of Christ, who would turn from Israel to the Gentiles, and who would be buried in the heart of the earth for three days and then be resurrected, becoming a sign to this generation for salvation.

In verse 41 the Lord seemed to be saying, "The Ninevites repented because of the sign of Jonah. Yet you, an evil and adulterous generation, which will see such a sign as that of the Son of Man buried in the heart of the earth for three days and three nights, will not repent." The Lord's word in verses 40 and 41 was not an ordinary word; it was a prediction. Before the Lord was buried in the heart of the earth, He prophesied in this way, telling the Pharisees that He would be three days and three nights in the heart of the earth. I believe that the Lord Jesus told them this in His mercy. He seemed to say, "I give you a prediction of My death and burial. This shall be a sign to you, just as Jonah was a sign to the Ninevites that caused them all to repent. I predict this now so that when you see it, you may repent." However, they did not repent. By this we see how stubborn the Pharisees were.

C. The King as the Greater Solomon in Resurrection

In the Lord's conversation with the Pharisees, suddenly another sign appeared: the sign of Solomon. Verse 42 says, "The queen of the south shall be raised in the judgment with this generation and shall condemn it, because she came from the ends of the earth to hear the wisdom of Solomon, and behold, a greater than Solomon is here." Christ, as the Son of David to be the King, is greater than Solomon the king. Solomon built the temple of God and spoke the word of wisdom, and to him the Gentile queen came (1 Kings 6:2; 10:1-8). This also is a type of Christ, who is building the church to be the temple of God and speaking the word of wisdom, and to Him the Gentile seekers turn.

Both of these types indicate that Christ, whether as the Prophet sent by God or the King anointed by God, would turn from Israel to the Gentiles, as prophesied in verses 18 and 21.

According to history, King Solomon preceded Jonah the prophet. But according to spiritual significance, Jonah came first, as recorded in Matthew. This also proves that Matthew's record is not according to the sequence of history, but according to the sequence of doctrine. According to doctrine, Christ must first die and be resurrected; then He builds the church and speaks the word of wisdom. This is the real sign to this generation, both to the Jews and to the Gentiles (1 Cor. 1:22, 24).

By His word in verses 40 through 42 the Lord prophesied fully concerning His death, burial, and resurrection. Jonah was a type of Christ in His death and burial, and Solomon was a type of Christ in His resurrection. If the Pharisees had not been stubborn, they would have realized that such words were not spoken lightly. Rather, the Lord's word was very serious, significant, and meaningful. The Pharisees should not have considered them as unimportant. If we had been there and had heard these words, we certainly would have considered them serious, weighty, and filled with significance. If the Pharisees had taken in the Lord's word, they would have repented and believed after the Lord was crucified, buried, and resurrected. In His answer to the Pharisees the Lord was merciful. Although it appears that He was rebuking them, He was more merciful than He was rebuking. He gave them the signs of Jonah and of Solomon, indicating that He was about to die, to be buried, and to be resurrected. His death and resurrection were to be the unique sign to this age and to that generation. This is also true today in the twentieth century. Christ's death and resurrection are still the unique signs to this age. His death is truly meaningful, and His resurrection is full of significance. Nevertheless, the stubborn Pharisees, representing that evil and adulterous generation, did not care.

The Lord's word concerning Jonah and Solomon also indicated that from that time onward He would not do any miracles for the Jewish people. Until He died and was resurrected, He would not give them any signs. His death and resurrection became the real sign to all the stubborn Jews. They were the unique signs to that generation.

V. THE REJECTING GENERATION BECOMING WORSE

Verses 43 through 45 indicate that the rejecting generation will become worse. Verse 43 says, "Now when the unclean spirit goes out from a man, it passes through waterless places, seeking rest, and does not find it." The unclean spirit, a demon (v. 22), seeks for rest but cannot find it in waterless places, because the lodging place of demons, after God's judgment by water in Genesis 1:2, is the sea. Since the demon cannot find rest in dry places, it returns into the man's body it originally possessed and makes its home there (vv. 44-45).

Verses 44 and 45 continue, "Then it says, I will return into my house from which I came out; and having come, it finds it unoccupied, swept, and decorated. Then it goes and takes with itself seven other spirits more evil than itself, and they enter in and make their home there; and the last state of that man becomes worse than the first. Thus shall it also be to this evil generation." Doctrinally, verse 43 continues verse 22. In between is a record of the Jews' rejection of Christ and Christ's forsaking of them. Here the Lord likened the evil generation of the rejecting Jews to the demon-possessed man. In the eyes of the Lord, the rejecting Jews were like demon-possessed people. The two signs of Jonah and Solomon indicated that the Gentiles would repent, but the case of the demon-possessed man indicated that the rejecting Jews would not repent. They will only sweep away the dirt and add good things to beautify themselves, but will not receive Christ to fill them. Rather, they will remain empty and unoccupied. This is the condition of today's Jews. Near the end of this age, they will be seven times more possessed by demons, and their state will become worse than ever.

The Lord Jesus likened that evil generation to a demon-possessed person out from whom a demon has gone. Because that person would not repent and accept Christ, he remained empty. Although the demon was cast out, Christ could not come in. Therefore that person was like a vacant house. The Lord Jesus said that this generation was like such a person. The Lord describes this house with three words: unoccupied, swept, and decorated. This word was also a prophecy, a prophecy that has been fulfilled and yet is still to be fulfilled. The Jews who have returned to form the nation of Israel are swept, decorated, and unoccupied. The entire nation of Israel today has been cleansed, and so many things have been cast out. Furthermore, they have been decorated with various good things; the Jewish people excel in science and other areas. However, the nation of Israel remains unoccupied. The Lord's word in these verses is a prediction of the stubborn generation of Jews today.

I love Israel, but I must speak according to God's revelation. In a recent visit to Israel, we saw that the Jews are swept, cleansed, and decorated, but they are unoccupied. I agree with the Lord's word. When the demon realized that the person was unoccupied, it took seven other spirits more evil than itself, and they all came to occupy the vacancy. This indicates that year by year the nation of Israel will become more and more devilish. More and more demonic things will be found there. The Jews are like a clean house, but they will not accept Christ and receive Him into them. Rather, they remain unoccupied. Consider the nation of Israel today. What is the Jews' goal? Many would say that they have no goal other than maintaining the existence of their nation. But that should not be their goal. Whether or not the nation of Israel exists does not depend upon the endeavor of the Jews; it depends upon God's mercy. I am not concerned for the existence of the nation of Israel. God has restored it, and no one can abolish it. All that the Arabs are doing is in vain because the restoration of the nation of Israel is the work of God. Nevertheless, the nation of Israel today has no goal; hence, it is unoccupied.

I became clear regarding this portion about Israel more than forty-five years ago. At that time, of course, I could not see the restoration of Israel or the return of Jerusalem. I will never forget the day in Shanghai when I read in the newspaper about the restoration of Israel; neither will I forget the day in 1967 when I heard that Jerusalem was returned to Israel. No doubt Israel will exist as a nation until the Lord comes back. My concern is that Israel remains empty. Why will the Jews not accept their Messiah? Why will they not allow Christ to occupy them? Today they remain unoccupied, and their situation will become worse and worse.

VI. REJECTION RESULTING
IN THE KING'S FORSAKING

After this, as the Lord Jesus was speaking to the crowds, His mother and His brothers stood outside, seeking to speak to Him, and someone said to Him, "Behold, Your mother and Your brothers are standing outside seeking to speak to You" (vv. 46-47). This also was an environment giving the Lord the opportunity to reveal something. The Lord said, "Who is My mother, and who are My brothers? And stretching out His hand over His disciples, He said, Behold, My mother and My brothers! For whoever does the will of My Father Who is in the heavens, he is My brother and sister and mother" (vv. 48-50). This indicates that the heavenly King forsook His relationship with the Jews in the flesh. In this chapter, the Jews' rejection of Christ, having reached its climax, resulted in Christ's full forsaking of them. At this point, the break between them and Christ began, and they were severed from Christ (Rom. 11:17, 19-20). After the break with the Jews, Christ turned to the Gentiles. Then His relationship with His followers was no more in the flesh, but in the spirit. Whoever does the will of His Father is His brother for helping, His sister for sympathizing, and His mother for tenderly loving.

In verses 46 through 50 we see a great turn, even a dispensational turn. From this point onward, Jesus' relationship with people is not based upon the natural birth, but upon the spiritual birth. Whoever does the will of the Father who is in heaven is a relative of Jesus. In other words, at the end of chapter twelve, the Lord indicated strongly that He had given up the entire race of Israel. After that, His relationship with people was to be based upon something spiritual. All those who do the will of the Father are His relatives. Hallelujah, we are not only Christ's relatives, but His members! We are His members not by our natural blood or natural birth, but by our spiritual birth in our spirit. He who is joined to the Lord is one spirit (1 Cor. 6:17). Now we are not only His brothers and sisters; we are one spirit with Him, one body in Him, and one new man in Him.

At the end of chapter twelve the Lord Jesus made a clear declaration to the whole universe that He was through with Israel according to the natural blood. Thus, Romans 11 says that Israel was cut off. This cutting off took place at the end of Matthew 12. Romans 11 also says that the Gentiles have been grafted in. This also took place at the end of Matthew 12. In the next message we shall see the mysteries of the kingdom. In that chapter we shall no longer see Israel, but the Gentiles who have been grafted in as the church.

LIFE-STUDY OF MATTHEW

MESSAGE THIRTY-FIVE

THE UNVEILING
OF THE KINGDOM'S MYSTERIES

(1)

In this message we come to chapter thirteen of Matthew. In order to understand this chapter, we must keep in mind that Matthew is concerned with the doctrine of the kingdom. Whatever is recorded in the Gospel of Matthew is according to the kingdom and according to the history of the kingdom. The sequence of doctrine in this book is according to the history of the kingdom.

We need to remember the main points covered in the first twelve chapters of Matthew. Chapter one covers Christ's genealogy and birth, and chapter two, the Gentile wise men seeking Christ and worshipping Him, the flight of Christ to Egypt and His return to Israel to be raised in Nazareth. In chapter three we see the recommendation and the anointing; in chapter four, the temptation and the beginning of the King's ministry to gain the crowds; and in chapters five, six, and seven, the decree of the constitution of the kingdom of the heavens. Chapter eight includes the continuation of the King's ministry in healing the leper, the centurion's servant boy, and Peter's mother-in-law, and the Lord's authority exercised over the wind, the sea, and the demons. Chapter nine covers the King's authority exercised in the forgiveness of sin; the calling of Matthew; the feast where the Lord is revealed as the Physician, the Bridegroom, the new cloth, the new wine, and the new wineskin; signs with dispensational significance; and the prayer to send reapers into the harvest. In chapter ten we have the appointment and sending out of the twelve apostles, and in chapter eleven, John's attempt to stir up the King, the King's answer and His appraisal of John, His rebuke of the stubborn generation, and the calling of people to come to His rest. Finally, chapter twelve covers the breaking of the Sabbath regulations to show that the Lord is the Head and that He cares for the members of His body, the battle for the kingdom, the climax of the King's rejection, the prophecy of the generation becoming worse, and the forsaking of the Jewish generation and the turning to the believers.

As the Lord continued His ministry, the establishing of the kingdom was accomplished to a certain degree. However, because the Jewish generation utterly rejected the Lord, He was forced to turn from them to His believers. This was a serious move, the turn from Israel to the Gentiles, the turn from the relationship according to natural birth to the relationship in the Spirit. Therefore, the end of chapter twelve marks a division in the Gospel of Matthew.

As we have seen, chapters five, six, and seven reveal the inward reality of the kingdom. We have pointed out that this constitution is divided into seven sections: the nature of the kingdom people (5:1-12); the influence of the kingdom people upon the world (5:13-16); the law of the kingdom people (5:17-48); the righteous deeds of the kingdom people (6:1-18); the dealing of the kingdom people with riches (6:19-34); the principle of the kingdom people in dealing with others (7:1-12); and the ground of the kingdom people's living and work (7:13-29). In these seven sections we see the heavenly and spiritual reality of the kingdom. This is not behavior or mere outward living; it is the kingdom of the heavens in reality. What is mainly revealed in chapter thirteen is the outward appearance of the kingdom of the heavens. The inward reality is one thing, and the outward appearance is another.

Throughout history, only a handful of Christians has seen this matter of the difference between the inward reality and the outward appearance of the kingdom. It was seen by Robert Govett and his student, D. M. Panton.

G. H. Lang, a teacher among the Brethren, also saw this matter to some degree, but he did not see it as accurately and clearly as Govett and Panton. We have received considerable help from the writings of Govett and Panton. But we thank the Lord that He has led us on in this matter. We have seen the kingdom of the heavens in more detail and in greater depth. I can testify that especially during the past fifteen years this matter has become very clear to me. In 1936 I put out my first writing on this subject. During the more than forty years since the publication of that little book, I have become more and more clear regarding the kingdom of the heavens.

The basic point concerning the kingdom is the need to differentiate between the inward reality of the kingdom and the outward appearance of the kingdom. If you do not differentiate between these two things, you will not be able to understand this book concerning the kingdom of the heavens.

In addition to the section on the reality of the kingdom, chapters five through seven, and the section on the outward appearance of the kingdom, chapter thirteen, there is a third section equally crucial in understanding the kingdom of the heavens: the Lord's prophecy given on the Mount of Olives recorded in chapter twenty-four. The reality of the kingdom was revealed on a mountain, the appearance of the kingdom was revealed by the seashore, and the manifestation of the kingdom was spoken of in prophecy also from a mountain. The mountain on which the reality of the kingdom was revealed was not in the region of the administrative center of the government, but in the region related to earning a living, because the reality is intimately related to our daily life. It is not a matter of administration or government.

The geographic features of the land in Israel are significant. The governmental center is in the hill country in the middle of the holy land. At the top of the hill country and in its center is Jerusalem, the capital. In this region the king exercises his administration. To both the north and the south are two regions for farming, for earning a living. The last time we went there I saw this matter clearly. Beersheba, which is in the south, is full of wheat and barley, indicating that is a rich land for farming. The land north of Jerusalem, rather close to Samaria, is a rich, green plain. This also is farming country where people may make a living. In the middle of these two regions is the governmental administration. We have pointed out that the reality of the kingdom was revealed not in the administrative region, but in the region of living. However, it was revealed on a mountain. The manifestation of the kingdom was prophesied on a mountain in the administrative region near the capital. This is meaningful, for the manifestation is related to administration, to government. Do not consider this matter as having no significance. The Lord Jesus deliberately went to these places to speak of the reality, the appearance, and the manifestation of the kingdom. If you are impressed with these three aspects of the kingdom, you will understand the Gospel of Matthew.

Thank the Lord that we have seen the reality of the kingdom. Now we must see the appearance of the kingdom. In chapters five, six, and seven there is no falsehood; everything is pure, genuine, heavenly, spiritual, and, to a certain extent, divine. In these chapters we see the nature of the kingdom people and the influence they exert upon the world. They are the salt of the earth and the light of the world. We also see the uplifted law of the kingdom people and the righteous deeds of the kingdom people. These deeds are pure, genuine, and real, performed in secret without any outward show. Furthermore, we see the attitude of the kingdom people toward material wealth and the fact that they have no anxiety regarding riches. Finally, we see the principle of the kingdom people in dealing with others and the ground of their living and work. In this section regarding the reality of the kingdom everything is real, pure, spiritual, and heavenly.

The situation in chapter thirteen, the chapter

concerned with the appearance of the kingdom, is altogether different. In this chapter we have the tares (vv. 25-30) and a great tree which is no longer according to its kind (vv. 31-32). In Genesis 1 God created everything, especially the plants and vegetables, according to its nature. For example, a peach is according to the peach nature, and a banana is according to the banana nature. But in Matthew 13 a mustard seed becomes a great tree. This indicates that it changes its nature, that it is no longer according to its nature. Therefore, in this chapter we see something of a façade, an appearance without reality. Along with the tares and the façade, there is also leaven (v. 33). All these things, found in the appearance of the kingdom, cause the appearance of the kingdom to be a mixture.

It is easy to see this mixture in today's Christendom. Today's Christendom exactly matches the portrait in Matthew 13 of the outward appearance of the kingdom of the heavens. In Christendom there are millions of tares, a great façade, and corrupting leaven. However, none of these things is found in chapters five, six, and seven, where everything is real, pure, spiritual, and heavenly. But what a mixture we see in chapter thirteen!

When we come to chapter twenty-four concerning the manifestation of the kingdom, we shall see that the manifestation is even more strict than the reality, just as the period of examination is a stricter time than that during the regular course of study. The students work diligently during the week in the reality of their schooling, but they may play, go dancing, or attend the movies during the weekend. That is like the appearance of the kingdom. The students should not be so happy and joyful, for they must consider the coming examinations. Furthermore, they must think of graduation, which will be the time of manifestation. By these three things — reality, appearance, and manifestation — we are able to understand the book of Matthew.

At the end of chapter twelve Israel was cut off and the

Gentiles were grafted in. At this point certain teachers, including Dr. Scofield, have made a great mistake. They say that after chapter twelve, due to the unbelief of Israel, the kingdom had been suspended. They do not see that, instead of being suspended, the kingdom was given over to another people. The Lord did not say, "From now on, I have no brothers, sisters, or mother." If He had said this, then the kingdom would have been suspended. What the Lord did was turn from one people to another. The Lord seemed to be saying, "The ones who do the will of My Father, who are born of My Father and live by His life, they are my brother, and sister, and mother." Hence, the kingdom has not been suspended. Rather, it has been shifted from one people to another.

I. THE PRELIMINARY WORK OF THE KINGDOM

A. The Heavenly King Going out of the House to Sit beside the Sea

Matthew 13:1 says, "On that day Jesus, going out of the house, sat beside the sea." To most Christian teachers, this verse is insignificant. When I read this verse as a young man, it meant nothing to me. But now I realize that this verse is very meaningful. At the end of chapter twelve, the heavenly King, having been fully rejected by the Jewish leaders, made a break with them. On that day He went out of the house to sit beside the sea. This is very significant. The house signifies the house of Israel (10:6), and the sea signifies the Gentile world (Dan. 7:3, 17; Rev. 17:15). The King's going out of the house to sit beside the sea signifies that after His break with the Jews, He forsook the house of Israel and turned to the Gentiles. It was after this that, on the seashore, He gave the parables concerning the mysteries of the kingdom. This signifies that the mysteries of the kingdom were revealed in the church. Hence, all the parables in this chapter were spoken to His disciples, not to the Jews.

The first three words of chapter thirteen, "On that day," join this chapter to chapter twelve, just as the words, "At that time," connect chapter twelve to chapter eleven. The words, "On that day," refer to the day that the Lord declared that He had forsaken Israel, the day He cut off Israel and grafted in the Gentile believers. On that day He went out of the house, signifying the house of Israel, to the sea, signifying the Gentile world. This move from the house to the sea corresponded to His declaration. He had declared that He no longer had anything to do with His natural relatives but that He had turned to the believing Gentiles. Now He was walking according to His declaration. Therefore, we see that this verse is very meaningful.

B. Great Crowds Gather to the King on the Seashore

Verse 2 says that great crowds were gathered to Him. But this does not mean that all those in these great crowds became His relatives.

C. The King Stepping into a Boat — the Church

Verse 2 also says, "He stepped into a boat to sit and all the crowd stood on the shore." The boat, which was in the sea but not of the sea, signifies the church, which is in the world but not of the world. The sea is the Gentile world, and the boat is the church in the Gentile world. It was in the boat, in the church, that the King of the heavenly kingdom, after forsaking the Jews and turning to the Gentiles, revealed the mysteries of the kingdom in parables. Hallelujah, today we are neither the house nor the sea — we are the boat! We are the boat with the King. One day the King stepped into our boat. Now we have the King in our boat, the church. But the crowd stood on the shore. Are you standing on the shore, or are you in the boat with the King? I can testify that I am not standing on the seashore — I am in the boat.

D. The King Speaking to the Crowds in Parables

Verse 3 says, "And He spoke to them many things in parables." He spoke these parables in the boat on the sea. Do you want to know the mysteries of the kingdom? If you do, then you must leave the house and not stand on the seashore, but get into the boat close to the Lord. This is the only place where we can understand the mysteries of the kingdom. Oh, we are in the church, in the boat! The church is neither the house of Israel nor the sea of the Gentiles; rather, it is the boat of the believers. In the church all the mysteries of the kingdom are revealed to us.

In order to know the mysteries of the kingdom, we must learn the skill of interpreting the parables. If you do not know how to allegorize the Bible, you will not be able to interpret the parables. For example, the boat is a parable. How can you interpret the boat if you do not know how to allegorize it? All the opposers need to follow this way. Then they will know the Bible. However, because they do not have the way to allegorize the Bible, they do not know it. Because we have the way to allegorize the Scriptures, we know the significance of the house, the sea, and the boat. Furthermore, we know all the parables. How happy I am to know the parables!

When I read Matthew 13 fifty years ago, I was bothered by so many things. I had many unanswered questions about what is found in this chapter. I bought some books on Matthew 13, but they were all worthless. These books even said that leaven refers to the power of today's Christianity and that the tree is the wonderful and magnificent organization of Christianity. But as I read those books, I did not have a good feeling within me; I did not believe what they said. However, I did not have a way to understand this chapter. Therefore I wrote to Brother Nee, telling him of my desire to know the Bible word by word and asking him to recommend the best book to help me in this matter. In his reply he told me that the best set of books was the *Synopsis of the Bible* by John Nelson

Darby. However, he pointed out that Darby's *Synopsis* was extremely difficult to understand. When I read Darby's *Synopsis* several years later, I discovered Brother Nee was right. I simply could not understand Darby's writing. To speak the truth, I did not receive any help from Darby's *Synopsis* as far as understanding Matthew was concerned. But through Brother Nee himself I received great help in knowing the parables. Now I can say with full assurance that we know the parables in Matthew 13. Nothing is hidden from us. To us, the mysteries of the kingdom are no longer mysteries, for these mysteries have all been opened to us.

1. The Mysteries of the Kingdom of the Heavens Hidden to the Crowds but Explained to the Disciples

Before we consider the parables in Matthew 13, I would like to impress you with some of the warnings found in this chapter. Verses 10 and 11 say, "And the disciples came and said to Him, Why are You speaking in parables to them? And He answered and said to them, Because to you it has been given to know the mysteries of the kingdom of the heavens, but to them it has not been given." The King of the heavenly kingdom revealed the things of the kingdom in parables (v. 34) in order to make them mysteries to the opposing and rejecting Jews, that they might not understand them. From the time the King came to sow the seed until He comes back to reap the harvest, everything concerning the kingdom is a mystery to the natural mind. Only the enlightened mind of a submissive heart can understand these mysteries.

When the disciples asked the Lord why He spoke of the kingdom in parables, the Lord seemed to say, "In order to keep it from them and to let you know. Everything depends on you and on them, not on Me. Whether or not you can understand what I speak in parables depends on you." In verse 12 the Lord continued, "For whoever has, it shall be given to him, and he shall be in abundance; but whoever does not have, even what he has shall be taken away from him." The words "whoever has" refer to the receiver and follower of the heavenly King, to whom the revelation concerning the kingdom will be given in abundance. But the one who does not have is the opposing and rejecting Jew, from whom what the heavenly King has spoken and done will be taken away. This is the real condition of the Jews today. They have no knowledge whatever concerning the kingdom of the heavens. It is altogether a mystery unknown to them.

Verses 13 and 14 say, "Therefore I speak to them in parables, because seeing they do not see, and hearing they do not hear, neither do they understand. And in them is being fulfilled the prophecy of Isaiah, which says, Hearing you shall hear and by no means understand, and seeing you shall see and by no means perceive."

Verse 15 says, "For the heart of this people has grown fat, and with their ears they have heard heavily, and their eyes they have closed; lest at any time they should perceive with their eyes and hear with their ears and understand with the heart and turn around, and I will heal them." The reason those in that stubborn generation could not understand lay in their heart, which had grown fat. Fat signifies the pride of having something. The heart of those in that stubborn generation was proud. That was the actual situation of the Pharisees. Because their heart had grown fat, their eyes and ears were affected. They could see, but not perceive; they could hear, but not understand. As a result, the mysteries of the kingdom meant nothing to them. All the parables were mysteries simply because of their pride.

This is exactly the situation today. If certain Christian teachers and leaders were to hear a message like this, they would condemn it, criticize it, and reject it. They would listen, but they would not understand. They would see, but they would not perceive. The reason they could not understand or perceive is the pride in their heart of having something. If the Brethren teachers heard this message, they would say, "No, the kingdom has been suspended. This is not the dispensation of the kingdom; it is the dispensation of the church. The dispensation of the kingdom will be in the millennium, in the coming age of a thousand years." This indicates the fatness of their heart, their pride in having something. This pride keeps people from understanding and perceiving. We must learn the first lesson given in the constitution of the kingdom of the heavens: "Blessed are the poor in spirit" (5:3). When we are poor in spirit, we have no pride in our heart. We are not proud of anything. Rather, we are unloaded, empty, and ready to receive something new from the Lord. We all need to prepare ourselves for what is revealed in this chapter.

I believe that the Lord has shown us the true interpretation of all these parables. Throughout these many years, I have not doubted anything regarding our understanding of them. In fact, in these days of working on the Gospel of Matthew I have been all the more confirmed that we have the correct interpretation, for our interpretation matches the history of the church and our experience. Because of the situation of today's Christianity, we all need to know this crucial chapter, a chapter that is even more crucial than chapters five, six, and seven. We need the enlightenment concerning this chapter in order not to be leavened, mislead, or corrupted.

2. The Disciples Being Blessed

The Lord also said that His disciples were blessed. According to verse 9, they were blessed to have a hearing ear. Moreover, verses 16 and 17 say, "But blessed are your eyes, because they see; and your ears, because they hear. For truly I say to you, that many prophets and righteous men have desired to perceive what you are seeing and did not perceive, and to hear what you are hearing and did not hear." What a blessing it is to see and hear the mysteries of the heavenly kingdom!

LIFE-STUDY OF MATTHEW

THE UNVEILING
OF THE KINGDOM'S MYSTERIES

(2)

We come in this message to the first mystery of the kingdom, covered in 13:3 through 8 and 18 through 23.

At the beginning of the first of the seven parables concerning the mysteries of the kingdom, the Lord did not say, "The kingdom of the heavens was likened unto," as He did in the other six parables (vv. 24, 31, 33, 44, 45, 47), because the kingdom of the heavens began with the second parable. In the first parable, the Lord was going out only to sow the seed for the kingdom. The seed had not yet grown to be the crop for the formation of the kingdom. Hence, the kingdom had not yet come, but had only drawn near in the Lord's preaching (4:17).

E. The Parable of the Sower —
the Preliminary Work of the King
for the Kingdom

When the Lord Jesus came, He came to do the preliminary work for the establishment of the kingdom. Throughout His human life, from His birth to His resurrection, the kingdom of the heavens still had not come. What He did in His life was a preparation for the establishment of the kingdom of the heavens.

1. The Sower Having Sown the Seeds

Verses 3 and 4 say that a sower went out to sow some seeds. In His preliminary work for the establishment of the kingdom of the heavens, the Lord Jesus came as a sower.

Several times the Lord was called a teacher. But here He likens himself not to a teacher, but to a sower. The sower in verse 3 is the Lord Himself (v. 37). Actually, the Lord did not come to teach, but to sow the seed. What is this seed? It is the word of the kingdom with the King in it as life (v. 19). The seed is also the sons, the people, of the kingdom (v. 38). If we check with our experience, we shall realize that the seed sown by the Lord Jesus into our humanity is just Himself as life to make us the seed of the kingdom. Here three things are interrelated: the word of the kingdom, the sons of the kingdom, and Christ Himself as the life within the seed. These three cannot be separated. The word of the kingdom actually is Christ Himself as the word of life. This seed eventually produces the sons of the kingdom, who are the believers. Therefore, the seed refers to the word of the kingdom, to Christ Himself as life, and to us, the sons of the kingdom. By Christ's being the living word of life sown into our being, we are made the sons of the kingdom.

In this parable we see that Christ establishes the kingdom of the heavens not by fighting or teaching, but by sowing Himself as the seed of life into believing people so that the kingdom of the heavens may grow up. The establishment of the kingdom of the heavens is absolutely a matter of growth in life. To establish the kingdom is to grow the kingdom. The kingdom is not established by outward working, but by inward growing. We need to emphasize this matter again and again. Because many Christian workers have not seen this, they still think that the church is built up by work and labor. But the church can be produced only by sowing Christ as the seed into humanity. This seed will grow within people and produce the church. The seed of life, Christ Himself in the word, sown into humanity will grow the church. The church is not produced by work; it is altogether produced by the growth in life. Therefore, the kingdom of the heavens is brought into being not by teaching or by working, but by sowing Christ as the living word of life into humanity. This seed will grow, and the life in it will produce the kingdom. The kingdom is absolutely a matter of life which has grown. The source of the kingdom is Christ as the seed of life. May we all be deeply impressed with the fact that the kingdom is a matter of life.

In this parable, which gives us a clear picture of the preliminary work of the kingdom, Christ came as a sower. Everyone who has sown seed knows that if there is no life in the seed, nothing will happen. Without life, it is impossible to have growth. In this parable Christ came neither as a great prophet to prophesy nor as a mighty king to rule. Yes, He was a prophet and a king, but in this parable He appears as a sower, not as a prophet or a king. In His hand there is not a scepter for ruling or for exercising authority, but seed for producing life. He came as a sower to sow Himself as the seed. Oh, may we all see this! This vision will revolutionize our concept and our Christian work. If we see this vision, we would no longer trust in what we do because we would know that the kingdom is a matter of life, that the church is a matter of growth in the life seed sown into our humanity. Therefore, we would trust completely in the growth of life. Those who have been with us for a number of years can testify that I do not teach others what they should do. I do not give them instructions regarding their behavior. But in meeting after meeting, conference after conference, and training after training, I have ministered Christ as the all-inclusive, life-giving Spirit. It has always been a matter of Christ, life, the Spirit, and the church.

We all need to see this basic vision that the kingdom is a matter of life growing in us. The young people who are burdened for the campuses must see this vision. Young people, if you go to the campuses to do a work, that will mean nothing. You should not go there to work, but to sow the seed, to be a sower. During the years I was with Brother Nee in China, I saw that he was not working; he was sowing Christ as a seed. He told me that Miss M. E. Barber did not come to China to work. She was in China sowing Christ, even sowing herself in Christ. She was a seed sown into that district in China. Eventually, something grew out of that seed. The Lord's recovery today is the produce of the seed sown by Sister Barber and Brother Nee. Do not think that our working means very much. No, our working does not mean anything. If you study the Gospels again, you will see that the first Christian worker was Christ Himself. However, He did not work very much. Instead, He was sowing.

In the parable of the sower the Lord gives us a picture of what He came to do. He came as a sower to sow the seed. To those who are proud this parable is a mystery. The Pharisees would probably say, "We know all about this and don't want to hear of it. We know what a sower is. We know that a sower simply sows seed and that this seed falls on various types of soil. This is elementary. We want to hear something deep, something philosophical. Speak to us about the laws of Moses. Jesus, have you never read Moses and the Psalms? We would like to hear about this, not about some seed falling on the wayside, rocky places, thorns, and good soil. You are just a kindergarten teacher." But to those who are poor in spirit and pure in heart this parable is much more profound than the teaching of Moses and all the Psalms. Hallelujah for the sower, the seed, and the good earth! This is altogether a matter of life. We need more hymns on the sower, the sowing, the seed, and the growth. Again I say, the kingdom grows; it is not built by our labor. Do not try to build the church, for what the church needs is growth. Day after day we need to sow Christ.

Recently an opposer told a brother, "We are going to stop you." He said that they were planning to stop the Lord's recovery. If the opposers try to do this, they will find themselves in trouble. Do not touch anything of life, for the more you touch it, the more it multiplies. If you leave it alone, it may remain dormant. But if you touch it, it will grow. Suppose you say to some seed, "Seed, I shall stop you. I shall bury you in the earth." How good that would be for the seed! But if you leave the seeds on a pedestal, appreciating them, looking at them, and treasuring them, that will be the most effective way to stop them. But if you try to terminate the seed by burying it in the earth, the seed will grow. The opposers simply do not know what the Lord's recovery is. The Lord's recovery is not work, teaching, or theology. It is a seed; it is the living Christ as a seed. I have the assurance to declare to the whole universe that the all-inclusive Christ as the life-giving Spirit has been sown into thousands of Americans. Do not touch them. If you try to persecute them or bury them, the one grain will be multiplied into many more grains. Who can stop the Lord's recovery? The seed has already been sown. The Lord came to the earth as a sower to sow Himself. Hallelujah, Jesus has been sown into humanity! The principle is the same in the Lord's recovery today. The recovery as the seed of life has been sown in America, Europe, Brazil, and many other places. No one and nothing can stop it. The Lord's recovery is not a movement. It is Christ Himself as the seed of life sown into our being. The sower is Christ, and the seed is also Christ, Christ in the word sown into us to make us the sons of the kingdom.

According to this parable and the Lord's own interpretation of it, this seed is sown into our heart (v. 19). In the past we have pointed out that our heart is not the receiving organ, but the loving organ, and that our receiving organ is our spirit. We say this based upon Ezekiel 36, where God promises to give us a new spirit and a new heart, a new spirit to receive God and a new heart to love Him. Here the Lord Jesus does not mention anything about the spirit; but He does say that the heart is the place where the seed is sown. Nothing can enter our spirit without first passing through our heart. In 1 Peter 3:4 our spirit is called the inner man of our heart. This indicates that our spirit is surrounded by our heart. The three main sections of the heart are the mind, the emotion, and the will. When we believed in the Lord Jesus, we had no awareness that we were exercising our spirit. But we did realize that we believed in Him with our heart. In other words, when we believed in Him, we opened our heart. The result, however, was that He came into our spirit. When we opened our heart to believe in Him, He came into our spirit. But our spirit is not the soil for growing Christ. The soil is our heart. This parable makes it perfectly clear that our heart is the soil, the earth, the very place where the seed is sown and where it grows. Therefore, in this parable the Lord does not deal with our spirit; He mainly touches our heart.

2. Some Seeds Falling Beside the Way

Verse 4 says, "And as He sowed, some seeds indeed fell beside the way, and the birds came and devoured them." Beside the way is the place close to the way. Because it is hardened by the traffic of the way, it is difficult for the seeds to penetrate it. This kind of wayside signifies the heart that is hardened by the worldly traffic and does not open to understand, to comprehend, the word of the kingdom (v. 19). The birds signify the evil one, Satan, who came and snatched away the word of the kingdom sown in the hardened heart.

If you compare the constitution of the kingdom of the heavens with the parable of the sower, you will see that this parable is based upon the concept of the constitution. The constitution covers the matters of being poor in our spirit and pure in our heart. Those who are the wayside cannot receive the seed because they are neither poor in spirit nor pure in heart. Because the wayside, part of the soil for farming, was so close to the traffic, it became hardened by the traffic. This made it impossible for the seed to penetrate it. Thus, the seed remained on the surface of the wayside. This signifies those who are not poor in spirit or pure in heart because they have so much worldly traffic. Education, commerce, politics, science, business, and other kinds of worldly traffic go back and forth within their mind, emotion, and will. They are occupied with promotion, position, and ambition. For this reason, it is very difficult to preach the gospel to those in politics. The politicians have too much worldly traffic in their being. Those seeking advancement in politics are ambitious to gain a position or to surpass others. Likewise, it is difficult to preach the gospel to those on Wall Street. Unless the Lord knocks them down, they are too hard to receive the word into them. Day and night they are preoccupied with figures, money, and business. They cannot be poor in spirit or pure in heart. The Wall Street traffic makes them hard in their heart. When you attempt to sow the seed into them, the seed cannot penetrate them. There is no room in them for the seed. This is also true among so many in education, especially those pursuing a doctoral degree. There has been so much traffic in their heart that their heart has been hardened, just like the wayside in the Lord's parable. Although they may hear the gospel of Christ, not a word can penetrate their heart.

We thank the Lord that, in His mercy, when the gospel was preached to us, we were poor in spirit and pure in heart. On the day I was saved by the Lord, I said to Him, "If the whole world could be mine, I would not take it. I don't want it and I don't like it. Lord, I want to keep my heart for You. I don't like to have any worldly traffic in my heart." It is never good to have traffic through farmland. No farmer would allow this. Are you part of the wayside? Do not stay close to the way. Stay in the center of the farm. Then the worldly traffic will not touch you.

3. Some Falling on Rocky Places

Verses 5 and 6 say, "And others fell on the rocky places, where they did not have much earth, and immediately they sprang up because they did not have depth of earth; but when the sun rose, they were scorched; and because they had no root, they were dried up." The rocky places that do not have much earth signify the heart that is shallow in receiving the word of the kingdom, because deep within are rocks — hidden sins, personal desires, self-seeking, and self-pity — which frustrate the seed from gaining root in the depth of the heart. The sun with its scorching heat signifies affliction or persecution (v. 21), which dries up the seed that is not rooted. The heat of the sun is for the growth and ripening of the crop once the seed is deeply rooted. But due to the seed's lack of root, the sun's growing and ripening heat becomes a death blow to the seed.

The things signified by the rocks correspond to what is covered by the complemented laws in the constitution of the kingdom of the heavens (5:17-48). The second type of earth corresponds to the temper, lust, self, and flesh — the things hidden in our heart. Perhaps not many among us are part of the wayside, but I am very concerned that a good number may be rocky places. In appearance they are the same as others, for the soil is on the surface. But they have no depth. Rather, they have lust, temper, self, and flesh. All these are rocks hidden beneath the soil. Therefore, the first type of soil corresponds to those who are not poor in spirit and pure in heart, and the second corresponds to those who still have their temper, lust, sin, self, and flesh beneath the surface. Some of you may still be hiding your lust, your selfishness, and your flesh. You may shout halle-lujahs in the meetings, but you do not have much depth. Instead of depth, there are rocks. Sooner or later, all these rocks will be exposed because the word that has been sown into you will not be able to be rooted in you. You may be happy and joyful, shouting praises to the Lord, but there is no root in you. Hence, when the affliction and perse-cutions come, you will be dried up like a plant without root that withers under the scorching heat of the sun. May the Lord have mercy upon us and dig out all the hidden rocks. May He dig out our temper, lust, self, flesh, and any other negative thing so that there may be room in our heart for the seed to be rooted deeply within us.

4. Some Falling on the Thorns

Verse 7 says, "And others fell on the thorns, and the thorns came up and choked them." The thorns here sig-nify the anxiety of the age and the deceitfulness of riches, which choke the word from growing in the heart and cause it to become unfruitful. The thorns, the anxiety of this age and the deceitfulness of riches, match the section in the constitution covering the attitude of the kingdom people toward riches (6:19-34). Several times in that section of the constitution the words "anxious" or "anxiety" are used. The Lord tells us not to be anxious about our living, about what we shall eat, drink, or wear. The third type of soil is not as bad as the second, but it is still difficult for the seed to grow in it because of anxiety and the deceitfulness of riches. All these thorns must be uprooted. If the anxiety of this age and the deceitfulness of riches are rooted out of our heart, the seed will grow.

The parable of the sower seems very simple, but it is actually deep and profound. It exposes the real condition of our heart in the presence of the heavenly King. Whatever is in us is exposed. This parable covers the hardness by the worldly traffic; the hidden lust, self, and flesh; and the anxiety of the age and deceitfulness of money. These are the wayside, the rocks, and the thorns. As long as you are either the wayside, the soil with hidden rocks, or the soil with thorns, the kingdom cannot grow in you. In other words, the church cannot grow in those types of soil. In order for the church to grow, the seed must fall on good earth.

5. Others Falling on Good Earth

Verse 8 says, "And others fell on the good earth and gave fruit, some indeed a hundredfold, and some sixty, and some thirty." The good earth signifies the good heart that is not hardened by worldly traffic, that is without hidden sins, and that is without the anxiety of the age and the deceitfulness of riches. Such a heart gives every inch of its ground to receive the word that the word may grow, bear fruit, and produce even a hundredfold (v. 23). The good heart is a heart which has no worldly traffic, no rocks, and no thorns. It has no hidden sins, selfishness, lust, or flesh and no anxiety of the age or deceitfulness of money. This kind of heart is truly pure to match the spirit. Such a heart is the good soil that grows Christ. Christ as the seed of life can grow only in this kind of heart, this kind of soil. This is the soil that can grow the kingdom.

In the United States of America there are millions of Christians. Recently a magazine said that there are fifty million regenerated Christians in this country. Only the Lord knows how many among this number are genuine Christians. Although there are so many Christians, I wonder how many are the good earth. How many have no worldly traffic, no hidden sins, flesh, lusts, or self, and no anxiety or deceitfulness of money? How many are poor in spirit and pure in heart? It is very difficult to find such Christians. Although we may be surrounded with Christians, we rarely find one who is truly poor in spirit and pure in heart. How about you? Do you still have worldly traffic in your heart? Are you truly poor in spirit and pure in heart? Are there any hidden rocks deep within? What about the anxiety of this age and the deceitfulness of money? Although we must consider these questions, we should not be discouraged. Rather, we should be encouraged. Nothing can stop God's economy. There will be at least some who are the good earth. According to the percentage indicated by the Lord's parable, this is twenty-five percent of the believers. I would be happy with even five percent. How good it would be if among all the real Christians five percent were poor in spirit and pure in heart, had no hidden self, flesh, or sin, and had no anxiety or deceitfulness of money! How wonderful it would be if five percent were pure for Christ to grow in them! Here and there, in so many major cities, the Lord will find the good earth. The Lord is merciful. We might have had too much traffic, but the Lord saved us from the wayside and placed us in the center of the farmland. I know of many brothers and sisters in whom the Lord has dug out all the hidden things and uprooted all the thorns to make their heart the good earth. Praise the Lord for this! There is no doubt that among us a good many are the good earth, the good soil. The kingdom and the church are growing here. Here in the church life we are growing Christ, and we are growing the kingdom. The kingdom does not come by our working. It comes only by the growth of Christ within us. May we all be impressed that today in the Lord's recovery the Lord is doing the work of sowing Himself into people so that He may have the good earth to grow Himself into the kingdom. This is the first parable, and this is the preliminary work for the establishment of the kingdom of the heavens.

LIFE-STUDY OF MATTHEW

MESSAGE THIRTY-SEVEN

THE UNVEILING
OF THE KINGDOM'S MYSTERIES

(3)

In the last message we saw that the good earth is the people according to the constitution of the kingdom of the heavens. The constitution is a complete description of the good earth, of one who is poor in spirit and pure in heart, who has no worldly traffic within him, whose being is not hardened, who has no hidden rocks of temper, lust, self, and flesh concealed within him. All this corresponds to the requirements given in the constitution. Those who are the good earth have no thorns, no anxiety of life, and no deceitfulness of riches. Therefore, they become the good earth in which the seed can grow. This good earth is the people who live according to the constitution of the kingdom of the heavens. In other words, their living exactly matches the constitution.

The kingdom of the heavens is built by the multiplication of the seed. The sower sows the seed, the seed grows and multiplies, and eventually the multiplication of the seed becomes the constituent of the kingdom. This reveals that the kingdom is not built by any kind of work, but that it is built by the multiplication of the seed sown by the sower. Christ came as the sower sowing Himself as the seed of life. This seed of life enters humanity to bring forth fruit, the sons of the kingdom. This is the multiplication of the seed. The kingdom is built by this multiplication. Therefore, the kingdom is the multiplication of the seed sown by the sower. The sower Himself is the seed, and the multiplication of the seed is the multiplication of the sower. Hence, the kingdom is built with the multiplication of

Christ. The kingdom is the enlargement of Christ, the multiplication of Christ as the seed sown into us. If we see this, we shall know what kind of living we should have and in what kind of situation we should be so that we may participate in the kingdom. Having seen this matter, let us now proceed to consider the second parable (13:24-30, 36-43).

II. THE ESTABLISHMENT OF THE KINGDOM AND ITS FALSE CONSTITUENTS

A. The Kingdom of the Heavens Likened to a Man Sowing Good Seed

Verse 24 says, "The kingdom of the heavens was likened to a man sowing good seed in his field." With the second parable the Lord began to say, "The kingdom of the heavens was likened to," because the kingdom of the heavens began to be established when the church was built (16:18-19) on the day of Pentecost, the time when the second parable began to be fulfilled. It was from that time, after the church was founded, that the tares, the false believers, were sown amidst the true believers, the wheat.

The kingdom of the heavens began with the second parable. This is the reason the Lord used the words "The kingdom of the heavens was likened to." These words were not spoken by the Lord in the first parable because at that time the kingdom of the heavens had not yet come. Rather, that parable was concerned with the preliminary work for the kingdom of the heavens. But at the time of the second parable, the kingdom of the heavens had come; thus, the Lord said that the kingdom of the heavens was likened to a man sowing good seed in his field.

B. The Heavenly King Having Sown Good Seed in His Field

The parable of the tares is easy to understand. In the first parable the seed sown by the sower was the word of the kingdom. Verse 19 says this clearly. But in the second parable we see that the seed has developed into the sons of the kingdom (v. 38). Firstly, this means that the seed was the word sown into humanity and, secondly, that it has grown into the sons of the kingdom. In the foregoing message I pointed out that the seed is the word with Christ in it as life. According to the second parable, this seed grows into us, the kingdom people, the sons of the kingdom. Therefore, the wheat is the sons of the kingdom, the real believers, those regenerated with the divine life.

C. The Enemy Having Come and Sown Tares amidst the Wheat

Verse 25 says, "But while the men slept, his enemy came and sowed tares amidst the wheat and went away." The men were the slaves (v. 27), referring to the Lord's slaves, mainly the apostles. It was when the Lord's slaves were sleeping, not watching, that the Lord's enemy, the Devil, came and sowed false believers amidst the true ones.

Verse 25 says that the enemy sowed tares amidst the wheat. A tare is a kind of darnel, a weed resembling wheat. Its seeds are poisonous, producing sleepiness, nausea, convulsions, and even death. The sprout and leaves of the tares look the same as those of the wheat. It is impossible to discern one from the other until the fruit is produced. The fruit of the wheat is golden yellow, but that of the tares is black.

In the Old Testament, the children of Israel in the kingdom of God were likened to grapes growing in the vineyard (21:33-34), whereas in the New Testament, the kingdom people in the kingdom of the heavens are likened to wheat growing in the field. The vineyard was fenced, limited only to the Jews; whereas the field is worldwide, unlimited, open to all peoples.

This parable discloses that not long after the establishment of the kingdom by the building of the church, the situation of the kingdom of the heavens changed. It was established with the sons of the kingdom, the wheat. But the sons of the evil one, the tares, grew up to alter the situation. Hence, a difference has arisen between the kingdom of the heavens and its outward appearance. Whereas the sons of the kingdom, the wheat, constitute the kingdom, the sons of the evil one, the tares, have formed the outward appearance of the kingdom, which today is called Christendom.

The wheat is the sons of the kingdom, the real believers regenerated with the divine life. The tares are the sons of the evil one, the Devil. In the early stages of their growth, the tares appear exactly the same as wheat in color and in shape. Even experts cannot discern the difference until the fruit appears. There is a great difference in the fruit of the tares and the fruit of the wheat, for the fruit of the tares is black and the fruit of the wheat is greenish yellow. The sons of the kingdom are the sons of God who have the divine life within them. The sons of the evil one are the false believers, believers only in name, who do not have the divine life in them.

D. The King's Slaves
Wanting to Gather Up the Tares,
but the King Allowing the Tares
to Grow with the Wheat until the Harvest

When the King's slaves wanted to gather up the tares (v. 28), He said, "No, lest while gathering the tares you may root up the wheat at the same time with them." Both the tares and the wheat grow in the field, and the field is the world (v. 38). The false believers and the true ones live in the world. To gather up the tares from the field means to take away the false believers from the world. The Lord did not want His slaves to do this, lest while taking away the false believers from the world, the true ones may be taken away from the world. The Catholic Church did much of this and by so doing killed many true believers.

Many Christian teachers have wrongly interpreted the field, saying that it is the church. According to this interpretation, in the church there are both false ones and real ones. But the Lord says clearly in verse 38 that the field is the world. The wheat and the tares are allowed to grow together in the world, not in the church. According to the Epistles, not even sinful ones are allowed to remain in the church. In 1 Corinthians chapter five the Apostle Paul charged the church at Corinth to excommunicate the sinful one. If even the real but sinful ones must be cast out, then how much more the false ones? The church is not to tolerate the false believers, but both the false and the true are allowed to grow together in the world. Please be clear that the field refers to the world. In the world there are both true and false believers, but this must not be so in the church.

The Lord told His slaves not to separate the wheat from the tares, but to allow them both to grow together until the harvest. Otherwise, the wheat may be rooted up with the tares. This means that the false believers must be allowed to exist in the world with the true believers. In the past centuries the Catholic Church has made the serious mistake of trying to uproot those who were considered tares. But most of those taken away by the Catholic Church were the real ones, even the best ones. This is the reason the Lord Jesus did not allow His slaves to do such a thing.

E. The Time of Harvest —
the Consummation of the Age

Verse 30 says, "Allow both to grow together until the harvest, and in the time of the harvest I will say to the reapers, Gather first the tares and bind them into bundles to burn them up, but the wheat bring together into My barn." The harvest is the consummation of the age, and the reapers are angels (v. 39). At the consummation of this age, the Lord will send the angels firstly to gather all the tares, all stumbling blocks, and those who do lawlessness, bind them into bundles, and burn them with the fire of the lake of fire (vv. 30, 40-42). Then the wheat, the righteous, will be brought together into the King's barn, the kingdom of their Father, to shine forth as the sun (vv. 30, 43).

In Galatians 2:4 and 2 Corinthians 11:26 Paul mentioned false brethren, saying that he was damaged by the false brethren. This indicates that in Paul's time the tares were present. Of course, a great many more tares have come in since Constantine made Christianity the state religion.

A CHART O

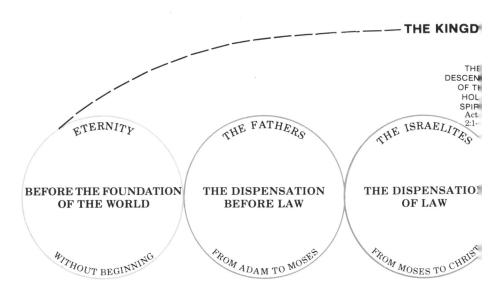

- - - - - - - - - - - - - - - THE KINGD

THE
DESCEN
OF TH
HOL
SPIR
Act
2:1-

ETERNITY

THE FATHERS

THE ISRAELITES

BEFORE THE FOUNDATION
OF THE WORLD

THE DISPENSATION
BEFORE LAW

THE DISPENSATIO
OF LAW

WITHOUT BEGINNING

FROM ADAM TO MOSES

FROM MOSES TO CHRIST

IN ETERNITY PAST	FROM ADAM TO MOSES	FROM MOSES TO CHRIST
Ephesians 1:4 1 Peter 1:20	Romans 5:13-14	John 1:17

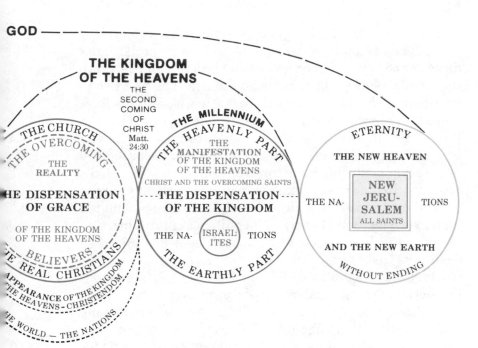

GOD

THE KINGDOM OF THE HEAVENS

THE SECOND COMING OF CHRIST Matt. 24:30

THE CHURCH

THE OVERCOMING

THE REALITY

THE DISPENSATION OF GRACE

OF THE KINGDOM OF THE HEAVENS

BELIEVERS

REAL CHRISTIANS

APPEARANCE OF THE KINGDOM

THE HEAVENS-CHRISTENDOM

WORLD — THE NATIONS

THE MILLENNIUM

THE HEAVENLY PART

THE MANIFESTATION OF THE KINGDOM OF THE HEAVENS

CHRIST AND THE OVERCOMING SAINTS

THE DISPENSATION OF THE KINGDOM

THE NA- ISRAELITES TIONS

THE EARTHLY PART

ETERNITY

THE NEW HEAVEN

NEW JERU-SALEM ALL SAINTS

THE NA- TIONS

AND THE NEW EARTH

WITHOUT ENDING

THE KINGDOM OF THE HEAVENS IS NEAR	THE MILLENNIUM Revelation 20:4-6:	THE NEW HEAVEN AND NEW EARTH WITH THE NEW JERUSALEM
	(1) THE HEAVENLY PART The manifestation of the kingdom of the heavens Matt. 24:46-47; 25:19-23; Luke 19:15-19; Rev. 2:26-27; 3:21; 2 Tim. 2:12	
Matthew 3:2; 4:17; 10:7	"The kingdom of the Father" Matt. 13:43 with Christ and the overcomers as the kings	Isaiah 65:17; 66:22 2 Peter 3:13 Hebrews 12:22 Revelation 21
THE BEGINNING OF THE ¦DOM OF THE HEAVENS	**(2) THE EARTHLY PART** The kingdom of Messiah 2 Sam. 7:13 "The tabernacle of David" Acts 15:16 The restored kingdom of Israel Acts 1:6	with all the redeemed and perfected saints, the sons of God, Revelation 21:6-7
Matt. 16:18-19; 13:24; 22:2	"The kingdom of the Son of Man" Matt. 13:41; Rev. 11:15 with the saved Israelites Rom. 11:26-27; Zech. 12:10; Ezek. 36:25-28	as the kings Revelation 22:5
THE REALITY OF THE ¦DOM OF THE HEAVENS	as the priests Zech. 8:20-23; Isa. 2:2-3 and the restored nations Acts 3:21	and the purged nations as the people Rev. 21:3-4, 24, 26; 22:2b
Matthew 5—7		
THE CHURCH		
. Tim. 3:15; Eph. 1:22b-23		
THE APPEARANCE OF THE ¦DOM OF THE HEAVENS	as the people Matt. 25:32-34	
Matthew 13:24-42		

In this parable the Lord points out the serious matter of the judgment upon the tares. This will be a special judgment, for the tares will be bound into bundles and cast into the furnace of fire, which is the lake of fire. The first two to be cast into the lake of fire will be Antichrist and the false prophet. Following them, the tares will be cast into the lake of fire at the time of the Lord's coming back. The judgment upon the tares will be so serious because they have been confusing, frustrating, and damaging God's economy. In the eyes of God, the tares are exceedingly evil.

The modernists of today are evil. They blaspheme the Lord by saying that He was an illegitimate child. They also say that the Lord Jesus was not the Redeemer, that His death was that of a martyr, and that His death was not for redemption. They also deny that Christ was resurrected. Furthermore, some modernists are very vague about God. It is difficult to determine what they believe concerning God. If you ask them about God, Christ, or the Spirit, they will respond that it is all a matter of definition. This answer is subtle and more than evil. Therefore, at the consummation of this age, the angels will bind the tares into bundles and cast them into the lake of fire. There will be no need for them to pass through the judgment at the white throne. By this judgment we can see how evil the tares are in the eyes of the Lord.

Although the tares have caused confusion, frustration, and damage, some so-called Christian groups actually boast of having tares among them, and they condemn us for not having any tares.

When the Lord Jesus came, He did not sow tares; He sowed only wheat. In His preliminary work for the establishment of the kingdom, He sowed only Himself, and He was very careful in so doing, sowing only one kind of seed. While the Lord's slaves were sleeping, the enemy, the evil one, Satan, came in to sow another seed, the seed of the tares. This took place not too long after the church was established on the day of Pentecost. The book of Acts indicates that certain false ones who had not received Christ into them as their life came in apparently as real ones. But they were tares, not wheat. In the early part of the fourth century Constantine the Great made Christianity the state religion of the Roman Empire. At that time tens of thousands of false believers came into Christianity. In order to Christianize the people, Constantine encouraged them to be baptized. Many who were baptized into Christianity were given a material reward of silver or clothing. This was the greatest opportunity for the evil one to sow his tares. At that time there were perhaps ten tares for every stalk of wheat. This has continued until the present. In Christendom there are millions of so-called Christians, but so many of them are not real believers.

Let me illustrate this from my own experience. I was born of a Southern Baptist mother. She taught us the stories of the Bible; however, at that time, although she was for Christianity, she herself definitely had not been saved. There were so many tares there it was difficult to find the wheat. The professor of world history in the American Presbyterian college where I studied came from a Jewish background. He was a false believer, believing neither in the Bible nor in the resurrection of Christ. Nevertheless, the Presbyterian mission sent him as a mission teacher to be a professor in their college. Some of the missionaries in China were modernists. Among both the Methodists and the Presbyterians, modernistic missionaries taught the people that the Bible was a book of fairy tales. They said that the Red Sea was not actually opened by God, but that the Israelites passed through a portion of the sea made shallow by the blowing of the wind. By now modernism might have penetrated the seminaries of even the Southern Baptists. Union Theological Seminary in New York treated John Sung like a mental case. After John Sung was saved, he was beside himself in the Lord, but those in that seminary, considering him a mental case, sent him to a mental hospital. Later John Sung returned to China, preached the gospel, and became probably the greatest evangelist in China. In today's Christendom there are thousands and thousands of tares.

In Matthew 13 we see a picture of the outward appear-

ance of the kingdom of the heavens. (Please refer to the
chart on pages 454 and 455.) The kingdom of God covers
everything from eternity past to eternity future. Between
the two eternities there is time divided into various ages or
dispensations. The first is the dispensation before law. After
Adam was created, he was placed in the garden where there
was no sin or darkness. From him, is the period of the
Patriarchs, the fathers, extending to Moses. This period of
the Patriarchs is known as the dispensation before law. Then
comes the dispensation of law. Following this are two
crucial dispensations, the first of which is the dispensation
of grace, the church age, and the other, the dispensation of
the kingdom, the millennium. As we have pointed out
already, the kingdom of the heavens covers only these two
dispensations. In the dispensation of grace there are a
number of complications, for the kingdom of the heavens has
three aspects: the aspect of reality, the aspect of appearance,
and the aspect of manifestation. As long as the church is
normal, it is the reality of the kingdom. In a normal situation
the church equals the reality of the kingdom. The third
aspect of the kingdom, the manifestation, is in the heavenly
part, the upper part, of the millennium. The lower part, the
earthly part, is the Messianic kingdom, the kingdom of the
Messiah, but the heavenly part is the manifestation of the
kingdom of the heavens. This heavenly part in 13:43 is also
called the kingdom of the Father, whereas the earthly part is
called in Matthew 13:41 the kingdom of the Son of Man.
Therefore, the kingdom of the Son is the kingdom of the
Messiah, and the kingdom of the Father is the manifestation
of the kingdom of the heavens.

In this message we are concerned with the appearance
of the kingdom. On the chart we have noted the appearance of the kingdom with a dotted line. It seems that
Christendom is different from the world, but actually there
is no difference at all. The appearance of the kingdom of
the heavens is today's Christendom. It is dark, devilish,
and even hellish, and we all must condemn it. Where are
you? Are you in the appearance of the kingdom or in the
reality of the kingdom? You used to be in the world, but

now you are in the church. But the church is no longer normal; rather, it has become abnormal. Therefore, there is the need of the dotted line within the church. The normal church is the reality, but the area in the dotted line indicates the abnormal church. All real Christians are in the church, but some of these Christians have become abnormal and defeated. You may say that you are neither in the world nor in Christendom, the appearance of the kingdom. You are in the church. But are you in the church in a normal situation or in an abnormal situation? The believers who are the thorny soil are abnormal. They are real Christians, but the growth of the seed is choked by the thorns so that it does not bring forth fruit. Fruit denotes both multiplication and expression. But those believers who are on the level of the constitution of the kingdom of the heavens are normal. They are poor in spirit, pure in heart; have all their temper, lust, self, and flesh dealt with; have no anxiety; and are not deceived by money. They are the good earth growing Christ into the kingdom. Therefore, they are in the normal church, which is the reality of the kingdom of the heavens.

When the Lord Jesus comes back, where will you be? If we have endured unto the end, that is, have kept ourselves in the spirit until the end, we shall be saved and shall be in the manifestation of the kingdom of the heavens, the heavenly part of the millennium. Those who are there will rule with Christ. According to 13:43, they will "shine forth as the sun in the kingdom of their Father." This is the real barn where all the wheat will shine over the nations. That shining will be the ruling, the reigning as kings.

We need to see that today's Christianity is in darkness. So many do not know where they are, where they should be, or where they will go. But in the Bible there is light, and the view is very clear. What we have seen is absolutely not according to human thought; it is a word according to the divine revelation. Everything in this chart is confirmed in the Bible. Everyone in the Lord's recovery must be deeply impressed with this chart. We are in an age of complications. Christ has come and has sown the seed, but the enemy has also come in and has done things to cause complications. Therefore, in this age we have the worldly people; the wheat, the sons of the kingdom, the children of God; and the tares, the false believers, the nominal Christians, the sons of the Devil, who are among the children of God. Many of the sons of the kingdom have become degraded and have fallen below the standard. Hence, they are abnormal.

Thus, there are four classes of people: the normal believers, the abnormal believers, the false believers, and the worldly people. Day after day, we are involved with all four categories. In the very place where you work all four types may be represented. We need to face this stiuation with a clear view of today's age. We would not stand with the world nor be a part of Christendom. Furthermore, we would not be real yet abnormal believers. Rather, we want to be real and normal believers, real sons of the kingdom who live according to the constitution of the kingdom of the heavens. We would grow Christ by living a life according to the constitution. Whatever we grow will be the multiplication which is the constituent of the kingdom of the heavens. Therefore, today we are not only in the reality — we are the reality. Then when the Lord Jesus, the King, comes again, we shall be in the manifestation of the kingdom of the heavens, shining over the world to reign as Christ's co-kings and enjoying the heavenly part of the millennium.

LIFE-STUDY OF MATTHEW

MESSAGE THIRTY-EIGHT

THE UNVEILING
OF THE KINGDOM'S MYSTERIES

(4)

In this message we shall continue to see the outward appearance of the kingdom of the heavens. As the parable of the tares reveals, the constituents of the kingdom are the sons of the kingdom, who have the divine life within them. However, the tares, the sons of the Devil, have come in. Because of these false ones among the constituents, the kingdom in its outward appearance has become Christendom. Formerly it was purely the kingdom of God, but now it has become Christendom with both real believers and false ones. When many people talk about Christianity, they are actually talking about Christendom. The kingdom of the heavens is not as large as Christendom, for the kingdom is smaller than Christendom and seems to be within it. The kingdom is real, composed of the genuine constituents who are the sons of the kingdom, the sons of God. But the tares sown by Satan have caused a mixture among the so-called Christians in the outward appearance of the kingdom of the heavens, which is Christendom.

III. THE ABNORMAL DEVELOPMENT OF THE
OUTWARD APPEARANCE OF THE KINGDOM

The Lord arranged the parables in Matthew 13 in a very good sequence. First we have the parable of the sower, who sows the seed to bring forth the constituents of the kingdom of the heavens. Then we have the parable of the tares sown by the enemy, the false ones among the constituents that cause the kingdom of the heavens to become Christendom. Following the parable of the tares, we have the parable of the mustard seed (13:31-32).

A. The Kingdom of the Heavens Being like a Grain of Mustard Seed

Verse 31 says, "The kingdom of the heavens is like a grain of mustard seed." The fruit, both of the wheat in the first two parables and the mustard here in the third parable, is for food. This indicates that the kingdom people, the constituents of the kingdom and the church, should be like a crop to produce food that satisfies God and man. Both wheat and mustard are good for food. In fact, it is very healthy and nourishing to eat wheat bread with mustard on it. However, in both the second and third parables we see the thought of the evil one, the subtlety of Satan. The evil one came in to sow tares among the wheat. As any farmer can tell you, tares greatly frustrate the growth of the wheat because they exhaust the fertility of the soil which is meant to nourish the growing wheat. Because the soil has been exhausted, wasted, by the tares, the wheat cannot grow properly. We may apply this to our present situation. Many false Christians have frustrated the growth of the genuine Christians. Wherever there are many false believers, it is difficult for the real believers to grow in life. This is the subtlety of the enemy. As we shall see, the subtlety of the enemy with respect to the mustard seed is to cause it to grow into a huge tree that is no longer good for food.

B. The Heavenly King Having Sown a Mustard Seed in His Field

On the one hand, what the Lord has sown is the grain of wheat. But on the other hand, it is a grain of mustard seed. Both the grain of wheat and the grain of mustard seed signify Christ as food to us in different aspects. He is both the wheat and the mustard for our nourishment.

C. The Mustard Seed Growing Greater than the Herbs and Becoming a Tree

Verse 32 says that after the mustard seed has grown, "It is greater than the herbs and becomes a tree." The church, which is the embodiment of the kingdom, should be like an herb to produce food, but it became a tree, a lodging place for birds, having its nature and function changed. (This is against the law of God's creation, that every plant must be after its kind — Gen. 1:11-12.) This happened when Constantine the Great mixed the church with the world in the first part of the fourth century. He brought thousands of false believers into Christianity, making it Christendom, no longer the church. Hence, this third parable corresponds to the third of the seven churches in Revelation 2 and 3, the church in Pergamos (2:12-17). The mustard is an annual herb, whereas the tree is a perennial plant. The church, according to its heavenly and spiritual nature, should be like the mustard, sojourning on the earth. But with its nature changed, the church became deeply rooted and settled in the earth as a tree, flourishing with its enterprises as the branches to lodge many evil persons and things. This has formed the outward organization of the outward appearance of the kingdom of the heavens.

For a mustard seed to become a tree is a violation of the principle ordained by God in His creation for living matter — that every plant must be according to its kind. This is what is referred to in Genesis 1, where we are told that every life grows according to its kind. A peach grows after the peach kind and an apple after the apple kind. This principle applies not only to plant life, but also to animal life and even to human life. Every type of life must develop according to its kind. A cow must be a cow, a donkey must be a donkey, and a horse must be a horse. A mule is an example of an animal not according to its kind. A mule is neither a horse nor a donkey; it is a hybrid between a horse and donkey. If a certain form of vegetable or plant life is not according to its kind, it will be abnormal and against the principle ordained by God in His creation. In keeping with this principle, a mustard must be according to a mustard, and a tree must be according to a tree. It is abnormal for a mustard to break God's principle and become a tree. But by growing into a tree, the mustard herb breaks this principle. This kind of growth is abnormal, a violation of God's regulation. Suppose human life developed without any regulation, and some Chinese grew into oxen, some Japanese grew into horses, and some Americans grew into elephants. How grotesque this would be! Thank God that in His creation He has put a governing principle into every type of life! However, when the Lord sowed the seed of a mustard herb, this herb grew into a tree. How abnormal is such a development!

When I was young, I read some books which said that this big tree was something positive. But this tree, although very large, is not positive at all. Suppose a man grew into an elephant. Would this be positive or negative? We all would be terrified of such an abnormal development. Today's Christendom is huge and devilishly abnormal. It is not only a tree, but a great tree. By this we see that not only the nature of the constituent of the kingdom has been changed, but that the size of the kingdom has become abnormal. If an herb is to be good for food, it should not grow too large. When an herb grows abnormally large, it is no longer tender, delicious, or good for food. In His economy God intends that His children be like wheat or mustard, the smaller and the more tender, the better. Furthermore, we should be annuals like wheat and mustard, neither of which remains more than a year. The church people must be annuals, not perennials. We should not be rooted deeply into the earth for a long period of time, for the Lord's intention is that we be sojourners on earth. As long as we are annuals like wheat and herbs, we shall produce the best foodstuff, grain to make loaves of bread and mustard to match the bread. This will afford others excellent food for their nourishment and satisfaction. However, the enemy has made the mustard a perennial tree that does not produce any foodstuff.

D. The Birds of Heaven Coming and Roosting in the Branches of the Tree

Verse 32 also says that the birds of heaven come and roost in the branches of this tree. Instead of producing foodstuff, this tree is a roost for birds. Because the birds in the first parable signify the evil one, Satan (vv. 4, 19), the birds of heaven in verse 32 must refer to Satan's evil spirits with the evil persons and things motivated by them. They lodge in the branches of the great tree, that is, in the enterprises of Christendom. The birds refer to the evil one and to evil persons, evil matters, and evil things — in short to all evil pertaining to the evil one. In today's Christendom, there are many evil persons, evil things, and evil matters. Christendom has become a big tree producing no fruit, but having become a lodging place for so many evil things.

When this parable was spoken by the Lord, it was prophecy; but today it has become history. In the Vatican we see the fulfillment of this parable. The Vatican is even an independent country, formed by an agreement between Mussolini and the pope. From that time onward, the Vatican and various nations of the world have exchanged ambassadors. This is a further indication that the Christian religion has become a big tree. Today there are approximately eight hundred million Catholics in the world, perhaps one fourth of the world's population, under the authority of the pope. Such a large number of people is under the papal system. Although Christianity has become a big tree, in Luke 12 the Lord Jesus called His church the "little flock." We should not be in the big tree, but remain in the little flock.

If you visit the Vatican, you will see that it is a huge tree, a lodging place filled with so many birds. The same thing is found in the Catholic churches in the United

States and in the large denominations. In the Catholic Church and in the denominations it is difficult to find a grain of wheat or a mustard seed. Instead of food, there is lodging for the birds. This is today's situation, the appearance of the kingdom of the heavens.

IV. THE INWARD CORRUPTION
OF THE OUTWARD APPEARANCE OF THE KINGDOM

A. The Parable of Leaven

With the appearance of the kingdom, there are three items: the changed nature, the tares; the changed outward appearance, the façade, the big tree; and the inward rottenness and corruption, the leaven. This brings us to the parable of the leaven.

1. The Kingdom of the Heavens Being like Leaven

Verse 33 says, "Another parable He spoke to them: The kingdom of the heavens is like leaven, which a woman took and hid in three measures of meal until the whole was leavened." Leaven in the Scriptures signifies evil things (1 Cor. 5:6, 8) and evil doctrines (Matt. 16:6, 11-12).

2. A Woman (the Apostate Catholic Church)
Having Taken the Leaven and Hidden It
in Three Measures of Meal

Verse 33 says that a woman took leaven and hid it in three measures of meal. The church, as the practical kingdom of the heavens, with Christ — the unleavened fine flour — as its content, must be the unleavened bread (1 Cor. 5:7-8). However, the Catholic Church, which was fully and officially formed in the sixth century and which is signified by the woman here, took many pagan practices, heretical doctrines, and evil matters and mixed them with the teachings concerning Christ to leaven the whole content of Christianity. This fourth parable corresponds to the fourth of the seven churches in Revelation 2 and 3, the church in Thyatira (2:18-29). This became the inward content of the outward appearance of the kingdom of the heavens.

Meal, for making the meal offering (Lev. 2:1), signifies Christ as food to both God and man. Three measures is the quantity needed to make a full meal (Gen. 18:6). Hence, to hide the leaven in three measures of meal signifies that the Catholic Church has fully leavened in a hidden way all the teachings concerning Christ. This is the actual situation in the Roman Catholic Church. This is absolutely against the Scripture, which strongly forbids putting any leaven into the meal offering (Lev. 2:4-5, 11).

The parable of the leaven reveals the matter of mixture. The three measures of meal refer to fine flour made of wheat grain. This fine flour was always used in the meal offering, the food for God's priests. Those who served God as priests fed on the fine flour of the meal offering. The meal offering was not only for the satisfaction of God's priests, but also for the satisfaction of God Himself. Thus, the meal offering was food both for the priests and for God. The meal offering is a full type of Christ in His humanity, with the fine flour signifying Christ. When the Lord appeared to Abraham, Abraham told Sarah, his wife, to prepare a full meal with three measures of fine flour. Hence, in the Bible, three measures denotes a full meal. The fact that three measures of meal have been leavened by the woman indicates that everything related to Christ has been leavened by this evil woman.

The woman of Matthew 13 is the Jezebel of Revelation 2. According to history, Thyatira signifies the apostate Roman Church. The apostate Roman Church is the woman of Matthew 13 and the Jezebel of Revelation 2. Eventually this evil woman will become the great prostitute, called Babylon the Great, seen in Revelation 17. Thus, the woman in Matthew 13, Revelation 2, and Revelation 17 is the apostate Catholic Church. After the papal system had been established, the many pagan practices which had been brought in were confirmed by that system. This is documented in Alexander Hislop's book, *The Two Baby-lons.*

3. The Whole Lump (Christianity) Having Been Leavened

According to 13:33, "the whole was leavened." The whole lump, indicating Christianity, has been leavened and corrupted. The author of *The Two Babylons,* a book written to expose the leaven of Roman Catholicism, himself used the term reverend, indicating that he himself was not completely purged of the leaven. If you read the history of Christianity, you will see that everything in it has been leavened. For example, in the Vatican there is a painting supposedly of the Trinity. Between the picture of an old man, who represents the Father, and a young man, who represents the Son, there is a young lady, called the mother of God. Above these three there is a dove, denoting the Holy Spirit. According to this picture, Mary is ranked in the deity, and the Trinity has become a quaternity. What leaven is this!

The Roman Catholic Church has leavened everything related to Christ. They do have Christ, the meal, but they have put leaven into the meal. They also have the golden cup, but it is filled with abominations (Rev. 17:4). There is no doubt that the Catholic Church has some amount of the divine things, signified by the golden cup, but they are mixed with abominations and all manner of devilish matters. This is today's Christendom. Without exception, everything in Christendom is a mixture. Consider the charismatic movement which has been brought into Catholicism and even mixed with the worship of Mary. Many Catholic charismatics think they are spiritual, yet they still worship Mary. The Roman Catholic Church also has what is called charismatic masses.

Whatever is not of the Spirit or of Christ is leaven. Leaven is something added to make things easy to eat.

Without leaven, bread would be hard, and it would be difficult to eat and digest. The Catholic Church uses this as an excuse for the use of leaven. They say they must make it easy for people to receive Christ. The Catholic Church says that Christ is mysterious, spiritual, and abstract and that people need pictures of Him in order to apprehend Him. Our natural being likes to use certain methods to make spiritual things easier to assimilate. This is what the Bible calls leaven, and we must be careful of it. We must be purged of all leaven.

Not only the Catholic Church has taken in leaven, but the Protestant denominations and groups have also. Rock music and drama are types of leaven used to make spiritual things easier for people to accept. When I was in China, I knew of some young men in a certain organization who mixed basketball with the preaching of the gospel. Using basketball for gospel preaching is also leaven. I doubt that very many were saved through this. The whole principle of the Y.M.C.A. is leaven, for the goal of the Y.M.C.A. is to bring the heavenly standard down to the earthly level, to bring the gospel to secular society in a worldly way. So many things in Christianity are leaven. These include Christmas, Easter, idols, pictures, images, rock music, drama, and the entire Y.M.C.A. system. We must be careful not to take anything other than Christ for God's purpose, because anything other than He is leaven. Oh, the subtle one is crouching nearby waiting for his prey! We can easily become his prey because in our human nature is the desire to make it easy for people to experience spiritual things. But whatever you use to help people to touch spiritual things is a type of leaven. The pure and sanctified way to preach the gospel and to bring people to Christ is prayer and the ministry of the Word. Do not take any other way. If after praying and ministering the Word, people will still not receive the gospel, that is up to the Lord. Whether or not people receive our word is a matter of the Father's will. We do not want to use any gimmicks to help in our preaching. Every gimmick is leaven. We are not for a work or for a movement — we are for the testimony of Jesus.

With the appearance of the kingdom of the heavens there are three matters: the tares, the changed nature of the constituents of the kingdom; the big tree, the false façade; and the leaven, the inward corruption and rottenness. We can apply this picture to today's Christianity. Throughout Christianity we can see tares, abnormal growth, and the corruption caused by leaven. In nearly every part of today's Christianity there is corruption. Although there is a certain amount of truth, it is mixed with leaven. Instead of purity, there is mixture. Those who oppose and criticize us, claiming to defend the truth, must deal with all these things. Praise the Lord that we have been called out of the façade and kept from the leaven! Nevertheless, we must be on the alert not to allow another kind of leaven to come in. Be careful not to take anything other than Christ. In building up the church and spreading the Lord's testimony, the only way is to pray and to minister the pure Word. In the eyes of God, any gimmick — anything other than Christ, the Word, prayer, and the Spirit — is leaven. We must pray until our preaching is in the power of the Spirit, and we must pray until our testimony is filled with the riches of Christ. This is the pure meal as food for God and man. This is what the Lord wants today.

I believe the reason the Lord gave all these parables showing the mysteries of the kingdom was to help the apostles and the early disciples to realize that this is the kingdom of the heavens. We must see the difference between the reality of the kingdom and the appearance of the kingdom. The reality is precious to God, but the appearance is abominable to Him. Therefore, we must treasure the reality and reject the appearance. We do not like the tares, the big tree, or the rottenness. We care for the pure wheat flour and the little mustard herb which are good for food. This is the church's testimony, which is food to God and man. Not until the hungry and seeking ones

come into the Lord's recovery can they find the pure food
for their spiritual satisfaction. Many of us can testify that
we were hungry for years, but that once we came into the
church, we were satisfied. Our spirit told us that here in
the church there is food. Here there are no gimmicks or
leaven, but fine flour with the mustard herb. This is the
Lord's recovery, and this is the dining table. This is the
Lord's testimony without the tares, the big tree, or the
leaven.

B. The Heavenly King Having Spoken Nothing to the Crowds but in Parables

Verse 34 says, "All these things Jesus spoke in parables
to the crowds, and apart from a parable He spoke nothing
to them." Because of the people's rejection, the heavenly
King spoke to them not in clear words, but in parables, in
order to keep the kingdom secret from them. The unveiling
of the kingdom became a mystery to them.

What the heavenly King did was a fulfillment of the
prophecy which said, "I will open my mouth in a parable"
(Psa. 78:2). By doing so, He uttered things hidden from the
foundation of the world. The kingdom people were chosen
by God before the foundation of the world (Eph. 1:4), but
the mysteries of the kingdom were hidden from the foundation of the world. The hidden things are the things concerning the kingdom. They are uttered by the heavenly
King, but uttered in a mysterious way in order to make
them still a secret from the people.

LIFE-STUDY OF MATTHEW

THE UNVEILING
OF THE KINGDOM'S MYSTERIES

(5)

In the Bible the number seven is composed of six plus one, three plus four, or four plus three. The seven churches in Revelation 2 and 3 are made up of three plus four. But the seven parables in Matthew 13 are made up of four plus three. The first four parables were given in the boat in the open air. These are the parables of the sower, the tares, the mustard seed, and the leaven. The last three were given privately to the disciples in the house. The previous three parables concerning the outward appearance of the kingdom were spoken publicly by the heavenly King in the boat to the crowds (vv. 2, 34), whereas the three parables following these were given privately in the house to the disciples (v. 36). This indicates that the things covered by these three parables are more hidden.

In each of the first four parables there was something related to eating. By this we see that the first four parables cover the matter of food. God's intention is to have a people on earth to be the constituents of His kingdom, and these people must be like food that is good to satisfy both God and man. But the enemy came in to plant tares among the wheat to frustrate the growth of the wheat and to damage it. Nevertheless some wheat has grown up and multiplied. Thus, in the fourth parable we have the meal. The fine flour composing the meal comes from wheat. The reason the Lord Jesus sowed wheat seeds was that God desires to have fine flour. Although Satan, God's enemy, sowed tares among the wheat to frustrate its growth, God cannot be defeated. Some wheat grew to produce grain, and the grain was ground into fine flour to make a loaf. While this was taking place, Satan caused the mustard herb, intended to be a source of food, to grow abnormally into a big tree and thereby to lose its function of producing food. Instead, it became an evil lodging place. This is a picture of Christendom today. In the various Christian organizations we see big buildings, offices, and complex hierarchies. We see the branches of the big tree, but nothing of the fine flour or the mustard herb. According to the fourth parable, Satan then took the further step of adding leaven to the fine flour. Here we see Satan's subtlety. Firstly, he sowed tares among the wheat to frustrate the growth of the wheat; secondly, he caused the mustard herb to grow abnormally and to lose its function; thirdly, seeing that some wheat was produced to make fine flour for a loaf to satisfy God and man, Satan added leaven to the meal.

The first four parables are all related to the farm. In 1 Corinthians 3:9 Paul says, "Ye are God's farm, ye are God's building" (Gk.). In this chapter we see that God's farm eventually produces gold, silver, and precious stones. How mysterious it is that the produce of God's farm becomes gold, silver, and precious stones, the materials for God's building. God's farm produces the things of life, and these things of life become the materials for God's building. Thus, God's farm is for God's building.

In the first four parables in Matthew we have the life growing, and in the next parable we have the treasure hidden in the field. The treasure must be made up of gold, silver, and precious stones, probably mainly precious stones. In the following parable we find the pearl. The New Jerusalem is built with gold, precious stones, and pearl. Gold is the material of the city proper, and precious stones and pearl are the two other building materials for the city of God. In the first four parables the Lord revealed the life that grows Christ into the kingdom. In the next two parables He revealed the matter of transformation for building. This brings us back to the basic thought of the

Bible — life and building. The parables in Matthew 13 reveal the matters of life and building. Life is Christ Himself as the seed sown into our humanity. This life grows within us, growing Christ into the kingdom. The growing of this life eventually produces precious stones and pearls.

After spending much time on Matthew 13, I found that its basic thought is the same as that of 1 Corinthians 3. In both chapters we have God's farm and God's building. The first four parables are related to God's farm for growing Christ into the kingdom, and the following two parables are related to transformation for producing precious materials for God's building. If we are not impressed with this matter, we shall not be able to understand the fifth and sixth parables.

We have consulted a number of books on Matthew 13, but none of them touch the depth of this chapter. None of the interpretations given in those books satisfied us. Even D. M. Panton says that the treasure hidden in the field is the kingdom and that the pearl is righteousness, for in 6:33 we are told to seek first the kingdom of God and His righteousness. The teaching prevalent among the Brethren did not get into the depth of this chapter. Although D. M. Panton saw that the treasure hid in the field referred to the kingdom, he was not clear about the pearl. In this message we need to consider these two parables in a definite way.

V. THE KINGDOM HIDDEN
IN THE GOD-CREATED WORLD

Verse 44 says, "The kingdom of the heavens is like a treasure hidden in the field, which a man found and hid, and in his joy goes and sells all, whatever he has, and buys that field." The treasure hidden in the field must consist of gold or precious stones, the materials for the building of the church and the New Jerusalem (1 Cor. 3:12; Rev. 21:18-20). Because the church is the practical kingdom today, and the New Jerusalem will be the kingdom in manifestation in the coming age, therefore the treasure hidden in the field signifies the kingdom hidden in God's created world.

A. The Kingdom of the Heavens
Being like a Treasure Hidden in the Field

The field in verse 44 is the earth, which signifies the world created by God for His kingdom (Gen. 1:26-28). In the Bible the earth signifies the world created by God, and the sea signifies the world corrupted by Satan. The earth also signifies Israel, the Jewish nation, because Israel was chosen by God, separated by God, and placed by God in a specific situation. Hence, the Jewish people stand before God as the earth created by Him. Based upon the same principle, the sea also signifies the Gentile world, for the Gentiles are the people corrupted by Satan. Therefore, in the Bible the earth and the sea stand for two things each.

The first four parables in Matthew 13 provide a clear picture of so-called Christianity. After giving forth these parables, the Lord privately spoke to His disciples the parables of the treasure hidden in the field and the pearl from the sea. If we understand the significance of the earth in the Bible, we shall know that the treasure hidden in the field must be the kingdom, and that the pearl produced out of the sea must be the church. The kingdom is truly a treasure to the Lord. How precious it is in His sight! The church is also a valuable pearl to Him. The Lord is continually seeking two things — the kingdom as the treasure and the church as the pearl. Ephesians 5:27 says that Christ will present to Himself a glorious church without spot, wrinkle, or any such thing. This is the church as a beautiful pearl produced out of the Gentile world.

Chapter one of Genesis says that God created the earth and that He created man in His own image with the intention that man would exercise His dominion over the animals, the fowl, and the fish. This is the kingdom on earth. However, man failed. But Psalm 8 follows with a prophecy. Verse 1 of this Psalm says, "O Lord our Lord, how excellent is thy name in all the earth." When the earth is God's dominion, His name will be sanctified and made excellent on the earth. Speaking of man, Psalm 8:6 says,

"Thou madest him to have dominion over the works of thy hands; thou hast put all things under his feet." The following verses reveal that man has dominion over the beasts of the field, the fowl of the air, and the fish of the sea. Hebrews 2 reveals that the man described in Psalm 8 firstly is Christ. Christ is the man who brings in God's dominion to earth and makes God's name excellent on earth. Then this man is Christ's Body. This is the treasure on earth, the kingdom.

Daniel 2 indicates that the earth will be under various forms of worldly power, but that Christ will be the stone coming from heaven to smash these worldly powers (Dan. 2:34-35, 44-45). This stone will eventually become a great mountain filling the entire earth. The stone is Christ, and the great mountain is Christ enlarged to be the universal kingdom on earth. All this is related to the treasure in the earth. Revelation 11:15 says, "The kingdom of the world has become the kingdom of our Lord and of His Christ, and He shall reign forever and ever." This will take place at the time of the millennium, when the whole earth will be Christ's kingdom. This surely is the treasure hidden in the field.

Verse 44 says that the kingdom of the heavens is like a treasure hidden in the field "which a man found and hid, and in his joy goes and sells all, whatever he has, and buys that field." The man here is Christ, who found the kingdom of the heavens in 4:12 to 12:23, hid it in 12:24 to 13:43, and in His joy went to the cross in 16:21; 17:22-23; 20:18-19; and 26:1 to 27:52 to sell all He had and buy that field — to redeem the created and lost earth — for the kingdom. Christ first found the treasure when He came out to minister, declaring, "Repent, for the kingdom of the heavens has drawn near." When the Jews' rejection of the Lord reached its peak, He forsook them. From that time onward, He hid the treasure. Then He went to the cross to buy not only the treasure, but also the field, and He thereby redeemed the earth created by God.

Christ went to the cross to redeem the God-created

earth because within the earth there was the kingdom, the treasure. For the kingdom, for this treasure, Christ redeemed the earth created by God. In order for Him to have the kingdom on earth, He must redeem the earth because it had been polluted and damaged by Satan's fall and by man's sin. The Lord sold all that He had and bought the earth; that is, He sacrificed all He had on the cross to redeem the earth for the treasure of the kingdom. No doubt this kingdom is realized in the church life. But its manifestation is related to the redeemed nation of Israel. During the millennium, the earth will become the kingdom of Christ. At that time, the nation of Israel will be the center of Christ's kingdom. Hence, the kingdom is mainly related to the nation of Israel and involved with Israel.

VI. THE CHURCH PRODUCED
OUT OF THE SATAN-CORRUPTED WORLD

A. The Kingdom of the Heavens
Being like a Merchant Seeking Fine Pearls

Verses 45 and 46 say, "Again, the kingdom of the heavens is like a merchant seeking fine pearls, and finding one pearl of great value, he went and sold all, whatever he had, and bought it." The merchant in verse 45 is also Christ, who was seeking the church for His kingdom. After finding it in 16:18 and 18:17, He went to the cross and sold all He had and bought it for the kingdom.

B. The Heavenly King's Work

In verse 46 we see the heavenly King's work in gaining the one pearl of great value. At the cross He sold all, whatever He had, and bought that pearl. The pearl, produced in the death waters (the world filled with death) by the living oyster (the living Christ), wounded by a little rock (the sinner) and secreting its life-juice around the wounding rock (the believer), is also the material for the building of the New Jerusalem. Since the pearl comes out of the sea, which signifies the world corrupted by Satan (Isa. 57:20; Rev. 17:15), it must refer to the church, which is mainly constituted with regenerated believers from the Gentile world, and which is of great value.

The Lord is not only seeking the kingdom; He also desires a beautiful church, the pearl. We have pointed out that, according to Revelation 21, the New Jerusalem is built with precious stones and pearls. In other words, the New Jerusalem is a combination of the treasure and the pearl. In Matthew 13 these are two, the treasure in the field and the pearl out of the sea. But in Revelation 21 they are combined in one entity. The New Jerusalem is both the kingdom and the church. In Matthew 16 the terms church and kingdom are used interchangeably. Firstly the Lord said, "I will build My church"; then He said, "I give to you the keys of the kingdom of the heavens." The fact that these terms are used interchangeably means that the church is equal to the kingdom and the kingdom to the church. Ultimately, in the New Jerusalem the kingdom and the church become one entity.

At this point some may be asking the following question: Since the kingdom is the church and the church is the kingdom, what is the difference between them? This brings us to a matter difficult to understand. Let me approach it by asking whether we in the Lord's recovery are in the church or the kingdom. It is correct to say that we are in both the church and the kingdom, but we must know in what sense we are the church and in what sense we are the kingdom. In other words, we must know in what sense we are the treasure and in what sense we are the pearl. As the kingdom, we are something of the earth created by God and redeemed by Christ; and as the church, we are something out of the world corrupted by Satan and condemned by God. The treasure, the symbol of the kingdom, is concealed within the earth. Hence, it is altogether related to the earth. But the pearl, the symbol of the church, has nothing whatever to do with the earth. It is something produced out of the sea. Out of the Satan-corrupted and God-condemned sea such a beautiful thing as a fine pearl has been produced. As the church, we have been produced out of the world, but we no longer have anything to do with the world. Although we are the pearl out of the sea, we are no longer in the sea. We have been regenerated to become a beautiful pearl. Being in another category, we have nothing to do with this rotten world. As the kingdom we have nothing to do with the Satan-corrupted world, but we are related to the God-created earth and Christ-redeemed earth. On the one hand, we are through with the world; on the other hand, we are building up something on earth. We are not building a tower of Babel; we are building the kingdom of the heavens. As Matthew 6:10 says, "Let Your kingdom come; let Your will be done, as in heaven, so on earth." God's kingdom cannot be established in the sea, and God's will cannot be done in the Satan-corrupted world. God's will must be done on the God-created earth, and God's kingdom must be established on the Christ-redeemed earth. At the same time we are both in the church and in the kingdom, in the pearl and in the treasure.

When the New Jerusalem comes, there will be no more sea, and the earth will be renewed (Rev. 21:1). On that new earth there will be a combination of the treasure and the pearl, of the kingdom and the church. In the New Jerusalem the treasure will no longer be hidden in the field, but built upon the surface of the field. In that combination of the treasure and the pearl, the treasure will be built up with the pearl. If you have this vision, you will see that even among us today the kingdom and the church are built up together. We do not have two entities, but just one entity. On the one hand, this entity is the treasure, the kingdom; on the other hand, it is the pearl, the church.

Among us in the Lord's recovery there should be no sea. Instead of the sea, we should have the renewed earth. But suppose you visit the church in Anaheim, and in many of the homes you hear nothing but gossiping. This would be a sign that the sea is still present with those brothers and sisters. Although a church filled with gossip is still a church, it is a church in the water of the ocean. Such a church cannot be the kingdom. It is the pearl, but not the treasure. But suppose in all the homes of the church in Anaheim there is no gossip, criticism, or idle words. Rather, there is nothing but the experience of Christ and the church. In such a case, there will be no sea. Instead, there will be life, light, and transformation. Such a church is the renewed land for the kingdom. In every home you see the proper humanity, and immediately you sense that there is no more sea, only the renewed earth. On this renewed earth there is the New Jerusalem composed of the pearl and the treasure. This is not only the church, but also the kingdom. In such a church you have the treasure in the field and the pearl out of the sea.

By this illustration we see that the church can be both the pearl and the treasure. When we are the pearl, we are out of the sea, out of the world. When we are the kingdom, we are on the earth. However, we are not on the earth in a subdued way, but in a reigning way, for we are on the earth as the heavenly kingdom. This should not be mere doctrine to us. It must be our genuine daily practice. If our conversation is filled with talk about worldly things, about money or the movies, it is a sign that we are filled with the things of the Satan-corrupted world. This is the sea. But if among us there is no gossip or criticism, but Christ, the church, and transformation, this is a sign that we are the new earth. Among us here in Anaheim we have the new earth. On this new earth we have the treasure, the kingdom, and the proper human life. Even today, this treasure is no longer hidden; it is on the surface of the earth. To the worldly people and to the unbelieving Jews, this treasure is hidden within the earth. Praise the Lord that we have such a treasure in the renewed earth! None of the outsiders or unbelievers understands this. Sometimes they say, "We don't understand those people. We don't know what they are doing. However, we realize that they are good people." This is the treasure, the evidence that we are living a proper human life on the God-created and Christ-redeemed earth. At the time of the millennium, in the eyes of God the entire earth will be a treasure.

In the first four parables in Matthew 13 we see only the growing of life: we see nothing of transformation. In these parables we have the wheat, the grain, the mustard, and the fine flour. Praise the Lord for the two following parables! We have not only four parables on the growing life, but also two parables on transformation. Transformation makes us pearls and precious stone, pearls for the church and precious stones for the kingdom. On the one hand, we are out of the world, having nothing to do with the corrupted world. On the other hand, we are living on earth as the proper humanity. For us, there is no more the sea, but the dry land created by God and redeemed by Christ. Now we are living and walking on this land. This is not only the church as the pearl, but also the kingdom as the treasure. I praise the Lord that I am part of the pearl and of the treasure. As part of the pearl, I have nothing to do with this rotten world. But as part of the treasure, I am very interested in this earth. I do not desire to go to heaven. I prefer to be here on this good earth where there is no more sea. We are the pearl and we are the treasure. We are out of the world, but we are still on the earth. This is the correct interpretation of these two parables.

LIFE-STUDY OF MATTHEW

THE UNVEILING
OF THE KINGDOM'S MYSTERIES

(6)

Before we consider the parable of the net, I would like to say a further word regarding the treasure and the pearl. In the Bible the number seven is composed of four plus three, three plus four, or six plus one. The first time the number seven is mentioned in the Bible, it is composed of the six days of creation plus one day, the Sabbath, for rest. In Revelation the seven churches are composed of three plus four. The seven seals are firstly composed of four plus three, then of six plus one. The principle is the same with the seven trumpets and the seven bowls. In Matthew 13 the number seven is composed firstly of four plus three, then of six plus one. The first four parables are all related to food-stuff, but the fifth and sixth parables are related to trans-formation for building. Although even the hardest bread can be leavened, pearl and precious stones cannot be leav-ened. Furthermore, although a wafer or even hard bread may be ruined by water poured upon it, this is not true of either precious stones or pearls.

The Lord's word in Matthew 13 is not merely a prophecy or a doctrine. It is also a vision of the practical situation of today's Christianity with respect to the church and the kingdom. The Lord's word about the mysteries of the kingdom is not idealistic or ethereal. It is practical. Thus, if we would understand these parables, we must look to the Lord for some practical application of them. Our understanding of the parables must match the practical situation.

If you look at today's Christendom, you will see that the real Christians are the wheat and that the false Christians have been mixed with the real ones to frustrate their growth. Everywhere on earth, especially in Europe, we see more false Christians than real ones. In Catholic countries like Italy and Brazil it is difficult to find one genuine Christian among many so-called Christians. Therefore, the interpretation of the tares as being false Christians is not only doctrinal, but also practical according to history and the present situation. Furthermore, the big tree stands before us. Every day we behold the huge façade of Christendom. This is neither doctrine nor mere prophecy. In front of our eyes we have the practical fulfillment of prophecy. We also see leaven everywhere. In Christendom there is leaven in everything. Every aspect and every corner of Christendom has been leavened. If there is a little truth, there is a great deal of leaven added to it. This is the actual situation today.

We can interpret the first four parables in a practical way and apply them in a practical way. Now we must do the same with the fifth and sixth parables. Recently the Lord has shown us the practical way to understand them. In order to understand any prophecy in a practical way we need the facts. Only when we see the facts can we understand the prophecy of these parables in a practical way. In the Lord's recovery we have the treasure and the pearl. In the first four parables we have the wheat, the tares, the mustard, and the leaven. We are not the tares; we are the wheat and the fine flour. However, in the Lord's recovery it is not adequate simply to be wheat or fine flour. If we are just wheat or fine flour, we shall not be satisfied. In the Lord's recovery there is also a pearl and the treasure, the precious stones. In His recovery the Lord must have a church that is pure, solid, and genuine like a pearl. In such a pearl there is no mixture or opaqueness. Rather, it is absolutely pure and bright. If you would know what the church in the Lord's recovery is, look at a pearl. By looking at a pearl, you will know what the church should be.

Although we are not yet completely satisfied, we can say that the churches in the Lord's recovery are like pearls. No matter how solid bread may be, it is still possible for it to be leavened. But when the church has become a pearl, it can no longer be leavened. Who could put leaven into pearl or precious stone?

In the Lord's recovery we on the one hand must be like a pearl and on the other hand like precious stone. Concerning life, we are the pearl; concerning our living, we are the treasure, the precious stone. Look at the New Jerusalem: all the gates are pearls, but the walls are built with precious stones. The pearl gates are for entrance, for the beginning; and the walls are for expression. The church is our life, and the kingdom is our living. As the church, we have been regenerated out of the Satan-corrupted world. But we are not only the pearl for the beginning, the entrance; we are also the precious stone for the expression. This signifies our living under the heavenly ruling. This is the kingdom. As the church, we are the pearl having life, a new start, and an entrance. As the kingdom, we are the treasure, the precious stone, standing there as something that has been built up to express Christ under the heavenly constitution. This is our living and our expression.

Some teachers say that the kingdom is related to Israel, but maybe no one says that the pearl is related to the church. Those who relate the kingdom to Israel are too doctrinal and dispensational, not at all practical. We need to apply the parables of the treasure and the pearl not only in a doctrinal way or a dispensational way, but also in a practical way. In order to apply them in a practical way, we must see that during the period of the existence of Christendom, the Lord is working to gain the treasure and the pearl. Christendom continues with the wheat, the tares, the big tree, and the leaven in the meal. But the Lord spoke not only the four parables for Christendom, but two parables for the genuine and proper church life. The churches in the Lord's recovery are in the fifth and sixth parables. The churches in the recovery today are the treasure and the pearl. As far as life is concerned, we are the pearl; and as far as our living is concerned, we are the treasure. For life, we are the pearl gates; for our living, we are the walls made of precious stones. This latter is the kingdom life, the living of the church under God's dominion.

This enables us to have a fuller understanding of the New Jerusalem. The twelve pearl gates signify the church as the entrance, and the walls built with precious stones signify the kingdom, the expression of living under the heavenly rule. When you say, "Lord Jesus, how I thank You that I have the divine life," that is the pearl. But when you say, "O Lord, grant me more grace that I may be poor in spirit and pure in heart, that I may be under Your ruling, that I may be dealt with by You so that I will not have any rocks or thorns within me, and that I may live under the heavenly constitution," you immediately become the treasure. On the one hand, we are the pearl; on the other hand, we are the treasure.

The fifth parable speaks of a man finding a treasure and the sixth, of the merchant seeking a pearl. For the kingdom, Christ is the man, and for the church, He is the merchant. This fits in with the concept of the entire Bible. The kingdom requires a man. In order to have God's kingdom on earth, there is the need of a man. Christ came as this man, not as the first man, but as the second man. Firstly this man found the kingdom. Then, because of the rejection of Israel, He hid the kingdom from the Jewish people. For the church, Christ is the merchant, one who is always seeking to gain something of high value. Regarding the kingdom, the man bought the field, the earth. The reason he bought the earth is that the kingdom is in the earth. However, in order to gain the pearl, the merchant did not purchase the sea; rather, he bought only the pearl. Christ is the One who bought the pearl directly, but He did not buy the treasure directly. Instead, He bought the field directly. Although Christ redeemed the church and the earth, He did not redeem the kingdom. The kingdom does not require a redeemer or a buyer. However, the lost earth the earth created by God and then lost, requires a redeemer. Furthermore, the church as God's chosen and predestinated people also requires a buyer because those people became lost. Therefore, the kingdom needs only a man, but the church needs a merchant and a redeemer.

VII. THE ETERNAL GOSPEL AND ITS RESULT

Verse 47 says, "Again, the kingdom of the heavens is like a net cast into the sea and gathering of every kind." This parable corresponds to 25:32-46. The net here does not signify the gospel of grace, which is preached in the church age, but the eternal gospel, which will be preached to the Gentile world in the great tribulation (Rev. 14:6-7). The sea into which this net is cast signifies the Gentile world, and "every kind" signifies all the nations, all the Gentiles (25:32).

Throughout the centuries, the parable of the net has been misunderstood and applied incorrectly. Many have said that the net signifies the gospel of grace. They have also likened this parable to the parable of the tares, saying that in the parable of the tares we have the real ones and the false ones, and that in the parable of the net we have the good ones and the bad ones. They claim that the good ones are the wheat and the bad ones are the tares. If this is true, then the Lord Jesus would have not been so wise, for He would have used two parables for the same thing.

Once again we need to consider the way the number seven is constituted. Firstly, it is composed of six plus one. The first six parables in Matthew 13 are related to the church. In the church there are the abnormal ones, and around the church there are the false ones. Thus, directly or indirectly, the first six parables are related to the church. But what happens to the people outside of the church, those in the world? Surely there is the need of a parable to cover them. If the seven parables in Matthew 13 covered only the church, then there would be no parable to cover the nations. In such a case, chapter thirteen would not be perfect. The seventh parable, the parable of the net, is related not to the church, but to the world, to the nations.

Those related to the church are classified into three groups: the real and normal Christians, the overcomers; the real, yet abnormal Christians, the defeated ones; and the false Christians. At the time of the Lord's coming back, the false Christians, the tares, will be bound into bundles and cast into the furnace of fire, that is, into the lake of fire. That will be the destiny of the tares. The normal, real Christians, the overcomers, will be transferred into the manifestation of the kingdom to be co-kings with Christ. The abnormal ones will be put in a certain place to be chastened, disciplined, and punished. These six parables give us a clear view regarding the real Christians and the false Christians. The seventh parable, the parable of the net, covers the destiny of the worldly people.

The net here is not the gospel of grace. Instead, it is the eternal gospel declared in Revelation 14:6 and 7. (See Life-study of Revelation, Message Forty-seven, pp. 541-547.) Most Christian teachers have neglected this gospel. During the tribulation, Antichrist, who will oppose all religion, will persecute both Christians and Jews. Christ will consider these persecuted Christians His brothers. Because Antichrist will persecute the Jews and the Christians, an angel will be sent forth to proclaim the eternal gospel. The eternal gospel is absolutely different in content from the gospel of grace. The gospel of grace is preached for repentance and faith in the Lord Jesus. The eternal gospel, however, will say that men should fear God and worship Him. It will not touch the matter of repentance nor will it require faith. Rather, because Antichrist will set himself up as God, erecting an image of himself and compelling people to worship it, the eternal gospel will tell people to worship God, the One who created the heavens, the earth, and the sea, not to worship the idol of Antichrist. Furthermore, the eternal gospel will command the people to fear God because Antichrist will be leading them to persecute and to kill God's people. Those who kill God's people must hear that God will come in to avenge them. Hence, they all must fear God.

The Bible says that Christ as a man has been appointed by God to judge the living and the dead (Acts 17:31; 2 Tim. 4:1). Christ will judge the living at the time of His coming back. This will take place before the millennium. In addition to the Jews and the Christians, there have been throughout the centuries a great many unbelievers, most of whom will have died before the Lord comes back. But a number will still be living at the time He comes again. These living ones will be the nations. When Christ comes back, He will exercise His judgment upon them. He will judge them not according to the law of Moses nor according to the gospel of grace, but according to the eternal gospel declared in the three and a half years immediately prior to Christ's coming back. In the Bible both the law of Moses and the gospel of grace are a basis for God's judgment. The eternal gospel declared in Revelation 14 will be the basis for Christ's judgment upon the living nations.

Matthew 25 says that when Christ comes back He will gather the nations together. This portion of the Word does not speak of either the Jews or the believers, but of the nations. Some have argued saying that the nations could not be the Lord's sheep. But Psalm 100 reveals that all the people on earth are the sheep of the Lord. Hence, in the Lord's eyes all the peoples on this earth are His sheep. When He comes back, He will gather them all before the throne of His glory, and there He will exercise His judgment upon them, based upon the eternal gospel. According to Matthew 25, the King will judge the nations according to the way they have treated His little brothers. During the tribulation, the Jews and the Christians will suffer a great deal. They will lack food and clothing, they will be sick, and they will be imprisoned. The ones who hear the eternal gospel and who fear God and worship Him will secretly help the believers, rendering them some financial or material assistance. Those who treat the believers favorably will be regarded by the King as sheep. But those who do not treat them well will be regarded as goats. The goats will be cast into eternal fire, but the sheep will be transferred to the millennium to be the citizens on the earth.

The first six parables cover various aspects related to the church. The worldly people are covered in the parable of the net. The church is a pearl out of the sea. After the church has been called out of the sea, what remains in the sea is the nations who will be living in the Gentile world. At the Lord's coming back, He will send out His angels to collect all the things in the sea. After they have been collected before the throne of His glory, they will be divided according to the way they have treated the believers during the tribulation. Those who have treated them well will be considered the sheep, the good ones, and those who have treated them poorly will be considered the goats, the evil ones. The good ones will be transferred to the millennial kingdom, which has been prepared for them from the foundation of the world (not before the foundation of the world). There these good ones will be the citizens of the coming kingdom. But the evil ones will be cast into the lake of eternal fire. This will close the age.

Matthew 13 presents us a clear vision. In this chapter we see that all seven parables close this age. The Lord will end this age by dealing with the church according to the first six parables and by dealing with the world, the nations, according to the last parable. In these parables we see all the aspects of the mysteries of the kingdom of the heavens. With this clear picture before us, we know where we are and where we are going. We also know where the unbelievers are, where they are going, and what their destiny will be.

VIII. THE TREASURE OF THINGS NEW AND OLD

At the end of this chapter the Lord spoke an additional parable. Verse 52 says, "And He said to them, Therefore, every scribe discipled to the kingdom of the heavens is like a man that is a householder, who brings forth out of his treasure things new and old." After giving the seven parables concerning the mysteries of the kingdom, the Lord likened the discipled scribe to a householder who has a treasure, a rich store, of things new and old, signifying not only the new and old knowledge of the Scriptures, but also the new and old experiences of life in the kingdom.

This added parable concerns a scribe who has been discipled into the kingdom of the heavens. A scribe was a scholar in the Old Testament, one who knew the books of Moses and the prophets. In this parable the Lord does not use the word "believed," but the word "discipled." Such a learned one has been discipled into the kingdom of the heavens. Formerly he was a scholar of the Old Testament dispensation, but now he has been discipled into the kingdom of the heavens. This means that he has been discipled into God's new economy. He knew God's old economy, but now he has been discipled into God's new economy. For this reason he is likened to a householder who brings forth out of his treasure things new and old. When the new things are put with the old things, we have the precious things. The Apostle Paul was such a person. He was an Old Testament scribe who one day was discipled into God's New Testament economy. Hence, Paul could bring forth the old things and the new things. This qualified him to write the book of Hebrews. In this book Paul brings forth many of the old things, with the new things as the interpretation.

In giving this parable the Lord was expecting that some of His listeners would be scribes, not all fishermen like Peter, John, James, and Andrew. The Lord Jesus is wise. At the turn of the new economy, He had to go to Galilee to find the unlearned fishermen. But after the turn had taken place, there would be the need of some learned ones to carry out all the mysteries. Although those Galileans heard the Lord speak all the mysteries, they were not scribes. In his writing, Peter did not refer to many things from the Old Testament; neither did John. But Paul was not a Galilean fisherman. He was a scribe who had been discipled into the kingdom. Therefore, he had a rich store, a rich treasure.

The Lord's recovery needs not only the unlearned Galileans, but also the scribes. After the Lord spoke the parables of the kingdom to the Galilean fishermen, He spoke another parable regarding the scribe discipled into the kingdom of the heavens. The Lord seemed to be saying, "You Galilean fishermen must listen to this. You are not adequate to carry out God's New Testament economy. I can use you to make the turn, but after the turn has been made, you will not be adequate. I need some scribes. I need one like Saul of Tarsus who studied at the feet of Gamaliel." In this matter we see the Lord's wisdom. Young people, you need to go to the best colleges and earn a degree. Then you will be scribes. Today the Lord needs not only the Galilean fishermen to make the turn; He also needs the scribes.

When the disciples heard the parables concerning the mysteries of the kingdom, they might have been very happy and said, "Hallelujah, we, the Galilean fishermen, know all the mysteries of the kingdom!" But the Lord might have said, "You are happy, but I still need some scribes. Sorry, none of you is a scribe. Peter, you will be good for the day of Pentecost, good for throwing the net and catching a large number of people. But after so many have been brought into the church, how will you deal with them? You Galilean fishermen do not have the ability for this. I need some scribes full of knowledge, some scribes discipled into My economy. These scribes will pull out the things new and old both from their knowledge and from their experience." Because Paul had advanced in religion, he could write the book of Galatians. Peter, however, could not write such a book. This is proved by Peter's word in his second book (2 Pet. 3:15-16). Perhaps he was the leading fisherman in casting the net, but he was not advanced in the Jewish religion. He did not know the books of Leviticus and Psalms as well as Saul of Tarsus did. Thus, all the Galilean fishermen were subdued by the parable of the scribe. If we apply this parable to Paul, we see what a rich treasure he had. Out of his treasure he could bring forth new doctrines and old doctrines, new experiences and old experiences. I hope that some of the young people will become scribes. For the Lord's recovery today we need both the fishermen and the scribes.

LIFE-STUDY OF MATTHEW

MESSAGE FORTY-ONE

THE TREASURE AND THE PEARL

In this message I have the burden to give an additional word concerning the treasure and the pearl (13:44-46). Throughout the centuries, these two parables have not been properly and thoroughly understood, nor have they been correctly applied. I want to approach these parables not in a doctrinal way, but in the way of application.

THE FACTS OF HISTORY

Firstly, we need to be reminded that Matthew 13 is a chapter on the mysteries of the kingdom of the heavens. The mysteries unveiled in these parables cover the entire span of Christian history. In other words, the mysteries of the kingdom of the heavens encompass the main points of Christian history between the Lord's first coming and His second coming. To interpret these parables properly, we need to take care of the facts of history. Otherwise, what we say about them will be imaginary and not practical. For example, in order to interpret Nebuchadnezzar's dream recorded in Daniel 2, we cannot afford to neglect the facts of history. We need to know what historical facts correspond to the golden head, the silver chest and arms, and the other parts of the great image Nebuchadnezzar saw in his dream. Revelation 6 also illustrates the need to know the facts of history in order to interpret the Scripture. In this chapter we have the four horses: the white horse, the red horse, the pale horse, and the black horse. Many interpretations of the four horses have been offered. However, none of them has satisfied us because those interpretations did not correspond to the facts of history. According to the historical facts, from the time of the ascension of Christ there has been the preaching of the gospel, the spreading of the glad tidings, represented by the white horse. Following that, there has been war signified by the red horse, famine signified by the black horse, and death signified by the pale horse.

A COMPLETE PICTURE OF CHRISTENDOM

With this principle in mind, we come to Matthew 13. As we have pointed out, the first four parables reveal the general situation of Christianity. The wheat signifies the real believers; the tares symbolize the false believers; the big tree represents Christendom with its huge organization; and the leaven added to the meal by the woman stands for the evil doctrines and heathen practices of the apostate church. We have seen that in the Bible the fine flour signifies Christ as the food to both God and His people. When all these items are put together, we have a complete picture of Christendom.

THE OVERCOMERS

The parables of the treasure hidden in the field and the pearl out of the sea are puzzling. What facts of history fit in with these parables? The true believers are the fulfillment of the wheat; the false believers, of the tares; Christendom, of the big tree; the apostate church, of the woman; the evil things of heathenism and various heretical teachings, of the leaven; and Christ as food for God and man, of the meal. But what is there in history that can be regarded as the fulfillment of the treasure and the pearl? As I was considering this matter before the Lord, He showed me that in history besides the real believers, the false believers, Christendom, the apostate church, the heresies and heathen practices, and Christ as food, there have been the overcomers, who are more solid, genuine, precious, and valuable in the eyes of God than the wheat. In God's eyes these overcomers are likened to the treasure hidden in the field and to the pearl out of the sea. From the first century until the present, among the many real Christians represented by the wheat, there have been a small number of more solid ones like the transformed precious stones hidden in the field. This is especially true today. In the Lord's recovery there are a good number of saints who love the Lord, who have given up the world, and who do not live by their natural life. Although they have had some failures, they still like to live in the spirit, spend time in the presence of the Lord, stay in the Lord's will, and be one with Him in a practical way. Those who are like this are not just the wheat, bulky in size and abundant in quantity; they are the transformed precious stones, smaller in quantity and hidden under the earth. Not many people can see them, but the Lord sees them.

REDUCED AND MADE SOLID

Many saints in the Lord's recovery can testify that they are not merely wheat, but something more solid, valuable, and precious. Before certain brothers and sisters came to the Lord's recovery, they were wheat. Outwardly, they were rather bulky and showy. But during the years they have been in the recovery, they have been constricted and reduced. They have become smaller year by year. When you were bulky, you were soft and light like cotton, easily ruined by a little water. But after you are reduced, constricted, and transformed, you have the assurance that you are more precious to the Lord. Many of us can testify of this. We in the Lord's recovery are not as bulky as we used to be. Instead, we are constantly being reduced, transformed, and made more solid. After you have become as solid as a precious stone, not even a flood can damage you. Instead of damaging a precious stone, water only makes it more clean and valuable.

If we examine Christian history, we shall find those who belong in the categories of the treasure and the pearl. The parables of the treasure and the pearl refer to the overcomers throughout the centuries. As an illustration of the genuine believers, the Lord uses the example of wheat grown from seed sown in the field. This, however, is a general illustration of the genuine believers. The Lord uses other illustrations to describe the overcoming members of the church. They used to be lifeless grains of sand. But they wounded Christ, the oyster living in the death water, and stayed at Christ's wound, where they participated in the secretion of Christ's life. This not only enabled them to be regenerated, but also caused them to become pearls. This is more than a seed sown in a field to produce wheat; it is something that has become precious through the secretion of the life of Christ.

THE CHURCH AND THE KINGDOM

We have pointed out that the treasure no doubt refers to precious stones. The New Jerusalem is the ultimate consummation of the church life and the kingdom life, for in this city the church life is combined with the kingdom. The building of New Jerusalem is mainly of the pearl gates and the precious stones which form the wall and its foundations. All this is set upon a golden base that upholds the entire building. In this message we are focusing on the pearl gate and the treasure wall. The pearl refers to the church, and the treasure, to the kingdom.

The church and the kingdom are spoken of in Matthew 13 in a mysterious way in parables. But in chapter sixteen the Lord speaks a clear word to His disciples regarding the church and the kingdom. In 16:18 He says, "On this rock I will build My church," and in the following verse, "I will give to you the keys of the kingdom of the heavens." In these verses we see the church and the kingdom. In order to understand the treasure and the pearl in Matthew 13, we must consider the church and the kingdom in Matthew 16. If you pray over these two chapters, you will spontaneously see that the treasure is the kingdom and that the pearl is the church. Both the treasure and the pearl are in the New Jerusalem.

According to Matthew 13, the Lord Jesus sold whatever He had and bought the pearl. Acts 20:28 says that the Lord purchased the church with His blood. This means that on the cross He sold all He had and bought the church. This verse is a strong proof that the pearl in Matthew 13 is the church, for the pearl was purchased by the merchant. No doubt the merchant is the Lord.

THE KINGDOM LIFE

We enter the realm of the kingdom by being regenerated, by being born again (John 3:5). Regeneration is related to the pearl, for the pearl is produced by the principle of regeneration. By being reborn we enter into the sphere of God, into the realm of the kingdom. After we were regenerated, we began to live by Him. Because we loved Him, we wanted to stay under His control and be restricted by Him. Many of us have experienced being restricted on every side. We are not limited by man, but by something inward that is invisible — by the life under the heavenly ruling. We may try to do certain things, but we are restricted from doing them by a mysterious, invisible, inward control. Our relatives or schoolmates are free to do those things, but we cannot do them. Something invisible exercises an inward control over us, and we live under this control. This is the treasure, the kingdom life.

Before we became Christians, we were sand. But we have been regenerated. This means that something living has entered into us. As more life juice is secreted over us, we become precious and begin to live under a mysterious control. This is the experience of the pearl and the treasure.

The local church in the Lord's recovery is a pearl. But in the eyes of the Lord, this church must also be a treasure hidden from the world. Neither the worldly people nor those in Christianity know what we are doing. But deep within we know that we are living a pearl life and a life under an invisible control. We are the pearl and the treasure.

The first four parables of chapter thirteen do not fully cover us. We are not just the wheat or the fine flour. We are more precious, solid, and genuine than this. We are the pearl and the treasure. This is the church life with the kingdom life in the Lord's recovery. If we did not have the second group of parables, we would not know where we should be. I am happy to say that I am no longer in the first group — I am in the second. Can you say this? Are you simply a believer who has a little of Christ? If this is your situation, then you must be a genuine Christian in Christendom. We thank the Lord that we are not in Christendom. Praise Him that many of us are the pearl and the treasure in the Lord's recovery!

TAKING HEED HOW WE BUILD

The parables of the pearl and the treasure match the verses which say, "Enter in through the narrow gate . . . for the gate is narrow and the way is constricted which leads to life, and few are those who find it" (7:13-14). The wide gate and broad way lead to destruction. At this point we need to refer to 1 Corinthians 3, where Paul admonishes us to take heed how we build upon the foundation of Christ. Are we building with gold, silver, and precious stones, or with wood, hay, and stubble? Gold, silver, and precious stones are materials that can withstand the test of fire. But the wood, hay, and stubble will be consumed. In today's Christianity there is a great deal of wood and dry grass, but there is very little gold. Among today's Christians it is difficult to find the gold, pearl, and precious stones. These materials are not bulky, but small. Look at Christianity: wood, hay, and stubble are everywhere; but where is the gold, and where is the precious stone? The way of Christianity is the broad way, but the way of the Lord's recovery is the constricted way. At times the enemy will attempt to lure us away from this constricted way into something that is outwardly big and bulky, something made of wood, hay, and stubble. However, in the New Jerusalem there will be nothing wooden, nothing that can be burned or consumed. Everything in the New Jerusalem will remain for eternity. Nothing can damage the gold, pearl, and precious stone. Our work and testimony must be like this.

I am burdened that we would all see that we are neither in Christendom nor on the broad way. We are in the Lord's recovery. We are not in the first four parables, but in the fifth and sixth parables. In the Lord's recovery the quantity is small, but the quality is higher and more solid, because here we have the treasure and the pearl.

STAYING IN THE CONSTRICTED WAY

Although a great many works have been performed in Christianity, will all this work be approved by the Lord? Toward the end of the constitution of the kingdom of the heavens, the Lord said, "Many will say to Me in that day, Lord, Lord, did we not prophesy in Your name, and in Your name cast out demons, and in Your name do many works of power?" (7:22). But the Lord Jesus will say, "I never knew you; depart from Me, workers of lawlessness" (7:23). The Lord may say, "I never approved you; I never allowed you to do these things. In My eyes everything you did was lawless." I do not believe that the works of Christianity will meet with the Lord's approval. But what about us? We need to be strengthened to remain in the constricted way. None of us should want to stay in the first group of parables, but we should go on to be in the second group. Let others gain a huge number and carry out a great work. We prefer to stay in the pearl and in the treasure where we are constricted.

Because many Christians have been leavened, they have become large and bulky. But from the day we turned to the Lord's recovery, we began to be constricted. We all can testify of this, especially those who were somewhat well-known in Christianity. Nothing in the Lord's recovery has made us greater. Instead, many things have taken place to reduce us. Christ will constrict us to the point that we shall be small enough to be put in a little bottle. But in this bottle there will be a treasure. Because our way is the constricted way, the Lord's recovery is His testimony. In today's Christendom the Lord can find a great deal of wheat and a small amount of meal, even in the Catholic Church. But He cannot find much of the pearl and the treasure in Christendom.

Although we are not proud, we realize that we in the Lord's recovery are different. I am a sinful human being, worse in my nature than you are. But I can testify, and the Lord can also testify for me, that there are many things that I simply cannot do because I have a constricting life within me. Day by day this life says "no" to certain things I want to do. This is the kingdom life mentioned in Romans 14:17. Because we are in the kingdom and under the reigning, we cannot do many of the things that other Christians are free to do. This is the treasure which is precious, valuable, and lovely in the eyes of the Lord. On the cross He sacrificed everything to buy both the pearl and the field in which the treasure is hidden. His buying the field and the pearl reveals that He is for the kingdom and the church. That we are in the Lord's recovery is not the result of our doing. We are here because the Lord has brought us together to be His living testimony. I have no doubt that, in the eyes of the Lord, the treasure and the pearl are here in the recovery.

In the first four parables the Lord covers Christendom in a general way, and in the next two parables He covers His overcomers in a particular way. The seventh parable, the parable of the net, covers the nations. At the time of the Lord's coming back there will be three peoples on earth: those in Christendom, those in the Lord's recovery, and those among the nations. In the parable of the net the nations are likened to fish in the sea. These "fish" are brought to the presence of the Lord, and the Lord exercises His judgment upon them. This will mark the completion of the age at the Lord's coming back. All this is covered by the seven parables concerning the mysteries of the kingdom of the heavens. We are neither in the first four parables nor in the seventh, but in the fifth and sixth. We are the treasure and the pearl. These parables of the treasure and the pearl are most precious. What a privilege it is to be the fulfillment of these parables!

LIFE-STUDY OF MATTHEW

THE PATHWAY TO GLORY

(1)

Because Matthew is a book on the kingdom of the heavens, Christ is here revealed as the heavenly King. In the other Gospels He is revealed as a man (Luke), as a slave (Mark), and as the Son of God (John).

The first thirteen chapters of Matthew cover many crucial items related to Christ. In chapter one we have the genealogy of Christ and the birth of Christ. In chapter two there is an account of the youth of Christ. In chapter three Christ is recommended by John the Baptist through baptism in water and anointed with the Spirit, and in chapter four He is tested and begins His ministry. After Christ was recommended, anointed, and tested, He came into His ministry. At the beginning of His ministry, He decreed, in chapters five, six, and seven, the constitution of the kingdom of the heavens. After issuing this decree, He came down from the mountain to continue His ministry. His ministry afforded Him excellent opportunities to reveal Himself to the people in many aspects. In chapter nine Christ revealed Himself as the Physician. As fallen people, we all are sick and have need of a physician. Because we stand in need of the Lord's healing, He firstly unveiled Himself as our Physician, our Healer. After this, He unveiled Himself as the Bridegroom, the most pleasant person; as our Shepherd, the One who takes care of us; and as the Lord of God's harvest. In chapter twelve Christ unveiled Himself as the real David, the greater temple, the Lord of the Sabbath, the greater Jonah, and the greater

Solomon. If we put all these titles together — the Physician, the Bridegroom, the Shepherd, the Lord of the harvest, the real David, the greater temple, the Lord of the Sabbath, the greater Jonah, and the greater Solomon — we shall realize that Christ as the King of the heavens is so much to us.

In addition to all these revelations of Christ, in chapter nine Christ unveiled that He is the new untreated cloth for the new garment, which is also Himself. Furthermore, He is the new wine and even the new wineskin. Do you not desire to enjoy Christ as the new cloth and as the new garment? Do you not want to drink Him as the new wine and preserve your enjoyment in Him as the new wineskin? I certainly desire this.

We have pointed out that Christ as the Savior and King is our Physician. Are you sick or even dying? I am concerned that some of those reading this message may be dying. But Christ is our Physician, our Healer. Any who are sick or dying can say, "Lord Jesus, thank You. You are my Physician, my Healer. I believe that You will grant me a complete healing." I have the assurance that we are all under His healing. Therefore, we are healthy and sound. How wonderful that Christ is our Physician!

Christ is so much to us. He is our Bridegroom. The most pleasant person is a bridegroom. We have the privilege of enjoying the best married life with Christ, our Bridegroom. As our Shepherd, Christ knows our needs and cares for them. Hence, we may forget our needs because He is our Shepherd. Christ is the Lord of God's harvest. He is also the real David, and we are His followers. In addition, He is the greater temple, and we are the priests serving, worshipping, and ministering within Him. We are not ministering in a religion; we are ministering in a Person who is the greater temple. Christ is also the Lord of the Sabbath, the Lord of rest. Thus, we have not only rest, but the Lord of rest. We do not need to seek for rest, for we have the Lord. Eventually, Christ is our greater Jonah and our greater Solomon. He is the Prophet, telling us what to do, guiding us, and leading us, and also the wonderful King, our beloved Solomon, within us. Oh, this is our Christ!

Although as a result of His ministry Christ was unveiled in such a way, His ministry resulted in complete rejection. At the end of chapter twelve, this rejection reached its climax. Christ was utterly rejected by that incurable generation of Jewish religionists. The rejection in chapter twelve exposed the fact that the rejecting nature of that generation was incurable and, in a sense, unforgivable both in this age and in the age to come. Because the Jews rejected the heavenly King to such an extent, He forsook them. He forsook the natural, fleshly relationship with the Jews and denied His natural relationships with His kindred. At the end of chapter twelve we see that the Jews firstly rejected the Lord and then that their rejection resulted in the King's forsaking them.

In chapter thirteen the King went into a boat on the sea. This signifies that He went into the church. In the church He unveiled the mystery of God's kingdom. In other words, He revealed the mystery of the church, which is the life-pulse, the reality, of the kingdom. Because the mystery of the kingdom was delivered in parables, only those who loved Him, followed Him, and were one with Him could understand it. We have seen that the Lord decreed the constitution of the kingdom to the crowd on the mountain. But in chapter thirteen He unveiled the mystery of the kingdom to His followers.

After we have seen the unveiling of the Lord Himself and the unveiling of the mystery of the kingdom of God, we as His followers need to know the way to follow Him. Peter, Andrew, James, and John, and all of the other disciples knew that the Lord was the Physician, the Bridegroom, and the Shepherd. They realized so many aspects of what He was. Furthermore, they heard the mystery of the kingdom. Now they needed to know the way to follow Him. Therefore, what is revealed beginning at the end of chapter thirteen is the pathway to follow this rejected King.

How can His followers follow Him after His rejection?

Remember that Matthew is not a book of history, but a book of doctrine. The record of Matthew is not according to historical facts; it is according to the sequence of doctrine. In his Gospel, Matthew presents the doctrine concerning the heavenly King and His genealogy, birth, youth, recommendation, anointing, testing, ministry, unveiling of Himself, and His unveiling of the mystery of the kingdom. After seeing all this, we may say, "How wonderful and marvelous! We know so many things about the King and the kingdom. What else do we need?" What we need is the way to follow Him. He is wonderful, and the kingdom is marvelous; but we need to know how we can get into this kingdom and follow Him. Therefore, the section from the end of chapter thirteen to the middle of chapter seventeen, a large section in this doctrinal book, gives us a clear map of the pathway to follow the rejected King.

If we are honest and faithful to Him, we must be on this way following the Christ who has been rejected by this age. Where are you today? You may say that you are in the Lord's recovery. But the Lord's recovery is a pathway on which we follow the rejected heavenly King. This King has been rejected by this generation and is still being rejected by it. Nevertheless, we would follow Him as those preferring to participate in His rejection. Hallelujah, we are the partakers of the enjoyment of Him and partakers of His rejection! He is the rejected King, and we are His rejected followers. He took the lead to be rejected and He is still taking it, and we are following Him on the pathway to glory. At the beginning of this pathway, there is nothing but rejection; however, at the end of it there is glory, the manifestation of the kingdom.

In this message and in the messages following I have the burden to show you how to walk on this pathway to glory. Although you are following Christ, you may not know how to walk on this pathway. In order to walk on it, you need a map. In these messages we shall learn how to read this map. We are following the rejected King, and our destination is glory. How we thank Matthew for including in his doctrinal book not only a diagram of the kingdom, but also a map of the pathway so that we may enter into the kingdom. From the end of chapter thirteen to the middle of chapter seventeen we have a clear map showing us how to walk on the pathway as we follow our beloved King into glory.

I. INCREASE OF REJECTION

The first thing we face on this pathway is rejection. Because Christ is the rejected One, we must be rejected also. We have no choice. Do not expect to be welcomed, for no one will welcome you until the glory comes. Instead, you must be willing to be rejected. In 13:53—14:13 we see the increase of rejection. Many of us have experienced some measure of rejection by those who opposed our coming into the church. But I need to tell you that this rejection will not decrease; rather, it will increase. There will be rejection upon rejection. Be prepared for this.

A. Rejection by the Galileans

1. Knowing Him according to the Flesh and Blinded by Their Natural Knowledge

The heavenly King was rejected firstly by the Jewish religionists. The religious leaders rejected Christ to the uttermost because they were fully occupied, possessed, and veiled by their religion. Because religion was everything to them, they could not recognize this heavenly King. Blinded by the religious veils, they rejected Him. After the Lord had been rejected in Jerusalem, the religious center, He turned to a geographical area that was not so religious — Galilee, the place where He was born and raised. Galilee was rather close to Gentile territory. However, He was not even welcomed in Galilee. Although the Galileans did not oppose Him, they rejected Him because of their natural knowledge. When they saw Him and heard Him speak, they said, "Is not this the carpenter's son? Is not his mother called Mary, and his brothers James and Joseph and Simon and Judas? And his sisters, are they not all with us? Where then did this man get all these things?'' (13:55-56). Here we see that the Galileans knew Him according to the flesh, not according to the spirit (2 Cor. 5:16). Thinking that they knew everything about Him, they were blinded by their natural knowledge. They saw the wonders, the miracles, He did, but they were preoccupied by their natural concepts. The religious people were preoccupied by their religion and by their religious concepts, and the Galileans were preoccupied by their natural knowledge

If we would know Christ and follow Him, we need to realize that religion and natural knowledge are both veils. Some of our opposers belittle us by saying that we do not have theological training. But the Lord Jesus, a carpenter's son, had no theological training Himself. Brother Nee, the one who helped me so much, much more than anyone else, had no theological training either. Religion and natural knowledge are two great obstacles frustrating people from recognizing who Christ is. If you follow religion, you will remain in Jerusalem, and if you follow your natural knowledge, you will be in Galilee. But Christ neither stays in Jerusalem nor remains in Galilee. As we shall see, He departs to the desert. Because Jerusalem was filled with religious concepts and Galilee was filled with natural knowledge, the Lord went to the desert. Are you in Jerusalem or Galilee, or are you in the desert? In the desert there is no religion, culture, or theological training. In Jerusalem there is religion and in Galilee there is natural knowledge, but in the desert there is the presence of Christ. Oh, in the desert we have Christ! This is our boast and enjoyment. We do not have religion or knowledge — we have Christ.

Because we belittle knowledge, we have been condemned and accused of being mind benders. But our minds are not being bent — they are being renewed from natural and religious knowledge. We must be bold to declare that we are no longer religious or natural. Instead of natural and religious knowledge, we have Christ as our wisdom, a wisdom that surpasses knowledge.

Any attempt to know Christ by natural knowledge will result in rejection. According to natural knowledge, Christ was the son of a carpenter and his mother was an ordinary woman. His countrymen knew all of His outward features, but they did not see that God was in Him. In 2 Corinthians 5:16 Paul says that, along with others, he knew Christ according to the flesh. When Paul was Saul of Tarsus, he knew Christ according to the flesh; he thought that Jesus was merely a little Nazarene. He did not realize that within Jesus was God. But one day on the road to Damascus the Lord Jesus said to him, "Saul, Saul, why persecutest thou me?" When Saul asked the Lord who He was, He responded, "I am Jesus." On the road to Damascus Saul realized that Jesus of Nazareth was now in the heavens. Jesus seemed to be saying, "I was not only the flesh — I was God, for the very God was in Me. Saul, you knew Me according to the flesh, not according to the spirit within."

It is the same today. We need to know other Christians not according to outward things, not according to their country, language, parentage, education, or outward appearance or qualification. If we know Christians according to these things, we know them according to the flesh. But we should know Christians according to the spirit, because Christ is in them. Several months ago, one of the opposers was invited to my home for lunch. We spent more than three hours together. At one point he said, "You don't have scholars among you, do you? We have more than a hundred scholars with us." However, eventually we, who are not supposed to have scholars among us, printed articles in the newspaper that the opposers are not able to answer. They have been troubled by so many carpenter's sons.

As we follow the Lord in His recovery, we should not know people according to the flesh or estimate them according to the flesh. We should know them according to one thing — according to the measure of Christ. Knowledge, intelligence, and outward appearance mean nothing. Perhaps a certain brother cannot speak well and uses poor grammar. Yet whenever he opens his mouth, Christ comes out. Even when you are sitting in his presence, you realize that some amount of Christ is with him. In the church life in the Lord's recovery we do not care for the outward appearance; we care only for the spirit within, where Christ is. This is the way to know Christ, the way to know other Christians, and the way to follow the Lord.

2. Causing the Heavenly King Not to Do Many Works of Power among Them

Verse 58 says, "And He did not do many works of power there because of their unbelief." The rejection of the Pharisees caused the heavenly King to forsake them. The unbelief of the Galileans caused the Lord not to do many works of power among them. Because of the Galileans' natural knowledge, the Lord Christ could not do anything with them. The Galileans did not say, "Jesus, we don't want You! Get away from here!" They simply asked, "Is this not the carpenter's son? Where did this man get this wisdom and these works of power?" These questions were sufficient. The heavenly King could no longer remain there, and His gracious works of power could no longer be enjoyed by them. Therefore, He departed from them to the desert where there was no culture, no religion, and, as we shall now see, no politics.

B. Rejection by the Heathen Tetrarch

In 14:1-13 we see the rejection by the heathen tetrarch. Politics is always alongside religion and culture. According to Matthew's presentation, after the rejection by religion and natural knowledge, there is the rejection by politics. Herod the tetrarch represents the rejection by politics. This is the basic principle of 14:1-13.

Herod had John the Baptist beheaded in prison. In 12:24 the Jewish religious leaders, representing the entire nation of the Jews, rejected the heavenly King to the utter-most. This forced Him to forsake His natural relationship with them (12:46-50). Then in 13:53-58 He was also rejected by the Galileans. Now in chapter fourteen, Matthew in his doctrinal arrangement unveils to us how Gentile politics treated the King's forerunner. Gentile politics were evil and full of corruption and darkness. Up to this point Matthew has given a full picture of how the Jews, Galileans, and Gentiles rejected the ministry of the kingdom of the heavens.

1. Heathen Politics Coinciding with Jewish Religion

Firstly, the rejection by religion reached its climax. Following this came the rejection due to natural knowl-edge. The rejection by politics coincided with the rejection by religion and natural knowledge. The religionists, those with natural knowledge, and the politicians did not hold a conference for the purpose of rejecting the Lord Jesus. Nevertheless, their rejection of Him coincided. Religion, natural knowledge, and politics all came together in the re-jection of Christ.

2. The Darkness of Politics Exposed

In chapter fourteen we see the darkness, rottenness, and injustice in politics. Our eyes need to be opened to see that in religion there is no welcome to our heavenly King. Neither is there a place for Him in natural knowledge nor in today's rotten, dark politics. In this generation there is no place for the heavenly King. Religion, culture, and politics are all one in rejecting the heavenly King. How I thank the Lord for the record in the Gospel of Matthew. If you read the chapters prior to fourteen, you will see the deceit-fulness in the Jewish religion. You will also see that natural knowledge has caused great damage to people. Further-more, you will see the rottenness and darkness in Roman politics, which was the leading political system on earth at the time. But even in the best political system there is nothing but rottenness and darkness.

3. *Causing the Heavenly King to Retreat to the Desert*

Thus far, we have seen the first two stations on the pathway to glory. The first station is the rejection by natural knowledge, and the second is the rejection by politics. The rejection both by culture and by politics compelled the heavenly King to retreat. When He heard of the execution of John the Baptist, "He departed from there in a boat to a desert place privately" (14:13). Due to the rejection by all the religious, cultured, political peoples, the heavenly King left them for a desert place. This indicates that henceforth He would hide Himself privately in a desert, in a place without culture, away from the religious, political, and cultured people. He did this in a boat, implying He would do this through the church. Due to the rejection of the civilized world, the Lord, through the church, has always been hiding Himself privately from the religious and political circles in a realm without much culture.

The remainder of 14:13 says, "And when the crowds heard of it, they followed Him on foot from the cities." In spite of the rejection of all peoples, there was still a good number who followed the heavenly King. They did this by leaving their cities. It was not that the King came to their cities to visit them, but that they left their cultured cities to follow Him in the desert. Through all the centuries, the true followers of Christ have left cultured spheres to follow their heavenly King outside the cultured world. We are among those who have followed Him. Where He is, we go. We follow Him through all manner of rejection to the desert.

LIFE-STUDY OF MATTHEW

THE PATHWAY TO GLORY

(2)

In this message we come to 14:14-21, the record of the Lord's miraculous feeding of the crowd in the wilderness.

II. LACKING IN NECESSITIES

A. At Evening Time in a Barren Desert

Many times after we have experienced rejection and have passed through it, we have been happy and released. But after we experience this release, we realize that we are in want and do not have anything to live on. We are lacking in necessities. This was the situation of the crowd that followed the Lord into the desert.

I believe that those who followed the heavenly King to the desert were enjoying a happy, pleasant time. They might have been so happy that they even forgot about eating. Verse 15 says, "Now when evening was come, the disciples came to Him, saying, This place is a desert, and the hour has already passed; therefore send the crowds away so that they may go into the villages and buy food for themselves." Peter might have taken the lead to remind Jesus that they were in the desert, that the hour was late, and that the crowds needed something to eat. He might have been the one to suggest that the Lord send the crowds away into the villages to buy food for themselves. The disciples seemed to be saying, "Lord, You see now that it is evening. Don't keep the crowd here. Send them away." Was not this a good idea that proceeded out of a good heart? Today's Peters all have good hearts. In the church life the good-hearted ones often make proposals. Do not be such a Peter.

B. Learning to Take Care of
the Need of Others

In reading the book of Matthew we need to take care of
the doctrinal arrangement of the book. Many readers consider Matthew either a storybook or a history book. But it
is not a history book; it is a book of doctrine. The Lord's
word in verse 16, therefore, is significant: "They do not
need to go away; you give them something to eat." The disciples asked the Lord to send the crowds away that they
might go and buy food for themselves. But the Lord told
the disciples to give the crowds something to eat. Their
concept was to ask people to do something; this was the
principle of the law. But the Lord's concept is to give people something to enjoy; this is the principle of grace. What
the disciples proposed was wholly based upon the principle of the law.

In verse 16 the Lord Jesus stopped the disciples. The
Gospels record a number of times that Peter was stopped.
He was very experienced in this matter of being stopped in
speaking. On the mountain, when he proposed building
three tabernacles, he was stopped by God. When he told
the man who collected the half-shekel tax for the temple
that his Master paid the tax, he was stopped by the Lord.
The Lord Jesus always stopped the good-hearted one. If
you do not have such a good heart, the Lord will not stop
you. But if you have a good heart, be prepared to be
stopped by Him. Your good heart needs to be stopped
because it is natural. The Lord Jesus stopped the disciples
by saying, "You give them something to eat." The Lord
seemed to be saying, "Do not ask the crowd to do something in order to get something. That is law. You should
give them something to eat. This is grace. I'm not here as
Moses telling people to do something in order to get something. I am Jesus Christ. I came with grace. I always give
people something. The law came through Moses, but grace
came with Me. Therefore, you must give the crowd something to eat. You disciples are completely wrong, for you
are still under the law, telling people to do certain things.

Are the people hungry? Certainly they are. I know this. I haven't done anything up to this point in order to expose you. I waited for evening to come just so that you might be exposed. If I had done something about their need, you would never have been exposed." Often in the Lord's recovery such instances occur. The Lord has deliberately done certain things to exhaust the patience of the natural ones. However, the good-hearted ones cannot bear this. Often, minutes before the end, they make a proposal. If they had waited for another few minutes, their folly would not have been exposed. Nevertheless, we must learn to get away from the regulations and commandments of the law. Instead, we must learn to know grace, to exercise grace, and to give to others according to the principle of grace.

When the Lord Jesus told them to give the crowd something to eat, the disciples said, "We have nothing here except five loaves and two fishes" (v. 17). When you are about to exercise grace, you will see that you have nothing. If you simply issue commandments to others, you will not realize how poor you are. You may think that you are very smart and say to yourself, "How smart I am! No one else has noticed that evening has come. But I know everything. I can even instruct Jesus. In the Lord's recovery I am the most intelligent one. I can tell others to do this and that. I know the time, I know the situation, I know what to say, I know what to do, I know everything. I even know how to command the Lord Jesus." However, when we are told by the Lord to exercise grace, we shall say, "When I am under the law, I am blind and don't know myself. Under the law, my poverty is not exposed. But now the Lord Jesus, speaking a word of grace, has told me to give them something to eat. This gracious word exposes my poverty. Immediately, I see that I have nothing. I have only a commanding mouth. I can give commands, I can instruct, and I can teach, but I have nothing to give." The law does not expose us that much. But whenever we are about to exercise grace, our poverty is exposed. We see that we have nothing to give to others, even nothing to feed ourselves.

May the Lord be merciful to us! Do not think that this

is merely a story about the Lord Jesus feeding five thousand men plus women and children with five loaves and two fishes. You may be familiar with the story of this miracle, but you may still lack the revelation or the light it contains. But today we are under the Lord's enlightenment. All of us are Peters. When we think that we know what to do and can tell others what to do, we are a Peter under the law. We are not one under grace. One who is under grace will always say, "Lord, I have nothing to give. There is a great need, but I cannot meet it. I realize that today is the day of grace, not the day of the law. Nevertheless, I have nothing to give. Grace exposes me." Are you under the law or under grace? If you are under the law, you will still feel that you have something to boast of — your smart mind, your foresight, your knowledge, your ability to instruct others. But when the Lord puts you under grace, your poverty and nothingness will be exposed, and you will have to admit that you have nothing to give, even nothing with which to feed yourself. Here we see clearly the principle of the law and the principle of grace.

C. Offering All to the Heavenly King

Speaking of the loaves and fishes mentioned in verse 17, the Lord said in verse 18, "Bring them to Me." Whatever we have of the Lord we need to bring to the Lord that it might become a great blessing to many others. The Lord often uses what we offer to Him to provide for the need of others. It is also in this way that He provides for the need of His followers today.

Although you may say that you do not have anything to offer to the Lord, you at least have yourself. Praise the Lord that we all can give ourselves to Him! We may have nothing but a poor, ugly self, but we can give our self to Him. Even a sick person can give himself to the Lord. Let us give whatever we are to Him. The Lord needs our consecration. If what we have is kept in our possession, it will be nothing. But if it passes out of our hands into the Lord's hands, it will become a great blessing. Consecrate yourself to the Lord. Offer what you have to Him. Then the Lord will have a way to bless many people, and you will be included in that blessing.

We all must see the doctrine in this portion of the Word. The doctrine is that we must not be under the law, but under grace. Grace exposes our poverty and our nothingness. Yet we have something — ourselves — to give to the Lord. No matter how little we have, we need to offer it to Him. If we put what we have into His hands, it will become a great blessing.

D. The Heavenly King Taking Care of All the Need by a Miraculous Blessing

1. Feeding the People

Verse 19 says, "And commanding the crowds to recline on the grass, He took the five loaves and two fishes, and looking up to heaven, He blessed, and break and gave the loaves to the disciples, and the disciples to the crowds." The Lord fed the people; He ministered the life supply to them. By having the crowds recline on the grass, He put the people into good order. This shows the Lord's wisdom and orderliness. By looking up to heaven the heavenly King indicated that His source was His Father in the heavens. Then He blessed the loaves and fishes and broke them. This indicates that whatever we bring to the Lord must be broken for it to become a blessing to others.

The Lord will break whatever is consecrated to Him. This means that after we consecrate ourselves to the Lord, we shall be broken by Him. However, many of us have prayed, "Lord, have mercy on me and do not break me. Lord, you know my wife is breaking me into pieces. Keep me whole, and save me from my wife's breaking hand." A number of sisters have also prayed to be saved from the breaking hand of their husbands. But the more you pray in this way, the more breaking there will be. We, however, are more like rubber than bread. It is easy to break bread, but difficult to break rubber. Therefore, with us, breaking is not enough. Sometimes the Lord also has to cut us. I am not joking, for I know my own case. Nevertheless, whatever you are and whatever you have must be offered to the Lord. If you do this, in His hand nothing will remain whole. Rather, everything will be broken. The Lord will break whatever is placed into His hands. If we are not broken, our consecration does not mean anything, and it is not effectual. Our consecration only works by our being broken by the Lord.

After the Lord broke the loaves, He gave them to the disciples. The loaves were from the disciples, and they brought them to the Lord. After being blessed and broken by the Lord, they were given back to the disciples for distribution to the crowds, to whom the loaves became a great satisfaction. This indicates that the disciples were not the source of blessing; they were only the channels used by the Lord, who was the source of the people's satisfaction. The broken bread was passed on to the disciples, and the disciples distributed it to the crowds. This broken bread became the satisfaction to all the hungry people, and there was great blessing. The principle is the same today. No doubt there has been great blessing in the Lord's recovery in this country. Nevertheless, we must realize that some dear ones have offered themselves to the Lord. In the Lord's hand, they all have been broken, and those broken pieces have brought in the blessing.

2. In Resurrection

John 6:9 tells us that the five loaves are barley loaves. In figure, barley typifies the resurrected Christ (Lev. 23:10). Thus, the barley loaves signify Christ in resurrection as food to us. While the loaves are of the vegetable life, signifying the generating aspect of Christ's life, the fishes are of the animal life, signifying the redeeming aspect of Christ's life. To satisfy our spiritual hunger, we need Christ's generating life as well as His redeeming life. Both of these aspects are symbolized by small items — loaves and fishes. This indicates that the heavenly King did not come to His followers in this age to reign over them as a great King, but as small pieces of food to feed them.

3. *With an Overflow*

Verse 20 says, "And they all ate and were satisfied; and they took up what was over and above of the fragments, twelve baskets full." Twelve baskets full of fragments indicate not only that the resurrected Christ is unlimited and inexhaustible, but also that the Lord's provision for us is abundant, more than sufficient to meet all our need. The five loaves and two fishes satisfied about five thousand men, apart from women and children (v. 21). What we offer to the Lord may be very little; but the blessing will be great, and the overflow, the surplus, will be greater than what we offered. What we offer to the Lord cannot be exhausted. Rather, it will be used by the Lord to bless others abundantly, even with a surplus, to testify that this is the Lord's marvelous doing. In this record of the miracle, the Holy Spirit's intention in His inspiration is to show that the real need of the followers of the heavenly King is the proper food to satisfy their hunger. The disciples of Christ did not know this, nor did the crowds who followed. The heavenly King knew this and would do something miraculously to impress them with their real need and His provision for that need. All they needed was His resurrection life to satisfy their spiritual hunger, as signified in this miracle.

What the heavenly King did also clearly indicates that He provides for the necessities of His followers while they follow Him in this rejecting world. This corresponds with His word in the heavenly constitution that the kingdom people need not be anxious concerning what they shall eat (6:31-33).

In following the rejected King, we must pass through many kinds of rejections. After these rejections, we shall be in want and have certain needs. But do not worry about your needs or be anxious concerning them, for the Lord takes care of them, even at the end of the day in a desert place. The Lord has a way to meet your need. Simply offer what you are and what you have into His hand, let Him break the offering, and let the broken offering feed the hungry ones. If you do this, you will enjoy satisfaction, and there will be a surplus remaining.

What the rejected King did in 14:14-21 was not merely a miracle to feed people. The miracle here indicates that as the rejected King, Christ has the adequate, sufficient, rich life supply for His followers. He not only takes care of our physical and material needs; He also affords the life supply to satisfy our hunger. Many of us can testify that after passing through rejection, we came into a situation where we had a shortage. Nevertheless, the Lord took care of us, and we did not lack anything. Eventually, we did not care about the material supply, but about the life supply to satisfy our spiritual hunger. As we follow the rejected King on the pathway to glory, we can testify that we are enjoying the life supply. Moreover, we are feeding others. And after such an enjoyment, there are still twelve baskets full of life supply.

Now we can say that this pathway is very good. Although here we have rejection and want, He is our life supply. He takes care of our physical needs and renders the rich life supply, even with an overflow, to meet our spiritual need. Therefore, we can say, "The Lord is my Shepherd; I shall not want." Not only are we without want — we are rich, we are satisfied, and we have twelve baskets full. With Him we have the material supply and the life supply. As we follow Him, even in the desert, we enjoy Him as our source of supply. Thus, we are not afraid of anything. Because He is with us, we shall not want. As long as we have His presence, everything is all right. We welcome the rejection and, in a sense, we even welcome the situation of being in want, for we have Him. Our need affords Him an excellent opportunity to do something for us.

LIFE-STUDY OF MATTHEW

THE PATHWAY TO GLORY

(3)

III. THE STORM ON THE WAY

As we follow the Lord on the pathway to glory, we first experience rejection, and then we suffer the lack of our daily necessities. After this, we experience the storm on the way (14:22-33). The storm in chapter fourteen indicates that on the pathway where we follow the rejected King there will always be troubles. From the end of chapter thirteen to the end of chapter sixteen, there are many negative things. Humanly speaking, as we follow the rejected King on the pathway to glory, there is nothing good. It seems that everything is a problem. Do you like rejection? Do you enjoy lacking the things you need for your daily living? Do you appreciate the storm on the sea? If on our pathway there is no rejection, shortage of daily necessities, or storm, it is an indication that we are not actually on the pathway. If we are truly on the pathway to glory, we shall have problems and hardships.

A. The Disciples Sailing in the Boat — the Church

Verse 22 says, "And immediately He compelled the disciples to step into the boat and to go before Him to the other side, until He send the crowds away." Suddenly, the Lord compelled the disciples to leave Him. However, He did not go with them. He compelled them to leave by boat in order that He might have more time to pray to the Father privately. As verse 23 indicates, He went up into the mountain to pray. Before the Lord sent them away, the disciples participated in the enjoyment of the

Lord's supply. The lack of necessities had issued in a very pleasant experience. The disciples were enjoying the Lord's supply, and they were happy. If we had been there, we would certainly have been joyful. I believe that Peter talked a great deal about what the Lord had done. He might have said, "John, isn't this wonderful? Look what the Lord did with five loaves and two little fishes!" Then the Lord seemed to say, "Don't talk. Step into a boat and go before Me to the other side. I realize you have been having an enjoyable time, but now you must go." The disciples might have said, "Lord, will You go with us?" Then the Lord might have answered, "No, you go by yourselves. I am going to the mountain to pray." Many times, immediately after a pleasant enjoyment of the Lord, He suddenly tells us to go to the sea. Then He leaves us. This is a portrait of today's situation. The Lord has gone to the mountain, to the heavens. However, He has charged His church to go ahead on the sea, where there often are contrary winds and storms.

B. The Heavenly King Praying on the Mountain

Verse 23 says, "And having sent the crowds away, He went up into the mountain privately to pray. And when evening came, He was there alone." The heavenly King, as the beloved Son of the Father (3:17), standing in the position of man (4:4), needed to pray privately to His Father who is in heaven, that He might be one with the Father and have the Father with Him in whatever He did on earth for the establishment of the kingdom of the heavens. He did this not in the desert, but on the mountain, leaving all the people, even His disciples, that He might contact the Father alone.

C. The Boat with the Disciples Distressed by the Waves under the Contrary Wind

Verse 24 says, "Now the boat was already many stadia away from the land, in the midst of the sea, distressed by the waves, for the wind was contrary." Surely the Lord took notice of the fact that the boat was distressed by a storm. When He compelled the disciples to step into the boat and to go before Him, He foresaw that a storm was coming. Nevertheless, He did not go with them. Rather, He went away to the mountain to pray. Today the Lord Jesus is on a mountain, that is, in the heavens (Rom. 8:34; Heb. 7:25), and the church is on the sea. Day by day we face the contrary winds. From the day we first came to Anaheim, the contrary winds have been blowing. We have not had one calm day. The church boat has constantly been distressed. However, this is our destiny. The fact that the Lord is in the heavens praying for us is a source of comfort and encouragement to us. We do not care how strong the contrary winds are, for we know that the Lord is on the mountain praying for us. The storm is not under the control of the opposition; it is under the Lord's feet.

Do not be afraid of the contrary winds. There is no need to be disturbed by them. Others can testify for me that, no matter what happens, I am not afraid of anything. My wife can testify that every night I sleep soundly and that every afternoon I have a good nap, free from worry. Sometimes my wife is surprised that I am not troubled by the problems. I have many things to do, and it is my duty to take a good rest. Because our destiny is in the Lord's hand, there is no reason for us to be afraid of anything. The contrary winds and the opposition are under His feet. The Lord is on a high mountain praying for us and interceding for us. He knows how strong the wind is. But He laughs at the wind and seems to say, "Little wind, you mean nothing to Me. What are you trying to do? You can't do anything with My church. Those in the boat are My followers. In fact, they are just Me. Although I am here in the heavens, I am also with them." What a marvelous picture this is of the high mountain, the troubling waves and contrary winds, and the little boat on the sea! The winds and the waves all work together for our good. Do you not believe that the opposition is working for our good? It certainly is.

In Anaheim we have seen how much good the opposition has accomplished for us.

Some have condemned me by saying that I do not believe that Jesus Christ is in the heavens. They accuse me of being too inward, of always telling you not to look to the heavens, but to look to Christ within you. The truth is we need to look in two directions. First, we must look to the Lord within us and say, "O Lord Jesus, are You happy with Your abode in me? Do You enjoy this place?" We all need to see that Christ is in us. In order to enjoy Him, we must know that He dwells within us. If He were far away, we could not enjoy Him. Second, in order to trust in the Lord, we must look to Him in the heavens where He sits with authority and intercedes for us. Soon He may be on His way to come to us. Hallelujah, He is both within us and in the heavens interceding for us! If we see this, we shall not be distressed, troubled, or bothered by any storm, for we shall have the assurance that the boat is His boat, that the church is His church. The sea cannot damage the boat. On the contrary, the sea serves the boat. As we shall see, the wind and the waves taught Peter a great deal.

D. The Heavenly King Walking on the Sea Coming to the Disciples

"And in the fourth watch of the night He came to them, walking on the sea" (v. 25). According to the Roman guards, there were four night watches, each of three hours, from sunset to sunrise. The first watch was the evening watch; the second, the midnight watch; the third, the cock-crowing watch; and the fourth, the morning watch (Mark 13:35). The fourth watch was probably from three to six o'clock in the morning.

Verse 25 says that the Lord came to His disciples, walking on the sea. While His disciples were distressed by the waves, the Lord walked on them. This testifies that He is the Creator and the Ruler of the universe (Job 9:8).

E. The Heavenly King Bringing Courage
to the Disciples by His Presence

Thinking that the Lord was a phantom, the disciples cried out for fear (v. 26). "But immediately Jesus spoke to them, saying, Have courage; It is I; do not fear" (v. 27). The heavenly King brought courage to the disciples by His presence. When they mistook Him for a phantom, a ghost, He encouraged them by saying, "It is I."

F. The Disciples Learning to Walk in the Storm
by Faith and Not by Sight

Verse 28 says, "And Peter answered Him and said, Lord, if it is You, command me to come to You on the waters." When the Lord said, "Come," Peter stepped out of the boat, "walked on the waters and came toward Jesus" (v. 29). Only Peter was bold enough to do this. I doubt that any of us would have been as bold as Peter. It was a miracle that Peter could walk on the waters. He walked on the waves by faith. Faith is our action upon the word of the Lord. To have faith does not mean that we are able to do things; neither does it mean that we make up our mind to go in a certain direction. Faith simply means that, although we may be very weak, we dare to act upon the Lord's word. The Lord said to Peter, "Come," and Peter took that word, acted upon it, and walked on the waves. Do not examine whether or not you have faith. If you examine yourself, your faith will disappear immediately. Do not ask yourself, "Am I strong in faith? Is my faith adequate?" If you question yourself like this, you will immediately sink beneath the waves.

Verse 30 says of Peter: "But seeing the strong wind, he was afraid; and beginning to sink, he cried out, saying, Lord, save me!" Peter came down from the boat and walked on the waves by faith in the Lord's word (v. 29); however, when he saw the strong wind, his faith vanished. He should have walked only by faith in the Lord's word, not by the sight of the circumstances (2 Cor. 5:7). When

Peter cried out for help, "Jesus stretched out His hand and took hold of him and said to him, You of little faith, why did you doubt?" (v. 31). Since the Lord said to Peter, "Come" (v. 29), Peter should have stood on that word and not doubted. Hence, the Lord rebuked him. Faith comes from the Lord's word and stands on the Lord's word. As long as we have the Lord's word, we should simply believe in His word and not doubt.

Do not be troubled by any storms, for we are in the boat, the Lord's church. Even if we cannot see the Lord or feel that He is with us, we may be assured that He is on the mountain interceding for us. Perhaps He is even on the way to the boat. Whether He is on the mountain interceding or on the waves walking toward us, we should not be disturbed. At times we may not only have peace inwardly, but even receive a word from Him to walk on the waves. When we receive such a word, we should simply walk on the stormy sea. Do not be bothered by the opposition and persecution. With the Lord's word we may walk to meet Him, even walking through all the opposition and upon it. This is faith.

We should not blame Peter for having little faith. Among all the disciples in the boat, Peter was the first to enjoy the Lord's presence. Some of us are too slow and too timid. Do not criticize others for being too quick. You need to be quick yourself sometimes. Which do you prefer — to be like Peter or to be like Thomas? Peter was bold, but Thomas was timid and cautious. In the churches there are many careful, cautious ones. But Peter was not cautious. As soon as he heard a word from the Lord, he stepped out of the boat and onto the water. However, the cautious ones may say, "But Peter had to cry out to the Lord to save him. There is no need for us to cry for help. We are safe here in the boat." Yes, you are safe in the boat, but you are not in the Lord's presence. You are not like Peter who was the first to get back into the presence of the Lord.

Peter caused a great deal of trouble. The quick ones always make trouble, whereas the timid ones never cause problems. The timid ones do not cause trouble, but neither do they bring in the presence of the Lord. With the cautious ones, nothing seems to happen. Year after year goes by, and everything remains calm. But those who are like Peter are always stirring things up. They may cause trouble, but they are rescued by the Lord and thereby are brought into His presence. Some of you cautious ones need to stir up a little trouble, then cry out to the Lord to be saved, and get into His presence. Who do you think enjoys the Lord more — the cautious ones or the quick ones? The answer certainly is the quick ones. Nevertheless, the timid ones may say, "Let us sleep. Sooner or later, the Lord Jesus will come. We don't need to jump in the water, cause trouble, and then cry out for rescue. We don't need to be so quick to get into the presence of the Lord. If we take it easy and be calm, the Lord will come." In one sense, the cautious ones are right and those like Peter are wrong. But the bold ones have more enjoyment of the Lord than the timid ones. Eventually, however, the Lord's presence is not just with Peter, but with all the disciples in the boat.

G. The Storm Ceasing
because of the Heavenly King's Presence

Verse 32 says, "And when they went up into the boat, the wind ceased." This was a miracle. This miracle not only testifies that the Lord is the Ruler of the heavens and the earth, but also that He cares for the hardships of His followers as they follow Him on the pathway to glory. When we have the Lord in our boat, the wind ceases. The record of the two miracles in this chapter implies that while Christ was rejected by the religious and political peoples, He and His followers were in the barren desert and on the stormy sea. Nonetheless, He is able to provide for their need and to carry them through hardships.

The Lord's presence caused the storm to cease. I have experienced this many times. I cannot tell you how many storms I have passed through during the past fifty years. But eventually every storm ceased. Not one storm lasted

more than three to five years. Three to five years actually is
not a long time. To the Lord, it is just a few minutes, for
with Him a thousand years are as one day. Do not be
alarmed — every storm will cease.

H. Worshipping the Heavenly King
and Recognizing Him as the Son of God

After the Lord had caused the wind to cease, "those
who were in the boat worshipped Him, saying, Truly You
are the Son of God" (v. 33). To recognize that the Lord is
the Son of God is to realize that He is equal to God (John
5:18). Hence, this indicates that the disciples acknowledged the Lord's divinity (Matt. 1:23; 3:17).

In 14:22-33 we see a portrait of ourselves. Some of us are
like Peter and others are like Thomas. Some are quick and
bold, always causing trouble and making mistakes; others
are timid, cautious, and sleepy. The timid ones may mur-
mur against the bold ones, "Brother So-and-So is too
quick. I don't agree with that. He is utterly wrong. But I
am slow and cautious." I am very clear about the situation
in the churches regarding the quick ones and the cautious
ones. I know those who are bold and who cause trouble and
those who are cautious and never cause problems. I
appreciate all the cautious ones; however, I do not agree
with them. Because they are so cautious, they never stir up
anyone or anything. People need to be stirred up to walk on
the waves so that they may get into the presence of the
Lord. Those who do this will bring the Lord to the boat. No
cautious one, timid one, slow one, or careful one has ever
brought the Lord Jesus to the boat. In the case of the
cautious ones, the Lord must come to the boat on His own.
If He does this, He will find the cautious ones sleeping. No
one will be waiting for Him. After waking from their
slumber, the cautious ones will say, "Lord, You are here.
This is rather good. Praise the Lord for this! Now it is time
to go back to sleep." Those who are slow and careful never
cause any trouble or problems. We need to be quick and
bold. However, in being quick and bold to step out of the

boat and walk on the sea, we must take care of four things: first, that we act upon the word of the Lord, not without hearing a word from Him; second, that our direction is toward the Lord Himself; third, that we get into the Lord's presence; and fourth, that we come back to the boat. If we take care of these four things, we shall be right, even if we appear to be wrong.

IV. THE POWER OF HEALING

After Jesus and the disciples came to Gennesaret, the people of that place brought to the Lord all who were ill. Verse 36 says, "And they besought Him that they might only touch the fringe of His garment; and as many as touched were made thoroughly well" (v. 36). The healing power went out, not from the inner being of Christ, but from the fringe of His garment. The Lord's garment signifies Christ's righteous deeds, and the fringe signifies the heavenly ruling (Num. 15:38-39). Out of Christ's heavenly-ruled deeds is the virtue that becomes the healing power. According to Numbers 15, the fringe of the garment signifies the virtue of God's people who walk according to His regulations. The fringe was made with a blue ribbon. This revealed that their daily walk was regulated by God's heavenly rule as indicated by the color blue, a heavenly color. When Jesus was on earth as a man, He walked in this way. His daily walk was regulated by God's heavenly commandments. Therefore, there was with Him a virtue that could flow out to heal others.

The healing that takes place in the church life does not mainly issue from the inner being of the Lord Jesus. Rather, it primarily issues from the virtue of the Lord's human life. In the church life we experience the Lord's presence with us on the sea in the midst of the contrary winds. His presence prepares the way for His virtue to flow out to reach the sick people and to heal them. This type of healing is different from the miraculous healing by divine power. The garment of Jesus does not signify His divinity.

Rather, it signifies the righteous deeds of His humanity. His humanity bore the mark of the blue ribbon, of being regulated by the heavenly ruling. This produced a virtue that was capable of healing the sick. This kind of virtue can be expressed only through the proper church life where Jesus is present.

Revelation 22:2 says that the leaves of the tree of life are for the healing of the nations. In typology, the fruit of the tree of life represents the Lord's divine life, and the leaves represent the Lord's human deeds. The fruit, the Lord's divine life, is for nourishing us, and the leaves, the Lord's human deeds, are for the healing of others. In the new heaven and the new earth the leaves of the tree of life will be for the healing of the nations, that is, the virtue of Christ's humanity will heal the people. In Matthew, after the boat reached its destination, the virtue of the Lord's human deeds became so prevailing that every manner of sickness was healed. Likewise when we have the proper church life with the Lord's presence today, there is among us the uplifted humanity of Jesus. This uplifted humanity has the virtue signified by the fringe of Christ's garment. If we, the church people, have the proper church life and live by Christ, we shall live out His uplifted humanity. In this kind of living there will be a virtue with the power to heal those around us.

In typology, the land visited by the Lord after the boat came to shore was a figure of the millennium. In the millennium there will be a great deal of healing. Nevertheless, the healing to be found in the millennium should be experienced today. The church people should have a foretaste of the millennium. We must live out the uplifted humanity of Jesus to have the virtue that can heal those surrounding us. For others to be healed means that their corrupted character is changed. Those around the church life are all in darkness and corruption. But if the church people live out the uplifted humanity of Christ, this will cause a healing power to flow into them. Even other Christians will be healed.

LIFE-STUDY OF MATTHEW

MESSAGE FORTY-FIVE

THE PATHWAY TO GLORY

(4)

As we follow the Lord on the pathway to glory, we experience rejection, the lack of necessities, and the storm on the sea. After this, we face the accusations from religion. In this message we shall see how the Lord dealt with the accusations of the traditional religionists (15:1-20).

V. KEPT AWAY FROM RELIGIOUS TRADITION

A. Accused by the Religionists of Not Washing Hands When Eating

Matthew 15:1 and 2 say, "Then there came to Jesus from Jerusalem Pharisees and scribes, saying, Why do your disciples transgress the tradition of the elders? For they do not wash their hands when they eat bread." Although the Lord had forsaken the rejecting religionists, they still would not cease to trouble Him. They came to Him from their religious center, Jerusalem, in order to discover His faults. However, their troubling afforded Him another opportunity to reveal the truth about how to be really clean (vv. 10-11, 15-20). The Pharisees and scribes asked the Lord Jesus why His disciples transgressed the tradition of the elders. This reveals that the disciples did not keep the old traditions in following the Lord. They cared only for the heavenly King's presence, not for anything else.

The elders spoken of in verse 2 were not the elders of the people, but the people of ancient times, those of bygone generations. In the past, some of those who claimed to be for God had certain practices, and their practices eventually became the traditions that were observed by the

Jews when the Lord Jesus was on earth. For example, certain of the ancients adopted the regulation of washing their hands whenever they ate. At the time of the Lord Jesus, this was a tradition. However, it was not a commandment in the Bible. Nothing commanded by God could ever become a tradition, for God's word is always fresh. A tradition, on the contrary, is something invented or initiated by man.

Some of the opposers have said that we should return to the so-called historic church and follow the traditional practices. Recently, a group of so-called fundamental Christians even published an article appealing to Christians to return to the historic church. But the historic church has adopted many regulations that are absolutely unscriptural, and it has made many decisions regarding things not found in the Bible. Consider, for example, the worship of Mary, which was sanctioned by the Council of Ephesus. There are more traditions in Christendom today than in Judaism when the Lord Jesus was on earth. Traditions are very prevailing in Christendom today. The traditional celebration of Christmas is an example. One of our critics has said that the origin of Christmas is not pagan. He even denied the fact that the Christmas tree is pagan. The Christmas tree is pagan, evil, and idolatrous. There can be no reconciliation between the Lord's living testimony and the traditional church. We are opposed because we, as the disciples following the Lord today, would not keep such traditions.

B. The Hypocrisy of the Religionists

1. Transgressing the Commandment of God because of Tradition

Verse 3 says, "And He answered and said to them, Why do you also transgress the commandment of God because of your tradition?" The Jewish religionists accused the Lord's disciples of transgressing their tradition, but the Lord condemned them for transgressing the commandment of God because of their tradition. They ignored God's commandment by caring for their tradition. In principle, the religious people today do the same. In many ways both the Roman Catholic Church and the Protestant denominations make void the word of God because of their traditions.

In verse 4 the Lord continued, "For God said, Honor your father and mother; and, he who speaks evil of father or mother, let him die the death." The Lord's dealing with the Pharisees and scribes here not only condemned them for making void the word of God because of their tradition, but also implied that man should honor his parents. God in His government among men has ordained that man should honor his parents. Among the ten commandments (Exo. 20:12), He has made this the first commandment concerning human relationships. Fallen human nature, however, always attempts to ignore the parents, that is, to rebel against God's government. The Lord as the heavenly King, in order to bring man back to God's government, emphasized that man should honor his parents. This corresponds to His word in the constitution of the kingdom of the heavens concerning the fulfillment of the law (5:17-19). Hence, the Apostle also emphasized this matter strongly (Eph. 6:1-3; Col. 3:20). We the kingdom people must honor our parents and not excuse ourselves as the Jewish religionists did. Any excuse indicates that we are not under the heavenly ruling, but that we are following our fallen human nature and the rebellious trend of today's generation.

In the Lord Jesus' encounter with the Pharisees, the Lord did not care for the traditions. On the contrary, He referred them to the word of God. In principle, we are doing the same today. Men are still making void God's word by means of their tradition, and we are being accused today of not keeping the traditions. Recently, one of our opposers twisted 1 Thessalonians 5:23, a verse that speaks of the three parts of man — the spirit and soul and body. He said that in this verse the Greek word translated "and" could also be rendered "even." But if we use "even" for the Greek conjunction in this verse, the spirit, soul, and body would equal one another. This is like a doctor saying that a person's legs are the same as his stomach and the stomach as the heart. What medical quackery that would be! In Christendom many still insist on the traditions, and in the so-called churches these traditions are very prevailing. But the Lord has raised us up to come back to the pure Word. We do not care for man's tradition, teaching, or practice. This has offended some, and we have been accused of damaging the "church." But the "church" we are accused of damaging is not actually the church; rather, it is the traditional church, the denominations, the sects.

Praise the Lord for the record in Matthew 15! All the aspects of this record coincide with our situation today. The Lord Jesus and His followers were accused by the traditionalists, and today we are accused by the religionists. In answering those who accused His disciples, the Lord seemed to say, "You Pharisees accuse My disciples of breaking your traditions. You need to see that you have broken God's commandment by holding to your tradition, and you continue to break it." In this way the Lord brought them back to the pure Word, telling them what was the commandment of God and what was man's tradition. It is the same today. We are accused of not following the historic church, that is, of not following the traditions. We answer that we must come back to the pure Word and not care for the traditions of the historic church. In the various councils and creeds of the historic church, there is no mention of the seven Spirits. This means that if we follow the traditional concept of the Trinity, we shall neglect the seven Spirits. Our critics say, "You don't honor the ancient councils which formulated the creeds regarding the Trinity." We respond, "We don't follow the creeds. They are man's teaching and tradition. Instead, we come back to the pure Word. In the Bible we find something more than what is included in the creeds, for the Bible speaks of the seven Spirits. Can you find a word about the seven Spirits in your creed?" This is merely one illustration of the gap between the Lord's recovery and traditional Christianity. This gap exists because the recovery is based wholly upon the pure Word, whereas Christianity is filled with traditions.

2. Honoring God with the Lips,
but the Heart Being Away from Him

In verses 7 and 8 the Lord Jesus said, "Hypocrites! Isaiah has well prophesied concerning you, saying, This people honors Me with their lips, but their heart is far away from Me." The heavenly ruling of the kingdom requires inward reality, not mere outward practice, in that it deals with the real condition of the heart, not the expression of the lips. The tradition of the Pharisees was outward, but the Lord's concern was for something inward. Some in today's religion oppose us because they are for the outward things. They do not know the inner life or the subjective truths. Some claim that because Christ is in the heavens, He cannot actually dwell in us but He is merely represented in us by the Holy Spirit. This indicates that they do not have the subjective Christ; they have only the objective Christ. But we in the Lord's recovery have both the objective Christ and the subjective Christ. Those who teach that Christ is merely represented in us do so because they believe that in the Godhead the Father, Son, and Spirit are three separate individuals. Because the Son is in the heavens, they insist that it is impossible for Him to be in us. Those who argue this way are in practice tritheists. They believe in the one-in-three, but not in the three-in-one. However, in the Bible there is not a hint to indicate that the three in the Godhead are separate. On the contrary, the Lord Jesus said to Philip, "Do you not believe that I am in the Father, and the Father is in Me?" (John 14:10). In the same verse the Lord continued by saying, "The words which I speak to you, I do not speak from Myself; but the Father Who abides in Me, He does His works." This verse reveals that when the Son speaks, the Father works.

John 7:29 says, "I know Him, because I am from Him, and He sent Me," and John 15:26 says, "But when the Comforter comes, Whom I will send to you from the Father, the Spirit of reality Who proceeds from the Father, He will testify concerning Me." The Greek preposition rendered "from" in these verses and in John 6:46 has the meaning of "from *with*." The Son is sent not only from the Father, but also from *with* the Father. In John 15:26 the Lord says that He will send the Spirit from *with* the Father. According to the human concept, the Spirit is sent from the Father, and the Father remains in the heavens. However, the Spirit of reality is sent by the Son, not only from the Father, but also with the Father. The Comforter comes from the Father and with the Father. The Father is the source. When the Spirit comes from the source, it does not mean He leaves the source, but that the source comes with Him. This Spirit, sent by the Son and coming with the Father, will testify concerning the Son. The three of the Godhead are three-in-one. The Father, the Son, and the Spirit are not three separate Gods, but the one unique God. This is the correct understanding of the Triune God according to the pure Word of God. However, those who hold the traditional concept of the Trinity in actuality have three Gods.

Those who say that Christ is not in us cannot have subjective experiences of Christ. How can they experience Him subjectively if they do not believe that Christ today is the life-giving Spirit indwelling our spirit? Because they lack the subjective experience of Christ, they accuse us of being heretical. Furthermore, they deny the fact, revealed in 2 Peter 1:4, that the believers are partakers of the divine nature. They teach that in this verse the phrase "divine nature" does not mean divine nature, but divine virtue. They also claim that to have the divine nature is to become God Himself. Furthermore, they accuse us of teaching evolution into God. Yes, we do say that we have the divine nature, because we have been born of our God. How ridiculous to say that a son does not have the nature of his father! Because we have been born of the divine Father, we certainly have His life with His nature. But this does not mean that we become or are becoming God Himself. According to the pure Word, we also say that the church today is the manifestation of God in the flesh (1 Tim. 3:15-16). Because we say this according to the Bible, we are again accused of making ourselves God and of teaching evolution into God. We are actually accused of making the church the fourth member of the Godhead! How evil is this charge!

In October, 1977, an international conference was held in Taipei. From January of that year I began to seek the Lord concerning the subject on which I should speak during that conference. By the first of October, I still had no idea what the subject would be. When asked about it, I could only say, "I don't know." But on October 2, 1977, a speech against us was delivered before a large congregation. Many of our brothers and sisters attended that meeting and gave us a report concerning it. Upon hearing their report, I immediately realized that I should speak on the subjective experiences of Christ. I realized that those opposing us do not know anything about the subjective experience of Christ. They care only for objective knowledge and doctrine of the Bible, of Christ, and of the church. Thus, I was burdened to tell all the churches represented in the conference that we need to experience Christ in a subjective way.

The problem between the Pharisees and the Lord Jesus and His followers was that the Pharisees cared only for outward tradition, ritual, and practice, for example, the washing of hands. They cared nothing whatever for inward reality. Therefore, the Lord Jesus pointed them to the inward matter of the heart. The Lord seemed to say, "Don't care for this outward practice of washing of hands. The dirt that needs to be cleansed away is within you." In the Lord's recovery today we likewise do not care for outward things; rather, we care for inward reality.

In 1968 many saints in Los Angeles were stirred up to be

buried in the water. As a result, a number of opposers condemned me for teaching rebaptism. However, I did not teach this. But I was happy to see the saints who felt they were old bury themselves in the water. Certainly this is much better than attending a casino. Certain Christians in Hong Kong played Mah-Jongg, and the pastors did not condemn it. However, when some leaped into the water to bury themselves, the pastors said that this was heretical. Today many of those who were buried in the water are very much with the Lord. The Lord cares for inward reality, not for the outward practice. To those who criticized the ones who were baptized again, I said, "The children of Israel crossed the Red Sea, which is clearly a type of baptism (1 Cor. 10:1, 2). But later they crossed the Jordan River. Was that not a burial? The children of Israel had to pass the River Jordan because they had become old. If, after they passed through the Red Sea, they had been faithful to the Lord and had entered into the good land, there would have been no need to cross the Jordan. But because of their unbelief and their years of wandering in the wilderness, they became old. Hence, they needed to bury the oldness and to be renewed by passing through the River Jordan. Twelve stones were buried in the river to represent the old Israel, and twelve stones were brought out of the river and set on the land to represent the renewed Israel. Yes, you were baptized years ago, but since that time you have been wandering in the wilderness. You need to be buried and renewed." The Lord does not care for outward rituals or regulations; He cares only for inward reality.

Because the Lord cares for inward reality, we are not concerned about the outward way of having our meetings. It means very little whether the meeting is loud or quiet. We care only for the inward experience of Christ, for inward reality. It is an insignificant matter whether our hands are dirty; it is the condition of our inward parts that is important.

Verse 8 says, "This people honors Me with their lips, but their heart is far away from Me." Those who follow the traditions may honor the Lord outwardly with their lips, but their heart is far away from God. The outward practice of the traditions seemingly is for God. Actually, however, the inward being of so many who follow the traditions is not for God. Do you believe the majority of Christians observe Christmas for God? Apparently they may be; actually, in the practice of Christmas, the heart of many is not for the Lord. They have the appearance, but not the reality. They have an outward professing lip, but their heart is away from the Lord. In the Lord's recovery we are not talking without inward reality. If we speak without reality, we are more than pitiful. Tradition is a matter of utterance from the lips without reality in the heart.

3. Worshipping God in Vain, Teaching the Commandments (Traditions) of Men

Verse 9 says, "But in vain do they worship Me, teaching as teachings the commandments of men." This reveals that some worship to God may be in vain. The main cause of this is the teaching of the commandments of men. We must worship God according to His word, which is the truth. Many of those who condemn our meetings for being too noisy have no heart for God. Again I say, in the eyes of God it is not a matter of the outward appearance, but a matter of the inward reality, not a matter of what we say, but a matter of what we are. Consider the so-called Christian services in which solos are sung by beautiful young ladies in short skirts. Where is the heart of many who are listening to them? It may be in fornication. Why are not these solos sung by old ladies instead of by attractive young women? Is this the worship of God? No, it is an abomination to our holy God! But our noise is not an abomination to Him. Let us make a joyful noise to the Lord (Psa. 100:1) from the spirit. We like to shout, "Praise the Lord! Amen! Jesus is Lord!" We do not care for the outward appearance; we care for the inward reality.

C. The Real Defiling Things

In verse 11 the Lord said that it is not "that which enters into the mouth" that "defiles the man, but that which goes out of the mouth, this defiles the man." In the kingdom of the heavens defilement is not of material things but of moral matters. Material things have nothing to do with the heavenly ruling, but moral matters do. All the evils that issue from the heart prove that we are not under the heavenly ruling.

D. The Hypocritical Religionists

1. Not Planted by the Heavenly Father

In verse 13 the Lord said, "And He answered and said, Every plant which My heavenly Father has not planted shall be rooted up." This word of the heavenly King indicates that the hypocritical Pharisees were not planted by the heavenly Father. By their rejection of the heavenly King, they were uprooted from the kingdom of the heavens.

2. Blind Leaders of the Blind

Verse 14 says, "Leave them alone; they are blind leaders of the blind; and if a blind man leads a blind man, both will fall into a pit." The self-righteous and arrogant religionists thought they were clear concerning the way to serve God, not realizing that they were blind leaders of the blind. Their eyes were veiled by their religious traditions; hence, they could not see Christ and the reality of God's economy that they might enter into the kingdom of the heavens. Their blindness led them to fall into a pit.

Those who follow the traditions are blind leaders of the blind. This is true today. Many opposers are also blind leaders of the blind. They may claim to know the Bible, but actually they are completely blind and have no light at all. Hence, they lead others into blindness. I feel very sad about all those who are being misled. I appeal to your conscience and ask this question: Can you deny that there is some amount of reality in the Lord's recovery? In the recovery genuine help has been rendered to assist you to experience Christ in a subjective way and to enjoy Him. I think that you all can say from your conscience that never before and in no other place were you helped so much to enjoy Christ. Nevertheless, a number are opposing us. But they have missed the blessing and enjoyment. As the Lord Jesus said, these blind leaders have not been planted by the Father. Rather, they are self-assuming ones, not God-planted ones. Their blindness will cause them to be uprooted. Their follies, quackery, and errors will uproot them.

Again we see that we are following the same way taken by the Lord Jesus and His disciples. They suffered rejection, experienced the lack of necessities, faced the stormy sea, and were accused by the traditionalists and religionists. It is the same with us today. This is the pathway to glory.

LIFE-STUDY OF MATTHEW

MESSAGE FORTY-SIX

THE PATHWAY TO GLORY

(5)

As we have pointed out many times, the Gospel of Matthew is not a book of history, but a book of doctrine. Matthew puts together certain historical facts for the purpose of revealing a doctrine. If you compare the four Gospels, you will see that Matthew presents the facts of history in an order different from that found in Mark or John. Mark and John were written according to the sequence of history. The arrangement of the facts in Matthew's record, however, is not according to history, but according to doctrine, because Matthew presents to us the doctrine concerning the kingdom. Thus, Matthew does not care for historical sequence; he cares for doctrinal sequence.

In chapter fifteen, immediately after the dispute regarding the washing of hands, there is a record of feeding on Jesus (15:21-28). Perhaps in your reading of chapter fifteen you have not found the way to connect verses 1 through 20 with verses 21 through 28. But these two sections go together. In the original text of the Bible, there were no paragraphs or verses. Thus, the second section was the immediate continuation of the first section. Matthew had a definite reason for putting these two sections together. His purpose was to show that what the Lord wants is not the washing of hands, but the eating of Him, the taking in of Him as food. He does not want us to wash outwardly; He wants us to eat, to take Him in. No matter how many times we may wash our hands, we shall still be hungry. In 15:21-28 we do not have washing; we see a dirty dog eating. The Lord does not care about the washing of hands. Whether you are outwardly dirty or not does not mean anything to Him. What truly matters to the Lord is that your hunger is satisfied. The Lord Jesus did not say to the Canaanite woman, "Yes, you have the right to eat of Me, but you are dirty. Wash yourself first and then come back to eat." No, the outward washing is in the foregoing section, not in this section. Here we see the matter of eating. In this chapter we see that what matters to the Lord is not outward practices, but the inward condition. We should not outwardly wash away the dirt; rather, we need to be cleansed from within.

The question is how we can be inwardly cleansed. In order to be cleansed from within, something must get into us, and the only way this can take place is by eating. As the nourishing food, the Lord Jesus is the best cleansing element. When He comes into us as food, He not only nourishes us, but also inwardly cleanses us. He does not wash our hands; He washes our system, our very being. This matter of inward cleansing through the eating of Jesus is the link that joins the first two sections of chapter fifteen.

In today's religion what is taught is mostly like the washing of hands. On Sunday after Sunday, sermons are given mainly on the outward washing. However, what people need is not the outward washing, but the inward cleansing, the cleansing in life and nature. They need a cleansing element that can get into their system, even into their vessels. They do not need the outward washing of hands, but the inward washing that comes from the proper eating. Jesus is not only the nourishing food; He is also the cleansing element. I can testify that day by day the Lord Jesus is getting into me to cleanse me from within. He is washing my inner being. In the church life we are not being washed outwardly; on the contrary, we are being cleansed and purified inwardly.

Many of the saints are willing to be purified from within. Often they pray, "Lord Jesus, come into me. I want to be purified more and more. Lord, I hate not only sin and the world, but also myself, my natural life, and my natural disposition. O Lord, I am so contaminated by my disposition. How I long to be cleansed from this defilement!" As we pray in this way, we spontaneously eat the Lord Jesus, and He comes into us both as the nourishing food and as the cleansing element. Deep within our conscience we can testify that, as we enjoy the Lord in the church life, we are purified, even when we do not have the intention of being purified. As long as we are enjoying the Lord, we are being purified from within. Therefore, what we have is not the washing of hands, but the cleansing of our being. In these days we have been falsely accused of brainwashing. However, we do not practice brainwashing, but we do experience the washing of our disposition. Not only our mind, but our entire being, needs to be cleansed. The Lord can testify for me that very often I pray, "Lord, I am still dirty. Lord, I sense that I am still so natural and so much in my disposition. Lord, I love You and I want to live by You. But even today, Lord, I have been in my natural disposition. O Lord, because I am dispositionally dirty, I need Your cleansing." This is the kind of cleansing we need. This is not a matter of outward washing of hands to make a display of how clean we are. It is a matter of the inward cleansing that comes from eating Jesus. We all need such an inward cleansing from the Lord.

VI. FEEDING ON CHRIST BY FAITH

A. Outside the Sphere of Religion

Verse 21 says, "And Jesus went from there and departed into the districts of Tyre and Sidon." The unbelief of the Galileans caused the Lord Jesus not to do many works of power among them (13:58), and the rejection of Herod caused Him to depart to the desert (14:13). In 15:1 the religionists came down from Jerusalem to spy on the Lord Jesus and to find fault with Him. The further opposition of the rejecting religionists caused the heavenly

King to depart farther from them, even into the districts of
Tyre and Sidon, Gentile country. The Galilean rejection
caused the Lord not to do many works of power among
them. Herod's rejection caused Him to depart from the
civilized cities to the desert. Now the opposition by the
religionists caused the Lord to go even farther away, to the
Gentile world.

B. Knowing Christ in a Proper Way

1. Incorrectly Calling Him Son of David

Verse 22 says, "And behold, a Canaanite woman came
out from those regions and cried out, saying, Have mercy
on me, Lord, Son of David; my daughter is badly demon-
possessed!" Due to the rejection of the religious Jews, the
opportunity to contact the heavenly King came to the Gentiles, even to a weak Gentile woman. The Canaanite
woman addressed the Lord Jesus as the Lord, the Son of
David. The title Lord implies Christ's divinity, and the
title, Son of David, His humanity. As a Gentile woman, it
was proper for her to address Christ as the Lord. However,
she had no right to call Him Son of David; only the
children of Israel were privileged to do so.

The disciples were troubled by the crying out of the
Canaanite woman, and they asked the Lord to send her
away. This indicates that once again they were instructing
the Lord, telling Him to do something. This also was the
principle of the law. The disciples seemed to be saying,
"Lord, she is crying out and troubling us. Can't you do
something, Lord? Please send her away." At this point the
Lord said, "I was not sent except to the lost sheep of the
house of Israel" (v. 24). If you read the Gospels carefully,
you will see that the Lord Jesus never took a word from His
disciples. When they made a proposal, the Lord always
refused to consider it. But whenever the disciples did not
want to do a particular thing, the Lord would tell them to
do it. Likewise, when we want to do something, the Lord
says no. But when we do not want to do anything, the Lord

says go. The purpose of this is to train us not to live and act according to the self or our natural concept. Peter could have said to the Lord, "Lord, if You have come to the lost sheep of the house of Israel, what are You doing here in Tyre and Sidon? Why have You come here?" But if Peter had said this to the Lord, the Lord still would have had a way to subdue him. No one can defeat the Lord Jesus. The disciples lost the case, and their mouths were shut.

Although the Lord was sent to the lost sheep of the house of Israel, at the time of 15:21-28 He was in a Gentile region. This afforded the Gentiles an opportunity to participate in His grace. This bears dispensational significance, showing that Christ came to the Jews first, but due to their unbelief, His salvation turned to the Gentiles (Acts 13:46; Rom. 11:11).

2. Rightly Calling Him Lord and Worshipping Him

In verse 25 the Gentile woman rightly called Jesus the Lord and worshipped Him, saying, "Lord, help me!" This second time she called Christ only Lord, not the Son of David, because she realized that she was not a child of Israel, but a heathen.

C. Feeding on the Lord

In verse 26 the Lord answered the Canaanite woman: "It is not good to take the children's bread and throw it to the dogs." The heavenly King's ministry in all His visits created opportunities for Him to reveal Himself further. In the situations created in chapters nine and twelve, He had opportunities to reveal Himself as the Physician, the Bridegroom, the new cloth, the new wine, the Shepherd, the real David, the greater temple, the Lord of the harvest, the greater Jonah, and the greater Solomon. Here another opportunity was created for Him to reveal Himself as the children's bread. The Canaanite woman considered Him the Lord, a divine Person, and the Son of David, a royal descendant, great and high to reign. But He unveiled Himself to her as small pieces of bread, good for food. This implies that, as the heavenly King, He rules over His people by feeding them with Himself as bread. We can be the proper people in His kingdom only by being nourished with Him as our food. To eat Christ as our supply is the way to be the kingdom people in the reality of the kingdom.

The Lord said that the children's bread should not be thrown to the dogs. This indicates that in the eyes of the Lord all the heathen are dogs, which are unclean in the eyes of God (Lev. 11:26).

Do you not believe that when the Lord Jesus was speaking to His disciples regarding this Canaanite woman He already had the intention to feed her? Certainly the Lord foreknew that He had to feed this woman. Why then did He not do it immediately? Although the woman came and cried to Him, He remained silent at first, saying nothing. It almost appeared as if He were dumb. His dumbness caused the disciples to implore Him to do something for her and to send her away. The reason the Lord Jesus did not do something right away was that He wanted to take this opportunity to teach His disciples. When the disciples came to Him, He said that He had come only for the lost sheep of the house of Israel. When the woman came to Him, He indicated to her that He had come as bread for the children and that it was not lawful to cast the children's bread to the dogs.

1. Standing in the Proper Position — as a Heathen Dog under the Table of the Master

When the Lord Jesus referred to the Canaanite woman as a dog, she said, "Yes, Lord; for even the dogs eat of the crumbs which fall from their masters' table" (v. 27). The Canaanite woman, not offended by the Lord's word, but rather admitting that she was a heathen dog, considered that at that time Christ, after being rejected by the children, the Jews, became crumbs under the table as a portion to the Gentiles. The holy land of Israel was the table on which Christ, the heavenly bread, came as a portion to the children of Israel. But they threw Him off the table to the ground, the Gentile country, so that He became broken crumbs as a portion to the Gentiles. What a realization this Gentile woman had at that time! No wonder the heavenly King admired her faith (v. 28).

The Gentile woman seemed to be saying, "Yes, Lord, I am a dirty, pagan dog. But don't forget, Lord, that even dogs have their portion. The dog's portion is not on the table like the children's portion. The children's portion is on the table, but the dog's portion is under the table. Now, Lord, You are not on the table, in the land of Israel. You are under the table, in the Gentile world. You are in the very place where I am. You are not on the table where the children are. You are now under the table where the dogs are. Lord, the dogs may eat the crumbs that are under the table." The Canaanite woman was keen, and the Lord Jesus was caught by her.

2. By Faith

Verse 28 says, "Then Jesus answered and said to her, O woman, your faith is great; let it be done to you as you desire. And her daughter was healed from that hour." This word indicates that the Canaanite woman's dealings with the Lord were by faith, and her faith was great, overcoming the apparent situation.

Because I am very careful in doctrinal matters, I have wondered why the Lord Jesus did not tell the Canaanite woman to wash herself and then come back and eat. If I had been the Lord, I would have said, "Yes, as a dog, you have your portion. But don't you realize how dirty you are? If you would eat Me as the crumbs, you need to wash yourself." According to doctrine, this woman definitely needed to be washed. But why did the Lord Jesus not ask her to wash herself before eating of Him? If the Lord had done this, He would have been acting contrary to what He had said in the foregoing verses when He belittled the matter of outward washing. Here the Lord is emphasizing the matter of eating. But this does not mean that we do not need to be washed. The blood is available. We may strike the blood and eat the Lamb. But in order not to confuse matters, in this section on eating, the Lord Jesus said nothing about washing. I believe that the Lord Jesus did this purposely to show His disciples that they needed only one thing — the eating. Even if we are as dirty as pagan dogs, we still have the right and the position to eat Jesus. Oh, we need to be uninhibited eaters! Do not wait until you have washed. Come to the Lord just as you are and eat of Him. As the words of a hymn say, "Just as I am, I come." We need to say, "Lord, I come just as I am. I don't need to change or to be cleansed. Lord, I need You, and I come to You to eat. Even if I am a dirty dog, I come to You just as I am." Eating is primary, and eating is everything.

The Canaanite woman did not come to the Lord because she was hungry; she came because her daughter was sick. But the Lord turned the situation to the matter of eating. The Lord did not say, "I came as a Physician to the children of Israel, and I cannot heal any heathen. I cannot cure dogs." Rather, the Lord seemed to be saying, "I came as bread to the children. It is not right to throw the children's bread to the dogs." Although the woman's request had nothing to do with eating, the Lord purposely related her case to the matter of eating to show us that what we need is not outward washing, but eating for the inward nourishing. In his doctrinal arrangement Matthew put these matters together that we might understand that for the kingdom of the heavens we do not need outward cleansing, but what we need is for Christ to get into us. Are you sick or weak? Do you have certain problems? Do not try to deal with these things in an outward way. Instead, deal with them in an inward way by eating Jesus. In fact, you should forget about all those things. What you need is not outward washing, but Christ coming into you. The Lord seemed to be saying to the Canaanite woman, "You don't need healing. You need Me! And you do not need Me outwardly; you need Me inwardly. You need to eat Me. I came as bread for people to eat, to digest, and to assimilate. I would like to get into your being, into your system, vessels, and fibers. I would like to get into your very constituent and become you. Thus, you need to eat Me. Don't deal with things in an outward way. Rather, deal with everything in an inward way by taking Me into you. As long as I can get into you to nourish you, every problem will be solved."

We do not need outward rituals or practices. In today's religion people are following outward practices. But God's economy is not a matter of outward things; it is a matter of Christ coming into us inwardly. For this, we need to take Christ in by eating Him.

When I came to this country, I came with a commission and a burden, with something that I had received from the heavens. Before you came into the church, you never heard a word about eating Jesus, for all the teachings in religion are concerned with the outward washing of hands, not with presenting the edible Jesus to people. But this ministry has come here with the commission to minister the edible Jesus to His believers. I do not care for the opposition and the attack. I know what I am doing. Thinking that I am too bold, some may say, "Why is this man so bold? Don't we have many scholars in this country, men with doctoral degrees from the best seminaries?" I do not care about those degrees. I care only for my burden. I have the strong assurance that I have something of the Lord from the heavens that is not found in today's religion. I am not here teaching or preaching — I am ministering the edible Christ. This is what the Lord's people need today. You do not need religious washings. Forget about such things! As dirty dogs, we need the eating of Jesus. We need to take Jesus in. Hallelujah, today Jesus is not on the table! He is under the table. He has been cast off the table by the Israelites, and now He is in the Gentile world. All of us, including me, are dirty, pagan dogs. Nevertheless, we can praise the Lord that we are dogs, because the very bread of life from the heavens is now where the dogs are. If the bread were on the table, it would not be available to us.

But today the bread is under the table where the dogs are. We need the edible Christ who is now so near to us.

How I appreciate this section of the book of Matthew! This section reveals that we must forget about outward washing and eat the Lord Jesus. Do not try to change yourself, to correct yourself, or to improve yourself. What we need is the eating of Jesus.

VII. HEALING FOR THE GLORIFICATION OF GOD

In 15:29-31 we have a record of healing for the glorification of God. Due to the rejection of the Jewish religion, the Lord remained in Galilee of the nations as the healing light. He would not go to Jerusalem, the religious center of the Jews, for them to be healed (13:15). According to the doctrinal arrangement of the record of chapter fifteen, healing comes after eating. In other words, the proper healing comes from inward eating. Dieticians say that if one eats properly, he will not have illness. Illness comes from improper eating, but healing comes from adequate, proper eating. This is the doctrinal point regarding healing in this portion of the Word.

VIII. FURTHER PROVISION FOR NECESSITIES

A. By the Compassion of the Heavenly King

In 15:32-39 we have the miracle of the feeding of the four thousand. Because the Lord had compassion on the multitude in the wilderness, He would not send them away fasting (v. 32). Christ will not allow His followers to hunger and faint in the way while following Him.

B. Because the Lesson of Faith Was Needed

When the disciples learned that the Lord intended to provide food for the people, they said to Him, "Where in a desert are there so many loaves for us as to satisfy so great a crowd?" (v. 33). Even in the barren desert the Lord was able to feed His followers and satisfy them, no matter how many there were. The disciples experienced this before, in

14:15-21; however, it seems that they had not learned the lesson of faith. They set their eyes on the environment instead of on the Lord. Yet the Lord's presence was better than a rich store.

C. The Offering of What the Disciples Had Bringing in the Blessing with an Overflow

The Lord asked the disciples, "How many loaves do you have?" This indicates that the Lord always wants to use what we have to bless others. Verse 36 says, "He took the seven loaves and the fishes, and giving thanks, He broke them and gave them to the disciples, and the disciples to the crowds." If we offer all we have to the Lord, He will take it, break it, and give it back to us for distribution to others, to whom it will become the satisfying and overflowing blessing (v. 37). Whatever we offer to the Lord, however little it is, will be multiplied by His blessing hand to meet the need of a great multitude (v. 38).

In 15:32-39 we see the corporate eating. When I was young, I was bothered by the fact that Matthew gives us two accounts that are almost the same (14:14-21; 15:32-39). However, if you read these two sections carefully, you will see that the purpose of each is different. The purpose of the section about the feeding of the five thousand is to show us that as we are following our rejected King on the pathway to glory, He is able to take care of us. But the purpose of the record of the feeding of the four thousand is to show that we should not simply eat Jesus as crumbs individually as dirty dogs. We also need to eat Him in a corporate way together with many others. Let us all eat Him together. In this corporate eating we do not eat the crumbs, but the whole bread, and a surplus remains. Today in the church life we are no longer dirty dogs eating. Rather, we are proper men eating Him in a corporate way. Every church meeting is a time of corporate eating. When we first came into the church life, we came as dirty dogs, and we ate under the table. But now we are no longer under the table; we are sitting at the table. Although we are in the desert, we are nevertheless at the table. This is the corporate eating, an eating that is complete. The full bread is on the table of the saved ones.

LIFE-STUDY OF MATTHEW

THE PATHWAY TO GLORY

(6)

The book of Matthew often joins things together which apparently have no connection. We see this at the end of chapter fifteen and the beginning of chapter sixteen. Why does 16:1 say that the Lord Jesus was tempted? What is the connection between this and the end of chapter fifteen? The last thing covered in chapter fifteen is the corporate eating. Four thousand men, apart from women and children, were fed by seven loaves and a few small fishes. It seems that 16:1-12 has nothing to do with chapter fifteen. However, when we probe into the depth of the doctrine revealed in Matthew, we see that there is a connection.

IX. BEING WARY OF THE LEAVEN
OF THE PHARISEES AND SADDUCEES

When it comes to the matter of eating, we must be careful not to eat any leaven. In 16:1-12 what is crucial is not the temptation presented by the Pharisees and Sadducees, but the leaven. Hidden within this temptation of the Lord Jesus, there was leaven. Yeast is a leavening agent, used in making bread. What we see, however, is not the leaven, but the bread. When we eat bread, we may not realize that we are also eating leaven, for leaven is hidden in the bread and thus is invisible. Although no one could see the leaven hidden in the temptation presented by the Pharisees and Sadducees, it was nonetheless concealed within it.

As we have seen, chapter fifteen deals with the matter of eating. From 15:1 through 16:12, Matthew's record is very much concerned with eating. Eating unclean things may defile us (15:1-20). What we need is not the outward washing, but the inward eating. Eating is the way to partake of Christ (15:21-28), and eating causes Gentile dogs to become children of God, even proper men. By eating we feed on the unlimited and inexhaustibly rich supply of Christ (15:32-39). Matthew 15 concludes with the record of corporate eating. However, we must beware of eating leaven (16:5-12), especially the religious leaven hidden within religious people, such as the Pharisees and the Sadducees. The Pharisees were the ancient fundamentalists, and the Sadducees were the ancient modernists. I am thankful that the Bible mentions them both. In today's religion there are also fundamentalists and modernists. The first group, the fundamentalists, have sound, scriptural beliefs. The second group, the Sadducees, deny what the Bible says.

In Matthew 16 Christ was present as bread, but the religious ones had hidden, damaging leaven. To repeat, Christ was the bread, and with the religious people, both the ancient fundamentalists and modernists, there was leaven. In the subtlety of religion, leaven tries to creep into the bread. Remember the parable of the leaven (13:33). Christ is the fine flour to feed God's people for God's satisfaction. But the woman, the apostate Roman Catholic Church, took leaven and hid it in the fine flour. Apparently leaven makes fine flour easier to take in; actually, it produces corruption. In chapter fifteen we see the bread available not only for Gentile dogs, but also for the men in the wilderness. In chapter sixteen the Lord warned His disciples and seemed to be saying to them, "Take care regarding your eating. It is right to eat Me, but you must beware of religious leaven." At the Lord's time there were the Pharisees and Sadducees, and today there still are Pharisees and Sadducees. These religious people, whether they are fundamentalists or modernists, have some secret, hidden leaven.

Now we can see the connection between chapters

fifteen and sixteen. We can see the reason Matthew speaks of leaven immediately after the record of corporate eating. Be careful. As you are enjoying the corporate eating, it is easy for leaven to secretly creep in. Eventually, leaven did creep into the church. The church was not very careful about this, and not too long after the day of Pentecost leaven came in. The bread on which the church had been feeding became completely leavened. Thus, the Lord's word in 16:6 and 11 was not only a warning, but also a prophecy.

By the end of chapter fifteen, the disciples were helped to realize that the Lord Jesus had come to be bread to the children of God. Firstly, the heathen were dirty dogs, but after eating Christ they had been regenerated and caused to become children of God, proper men to enjoy Christ in a corporate way. When all this was made clear to the disciples, they must have been happy. However, then the Lord seemed to say, "It is good to eat Me and to enjoy the corporate eating. But there are religious people who in the name of God, under the cloak of worshipping God, and presumably for the purpose of glorifying God, will bring in leaven. They will be utilized by the enemy to secretly bring in some damaging and corrupting thing. You must beware of this."

The Lord Jesus came as bread to be taken in by sinners so that they may be regenerated to be the children of God and transformed into the proper men to feed on Christ corporately. Although this is wonderful, there is the danger of religious leaven that comes from religious people. In Christianity religious people are highly respected. But I speak of them in a negative way because I realize that the religious ones always have some leaven. Under the cloak of religion, they bring in certain matters that corrupt and damage the things of God. Therefore, we must learn to beware of leaven as we are enjoying Christ as our heavenly bread.

This leaven always comes from religion, from the Pharisees and Sadducess. Mark 8:15 speaks also of the leaven of Herod. Matthew does not mention this type of leaven because his purpose is to show that in feeding on Christ there is the danger of taking in something religious. Anything religious may have leaven in it. The leaven of the Pharisees and Sadducees was their teaching (16:12). None of the Pharisees taught in a way that would obviously damage people. If they did this, no one would listen to them. The same was true of the Sadducees. If they did not give people the impression that their teaching would help them, no one would listen to them. The principle is the same today. In today's Christendom there is teaching upon teaching. Every teaching appears to help people. No one will ever tell you that the teaching he is about to give you may damage you or lead you astray. On the contrary, everyone with a certain teaching pretends that his teaching is good and helpful. This is the reason people like teachings. But we need to realize that leaven may often be concealed under the cloak of religious teachings.

Christ is the bread of heaven sent by God and from God. Leaven, however, is something sent by Satan and from Satan. Thus, God sent bread, and God's enemy sent leaven. God is endeavoring to put Christ into His people, and the enemy is working to put in leaven as God's children are taking in Christ. This principle is evident in today's Catholicism. Take the example of Christmas. The birth of Christ and the incarnation of Christ are the fine flour as food to us. But Christmas is leaven. The birth of Christ is pure. How pure it is that God has been incarnated! But consider how defiled and corrupt is the practice of Christmas today. There are even such things as Christmas dancing parties. What leaven there is in this matter of Christmas! Christmas is so full of leaven that it is difficult to find any fine flour at all.

We may apply this principle to nearly everything in today's Christendom. For example, there is nothing wrong with being a servant of God. But why should people use the title Reverend? To call yourself Reverend is to bring in leaven. It is also leaven to use denominational names, such as Lutheran and Baptist. All these titles are leaven.

Furthermore, it is pure to sing praise to the Lord, but to have a soloist is to add leaven. Although we enjoy the corporate eating of Jesus, we need to beware of hidden, religious leaven. Even some of the dear saints in the Lord's recovery may wonder what is wrong with having a soloist in the meeting. Oh, how we must beware of every kind of leaven! It is not easy to discern that leaven is hidden in the bread.

A. Temptation of the Pharisees and the Sadducees

1. Asking for a Sign

Matthew 16:1 says, "And the Pharisees and Sadducees came, and tempting Him asked Him to show them a sign out of heaven." Those who bring in leaven desire to see signs, miracles. Nothing is more deceitful than miracles. Suppose Antichrist appeared and set up his image in front of you, and the false prophet was able to make this image speak to you. You could easily be deceived by this and say, "This is marvelous. If this were not a miracle, how could he make the image speak?" Leaven always creeps in through the subtlety of miracles. In 16:1-12 the two key words are sign and leaven. The religionists, the Pharisees and Sadducees, came to the Lord Jesus and asked Him to show them a sign from heaven. However, the Lord Jesus refused to show them such a sign. The pure bread, the pure Christ, does not perform signs. As we shall see, He Himself is the unique sign.

2. Not Being Able to Discern the Signs of the Times

In verses 2 and 3 the Lord indicated to the Pharisees and Sadducees that although they knew how to discern the face of heaven, they could not discern the signs of the times. The signs of the times were on the one hand that the generation was evil and adulterous and on the other hand that Christ was to die and be resurrected for that evil generation. The Pharisees and Sadducees could not discern these things.

3. Only the Sign of Jonah Being Available to the Evil and Adulterous Generation

Verse 4 says, "An evil and adulterous generation seeks a sign, and a sign shall not be given to it, except the sign of Jonah. And He left them and went away." Jonah was the prophet who turned from Israel to the Gentiles and was put into the belly of the great fish. After remaining there for three days, he emerged to become a sign to that generation for repentance (Jonah 1:2, 17; 2:2-10). This was a type of Christ, the prophet sent by God to His people (Deut. 18:15, 18), who would turn from Israel to the Gentiles, and who would be buried in the heart of the earth for three days and then be resurrected, becoming a sign to this generation for salvation. The Lord's word here implies that to that evil and adulterous, Jewish and religious generation, the Lord would do nothing but die and be resurrected as a sign, the greatest sign to them, that they might be saved if they would believe. In speaking of the sign of Jonah, the Lord seemed to be saying, "You Pharisees and Sadducees do not need miracles. You need to discern that this generation is evil and to believe in Me and take Me into you as the crucified and resurrected One. You need to repent as the people of Nineveh did, and you need to believe that I will die for your sins and be resurrected to impart Myself into you as life. This is the sign for this generation. No other sign will be given. I am the sign to you, the sign of the crucified and resurrected Christ. You need to repent and to receive Me into you as your bread."

B. The Leaven of the Pharisees and Sadducees

At this juncture the Lord brought in the matter of leaven, saying, "Take heed and beware of the leaven of the Pharisees and Sadducees" (v. 6). As we have pointed out, this leaven is the teaching of the Pharisees and Sadducees (v. 12). The teaching of the Pharisees was hypocritical (23:13, 15, 23, 25, 27, 29), and the teaching of the Sadducees was like today's modernism, denying the resurrection, angels, and spirits (Acts 23:8). Hence, the teachings of both the Pharisees and Sadducees were impure and evil, and were likened to leaven, which was forbidden to be seen with God's people (Exo. 13:7).

Again I say that the words sign and leaven are the two crucial words in this section. We should not believe in any miracle that does not have in it the essence of Christ's crucifixion and resurrection. I have seen the so-called healing services in the Pentecostal movement. However, to speak truly there was a great deal of leaven there. The essence of the crucifixion of Christ and of the resurrected life of Christ was lacking. Every miracle, every sign, must be based upon the principle of the crucifixion and the resurrection. The sign of Jonah, the sign of the crucified and resurrected Christ, must accompany every genuine miracle. Otherwise, the miracles will simply be a type of leaven. A great many Christians have been leavened by miracles. Today the so-called speaking in tongues has become a type of leaven, and so many of those who speak in tongues have been leavened by this practice. When some come to a meeting, they care only for speaking in tongues, no matter whether or not the tongues are real and genuine. As long as there is the manifestation of "tongues," they are happy. This shows how leavened they are. They have no heart for the pure bread, for the pure sign with the essence of Christ's crucifixion and resurrection. On the contrary, they are leavened. Again I say, beware of every kind of leaven.

X. RECEIVING THE REVELATION
CONCERNING CHRIST AND THE CHURCH

In 16:13-20 we come to a section of the Gospel of Matthew concerned with the revelation of Christ and the church. Before we consider the details of this section, we need to consider the connection between it and the foregoing section, verses 1-12.

A. In the District of Caesarea Philippi

Verse 13 says that the Lord Jesus came into the district of Caesarea Philippi with His disciples and there asked them, "Who do men say that the Son of Man is?" It seems that this is not related to the matter of leaven. Caesarea Philippi is in the northern part of the Holy Land, close to the border, at the foot of Mount Hermon, on which the Lord was transfigured (17:1-2). It was far from the holy city with the holy temple, where the atmosphere of the old Jewish religion filled every man's thought, leaving no room for Christ, the new King. The Lord brought His disciples purposely to such a place with a clear atmosphere that their thought might be released from the effects of the religious surroundings in the holy city and holy temple, and that He might reveal to them something new concerning Himself and the church, which is the pulse of His heavenly kingdom. It was here that the vision concerning Him as the Christ and the Son of the living God came to Peter (vv. 16-17). It was also here that the church was revealed and mentioned for the first time as the means of bringing in the kingdom of the heavens (vv. 18-19).

Several months ago, some other brothers and I visited both Jerusalem and Caesarea Philippi. The religious atmosphere of Jerusalem was foul and terrible. Physically, mentally, and spiritually, the atmosphere was stuffy. We were disgusted with what we saw there. One day we drove to the north, to Caesarea Philippi. How fresh the air was there! We saw a fountain which was one of the three sources of the Jordan River. We lingered there for a while, enjoying our lunch and having a pleasant time. The reason the Lord Jesus brought His disciples to Caesarea Philippi was to clear them of the foggy religious atmosphere of Jerusalem and the Jewish religion. Only after the Lord had brought the disciples to Caesarea Philippi did He begin to ask them questions regarding who He was. Caesarea Philippi was the right place for the Lord Jesus to be revealed to His disciples. It was also the right place for the revelation to be given regarding the church.

However, we still have not seen the connection between these two portions of the Word. The connection is that if we are still under the influence of religious leaven, we shall never be clear about Christ or the church. In order to be clear about Christ and the church, you need to eliminate all leaven. You not only need to get away from the religious center, from the holy city with the holy temple, with the stuffy, foul, atmosphere filled with religious concepts, but you also need to be purged of the religious leaven. If there is still leaven within you, you will be under a veil, and your eyes will not be able to see Christ and the church. To see Christ and the church you need to get away from the religious center and all the so-called holy things, places, and persons, and you need to eliminate every kind of leaven.

Although certain Christians have a heart for God, they still cannot see the church. Neither can they see Christ in a pure and genuine way because they are saturated with religious leaven. Now we can see the reason Matthew placed the first part of chapter sixteen immediately after his account of the corporate eating. In our eating we need to beware of leaven. Moreover, if we would see Christ and the church, we should not have any religious leaven. We need a clear sky and a clear atmosphere; we also need a clear mind and a clear understanding, an understanding not under the influence of religious leaven. If we still hold the concept that there is nothing wrong with Christmas or with the denominations, it is an indication that our understanding is saturated with hidden religious leaven. This leaven creates not an outward fog, but an inward mist. If there is such a mist within us, our vision will be blurred. The inward condition of some saints is like this. They are filled with mist. But every once in a while a little hole appears, and a portion of clear sky can be seen. However, immediately afterward the mist covers the clear spot. Some of these saints may say, "What's wrong with the title Southern Baptist? A denomination is not a gambling casino, is it?" If you think like this, your vision will be blurred. Questions like these indicate that you still hold on to leavened, religious concepts.

Many of us have been leavened from the time we were born. Throughout our childhood we were constantly under the influence of leaven. Although you knew nothing of Christ, you were familiar with Santa Claus, Christmas stockings, and trees decorated with colored lights. Your thought and feeling were completely leavened. To you, the church was a bungalow with a high tower and bell. This shows that unconsciously and subconsciously you were leavened. Moreover, the more you were educated and trained in school, the more the leaven saturated your being. Therefore, we need to leave the religious center and go far to the north, to the region of Caesarea Philippi, where the sky is clear. Also, we need to say to the Lord inwardly, "Lord Jesus, purify me of every kind of leaven. I don't want there to be fog without or mist within. I want to be a clear person under a clear sky."

Again I say that the bread in Christendom is impure; it is leavened. The very Christ preached and taught by today's religion has been leavened. Consider how much leaven there is in the preaching of Christ and in the teaching regarding the church. The "bread" of the church, that is, the truth concerning the church, has been especially leavened. Recently I was grieved to hear that some Christian preachers have issued a call for Christians to come back to the so-called historic church. Do they not know that the councils of the historic church made many evil decisions, one of which made at the Council of Ephesus (A.D. 431) was to sanction the worship of Mary? As you know, the charismatic movement has penetrated the Catholic Church and has even been mixed with the worship of Mary. How can those who have had the charismatic experience tolerate such idolatry? But today some are saying, even over the radio, that there is no idolatry in Catholicism. A certain group in Berkeley is striving to investigate us. I wonder why they do not investigate the Catholic Church. Why do they not go to the Vatican and see the paganism, idolatry, and heresy there? The fact that they investigate us but not the Catholic Church exposes their evil intention, which is to suppress us and to terminate us. In every corner of today's Christendom there is hidden leaven. Nothing there is pure. The whole of Christendom has been leavened. This is not my word; it is the prophetic word of the Lord Jesus in 13:33, where the Lord said that "the whole was leavened." We, however, stand against the leaven and we are testifying the pure Jesus. Although this is offensive to many, there is nothing we can do about it. We must testify the pure Christ and stand against all leaven.

B. Receiving the Revelation concerning Christ

In verse 13 the Lord asked His disciples a question: "Who do men say that the Son of Man is?" As a man, Christ was a mystery, not only to that generation, but also to people today.

1. Christ Not Being John the Baptist, Elijah, Jeremiah, or One of the Prophets

Verse 14 says, "And they said, Some, John the Baptist; and others, Elijah; and still others, Jeremiah, or one of the prophets." At most, people can only recognize that Christ is the greatest among the prophets. Without heavenly revelation, no one can know that He is the Christ and the Son of the living God (v. 16).

2. Christ, the Son of the Living God

After the Lord asked His disciples to say who they thought He was, Simon Peter answered and said, "You are the Christ, the Son of the living God" (v. 16). The Christ, as the anointed One of God, refers to the Lord's commission; whereas the Son of the living God, as the second of the Triune God, refers to His person. His commission is to accomplish God's eternal purpose through His crucifixion, resurrection, ascension, and second advent, whereas His person embodies the Father and issues in the Spirit for a full expression of the Triune God.

The living God is in contrast to dead religion. The Lord is the embodiment of the living God, having nothing to do with dead religion.

3. Revealed by the Heavenly Father under His Blessing, Not by Flesh and Blood

Verse 17 says, "And Jesus answered and said to him, You are blessed, Simon Bar-jona, because flesh and blood did not reveal this to you, but My Father Who is in the heavens." Flesh and blood refer to man, who is composed of flesh and blood. Only the Father knows the Son (11:27); hence, only He can reveal the Son to us.

C. Receiving the Revelation concerning the Church

In verse 18 the Lord said, "And I also say to you that you are Peter, and on this rock I will build My church, and the gates of Hades shall not prevail against it." The Father's revelation concerning Christ is just the first half of the great mystery, which is Christ and the church (Eph. 5:32). Hence, the Lord needed also to reveal to Peter the second half, which is concerning the church.

1. The Building of the Church

a. By Christ

In verse 18 the Lord said, "I will build My church." The Lord's building of His church began at the day of Pentecost (Acts 2:1-4, 41-42). Yet the Lord's prophecy here has still not been fulfilled, even by the twentieth century. Christendom, composed of the apostate Roman Catholic Church and the Protestant denominations, is not the Lord's building of His church. This prophecy is fulfilled through the Lord's recovery, in which the building of the genuine church is accomplished.

The words "My church" indicate that the church is of the Lord, not of any person or thing; it is not like the denominations, which are denominated after some person's name or according to some thing.

b. Upon the Rock

The Lord told Peter that He would build His church upon "this rock." The words "this rock" refer not only to Christ, but also to this revelation of Christ, which Peter received from the Father. The church is built on this revelation concerning Christ.

Roman Catholicism claims that the rock in verse 18 refers to Peter, whereas most fundamental Christians say that it refers to Christ. Although it is correct to say that the rock denotes Christ, not even this understanding is adequate. The rock here refers not only to Christ, but even the more to the revelation concerning Christ. In this chapter the Father reveals something from the heavens to Peter. This heavenly revelation from the Father is the rock. It is not an insignificant matter that the church is built both upon Christ and upon the revelation concerning Christ. The denominations are not built upon this rock. For example, the Southern Baptist denomination is built upon the revelation of baptism by immersion, not upon the revelation of Christ. In the same principle, the Presbyterian denomination is built upon the doctrine of presbytery. Likewise, the charismatic churches or groups are not built upon this revelation concerning Christ; they are built upon their knowledge of the charismatic things and on their experience of them. Thus, the Foursquare denomination is built upon the revelation of the foursquare gospel, not on the revelation of Christ.

The church that is built upon the revelation concerning Christ is the genuine church, and it is not sectarian. The problem today is that Christians like to form groups or so-called churches according to their concept and viewpoint. But their concept is not the revelation concerning Christ. The church must be built upon "this rock," that is, upon the revelation of Christ. If we see this, we shall be saved from division. Only one thing is built upon the revelation of Christ, and that is the church. Any group that is built upon doctrines, views, practices, or concepts is not the church built upon the revelation concerning Christ. The revelation concerning Christ is the rock upon which the Lord Jesus is building His church.

c. With the Stone

The Greek word rendered "Peter" in verse 18 may also be rendered "a stone," which is the material for God's building. Like Peter, all the believers need to be transformed into stones for the building of the church (1 Pet. 2:5).

d. The Gates of Hades Not Prevailing against It

In verse 18 the Lord also said that the gates of Hades would not prevail against His church. The "gates of Hades" refers to Satan's authority or power of darkness (Col. 1:13; Acts 26:18), which cannot prevail against the genuine church built by Christ upon this revelation concerning Him as the rock, with stones such as Peter, a transformed human being. This work of the Lord also indicates that Satan's power of darkness will attack the church; hence, there is spiritual warfare between Satan's power, which is his kingdom, and the church, which is God's kingdom.

When we were in Rome several months ago, we visited Saint Peter's Cathedral. On the dome there were written some words from Matthew 16:18: "I will build my church upon this rock." However, the last part of this verse — "And the gates of Hades shall not prevail against it" — was not written there. Perhaps this indicates that the gates of Hades have totally defeated the Catholic Church. The church in the Lord's recovery, however, is truly built upon the revelation concerning Christ, and against this church the gates of Hades cannot prevail.

2. The Church Being the Kingdom of the Heavens

Verse 19 speaks of the kingdom of the heavens. The words "the kingdom of the heavens" here are interchangeably used for the word "church" in the previous verse. This is a strong proof that the genuine church is the kingdom of the heavens in this age. This is confirmed by Romans 14:17, which refers to the proper church life.

a. The Keys Given to Peter

In verse 19 the Lord said to Peter, "I will give to you the keys of the kingdom of the heavens." According to history, the keys have been two: Peter used one to open the gate for the Jewish believers to enter the kingdom of the heavens on the day of Pentecost (Acts 2:38-42); and he used the other to open the gate for the Gentile believers to enter the kingdom of the heavens in the house of Cornelius (Acts 10:34-48).

b. Binding and Loosing on Earth
What Has Been Bound and Loosed in the Heavens

In verse 19 the Lord also said to Peter, "Whatever you bind on the earth shall be what has been bound in the heavens, and whatever you loose on the earth shall be what has been loosed in the heavens." The Gospel of Matthew is concerned with the kingdom of the heavens, which is a matter of authority. The church revealed in this book represents the kingdom to reign. Hence, the authority to bind and to loose is given not only to Peter, the apostle for the church here, but also to the church itself (18:17-18). Whatever the church people bind or loose on earth must be what has been bound or loosed in the heavens already. We can only bind or loose what has already been bound or loosed in the heavens.

D. The Revelation concerning Christ and the Church Kept Secret

Verse 20 says, "Then He charged the disciples that they

should tell no one that He is the Christ." The revelation concerning Christ with His church is always hidden from religious people.

LIFE-STUDY OF MATTHEW

MESSAGE FORTY-EIGHT

THE PATHWAY TO GLORY

(7)

On the pathway to glory we have rejection, the lack of necessities, the storm on the sea, and the accusation from religion, and then we learn how to eat Christ. As the result of eating Christ, there is the healing for the glorification of God. Following this, there is the corporate eating, the warning regarding leaven, and the clear revelation concerning Christ and the church. In this message we come to the last station of the pathway to glory: the way of the cross. Only when people have learned how to eat Christ and to beware of religious leaven and are under a clear sky, can the revelation of Christ and the church be given. Many of us can testify that before we came to such a place, the revelation of Christ and the church did not come. It comes only in Caesarea Philippi. We feed on Christ not only as the crumbs, but also in a corporate way as the rich, unlimited, inexhaustible supply of life. Only then can we see the revelation of Christ and the church. Thus, three things are vital: that we know how to feed on Christ and to enjoy the inexhaustibly rich supply of Christ; that we are purged of all religious leaven; and that we are in Caesarea Philippi under a clear sky. Here the fog is driven away. We cannot afford to stay in a situation where there is religious fog. If we remain in that kind of place, we shall not see the revelation given in Caesarea Philippi. Hallelujah, we have the rich supply, we have a clear sky, and we have no fog! Therefore, we see the vision of Christ and the church.

XI. TAKING THE WAY OF THE CROSS

A good number of Christian teachers have seen the connection between Matthew 16:13-20 and 16:21-28, the connection between the portion of the Word concerning Christ and the church and that concerning the way of the cross. In order to experience Christ and to have the church built upon Christ, we need to take the way of the cross. Christ was the Pioneer, the Forerunner, in taking the way of the cross. This is the unique way for Christ to be released, and it is also the unique way for the church to be built with Christ and upon Christ.

A. Christ Going to Jerusalem to Suffer Crucifixion and to Be Resurrected

Verse 21 says, "From that time Jesus began to show to His disciples that He must go to Jerusalem and suffer many things from the elders and chief priests and scribes, and be killed, and be raised on the third day." After the revelation of the great mystery concerning Christ and the church, the crucifixion and resurrection of Christ are unveiled. For Christ to build His church, He must go to the religious center, pass through crucifixion, and enter into resurrection. In verse 21 the Lord first revealed to His disciples His crucifixion and resurrection. Before this time, He had not mentioned anything about these things. Following the revelation of Christ and the church, the Lord Jesus revealed to His enlightened disciples His crucifixion and resurrection. This is very meaningful. After we see Christ and the church, we must be prepared to take the way of the cross. You may be wondering what the way of the cross is. To take the way of the cross is not to reserve anything of the self. No matter how good, right, or profitable you may be, you need to be crucified. For the enjoyment of Christ and for the building of the church, we must be crucified. Nothing of our being should be reserved.

In verse 21 the Lord Jesus spoke both of His crucifixion

and His resurrection. The disciples, however, picked up the matter of crucifixion, but neglected the matter of resurrection. The disciples heard that the Lord was to be killed, but it seems that they did not hear that He would be resurrected. Nevertheless, the Lord did say that He would be raised on the third day. They did not grasp this part of the Lord's word because they had no concept of resurrection. Within them was the fear that the Lord Jesus would be killed. Thus, when the Lord spoke about His resurrection, the disciples did not apprehend it. It is the same with us today. We immediately take in whatever corresponds to our concept. But if a certain thing does not correspond to what is already within us, we do not take it in. Some people wonder why in my speaking I repeat things again and again. Although I may repeat certain things, some people still do not get them. Again I say that although the Lord Jesus spoke of two matters, crucifixion and resurrection, the disciples grasped the first, but not the second.

B. Satan's Frustration of Christ through Peter's Natural Concept

Verse 22 says, "And Peter, taking Him to him, began to rebuke Him, saying, God be merciful to You, Lord; this shall by no means happen to You!" Peter's word reveals that the natural man is never willing to take the cross. Peter was bold and had a good heart toward the Lord. Without Peter, we would not have so many revelations, for through his boldness in making mistakes a number of revelations were given. Here Peter was bold enough to rebuke the Lord. As Peter was rebuking the Lord, his expression might have been that of Satan. Peter's words — "God be merciful to You, Lord" — sound very nice, but they were actually a rebuke. Peter had been offended by the Lord's word about being killed. Because he was fully in himself, he actually rebuked the Lord Jesus.

In verse 23 we see the Lord's response: "But He turned and said to Peter, Get behind Me, Satan! You are a stumbling block to Me; for you are not setting your mind on the things of God, but on the things of men." Christ perceived that it was not Peter but Satan who was frustrating Him from taking the cross. This reveals that our natural man, which is not willing to take the cross, is one with Satan. When we are setting our mind, not on the things of God, but on the things of men, we become Satan, a stumbling block to the Lord in the fulfillment of God's purpose.

C. Following Christ by Denying the Self and Taking Up the Cross

Verse 24 says, "Then Jesus said to His disciples, If anyone desires to come after Me, let him deny himself, and take up his cross, and follow Me." Here the Lord speaks about denying the self. To deny our self is to forfeit our soul-life, the natural life (v. 26; Luke 9:25).

In verse 25 the Lord continues: "For whoever desires to save his soul-life shall lose it; but whoever loses his soul-life for My sake shall find it." In verses 23 through 25, three things are related to one another: mind, himself, and soul-life. Our mind is the expression of our self, and our self is the embodiment of our soul-life. Our soul-life is embodied in and lived out by our self, and our self is expressed through our mind, our thought, our concept, our opinion. When we set our mind, not on the things of God, but on the things of men, our mind grasps the opportunity to act and express itself. This was what happened to Peter. Hence, the Lord's following word indicated that he had to deny himself and not save his soul-life, but rather lose it. To lose the soul-life is the reality of denying the self. This is to take up the cross.

Actually, in these verses four things are related: Satan, mind, self, and soul-life. This message is concerned mainly with these four things, which begin with the mind and ultimately consummate with Satan. The mind is the expression of the self, and the self is the embodiment of the soul-life. The soul-life is lived out by the self, and the self is expressed through the mind. What the mind thinks or considers is an opinion, idea, or concept. The mind's opinion, concept, or idea is the expression of the self, the embodiment of the soul-life. The soul-life is embodied in the self, just as the Father is embodied in the Son. The soul-life is like the Father, the self is like the Son, and the mind is like the Spirit. Thus, we have here a trinity of mind, self, and soul-life.

The soul-life, the source, is embodied in the self, which is expressed in the mind. Perhaps you have never before considered your mind the expression of the self. If you saw this, you would probably not use your mind so much. Your opinion is the expression of your self. Beware of your opinion, for it is not a positive thing. Natural opinions, concepts, ideas, and thoughts are negative things, for they are the expression of the self. The soul is embodied in the self and lived out through the self, and the self is expressed in opinions. When the self is expressed through the mind as opinion, that is Satan.

I have learned to be afraid of my opinions. During the years, I have been enlightened to see that the natural opinion or concept is the incarnation of Satan. If this were not so, how could the Lord Jesus have rebuked Peter and called him Satan? The first time I read this in the Bible, I was shocked. In verse 23 Peter and Satan had become one in Peter's selfish opinion. Peter's opinion was Satan. To repeat, the soul-life is embodied in the self, and the self is expressed through the mind. When the mind expresses an opinion, that is the incarnation of Satan.

Have you ever realized that often your opinion has been the expression of Satan? I doubt that you have ever understood the matter in this way. It is crucial that we see that our natural opinion is the incarnation of Satan. Nothing damages your Christian life more than your opinions. The expression of the natural opinion is the product of satanic inspiration. Because your natural opinion comes from Satan's inspiration, you need to beware of it. If you use your mind excessively, the Lord Jesus will call you Satan. If you exercise your mind too much, you will be the expression of Satan, and the Lord Jesus will say to you, "Get behind Me, Satan."

To take the way of the cross to enter into glory requires that we not use our mind in a natural way. We must deny the self, bear the cross, and follow Christ. I do not believe that anyone who exercises his mind in a natural way can be a good follower of Christ. When we exercise our mind too much, we do not follow Christ. Christ is not in our mind, but in our spirit. If you examine these verses in their context, you will see that the mind is the expression of the self, that the self is the embodiment of the soul-life, and that all this must be put on the cross.

In verse 24 the Lord said, "If anyone desires to come after Me, let him deny himself, and take up his cross, and follow Me." The cross is not merely a suffering; it is primarily a killing. It kills and terminates the criminal. Christ first bore the cross and then was crucified. We, His believers, have first been crucified with Him and then bear the cross today. To us, bearing the cross is to remain under the killing of the death of Christ for the terminating of our self, our natural life, and our old man. In so doing we deny our self that we may follow the Lord.

Many Christians have a mistaken concept of the cross. They think that the cross is just for suffering. In this section of the Word, however, the cross does not denote suffering, but killing. The ultimate purpose of the cross is not to cause you to suffer; it is to terminate you, to kill you. The Lord's word here does not have the concept of suffering; His concept concerning the cross is that of killing.

The Lord Jesus firstly bore the cross and then He was crucified on the cross and terminated. As the Lord Jesus was bearing the cross, He was constantly under the killing, not under suffering. It is a wrong concept to associate the cross merely with suffering. The Lord Jesus began to bear the cross immediately after His baptism. Baptism means that a person is put into death, terminated, and buried. From the moment of His baptism, the Lord Jesus was constantly putting Himself under the cross and keeping Himself there. He was a person who was constantly being put to death. With Him, the bearing came first and the killing followed. With us it is just the opposite, for we are first crucified with Him and then we bear the cross.

As a youth, I was taught that to bear the cross is to suffer. This erroneous concept comes from Catholicism. I repeat, the concept of bearing the cross in Matthew 16 is not that of suffering, but of being put to death. In order to bear the cross, we must realize that we have already been crucified. We have been killed on the cross with Christ, and now we must remain under this killing. I am a person who has been killed. My self-life, my mind, my natural life, and my whole being have been killed. Now I need to remain under this killing. This is what it means to bear the cross.

When I was a young person, I heard certain exhortations given to others related to bearing the cross. A wife who was suffering the unkindness of her husband was told to bear the cross. In other words, she was told that to suffer the unkindness of her husband was to bear the cross. But suffering cannot build up the church. However, the genuine bearing of the cross builds up the church, because it puts to death the self, the soul-life, and the natural life. We all have been buried, baptized, and terminated. Now we need to stay in this termination. This is to take the way of the cross.

A dead man has no opinion. It is impossible to bend his mind because his mind no longer functions. If your mind can be bent, it means that it is still alive, active, and aggressive. If you tried to bend the minds of those buried in a cemetery and they could speak, they would say, "You have come to the wrong place. We all are dead, and our minds have stopped functioning. There is no need for you to come to bend our minds." If we bear the cross, we shall be like those buried in the cemetery. We shall remain in a state of termination and lie there under death. This is the correct meaning of bearing the cross.

In Matthew 16 Peter was very active and aggressive. On the one hand, it is good to stir up things by being aggressive. However, all the quick brothers need to be killed. I love the quick ones, the bold ones, the troublesome ones, because they stir up things. If there were no brothers like this in the Lord's recovery, no one would cause trouble. Because of brothers like this, there are always troubles in the recovery. Without these troubles, the Lord Jesus could not be revealed to such a great degree. Eventually, however, the Lord called Peter, the quick one, Satan. All the quick Peters must be terminated. They need to be killed and stay under the killing of the cross. Otherwise, there will be no way for the church to be built.

To take the pathway to glory ultimately means to put ourselves to death. This pathway is not only a matter of rejection, of experiencing the lack of necessities, of facing the storm on the sea, of encountering the accusations of religion, of learning to eat the Lord Jesus as the inexhaustible life supply, of being warned to beware of the leaven, and of seeing the vision of Christ and the church. In addition to all this, we need to be terminated. The last station of the pathway to glory is the station of self-termination. The view presented in the Gospel of Matthew is marvelous. Matthew's view covers rejection, necessity, the storm, the accusation from religion, the leaven, Satan, the self, the mind, and the soul-life. If you do not know how to face these things, it will be difficult for you to enter into glory. The last step before entering into glory is the termination of the self. It is not sufficient merely to pass through rejection or to experience the Lord's supplying our material necessities. Also, it is not adequate to endure the stormy sea, to deal with the religious accusation regarding outward things, to feed on Christ, and to beware of leaven. Ultimately, the pathway to glory is a matter of being terminated.

You may think that Satan is in the rejection, the storm, or the accusation. Actually, Satan is not in these things; instead, only demons are there. The demons are behind the rejection, the storm, and the religious accusations. But Satan, the king of the demons, is in your mind, your self, and your soul-life. Therefore, you must hate your self more than you hate rejection. Martin Luther once said that he was more afraid of himself than he was of the pope, for he knew that he had the strongest pope, the self, within him. The subtle, concealed enemy, even the adversary, is our self. Thus, the last dealing along the pathway to glory is to deal with this self.

As we have seen, the self is active in the opinions, concepts, and ideas expressed by our mind. Christians today fight and are divided because of differing opinions. For this reason, the Apostle Paul said that we all need to be attuned to the same opinion (1 Cor. 1:10). Hence, to take take the pathway to glory is ultimately to deal with our self.

I believe that we have seen a clear vision that bearing the cross is not a matter of suffering, but of keeping the self under the termination of death. The cross of Christ is the terminating death, and we must stay in the place of this termination. To remain there is to bear the cross. I am bearing the cross, for I keep myself under Christ's termination. Therefore, because I have been terminated, I have no idea, no concept, no opinion. By the Lord's grace, I wish to remain in the place of termination for my whole life.

Resurrection follows termination. When we keep ourselves under Christ's termination, spontaneously there will be a reaction in our spirit. This reaction is resurrection. Resurrection is what is needed for the building up of the church. To experience termination and resurrection is the way to enjoy Christ and to build up the church. In verse 24 the Lord tells us to follow Him. Before the Lord's crucifixion, the disciples followed Him in an outward way. But since His resurrection, we follow Him in an inward way. Because in resurrection He has become the life-giving

Spirit (1 Cor. 15:45) dwelling in our spirit (2 Tim. 4:22), we follow Him in our spirit (Gal. 5:16-25).

1. Saving the Soul-life Being to Lose It, But Losing the Soul-life for Christ's Sake Being to Find It

In verse 25 the Lord says, "For whoever desires to save his soul-life shall lose it; but whoever loses his soul-life for My sake shall find it." In following the Lord we should not save our soul-life, that is, we should not let the soul have its enjoyment. If we save it in this age, we shall lose it in the coming age. But if we lose it for Christ's sake, we shall find it in the enjoyment of the kingdom in the coming age.

2. Gaining the Whole World by Forfeiting the Soul-life Profiting Nothing

In verse 26 the Lord asked, "For what shall a man be profited if he should gain the whole world, but forfeit his soul-life? Or what shall a man give in exchange for his soul-life?" The enjoyment of the soul-life today is wrapped up with the world. To gain the world for the enjoyment of the soul is to forfeit the life in the enjoyment of the kingdom in the coming age. Even if we gained the whole world for the enjoyment of the soul-life in this age by forfeiting the enjoyment of the soul-life in the coming age, it would profit nothing. Nothing is worthy to be given in exchange for the enjoyment of the soul-life in the kingdom.

D. The Reward of the Kingdom

Verse 27 says, "For the Son of Man is about to come in the glory of His Father with His angels, and then He will reward each man according to his doings." The word "For" at the beginning of this verse indicates that the Lord's rewarding of His followers at His coming back in verse 27 will be according to whether they lose or save their soul, as mentioned in verses 25 and 26. The reward will be given according to how we have borne the cross. It depends on whether or not we keep ourselves under the killing of the cross, on whether we save our soul-life in this age or lose it.

1. At the Coming of Christ
in the Glory of the Father

This will be judged by the Lord at His coming in the glory of His father. If we do bear the cross to follow Him by losing the enjoyment of our soul in this age, He will reward us with the enjoyment of the soul in the kingdom.

2. According to the Believers' Doings

In verse 27 the Lord says that "He will reward each man according to his doings," that is, according to whether or not we lose our soul-life's enjoyment in this age. This will have nothing to do with our eternal salvation; however, it has very much to do with the Lord's dispensational reward to us.

3. At the Judgment Seat of Christ

The reward will be given to every man at the judgment seat of Christ when Christ comes back (2 Cor. 5:10; Rev. 22:12). This indicates that this will transpire in the air after all the believers have been raptured into the presence of the Lord there.

4. To Be Enjoyed
at the Manifestation of the Kingdom

The Lord's reward will be the entering into the kingdom, which will be at the manifestation of the kingdom. The Lord refers to the manifestation of the kingdom in verse 28: "Truly I say to you, There are some of those standing here who shall by no means taste death until they see the Son of Man coming in His kingdom." This was fulfilled by the Lord's transfiguration on the mountain (17:1-2). His transfiguration was His coming in His kingdom, which was seen by His three disciples, Peter, James, and John. In the next message we shall point out that the transfiguration of Christ was a miniature of the manifestation of the kingdom. The manifestation of the kingdom in the millennium will be the reward to the followers of Christ who remain under the killing of the cross on the pathway to glory. All the dear ones who follow Christ in this way will be rewarded with the manifestation of the kingdom.

LIFE-STUDY OF MATTHEW

MESSAGE FORTY-NINE

THE MINIATURE OF THE MANIFESTATION
OF THE KINGDOM

From 13:53 to 17:8 the record of the Gospel of Matthew portrays the way to follow the heavenly King, from His rejection to the entering in of the manifestation of the kingdom. His followers not only shared His rejection by the Jews (13:53-58), but were also persecuted and even martyred by Gentile politics (14:1-12). Therefore, they were in the desert with Him in a situation of poverty, yet they were richly cared for by Him (14:13-21). When they were on the stormy sea under the contrary wind, He walked on the sea, calmed the storm, and brought them through (14:22-34). At that point, many sick ones were healed by touching Him (14:35-36), but the hypocritical worshippers of God came to accuse Him because His followers transgressed their tradition (15:1-20). Then His disciples followed Him through Gentile country, where a demon-possessed Gentile was healed (15:21-28). After this, they followed Him along the sea of Galilee and up the mountain, where those with all kinds of sicknesses were healed and the need of His followers in the crowd was again richly provided for in a barren desert (15:29-39). Following this, both the fundamentalists and modernists of that day came to tempt Him, and He indicated that He would die to be a unique sign to them (16:1-4). Then He charged His followers to beware of the leaven of both the fundamentalists and modernists (16:5-12). After all this, He brought His followers to the border of the holy land, close to Gentile country, that they might have a revelation of Him, of the church, and of the cross as the way for them to enter into the kingdom (16:13-28). Finally, He brought them into glory in the manifestation of the kingdom (17:1-8). In this message we shall see that the Lord's transfiguration was a miniature of the kingdom (16:28-17:13).

If we compare all the things mentioned above with our experience, we shall see that our way today is exactly the same as that revealed in 13:53—17:8. On the pathway to glory we face rejection, the storm, and the accusations. We experience the eating, we beware of leaven, and we have a revelation of Christ and the church. Furthermore, we take the way of the cross and deny the self and the soul-life. These are the steps along the pathway to glory.

Matthew 13:53—17:8 is a marvelous doctrinal section. Thirty-four years ago, I gave a message on this portion of the Word in Shanghai. I had just arrived there as a newcomer in the work with Brother Nee. I was asked to give the message one Sunday morning. Then I received the burden to minister on the subject of the pathway to glory. I asked the congregation to read more than three chapters of Matthew, from the end of chapter thirteen to the first part of chapter seventeen. Then I gave a long message on these chapters. Nearly all the points in that message were the same as those covered in these messages on the pathway to glory. Although I had not yet seen the matter of eating, the structure of the message was the same as that of these messages. How wonderful it is to be on the pathway to glory! I can testify that during the past forty-four years I have taken every step of this pathway. I have experienced rejection, the lack of material necessities, the storms, and the accusations. Moreover, I have seen the revelation concerning Christ and the church. Because I have been walking this pathway for such a long time, in a sense I have already entered into glory. Others of us are either in the glory or are very close to it. Although some of us may be in the glory, we are still on the pathway to a greater degree of glory. We all need to keep walking on this pathway until the Lord comes back.

I. THE KINGDOM HAVING COME

Matthew 16:28 says, "Truly I say to you, There are some of those standing here who shall by no means taste death until they see the Son of Man coming in His kingdom." This was fulfilled by the Lord's transfiguration on the mountain (17:1-2). His transfiguration was His coming in His kingdom, which was seen by three of His disciples, Peter, James, and John.

II. CHRIST TRANSFIGURED
ON A HIGH MOUNTAIN

Matthew 17:1 says, "And after six days Jesus takes with Him Peter and James and John his brother, and brings them up into a high mountain apart." Since the Lord's transfiguration transpired six days after the revelations concerning Christ and the church in chapter sixteen (given at the very foot of Mount Hermon), the high mountain here must be Mount Hermon. To receive the revelation concerning Christ and the church we must be far away from the religious environment; but to see the vision of the transfigured Christ we need to be on a high mountain, far above the earthly level.

Verse 2 says, "And He was transfigured before them, and His face shone as the sun, and His garments became white as the light." Not many Christians realize that Christ's transfiguration was His coming in His kingdom. In the past we pointed out that the Lord's coming will not take place suddenly; rather, it will come gradually. In a sense, the Lord will come back from heaven; but in another sense, He will come out of us. When He fully lives Himself out of us, that will be the time of His coming. According to Matthew 17:1 with 16:28, His coming was His transfiguration, and His transfiguration was His glorification. When He was transfigured, He was glorified.

Now we must see what it means to be glorified. When Christ, who is God, became a man, His divinity was incarnated in His humanity. He was a unique person, one possessing both divinity and humanity. His divinity was concealed within His humanity. Outwardly, He was a man, but inwardly He was the very God. God was hidden, contained, concealed, within this man. Glory is God manifested, God expressed. It is nothing other than God Himself manifested and seen by man. The God hidden within the humanity of Jesus was the very glory. Thus, the glorious divine element was concealed within the human element of Jesus. As He walked on earth, no one could see His glorious divinity. Many saw the miracles and realized that He was someone extraordinary, but prior to His transfiguration no one had ever seen the glory concealed within Him. Then one day He brought three of His most intimate disciples to a high mountain, and was there transfigured before them. For the Lord Jesus to be transfigured meant that His humanity was saturated and permeated with His divinity. We may say that His humanity was soaked with divinity. This transfiguration, which was His glorification, was equal to His coming in His kingdom. This indicates that Christ's coming in His kingdom is linked with His transfiguration. Where His transfiguration is, there the coming of the kingdom is also. The coming of the kingdom is the Lord's glorification, His transfiguration; and His glorification is the saturation of His humanity by His divinity. This is the meaning of transfiguration. Because the Lord has been transfigured, He is now in glory.

In Christ's transfiguration, His humanity was glorified; it was brought into God's glory. Before that time, God was in Him, but His humanity was not in God's glory. In His transfiguration His humanity was thoroughly saturated with His glorious divinity. In the coming manifestation of the kingdom, Christ will be like this. He will be the very Christ with both divinity and humanity, but His humanity will be soaked with His divinity.

The day is coming when we shall not only see this, but also experience it ourselves. We now have the divine life with the divine nature within us. However, we still have our natural humanity. No matter how spiritual and holy we may be, our humanity is still natural. It has not yet been saturated with the divine glory. But at the time of the manifestation of the kingdom, our humanity will be glorified by the glorious divinity within us.

Perhaps the opposers will label this evolution into God. But this is not evolution into God — it is glorification. The opposers need to read Romans 8:30: "And whom He predestinated, these He also called; and whom He called, these He also justified; and whom He justified, these He also glorified." I would like to ask the opposers what they think it means to be glorified. Do they think that to be glorified is merely to enter the realm of glory? This is a very superficial understanding of glorification. To be glorified is to be saturated with God's glory. It is to be transfigured, not from without, but from within. One day we shall be a great surprise to the unbelievers. Second Thessalonians 1:10 says, "When he shall come to be glorified in his saints, and to be admired in all them that believe." The unbelievers will be shocked by our glorification. Because in our humanity we are the same as the unbelievers, they can see no difference between us and them. But the day is coming when they will see a glorious difference, for our humanity will be saturated with divinity, and we shall become a glorious people. We shall not just be spiritual, holy, pure, and clean. We shall be glorious. This is the coming of the kingdom. We are waiting for this to take place.

III. MOSES AND ELIJAH, REPRESENTING THE OLD TESTAMENT OVERCOMERS, TO BE IN THE MANIFESTATION OF THE KINGDOM

Verse 3 says, "And behold, Moses and Elijah were seen by them, conversing with Him." Moses and Elijah represent the Old Testament overcomers who will be in the manifestation of the kingdom. They both appeared in the coming of the kingdom, that is, they were present in the manifestation of the kingdom.

IV. PETER, JAMES, AND JOHN, REPRESENTING
THE NEW TESTAMENT OVERCOMERS,
TO BE IN THE MANIFESTATION OF THE KINGDOM

In this miniature of the manifestation of the kingdom we have not only the Old Testament overcomers, but also New Testament overcomers, represented by Peter, James, and John. In this manifestation we have a glimpse of the full manifestation of the kingdom in the future.

V. MOSES AND ELIJAH,
REPRESENTING THE LAW AND THE PROPHETS,
BEING WRONGLY RANKED WITH CHRIST

Moses died, and God hid his body (Deut. 34:5-6); and Elijah was taken by God into heaven (2 Kings 2:11). God purposely did these two things so that Moses and Elijah might appear with Christ on the mount of His transfiguration. They were also preserved by God to be the two witnesses in the great tribulation (Rev. 11:3-4). Moses represents the law, and Elijah, the prophets. The law and the prophets were the constituents of the Old Testament as a full testimony of Christ (John 5:39). Now Moses and Elijah appeared to converse with Christ concerning His death (Luke 9:31) according to the Old Testament (Luke 24:25-27, 44; 1 Cor. 15:3).

We have pointed out that God hid Moses' body and that Elijah was taken to heaven. However, Elijah was not taken to the third heaven. Acts 2:34 indicates that apart from Christ no one has ascended into heaven. Thus, Elijah was not in the third heaven. God hid Moses' body and He kept Elijah until the day of Christ's transfiguration. When Christ was transfigured, these two appeared with Him.

In verse 4 Peter said, "Lord, it is good for us to be here; if You are willing, I will make three tabernacles here, one for You, and one for Moses, and one for Elijah." This indicates that Peter recognized Moses and Elijah. Perhaps you are wondering how Peter was able to recognize them. In the

Lord's conversation with Moses and Elijah there must have been some indication of their identity that made it possible for Peter to recognize them. Peter might have said, "This is Moses and this is Elijah! How happy I am to see you! Oh, it is wonderful to be here!"

A. Peter's Natural Concept

In his excitement Peter made the absurd proposal that he make three tabernacles, one for the Lord, one for Moses, and one for Elijah. The effect of Peter's absurd proposal was to put Moses and Elijah on the same level with Christ, which means to make the law and the prophets, represented by Moses and Elijah, equal to Christ. This was absolutely against God's economy. In God's economy the law and the prophets were only a testimony to Christ; they should not be put on the same level with Him.

B. The Father's Revelation

Verse 5 says, "While he was still speaking, behold, a bright cloud overshadowed them, and behold, a voice out of the cloud, saying, This is My beloved Son, in Whom I delight; hear Him!" This declaration of the Father to vindicate the Son was given firstly after Christ's rising from baptism, which signified His resurrection from the dead. This is the second time the Father declared the same thing, this time to vindicate the Son in His transfiguration, which prefigures the coming kingdom. In God's economy, after Christ came, we should hear Him, no longer the law or the prophets, since the law and the prophets were all fulfilled in Christ and by Christ.

C. No One except Christ Alone

When the disciples heard the voice out of the cloud, "they fell on their face and feared exceedingly" (v. 6). After the Lord Jesus came to them, touched them, and told them to arise and not to fear, they lifted up their eyes and "saw no one except Jesus Himself alone" (v. 8). Peter proposed to rank Moses and Elijah, that is, the law and the prophets, with Christ, but God took Moses and Elijah away, leaving no one except Jesus Himself alone. The law and the prophets were shadows and prophecies, not the reality, which is Christ. Now that Christ is here, the shadows and prophecies are no longer needed. No one except Jesus Himself alone should remain in the New Testament. Jesus is today's Moses, imparting the law of life into His believers. He is also today's Elijah, speaking for God and speaking forth God within His believers. This is God's New Testament economy.

God took Moses and Elijah away because He would not tolerate seeing His children rank anyone on the same level as His Son Jesus Christ. Therefore, when the disciples saw the Lord Jesus, they saw no one except Him alone. This was a lesson to them. In the kingdom God will not allow the law or the prophets to be held equal to Christ. Since the kingdom has come, there should be nothing but Christ.

In God's economy today Christ is the living lawgiver, the One who has imparted Himself into our being as the Giver of the law of life. Thus, Christ is our real Moses, who was a type, a shadow of Christ. The law Moses gave was not the real law; rather, it was the law of dead letters. The real law is the law of life, which only Christ can give us. Because He has given us the law of life, He is the real lawgiver. Furthermore, in God's economy Christ is the real prophet. Elijah also was a type, a shadow, of Christ, who is the true prophet (Acts 3:22). Christ is within us not only to impart the law of life into our being, but also to speak for God. Christ speaks forth God. Because we have Christ as the real Moses and the real Elijah, we do not need any other Moses or Elijah in God's New Testament economy.

As we await the coming of the kingdom, we must learn not to rank Moses, Elijah, or anyone else on the same level as Christ. Instead, we need to learn to experience Christ as our Moses and Elijah. He is the One imparting the law of life into us. In other words, as our present, real, subjective

Moses He is regulating us from within. Moreover, He is also our present and subjective Elijah, constantly speaking for God and speaking forth God within us. We must listen to Him.

After the Lord had been transfigured before the disciples, Peter might have felt both happy and sorrowful. He might have felt sad about being rebuked. It was a serious matter to be rebuked in such a glorious situation. While everyone was having an enjoyable time, Peter spoke nonsense, and he was rebuked for it. Perhaps James and John said to him, "Peter, you are always doing things like this. Perhaps by now you have learned your lesson. When we were having a good time with the Lord Jesus on the mountain, you spoke nonsense, and you were rebuked. But, Peter, we shared the shock of this with you. We would not have been shocked, if you had not been shocked first. But please don't do that again."

VI. THE MANIFESTATION OF THE KINGDOM
KEPT SECRET

Verse 9 says, "And as they were coming down from the mountain, Jesus commanded them, saying, Tell the vision to no one, until the Son of Man is raised from among the dead." The vision of the transfigured, glorified Jesus cannot be realized by anyone except in the resurrection of Christ. Here we see the principle that the manifestation of the kingdom can be revealed only in resurrection. Anyone who is not in resurrection is not qualified to see it. If we believe in resurrection and live in resurrection, we shall be in glory, even though the manifestation of the kingdom has not yet come. When we live and walk in resurrection, we have the sense that we are in glory and that we can see the glorious manifestation of the kingdom. Thus, the manifestation of the kingdom can be revealed only to those in resurrection. For this reason, the Lord Jesus charged the disciples not to talk about His coming in His kingdom.

VII. JOHN THE BAPTIST BEING ELIJAH
COMING BEFORE THE KINGDOM

In verse 10 the Lord's disciples asked Him, "Why then do the scribes say that Elijah must come first?" The matter of Elijah coming first is according to Malachi 4:5-6. In verse 11 the Lord replied, "Elijah indeed is coming and will restore all things." This will be fulfilled at the time of the great tribulation, when Elijah will be one of the two witnesses (Rev. 11:3-4), as prophesied in Malachi 4:5-6. In verse 12 the Lord continued, "But I say to you that Elijah already came, and they did not recognize him, but did to him whatever they wished; thus also the Son of Man is about to suffer by them." This refers to John the Baptist (v. 13), who came in the spirit and power of Elijah (Luke 1:13-17) and was rejected (11:18) and beheaded (14:3-12).

The disciples had a theological problem. They seemed to be saying to the Lord, "Lord Jesus, Your kingdom has come, and we have seen it. But the scribes told us that Elijah would appear before the coming of the kingdom. We saw You coming in Your kingdom, but Elijah has not appeared. How can this be?" The disciples were bothered because they had some knowledge of scriptural doctrines. If I had been one of them, I would have asked the same thing. In contrast to Peter's nonsensical proposal on the mountain, the disciples' question was logical. Often when we are in a glorious situation, we do nonsensical things. But after we become clear and sober, we are very logical.

The Lord Jesus told the disciples that Elijah would come and restore all things (v. 11). This word indicates that the coming of the kingdom was not yet in full. In the future there will be a full manifestation of the kingdom. Before this, Elijah will come. On the one hand, Elijah has come; but on the other hand, he has not yet come in full. John the Baptist was Elijah, but he was not Elijah in full. The full coming of Elijah will take place in the future. The Elijah who had already come was rejected and killed. The disciples understood that the Lord was speaking of John the Baptist. Just as the transfiguration of Christ was the coming of the kingdom, but not in full, so the coming of John the Baptist was the coming of Elijah, but not his coming in full. Before the full coming of the kingdom, Elijah will come in full.

In the Bible the fulfillment of prophecy is often like this. First there is a partial fulfillment, then the complete fulfillment. The same is true in principle with our experience of being in glory. During the past years, I have experienced being in glory, but this experience was not in full. At the time of the full manifestation of the kingdom of Christ, we shall all enter fully into glory. But today we see in Christ's transfiguration a miniature of the coming manifestation of the kingdom. The miniature assures us that the full manifestation will come.

LIFE-STUDY OF MATTHEW

MESSAGE FIFTY

APPLICATION OF THE REVELATION
AND VISION CONCERNING CHRIST

Immediately after the record of the Lord's transfiguration on the mountain, we have the record of the healing of a demon-possessed person (17:14-21). Following this, the Lord spoke to His disciples the second time about His crucifixion and resurrection (17:22-23). Then we have the incident regarding paying the half-shekel (17:24-27). As we read chapter seventeen, it may be difficult to understand the connection between all these things. If we would understand the Gospel of Matthew, we need to remember that Matthew puts different facts together to reveal a doctrine. Although the three disciples, who represented the other disciples, had been in the miniature of the manifestation of the kingdom, there was still the need for three things: the dealing with the demon-possessed person, the revealing of the Lord's crucifixion and resurrection, and the paying of the half-shekel to the tax gatherers.

I. THE POWER OF DARKNESS OUTSIDE THE KINGDOM

We have pointed out that the coming of the kingdom in 16:28—17:2 was not the coming of the kingdom in full; it was simply a miniature and a foretaste. The prophecies concerning the manifestation of the kingdom have not yet been completely fulfilled. When we get out of the sphere of the transfiguration, out of the atmosphere of the manifestation of the kingdom, we face the power of darkness outside the kingdom. Demon possession signifies the power of darkness. In the realm of the Lord's transfiguration there is glory, but outside this realm there is the power of darkness. While we are enjoying the transfiguration on the mountaintop, others are in the valley suffering from demon possession. During an inspiring conference or training, we may have the sense that we are on the mount of transfiguration. However, when we return home, we realize that the power of darkness is still all around us. To deal with the power of darkness there is the need of the exercise of the authority of the heavenly King (17:18). We can exercise this authority only through prayer and fasting. As the heavenly King, the Lord has such authority, but we need to pray, even with fasting, to execute the Lord's authority.

II. CHRIST'S CRUCIFIXION AND RESURRECTION

In 17:22 and 23 the Lord said to His disciples, "The Son of Man is about to be delivered into the hands of men, and they shall kill Him, and on the third day He shall be raised up." When the disciples heard this, "they were exceedingly grieved." The transfiguration on the mountaintop was not the full transfiguration. Christ still had to pass through crucifixion and enter into resurrection. Matthew specifically says that the disciples "were exceedingly grieved." According to the concept of Peter, James, and John, the Christ who had been transfigured on the mountaintop did not need to be crucified. Thus, they might have said, "Christ has already been transfigured. Why does He still need to pass through crucifixion and resurrection?" Because the disciples had a mistaken concept, they were grieved at the Lord's word.

We also may have times when we have a foretaste of the transfiguration. Afterward, however, we still need to descend from the mountain and bear the cross in the presence of our husband or wife. No matter how excellent the experience of transfiguration might be, we still need to stay under the killing of the cross. By bearing the cross we pass through crucifixion into resurrection. This is the connection between these three sections of Matthew.

III. APPLICATION OF THE REVELATION
AND VISION CONCERNING CHRIST

Unless we receive light from the Lord, it is difficult to see the connection between verses 1 through 23 and verses

24 through 27. In 17:24-27 we have the matter of paying the half-shekel to the poll-tax gatherers. This is a test to determine whether or not we know how to apply the revelation and vision concerning Christ. In chapter sixteen Peter received a clear revelation from the heavenly Father regarding Christ as the Son of the living God. From that time onward, Peter was certain that Christ was the Son of the living God. Following this, on the mountaintop he saw a vision of Christ manifested as the Son of the living God. Therefore, he both received the revelation and saw the vision. It is possible to have a revelation without having a vision. What Peter received from the heavenly Father in chapter sixteen was merely the revelation. In chapter seventeen he saw the Son of God manifested and expressed through the man Jesus of Nazareth. Nothing could have been more clear than this revelation and vision.

Peter, however, had to be tested regarding the application of the revelation and the vision. To receive the revelation and to see the vision is one thing, but to apply them in a practical way is another. For example, we probably all have received the revelation from Galatians 2:20 that we have been crucified with Christ and that Christ lives in us. Perhaps even the weakest one among us has received this revelation. However, when your wife or husband gives you a difficult time, can you still say, "It is not I, but Christ"? When you are with your wife or husband, the revelation of having been crucified with Christ and of Christ living in you may vanish. Very few who have received this revelation apply it to the practical matters in their daily living. Peter might have been like this. He might have said, "I have received the revelation that Jesus is the Son of the living God, and I saw Him transfigured on the mountain. This is very clear to me. Perhaps you have not seen this vision, but I have." For Peter to receive the revelation and see the vision was wonderful. But now he had to be tested by those who collected the poll tax.

A. Peter's Natural Concept

Verse 24 says, "And when they came to Capernaum,

those who received the half-shekel came to Peter and said,
Does not your teacher pay the half-shekel?" The half-
shekel was a Jewish poll tax for the temple (Exo. 30:12-16;
38:26). When Peter was asked this question, he immediately said, "Yes." Peter did not know how to apply the
revelation and the vision, and he was exposed. On the
mount of transfiguration, Peter heard the voice from
heaven charging him to hear Christ (17:5). If he had still
remembered what had taken place on the mountain, he
would have referred the question to Christ to hear what He
would say. But instead of listening to Christ, he gave his
own answer. On the mountain Peter heard the Father say,
"This is My beloved Son, in Whom I delight; hear Him!"
At that time, Peter talked too much, and he was rebuked
for it. Now when the poll-tax gatherers asked him whether
or not the Lord paid the half-shekel, he still had too much
to say and did not hesitate to answer. If he had learned the
lesson, he would have said, "Gentlemen, let me go to Him
and hear Him. I need to ask Him whether or not He pays
the half-shekel. I don't have the right to say anything."
Peter, however, did not respond this way, and he was
exposed by this test. It is the same with us today. After a
conference or training, we may proclaim that we shall
never be the same. But I assure you that after you return
home, you will be exactly the same. However, do not let
this disappoint you.

B. Christ's Correction

Verses 25 and 26 say, "And when he came into the
house, Jesus anticipated him, saying, What do you think,
Simon? From whom do the kings of the earth receive
custom or poll tax, from their sons or from strangers? And
when he said, From strangers, Jesus said to him, Then the
sons are free." The poll-tax gatherers came to Peter
because he was so prominent, like the nose on our face. The
quick ones, the bold ones, are the "nose" in the church life.
Whenever the church undergoes a test, the "nose" is the
part that gets hurt because it is the first to bump into
things. Because he stood out so much, Peter got into

trouble. After telling the tax gatherers that the Lord Jesus paid the half-shekel, Peter came into the house. But as verse 25 says, Jesus "anticipated him." Peter was quick, but the Lord was sovereign and did not give him a chance to say anything. On the mountaintop Peter was interrupted by a voice from heaven, and in the house he was stopped by the Lord. Peter had spoken presumptuously. Hence, the Lord stopped him and corrected him before he could speak to Him.

The Lord asked Peter whether the kings of the earth receive custom or poll tax from their sons or from strangers. The sons of kings are always free from paying custom or poll tax. The half-shekel was paid by God's people for His temple. Since Christ is the Son of God, He was free from paying it. This was contrary to what Peter had just answered.

Peter had received the revelation concerning Christ being the Son of God (16:16-17) and he had seen the vision of the Son of God (17:5). Now, in application, he was put to the test by the poll-tax gatherers' question. He failed in his answer by forgetting the revelation he had received and the vision he had seen. He forgot that the Lord was the Son of God who did not need to pay the poll tax for His Father's house.

When the Lord asked Peter whether the kings of the earth received tax from their sons or from strangers, Peter answered, "From strangers." Doctrinally and theologically Peter answered correctly. When the Lord said to him, "Then the sons are free," Peter must have been stunned. It seems that the Lord was saying, "Peter, have you forgotten the revelation that I am the Son? On the mountaintop you saw Me as the Son." The half-shekel was not a tax paid to the secular government. It was collected for the purpose of meeting the expenses of the temple of God, God's house on earth. According to Exodus 30 and 38, every Israelite had to pay a half-shekel to care for the Lord's house. Because Jesus is the Son of God, there is no need for Him to pay this tax. When the Lord said that the sons are free, He was indicating that He, as the Son of God, was free from paying the poll tax. After hearing this, Peter did not know what to say. He might have just agreed and said, "Yes, the sons are free. Since You are the Son of God, You are free. Lord, I am sorry for answering the way I did. I forgot the revelation and the vision. I received the revelation that You are the Son of God, and I saw the vision of You as the Son of God. But when the test came, I forgot all about it. Lord, please forgive me."

C. Flexibility by Christ
as the Living Law-giver Replacing Moses

Verse 27 says, "But that we may not stumble them, go to the sea and cast a hook, and take the first fish that comes up, and when you open its mouth you will find a shekel; take that and give it to them for Me and you." After convincing Peter that He did not need to pay the half-shekel, the Lord, as the New Testament Law-giver, today's Moses, gave the command to Peter to pay it for Him. The Lord did this purposely to teach Peter that in God's New Testament economy, He is the unique One; neither Moses, Elijah, Peter, nor anyone else has the position to speak or to give a command.

D. Application through a Miracle
Prophesied by Christ
as the Living Prophet Replacing Elijah

After shutting Peter's mouth, the Lord, as the New Testament prophet, today's Elijah, told him to go fishing to obtain a shekel in order to pay the tax. This prophecy was fulfilled. No doubt Peter was troubled about having to go fishing and perhaps having to wait a long time for a fish to appear with a shekel in its mouth. While the Lord was correcting and teaching Peter, He took care of his need. This is always the Lord's way in dealing with us.

When Peter answered yes, the Lord said no. But when Peter was convinced that the Lord did not need to pay the tax, the Lord told him that He would pay it. Perhaps Peter was about to go after the poll-tax gatherers and tell them that the Lord did not need to pay the tax. Peter might have

been considering this when the Lord charged him to catch
a fish with a shekel in its mouth and to use that shekel to
pay the tax. The tax had to be paid in order not to stumble
others. We cannot subdue the Lord Jesus. Whatever He
says is always right, and whatever we propose to Him is always wrong. Christ is today's Moses; He makes the laws.
When He says yes, the answer is yes; and when He says no,
it is no. What we say means nothing. It is what He says
that counts. The meaning of the vision on the mountaintop is that we should hear the Lord Jesus and not anyone
else, including ourselves. Christ, not Moses, is the One to
say yes or no. Regarding the same matter, the Lord may
say yes to someone else and no to you. If he does this, do
not argue with Him.

When Peter had to go fishing in order to find a half-
shekel, he learned a lesson. Don't you think that Peter was
troubled by having to go fishing? Certainly he was. Although the Lord Jesus is kind and merciful, One who will
not break a bruised reed or quench smoking flax, He sometimes deals with us in a hard way. When the Lord indicated to Peter that He would pay the temple tax, He did
not reach into His pocket, take out a shekel, and give it to
Peter. If He had done that, He would have been too easy on
Peter. A shekel had been prepared by the Lord, but Peter
had to fish for it. I wonder how Peter felt. Did he feel like
laughing or weeping? I believe that as Peter was fishing, he
was unhappy and very troubled. If I had been Peter, I
might have said to the Lord, "Lord, since You can provide
a shekel out of the mouth of a fish, why don't You just
reach into Your pocket and give me one? Why are You so
troublesome? Now I must go down to the sea and fish.
Maybe a storm will come while I am fishing. Lord, if You
intend to perform a miracle, why not do it now?" Peter,
however, had learned a great deal; and this time, instead of
saying a word, he did what the Lord had told him.

I do not believe that the fish came immediately.
Rather, I believe that the Lord exercised His sovereignty to
keep the fish away for a period of time. Thus, Peter was
waiting without any sign of a fish. As he was waiting, he

might have rebuked himself and said, "Why did I answer so quickly? I shouldn't have faced those tax gatherers. James and John didn't get into trouble. But because I am so bold and so quick, I got myself into trouble." Eventually, the fish came with a shekel in its mouth. This was sufficient to take care of both the Lord and Peter.

The record here is very simple, but the story is rich in its implications. It implies that Christ is the Prophet, for He told Peter to go fishing and that the first fish would have a shekel in its mouth. Was that not a prophecy? The Lord's prophecy was practical, and it was fulfilled exactly as He had spoken. Thus, Peter's experience here was a proof that the Lord is the real Elijah and that we should hear Him. This story also implies that the Lord is today's Moses. It is not up to us to say yes or no; it is altogether up to Him. We simply need to do whatever He says. Moreover, we should not do what He doesn't tell us to do.

Through this incident, Peter was tested that he might know how to apply the revelation and the vision concerning Christ. Through this experience, he came to learn what it means to "hear Him." He realized that he did not need to hear Moses or Elijah, but to hear Him. For us today, Christ is our Moses and Elijah. He is our present, living Law-giver and our Prophet. Whatever He says, that is the law, the law of life. Furthermore, what He says is today's prophecy to meet our present, practical situation. This is not merely a story; it is a lesson for Peter and for us as well.

LIFE-STUDY OF MATTHEW

MESSAGE FIFTY-ONE

RELATIONSHIPS IN THE KINGDOM

(1)

Chapters eighteen, nineteen, and twenty are a distinct section of the Gospel of Matthew dealing with the relationships among the kingdom people. In previous chapters we have seen the King's decree of the constitution of the kingdom, the King's ministry, and the revelation of the mystery of the kingdom. We have also seen the pathway to glory and the practical matters that followed the Lord's transfiguration. Now we must see the relationships among the kingdom people, that is, how to be related to one another in the kingdom. This is a practical matter. It is not merely doctrinal, as the constitution of the kingdom, or prophetic, as the mystery of the kingdom. In particular, chapter eighteen deals with how to be in the kingdom of the heavens: it is to become as little children (vv. 2-4); not to stumble others or to set up any stumbling block (vv. 5-9); not to despise even a little believer (vv. 10-14); to hear the church and not be condemned by it (vv. 15-20); and to forgive a brother to the uttermost (vv. 21-35). All this indicates that to enter into the kingdom of the heavens we must be humble and not despise any believer, but love our brother and forgive our brother.

Before we consider 18:1-20, we need to have an overall view of these three chapters, which cover five matters. The first is pride. If we would relate to others in a proper way in the kingdom, our pride needs to be dealt with. We need humility. Not one of us is a humble person. Every fallen person is proud. In the past certain brothers and sisters have told me that their wives or husbands were humble.

Later these brothers and sisters had to admit that their wives or husbands were not that humble. Some brothers who had told me that their wives would never give them a problem later came to me in tears telling me of the trouble they were having with their wives. There is no such thing as a humble person.

Being in the kingdom is a corporate matter, not an individual matter. However, whenever we come together as a company, there will be difficulties. This is the reason certain young people do not want to get married. Although it will cause them problems, the young people nevertheless need to get married. Because it is difficult to be together in company, Matthew includes these chapters covering our relationships with one another. We have no choice concerning this. If I had my choice, I would prefer to stay by myself, devote all my time to prayer, and wait alone for the kingdom to come. But we have been predestinated to be together. However, in our being together pride is the first problem.

The second problem is our inability to forgive others. The matter of forgiveness is covered in the second half of chapter eighteen. We all must learn to forgive others, something that none of us enjoys doing. Deep within our heart, we do not want to forgive others.

According to the Bible, to forgive is to forget. For us, to forgive a person may mean that we simply do not care about the particular offense. However, we still remember it. How difficult it is to forget an offense against us! Without the Lord's mercy and grace, we would remember others' offenses even in eternity. But when God forgives, He forgets. Hebrews 10:17 says, "And their sins and their lawlessnesses I will by no means remember any more." To forgive something absolutely is to forget it. Our Father in heaven considers us as if we have never sinned, for He has forgiven and forgotten our sins. But when we forgive an offense, we often remind others of it. For example, a sister may say, "The elders treated me very poorly; however, I have forgiven them. But let me tell you a little about what happened." Genuine forgiveness means that we forget the offense.

The root of our unwillingness to forgive others lies in our dispositional anger. No matter how nice you may be, you still have dispositional anger. The reason you are offended is that you have such a disposition. I may strike a chair again and again, but the chair will not be offended because it has no disposition. But if I strike you, you will be offended because of the dispositional anger hidden within you. We all are subject to dispositional anger. Sometimes when I have offended a brother, he has said that he does not care about the offense. Actually, we all care when we are offended. The outward reaction or appearance may be different, but the dispositional anger, the anger hidden in our disposition, is the same. Because of our dispositional anger, it is difficult to forgive others.

This dispositional anger shows up between husbands and wives. I advise the young sisters never to offend their husbands. If they do, it will be hard for their husbands to forget that offense. Although your husband may say that he has forgiven you, deep within he has not done so. Every man has a disposition that makes it easy for him to be offended, especially by his wife. Women find it easy to complain to their husbands. The reason there are so many separations and divorces is that the women complain and that the men find it difficult to forgive. Sisters, try your best not to complain to your husband. If he is late, forget about it. Do not make an issue of it. Brothers, I advise you to ignore the complaints of your wife. I advise the sisters not to complain and the brothers not to be offended.

We have seen the matters of pride and of our inability to forgive others. Now we come to the problem of lust, which is indicated in chapter nineteen. In the constitution of the kingdom of the heavens lust was thoroughly dealt with. It was also touched in chapter thirteen, the chapter concerning the mystery of the kingdom of the heavens. Lust is a great problem to the kingdom people. Many separations and divorces are related to lust. Therefore, in chapter nineteen the Lord Jesus touched this matter of lust. Apart from the Lord's grace, none of us is able to overcome it.

The fourth problem is the problem of riches. It is very difficult for a rich man to enter into the kingdom of the heavens, even more difficult than for a camel to pass through the eye of a needle. The matter of riches is a great frustration to the kingdom life, and it is also dealt with in the constitution of the kingdom of the heavens and in the parable of the sower in chapter thirteen.

The last problem is ambition, which is covered in chapter twenty. Zebedee's wife, ambitious that her two sons would enjoy a high position in the kingdom, said to the Lord, "Say that these two sons of mine may sit, one on Your right hand and one on Your left, in Your kingdom" (20:21). The Lord told her that she did not know what she was asking. Matthew records the story of Zebedee's wife making requests for her sons, but John does not record it because his Gospel is not the Gospel dealing with the kingdom. Matthew records this incident because in the kingdom there is the problem of ambition for position.

Ambition has been a problem both in the East and in the West. Many times when elders were appointed in the churches, brothers were offended because others were appointed instead of them. Although, at the most, a church needed three or four elders, the number of self-appointed candidates for eldership might have been more than fifteen. Whether or not those brothers prayed about being appointed elders, I do not know. But I am rather certain that they expected to be appointed. When they realized that they had not been appointed elders, they began to speak negatively about the church, simply because they did not receive the position they desired. We have encountered this problem in the church in Taipei, a church with more than twenty thousand members. Every time a new home meeting was opened, there was a need to appoint two or three leading brothers and leading sisters to manage the practical affairs of that home meeting. Nearly every time the leading ones were appointed, some sister was offended because she was not among those appointed. Because they were offended, they stopped coming to the meetings for a period of time. This exposes the problem of ambition.

These three chapters actually cover these five things. They deal thoroughly with pride, dispositional anger, lust, riches, and ambition. All these problems are within us. If we would get into the depths of these chapters, we would certainly be touched. For instance, we would see that we are people full of pride and that anger is hidden in our disposition. No matter how patient or forbearing we try to be, anger is still deeply rooted in our disposition. This is what makes it difficult for us to forgive others. Furthermore, we are troubled by lust and riches, both of which damage the kingdom life. Finally, there is the problem of ambition. Matthew purposely covers these five problems in his Gospel to show that we must take care of them in order to be in the kingdom. Pride, dispositional anger, lust, riches, and ambition are all "scorpions." We need a divine pest control to kill these "scorpions." Under God's inspiration, Matthew selected various cases and put them together in order to expose these things. Now we need to consider them one by one.

I. HUMILITY REQUIRED

In the kingdom life, humility is required (18:1-4). In principle, all the kingdom people must be little children. To be humble is to be like a little child. If we are not humble, we shall either be offended by others or we shall offend others, that is, we shall either be stumbled by others or stumble others. All stumbling takes place because of pride. If we were not proud, we would not be stumbled. The fact that we can be stumbled proves that we are proud. If a little child is offended, the offense will be forgotten in just a few minutes. But once adults are offended, they are stumbled because of their pride. Furthermore, the stumbling we cause to others also issues from our pride.

II. STUMBLING ABANDONED

It is a serious matter to stumble someone. Verse 6 says, "And whoever stumbles one of these little ones who believe in Me, it is better for him that a great millstone be hanged around his neck, and that he be drowned in the depth of the sea." In these verses the Lord warns us to deal with this matter. If the hand, the foot, or the eye causes us to stumble, we must deal with these causes of stumbling in a serious way. Otherwise, we shall not be one in the proper kingdom life. In order to be in the proper kingdom life, we need to be humble. Then we shall not be stumbled or be a cause of stumbling to others. All stumbling must be abandoned.

III. THE HEAVENLY FATHER'S CARE
FOR THE LITTLE ONES

No matter how small we are, we are lovely in the eyes of the Father, and He cares for us. He does not like to see anyone stumbled. We so easily offend the little ones for whom the Father cares, and as little ones ourselves we are easily stumbled. If we would avoid being stumbled and stumbling others, we need to be humbled. Humility will rescue us.

IV. DEALING WITH AN OFFENDING BROTHER

A. By Direct Rebuking

Verse 15 says, "Now if your brother sins, go, reprove him between you and him alone. If he hears you, you have gained your brother." In this section we also see how to deal with an offending brother. If a brother sins or offends us, we must first go to him in love and point out his offense.

B. By the Testimony of Two or Three

Verse 16 says, "But if he does not hear you, take with you one or two more, that by the mouth of two or three witnesses every word may be established." If the brother will not listen to you, you should not give up. Rather, you should go to him with one or two witnesses, hoping that the brother will listen to you and be rescued.

C. By the Church

Verse 17 says, "But if he refuses to hear them, tell it to the church." If a brother sins, we need firstly to deal with him by ourself in love (v. 15), then with two or three witnesses (v. 16), and finally through the church with authority (v. 17).

D. By Cutting Off the Fellowship

The last part of verse 17 says, "And if he refuses to hear the church also, let him be to you as the Gentile and the tax collector." If any believer refuses to hear the church, he will lose the fellowship of the church like the Gentile, the heathen, and the tax collector, the sinners who are outside the fellowship of the church. A Gentile or tax collector is someone who does not have fellowship in the kingdom life or in the church life. To consider someone a Gentile or a tax collector does not mean to excommunicate him. It means that he is considered as one cut off from the fellowship of the church. Excommunication is mentioned in 1 Corinthians 5. The church must excommunicate fornicators and idolaters. But the offending brother who will not listen to two or three or to the church may not necessarily require excommunication. Although the situation with him is unpleasant, it is not in the same category as fornication or idolatry. He is cut off from the fellowship of the church in order that this loss of fellowship may encourage him to repent and to recover his fellowship with the church.

E. By Exercising the Kingdom Authority

In order to deal with such an offending brother, we must exercise the kingdom authority. Because the church today is weak, it does not realize its need to exercise this authority. The brother mentioned in this portion of the Word is first offending and then rebellious. First he offends someone. Then because he will not listen to the one he has offended, to two or three witnesses, or even to the church, he becomes rebellious. Because he rebels against the church, the church must exercise its authority to bind and to loose. It binds when he is rebellious and looses when he repents. In verse 18 to bind means to condemn, and to loose means to forgive. Because such a rebellious brother will not listen to the church, the church must exercise the kingdom authority to bind him until he repents. But when he repents, the church must exercise the kingdom authority to forgive him and to restore him to the fellowship of the church.

F. By Prayer in One Accord

The dealing with the offending brother must be carried out by prayer in one accord. Verse 19 says, "Again I say to you that if two of you agree on earth concerning anything, whatever they may ask, it shall come to them from My Father Who is in the heavens." Strictly speaking, in verse 19 "ask" refers to prayer which deals with the brother who refuses to hear the church. If we pray according to the Lord's promise, our prayer will be answered, and the offending brother may be recovered.

G. In the Lord's Presence

All this should be done in the Lord's presence. If you attempt to exercise the kingdom authority without His presence, it will not work. Verse 20 points out the need for the Lord's presence: "For where two or three are gathered together in My name, there I am in their midst."

V. THE UNVEILING OF THE LOCAL CHURCH

A. The Church in Locality

Verse 17 says, "But if he refuses to hear them, tell it to the church." The church revealed in 16:18 is the universal church, which is the unique Body of Christ, whereas the church revealed here is the local church, the expression of the unique Body of Christ in a certain locality. Chapter sixteen relates to the universal building of the church, whereas chapter eighteen relates to the local practice of the church. Both indicate that the church represents the kingdom of the heavens, having authority to bind and to loose.

In order to be in the kingdom of the heavens in a practical way, we need to be in a local church. According to the context of verse 17, both the reality and the practicality of the kingdom are in the local church. In a chapter dealing with relationships in the kingdom, the Lord speaks eventually of the church. This proves that the practicality of the kingdom today is in the local church. Without the local church, it is impossible to have the practicality and reality of the kingdom life. Many Christians today talk about the kingdom life, but without the practical local church life, this talk is in vain.

In chapter sixteen the Lord revealed the universal church. But the universal church requires the practicality of the local church. Without the local church, the universal church cannot be practiced; rather, it will be something suspended in the air. The local church is the reality both of the kingdom and of the universal church.

B. Other than the Two or Three Meeting in the Lord's Name

Many Christians think that as long as two or three meet in the name of the Lord and have His presence, they are the church and the reality of the church is there. However, if you read this portion of the Word carefully, you will see that the two or three mentioned in verse 20 are not the church. These two or three are the two or three in verse 16. They may gather together in the Lord's name, but they are not the church; for if there is some problem, they need to tell it to the church (v. 17). If those two or three were the church, there would be no need for them to take the problem to the church. The fact that they need to "tell it to the church" proves that they are not the church, but rather part of the church. They belong to the church and they are members of the church, but they are not the church.

Do not think that two or three meeting in the name of the Lord with the Lord's presence are the church. If we believe this, then it is possible for a church of three hundred members to be divided into one hundred churches, with every group of two or three thinking that it is a church. What a mess this would be! Two or three may meet in the name of the Lord and the Lord may truly be in their midst, but this does not mean that they are the church.

C. Being the Kingdom
with the Heavenly Authority

The church has the authority, and we must listen to the church and submit to the church. If we do not submit to the church, we are through with the kingdom, for the kingdom life is a life of submission to the church.

D. Having the Lord's Presence as Its Reality

The context of Matthew 18 indicates that the reality of the church is the Lord's presence. The Lord's presence is the authority of the church. The church must be certain that it has the presence of the Lord as its reality; otherwise, it has no genuine authority. The real and practical authority of the church is the Lord's presence. If anyone does not listen to the church, he rebels against the Lord's presence. The church has the ground to exercise authority in the presence of the Lord over any case of rebellion.

The basic factor that causes trouble in the church is pride. Pride is what causes a brother to offend the one who comes to him in love, it is what makes him unwilling to listen to two or three or even to the church, and it is what causes him to rebel against the church. We all must kill the "gopher" of pride. Let us humble ourselves and always listen to the church and submit to the church. May the Lord grant us mercy for this.

LIFE-STUDY OF MATTHEW

RELATIONSHIPS IN THE KINGDOM

(2)

It may seem that Matthew 18 is not a deep chapter and that the parable in verses 23 through 35 is shallow. Actually, what is revealed in this chapter is very deep. When most Christians read Matthew, they do not realize that this book deals not only with the doctrine of the kingdom, but with the practical kingdom life. If we would understand any portion of Matthew, we need to keep this fact in mind. When I was young, I did not care to read Matthew 18 because I did not see that this chapter deals with the kingdom life. Although you have read this chapter before, you probably have not seen what it really deals with. Rather, you may have thought that it is merely concerned with Christian behavior, that it is merely a word about forgiving our brothers. Because of our natural concept, we do not see that this chapter is deeply concerned with the kingdom life.

The fact that this portion of the Word deals with the practical kingdom life is proved by verse 1: "In that hour the disciples came to Jesus, saying, Who then is greatest in the kingdom of the heavens?" To enter into the kingdom of the heavens means to enter into the manifestation of the kingdom of the heavens. Therefore, this chapter, along with chapters nineteen and twenty, deals with the kingdom life.

In order to remain in the kingdom life, we must have humility. If we have humility, we shall neither offend others nor be offended by others. We shall neither stumble others nor be stumbled by them. All stumbling, of ourselves or of others, comes from pride. We need to hate pride and treat it as a "gopher" that must be killed. Otherwise, the "gopher" of pride will ruin the kingdom life.

In chapter eighteen we see how to deal with someone who offends others. If a brother offends us, we should go to him directly in love. If he does not listen to us, we should go to him again with one or two witnesses. If he still does not listen to us, even in the presence of witnesses, we should tell the matter to the church and let the church deal with him. If he refuses to hear the church, then the church should consider him a heathen or a tax collector and cut off his fellowship with the church. Although this is a word telling us how to deal with a brother who causes offenses, it is also a word indicating that it is a serious matter to offend others. The seriousness of this is shown by the danger of being cut off from the fellowship of the church. To be cut off from the fellowship of the church means to be put out of the kingdom life. This is serious.

In the Lord's word about dealing with an offending brother, the authority of the kingdom is involved. Verse 18 says, "Truly I say to you, Whatever you bind on the earth shall be what has been bound in heaven, and whatever you loose on the earth shall be what has been loosed in heaven." If someone offends the brothers and rebels against the church, the heavens will bind him. Notice that verse 18 says that the church binds what has already been bound in the heavens. This indicates that the offense and the rebellion cause the heavens to bind the one responsible for the offense. If you reject the church and rebel against the church, the heavens will bind you. Because the heavens have bound you already, the church executes what the heavens have already bound. If you consider verse 18 in its context, you will realize that it is not an insignificant matter to rebel against the church. The church simply follows the heavens to bind what the heavens have already bound. The church's binding is the execution of the heavens' binding. Before the church says, "Lord, we bind this rebellious brother," he has already been bound in the heavens.

The same is true regarding repentance. To repent to the church for your rebellion is a matter of great significance. If you repent to the church, the heavens will immediately loose you, and then the church will loose what has been loosed in the heavens. To rebel against the church is serious, and to repent to the church is very significant. By this we see that Matthew 18 covers the kingdom life.

What is found here is not simply a matter about offending someone or listening to the church. It is a matter of whether or not we shall remain in the kingdom. If we rebel against the church, the heavens stand behind the church and support it. Hence, if you rebel against the church, the heavens will say, "I bind you." Then the church will rise up to bind what the heavens have bound. But if you repent, the heavens will say, "You are loosed." Then the church will carry out what has been loosed in the heavens. Whether we rebel against the church or repent to the church, both are serious. Both reveal that our relationship with the brothers and with the church has a great deal to do with the kingdom life.

VI. FORGIVING FOR BEING FORGIVEN

A. Forgiving the Offending Brother Even Seventy Times Seven

After listening to the Lord's word about the kingdom life, Peter asked Him a question: "Lord, how often shall my brother sin against me and I forgive him? Until seven times?" (v. 21). Peter did not ask this on behalf of others; rather, being quick and bold, he asked it according to what was in him. Those who are quick often offend others. The more active, quick, and bold we are, the more we offend others. But those who are cautious and slow rarely offend anyone. Why was it not John who asked this question? It was Peter who was concerned about the Lord's word regarding the offending brother. Because Peter often offended others, he was very concerned and asked the Lord about forgiveness.

Verse 22 says, "Jesus says to him, I do not say to you until seven times, but until seventy times seven." Seventy times seven means that we must forgive others an unlimited number of times. There is no need to count or keep a record of the number of times you forgive others. Over and over and over, you need to forgive them.

B. Forgiving Others as the Lord Has Forgiven Us

1. Our Debt to the Lord Being Impossible to Pay Off

In verses 23 through 35 the Lord gives a parable as an illustration. Verses 23 and 24 say, "Therefore, the kingdom of the heavens is likened to a man, a king, who desired to settle accounts with his slaves. And when he began to settle them, one was brought to him who owed him ten thousand talents." According to the context of this parable, the settling of accounts here refers to the Lord's dealing with us in this age through such things as severe illness or certain extreme hardships which cause us to realize how much we owe the Lord and to beg Him to forgive us. According to verse 24, one slave owed him ten thousand talents, that is, about twelve million dollars. It was impossible for the debtor to pay off this debt. This refers to the heavy debt of our failures accumulated after we were saved.

2. The Lord's Forgiveness by His Mercy

After the slave begged the king to be patient with him until he repaid the debt, "the lord of that slave was moved with compassion and released him and forgave him the loan" (v. 27). This refers to the forgiveness of our debts in our defeated Christian life for the restoration of our fellowship with the Lord.

3. Another's Debt to Us Being Very Small Compared with Our Debt to the Lord

Verse 28 says, "But that slave went out and found one of his fellow slaves who owed him a hundred denarii, and he seized him and took him by the throat, saying, Pay, if you owe anything." This definitely refers to things that take place in this age. The hundred denarii spoken of in this verse is less than a millionth part of ten thousand talents. This refers to a brother's sin against us after we have been saved. How small is any brother's debt to us compared to our debt to the Lord!

4. We Being Unwilling to Forgive

Nevertheless, we may not be willing to forgive. Verses 29 and 30 say, "His fellow slave therefore fell down and entreated him, saying, Have patience with me, and I will repay you. And he would not, but went away and threw him into prison until he should pay what was owed." The offended brother, the one not willing to forgive others, was certainly saved. Thus, in this parable the Lord is dealing not with sinners, but with believers, with saved ones. He deals with a brother who has been offended, yet who is not willing to forgive.

5. The Brothers Being Grieved by Our Unwillingness to Forgive

Verse 31 says, "His fellow slaves, having seen what had taken place, were exceedingly grieved and came and explained to their lord all that had taken place." If we do not forgive the brother who sins against us, it will grieve the other brothers, and they may bring this matter to the Lord.

6. Punished by the Lord for Our Unwillingness to Forgive

Verse 34 says, "And his lord was angry and delivered him to the tormentors until he should pay all that was owed to him." This refers to the Lord's dealing with His believers at His coming back. If we do not forgive the brother who sins against us, we shall be disciplined by the Lord until we forgive him from the heart, that is, until we have paid everything we owe. Then the Lord will forgive us. This is forgiveness in the kingdom. This implies that if we do not forgive a brother from our heart today, we shall not be allowed to enter into the kingdom in the coming age.

Many Christians do not understand this portion of the Word. Verses 34 and 35 indicate that the one who does not forgive his brother from his heart will be under the hand of the tormentors until he forgives everything. Certainly such a one is a saved one. Nevertheless, he is given over to the tormentors for a period of time. This does not mean, however, that he is cast into prison forever. Rather, he will be tormented until he pays the debt, that is, until he forgives his brother from his heart.

Today most Christians believe that as long as they are saved, there will be no problem in the future. But in this parable the one who refuses to forgive his fellow slaves is not a false Christian, but a real Christian. You need to realize that it is possible for a real Christian one day to be delivered to the tormentors. Perhaps you will say, "The Lord Jesus will not do this to me. I have never robbed a bank. I have always been righteous and have not mistreated others." But the Lord may say, "No, you didn't rob a bank or damage anyone, but you have not forgiven your brother from your heart." Do you think that such an unforgiving brother is actually in the kingdom in a practical way? According to God's mathematics, to forgive is to forget. However, you may not be willing to forgive those who have offended you. This is a serious matter. If you claim to be in the kingdom life in a practical way, why then are you not willing to forgive others from the heart? Your unwillingness to forgive causes you to lose the kingdom life.

In verses 15 through 20 the emphasis is on the offending brother needing to repent. But in the parable the emphasis is on the offended one needing to forgive. Both our unwillingness to repent and our unwillingness to forgive will keep us out of the kingdom. If we offend someone but are not willing to repent and ask for forgiveness, we shall be kept out of the kingdom. In the same principle, if we are offended but are unwilling to forgive, we shall also be kept out of the kingdom. Often we think that we are in the kingdom when, according to God's mathematics, we are not. It depends on whether or not we are willing, on the one hand, to repent and ask for forgiveness and, on the other hand, to forgive others from our heart.

I have observed these two problems in the church life throughout the·years. When certain brothers offended others, they were not willing to repent and ask for forgiveness. As a result, they were out of the church life. By being out of the church life, they were out of the kingdom. I also saw those who were offended but who were not willing to forgive the one who had offended them. They also were kept from the church life. Apparently those who do not repent and those who do not forgive others are in the kingdom. Actually, according to God's reckoning, they are not.

Whenever a church is newly established, the church experiences a honeymoon. During the honeymoon, everything is wonderful. The brothers and sisters say, "How marvelous it is to be in the church! We used to be scattered and divided in the denominations. But now the captives have returned home. Praise the Lord for bringing us back!" However, as time goes by, there will be offenses. In the church life we simply cannot avoid offending one another, for we are daily in close contact with one another. We may offend others without having any intention of doing so. From the day I first came into the ministry until now, I have not had any intention to offend anyone. I have even prayed that the Lord would give me wisdom to know how to go in and out among the Lord's people. But no matter how much I prayed to the Lord regarding this, I have unconsciously and unintentionally offended others. The same is true in married life. I do not believe that there is one couple who has not had offenses between them. Offenses are unavoidable.

During the years, I have visited church after church. Everyone in a new church is happy, and all the faces are smiling. But when I visited the same church two years later, I saw many unhappy faces there. Privately I contacted some of those who seemed the most unhappy and asked what had happened to them and why they were silent in the meetings. They told me of the offenses and the unhappy feelings toward the elders or toward others. Whenever I heard this, I prayed desperately for the church and said, "Lord, the church simply cannot go on like this." Then I contacted the elders and asked them about the situation. Sometimes the elders said, "Brother Lee, forget about that person. Although he was one of the pioneers of the church life here, he has offended almost everyone." Upon hearing this, I asked the elders if they would forgive him. In many cases, they were unwilling to do so. Thus, one side was unwilling to repent, and the other side was unwilling to forgive. If such a situation continues, the church life is over. The saints may still come together and sing a few hymns, but because of the offenses, the judgment, and the unwillingness to repent or to forgive, there is no kingdom life in that place. God who sees everything knows what is hidden beneath the surface of the church life. We may meet as a church, but among us there may not actually be the kingdom life. Because of the unwillingness to repent and to forgive, the kingdom life vanishes.

C. Forgiveness in the Kingdom

1. Forgiveness in the Present Age

In God's governmental administration, His forgiveness is dispensational. For His administration, He has planned different ages. The period from the first coming of Christ to eternity is divided dispensationally into three ages: this age, the present one, from Christ's first to His second coming; the coming age, the millennium, the one thousand years for restoration and heavenly reigning, from Christ's second coming to the end of the old heaven and the old earth; and eternity, the eternal age of the new heaven and new earth. God's forgiveness in this age is for sinners' eternal salvation (Acts 2:38; 5:31; 13:39). If a believer, after being saved, commits any sin, but will not make a clearance through confession and the cleansing of the Lord's blood (1 John 1:7, 9) before he dies or the Lord comes back, this sin will not be forgiven in this age, but will remain to be judged at the judgment seat of Christ. He will not be rewarded with the kingdom to participate in the glory and joy with Christ in the manifestation of the kingdom of the heavens, but will be disciplined to make a clearance of this sin and be forgiven in the coming age. This kind of forgiveness will maintain his eternal salvation, but will not qualify him to participate in the glory and joy of the coming kingdom.

2. Forgiveness in the Kingdom Age

If anyone offends the church and is not willing to repent or if he is offended and is not willing to forgive the one who has offended him, he will be out of the kingdom not only in this age but in the coming age. This means that he will not share in the manifestation of the kingdom. Do not listen to the mistaken teachings that Christians cannot have any problems in the coming age. Some will have great problems and will be excluded from the glory and joy which the overcomers will share with the Lord Jesus during the millennium. Furthermore, they may be put under the hands of the tormentors. If today you can be considered by the church as a heathen or a tax collector, then what will happen to you during the manifestation of the kingdom? It is a very serious matter to offend the saints or the church and to rebel against the church. If you remain in such a state, where will you be at the time of the manifestation of the kingdom? Also, what about those who are unwilling to forgive those who have offended them? Yes, certain ones may have offended you, but you need to remember how much God the Father has forgiven you. Why will you not conduct yourself as a beloved son of the Father and forgive others as He has forgiven you? We all have a weakness here, for we all are unwilling to forgive others. If you still remember a brother's offense against you, it indicates that you have not forgiven him from your heart. If this is your situation when the kingdom comes, you will be delivered to the tormentors.

Perhaps you have not heard such a serious word before and were misled concerning this matter. Many Christians do not know how to interpret this part of the Word because they have not seen God's dispensational administration. They do not realize that God has ordained three ages: the present age, the coming age, and the eternal age. According to Matthew 12:32, certain sins cannot be forgiven either in this age or in the coming age. This indicates that other sins can be forgiven in this age or in the next age. If you offend the church and rebel against the church, you commit a sin. But if you repent to the church, this sin will be forgiven in this age. However, if you do not repent to the church, this sin will not be forgiven in this age. Rather, you will need to wait until the coming kingdom age before this sin is forgiven. During the kingdom age, you will be under the discipline of God. Then you will repent and be forgiven. Although you may be disciplined in the coming age and dealt with by God, you will not be lost. After you have been dealt with, you will repent and apply the blood. Then, in that age, you will be forgiven. We need to be very serious about this matter. Have you offended anyone? If you have, you need to repent. Has anyone offended you? If so, by the Lord's grace you must forgive that offense and forget about it. If we do this, there will be no friction among us. All offenses will be removed by our repentance and forgiveness.

If we do not practice the way of repentance and forgiveness, the longer we stay in the church life, the more offenses there will be. The offenses will accumulate until they are as high as a mountain. This will annul the kingdom life and cause us to forfeit the church life. May the Lord grant us the grace we need. If I offend you, I need to go to you and repent. If you offend me, I need to look to the Lord for the grace to forgive you from my heart. And once I have forgiven an offense, I should forget it and never mention it again. If we do this, we shall have the proper kingdom life. Then we shall share in the manifestation of the kingdom. Otherwise, during the millennium we shall be under God's discipline so that we will repent of our offense or forgive the one who offended us.

LIFE-STUDY OF MATTHEW

MESSAGE FIFTY-THREE

THE KINGDOM REQUIREMENTS

In this message we come to 19:1-22, a portion in which Matthew places together certain incidents in Christ's life to show the requirements of the kingdom. In 19:3-12 the Pharisees tempt the Lord by asking Him about divorce, and in 19:16-22 a rich man inquires of Him concerning eternal life. The Gospel of John does not mention either of these cases. But in Matthew they are not only recorded; they are put in the same portion of Matthew's Gospel. In chapter nineteen we see the matter of divorce and the matter of loving riches. Between these two things we have the matter of receiving the little children (vv. 13-15). Apparently, these three things are not related. But when we get into the depths of the significance of these things, we see that all are related to entering the kingdom of the heavens. Hence, they are the requirements of the kingdom.

I. UNVEILED IN THE DISTRICTS OF JUDEA
ACROSS THE JORDAN WITH THE POWER OF HEALING

Matthew 19:1 and 2 say, "And it came to pass when Jesus had finished these words, He withdrew from Galilee and came into the districts of Judea across the Jordan. And great crowds followed Him, and He healed them there." Due to the rejection of the Jews, the heavenly King left them and went to Galilee in the north. Now He was coming back to Jerusalem to accomplish His death and resurrection, as He had prophesied in 16:21 and 17:22 and 23, for the establishment of the kingdom. He came back still with the power of healing indicating that, as the King of the heavenly kingdom, He had authority over the negative things that damaged God's creation.

II. FROM THE WRITTEN LAW BACK TO
GOD'S ORDINATION FROM THE BEGINNING

A. Dealing with Lust

If we mean business with the Lord concerning the kingdom, we must deal with lust, pride, and the love of wealth. The Gospel of John says nothing about dealing with lust because John is a book of life. But because Matthew is a book on the kingdom, it speaks of dealing with lust and other things as well. The kingdom is a matter of exercise, and most of this exercise involves various kinds of dealings. Lust, pride, and the love of wealth keep us from entering into the kingdom. The love of money is no doubt related to the self. By nature, we all love money for ourselves. However, if we would enter into the kingdom of the heavens, we must deal with this love of money. Again and again, the Gospel of Matthew deals with lust. In the constitution of the heavenly kingdom, the King explicitly mentions dealing with lust. The reference to plucking out our eyes or cutting off our hands in Matthew 5:29 and 30 shows how strict and serious we must be in this matter. Otherwise, there is no way to enter the kingdom of the heavens. The thorough dealing with lust has been neglected by today's Christians. Very few Christians have ever heard a sober word from Matthew 5 and 19 regarding lust. Because of this lack, there is no genuine church life or kingdom of the heavens among today's Christians. How the Lord needs a testimony on earth! For His testimony the Lord must have a recovery. We are not concerned about having a large number. At the time of Elijah, the Lord had only seven thousand. If the Lord had seven thousand in this country, He would have a prevailing testimony against all adulterous things.

Matthew 19:3 says, "And the Pharisees came to Him, tempting Him, and saying, Is it lawful for a man to put away his wife for every cause?" The religionists did not let the Lord go, but came again and again to tempt Him. However, their tempting always afforded the Lord an opportunity to unveil Himself and God's economy. Here the opposition of the religionists afforded the Lord the opportunity to expose the seriousness of divorce. The source of divorce is lust. If there were no lust, there would not be any divorce.

The Lord's word in 19:4-6 not only recognizes God's creation of man, but also confirms God's ordination of marriage, that is, one man and one woman joined and yoked together as one flesh, inseparable by man. Marriage is the union of one man and one woman. This is God's ordination, and it is very serious for anyone to break it. God's ordination here involves not only physical things, but also spiritual things; for the union of one man and one woman in marriage signifies the oneness of Christ and the church. As there is one husband for one wife, so there is one Christ for one church. There should not be more than one wife for one husband, or more than one husband for one wife. How serious it would be if there were one Christ and many churches, or one church and more than one Christ! God's ordination is to have one Christ and one church. In figure and in shadow, there must be one wife for one husband. That this was God's ordination in creation is clearly recorded in the Word.

In verse 7 the Pharisees asked the Lord, "Why then did Moses command to give her a writing of divorce and to put her away?" This commandment was not a part of the basic law, but a supplement to the law. It was given by Moses, not according to God's ordination from the beginning, but temporarily because of the hardness of man's heart.

Instead of arguing with the Pharisees, the Lord said, "Moses, because of your hardness of heart, allowed you to put away your wives; but from the beginning it has not been so." The commandment concerning divorce given by Moses was a deviation from God's original ordination, but Christ as the heavenly King recovered it back to the beginning for the kingdom of the heavens. This indicates that the kingdom of the heavens, corresponding with God's ordination from the beginning, does not allow any divorce.

In verse 8 we see the principle of recovery. Recovery means to go back to the beginning. Things that exist may not date back to the beginning. We need to go back to the beginning. In the beginning, God ordained one husband and one wife, and there was no divorce. Because of the hardness of the people's hearts, Moses tolerated divorce and allowed a man to divorce his wife by giving her a writing of divorce. The Lord was asking the Pharisees if they would care for God's ordination or for the hardness of their heart. Every seeker of God should say, "O Lord, have mercy upon me that I may care for Your original ordination. I do not want to care for the hardness of my heart. I condemn and reject the hardness of my heart and return to Your original ordination." This is what is meant by recovery.

Today many Christians are arguing for certain things. Because of the hardness of the fallen human heart, the Lord tolerates some of those things. Should we agree with this toleration and the hardness of the human heart? Certainly not. Rather, we must receive the Lord's grace to go back to God's original ordination. We must go back to the beginning.

Verse 9 says, "But I say to you that whoever puts away his wife, except for fornication, and marries another, commits adultery; and he who marries her who has been put away commits adultery." The Greek word for fornication means harlotry, whoredom, which is worse than adultery. The Lord's word here indicates definitely that nothing but fornication breaks the marriage tie. (Of course, death automatically breaks it.) Except for fornication, there is no ground for divorce.

B. By God's Gift

Verse 10 says, "The disciples say to Him, If the case of the man is thus with the wife, it is better not to marry." Now the disciples realized that according to God's ordination, marriage is the strictest bond. Once one is married, he is fully bound, without any way to be released, unless the other party commits fornication or dies. It was such a realization that caused the disciples to think that it was better not to marry. But it is not up to them.

In verse 11 the Lord said to His disciples, "Not all men can accept this word, but those to whom it has been given." Not all men, but those to whom God has given the gift, are able to refrain from marriage. Without God's gift, any attempt to remain unmarried will meet with temptations.

Verse 12 continues, "For there are eunuchs who were born thus from their mother's womb, and there are eunuchs who were made eunuchs by men, and there are eunuchs who made themselves eunuchs because of the kingdom of the heavens." Those who are made eunuchs because of the kingdom of the heavens are those to whom God has given the gift not to marry for the sake of the kingdom of the heavens. Paul was such a one (1 Cor. 7:7-8; 9:5).

In ourselves we are not able to keep God's original ordination. For this, we need grace; we need God's gift. Only those who have received the gift of grace can accept the Lord's word regarding God's original ordination.

A eunuch is one who deals thoroughly with lust. In order to be such a spiritual eunuch, we need grace. Only grace can afford us the strength and the supply to have a thorough dealing with lust. Lust is a great problem in our life. Because in ourselves we are not able to deal with this "scorpion," we need to look to the Lord and pray, "Lord, have mercy on me and grant me the grace I need." By grace it is possible to deal with the subtle, evil "scorpion" of lust that damages our life.

Lust damages not only the kingdom life and the church life, but also human life. It ruins marriages and society. It damages the spirit, mind, and body. Anyone who is under the dominion of the "scorpion" of lust will be ruined for the proper human life, family life, social life, church life, and kingdom life. Lust damages every kind of life. The corruption in today's society mainly comes from lust. If lust is dealt with, most of this corruption will disappear. We in the church life must deal with lust in a serious way. For this, we must depend on the Lord's grace.

The religionists' temptation here afforded an opportunity for the Lord to unfold a further matter concerning the kingdom of the heavens. Chapter eighteen reveals how we must deal with the brothers that we may enter into the kingdom of the heavens, whereas chapter nineteen reveals that firstly married life (vv. 3-12) and then our attitude toward riches (vv. 16-30) are related to the kingdom of the heavens. Married life involves lust, and our attitude toward riches involves covetousness. The kingdom of the heavens rules out every trace of our lust and covetousness.

III. THE KINGDOM BLESSING
COMING THROUGH HUMILITY

When the disciples rebuked those who were bringing some little children to the Lord, the Lord Jesus said, "Permit the little children and do not prevent them from coming to Me, for of such is the kingdom of the heavens" (19:14). Then He laid His hands on them. Here the Lord stresses again that to participate in the kingdom of the heavens, we must be like little children.

On the surface, 19:13-15 seems to deal with an insignificant matter. Actually, these verses are concerned with pride. The Lord seemed to be saying to His disciples, "You should not reject these little ones. On the contrary, you must become a little one yourself. Pride is hidden within you. You must condemn and reject your pride. If you reject your pride and become as little children, you will be in the kingdom of the heavens."

Matthew placed the dealing with pride between the dealing with lust and money. This arrangement is meaningful. Every fleshly person who is a lover of money is a proud person. Pride is always found between lust and the love of money.

IV. HIGHER THAN THE LAW

Verse 16 says, "And behold, one came to Him and said, Teacher, what good thing shall I do that I may have eternal life?" To have eternal life in Matthew differs from having eternal life in John. Matthew is concerned with the kingdom, whereas John is concerned with life. To have eternal life in John is to be saved with God's uncreated life that

man may live by this life today and for eternity, whereas to
have eternal life in Matthew is to participate in the reality
of the kingdom of the heavens in this age and to share in its
manifestation in the coming age.

In the Gospel of John the eternal life is mainly for
regeneration, for the new birth. By regeneration, we
become the children of God. Furthermore, the Gospel of
John reveals that by the eternal life, the life of God within
us, we may bear fruit. Hence, the eternal life in John is for
reproduction. But in the Gospel of Matthew, eternal life is
not for the new birth, but for the kingdom. Many Christians confuse the eternal life in John with the eternal life in
Matthew. It is the same eternal life in both John and
Matthew, but with different purposes. To repeat, in John
the eternal life is for the new birth, but in Matthew it is for
the kingdom. No one can have the kingdom life without
God's eternal life.

A. Realizing Only God is Good

In verse 17 the Lord answered the one who had asked
Him what good thing he should do to have eternal life:
"Why are you asking Me concerning that which is good?
One is good." This One is God. Only God is good. This
indicates not only that the young man asking the question
is not good, but also that the Lord Jesus is God, who is
good. If He were not God, He also would not be good.

B. Keeping the Law's Commandment

The Lord also said to this young man, "If you want to
enter into life, keep the commandments." Here the Lord
speaks about entering into life. To enter into life means to
enter into the kingdom of the heavens (v. 23). The kingdom of the heavens is a realm of God's eternal life. Hence,
when we enter into it, we enter into God's life. This differs
from being saved. To be saved is to have God's life enter
into us, whereas to enter into the kingdom of the heavens is
to enter into God's life. The former is to be redeemed and
regenerated with God's life; the latter is to live and walk by
God's life. One is a matter of birth; the other is a matter of
living.

According to the Gospel of John, to have eternal life is to receive eternal life into us. But according to Matthew, to have eternal life is to enter into eternal life. The eternal life enters into us to give us the new birth to become God's children. Then we enter into eternal life to have the kingdom life. Thus, in John eternal life involves salvation, but in Matthew it is not related to salvation.

"If you want to enter into life," the Lord said to the young man, "keep the commandments." Keeping the commandments is not the requirement for salvation; it is related to entering into the kingdom of the heavens. According to the constitution of the kingdom of the heavens, to enter into life requires us to meet not only the standard of the old law, but also the standard of the complemented new law (5:17-48). Salvation requires only faith, whereas the kingdom of the heavens requires a surpassing righteousness, which issues from the keeping of the old law plus its complement given by the heavenly King.

The disciples' question in verse 25 — "Who then can be saved?" — indicates that they thought entering into the kingdom of the heavens was the same as being saved. Many Christians today have the same concept. They know only about salvation; they know nothing about the kingdom of the heavens. When we first preached the kingdom more than forty years ago, we proclaimed the assurance of salvation. Although missionaries had been in China for more than a hundred years, they had not made the assurance of salvation clear to the Chinese saints. Thus, wherever we went, we tried to help the believers to be sure of their salvation. When we preached the assurance of salvation, many pastors opposed us and condemned us for being proud. Some said, "We have been pastors for many years, and not even we dare to say that we are saved. How can you claim to be saved? You are too proud. We all must believe in the Lord Jesus, behave ourselves, and wait until we die and go to the Lord. Then the Lord will tell us whether or not we are saved." But we fought the battle for the assurance of salvation, giving the people verse after verse to prove that we can know that we have been saved and that there is no need to wait for us to die and go to the Lord. After a few years of fighting, we gained the victory.

After winning this battle, we preached the kingdom reward. We began to say to people, "Yes, there is no doubt that you have been saved. But to be saved is one thing and to receive the kingdom reward is another." Although this word did not offend very many pastors, it offended many careless Christians. When we preached the assurance of salvation, all the careless Christians were happy and said, "Hallelujah, we are saved! The Bible tells us so. As long as we believe in the Lord Jesus, we are saved." But their happiness did not last very long, for the same ones who preached to them the assurance of salvation told them that they may have a problem, lose the kingdom reward, and be disciplined. None of the careless, worldly Christians wanted to hear this. After a message on the kingdom, a wealthy woman once said to me, "Brother Lee, is what you are talking about related to my going to heaven? I don't care about anything else. If I can only be a doorkeeper at the gate of heaven, I shall be satisfied." Many Christians have this idea. As long as they are saved and bound for heaven, they are happy. Those who say this have been drugged, caring only for salvation and heaven. But in Matthew 19 the Lord speaks about entering into the kingdom of the heavens. Although you may be saved, you may be in danger of not entering into the kingdom of the heavens. Surely the Lord's word about it being easier for a camel to go through the eye of a needle than for a rich man to enter into the kingdom of God is not concerned with salvation. This word is concerned with the kingdom of the heavens. It is very difficult for one who loves riches to enter into the kingdom of the heavens.

C. To Be Perfect by Laying Up Treasure in the Heavens and Following Christ

When the young man told the Lord that he had observed all the commandments, the Lord said to him, "If you want to be perfect, go, sell what you have and give to the poor, and you shall have treasure in heaven, and come, follow Me" (v. 21). Even if the young man had observed the commandments of the old law as he had claimed, he was still not perfect, not up to the standard of the requirement of the complemented law; for he was not willing to sell what he had and lay up treasure in heaven, as the constitution of the kingdom required (6:19-21). To follow the Lord is to love Him above all things (10:37-38). This is the supreme requirement for entering into the kingdom of the heavens.

Verse 22 says, "But the young man, hearing this word, went away sorrowing, for he had many possessions." Loving material possessions above the Lord causes one to sorrow, but those who love Christ above all things are joyful in losing their possessions (Heb. 10:34).

There are two kinds of rich men: those who are rich with many material possessions and those who dream about being rich although they actually are not rich. In the past, some of us may have dreamed of being a millionaire. In the sense of dreaming about riches, everyone is a rich man. The desire of some young women is to marry a rich man. This is their dream. If you are not the first kind of rich person, then you probably are the second.

The Lord said that it is more difficult for someone who loves money to enter into the kingdom than it is for a camel to go through the eye of a needle. This illustration reveals the seriousness of the love of money as far as the kingdom is concerned. The love of money is the greatest hindrance to entering into the kingdom.

The Lord dealt with the young man in chapter nineteen in a wise manner. He had come to the Lord to ask Him what he should do in order to have eternal life, that is, to live in the kingdom. Knowing the young man's heart, the Lord told him to keep the commandments. When the Lord was asked which commandments, He listed six of them: the commandments regarding murder, adultery, stealing, bearing false witness, honoring father and mother, and loving our neighbor as ourself (vv. 18-19). Then the young man said, "All these things I have observed; what do I lack yet?" The Lord was ready to answer him and told him what to do in order to be perfect. In His answer the Lord seemed to be saying, "Even if you have kept all the commandments, you still are not perfect. You may be perfect according to the law of Moses, but not according to the constitution of the kingdom of the heavens. To be perfect according to the constitution of the kingdom, you must sell your possessions, give them to the poor, and follow Me." This was a killing word. When the Lord mentioned six of the commandments, the young man was very encouraged, for he was one who kept the law. But when the Lord told him to uproot his love for money and to follow Him, he went away sorrowful.

When I was young, I was troubled by the Lord's word in chapter eighteen concerning forgiveness. I regarded it as a sobering word, and I took it seriously. I asked myself if I was willing to forgive everyone. When I came to chapter nineteen, I asked myself whether or not I could uproot the love of money. Like most students in China at the time, I was quite poor. But even a poor Chinese student could dream of becoming rich. At that time I did not have the boldness to say, "Yes, Lord, I can uproot the love of money." I realized that probably I could not succeed in doing this. The love of money exposes how far off the course many of today's Christians are. To them, the Gospel of Matthew is a story book. When they read it, it seems that nothing touches them. But we must be touched by the Lord's sobering word in chapter nineteen regarding the requirements of the kingdom. Do you mean business with the Lord for His kingdom? If so, then what about the love of money? Is there still room in you for the love of money? This is a serious matter.

Only by the divine life can we fulfill the requirements of the kingdom. It is easy to fulfill these requirements when we have the grace to do so. By our human life it is impossible, but by the divine life with the divine grace it is easy. In fact, it is a joy. What a joy to lay up treasure in the heavens!

We, the people in the kingdom, are altogether different from the worldly people. We are even different from those in Christianity. Our heart has been touched, and we are serious with the Lord concerning His kingdom. Riches and material possessions do not mean much to us. By our natural life it is very difficult to have such an attitude toward riches. But by the divine life with the divine grace, we can say that it is a joy for us to lay up treasure in the heavens.

We have seen three requirements for entering into the kingdom of the heavens: dealing with lust, dealing with pride, and dealing with the love of riches. To deal with the love of riches is to deal with the self. Those who love money do so for two reasons: for security and for pleasure. People in this country are worried about their security. They are anxious to provide for their future and their old age. Others love money for the pleasure it gives them. They enjoy counting how much money they have in the bank. Both security and pleasure are related to the self. Thus, the love of money is a matter of the self. To deal with the love of money is to deal with the self, although the self is dealt with indirectly.

The Lord's sober word regarding the requirements of the kingdom should not merely be doctrine to us. We need to take the Lord's word in a serious way and open ourselves to the Lord concerning lust, pride, and the hidden love of riches for the sake of the self. May the Lord have mercy upon us to give us a thorough dealing with these matters for the kingdom of the heavens.

LIFE-STUDY OF MATTHEW

MESSAGE FIFTY-FOUR

THE KINGDOM REWARD
AND
THE PARABLE OF THE KINGDOM REWARD

In Matthew 19:1-22 we have the requirements of the kingdom, and in 19:23-30, the reward of the kingdom. Matthew 20:1-16 is the parable of the kingdom reward. In this message we shall consider the reward of the kingdom and the parable of the kingdom reward.

I. IMPOSSIBLE FOR THE RICH MAN
TO ENTER INTO THE KINGDOM

Verses 23 and 24 say, "And Jesus said to His disciples, Truly I say to you, it is difficult for a rich man to enter into the kingdom of the heavens. And again I say to you, It is easier for a camel to go through the eye of a needle than for a rich man to enter into the kingdom of God." The kingdom of God is used in verse 24 instead of the kingdom of the heavens mentioned in verse 23. At this point, the kingdom of the heavens had not come, but the kingdom of God was present. Hence, the Lord used the term the kingdom of God.

The Lord's word about it being easier for a camel to go through the eye of a needle than for a rich man to enter into the kingdom of God indicates the impossibility of entering into the kingdom of God by our natural life.

II. THE IMPOSSIBILITY BECOMING
A POSSIBILITY WITH GOD

Verse 25 says, "And when the disciples heard this, they were exceedingly astonished and said, Who then can be saved?" The disciples, like most Christians today, confused salvation with the kingdom of the heavens. The Lord's word to the young man concerned entering into the kingdom of the heavens, but the disciples considered that it referred to salvation. They had the natural, common concept of being saved. They did not grasp the Lord's revelation concerning entering into the kingdom of the heavens.

In verse 26 the Lord said to them, "With men this is impossible, but with God all things are possible." By our human life it is impossible to enter into the kingdom of the heavens, but it is possible by the divine life, which is Christ Himself imparted into us that we may live the kingdom life. We can fulfill the requirements of the kingdom by Christ, who empowers us to do all things (Phil. 4:13).

III. THE KINGDOM REWARD

In verse 27 Peter said to the Lord, "Behold, we have left all and followed You; what then is there for us?" Peter seemed to be saying, "No matter how difficult it is to enter into the kingdom, we, like the camel, have passed through the eye of the needle. Since we have left all and followed You, what is there for us?" Peter's concept was quite commercial. The Lord answered him, as usual, in a clear, definite way.

A. To Receive a Hundredfold in This Age

The kingdom reward is of two parts. The first part is in this age, and the second part is in the coming age. The first part of the kingdom reward is mainly related to material things and natural things. If, for the kingdom's sake, or for the sake of the Lord's name, we leave all these things, the Lord will reward us a hundredfold. In verse 29 the Lord said, "Everyone who has left houses, or brothers, or sisters, or father, or mother, or children, or lands for My name's sake, shall receive a hundredfold and shall inherit eternal life." To receive a hundredfold, houses, lands, and relatives, is to be rewarded in this age (Mark 10:30). This refers to the enjoyment of the brothers and sisters in the Lord with their possessions today. I can testify that I have left everything to follow the Lord, including my relatives. I hardly have a friend outside the local church. But I have hundreds of brothers, sisters, and mothers. In the church life we all have many mothers, brothers, and sisters. In a sense, those in the church life love me more than my relatives do. This is a reward. We need to believe the promise of the Lord that if we leave everything behind us to follow Him, we shall receive a reward, even in this age.

B. To Inherit Eternal Life in the Coming Age

In verse 29, the Lord also speaks of inheriting eternal life. To inherit eternal life is to be rewarded in the coming age (Luke 18:29-30) with the enjoyment of the divine life in the manifestation of the kingdom of the heavens. In the manifestation of the kingdom, we shall participate in the enjoyment of eternal life in the millennial kingdom with the Lord Jesus. This will be greater than the first aspect of the kingdom reward, which we receive in this age.

C. In the Time of Restoration to Be Co-kings with Christ

In verse 28 the Lord said, "Truly I say to you that you who have followed Me, in the regeneration, when the Son of Man shall sit on the throne of His glory, you also shall sit on twelve thrones, judging the twelve tribes of Israel." The regeneration is the restoration of the coming kingdom age (Acts 3:21) after the Lord's second coming. In the coming kingdom, the overcomers will sit on thrones to reign over the earth (Rev. 20:4). The first twelve apostles, including Peter, will judge the twelve tribes of Israel, while the others will rule over the nations (Rev. 2:26).

D. Not Being a Legal Matter

After hearing the Lord's answer, Peter had nothing more to say. His mouth was shut. But the Lord went on to say, "But many that are first shall be last, and the last first" (v. 30). Many Christians use this verse, but most use it incorrectly. I am concerned that many of us do not understand this verse properly. Some say that a person who has just been saved but who has considerable experience is an example of the last becoming first. This is a natural interpretation. Others say that the young ones, who are last, have become the first, and that we, the older ones, are out of date and have become the last. This also is a natural understanding. Knowing that we would take His word in a natural way, the Lord gave the parable in 20:1-16 to explain the meaning of this verse. The word "For" at the beginning of 20:1 indicates that this parable is an explanation of 19:30. Furthermore, in 20:16 the Lord again says that the last shall be first and the first last. This also proves that the parable is an interpretation of the Lord's word.

In order to understand 19:30 and the parable in 20:1-16, we need to see that Peter had a commercial mentality. His commercial mentality was exposed in 19:27, when he asked, "What then is there for us?" In other words, Peter was saying, "Lord, we have paid the price. Now what will You give us?" At the supermarket we pay a certain price and receive in exchange something with a certain value. We get what we pay for. This was Peter's concept. He said that they had left everything to follow the Lord, that is, they had paid the full price. Now he wanted to know what he would get in exchange for the price he had paid. The Lord Jesus was fair and answered Peter in a clear way in 19:28 and 29. The Lord seemed to say, "When I sit on the throne of My glory, you will sit on twelve thrones. Peter, this is what you have paid the price for. Everyone who has left houses or relatives for My name's sake will receive a two-part reward, the first part in this age and the second part in the coming age. In this age you will receive a hundredfold to replace the material things you left. In the coming age you will have the full enjoyment of eternal life." The Lord's answer was clear and fair, and I believe Peter was very satisfied with it.

The Lord, however, did not let Peter go, for he needed a

further lesson. Therefore the Lord said that many (but not all) who are first shall be last, and the last first. This indicates that many, like Peter, who were the first would be the last to receive the reward. The Lord said this in order to revolutionize Peter's commercial mentality. The Lord seemed to be saying to Peter, "Those who are the first will be last, and those who are the last will be first. I say this to show you that what I give you is not based upon your commercial sense. Although you must pay in order to receive the reward of the kingdom, receiving the reward is not a commercial matter. Actually, the price you have paid means nothing."

The same, of course, is true of us today. What we have given up does not mean anything. Even if the President of the United States were to give up his presidency in order to have the kingdom reward, that would not mean anything. However, what the Lord gives means a great deal. If you pay a dollar for something at the department store, you receive something worth a dollar; and if you pay a hundred dollars, you receive something worth a hundred dollars. But, in the eyes of the Lord, the price we pay for the reward is just a few cents, but the reward He gives is worth millions. What could we pay to receive the full enjoyment of eternal life? The full enjoyment of eternal life in the manifestation of the kingdom is priceless. The price we pay cannot compare with the reward we shall receive. Receiving the reward is not a commercial transaction. It is not a matter of paying a certain amount and of receiving something equal to that in value.

Actually, what we pay is dung (Phil. 3:8). Everything apart from Christ is dung. The Lord seemed to be saying to Peter, "Peter, in the kingdom you will be sitting on the throne ruling over the children of Israel. This is the kingship. Peter, all you have given up to obtain this is dung. Do you think you can buy the kingship with dung? If you attempt to pay Me with dung, I would not accept it. Rather, I would tell you to get rid of those things. Although the price you pay is dung, I shall reward you with the kingship." Peter, who had a commercial mentality, needed to be reeducated by the Lord Jesus. The Lord was wise and patient with him and gave a long parable to explain what He meant when He said that the first would be last and the last first.

IV. A HOUSEHOLDER HIRING WORKMEN
FOR HIS VINEYARD

A. Early in the Morning

Mattew 20:1 and 2 say, "For the kingdom of the heavens is like a man, a householder, who went out early in the morning to hire workmen for his vineyard. And having agreed with the workmen for a denarius a day, he sent them into his vineyard." The householder is Christ. The morning here is 6:00 a.m., denoting the earliest part of the church age, when Christ came to call His disciples into the kingdom. The workmen are the disciples, and the vineyard is the kingdom. The agreement referred to in verse 2 denotes the agreement He made in 19:27-29. The denarius is the reward the Lord offered Peter in His agreement with him in 19:28 and 29.

B. About the Third Hour

Verses 3 and 4 say, "And he went out about the third hour and saw others standing idle in the market place, and to those he said, You go also into the vineyard, and whatever is right I will give you. And they went." The third hour was 9:00 a.m., denoting the second part of the church age. The word "idle" indicates that whoever does not work in the kingdom of the heavens is standing idle in the world, which is denoted by the market place.

C. About the Sixth Hour and about the Ninth Hour

Verse 5 says, "Again he went out about the sixth and the ninth hour and did likewise." The sixth hour, 12:00 noon, denotes the middle part of the church age, and the ninth hour, 3:00 p.m., denotes the fourth part of the church age.

D. About the Eleventh Hour

Verses 6 and 7 say, "And about the eleventh hour he went out and found others standing, and said to them, Why are you standing here all the day idle? They said to him, Because no one has hired us. He said to them, You go also into the vineyard." The eleventh hour was 5:00 p.m., denoting the fifth part of the church age. Those hired at the eleventh hour said they were standing around idle because no one had hired them. Outside the kingdom of God, no human beings are employed by God. Although the hour was late, the Lord still sent them into the vineyard. Even near the end of the church age, the Lord still calls people to work in His kingdom.

V. THE HOUSEHOLDER REWARDING THE WORKMEN

A. At Evening

According to verse 8, the householder rewarded the workmen at evening, that is, at 6:00 p.m. This denotes the end of the church age.

B. Beginning from the Last to the First

Verse 8 says, "And when evening was come, the lord of the vineyard said to his steward, Call the workmen and pay them their wages, beginning from the last to the first." For the lord to begin from the last to the first was against the natural and commercial concept. It indicates that what is paid to the latest workmen is not according to their work, but according to the gracious wish of the lord of the vineyard.

C. The Last and the First
Receiving the Same Reward

Verses 9 and 10 say, "And when those hired about the eleventh hour came, they received each a denarius. And when the first came, they supposed that they would receive more; and they themselves also received each a denarius." Here we see that the last and the first received the same reward. The first workmen mentioned in verse 10 included Peter, who made a deal with the Lord in 19:27-29.

D. The First Murmuring according to Legality

Much to the surprise of those hired first, the last were the first to receive the reward, although they worked just one hour, not during the heat of the day. Thus, when those hired first saw that the last received a denarius, they expected to receive a great deal more. However, they also received a denarius. Verses 11 and 12 say, "And when they received it, they murmured against the householder, saying, These last have worked one hour, and you have made them equal to us who have borne the burden of the day and the scorching heat." Those hired first should remember Romans 9:14-15 and 20. There is no unrighteousness with the Lord. He will have mercy on whom He will have mercy. Who are they to reply against the Lord? But Peter's natural concept, representing that of all believers, was commercial; he did not know the Lord's gracious wish. Thus, he murmured against the Lord according to legality.

E. The Householder's Answer Showing Grace according to His Desire

Verse 13 says, "But he answered and said to one of them, Friend, I am not wronging you; did you not agree with me for a denarius?" By "one of them" the Lord was no doubt referring to Peter. The agreement mentioned in this verse was the agreement the Lord made with Peter in 19:27-29. Here the Lord seemed to be saying, "Peter, we signed an agreement. I don't owe you anything, for I have given you what I promised. However, I'd like to show you that My reward is not a commercial matter, but a matter of grace. Peter, you need to learn the lesson of grace. The reward is a matter of grace according to My desire. Out of grace, I desire to give those hired last the same reward that I promised to give you. What is wrong with this?"

Verse 14 continues, "Take what is yours and go. I desire to give to this last one even as to you." This was a strong answer to Peter from the Lord, indicating that the Lord had given him what He thought he deserved. But the Lord has the right to give the same thing to the latest workmen according to His own wish, in the principle not of work but of grace. This shattered and corrected Peter's natural and commercial mind.

Verse 15 says, "Is it not lawful for me to do what I wish with what is mine? Or is your eye evil because I am good?" Peter's concept, in dealing with the Lord in 19:27, was altogether commercial, according to the principle of work, not of grace. In His answer to Peter, the Lord strongly indicated that His reward to His followers is not commercial, but according to His desire and grace. For the disciples to gain the kingdom of the heavens, they need to leave all and follow the Lord. But what He will give them as a reward is more than they deserve. It is not according to the principle of commerce, but according to the Lord's good pleasure. This is an incentive to His followers.

F. Not a Legal Matter but a Matter of Grace

In verse 16 the Lord concludes this parable: "Thus shall the last be first and the first last." The last are the latest workmen, and the first are the earliest ones. In working, the earliest ones came first, but in receiving the reward, the last became the first. It is this way that the Lord makes the last first and the first last. Therefore, the reward is not a legal matter, but a matter of grace.

We should not have a commercial mind. Salvation is based upon grace. The Lord Jesus has done everything for us, and there is no need for us to work. The kingdom reward, however, is according to our work, according to the price we pay. If we pay the price, then the Lord will give us a reward. It may seem that the reward is purchased by our work. If we think this, then we are like Peter with a commercial mentality. We need to be reeducated to see that even the reward is based upon grace. The way to

receive the reward is not to pay the price, but to enjoy
grace.

To be saved is to receive grace, and to gain the reward is
to enjoy the grace we have received. When we believed in
the Lord, we received grace and were saved. After receiving grace we must learn to enjoy grace. To leave all things
behind and follow the Lord is not to pay a price; it is to
enjoy the grace we have received. Do not think that you
have sacrificed anything. What you sacrifice is just dung;
it is vanity of vanities. Everything under the sun is vanity.
Your education, position, and future are all vanity. Dung
cannot be considered a price. To leave all things behind is
to be unloaded and released. You have been under the
heavy load of your position, wealth, and concern for your
future. Thus, you need to be unloaded, and the way to be
unloaded is to enjoy grace. Grace unloads us. To be
unloaded through the enjoyment of grace, however, is not
to pay a price. We are not here paying a price. Rather, we
are enjoying liberation. Hallelujah, I have been liberated! I
have been liberated from my relatives, fame, position,
future, and everything; I am completely free. I am not paying a price — I am enjoying grace.

We all need to give up the commercial mentality. Some
saints have said, "I have left everything for the church. I
have suffered very much, and now I have nothing." Whenever I have heard this kind of complaint, deep within me I
said, "You cannot receive anything, because your giving up
of all things and your suffering have not been done in the
proper spirit. If you were in the right spirit, you would be
thankful, joyful, and praise the Lord that you are no longer
burdened." If we have given up all things for the Lord in a
proper spirit, we would say, "O Lord, I thank You that I
am not bearing the load of position, ambition, or concern
for the future. All the worldlings are under a heavy load.
But, Lord, I praise You that I have been unloaded and
liberated. I am not paying a price — I am daily enjoying
grace. Lord, whatever You give me is not a reimburse-
ment, but a further enjoyment of Yourself."

I believe that we are in the last group of workmen, those hired at five o'clock in the afternoon. But we shall be the first to be rewarded, although we shall not work as long as Peter, James, John, and Paul, who have been working for nearly twenty centuries. They have labored the entire day, bearing the scorching heat. But we have labored for such a short time, at the most a number of years. Perhaps as we are receiving the reward, Peter will say to John, "Look, these people are receiving the reward before us." But that will be the fulfillment of the Lord's word that the last shall be the first and the first last. Perhaps John will say to Peter, "Peter, be patient. If these last ones are receiving such a reward, we shall certainly receive much more." However, Peter and John may be surprised to receive the same reward as those hired last. But the Lord may say to Peter and to all those hired first, "Didn't I make an agreement with you? Was not My promise satisfactory? Do not complain, but take your reward and go to the throne. Do I not have the right to do things according to My desire? Am I wrong for being good?" One day, we shall receive the same reward as Peter, and we shall receive it first. Peter's reward will be a denarius, and ours will be the same. This denarius denotes the full enjoyment of the divine life in glory in the manifestation of the kingdom. This will be our reward.

LIFE-STUDY OF MATTHEW

THE THRONE OF THE KINGDOM
AND
THE CUP OF THE CROSS

After the Lord spoke regarding the requirements of the kingdom and the kingdom reward, He was still concerned about the spiritual situation of His followers. Therefore, after giving His disciples a definition of the kingdom reward, He spoke to them again about His coming crucifixion and resurrection. The Lord also knows our real situation today. Although we may not think that we need a further word or a further revelation, the Lord knows our need.

I. KNOWING CHRIST'S
CRUCIFIXION AND RESURRECTION

In 20:17-19 the Lord unveiled for the third time His crucifixion and resurrection. The first was in Caesarea Philippi, before His transfiguration (16:13, 21). The second was in Galilee, after His transfiguration (17:22). This time was on the way to Jerusalem. This revelation was a prophecy, altogether strange to the natural concept of the disciples, yet fulfilled literally in every detail.

It seems to me rather unusual that after the definition of the kingdom reward the Lord would once again unveil His crucifixion and resurrection. Apparently this has no significance. However, if you get into the depth of this book, you will see that this is a very significant continuation. In order to receive the kingdom reward, we need to experience the cross and the resurrection. Although we may know everything regarding the kingdom, we must still have a proper grasp of the Lord's crucifixion and resurrection. Apart from experiencing the Lord's cross and resurrection, it is impossible to experience the Lord's life for the reward of the kingdom. In Philippians 3 Paul said that for Christ's sake he counted all things but dung. Then he said that he desired to know Christ and the power of His resurrection that he might be conformed to Christ's death. Paul had an adequate understanding of the Lord's death and resurrection. This understanding is for us to experience Christ as our life for the kingdom. For the kingdom reward, we need the experience of the Lord's crucifixion and resurrection. Thus, 20:17-19 is a continuation of the foregoing section.

The third time the Lord revealed His crucifixion and resurrection He did so to His disciples again. As He was going to Jerusalem, He took the twelve disciples aside and told them about His coming crucifixion and resurrection. The Lord must have had a specific purpose in doing this. He specifically told the twelve that He needed to go to Jerusalem, to be delivered to the chief priests and scribes, to be condemned to death, to be delivered to the Gentiles, to be mocked, scourged, and crucified, and to be resurrected on the third day. He spoke to His disciples concerning His death and resurrection in a detailed way.

II. THE THRONE OF THE KINGDOM

What was the disciples' reaction to the Lord's full unveiling of His crucifixion and resurrection? They did not say, "Amen, Lord. The first and second times we didn't see this. Thank You, Lord, for taking us aside this time and purposely telling us about this. Now we realize that You must pass through death and resurrection. No doubt this includes all of us. Eventually, we also shall experience this wonderful death and resurrection." The disciples definitely did not react like this. Rather, verses 20 and 21 say, "Then the mother of the sons of Zebedee came to Him with her sons, worshipping and asking something of Him. And He said to her, What do you desire? She said to Him, Say that these two sons of mine may sit, one on Your right hand

and one on Your left, in Your kingdom." The mother of the sons of Zebedee was the Lord's aunt, His mother's sister, and Zebedee's sons, James and John, were His cousins. Thus, there was a natural relationship between them and the Lord. Immediately after the Lord had unveiled His death and resurrection for the third time, the mother of James and John came to Him asking that her two sons might sit on His right hand and left hand in the kingdom. Although the Lord had spoken of the crucifixion and the resurrection, their mind was set on the throne. Often we are exactly like James and John. Again and again they heard about the crucifixion and the resurrection. But in them and in their mother there was the desire for the throne. This is the ambition for position. The mother of James and John might have said to herself, "One day, when the Lord is enthroned, maybe my two sons will be sitting one on His right hand and the other on His left hand. How glorious this would be!" This was their reaction to the Lord's word about His death and resurrection.

III. THE CUP OF THE CROSS

In verses 22 and 23 the Lord replied, "You do not know what you are asking. Are you able to drink the cup which I am about to drink? They said to Him, We are able. He said to them, My cup you shall indeed drink, but to sit on My right hand and on My left is not Mine to give, but it is for those for whom it has been prepared by My Father." If we want to sit on the throne in the kingdom, we must be prepared to drink the cup of suffering. To suffer the cross is the way to enter into the kingdom (Acts 14:22). The selfish entreaty of the mother of John and James afforded an opportunity for the Lord to reveal the way to enter into the kingdom.

In answering the mother of James and John the Lord said, "To sit on My right hand and on My left is not Mine to give, but it is for those for whom it has been prepared by My Father" (v. 23). These words indicate that the Lord had a submissive spirit. He did not assume anything, but gave place to the Father. Standing in the position of man, the Lord was fully subject to the Father, not assuming the right to do anything outside the Father. We all need to learn to give everything to the Lord. We have no place to say anything regarding position.

IV. THE FLESHLY RIVALRY OF THE DISCIPLES

In verse 24 we see the fleshly rivalry of the disciples: "And when the ten heard it, they were indignant concerning the two brothers." The disciples were more than angry; they were indignant, apparently fearing that nothing would remain for them. The twelve were filled to the brim with ambition for position, and nothing regarding the Lord's death and resurrection penetrated them. What a pitiful situation! If this had taken place in chapter four, we might sympathize with them. But this was their reaction after the decree of the constitution of the kingdom, after so many revelations concerning Christ, after the unveiling of the mystery of the kingdom, and after experiencing the many negative factors on the pathway to glory. After all this, the twelve were still fully occupied with the matter of position. Luke 22:24 says that the disciples were striving among themselves concerning who would be the greatest. Peter, Andrew, James, John, and all the others were fighting for greatness.

Matthew mentions the rivalry among the disciples in order to expose the same ambition for position that is still hidden within us today, even though we are in the church. Some are ambitious to be elders or deacons. If they cannot be an elder or a deacon, they at least aspire to be a group leader.

V. THE EXERCISE OF THE KINGDOM LIFE

There are times when the Bible apparently contradicts itself. For example, in Matthew 23 the Lord says that we should not be called a teacher. But in Ephesians 4 Paul says that Christ gave some teachers. Furthermore,

Matthew 23 says that we should not have any leaders. But in the Epistles we are told that there are leaders in the church (Heb. 13:17, 24). The Bible, however, is not contradictory. We need to see that what is in the mind of the Lord is utterly different from what is in our natural mentality. In the mind of the Lord the elders or the leaders should not control others. In the church life there should not be any control. But this does not mean that there is no governing, no ruling. To rule is one thing and to control is another. All the leaders in the churches must be clear about this. In the Lord's churches we need ruling, but not controlling.

At this point we need to read 1 Corinthians 12:28. "And God hath set some in the church, first apostles, secondarily prophets, thirdly teachers, after that miracles, then gifts of healings, helps, governments, diversities of tongues." The "helps" mentioned in this verse refer to the service of the deacons. These "helps" are mentioned before governings, which refer to the function of the elders. Hence, in the New Testament there is a verse telling us that the governing of the elders is lower than the help of the deacons. You may find this fact very surprising. According to our natural concept, the elders are much higher than the deacons. But the Apostle Paul, under the inspiration of God, lists the function of the elders after the function of the deacons. In this verse, Paul deliberately reverses the order of the elders and deacons, listing the office of the elders next to the last item, which is speaking in tongues. When Paul wrote this book from Ephesus, Corinth was a hotbed of Pentecostalism. In writing this book, he purposely diminished the significance of speaking in tongues, making it the last item, and listed the function of the elders after the function of the deacons.

Everyone who is put into eldership becomes a slave. The elders are not kings; they are slaves. As one in the Lord's ministry, I also am a slave. Others may enjoy their freedom, but I have no freedom because I have been purchased to be a slave. Likewise, every elder is a slave. In the world, to have a position means to have glory. But in the church, to have a position means to be in slavery. In Catholicism there is a hierarchy of priests, bishops, archbishops, cardinals, and the pope, all of whom are above the laity. This is vainglory. In the church there is no such vainglory; instead, there is slavery.

It is a shame that some are ambitious for position in order to have honor and glory. This is a "scorpion" creeping into the church life. If it were not a matter of function, I would not sit in the front row. Do not think that it is glorious to sit in the front. I much prefer to sit in the back. However, if the elders began to sit in the back, then in your eyes the rear seats would become the most honorable. This indicates that it is not a matter of where the elders sit, whether in the front or in the back, because the honor of their seats exists only in our mentality. Oh, how our mind needs to be renewed! For the new man, we need to be renewed in the spirit of the mind and drop the hellish concept of position.

During the years I was with Brother Nee, I observed that no one who desired to be an elder was appointed to be one. For the kingdom life we must kill the ambition for position. It is a shame to talk about position, about who is higher than others. To seek a position in the church life is not a glory, but a shame.

Regarding the matter of ambition for position, two things are clear: first, in 1 Corinthians 12:28 Paul lists the function of the elders after the function of the deacons; second, to be an elder is to be a slave. The matter of the leading ones being slaves corresponds to the Lord's word in 20:25 through 27: "Jesus called them to Him and said, You know that the rulers of the nations lord it over them, and the great exercise authority over them. It is not so among you; but whoever wants to become great among you shall be your servant, and whoever wants to be first among you shall be your slave." How contrary this is to the natural, self-seeking mind! The eldership is a form of slavery. Every leader must be a slave. Therefore, there should be no hierarchy among us. Rather, we all are brothers on the same level. The indignation of the ten disciples afforded the Lord an opportunity to reveal the way to be in the kingdom, that is, to be willing to serve others as a servant, even as a slave, rather than to rule over others.

Verse 28 says, "Even as the Son of Man came not to be served, but to serve and to give His life a ransom for many." In this book, the book of the kingdom, the Lord always stands in the position of a man. Although the kingdom of the heavens is constituted with the divine life, it is carried out in humanity.

It is helpful to see the difference between rule and control. To control others means to make decisions for them and to tell them what to do or not to do. It is to put people under your direction. In the Lord's recovery, we must hate this kind of control. No one should exercise control, because we all are under the one Lord and have the one Spirit living in us and leading us. However, there is a need for ruling. If in a meeting the saints are told what to do, that is control. But there must be some ruling in the meeting. Suppose, for example, someone worships an idol and claims the freedom to do so. This must be ruled out. We even need some ruling in deciding the times of the meetings. If we are democratic and there is no rule, some may insist on meeting at 4:30 a.m., while others may want to meet at an equally inconvenient time in the afternoon. Thus, the elders need to go to the Lord in prayer, fellowship with the saints, and use their spiritual nose to discern the feeling of the saints so that they can determine what time is best for the meetings. Then the elders should make a decision. This is not control; it is ruling.

It is not easy to be an elder. In order to be an elder, you need to have a good spiritual nose to sense the situation of the saints. You also need to have a living, keen spirit with a sharp intuition to know God's will. Then you will be able to make the right decisions. Sometimes the elders make decisions concerning the time of the meetings according to their convenience. This is a mistake. The time of the meetings should not be decided according to the elders' convenience, but according to the situation of the saints. For this, you must exercise your intuition toward God to know what He wants.

Decisions such as these are made by the elders because the government is in their hands. But do not think that governing is higher than helps. Our concept regarding this needs to be revolutionized. We need to have a spiritual understanding and a heavenly concept concerning the things of the church. What is revealed in the Bible is absolutely different from our natural understanding. Do not think that to be an elder is to occupy a high position. I repeat, to be an elder is to be a slave. When a brother is made an elder, he should say, "I have been drafted into the eldership, and I have no choice. I don't want to be an elder, but there is nothing I can do about it. The Lord has drafted me and has made me an elder." The sisters whose husbands are elders should say, "When my husband became an elder, he became a slave. But I am happy that the Lord has drafted him in such a heavenly way." When our concept has been thoroughly revolutionized, the shame of ambition for position will be slain.

In Matthew 23 the Lord Jesus said that among us there should be no teachers or leaders, but that we should all be brothers. But when the Apostle Paul refers to teachers and leaders, he does not mean kings or a hierarchy. Thus, both the Lord Jesus and the Apostle Paul spoke the same thing, and the Bible is not contradictory. I am thankful for Paul's word in 1 Corinthians 12:28 and for the Lord's word that those who take the lead should become slaves. Because ambition for position kills the kingdom life, we need to slay the concept of position and hierarchy.

VI. BLINDNESS NEEDING TO BE HEALED

In 20:29-34 we have a record of the healing of the two blind men. The fact that this incident immediately follows the record of the mother of James and John indicates that James and John were blind. They might have thought that they were following Christ, but actually they were on the wayside, for they had not yet seen the way. Instead of having a proper understanding of the Lord's crucifixion and resurrection, they were still seeking a position. Because they were blind, they needed to be healed.

According to the Old Testament, the healing of blindness is related to the millennium. The principle is the same in the New Testament. Acts 26:18 says, "To open their eyes, to turn them from darkness to light and from the authority of Satan to God." This indicates that the healing of blindness is for the kingdom. No one who is blind is on the way to the kingdom. Apparently James and John were on the way; actually, they were blind and on the wayside. Their eyes had not yet been opened to see the way of the cross.

In 20:17-34 we see three things: the unveiling of the cross and the resurrection, the disciples' poor response because of their ambition for position, and the healing of the two blind men. Anyone who is ambitious is blind. As long as we are ambitious, we are on the wayside and need healing. As soon as the two blind men received their sight, they followed the Lord on the way. This indicates that when we see the cross and the resurrection, we are on the way following the Lord. When the two blind men who had been healed began to follow the Lord Jesus, they were on the way, no longer on the wayside. It was from the time these two men were healed that James and John began to follow the Lord.

The Lord had asked them if they were able to drink of the cup which He was about to drink, and they said that they were able (20:22). The Lord's word here may be considered prophecy. To drink the cup of the cross means to become a martyr. James was the first of the twelve disciples to be martyred, and John was the last.

The cross and the resurrection mean a great deal to us, but the ambition for position must be crossed out. If we are ambitious, we are still blind and on the wayside; we are not on the way following Christ. Because we are blind, we need to be healed. We are not in the Lord's recovery to gain a position; we are here to follow Him to the cross. Instead of talking about the throne, we prefer to drink the cup of the cross, and we are ready to be martyred.

LIFE-STUDY OF MATTHEW

THE WARM WELCOME OF THE HEAVENLY KING, THE CLEANSING OF THE TEMPLE, AND THE CURSING OF THE FIG TREE

In this message we come to 21:1-22, where three matters are covered: the welcoming of the meek King (vv. 1-11); the cleansing of the temple (vv. 12-17); and the cursing of the fig tree (vv. 18-22).

Chapter sixteen is a crucial turning point in the Gospel of Matthew. Prior to this chapter, the Lord Jesus went to Jerusalem a number of times. But in chapter sixteen, He brought His disciples to the north, far away from Jerusalem, which was in the center of the Holy Land, in the territory of Benjamin. After chapter sixteen, the Lord gradually returned from the north to Jerusalem.

In 16:13—23:39 Matthew gives us a record of the pathway of the Lord's rejection. In this section we see the Lord's activities in various regions: before going to Judea (16:13—18:35); from Galilee to Judea (19:1—20:16); on the way to Jerusalem (20:17—21:11); and in Jerusalem (21:12—23:39). Thus, Matthew 21:1 says, "And when they drew near to Jerusalem and came to Bethphage, to the Mount of Olives." They began the journey from Galilee in 19:1. They were on the way in 20:17, and passed through Jericho in 20:29. Now in chapter twenty-one they have come to the Mount of Olives, which was just outside the city of Jerusalem, in a suburb of that city. This chapter marks the beginning of the Lord's last week on earth.

The Lord purposely went back to Jerusalem not to minister, preach, teach, or perform miracles, but to present Himself as the Lamb of God to be slaughtered, to be crucified.

I. A WARM WELCOME TO THE MEEK KING

A. The Coming of the Meek King

According to the four Gospels, the Lord Jesus did not do things to insure Himself a warm welcome. Instead, He was always prepared for rejection. But in 21:1-11 He made some preparations to be warmly welcomed.

1. Under the Lord's Sovereignty

The welcome given to the Lord here was carried out under His sovereignty. In verses 2 and 3, the Lord told two of His disciples, "Go into the village opposite you, and immediately you will find a donkey tied and a colt with her; loose them and lead them to Me. And if anyone says anything to you, you shall say, The Lord has need of them, and immediately he will send them." If I had been there, I would have said, "Lord, how do You know there will be a donkey tied there and a colt with her? And how do You know that the man will allow us to take them?" Here we see the Lord's omniscience and sovereignty. He wanted His disciples to know that He was the sovereign King who owned all things. Thus, the donkey and the colt belonged to Him. The Lord also indicated to them that He was omniscient, for He could see things clearly without physically being in a certain place. In exercising His authority as King, the Lord is both omniscient and sovereign.

2. Fulfilling the Prophecy

Verses 4 and 5 say, "Now this took place that what was spoken through the prophet might be fulfilled, saying, Say to the daughter of Zion, Behold, your King is coming to you, meek and mounted on a donkey and on a colt, the foal of a beast of burden." The way the King came into Jerusalem fulfilled the prophecy of Zechariah 9:9. The term "the daughter" of Zion in 21:5 means the people of Jerusalem (cf. Psa. 137:8; 45:12). This prophecy was being fulfilled to them.

3. On a Donkey and on a Colt

Verse 5 says that the King came "mounted on a donkey and on a colt, the foal of a beast of burden." This signifies the meek and lowly state in which the Lord was willing to present Himself. The Lord did not tell His disciples to get a carriage or a wagon, but a donkey and a colt. He did not even choose to ride on a horse, but on a little donkey. I have spent considerable time to find out why the Lord was mounted on a donkey and a colt. Was He riding on the donkey or on the colt? Why did the Lord Jesus need both the donkey and a colt, a baby donkey? The colt must have been a baby donkey because it is called a foal of a beast of burden, and this beast of burden must have been a donkey. The donkey was probably the mother, and the colt was probably her offspring. Both the mother and the offspring worked together to bear the King, for He was mounted on both the donkey and the colt. Perhaps the Lord rode upon the donkey first and shifted to the colt when He was close to the city. Mark and Luke mention only the colt, not the donkey (Mark 11:1-10; Luke 19:29-38), whereas John speaks of a young donkey, a donkey's colt (John 12:14-15). Thus, the emphasis of the four Gospels seems to be on the colt.

The donkey and the colt together give us an impression of meekness and humility. If the Lord has been mounted only upon a donkey, the impression of meekness would not have been so striking. Suppose a very small sister stands before us holding a tiny baby in her arms. This would give us a deep impression of smallness, for the tiny baby would strengthen the impression of smallness. The significance of the Lord's riding on a donkey is not smallness, but meekness. The heavenly King came not with haughty splendor, but with gentle, humble meekness. This impression of meekness is strengthened by the colt accompanying a donkey to bear the meek King. The Lord Jesus did not ride into Jerusalem proudly on a horse. He came mounted upon a little donkey, even a small colt. No earthly king would do this. The Lord Jesus seemed to be telling His disciples, "Take the donkey and the little colt. I shall ride upon the beast of burden, but the colt must go along too in order to show My meekness. This will help the people see how meek the heavenly King is."

The Lord Jesus came not to fight or to compete, but to be a meek King. The presence of the baby donkey testified that the Lord did not care to fight or compete with anyone. Rather, He was humble and meek. I believe that this was the impression the Lord Jesus wanted to convey to the people. Yes, He was the heavenly King, but He had no intention to come as a great King fighting or competing with others. Instead, He came as a meek King who did not fight against anyone or compete with anyone.

B. The Warm Welcome of the Crowds

1. Spreading Their Garments on the Road

In verse 7 we see that the disciples put their garments on the donkey and the colt, and verse 8 says, "And most of the crowd spread their own garments in the road." Garments signify the human virtues of people's conduct. The disciples honored the lowly King by putting their garments on the donkey and colt for Him to ride on, and the crowd honored Him by spreading their garments in the road for Him to pass through. The people honored the Lord with their clothing, that is, with whatever they had. No matter how poor a man is, he at least has some clothing with which to cover himself. We need to honor the Lord, the meek King, with whatever we are. No matter what our condition may be, we have something with which to honor Him. I do not believe that the garments put on the donkey and on the road were splendid or beautiful. Nevertheless, the people used what they had. Although we are sinful, pitiful, and even evil, the Lord likes to be honored with what we are. Even sinners can honor the Lord with what they are, if they have a heart to honor Him.

2. Spreading Palm Branches in the Road

Verse 8 also says, "Others cut branches from the trees and spread them in the road." The branches are the branches of the palm tree (John 12:13), signifying the victorious life (Rev. 7:9) and the satisfaction of enjoying the rich produce of this life as typified by the feast of tabernacles (Lev. 23:40; Neh. 8:15). The crowd used both their garments and the palm tree branches to celebrate the lowly King's coming. A palm tree, signifying the victorious life, is rooted deeply in hidden springs and grows prevailingly upward into the air. This signifies the victorious life. In honoring the meek King with whatever they were, the people recognized that He was the One with the victorious life.

3. Crying Hosanna to the Son of David

Verse 9 says, "And the crowds who went before Him and those who followed cried out, saying, Hosanna to the Son of David; Blessed is He Who comes in the name of the Lord; Hosanna in the highest!" The Hebrew word Hosanna means "save now" (Psa. 118:25). The title "the Son of David" was the royal title of the lowly King. In the warm welcome of the heavenly King, the people shouted out a quotation from Psalm 118: "Blessed is He Who comes in the name of the Lord" (v. 26). According to Psalm 118, only the One who came in the name of the Lord was qualified to be praised in such a way. Thus, the spontaneous praise of the people sovereignly indicated that this meek King came not in His own name, but in the name of Jehovah. Those who welcomed the King indicated through their praise that He was the One sent by the Lord, thus the One who came in the name of the Lord.

4. Still Knowing Him as the Prophet from Nazareth of Galilee

When the heavenly King entered into Jerusalem, the whole city was stirred up, but the crowd still said, "This is the prophet Jesus, who is from Nazareth of Galilee"

(v. 11). On the one hand, the crowds praised Him as the Son of David, the One who comes in the name of the Lord; on the other hand, some still recognized Him in a natural way as a prophet from a despised city.

II. CLEANSING THE TEMPLE

Verse 12 says, "And Jesus entered into the temple and cast out all those who were selling and buying in the temple, and He overturned the tables of the money-changers and the seats of those who were selling the doves." When the Lord entered the city of Jerusalem, the first thing He did was cleanse the temple. Any earthly king, upon entering the capital, would immediately have ascended to the throne. But the Lord did not do this because He was not for His own interests, but for God's interests. His heart was not for His kingdom, but for God's house.

It is the same in principle with us today. When we welcome the Lord into us as our King, He does not go immediately to the throne; rather, He goes to our spirit and cleanses it. Many of us have experienced this. When we received the Lord as life, we also received Him as the King. On the day He came into us to be our life and our King, He did not enthrone Himself, but cleansed God's temple, which today is our spirit, the habitation of God (Eph. 2:22).

A. Cleansing, Healing, and Praising

Our spirit should be a house of prayer, but because of the fall it has been made a den of robbers. But when Jesus comes into us He drives all the robbers away and cleanses the temple of our spirit. After the cleansing, the Lord healed the blind and the lame in the temple (v. 14). This indicates that His cleansing of the temple causes people to have the sight to see and the strength to move. It is the same with us today. Verse 15 says that the children were "crying out in the temple and saying, Hosanna to the Son of David." At least a few times the Gospel of Matthew mentions children, for this book stresses that the kingdom people need to become as children. Only those who have become children will praise God. This was after the healing of the blind and the lame. When our blindness and lameness are healed, we also shall praise the Lord as little children.

B. The Religious People Being Offended

The stubborn chief priests and scribes were indignant, even after they saw the wonders the lowly King performed. Their indignation was due to their pride and jealousy, which blinded them from seeing any vision concerning the heavenly King.

C. The Heavenly King Staying Away from Jerusalem to Lodge in Bethany

Verse 17 says, "And leaving them, He went out of the city to Bethany and lodged there." In His last visit to Jerusalem, the Lord remained there only during the day for His ministry. Every evening He departed to lodge in Bethany, on the eastern slope of the Mount of Olives (Mark 11:19; Luke 21:37), where the house of Mary, Martha, and Lazarus and the house of Simon were (John 11:1; Matt. 26:6). In Jerusalem He was rejected by the leaders of Judaism, but in Bethany He was welcomed by His lovers.

After the Lord Jesus comes into us and cleanses our spirit, we may sense that He leaves us, just as He left Jerusalem for Bethany after cleansing the temple. The Lord may come into you, cleanse your spirit, which is the temple of God, and leave for another place. Perhaps you will say, "This is not my experience. My experience is that after the Lord Jesus has cleansed my spirit, He stays with me." If this is your experience, then you must be one of the lovers of Jesus like Mary, Martha, Lazarus, or Simon. However, after many Christians receive Christ into them and experience His cleansing of their spirit, they do not love Him.

Thus, in their experience the Lord leaves them to lodge in another place, a place called Bethany.

According to the New Testament, Bethany is the place of the Lord's lovers. In the New Testament we read of two houses in Bethany: the house of Mary, Martha, and Lazarus and the house of Simon the leper. All these dear ones were lovers of the Lord Jesus. During the last week of His life on earth, He went every day into Jerusalem, but every night He went out of Jerusalem and lodged in Bethany. Jerusalem was the place where He was examined, tested, and slaughtered; but Bethany was His lodging place.

In a very definite sense, today's religion is a Jerusalem to the Lord Jesus; it is not His lodging place. The lovers of Christ are not in Jerusalem, but in Bethany. Are you in Jerusalem or in Bethany? We should not be the Jerusalem people, but the Bethany lovers. If you are among the Jerusalem people, Jesus will come to be tested and examined by you. But if you are among His lovers in Bethany, He will come to lodge with you. If the Lord Jesus comes into you and cleanses your spirit, yet you still do not love Him, it means that you remain among the Jerusalem people. You are not one of the Bethany lovers. Although He cleanses the temple in Jerusalem, He does not lodge there. Rather, He goes out of the city to lodge in Bethany. How meaningful this is!

III. CURSING THE FIG TREE

A. Christ Being Hungry

Verse 18 says, "Now in the morning as He returned into the city, He was hungry." This signified that the Lord was hungry for fruit from the children of Israel that God might be satisfied.

B. The Fig Tree — the Nation of Israel — Having Leaves but No Fruit

Verse 19 says, "And seeing one fig tree on the way, He came to it and found nothing on it but leaves only." Just as the eagle is a symbol of the United States, so the fig tree here is a symbol of the nation of Israel (Jer. 24:2, 5, 8). The fig tree the Lord saw was full of leaves but fruitless, signifying that at that time the nation of Israel was full of outward show, but had nothing that could satisfy God. According to the Bible, leaves are an outward show, but the fruit is something real and solid to satisfy God and man. At that time, the Lord Jesus came from God to Israel hungry for some fruit to satisfy God's hunger. However, instead of fruit, He found only leaves.

C. The Fig Tree Being Cursed

Verse 19 also says, "And He says to it, Let there no longer be fruit from you forever. And the fig tree was instantly dried up." This signifies the curse on the nation of Israel. From that time, the nation of Israel was truly dried up. According to history, from the last few days the Lord Jesus was on earth, there has been a curse upon the nation of Israel. As we shall see, the fig tree is mentioned again in chapter twenty-four, where the fig tree signifies the restoration of Israel, which took place in 1948.

According to our experience, we can testify that first the meek King comes into us, and we welcome Him. However, He comes in not to be enthroned, but to cleanse the temple of God, because He cares for God's house. Caring also for God's satisfaction, He desires fruit from God's people. But most of His people cannot afford Him any fruit. As a result, they are dried up. Many of us have experienced this. The meek King came into us, we welcomed Him, and He cleansed the temple of God. But because we did not bear fruit, we were dried up. Perhaps you will say, "Isn't the Lord merciful and gracious? Since He is merciful and gracious, how could He curse us in such a way?" Nevertheless, when we do not bear fruit, we are dried up.

Most Christians today have become dried up. Although they have welcomed the heavenly King and He has cleansed their temple, they have no fruit for God's satisfaction, and thus they are dried up. How many Christians today are living and bearing fruit? Very few. Whenever someone is dried up, his spirit does not function. Hence, there is no temple and no fruit, no proper worship and no satisfaction to God.

The concern of the meek King is for God's house and God's satisfaction. He cleanses us that we may offer proper worship to God, and He deals with us that we may bear fruit for God's satisfaction. In the practical kingdom life in the church today, Christ must be welcomed as the King. Then He must cleanse God's temple, that is, He must purify our spirit. Then we, as the kingdom people, shall bear fruit for God's satisfaction. Otherwise, we shall be cursed until the day of restoration. This was the situation with the nation of Israel when the Lord was on earth, and it is the situation among Christians today. Because the nation of Israel was dried up, the kingdom was taken away from them and given to another people. If we are not cleansed in our spirit to offer God the proper worship and to bear fruit for His satisfaction, the kingdom will also be taken away from us and given to others.

D. The Frustrating Mountain
Removed by Believing Prayer

Verses 20 through 22 indicate that the Lord cursed the fig tree by faith. Faith can move the frustrating mountain through believing prayer.

LIFE-STUDY OF MATTHEW

THE HEAVENLY KING BEING TESTED

(1)

I. IN THE LAST WEEK OF HIS LIFE ON EARTH

The events in chapter twenty-one took place during the last week of the Lord's life on earth (John 12:1). In this period of time He willingly presented Himself to the children of Israel for a thorough examination.

II. AS THE PASSOVER LAMB
BEING EXAMINED BEFORE THE PASSOVER

We have seen that the last time the Lord Jesus came to Jerusalem He came not to work, but to present Himself to those who were to slaughter Him. In 21:23—22:46 the Lord was tested and examined. According to Exodus 12, the passover lamb had to be examined four full days. In the Jewish calendar, four days could also be considered six days, for part of a day was counted as one day. Thus, Matthew says that Christ ascended the Mount of Transfiguration after six days, but Luke says that He did so after eight days (Matt. 17:1; Luke 9:28). During the last week of His life, Christ was examined for six days. Then He was crucified on the day of the Passover. This indicates that He was the real Passover Lamb; the lamb in Exodus 12 was a type.

III. BY THE CHIEF PRIESTS AND ELDERS
OF THE PEOPLE

A. Asking Him about the Source of His Authority

First the Lord was examined by the chief priests and the elders. Matthew 21:23 says, "And as He came into the temple, the chief priests and elders of the people came to Him as He was teaching and said, By what authority are you doing these things? And who gave you this authority?" The chief priests represented the religious power, and the elders represented the civilian power. These two powers came together to test Christ, who was standing before them as the Passover Lamb to be examined by the children of Israel. These Jewish leaders asked the Lord where He had received His authority and who had given it to Him. The Lord Jesus did not answer them directly, but with another question.

B. Christ Asking Them about the Baptism of John

In verse 24 we see the Lord's answer: "I also will ask you one question, which if you tell Me, I also will tell you by what authority I do these things: The baptism of John, whence was it? From heaven or from men?" This was a difficult question for the chief priests and elders to answer. If they had said that John's baptism was from heaven, the Lord would have asked them why they did not believe him. But because they were afraid of the crowds, who regarded John as a prophet, they did not dare to say that it was from men.

C. The Chief Priests and Elders Lying to Him

The chief priests and elders told the Lord Jesus that they did not know whether John's baptism was from heaven or from men (v. 27). Their answer was a lie. Children often lie by saying that they do not know. This is the best way for them to escape an accusation. The children are not taught to lie in this way; they do it naturally. Thus, the chief priests and the elders were like children who lie by saying that they do not know.

D. The Lord Answering Them, Exposing Their Lie, and Avoiding Their Question

Verse 27 says, "He also said to them, Neither do I tell you by what authority I do these things." This indicated that the Lord knew the Jewish leaders would not tell Him what they knew; hence, neither would He tell them what they asked. They lied to the Lord in saying that they did not know. But the Lord spoke the truth wisely to them, exposing their lie and avoiding their question. In this way, the Lord Jesus passed the first test, and no defect was found in Him.

E. The Parable of Two Sons

After the Lord Jesus had dealt with the chief priests and elders in such a wise manner, He gave them a parable about a man who had two children (vv. 28-32). The man told the first child to work in the vineyard. At first the child refused, but later he regretted it and went. The man told the second child to do the same. But after saying that he would go, he eventually did not go. The Lord Jesus then asked His hearers which of the two did the will of the father. When they said the first, the Lord said to them, "Truly I say to you, that the tax collectors and the prostitutes are going into the kingdom of God before you" (v. 31).

In Luke 15:1-2, 11-32, the Lord likened the leaders of Judaism to the firstborn son, and the tax collectors and sinners to the second son; but here the Lord likened them in the opposite order. This indicates that the Jews were the firstborn of God (Exo. 4:22), having the birthright, but due to their unbelief the birthright was shifted to the church, which has become God's firstborn (Heb. 12:23). Thus, the Lord's word here implies a shifting of the birthright. In God's economy the birthright was taken from Israel and given to another people, a people composed of saved sinners and tax collectors. This means that the birthright of God has been transferred from Israel to the church.

Verse 32 says, "For John came to you in the way of righteousness, and you did not believe him; but the tax collectors and the prostitutes believed him; and you, when you saw it, did not later regret it so as to believe him." The Lord seemed to be saying, "You chief priests and elders are the second sons. Apparently you obey God, but actually you disobey Him. In the eyes of God, the sinners, tax collectors, and prostitutes are much better than you, because they received the preaching of John the Baptist. Because they received John's way of righteousness, they will enter into the kingdom of the heavens, but you will be shut out." This means that the birthright was taken from Israel and given to the saved, repentant, and forgiven sinners who constitute the church.

Verse 32 speaks of the way of righteousness. The Gospel of Matthew, as the book on the kingdom, stresses the matter of righteousness, for the kingdom life is one of strict righteousness, after which we must seek (5:20, 6; 6:33). John the Baptist came in the way of such righteousness, and the Lord Jesus was willing to be baptized by John to fulfill such righteousness (3:15).

F. The Parable of the Vineyard

1. A Householder Planting a Vineyard and Leasing It to Husbandmen

In verses 33 through 46 the Lord continues with another parable concerning the transfer of the kingdom of God. Verse 33 says, "There was a man, a householder, who planted a vineyard and put a hedge around it, and dug a winepress in it, and built a tower, and leased it out to husbandmen, and went into another country." The householder is God, the vineyard is the city of Jerusalem (Isa. 5:1), and the husbandmen are the leaders of the Israelites (21:45).

2. The Householder Sending His Slaves Again and Again to Receive Fruits, but the Husbandmen Flogging and Killing Them

When the householder sent his slaves to the husbandmen to receive his fruits, the husbandmen flogged them and killed them (vv. 34-36). These slaves were the prophets sent by God (2 Chron. 24:19; 36:15). The flogging, killing, and stoning mentioned in verse 35 were the persecutions suffered by the Old Testament prophets (Jer. 37:15; Neh. 9:26; 2 Chron. 24:21).

3. The Householder Later Sending His Son but the Husbandmen Casting Him Out of the Vineyard and Killing Him

Later, the householder sent his son. The son, of course, was Christ. When the husbandmen saw the son, they said, "This is the heir; come, let us kill him and possess his inheritance" (v. 38). This word indicates that the Jewish leaders were jealous of Christ's rights and wanted to maintain their false position. Thus, "they took him and cast him out of the vineyard and killed him" (v. 39). This refers to Christ's being killed outside the city of Jerusalem (Heb. 13:12).

4. The Householder Destroying the Evil Husbandmen and Leasing the Vineyard to Other Husbandmen

Verses 40 and 41 say, "When therefore the lord of the vineyard comes, what will he do to those husbandmen? They say to Him, He will miserably destroy those evil men, and will leave the vineyard to other husbandmen, who will render the fruits to him in their seasons." Verse 41 was fulfilled when the Roman prince, Titus, and his army destroyed Jerusalem in A.D. 70. The other husbandmen spoken of in this verse were the Apostles.

5. Christ as the Cornerstone Rejected by the Jewish Builders

In verse 42 the Lord Jesus says, "Have you never read in the Scriptures, The stone which the builders rejected, this has become the cornerstone; this was from the Lord, and it is marvelous in our eyes?" The stone here is Christ for God's building (Isa. 28:16; Zech. 3:9; 1 Pet. 2:4), and the builders are the Jewish leaders, who were supposed to work on God's building. In this verse the Lord said that the stone rejected by the builders has become the cornerstone (Gk., the head of the corner). Christ is not only the foundation stone (Isa. 28:16) and the topstone (Zech. 4:7), but also the cornerstone.

6. The Kingdom of God Having Been Taken from the Jews and Given to the Church

Verse 43 says, "Therefore I say to you that the kingdom of God shall be taken from you and shall be given to a nation producing the fruits of it." The kingdom of God was already there with the Israelites, whereas the kingdom of the heavens had only drawn near (3:2; 4:17). This proves that the kingdom of the heavens is different from the kingdom of God. In this verse the Lord says that the kingdom of God will be given to another nation, which is the church.

7. The Jews Stumbling at Christ and Being Broken to Pieces

The first part of verse 44 says, "And he who falls on this stone shall be broken to pieces." This refers to the Jews who stumbled at Christ and were broken to pieces (Isa. 8:15; Rom. 9:32).

8. Christ as God's Building Stone to Fall on the Gentile Nations

The last part of verse 44 says, "But on whomever it falls, it shall scatter him as chaff." This refers to the nations which Christ will smite at His coming back (Dan. 2:34-35). To the believers, Christ is the foundation stone in whom they trust (Isa. 28:16); to the unbelieving Jews, He is the stumbling stone (Isa. 8:14; Rom. 9:33); and to the nations, He will be the smiting stone.

At the end of this parable, the Lord Jesus not only indicated that the kingdom would be taken from Israel and given to the church; He also referred to God's building. Very few Christians today are clear about God's building. Although you may have been in Christianity for years and may have heard that Christ was the Son of God, the Savior, the Redeemer, and perhaps even your life, you probably never heard that Christ is also God's building stone. As we have pointed out, He was the stone rejected by the builders. The Jewish leaders must have been shocked to hear that Christ was a stone. In talking with them concerning the vineyard, indicating thereby that He was the son of the owner of the vineyard, Christ eventually referred to Himself as the stone rejected by the builders. Today, hardly any Christians have the concept that our Savior is a stone for God's building.

In Acts 4:10 and 11 Peter referred to Jesus Christ of Nazareth as the stone rejected by the builders. Then in verse 12 he said, "And there is no salvation in any other; for neither is there another name under heaven given among men in which we must be saved." Christians often use Acts 4:12 in preaching the gospel, but rarely, if ever, do they tell people that Christ is not only the Savior but also the stone. That our Savior is a stone reveals the fact that God's salvation is for God's building. The Savior is related to salvation, and the stone is related to building. But today's Christians have not seen this matter adequately. God's intention on earth is not simply to have a vineyard — it is to have a building. In the ancient times the nation of Israel was a vineyard; however, today the church is not merely a vineyard, but also a building. The church is a farm that produces materials for God's building (1 Cor. 3:9). Whatever this farm grows is for the building. Although this matter has been missed by both Jews and Christians, the light has come to us in these last days so that this truth may be recovered. We have come to know that Christ is not only the Savior, but also the stone.

In the life-study of Revelation, we saw that Christ is the Lion-Lamb-stone. He is the Lion for victory, the Lamb for redemption, and the stone for building. In a sense, both Jews and Christians see the matter of redemption. However, they have not progressed to see the building. Christians today simply do not realize that Christ is a stone. In verse 42 the Lord said that the stone, not the Savior, would be rejected by the builders. Eventually, in resurrection, this rejected stone became the cornerstone. This is seen clearly in Acts 4, a chapter dealing with the resurrection of Christ.

The cornerstone is the stone that joins the walls. As the cornerstone, Christ connects the Jews and the Gentiles. Through Christ as the cornerstone the Jewish believers and the Gentile believers are brought together as one building for God. Thus, Christ is not only the foundation stone to support the building, but also the cornerstone to join the two main walls.

In verse 44 we see that Christ is not only the building stone, but also the stumbling stone. Whoever falls on this stone will be broken to pieces. In Romans 9:32 Paul says that the Jews "stumbled at the Stone of stumbling." The Jews that have rejected the Lord Jesus have fallen upon this stone and have been broken to pieces.

In verse 44 the Lord also says that this stone will fall on certain ones and scatter them as chaff. Thus, the Lord is also a smiting and scattering stone to the Gentiles. Daniel 2:34 and 35 say, "Thou sawest till that a stone was cut out without hands, which smote the image upon his feet that were of iron and clay, and brake them to pieces. Then was the iron, the clay, the brass, the silver, and the gold, broken to pieces together, and became like the chaff of the summer threshingfloors." These verses indicate that when Christ comes the second time, He will be a stone cut without hands falling from the heavens upon the great image. Daniel 2:35 also says, "The stone that smote the image became a great mountain, and filled the whole earth." The great image signifies the worldly powers from Babylon down to the ten kingdoms of the restored Roman Empire, which will exist at the time of Christ's coming back. Christ will be the smiting stone that will scatter all the broken nations as chaff. Then He will become a great mountain, that is, the kingdom of God on earth.

Therefore, Christ is a stone to three categories of

people: for the believers, He is the building stone; for the rejecting Jews, He is the stumbling stone; and for the Gentiles, He is the smiting stone. If you believe in Him, He will be to you the building stone. If you are a Jew and reject Him and are stumbled by Him, you will experience Him as the stumbling stone and be broken to pieces. If you are an unbelieving Gentile fighting against God, you will know Him one day as the smiting stone, for He will smite you and scatter you like chaff driven by the wind.

As a believer, Christ to you is a building stone. But how much building have you actually experienced? Although we are believers and although Christ is the building stone, we may not have very much building. Some genuine believers have even stumbled at Christ. On the one hand, they believe in Christ; but on the other hand, they say that they cannot take the way of Christ, and they shake their head at Him. In other words, they were stumbled at Him. Thus, instead of being built up by Christ, they have been stumbled by Him. Furthermore, some true believers have been smitten by Christ and blown away like chaff. It is rare to find genuine believers who are truly being built together. Such a building cannot be found in today's Christianity. If you look for it in Catholicism, you will find abominations and fornication instead of building. Neither can the building be found in the denominations. On the contrary, today's Christianity is full of stumbling and breaking. Yes, many have been brought to the Lord in Catholicism and in the denominations. But after they were brought to the Lord, they were spoiled. Instead of being built, they were stumbled or smitten.

We need to examine ourselves and ask how much of the building there is among us. Matthew was the only one among the four writers of the Gospels to give us a clear record of Christ as the stone. His record is complete. In no other portion of the Bible can we find Christ presented as a stone in three aspects: the building stone, the stumbling stone, and the smiting stone. All three aspects are found in Matthew for the kingdom.

The church is the life-pulse of the kingdom. This means
that just as the body dies when the pulse stops, so the kingdom is wholly dependent upon the church. The church, in
turn, is completely dependent upon the building. If there is
no building, there is no practical church life. The church
life is not simply a matter of meeting together or of having
a little fellowship. In whatever locality we are, we need to
be builded. For this, we must enjoy and experience our
Christ as the stone. He is not only the foundation stone
that bears us up, but also the cornerstone that joins us
together. In Him and through Him we are built together.

Apart from such a building the church is vain, and
without the church the kingdom has no life. The church is
the kingdom life, and the reality of the church is the building. How we need to experience Christ as the building
stone! He is the building element, the building life. Christ
is life to us not only for victory, but all the more for building. The inner life people have spoken a great deal about
Christ as the victorious life. But I never heard any one of
them give a message saying that Christ is the building life.
He is not only the victorious life, but also the building life.
If you simply experience victory through Christ as life,
your experience is not yet adequate. You must go on to
experience the building life of Christ. Ultimately, Christ as
life within us is for God's building. You may be victorious,
but still not be built. We need to be built. When we
are built, we shall have the reality of the church life, and
the church will be the life-pulse of the kingdom. Then the
kingdom will be here in actuality.

To repeat, the actuality of the kingdom is the church,
and the reality of the church is the kingdom. In other
words, the kingdom depends upon the church, and the
church depends upon the building. We need to consider to
what extent we have experienced Christ as the building
stone. I believe that in the days to come the Lord will show
us much more concerning the building. This building is
closely related to the new man. On the one hand, the new
man has been created, but on the other hand, the new man

is being built. In order to have this new man, we need to experience Christ as the building stone.

9. The Jewish Leaders
Seeking to Seize the Heavenly King

After such a marvelous revelation, the Jewish leaders sought to seize the heavenly King that they might kill Him (vv. 45-46). This indicated that they, as the builders, fully rejected Christ as God's building stone.

LIFE-STUDY OF MATTHEW

THE HEAVENLY KING BEING TESTED

(2)

In this message we come to 22:1-14, the parable of the marriage feast. This parable is the continuation of the Lord's answer to the chief priests and elders of the people. In His answer to their question regarding His authority, He spoke three parables: the parable of the shifting of the birthright, the parable of the vineyard, and the parable of the marriage feast. The parable of the shifting of the birthright reveals that the birthright, which had belonged to the nation of Israel, has been taken away and given to the church. The parable of the vineyard indicates that the kingdom of God was about to be taken away from Israel and given to the church. Thus, these two parables are parallel to each other. If you do not have the birthright, you cannot participate in the kingdom. By this we see that the birthright and the kingdom go together. These first two parables refer to Israel on the negative side, for both the birthright and the kingdom were taken away from Israel.

If the Lord's answer had stopped here, it would have been imcomplete. It would have dealt only with the negative side and had no positive issue. As we come to the end of chapter twenty-one, we have the realization that there must be something more. Therefore, after the first two parables, the Lord added the parable of the marriage feast as the completion of His answer. In giving this parable, He turned from the negative side to the positive side.

G. The Parable of the Marriage Feast

1. A King Making a Marriage Feast for His Son

Matthew 22:2 says, "The kingdom of the heavens was likened to a man, a king, who made a marriage feast for his son." The parable of the vineyard in chapter twenty-one refers to the Old Testament, in which there was the kingdom of God (21:43), whereas the parable of the marriage feast in this chapter refers to the New Testament, in which there is the kingdom of the heavens. The king here is God, and the son is Christ.

In the foregoing parable (21:33-46), the Lord illustrated how the Jews would be punished, and how the kingdom of God would be taken from them and given to the kingdom people. Another parable is needed for Him to illustrate how the kingdom people in the kingdom of the heavens will be strictly dealt with. Both parables indicate that the kingdom is a serious matter.

In the foregoing parable, the Old Testament was likened to a vineyard, with the focus mainly on the matter of labor under the law; in this parable, the New Testament is likened to a marriage feast, with the focus mainly on the matter of enjoyment under grace. The vineyard is not mainly for enjoyment, but for labor. But in a marriage feast there is no labor. Instead, there is full enjoyment. No one attends a marriage feast for the purpose of laboring; all attend for enjoyment. Thus, the parable of the vineyard depicts labor under the law, and the parable of the marriage feast depicts enjoyment under grace. We in the Lord's recovery are not laboring under law, but are enjoying under grace. What a contrast between these two parables! Today, we are not under law, but under grace. We are not laboring, but enjoying. This is the basic principle in understanding these parables.

2. The King Sending His Slaves Again and Again to Call Those Invited to the Marriage Feast

Verse 3 says, "And he sent his slaves to call those who

were invited to the marriage feast, and they would not come." The slaves mentioned in this verse are the first group of the New Testament apostles. Verse 4 continues, "Again he sent other slaves, saying, Tell those who were invited, Behold, I have prepared my dinner; my oxen and my fatted beasts are killed, and all things are ready; come to the marriage feast." The slaves here are the apostles sent later by the Lord. This verse speaks of oxen and fatted beasts, both of which refer to Christ as the One killed that God's chosen people might enjoy Him as a feast. Christ has many aspects for our enjoyment. As the oxen and the fatted beasts, He has been killed and prepared for our enjoyment. Although everything had been prepared and although the slaves went out again and again, the people refused to come, even laying hold of the slaves, treating them shamefully, and killing them (vv. 5-6).

3. The King Sending His Troops to Destroy the Murderers and Burn Their City

Verse 7 says, "And the king was angry; and he sent his troops and destroyed those murderers and burned their city." These were the Roman troops under Titus which destroyed Jerusalem in A.D. 70. The fact that the troops here are described as the king's troops indicates that all the armies on earth are the Lord's. Thus, the army of the Roman Empire was actually God's army. God sent the Roman army as His forces to accomplish His purpose to destroy Jerusalem.

During the transitory period between the Old Testament and the New Testament, the old and the new overlapped. In the parable of the vineyard, the owner destroyed the evil men because they rejected, persecuted, and killed his servants. They even killed Jesus Christ, the Son of God. The parable of the marriage feast says that God will destroy the city because, after killing Christ, they also killed the apostles sent to invite them to the marriage feast. God did not destroy them immediately after they had killed the Son of God. By killing Him they helped to prepare the fatted beasts for the feast. But after the apostles had been rejected and killed, the Lord sent the Roman army under Titus to destroy the city of Jerusalem. Titus was cruel and merciless, tearing down the temple and burning the city. As the Lord Jesus had said, not one stone of the temple was left upon another. Furthermore, Titus killed a large number of Jews, the leaders in particular. This was the complete fulfillment of the Lord's prophecy in this parable.

4. The King Sending His Slaves to the Thoroughfare to Call People to the Marriage Feast

After the destruction of Jerusalem, God turned from the Jews to the Gentile world. Verses 8 and 9 say, "Then he says to his slaves, The marriage feast is ready but those who were invited were not worthy. Go therefore to the thoroughfares, and as many as you find, call to the marriage feast." Because of the Jews' rejection of the gospel, they were not worthy of the enjoyment of the New Testament (Acts 13:46). Therefore, the preaching of the New Testament was turned to the Gentiles (Acts 13:46; Rom. 11:11). Here the Gentile world is signified by the thoroughfares. Throughout the centuries, the preaching of the gospel in the Gentile world has been successful, although there has been some opposition and rejection.

5. Many, Both Evil and Good, Coming to the Marriage Feast

Verse 10 says, "And those slaves went out into the streets and gathered together all whom they found, both evil and good; and the marriage feast was filled with those reclining at the table." Because the proclamation was so prevailing, the marriage feast was filled with the called and invited ones.

6. A Man Being Found Not Clothed
with the Marriage Garment

Verse 11 says, "But when the king came in and beheld those reclining at the table, he saw there a man not clothed with a marriage garment." The man without a marriage garment must surely have been a saved one. How could anyone answer God's calling, yet not be saved? As long as we have answered God's calling, we have been saved. In verse 14 the Lord Jesus speaks of many being called, and in Ephesians 4:1 Paul points out that we, the saved ones, are the called ones. We have been called to be saved. Although the man in verse 11 was called and saved, he nevertheless lacked the marriage garment.

This marriage garment is typified by the raiment of embroidery in Psalm 45:14 and signified by the fine linen in Revelation 19:8. This is the surpassing righteousness of the overcoming believers in Matthew 5:20. The man not clothed with a marriage garment is saved, because he has come to the marriage feast. He has received Christ as his righteousness that he might be justified before God (Phil. 3:9; 1 Cor. 1:30; Rom. 3:26), but he has not lived Christ out as his subjective righteousness that he might participate in the enjoyment of the kingdom of the heavens. He has been called to salvation, but he is not chosen for the enjoyment of the kingdom of the heavens, which is only for the overcoming believers.

The wedding garment signifies our qualification to participate in the marriage feast. The New Testament mentions this feast at least twice, in Matthew 22 and in Revelation 19. According to Revelation 19, those invited to the marriage feast are clothed in white linen. The white linen in Revelation 19 is the marriage garment in Matthew 22. This white linen signifies the surpassing righteousness. Matthew 5:20 says, "For I say to you, that unless your righteousness surpass that of the scribes and Pharisees, you shall by no means enter into the kingdom of the heavens." This surpassing righteousness which qualifies us to participate in the manifestation of the kingdom in the coming age is typified in Psalm 45, where we are told that the queen has two garments. We, the believers, should also have two garments. We all have the first garment, the garment that qualifies us to be saved. This garment is the objective Christ whom we received as our righteousness before God. In Christ, who is our righteousness, we have been justified and saved. But after receiving Christ, we need to live Him out. We need to live by Christ so that Christ may become our subjective righteousness. This subjective righteousness, Christ lived out of us in our daily life, is the white linen, the second garment, the marriage garment that qualifies us to participate in the marriage feast.

In the parable of the vineyard, the Lord was strict with the husbandmen, requiring that their labor reach a certain standard. We need to drop the idea that because we are under grace the Lord is not strict with us. Many misunderstand the Lord and misuse His grace. Most Christians think that the Lord is not strict with us and that as long as we have His grace, everything is all right. However, the Lord is more strict with those who are under grace. Both the parable of the vineyard and the parable of the marriage feast reveal the strictness of the Lord in dealing with His people, whether Jews under the law or believers under grace. Do not think that because we have been invited to the marriage feast, we can afford to be careless. On the contrary, the Lord may come into the feast and pick you out as one not having the second garment. Yes, you have received Christ as your righteousness to be justified before God. But are you living by Christ? Is He your subjective righteousness?

The requirements of the second garment are strict, more than a matter of keeping a few commandments or regulations. Rather, day by day we need to live by Christ and live out Christ. This is not a matter of doing, but of living. In the New Testament economy, God does not mainly deal with our doings, but with our living, by whom and by what way we live. The small things in our daily living expose whether or not we live by Christ. It is easy to grasp the doctrine that we have been crucified with Christ, that we live no longer, and that Christ lives in us. But do we experience this as a reality in our daily life? Whenever we are careless in our daily living, we are not living by Christ. If we live in a loose, careless manner, we are not those with the marriage garment.

There is no problem regarding our salvation, for we have been called and justified. But what will be your situation before the judgment seat of Christ? Will you be qualified to enter the marriage feast? If you believe the first part of the gospel, then you must also believe the second part. How we need to look to the Lord for His mercy! We need to pray, "Lord, have mercy on me. I have received You, Lord, but I need more grace to live by You. Lord, because You are my Savior, I know that I am eternally saved. But I need Your grace that I may live by You as my life." We need to speak by Christ, and even our anger must be according to Christ. When we are about to lose our temper, we should consider whether or not we are losing our temper by Christ. If we do this, we shall have a proper Christian living by Christ.

The second garment has been neglected by today's Christians. Martin Luther helped us to know the first garment, Christ as righteousness for us to be justified by God. This truth was recovered more than four hundred years ago. But in the Lord's recovery today we have come to the second garment. We need both the objective and subjective righteousness. This is an important matter in the Gospel of Matthew, for it is a requirement of the kingdom.

7. The Man without the Marriage Garment Being Cast Out into the Outer Darkness

Verses 12 and 13 say, "Friend, how did you come in here not having a marriage garment? And he was speechless. Then the king said to the servants, Bind his feet and hands, and cast him out into the outer darkness; there shall be the weeping and the gnashing of teeth." The servants mentioned in verse 13 must be angels (13:41, 49). To be cast out into the outer darkness is not to perish; it is to be dealt with dispensationally for not having lived an overcoming life by Christ to qualify for participation in the enjoyment of the kingdom during the millennium. At that time, the overcoming believers will be with Christ in the bright glory of the kingdom (Col. 3:4), whereas the defeated ones will suffer discipline in outer darkness.

Because the man without a marriage garment is cast into outer darkness, many Christian teachers say that he is a false believer. But how could a false believer be admitted to the marriage feast of Christ in the air? The reason many Christian teachers say that this man is an unbeliever is that they do not believe that a saved one can be punished by being cast out into outer darkness. However, according to the Gospel of Matthew, believers may be subject to dispensational punishment, a subject covered more than once in this Gospel. Few Christians believe that there will be such a punishment for the saved ones. But for more than forty years we have been teaching that we need to be overcomers. Those who are not overcomers will be excluded from the enjoyment of the kingdom during the millennium and will probably be punished.

We have seen that the man without a marriage garment is cast out into outer darkness. Notice that the Lord Jesus did not just say darkness, but outer darkness. The Bible says clearly that when the Lord Jesus comes back, He will come in glory. Thus, there will be a sphere, a realm, of glory, and all the believers will be raptured to Him in His glory. In the air the Lord will set up the judgment seat. After the believers have been judged, the defeated ones will be put into outer darkness. This refers to the darkness outside the realm of the Lord's glory. For this reason the Lord used the word "outer" to describe that darkness.

To be cast out into outer darkness is not to suffer eternal perdition. The New Testament reveals that once a person has been saved, he is saved for eternity and can never perish. However, the so-called Arminian theology teaches that a person can be saved and then lost again. This, however, is contrary to the Scriptures. Although we cannot be lost, God may deal with us dispensationally. In the past some have argued with me about this and said, "How can a blood-washed and redeemed person still be punished by God?" I replied, "After you were washed by the Lord's blood and redeemed, did you not experience God's chastening for your wrongdoings? Has not God punished you?" Knowing that God may chastise those who sin after they have been saved, they lost the case. Others have argued that God chastises us only in this age while we are in the flesh; after the Lord comes back and we are raptured, they think there will be no problem. To this I have said, "Please do not hold this concept. Do not think that there can be no problems after resurrection and rapture. After the sinners have died and are resurrected, they will be brought to the white throne for judgment. This proves that resurrection does not solve all problems. Do not think that death and resurrection will automatically rescue you from having problems in the future. God may still deal with you after your resurrection. Do not be deceived." Most Christians today reject the teaching concerning the dispensational punishment of believers. This is why so many are loose and careless in their daily living. Instead of fearing God's dispensational discipline, they say, "I am saved, and the blood has washed me. If I do something wrong, the Lord may correct me a little. But there will be no problems for me in the future." How misleading it is to hold a concept so contrary to the pure word of God! When we come back to the pure Word, we see that it is a serious matter to come to the marriage feast without the marriage garment.

We need to read the book of Matthew with a sober mind and consider its teachings seriously. Although this book has been buried for centuries, the Lord has opened it to us. Some may argue that we do not adequately know the love of God and that we present God as One who is too hard and cruel. But if God were loving according to their concept, how could He send an army to destroy the city of Jerusalem? In Romans 11 Paul says that God is kind, but also that He is severe and that we need to be serious with Him. When God is kind, He is truly kind; and when He is severe, He is very severe. God has been severe with the Jews, and He will also be severe with us.

Today there are many sugar-coated teachings in Christianity. Some preachers dare not teach what they see in the Bible because they are concerned about losing their audience or offending others. Therefore, they sugar-coat many of their teachings. But we must strip away the sugar-coating, come back to the pure Word, and see what the Lord has to say. We need the sober word found in the Gospel of Matthew. Remember, one day you will be examined to see whether or not you have the second garment to qualify you for the marriage feast. Get ready for this by preparing the second garment, the white linen, the surpassing righteousness. May the Lord have mercy upon us for this!

My burden in this message is not to threaten you; it is to open the pure Word and give you a healthy dose that has no sugar-coating. We all are responsible to read the Lord's word and to give it thoughtful consideration. The Lord's parable in 22:1-14 is very significant. Anything given in a parable is important. The Lord would not have given this parable if what is conveyed in it were not significant.

8. Many Being Called but Few Being Chosen

In verse 14 the Lord concludes: "For many are called but few are chosen." To be called is to receive salvation (Rom. 1:7; 1 Cor. 1:2; Eph. 4:1), whereas to be chosen is to receive a reward. All believers have been called, but few will be chosen as overcomers. The overcomers, the chosen ones, will be rewarded and qualified to participate in the marriage feast of the Lamb.

LIFE-STUDY OF MATTHEW

MESSAGE FIFTY-NINE

THE HEAVENLY KING BEING TESTED

(3)

IV. BY THE DISCIPLES
OF THE PHARISEES AND THE HERODIANS

After the Lord Jesus had been examined by the chief priests and the elders of the people concerning the source of His authority, the disciples of the Pharisees with the Herodians questioned Him about giving tribute to Caesar (22:15-22). The Herodians were those who took sides with King Herod's regime and took part with him in injecting Grecian and Roman manners of life into the Jewish culture. Normally they sided with the Sadducees, but were opposed to the Pharisees; here they united with the Pharisees to ensnare the Lord Jesus.

The Herodians opposed the Pharisees because the Pharisees were very conservative, whereas the Herodians were modern, standing with the Sadducees who also were modernistic in their thinking. However, on this occasion the Herodians and Pharisees conspired to trap the Lord Jesus. They expected Him to fall into their snare. In verse 17 they said to the Lord, "Tell us therefore, What do you think? Is it lawful to give tribute to Caesar, or not?" This is really an ensnaring question. All the Jews opposed giving tribute to Caesar. If the Lord Jesus had said that it was lawful to do this, He would have offended all the Jews who followed the Pharisees. But if He said that it was not lawful, this would have given the Herodians, who stood with the Roman government, strong ground to accuse Him. The matter of paying tribute to Caesar was very unpleasant to the Jews; they hated it. The Pharisees were especially against it. However, the Herodians agreed with paying tax to the Roman government. Thus, one of the two parties opposed this matter, and the other favored it. According to their concept, no matter how the Lord answered their question, He would still fall into their snare.

The Lord Jesus, however, is wise and knows how to handle every person and every situation. In verse 19 He said, "Show Me the tribute money." Then they brought to Him a denarius. The Lord did not show the Roman coin, but asked them to show one to Him. Since they possessed one of the Roman coins, they were caught. By having a Roman coin, they had lost the case already.

Verses 20 and 21 say, "And He says to them, Whose is this image and inscription? They say, Caesar's. Then He says to them, Pay then what is Caesar's to Caesar, and what is God's to God." To pay Caesar what is Caesar's is to pay tribute to Caesar according to his governmental regulations. To pay to God what is God's is to pay the half shekel to God according to Exodus 30:11-16, and to offer all the tithes to God according to the law of God. The Jews were under two authorities, the political authority of Rome and the spiritual authority of God. In Jerusalem there was not only the Roman government, but also the temple of God. For this reason, the Jewish people had to pay tax to both systems, to the Roman government and to God's temple. Therefore, the Lord told them to pay to Caesar what is Caesar's and to God what is God's. This answer shocked the Pharisees and the Herodians, and they were defeated.

V. BY THE SADDUCEES

In 22:23-33 we see the Lord's test at the hands of the Sadducees. The Sadducees were ancient modernists who did not believe in angels or in resurrection (Acts 23:8). They were exactly like the modernists and higher critics of today who do not believe in the Scriptures, in angels, or in miracles. These ancient modernists came to the Lord with a question regarding the resurrection. It seemed that they were quite clever. They told the Lord of a woman who had married seven brothers and asked Him, "In the resurrection, therefore, of which of the seven will she be the wife? For they all had her" (v. 28). From the human point of view, this was a difficult question. No doubt the Pharisees, the ancient fundamentalists, would have found it hard to answer. The Lord Jesus, however, gave the Sadducees a strong answer.

Verse 29 says, "But Jesus answered and said to them, You are deceived, not knowing the Scriptures nor the power of God." Knowing the Scriptures is one thing, and knowing the power of God is another. We need to know both. The Scriptures here refer to the verses of the Old Testament concerning the matter of resurrection, and the power of God refers to the power of resurrection. In His answer to the Sadducees, the Lord did four things: firstly, He condemned them; secondly, He rebuked them; thirdly, He taught them; and fourthly, He muzzled them. He condemned them by telling them that they were deceived. Every modernist has been deceived. For this, they need to be condemned. Today's modernists must be condemned for denying the resurrection, angels, and miracles. When I was young, such teachings were spreading in China. For example, the modernists said that the water of the Red Sea was not divided and that the people did not cross over on dry land. They claimed that the shallow water of the sea was blown apart by a strong wind and that this enabled the people to walk on land. What a demonic teaching! The ancient modernists, like those of today, thought they were so clever, but actually they were deceived. Therefore, the Lord rebuked them by saying that they did not know the Scriptures or the power of God.

After the Lord condemned and rebuked the Sadducees, He taught them. In verse 30 He said, "For in the resurrection they neither marry nor are given in marriage, but are as angels of God in heaven." This means that in resurrection there will be no male or female. Hence, there will be no marriage. This will take place by the power of God. Those who deny the resurrection do not know the power of God.

In order to help the Sadducees know the depth of truth

implied in the words of the Scriptures, the Lord said, "But concerning the resurrection of the dead, have you not read that which was spoken to you by God, saying, I am the God of Abraham, and the God of Isaac, and the God of Jacob? He is not the God of the dead, but of the living." Since God is the God of the living and is called the God of Abraham, Isaac, and Jacob, these three who have died will be resurrected. This is the way the Lord Jesus handled the Scriptures — not only by the letter, but by the life and power implied within them.

I appreciate the Lord's interpretation of the Bible. He said that God was the God of Abraham, Isaac, and Jacob. If there were no resurrection to come, then God would have to be the God of the dead. The fact that God is the God of the living and that He is the God of Abraham, Isaac, and Jacob proves that Abraham, Isaac, and Jacob will be resurrected. If they are not to be resurrected, then how could God be the God of the living? This is the genuine, honest, living, trustworthy exposition of the Bible. By giving the Sadducees such an answer, the Lord muzzled them.

VI. BY A LAWYER OF THE PHARISEES

When the Pharisees learned that the Lord had silenced the Sadducees, they held a council about what to do next. Then one of them, a lawyer, tempted the Lord by asking Him a question about the great commandment in the law. A lawyer was one versed in the law of Moses, a professional interpreter of the law of the Old Testament. The Lord said that the great and first commandment was to love the Lord with all our heart, soul, and mind (vv. 37-38). Then He continued, "And the second is like it: You shall love your neighbor as yourself. On these two commandments hang all the law and the prophets." These two commandments are both a matter of love, either loving God or loving man. Love is the spirit of God's commandments.

In all these tests the Lord Jesus was questioned regarding four things: religion, politics, belief, and the law. Regarding religion, He was questioned concerning the source of authority in religious activities. Regarding politics, He was asked about paying tribute to the Roman government. Regarding belief, He was questioned about the belief in the resurrection. Regarding the law, He was asked which was the great commandment. From all four directions those who tested the Lord Jesus were muzzled and had nothing more to say.

VII. MUZZLING ALL THE TESTERS BY THE QUESTION OF QUESTIONS

After He had been questioned, the Lord had a question for the Pharisees. Verses 41 and 42 say, "Now while the Pharisees were gathered together, Jesus questioned them, saying, What do you think concerning the Christ? Whose Son is He?" From 21:23 to 22:46, during His last visit to Jerusalem, the center of Judaism, Christ was surrounded by the chief priests, elders, Pharisees, Herodians, Sadducees, and a lawyer, who endeavored to ensnare Him by asking puzzling and crafty questions. Firstly, the chief priests, representing the authority of the Jewish religion, and the elders, representing the authority of the Jewish people, asked Him concerning His authority (21:23). This was a question according to their religious concept. Secondly, the fundamental Pharisees and political Herodians asked Him a question related to politics. Thirdly, the modernistic Sadducees questioned Him concerning the fundamental belief. Fourthly, a self-qualified lawyer asked Him a question concerning the law. After answering all their questions wisely, He asked them a question concerning Christ. This is the question of questions. Their questions were related to religion, politics, belief, and the law. His question was concerning Christ, who is the center of all things. They knew religion, politics, belief, and the law, but they paid no attention to Christ. Hence, He asked them, "What do you think concerning the Christ?" This question of questions must be answered by everyone.

People today have many questions, but all their questions can be classified into the four categories of religion, politics, belief, and the law. Just as in ancient times, peo-

ple today care for these things, not for Christ. They simply
have no concept concerning Him. But God's concern is for
Christ, and Christ's concern is for Himself. Hence He asks,
"What do you think about Christ? Whose Son is He?" This
question touches Christ's Person, which is a mystery, the
most perplexing matter in the universe.

Christology is the study of the Person of Christ. From
the second century onward, Christian teachers have been
fighting with one another concerning Christology. Today
the battle between us and the opposers is also related to
this matter. For example, one of the leading opposers
teaches that Christ is not in us, but is merely represented
in us by the Holy Spirit. According to him, Christ is at the
right hand of God in the third heaven, and the Holy Spirit
represents Him in us. This concept is related to tritheism,
the teaching that the three of the Godhead are separate
individuals. Those who teach that Christ is merely represented in us by the Holy Spirit actually have three Gods.
Deep within, many fundamental Christians subconsciously have this concept. Recently, some opposers have
said that Christ's divinity is in the believers, but His
humanity is in heaven. How ridiculous! Now some not only
have three Gods, but two Christs, a material Christ and a
spiritual Christ. Such peculiar concepts are the issue of our
fallen mentality. What a dreadful thing to separate
Christ's humanity from His divinity! This illustrates the
fact that the question regarding Christ is still the question
of questions today.

When the Pharisees were asked this question by the
Lord, they replied that Christ was David's son (v. 42). No
doubt, according to the Scriptures, this answer was correct. Then the Lord said, "How then does David in spirit
call Him Lord, saying, The Lord said to My Lord, Sit on
My right hand until I put Your enemies underneath Your
feet? If then David calls Him Lord, how is He his Son?"
(vv. 43-45). The question here is how a great-grandfather
could call his great-grandson Lord. This was one question
the Pharisees did not know how to answer. As God, in His
divinity, Christ is the Lord of David; as a man, in His

humanity, He is the Son of David. The Pharisees had only half the scriptural knowledge concerning Christ's Person, that He was the Son of David according to His humanity. They did not have the other half, concerning Christ's divinity as the Son of God. The mention of the spirit in verse 43 indicates that Christ is only known by us in our spirit through God's revelation (Eph. 3:5, Gk.).

Verse 46 says, "And no one was able to answer Him a word, nor did anyone from that day dare to question Him any more." Christ's question of questions concerning His wonderful Person muzzled the mouths of all His opposers. The Pharisees had studied the Old Testament, and they had seen clearly that Christ was to be the Son of David. But they did not see that Christ was also the Son of God.

Even those who have admitted that Christ is both the Son of God and the Son of David have argued whether His two natures were separate or mingled. Instead of arguing about Christ's Person, we should say, "Hallelujah, we have a Person who is glorious and mysterious! He is so wonderful that we cannot adequately understand Him." Consider Isaiah 9:6: "For unto us a child is born, unto us a son is given . . . and his name shall be called Wonderful, Counselor, The mighty God, The everlasting Father, The Prince of Peace." It will take eternity for us to understand this verse. Christ is a child, yet He is the mighty God. He is the Son, yet He is called the everlasting Father. Do not think that we can understand Christ adequately today. No, He is too wonderful and too far beyond our comprehension. We do not even fully understand ourselves, much less Christ. Do you know where your spirit is, or where your soul is? Can you locate your heart? The more you analyze yourself, the more you will find yourself in a maze. When I was very young, I thought I knew myself thoroughly. But the longer I have lived, the more I realize how little I know. If we cannot understand ourselves, how can we adequately understand Christ, the embodiment of the Triune God?

How wonderful Christ is! He is both God and man, both the Son of God and the Son of David. Furthermore, He is both in the heavens and in us. He is inside and outside; He is on the top and on the bottom; He is the greatest and the smallest. Oh, Christ is everything! We need to know Him to such a degree. Then we shall say, "Lord Jesus, I cannot exhaust the knowledge of You. Lord, You are the only worthy One. If there is a God, this God must be You. If there is a genuine human being, this person must be You. Lord, You are the Savior, the Redeemer, the life, and the light." We today must come to know how inexhaustible the Lord Jesus is as the Son of David and the Son of God. Both the experience of Him and the knowledge of Him are inexhaustible. Because Christ is the all-inclusive One, the enjoyment of Him is inexhaustible.

Do not be led into the devilish snare of debate concerning the Person of Christ. Thinking you know everything concerning Christ's Person is an indication that you have been snared already. Although we can know Christ, we cannot understand Him thoroughly. We know that Jesus Christ is the Son and that He is also called the Father, for the Bible tells us so. But we cannot comprehend this adequately. We also know that Christ is the Son of God and the Son of man and that He has both the divine nature and the human nature in one Person. Thus, He is one Person with two natures and two lives. However, it is beyond our ability to understand this thoroughly. We simply believe whatever the Bible says and praise Him for being so wonderful! We need to worship Him, take Him in, enjoy Him, and experience Him as the wonderful One.

LIFE-STUDY OF MATTHEW

REBUKING THE JEWISH RELIGIONISTS
AND FORSAKING JERUSALEM WITH ITS TEMPLE

After the Lord had been examined and tested by the religious leaders, in His wisdom He muzzled them. Eventually, He reached the point where He did not talk to them any further. Rather, in chapter twenty-three, He gave them a final word. In this message we shall consider the Lord's rebuking of the Jewish religionists and His forsaking of Jerusalem with its temple.

I. REBUKING THE JEWISH RELIGIONISTS

A. Their Hypocrisy

In His rebuke of the Jewish religionists, the Lord first spoke against their hypocrisy (23:1-12).

1. Seating Themselves in Moses' Seat
and Saying but Not Doing

In verses 2 and 3 the Lord said, "The scribes and the Pharisees have seated themselves in Moses' seat. All things therefore, whatever they tell you, do and keep; but do not do according to their works, for they say and do not do." The scribes and Pharisees said certain things concerning the law, but they did not do them. For this reason, the Lord told His disciples to do whatever the scribes and Pharisees said, for their speaking was according to the Bible. However, He told His disciples not to follow what they did, for their deeds were hypocritical.

2. Binding Heavy Burdens and Laying Them on the Shoulders of Others, but Not Moving Them with Their Finger

Verse 4 says, "And they bind heavy burdens and hard to bear, and lay them on men's shoulders, but they themselves will not move them with their finger." The scribes and Pharisees put the burden of law on others, but they would not use even their finger to lift it.

3. Doing All Their Works to Be Seen by Men

In verse 5 the Lord said, "And all their works they do to be seen by men." The scribes and Pharisees did everything to make an outward show so that others could see them. They did this because of their pride and because they wanted to receive the praises of men.

4. Broadening Their Phylacteries and Enlarging the Fringes of Their Garments

Verse 5 also says, "They broaden their phylacteries and enlarge the fringes of their garments." A phylactery is a part of the law written on parchment and worn upon the forehead as a frontlet and upon the left arm, according to Deuteronomy 6:8 and 11:18. The scribes and the Pharisees broadened it to make it a charm. They also broadened it for the purpose of making a display of how they loved the law, were for the law, and kept the law. This reveals how much they desired to maintain a good appearance in the eyes of others.

The law required the Israelites to make fringes on the borders of their garments with a band of blue, signifying that their conduct (typified by the garment) was regulated by the heavenly rule (indicated by the band of blue), and reminding them to keep God's commandments (Num. 15:38-39). The scribes and Pharisees enlarged the fringes, pretending that they kept God's commandments and were regulated by them to a surpassing degree. They did this in order to glorify themselves.

5. Loving the Chief Place at Dinners and the Chief Seats in the Synagogues

Verse 6 says that the scribes and Pharisees "love the chief place at the dinners and the chief seats in the synagogues." This indicates that they enjoyed being above others and that they desired to be great among the people.

6. Loving the Salutations in the Market Places and Being Called Rabbi by Men

Verse 7 indicates that they loved "the salutations in the market places and to be called by men, Rabbi." The scribes and Pharisees liked to be saluted by the people in the market places. They also enjoyed being called Rabbi, a title of honor which means teacher, master.

7. In Contrast with the Humility of the Kingdom People

The behavior of the scribes and Pharisees is in contrast to the humility of the kingdom people. The kingdom people must be the exact opposite of them. For example, in verse 8 the Lord says, "But you, do not be called Rabbi; for One is your Teacher, and you are all brothers." This indicates that Christ is our only teacher and master. Verse 9 says, "And do not call anyone your father on the earth; for One is your Father, He Who is in the heavens." This verse reveals that God is our only father. We all have one heavenly Father, and that is God Himself. In verse 10 we see that Christ is our only Leader, Guide, Instructor, and Director. This verse says, "Neither be called leaders, because One is your Leader, the Christ." The Greek word rendered "leaders" can also be translated "guides," "instructors," "directors." In verses 11 and 12 we see that the greater among us should be our servants, that whoever exalts himself will be humbled, and that whoever humbles himself will be exalted. Thus, the self-exalted one will be humbled, and the self-humbled one will be exalted.

B. Their Eightfold Woe

In 23:13-36 the Lord pronounces an eightfold woe upon the scribes and Pharisees. In chapter five we have a ninefold blessing, but here we have an eightfold woe.

1. The First Woe

Verse 13 says, "But woe to you, scribes and Pharisees, hypocrites, because you shut the kingdom of the heavens in the face of men; for you do not enter in yourselves, nor do you allow those who are entering to enter." The Pharisees shut up the kingdom of the heavens. They neither entered in themselves nor allowed those who were entering in to enter. Among today's Christians, some are just like this. They do not have the heart to enter into the kingdom of the heavens, and at the same time they do not allow those who desire to enter in to do so. Nearly all the opposition against us comes not from unbelievers, but from devoted Christians who desire to frustrate those who want to come this way. In the eyes of the Lord this is a most subtle thing.

2. The Second Woe

Verse 14 says, "Woe to you, scribes and Pharisees, hypocrites, because you devour widows' houses, even while for a pretense you make long prayers; therefore, you shall receive greater condemnation." While they were pretending to make long prayers, they devoured widows' houses.

3. The Third Woe

Verse 15 says, "Woe to you, scribes and Pharisees, hypocrites, because you compass the sea and the land to make one proselyte, and when he becomes one, you make him twofold more the son of Gehenna than yourselves." This also happens today. In the Far East I observed that the Catholics made proselytes of some Buddhists only to make them twofold more a son of Gehenna than themselves.

4. The Fourth Woe

Verse 16 says, "Woe to you, blind guides, who say, Whoever swears by the temple, it is nothing; but whoever swears by the gold of the temple, he is a debtor." Their blindness is exposed here. In verse 17 the Lord continues, "Fools and blind, for which is greater, the gold or the temple which sanctifies the gold?" To sanctify the gold is to make the gold holy positionally by changing its position from a common place to a holy one. The temple is greater than the gold because it sanctifies the gold. Sanctification has two aspects, the positional aspect and the dispositional aspect. Here we see that the gold is sanctified by the temple. This is positional sanctification, not dispositional sanctification. Perhaps the gold was once in the market place. When it was there, it was common, not holy, not separated to God. But when the gold was taken from the market place and put into the temple, it was positionally sanctified by being in the temple. Formerly it was the common gold in the market place; now it is the sanctified gold in the temple of God. Although the position of the gold has been changed, its nature remains the same. This is positional sanctification.

The principle is the same with respect to the altar and the gift in verses 18 and 19. The sanctification of the gift by the altar is also a kind of positional sanctification. The sanctification of the gift comes about by changing the gift's location from a common place to a holy one. Because the altar was greater than the gift, the altar sanctified the gift. For example, when a lamb was with the flock, it was common, not separated to God or sanctified. But once it was offered upon the altar, the altar sanctified the lamb to God. However, as in the case with the gold, the nature of the lamb remained the same. Only its outward position was changed. Formerly it was with the flock; now it is on the altar for God. This type of sanctification, positional sanctification, does not affect our nature. The sanctification spoken of in Romans 6, however, is dispositional sanctification; it touches our being, our inward nature.

In verses 20 through 22 the Lord says that he who swears by the altar, swears by it and by all things upon it; that he who swears by the temple, swears by it and by Him who dwells in it; and that he who swears by heaven, swears by the throne of God and by Him who sits upon it.

5. The Fifth Woe

Verses 23 and 24 contain the fifth woe. The scribes and Pharisees tithed mint, anise, and cummin, but left aside the weightier matters of the law, judgment and mercy and faith. The Lord said they were blind guides, who strained out a gnat, but swallowed a camel.

6. The Sixth Woe

Verses 25 and 26 say, "Woe to you, scribes and Pharisees, hypocrites, because you cleanse the outside of the cup and the dish, but within they are full of robbery and self-indulgence. Blind Pharisee, cleanse first the inside of the cup and the dish, so that their outside may become clean also." The scribes and Pharisees cared only for the outside. The situation was the same in chapter fifteen. Although they washed their hands, they were inwardly full of robbery and self-indulgence. Robbery is related to the love of money, and indulgence is related to lust. Thus, although the scribes and Pharisees cleansed themselves outwardly, inwardly they were full of the love of money and lust.

7. The Seventh Woe

Verses 27 and 28 say, "Woe to you, scribes and Pharisees, hypocrites, because you resemble white-washed graves, which outwardly appear beautiful, but within are full of dead men's bones and all uncleanness. So also you outwardly appear righteous to men, but within you are full of hypocrisy and lawlessness." The Pharisees were like tombs. Have you ever thought that fallen people are like tombs? Outwardly they may be beautiful and appear righteous to men, but within they are full of dead men's bones and uncleanness, full of hypocrisy and lawlessness.

8. *The Eighth Woe*

In verses 29 through 36 we have eighth woe. Verse 29 says, "Woe to you, scribes and Pharisees, hypocrites, because you build the graves of the prophets and adorn the monuments of the righteous." Monuments here refer to the tombs of the righteous. Outside of Jerusalem there are a number of monuments. The Pharisees remodeled the graves of the prophets and adorned them in order to make a show. The Lord said that by doing this they were proving that they were the sons of those who murdered the prophets (v. 31). Thus, the Lord called them "serpents" and the "brood of vipers" (v. 33). As verse 34 indicates, the scribes and Pharisees later scourged and killed the New Testament apostles sent out by the Lord.

The Lord's rebuke of the scribes and Pharisees affords us an accurate picture of today's religion. Everything found in 23:1-36 resembles the situation today. Remember, this rebuke is found in the book of the kingdom. Matthew's intention is certainly to present the negative in order to reveal the positive. The kingdom life must be the opposite of what is exposed in 23:1-36. It must be an absolute contrast to this black and hellish picture. Only by the mercy and grace of the Lord can we escape the situation portrayed here. Thus, we all need to pray, "O Lord, save me! Rescue me! Take me away from this terrible situation."

II. FORSAKING JERUSALEM
WITH ITS TEMPLE

After the Lord had been tested and examined and after He had rebuked the scribes and Pharisees, He forsook

Jerusalem with its temple. In 23:37-39 the Lord spoke a final word to Jerusalem. After this word, the Lord had nothing more to do with her.

A. Jerusalem Killing the Prophets

Verse 37 says, "Jerusalem, Jerusalem, who kills the prophets and stones those who are sent to her!" Jerusalem and her children were chosen by God to fulfill His purpose. However, when God sent His prophets to them, they killed them.

B. The Lord as a Hen
Desiring to Gather Her Children
Together under Her Wings

Verse 37 also says, "How often I desired to gather your children together as a hen gathers her young under her wings, and you would not!" It has always been God Himself who cared for Jerusalem, like a bird fluttering over her young (Isa. 31:5; Deut. 32:11-12). Hence, when the Lord Jesus said, "I desired to gather your children together as a hen gathers her young under her wings," He indicated that He was God Himself. The Lord is like a loving bird, fluttering, brooding, over her young. Often He desired to gather the children of Jerusalem together, but they were not willing. As the Lord Jesus was declaring this final word to them, He was still like a loving hen, stretching out His wings to brood over the little ones. But they were not willing to be gathered under His wings.

C. The House — the Temple — Left Desolate

In verse 38 the Lord said, "Behold, your house is left to you desolate." Since "house" here is singular, it must denote the house of God, which was the temple (21:12-13). It was the house of God, but now it is called "your house," because they had made it a den of robbers (21:13). The prophecy about the house becoming desolate corresponds with that in 24:2, which was fulfilled when Titus destroyed Jerusalem with the Roman army in A.D. 70.

According to the context of the whole Bible, the house here refers to the temple, the unique house, the house of God. But at this point the house of God had become "your house"; it was no longer the house of God, but the den of robbers. When the Lord was cleansing the temple, He said, "My house shall be called a house of prayer, but you are making it a den of robbers" (21:13).

In ancient times, according to the book of Ezekiel, God left His temple. The same thing was happening here. In chapter ten Ezekiel saw in a vision the glory of God leaving the temple. Thus, the temple was left desolate for the rebellious Jews, and eventually it was burned and destroyed. Here in Matthew 23 the Lord was once again about to leave the house desolate. Not too long afterwards, the temple was destroyed by the Roman army under Titus. Thus 23:38 corresponds to 24:2, which indicates that not one stone was to be left upon another. Both of these verses refer to the desolation of the temple in Jerusalem. At the time the temple was destroyed, it was no longer the house of God; rather, it had become the house of rebels.

D. Not Seeing the Lord until His Coming Back

Verse 39 says, "For I say to you, You shall by no means see Me henceforth until you say, Blessed is He Who comes in the name of the Lord." This will be at the Lord's second coming, when all the remnant of Israel will turn to believe in Him and be saved (Rom. 11:23, 26). Ezekiel saw the glory leaving the temple. This glory typified the Lord Jesus, who is the real glory, the manifestation of God. Israel will not see Him again until His second coming. According to Zechariah 12, the remnant of Israel will repent when the Lord comes again. Then they will say to Him, "Blessed is He Who comes in the name of the Lord."

The Lord's word here is brief, but it includes a number of things from the destruction of Jerusalem until the Lord's second coming. Here the Lord made a clear declaration that He, the very glory of God, was leaving the nation of

Israel and that they would not see Him until His coming again. Nearly two thousand years have passed since that time, and Israel still has not seen the Lord Jesus. Some may ask, "Does this mean that the Jews have no opportunity to believe in the Lord Jesus?" As individuals, the Jews still have the opportunity to believe, but as a nation they do not have this opportunity today. As a nation, Israel is through with the Lord. Thank the Lord that He is still merciful to the Jews. Even though He has left the nation of Israel, the back door is still open for individual Jews to come to Him. Today no Jew has the position to come to God as a representative of his nation. But when the Jews are persecuted by their enemies at the end of this age, they will cry out to their God. Then Christ will descend and place His feet on the Mount of Olives, which will be cleft like the waters of the Red Sea. This will enable the Jews to escape from persecution. At that time they will repent to the Lord and call upon Him, and the nation will be saved. This salvation will be not only for individuals, but for the entire nation. However, before the Lord's coming back, it is impossible for the nation of Israel to repent. But, as we have pointed out, individual Jews can still repent today and come into God's grace.

LIFE-STUDY OF MATTHEW

PROPHECY OF THE KINGDOM

(1)

The knowledge most Christians have of Matthew 24 and 25 is vague and indefinite. As we come to these chapters, we need to drop this kind of vague knowledge. For the basic understanding of these chapters we are standing upon the shoulders of many great teachers who have gone before us. These great teachers include Darby, Newton, Pember, Govett, and Panton. According to church history, not until about one hundred fifty years ago were these chapters opened to the Lord's people. After 1829, when the Brethren were raised up, these chapters began to be opened to the seeking saints. If you collect the various writings regarding Christ's second coming, the great tribulation, the prophecy concerning the seventy weeks in Daniel, and the rapture, you will see that during the past one hundred fifty years the knowledge of Matthew 24 and 25 has progressed.

When Brother Nee was young, he was helped a great deal by reading the books of Pember, Govett, and Panton. Of course, he saw something even further, and before 1930 he conducted a study of the book of Revelation, upon which our study of Revelation was based. Later, Brother Nee held a study of Matthew in which he gave several messages on chapters twenty-four and twenty-five. He also had studies on the matters of the rapture and the tribulation. After he conducted these studies, Brother Nee saw something further. During the last twenty years, I myself also have gone on a little in understanding these matters. Therefore, what I shall present to you in these messages on

chapters twenty-four and twenty-five is not merely the
result of my own study, but the product of knowledge that
has progressed throughout the past one hundred fifty
years. It is not something superficial, but the cream of the
labor of many others. The more I have ministered on the
Lord's coming, the rapture, and the tribulation, the more
convinced I have become that we have the proper understanding of these things.

Prophecy in the Bible is like a jigsaw puzzle. We need
to find the various pieces that are scattered throughout the
Bible and see how they fit together. I have been doing this
for more than fifty years. What I am presenting in these
messages is the result of all these years of study.

I. CONCERNING ISRAEL

A. From Christ's Ascension
to the End of the Age

Matthew 24:1-31 is concerned with Israel. Verses 1-14
cover the time from Christ's ascension to the end of the
age.

1. The Temple About to Be Destroyed

The prophecy of the kingdom given on the Mount of
Olives is a continuation of the Lord's declaration regarding His forsaking of Israel. This declaration is given at the
end of chapter twenty-three. Chapter twenty-four continues, "And Jesus came out from the temple and was
going away, and His disciples came to Him to show Him
the buildings of the temple" (v. 1). Notice that chapter
twenty-four begins with the word "And." This indicates
that this chapter is a direct continuation of the last part of
chapter twenty-three. In 23:37-39 the Lord said that He
desired to gather Jerusalem, that the house was left desolate, and that they would not see Him until they say,
"Blessed is He Who comes in the name of the Lord." Then,
immediately after this, chapter twenty-four continues with
the words, "And Jesus came out from the temple." This

indicates that as soon as the Lord had declared that He was forsaking Israel, He came out of the temple and began to go away. The word "away" is very strong, showing that the Lord was not merely going, but going away. The fact that the Lord had come out from the temple indicates that He had left the temple. This was to fulfill His word in 23:38 concerning leaving the temple to the rejecting Jews as their house of desolation. This is equivalent to God's glory leaving the temple in the time of Ezekiel (Ezek. 10:18).

As the Lord Jesus was going away from the temple, "His disciples came to Him to show Him the buildings of the temple." The word "temple" here denotes the entire precincts of the temple. As the Lord was going away, there might have been a distance between Him and His disciples, who were probably still lingering by the temple. Therefore, they came to Him to show Him the buildings of the temple. This indicates that the disciples did not agree with the Lord's forsaking of the temple. The Lord had forsaken the den of robbers, leaving the temple to be a house of desolation. But the disciples still appreciated the temple and were trying to bring Him back to it by pointing out the buildings, perhaps by pointing them out one by one.

Verse 2 says, "But He answered and said to them, Do you not see all these things? Truly I say to you, A stone shall by no means be left upon a stone which shall not be thrown down." This was fulfilled in A.D. 70 when Titus with the Roman army destroyed Jerusalem.

Notice that the Lord did not say, "I have seen these things"; instead, He said, "Do you not see all these things?" This indicates clearly that the Lord Jesus would not turn His eyes back to look at the buildings. He seemed to be saying, "I don't like to look at these things, but you have seen them. To you, they are complete, beautiful, splendid, and perfect. But there will not be one stone left upon another which will not be thrown down. Now you point out these things to Me building by building. But the day is coming when all this will be leveled." We need to visualize the situation here. The disciples kept their eyes upon the buildings and pointed them out to the Lord. But the Lord would not turn to see them. Rather, He told His disciples that the buildings would be torn down. His answer must have shocked the disciples. As they all walked from the temple to the Mount of Olives, neither the Lord nor the disciples had anything more to say. Because the matter was too serious, the disciples asked Him nothing further until they came to the Mount of Olives.

Verse 3 says that after the Lord came to the Mount of Olives and sat down there, the disciples came to Him privately to ask Him about these things. Their meeting with the Lord on the mountain reveals that in order to receive the vision of the Lord's prophecy concerning this age, we need to climb to the high mountain to enter into His presence.

The disciples came to the Lord privately. Having heard the terrible news that the buildings of the temple would be leveled, they wanted to keep this matter confidential. Perhaps as we read these verses today, we do not sense the seriousness of them. But when the disciples heard this word from the Lord Jesus, they were shocked and dared not talk about it openly. Not until the Lord had come to the Mount of Olives and sat down were they bold enough to ask Him about these things.

In verse 2 the word "things" refers to the buildings of the temple. But the same term used in verse 3 refers to matters, which include the things covered from verse 32 of the foregoing chapter: the Jews' filling up the measure of their fathers, the coming of the judgment of God upon them, their persecution of the Lord's sent ones, and the destruction of the temple. In verse 3 the disciples were asking the Lord Jesus when these things would transpire.

In verse 3 the disciples said, "Tell us, When shall these things be, and what is the sign of Your coming and of the consummation of the age?" The question of the disciples consists of three points: when these things will be, including not only the destruction of the temple (v. 2), but also the things mentioned in 23:32-39; the sign of Christ's coming; and the sign of the consummation of the age. The Lord's word from verse 4 through 25:46 answers the disciples' question concerning these three points.

The Greek word rendered "coming" in this verse is *parousia*, which means presence. Christ's coming will be His presence with His believers. This parousia will begin with His coming to the air and end with His coming to the earth. Within His parousia, there will be the rapture of the majority of the believers to the air (1 Thes. 4:15-17), the judgment seat of Christ (2 Cor. 5:10), and the marriage of the Lamb (Rev. 19:7-9). The question asked here is concerning the sign of the Lord's parousia and the sign of the end of this age. Hence, His answer in chapter twenty-four deals mainly with the sign of His parousia and with the sign of the end of this age.

The disciples did not ask, "What is Your coming?" They asked, "What is the sign of Your coming?" Thus, chapters twenty-four and twenty-five deal with the Lord's answer regarding when these things would take place, the sign of His coming, and the sign of the consummation of the age. The consummation of the age denotes the very end of this present age. As we read chapters twenty-four and twenty-five, we need to be clear that the Lord's answer is directed to the disciples' three questions.

2. Many Deceivers Coming

Verses 4 and 5 say, "And Jesus answered and said to them, See that no one leads you astray. For many shall come in My name, saying, I am the Christ, and they shall lead many astray." The Lord's answer is of three sections: the first section (24:4-31) concerns the Jews who are the elect; the second (24:32—25:30) concerns the church; and the third (25:31-46) concerns the Gentiles, the nations. The first section, concerning the Jews, should be literally interpreted; whereas the second section, concerning the church, should be spiritually interpreted, because it is spoken in parables for the reason given in 13:11-13. For instance, the winter in 24:20 is a literal winter, but the summer in 24:32 is a symbol signifying the time of restoration. But the third section, concerning the Gentiles, should again be literally interpreted.

Some aspects of the prophecy in verses 4 through 14 have been fulfilled, and some will be in the process of being fulfilled until the time of the great tribulation, which will be the consummation, the end, of this age.

In verses 4 and 5 the Lord said that many deceivers would come in the name of Christ and lead many astray. History tells us that this has been so. Since the time that Christ ascended to the heavens, many have come claiming to be Christ.

3. Wars, Rumors of Wars, Famines, and Earthquakes

Verse 6 says, "And you shall hear of wars and rumors of wars; see that you are not disturbed; for these things must take place, but the end is not yet." The wars here refer to all the wars from the first century to the present. They are signified by the red horse of the second seal in Revelation 6:3-4. Many wars have been fought in the region of the Mediterranean, the place where the good land is.

The "end" in verse 6 is the consummation of this age (v. 3; Dan. 12:4, 9, 6-7), which will be the three and a half years of the great tribulation. Remember, in these verses the Lord is giving the indicators of the end of this age.

Verse 7 says, "For nation shall rise against nation, and kingdom against kingdom, and there shall be famines and earthquakes in various places." "Nation" refers to the peoples, the Gentiles, and "kingdom" refers to the empires. The rising of nation against nation, or people against people, refers to civil war, whereas the rising of kingdom against kingdom refers to international war. From the time of the Lord's ascension there have been both civil war and international war. Moreover, there have been many famines, which are mostly the issue of war. According to history, war has always brought famine, signified by the black horse of the third seal in Revelation 6:5-6. For example, Germany was defeated in World War I because of the shortage of bread. Thus, the sequence is war, famine, and death.

The Lord also said that there would be earthquakes in various places. Since Christ's ascension, earthquakes have been increasing throughout all the centuries and will be intensified at the end of this age (Rev. 6:12; 8:5; 11:13, 19; 16:18). It seems that each year there are more earthquakes than in the previous year.

In verse 8 the Lord said, "But all these things are the beginning of birth pangs." This verse refers to the nation of Israel as a woman. The Jews, as God's elect, will suffer birth pangs like a woman in travail to bring forth a remnant who will participate in the Messianic kingdom, the earthly section of the millennium. Then the nation of Israel will rejoice.

As we have seen, the Lord's answer in chapters twenty-four and twenty-five is in three sections, the sections concerning the Jews, the church, and the Gentiles. On earth today there are these three categories of peoples. Thus, in order to give the disciples a full answer to their question, the Lord covers these three peoples in a good sequence, beginning with the Jews and then continuing with the church and the Gentiles. When the Lord spoke this prophecy, His audience, composed of the disciples, had a dual status. On the one hand, they were Jews; on the other hand, they were the disciples of Christ, the representatives of the church. Hence, the Lord spoke to them both about the Jews and about the church. However, we must be careful not to apply the verses in the section dealing with the Jews to the Christians in the church.

We have pointed out that the Lord's word in the section concerning the Jews is a plain word and requires no interpretation. For example, when the Lord speaks of winter, He means a literal winter; and when He mentions the Sabbath, He is talking about an actual Sabbath. But the second section, the section concerning the church, requires a great deal of interpretation because in this section the Lord speaks in parables. In Matthew 13 we see that the church is a mystery. Thus, in order to preserve the mystery of the church, the Lord could not speak in plain words, but needed to speak in parables, which require interpretation. For example, the summer spoken of in this section is not an actual summer; rather, it is a symbol of the restored kingdom of the Jews. Likewise, the fig tree is a symbol of the nation of Israel, and the virgins are symbols of the believers. The third section, the section concerning the Gentiles, is spoken in plain words and does not require interpretation.

The section regarding the Jews is full of suffering because the nation of Israel is compared to a woman giving birth to a child. The process of delivering the child has gone on for nearly two thousand years. What a prolonged delivery! According to the Bible, this long delivery is a form of punishment to the woman. Thus, the nation of Israel, the woman delivering the child, is still suffering. Everything mentioned in verses 4 through 7 is the beginning of birth pangs, not the actual sufferings. The time of suffering will be the great tribulation spoken of in verse 21. Hence, the sufferings in verses 4 through 7 are not the great tribulation, but the beginning of birth pangs. Throughout the centuries, the Lord has dealt with the Jews in a sovereign way. Nevertheless, the Jews have passed through one suffering after another. Even today, the nation of Israel is suffering. Many Arab countries are opposing her.

Although the nation of Israel has been in the process of delivering a child for such a long time, the child still has not come forth. This child will be the remnant of Israel that will be saved and restored. The nation of Israel today has not come up to God's intention. Some of us visited Israel this year; the sin, immorality, and superstition we saw there were disgusting. The Bible prophesied that the Jews would return to the good land in unbelief. Nevertheless, the Lord will take care of them.

4. The Disciples to Be Persecuted and Hated by the Nations

Verse 9 says, "Then they shall deliver you up to affliction and shall kill you, and you shall be hated by all the nations because of My name." The "you" here refers to the Jewish disciples, who were the prophets and wise men sent to the Jews (23:34). The first martyrs were all Jews. They were slain not only by the Jewish nation, but by the nations. Wherever they went, they were persecuted.

5. Many Being Stumbled, Delivering Up One Another, and Hating One Another

Verse 10 says, "And then many shall be stumbled and shall deliver up one another, and they shall hate one another." This refers to the believing Jews. Among the believing Jews, many will be stumbled and deliver up one another. This indicates that the Jewish Christians will fight against one another and hate one another. This is the degradation of the Jewish believers.

6. Many False Prophets Arising and Leading Many Astray

Verse 11 says, "And many false prophets shall arise and shall lead many astray." This began to happen after Christ's ascension and will continue until the end of this age.

7. Lawlessness Being Multiplied and the Love of Many Growing Cold

Verse 12 says, "And because lawlessness is multiplied, the love of the many shall grow cold." Do not apply this verse directly to the members of the church. Although you may borrow it and use it for the church, the direct application must be to the Jewish believers who have become cold in their love.

8. *The One Enduring to the End to Be Saved*

Although the love of the many shall grow cold, "he who endures to the end, he shall be saved" (v. 13). Because the Jewish believers are to suffer persecution, they are called upon to endure to the end in order to be saved. They need to exercise their endurance in the Lord and not give up their faith. To be saved here implies to be saved into the manifestation of the kingdom. Suppose, because of persecution and hatred, some Jewish believers are defeated. Those who are defeated will not participate in the manifestation of the kingdom of the heavens. Therefore, in this verse, to be saved is not to receive eternal salvation; it is to be saved out of persecution and it is to be saved into the manifestation of the kingdom.

9. *The Gospel of the Kingdom Being Preached in the Whole Inhabited Earth to All the Nations*

Verse 14 says, "And this gospel of the kingdom shall be preached in the whole inhabited earth for a testimony to all the nations, and then the end shall come." The gospel of the kingdom, including the gospel of grace (Acts 20:24), not only brings people into God's salvation, but also into the kingdom of the heavens (Rev. 1:9). The emphasis of the gospel of grace is on forgiveness of sin, God's redemption, and eternal life; whereas the emphasis of the gospel of the kingdom is on the heavenly ruling of God and the authority of the Lord. This gospel of the kingdom will be preached in the whole earth for a testimony to all the nations before the end of this age comes. The gospel of the kingdom is a testimony to all the nations, the Gentiles. This testimony must spread to the whole earth before the end of this age, the time of the great tribulation.

In verses 4 through 14 we see the actual history concerning the Jews from Christ's ascension until the end of this age, the three and a half years of the great tribulation. Before the great tribulation comes, everything in these

verses will transpire. The last item will be the preaching of
the gospel of the kingdom. I believe that the churches in
the Lord's recovery will bear the burden to bring this gospel to all the inhabited earth. The gospel of grace has been
preached in every continent, but not the gospel of the kingdom. The gospel of grace is the lower gospel, but the gospel of the kingdom is the higher gospel. This higher gospel
will be brought to every continent through the churches in
the Lord's recovery. This, the strongest sign of the consummation of the age, will take place before the great tribulation. Thus, the most important sign of the consummation of the age is the preaching of the gospel of the kingdom to all the inhabited earth.

LIFE-STUDY OF MATTHEW

PROPHECY OF THE KINGDOM

(2)

We have seen that the Lord's answer to His disciples' question is of three sections: the section concerning the Jews (24:4-31), the section concerning the church (24:32—25:30), and the section concerning the Gentiles (25:31-46). The section concerning Israel is divided into two parts: from Christ's ascension to the end of the age (24:1-14) and during the end of the age (24:15-31). In order to understand 24:1-31, we must keep these subsections in mind. We must also be careful not to misapply the verses, that is, not to apply them to the wrong time or to the wrong people.

Many Christian teachers do not understand the significance of the term "the end of the age." The Greek phrase here can also be translated "the completion of the age" or "the consummation of the age." The end of the age denotes the three and a half years of the great tribulation that will terminate this age. Therefore, the end of the age is not the close of the age, but the very last period of the age. In order to understand the prophecies in the Old and New Testaments, we must have a clear understanding of this matter. Many Christian teachers are confused regarding the prophecies because they are not clear about the end of this age.

This term "the consummation of the age" is found in the last verse of Matthew (28:20). Because we hope to be raptured, we expect the Lord to be with us until the end of this age, not until the close of the age. At the close of the age, the Lord will descend to the earth and place His feet on the Mount of Olives. Before this takes place, there will be a period of time which the Bible calls the end of the age, a period of time which will last three and a half years. In 24:6 the Lord told His disciples that they would hear of wars and rumors of wars, but that "the end is not yet." He told them not to be disturbed, for such things were but the beginning of birth pangs. The end of the age, the great tribulation, was not yet. In verse 14 He said that the gospel of the kingdom would be preached in the whole inhabited earth for a testimony to all the nations and then the end would come. In verse 6 He said that the end was not yet, but in verse 14 He said that the end would come.

We need to remember that 24:1-14 speaks of the things between Christ's ascension and the end of the age. All these verses must be applied to the Jews during this period of time.

B. At the End of the Age

Now we come to 24:15-31. These verses describe the things that will happen at the end of the age, during the last three and a half years. The end of the age begins with verse 15. Remember, this chapter speaks especially about the sign of the Lord's coming and the sign of the end of the age. Verse 14 indicates that a strong sign of the end of the age is the preaching of the gospel of the kingdom to the whole world. When this has been accomplished, we should realize that the last three and a half years are about to begin. Thus, the preaching of the gospel of the kingdom will be the greatest sign of the end of this age. Prior to this preaching, many other things will have taken place. But these things are not the signs of the end of the age, for in speaking about them the Lord said that the end was not yet. Therefore, the preaching of the gospel of the kingdom to all the inhabited earth will be the unique sign of the end of this age. Immediately after the preaching of the gospel of the kingdom, the events described in verse 15 will take place.

1. The Great Tribulation

a. The Image of the Antichrist
Standing in the Temple

Verse 15 says, "When therefore you see the abomination of desolation, spoken of through Daniel the prophet,
standing in the holy place (let him who reads understand)." How long the period of time will be for the events
covered in verses 4 through 14, no one knows. But the
prophecy in verses 15 through 31 concerning the remnant
of the Jews will definitely be fulfilled in the last three and a
half years of this age, the time of the great tribulation, the
second half of the last week prophesied in Daniel 9:27. It
will begin with the setting of Antichrist's image (the idol)
in the temple (v. 15) and end with Christ's open coming
(v. 30).

"Abomination" means an idol (Deut. 29:17). Here it
refers to Antichrist's image set up in the temple of God as
an idol (Rev. 13:14-15; 2 Thes. 2:4) at the beginning of the
great tribulation (v. 21). Antichrist with his false prophet
will force people to worship this idol. The setting up of the
idol will mark the beginning of the great tribulation, the
end of the age.

There are many Christians who are not clear about the
phrase "the abomination of desolation." As we have seen,
the abomination here refers to an idol, the image of Antichrist set up in the holy place. According to Revelation 13,
this image will be able to speak. Before that time, no idol
will be able to speak. The Greek word rendered "desolation" means "causing desolation," "desolating." The
abomination, the idol of Antichrist, will cause desolation.
Antichrist is called the destroyer (Apollyon, Rev. 9:11); he
will do much destroying (Dan. 8:13, 23-25; 9:27). As soon as
Antichrist sets up his image and forces people to worship
it, he will begin to destroy all religious things. Furthermore, this idol will provoke the Lord's anger, and He will
come in to destroy Antichrist and his army. This is what is
indicated by the phrase "abomination of desolation."

This idol will stand in the holy place. Here the holy place refers to the temple (Psa. 68:35; Ezek. 7:24; 21:2). This indicates that Antichrist will set up his image in the temple.

b. The Jews Needing to Flee

When the abomination of desolation is set up in the holy place, the Jews will need to flee. Verse 16 says, "Then let those who are in Judea flee to the mountains." One who is on the housetop should not even come down to take the things out of his house, for the great tribulation has come. The situation will be so urgent that the Jews should not return to their houses for anything. Those who are in the field should not even turn back to take their garments (v. 18). Verse 19 says, "But woe to those who are with child and those who nurse babes in those days." Either to be with child or to nurse babes is inconvenient for escape. It will be necessary for the Jews to run as quickly as possible.

Verse 20 continues, "And pray that your flight may not be in winter, nor on a Sabbath." Winter is a difficult time for escape, and on the Sabbath travel was limited. On the Sabbath, one was allowed to walk only a short distance (Acts 1:12), not adequate for escaping. The mention of Sabbath here indicates that the Jews will keep it after the restoration of the nation of Israel. The disciples, the audience for the Lord's word here, had a twofold status, one representing the remnant of the Jews and the other representing the New Testament believers, who constitute the church. In the section of the Lord's word concerning the Jews (24:4-31), they represent the remnant of the Jews; whereas in the section concerning the church (24:32—25:30), they represent the New Testament believers. In the Gospels, in things regarding circumstances, the Lord treated His disciples as Jews, but in things concerning spirit and life, He considered them New Testament believers.

c. There Being Great Tribulation

Verse 21 says, "For then there shall be great tribulation, such as has not occurred from the beginning of the world until now, nor ever shall be." The great tribulation will occur in the last three and a half years of this age. The great tribulation will have Jerusalem as its center and Judea as its circumference, whereas the trial in Revelation 3:10 will have Rome as its center and the whole inhabited earth as its circumference. No other tribulation will be able to compare with this great tribulation which will take place under the hand of Antichrist.

Jerusalem has already been destroyed more than once, and it will be destroyed again. The first time Jerusalem was destroyed was under Nebuchadnezzar with the Babylonian army. Later, in the second century B.C., after the rebuilding of the temple, the temple was polluted by Antiochus Epiphanes. Many Bible students realize that he was a type of Titus, who came to destroy Jerusalem in A.D. 70. Certain portions of Daniel refer both to Antiochus and Titus, and it is sometimes difficult to discern which verses refer to Antiochus and which to Titus. Luke 21 indicates that the destruction of Jerusalem under Titus is connected to the destruction under Antichrist. For this reason, readers of the New Testament find it difficult to determine which verses refer to the destruction under Titus and which refer to the destruction under Antichrist. Thus, Antiochus Epiphanes was a type of Titus, and Titus was a type of Antichrist.

We must be careful not to confuse the verses in Matthew 24 with those in Luke 21, for they do not refer to exactly the same thing. In Matthew there is no reference to the destruction under Titus, which was a shadow of the destruction recorded here. The destruction of Jerusalem under Titus in A.D. 70 was a shadow of the destruction to come under Antichrist. Do not apply 24:15-31 to any time other than the last three and one half years of this age, when Antichrist will rise up to persecute the Jews.

Verse 22 says, "And except those days were cut short, no flesh at all would be saved; but because of the elect, those days shall be cut short." As we have seen, the great tribulation will last only three and one half years. The elect spoken of in this verse are the Jews, God's chosen people (Rom. 11:28).

How do we know that the great tribulation will last three and one half years? Daniel 9 speaks of the last week of the seventy weeks. The last week will be the last seven years of Israel's history in this age. At the beginning of these seven years, the Jews will make a covenant with Antichrist. But at the middle of these seven years, Antichrist will change his mind and turn his back upon them. In his agreement with the Jews, Antichrist will allow them to worship God according to the Jewish religion. But at the end of the first three and one half years, Antichrist will begin to persecute every kind of religion, set up his image in the temple, and force people to worship him. That will be the beginning of the great tribulation, the end of this age, the last three and one half years. In God's sovereignty and mercy, this time has been cut short. The tribulation under Antichrist will be so severe that no one will be able to bear it. If God had not cut it short, no flesh at all would be saved. But for the sake of the elect, those days will be limited to three and one half years.

d. False Christs and False Prophets
Arising and Showing Great Signs and Wonders
to Lead the Jews Astray

Verse 23 says, "Then if anyone says to you, Behold, here is the Christ, or, Here; do not believe it." The Jews rejected Jesus as their Messiah and are expecting a Messiah to come. They need to be warned that Messiah, the Christ, will not arise here or there on earth, but will descend on the cloud from heaven. If some say that Christ is in Bethany or others claim that He is in Bethel, the Jews are not to believe them.

Verse 24 continues, "For false Christs and false prophets shall arise and shall show great signs and wonders so as to lead astray, if possible, even the elect." Antichrist will be the last of the false Christs and will work signs and lying wonders with the power of Satan to deceive the perishing (2 Thes. 2:3, 9-10). Another beast, the false prophet, in Revelation 13:11 will be the last of the false prophets (Rev. 19:20) and will do great signs to deceive the earth dwellers (Rev. 13:13-14).

Verses 25 and 26 say, "Behold, I have told you beforehand. If therefore they say to you, Behold, He is in the wilderness, do not go forth; Behold, He is in the inner rooms; do not believe it." The wilderness is where a person separates himself from the world so that he may easily cause people to wonder whether he is the Messiah, as happened in the case of John of Baptist (3:1; John 1:19-20). The private rooms are where a person can make himself mystical and charm others.

2. Christ's Coming to the Earth

a. Christ's Coming Being like the Lightning from the East to the West

Verse 27 says, "For as the lightning comes forth from the east and shines to the west, so shall the coming of the Son of Man be." This indicates that the Christ who will be coming to earth will not be on earth or in the wilderness or in the inner room, but in the air. As the lightning flashes from the east to the west, so will the coming of the Son of Man be.

The coming (parousia) of Christ has two aspects: one is the secret aspect toward His watchful believers; the other is the open aspect toward the unbelieving Jews and Gentiles. The lightning here signifies the open aspect after the great tribulation (v. 29), whereas the thief's coming in verse 43 signifies the secret aspect before the great tribulation. Lightning is concealed in a cloud, waiting for an opportunity to flash forth. Christ will also be clothed with a cloud (Rev. 10:1) in the air for a time and then will suddenly appear like a flash to the earth.

The Greek word *parousia* is a specific word used in the New Testament to describe the Lord's coming. Parousia means the Lord's presence. This presence of the Lord begins with His coming to the air. It is difficult to determine when He will come from heaven to the air. Between the two aspects of the Lord's coming, His coming to the air and His coming to the earth, there is the parousia, the Lord's presence. This is the reason the Lord's coming has a secret aspect and an open aspect. His coming to the air is secret, but His coming to the earth is public. Twelve hundred sixty days after Antichrist sets up his image, Christ will come to earth. Thus, His open coming can be calculated, but His secret coming is not known by anyone. When He comes to the air, He will be enveloped in a cloud. But when He comes to the earth, He will be upon the cloud.

b. The Vultures Being Gathered
Where the Corpse Is

Verse 28 says, "Wherever the corpse is, there the vultures shall be gathered together." We have spent a great deal of time to learn what the corpse is and what the vultures are, and I believe that the Lord has given us the proper understanding. In the context, verses 15 and 21 imply that at the end of this age Antichrist will be the cause of the great tribulation. It is he who needs to be judged and destroyed. As all people in Adam are dead (1 Cor. 15:22), so in the eyes of the Lord the evil Antichrist with his evil army, who will war against the Lord at Armageddon (Rev. 19:17-21), is the stinking corpse, good for the vultures' appetite. And as in the Scriptures both the Lord and those who trust in Him are likened to the eagle (Exo. 19:4; Deut. 32:11; Isa. 40:31), and the swift destroying armies are also likened to flying eagles (Deut. 28:49; Hos. 8:1, NASV), so the vultures here, of the same raptorial kind as the eagle, must refer to Christ and the overcomers, who will come as a swift-flying army to war against Antichrist and his armies and destroy them, thus executing God's judgment upon them at Armageddon. This indicates not only that at His appearing to the earth Christ with His overcoming saints will be where Antichrist is with his armies, but also that Christ with the overcomers will appear swiftly from the air like the vultures. This corresponds with the lightning's flash in the foregoing verse.

According to the previous verses, we can learn what day the Lord Jesus will come to earth, but we cannot find out where. Verse 28 tells us where: the place where the corpse is, there the vultures will be gathered together. When Antichrist sets up his image, we may begin to count twelve hundred sixty days until Christ descends publicly to the earth. But this does not mean that we can know the day of His secret coming. Never be so foolish as to try to find out this day. During the past century, a number of people have tried to do this. Some even bathed, put on clean garments, and went to a housetop to wait for His coming; however, nothing happened. To repeat, the Lord's coming to the air is secret. He will come as a thief to steal you secretly. No one can give the day or the hour of this coming. But His coming to the earth will be open and the day is revealed: twelve hundred sixty days after the idol is set up. As we have pointed out, verse 28 indicates the place — the place where the armies of Antichrist are. That is the place where Christ will come to the earth with His overcomers.

c. Immediately after the Tribulation the Sun Being Darkened, the Moon Not Shining, the Stars Falling, and the Powers of the Heavens Being Shaken

Verse 29 says, "And immediately after the tribulation of those days, the sun shall be darkened, and the moon shall not give her light, and the stars shall fall from heaven, and the powers of the heavens shall be shaken." This is a strong proof that the open coming of Christ will be after the great tribulation. This supernatural calamity in heaven will follow the great tribulation at the close of this age. This differs from the fourth trumpet (Rev. 8:12), which will occur very close to the great tribulation.

d. The Sign of the Son of Man Appearing in Heaven

Verse 30 says, "And the sign of the Son of Man shall appear in heaven, and then all the tribes of the land shall wail, and they shall see the Son of Man coming on the clouds of heaven with power and great glory." What this sign is we have no way of knowing. However, it must be supernatural and clearly visible (perhaps like the lightning in verse 27), appearing in heaven.

The tribes here refer to the tribes of the nation of Israel, and the land to the holy land. At the Lord's appearing, all the tribes of Israel will repent and wail (Zech. 12:10-14; Rev. 1:7).

This verse says that the Son of Man will come on the clouds of heaven with power and great glory. By this time the Lord is no longer in the cloud, but on the cloud, appearing to the people on earth. This is the open aspect of His second coming. In Christ's first coming, His authority was manifested in such things as casting out demons and healing diseases (7:29; 8:8-9; 9:8; 21:23-24) to vindicate Himself as the heavenly King; whereas in His second coming, His power will be exercised to execute God's judgment, to destroy Antichrist and his armies, and to bind Satan for the establishment of His kingdom on earth.

3. The Gathering of Israel

Verse 31 says, "And He shall send His angels with a loud trumpet, and they shall gather together His elect from the four winds, from the extremities of the heavens to their extremities." After the great tribulation, at His coming back to earth, the Lord will gather together the scattered Jews from all parts of the earth to the holy land. This will be the fulfillment not only of the Lord's word in 23:37, but also of God's promise in the Old Testament.

Matthew 24:4-31 is a sketch of twenty centuries of Jewish history. Like those on the Mount of Olives with the Lord, we have a clear view of this. Therefore, sitting with the greatest Prophet, we know what the situation is. Not even the leaders of nations are as clear as we are. We have seen the events from Christ's ascension to the end of this age and the events during the end of this age, the period of the great tribulation. At the end of the great tribulation, there will be supernatural calamities, and Christ will appear openly and publicly to the inhabitants of the earth, especially to the Jews in the holy land. Christ will descend where Antichrist and his armies are gathered. Like vultures devouring a corpse, Christ and His overcomers will defeat Antichrist and his army. Then Christ will gather all the remaining Jews into the Messianic kingdom.

LIFE-STUDY OF MATTHEW

PROPHECY OF THE KINGDOM

(3)

Matthew 24:32—25:30 is concerned with the church. In this portion of the Word, everything spoken by the Lord is related to two matters: watchfulness and readiness, and faithfulness and prudence. In chapter twenty-four watchfulness and readiness is covered in verses 32 through 44, and faithfulness and prudence in verses 45 through 51. In chapter twenty-five, the parable of the virgins illustrates watchfulness, and the parable of the talents illustrates faithfulness. All this is related to us. We need to watch and be ready for the Lord's coming back so that we may be raptured earlier. We also need to be faithful and prudent in serving the Lord so that we may receive the reward. Thus, watchfulness is for the early rapture, and faithfulness is for reward. This is a very clear general sketch of 24:32—25:30.

II. CONCERNING THE CHURCH

A. Watching and Being Ready

The word "But" at the beginning of verse 32 indicates that from verse 32 through 25:30 is another section, the section concerning the church. The word "But" indicates that in His prophecy the Lord turns from the Jews to the believers.

1. The Restored Nation of Israel Being a Sign of the End of This Age and a Sign to the Believers

Verse 32 says, "But learn the parable from the fig tree: when its branch has already become tender and puts forth its leaves, you know that the summer is near." The fig tree, signifying the nation of Israel, was cursed in 21:19. It passed through a long winter, from the first century to A.D. 1948, when the nation of Israel was restored. That was its branch becoming tender and putting forth its leaves. This fig tree is a sign of the end of this age and a sign to the believers. To become tender signifies that life has come back, and to put forth leaves signifies outward activity. Winter signifies the time of being dried up, the time of tribulation (24:7-21). Summer signifies the age of the restored kingdom (Luke 21:30-31), which will begin at the Lord's second coming.

Verse 33 says, "So you also, when you see all these things, know that it is near, at the doors." All these things refer to the things predicted in verses 7 through 32. "It" refers to the restored kingdom of Israel (Acts 1:6), signified by the summer in verse 32.

We have pointed out that the fig tree symbolizes the nation of Israel. Israel is a sign to us, just as the preaching of the gospel of the kingdom is a sign to the Jews. When the Jews see the preaching of the gospel of the kingdom, they should realize that it is a sign of the coming tribulation. Likewise, Israel as a fig tree is a sign to us concerning the Lord's coming. The disciples had asked the Lord concerning the sign of His coming and the sign of the consummation of the age. In the foregoing section the Lord gives the sign of the consummation of the age. This sign is the preaching of the gospel of the kingdom. Now the Lord gives another sign, the sign of His coming. This sign is the fig tree. When its branches become tender and it puts forth its leaves, we know that summer, the full restoration of the Messianic kingdom, is near.

Today the restoration of Israel is not yet in fullness. As far as both population and geography are concerned, there has not been a full restoration of Israel. The Israelis and the Arabs are quarreling about the land west of the Jordan and about the Golan Heights. According to the Bible, the Golan Heights, close to Mount Hermon, and the land west of the Jordan belong to the good land and will belong to Israel. The Lord is sovereign and He knows the situation between Israel and the Arabs. He realizes that the restoration of the nation of Israel is not yet in full. The restoration of the nation of Israel is becoming more and more full. At the time of the millennium, it will reach its fullness.

2. All Things Predicted
Concerning Israel Taking Place

Verse 34 says, "Truly I say to you, This generation shall by no means pass away until all these things take place." These things refer to the fig tree becoming tender and putting forth its leaves. These things will take place before this generation is over.

It is not the generation according to age or people, as the generation in 1:17; it is the generation according to the moral condition of the people, as the generation in 11:16; 12:39, 41, 42, 45; and Proverbs 30:11-14. This means that from the time the Lord Jesus delivered this prophecy until the full restoration of Israel, the moral situation of that generation will not be changed. This generation shall not pass away until the full restoration of the nation of Israel takes place. Then the generation will change, and the moral situation will turn from evil to good.

3. No One Knowing That Day and Hour
except the Father

Verse 36 says, "But concerning that day and hour no one knows, neither the angels of the heavens, nor the Son, but the Father only." The Son, standing in the position of the Son of Man (v. 37), does not know the day and hour of His coming back.

4. The Coming of Christ
Being as the Days of Noah

Verse 37 says, "For as the days of Noah were, so shall the coming of the Son of Man be." Many Christians have misunderstood this verse. The Lord's coming (parousia) will be as the *days* of Noah. This indicates that the Lord's parousia will be a period of time. This period will be as the days of Noah; that is, the situation of the Lord's parousia will be like that in the days of Noah.

Verses 38 and 39 say, "For as they were in those days before the flood, eating and drinking, marrying and being given in marriage, until the day in which Noah entered into the ark, and they did not know until the flood came and took all away; so also shall the coming of the Son of Man be." "For" indicates that this verse is the explanation of why and how the Lord's parousia will be as the days of Noah. It is because in the days of Noah the following conditions existed: people were befuddled by eating, drinking, marrying, and being given in marriage; and they did not know until the flood came and took them away. During the Lord's parousia, people will be the same; befuddled by the necessities of this life and not knowing that God's judgment (signified by the flood) will come upon them by the Lord's coming. The believers, however, should be de-drugged and soberly know that Christ is coming to execute God's judgment upon this corrupted world.

Eating, drinking, and marriage were originally ordained by God for man's existence. But due to man's lust, Satan utilizes these necessities of human life to occupy man and keep him from God's interests. Toward the end of this age, this situation will be intensified and will reach its climax during the Lord's parousia.

The most striking features of the days before the flood were eating, drinking, marrying, and being given in marriage. This indicates that the people of those days were drugged by their fleshly, worldly enjoyment. The same thing is happening in society today. The enemy of God, Satan, utilizes the necessities of life to poison the people created by God. The entire human race has been poisoned. However, this does not mean that there is no need for us to eat, drink, or get married. All this is necessary for our existence. But we must not allow these things to drug us and to dull our senses. In human society today the senses of every person, high or low, old or young, are numb, indicating that the people have been poisoned by the way of this age in eating, drinking, and giving in marriage. This was the situation in the days of Noah, and it will be the situation at the time of the Lord's parousia.

People today are studying and working for the purpose of enjoying good eating, good drinking, and a good marriage. They have no thought concerning the things of God. How prevailing is this lack of sense concerning God today! It is prevailing especially in the educational sphere and the commercial sphere. So many in the universities have been drugged by their pursuit of an education. Their education is merely for eating, drinking, and marriage. Those in the commercial field have also been drugged by the desire to make money, also for the purpose of having better eating, drinking, and marriage. This has caused many divorces. When a young man is poor, he may marry a certain woman. But when he makes more money, he may divorce his wife and marry another in his desire for a better wife. This situation will continue until it reaches the climax during the Lord's parousia. During the days of Noah, this climax was reached a little before the flood which came in with the judgment of God. In a sense, the parousia of Christ will be like the flood coming with God's judgment. The flood brought judgment upon the drugged people of Noah's day. The parousia will bring God's judgment upon this drugged world. Christ will descend to earth and execute God's righteous judgment upon this drugged and rebellious world.

5. Before the Coming of Christ, One Being Taken and the Other Left

Verses 40 and 41 say, "Then shall two men be in the field; one is taken, and one is left. Two women shall be grinding at the mill; one is taken, and one is left." According to the context, "Then" here means "by that time." It indicates that while the worldly people are befuddled by

the material things, with no sense of the coming judgment, some of the sober and watchful believers will be
taken away. To the befuddled people, this should be a sign
of Christ's coming.

The two men in verse 40 must be brothers in Christ,
and the two women in verse 41 must be sisters in the Lord.
This is indicated by verse 42, which tells us to watch
because we do not know on what day our Lord comes. Both
"watch therefore" and "your Lord" prove that the two men
and the two women in verses 40 and 41 are believers. The
Lord would not charge unsaved people to watch, nor is He
the Lord of the unsaved.

To be taken means to be raptured before the great
tribulation. This rapture is a sign of the Lord's coming and
a sign to the Jews. It is very interesting to see that the two
men are working in the field and that the two women are
grinding at the mill. Both working in the field and grinding are for eating. There is a difference between our eating
and the eating of the worldly people. The worldly people
study and work, and we also study and work. The worldly
people, however, have been drugged. But we have not been
drugged. Rather, we are simply fulfilling our duty to make
a living. We are not for eating, drinking, and marriage; on
the contrary, we maintain our existence in order to take the
way of the cross to fulfill God's purpose. Our concern is not
for our education, employment, or business.

When some of the young people hear this, they may
say, "How glad we are to hear this word! Let's not care any
more for study or for work. Let us spend all our time praying and having fellowship with one another." Such an attitude is wrong. Remember, according to verse 40 the
brothers were farming, and according to verse 41 the sisters
were grinding. Grinding grain is very hard work. This indicates that we Christians should not take easy jobs. We
need to work hard in order to make a living. The eating and
drinking in verse 38 is worldly, but the farming and grinding in verses 40 and 41 are holy. If the ones taken were not
doing something holy, they could not have been raptured.

Do you realize that farming can be holy, but working as a pastor can be very worldly? A Bible teacher may be worldly; yet a sister who grinds grain may be holy. Many of the sisters who work at cooking the meals are holy sisters. It is not those who talk about holiness who are necessarily holy. Sometimes the more certain sisters talk about being holy, the less holy they are. It is better for such sisters to spend more time cooking to serve excellent food to their husbands, their children, and those to whom they give hospitality. The sisters who do this will be holy. Some sisters know how to have fellowship about being holy, but they do not know how to do a good job in their cooking. They always cook plain meals for their families, excusing themselves by saying that there is no need for them to waste time in cooking. But after a period of time, their husbands and children are discontent with such cooking. The more these sisters talk about being holy, the less holy their husbands and children become. They talk about holiness, but they do not take proper care of their families. We need more holy sisters to grind at the mill to produce fine flour. We are not drugged, but we do need to be properly nourished.

The principle is the same with the brothers in their jobs. A brother should not talk about holiness and neglect his job. If he does this, he will be fired. Notice, the rapture does not take place when the two brothers and the two sisters are praying, but when they are working. When I was young, I was told how wonderful it would be to be raptured while we were praying or reading the Bible. But the Lord Jesus does not speak this way. Instead, He says that two men were farming and that two women were grinding. They were not fasting, praying, or reading the Bible; they were doing their ordinary work.

The Lord Jesus certainly spoke this word with a definite purpose. He wanted to show us that as we wait for His coming and expect to be raptured, we must be very faithful in our daily duties. We need to do the best farming and the best grinding. We need a properly balanced human life, not the life of monks who devote themselves to spiritual things and expect others to take care of them. It is the brothers working in the field and the sisters grinding in the mill who will be raptured.

There used to be a proverb that anyone who becomes a preacher becomes useless. The reason for this proverb is that preachers do not need to work to earn a living. Rather, the burden for their living is placed upon others. It is a shame for us to be like this. We need to work diligently and do our duty in a proper way. When we are in the field or at the mill, we may be raptured. The sisters who are wives and mothers must do the best grinding and learn how to prepare the most healthy meals for their families. Sisters, if your husband and children are not healthy, you will be held responsible for this before the Lord. If you take care of this matter before the Lord, you will be truly holy. Do not spend your time in talking about holiness, but spend it in cooking healthy, digestible, delicious meals. You need to prepare good meals to preserve the life of your husband and to build up the health of your children. This matter is included in the Lord's reference to grinding at the mill.

The brothers who are fathers and husbands also need to work diligently at their jobs to earn the money needed to take care of their families. Those who work simply to have a great deal of money in the bank are drugged. But we need to labor in order to provide the best things for our children. Otherwise, we are faithful neither to God nor to our children. As parents, we must do the best to educate our children. We should not have the attitude that it is good enough for them to graduate from high school and work in a menial job. To be in the field means that we care that our children are fed well and educated in the best way. We should not be those who love the world and work to make money for ourselves. But we should be those who work diligently to earn money for our family. As those with a fallen human nature, it is easy for us to excuse ourselves for not spending so much time in the field or at the grinding. If you do this, you will not be raptured. I repeat, you will be raptured while you are working in the field or grinding out the grain.

Of the two men in the field, one is taken and the other is left; and of the two women grinding at the mill, one is taken and the other left. The reason for this is that there is a difference between them in the matter of life. I believe that the one taken is mature and that the one left is immature. The life makes the difference. The rapture of the overcomers, those who are mature in life, will be a sign to those who are left. Suppose you are working in the field with a brother and he is suddenly taken away to the heavens. That would certainly be a sign to you. Suppose two sisters are grinding at the mill, and one is taken away to the Lord. Surely that would be a sign to the sister who was left!

6. Watching and Being Ready
Because Christ Will Come as a Thief

In verse 42 the Lord tells us to watch, for we do not know on what day the Lord will come. Then verse 43 says, "But know this, that if the householder knew in what watch the thief was coming, he would have watched and would not have allowed his house to be broken into." The householder refers to the believer, and the house, to the believer's conduct and work which he has built up in his Christian life. A thief comes to steal precious things at an unknown time. The Lord will come secretly as a thief to those who love Him and will take them away as His treasures. Hence, we should watch. "Therefore," as the Lord says in verse 44, "you also, be ready, for the Son of Man comes in an hour that you think not." This refers to the Lord's secret coming to the watchful overcomers.

B. Being Faithful and Prudent

1. The Faithful and Prudent Slave Giving Food to the Lord's Household at the Appointed Time

Verses 45 through 51 are concerned with faithfulness and prudence. Verse 45 says, "Who then is the faithful and prudent slave, whom the master has set over his household to give them food at the appointed time?" Faithfulness is toward the Lord, whereas prudence is toward the believers. Watchfulness is for rapture into the Lord's presence, but faithfulness is for reigning in the kingdom (v. 47).

The household spoken of in verse 45 refers to the believers (Eph. 2:19), who are the church (1 Tim. 3:15). To give them food is to minister the Word of God with Christ as the life supply to the believers in the church. We all must learn how to minister the life supply to the household of the Lord at the appointed time.

Verses 46 and 47 say, "Blessed is that slave whom his master when he comes shall find so doing. Truly I say to you, that he will set him over all his possessions." To be blessed here is to be rewarded with ruling authority in the manifestation of the kingdom. The faithful slave of the Lord will be set over all His possessions as a reward in the manifestation of the kingdom of the heavens.

2. The Evil Slave Beating His Fellow Slaves, Eating and Drinking with the Drunken, and Being Cut Off from the Lord in His Coming Glory

Verse 48 says, "But if that evil slave says in his heart, My master is delaying his coming." The evil slave is a believer, because he is appointed by the Lord (v. 45), he calls the Lord "my master," and he believes that the Lord is coming. Verse 49 says that the evil slave beats his fellow slaves and eats and drinks with the drunken. To beat the fellow slaves is to mistreat the fellow believers, and to eat and drink with the drunken is to keep company with worldly people, who are drunk with worldly things.

Verses 50 and 51 say, "The master of that slave shall come on a day when he does not expect him, and in an hour which he does not know, and shall cut him asunder and appoint his portion with the hypocrites; there shall be the weeping and the gnashing of teeth." The problem with the evil slave is not that he does not know that the Lord is coming, but that he does not expect Him. He does not like to live the kind of life that is prepared for the Lord's coming. Therefore, when the Lord comes back, He will cut him asunder and appoint his portion with the hypocrites. To cut him asunder means to cut him off. This signifies a separation from the Lord in His coming glory. This corresponds to being cast out into the outer darkness in the conclusion of the parable of the talents (25:14-30), which is a completion to this section. The Lord will not cut the evil slave in pieces; rather, He will cut him off from the glory in which He Himself will be. This is equal to being cast out into outer darkness.

Whoever is cast into outer darkness will be cut off from the Lord, from His presence, from His fellowship, and from the glorious sphere in which the Lord will be. This is not to perish eternally, but to be chastened dispensationally. Who can say that the evil slave is not a genuine believer? If he were not a brother, how could his work have been assigned by the Lord? The Lord would not assign duties to a false believer. Certainly the evil slave is a saved one. In Matthew, the book of the kingdom, the issue is not salvation. The issue is the kingdom: whether we shall receive a reward to enter into the kingdom, or whether we shall lose the reward, miss the enjoyment of the kingdom, and suffer punishment and discipline where there will be weeping and gnashing of teeth.

LIFE-STUDY OF MATTHEW

MESSAGE SIXTY-FOUR

PROPHECY OF THE KINGDOM

(4)

We have seen that the section of the prophecy of the kingdom concerning the church covers two aspects: the aspect of being watchful and ready and the aspect of being faithful and prudent. Watchfulness and readiness are related to our Christian life. We all need to be watchful and ready for the Lord's coming. However, a proper Christian should take care not only of the aspect of life, but also of the aspect of service. For service, we need faithfulness and prudence. Thus, we need to be faithful toward the Lord and prudent toward our fellow believers. As we have seen, in chapter twenty-four both aspects are covered. In life we need to be watchful and ready, and in service we need to be faithful and prudent.

Although both these aspects are covered in chapter twenty-four, they are not covered fully. Thus, in chapter twenty-five there is the need of a complementary word for each aspect covered in chapter twenty-four. Matthew 25:1-30 completes the section in chapter twenty-four concerning the believers. The parable of the virgins (25:1-13) completes the matter of watchfulness and readiness. How to watch and be ready is revealed in the parable of the virgins. Matthew 25:13, the last verse of the parable of the virgins, says, "Watch therefore, for you do not know the day nor the hour." This word, very similar to 24:42, indicates that 25:1-13 is a completion to 24:40-44 concerning watchfulness for rapture.

Matthew 24:32-44 is a section on watchfulness and readiness. Matthew 25:1-13 is also a section on watchfulness and readiness, the completion of the foregoing section. In the same principle, both 24:45-51 and 25:14-30 are sections on faithfulness and prudence. Matthew 25:30, which speaks of casting the useless slave into outer darkness, is parallel to 24:51. This indicates that 25:14-30 is a completion to 24:45-51, which concerns faithfulness for the Lord's work. Matthew 24:45-51 deals with the slave's unfaithfulness in fulfilling the Lord's commission. Matthew 25:14-30 is still needed to deal with the slave's unfaithfulness in using the Lord's talent. Although 24:45-51 tells us to be faithful and prudent, it does not show us how to be faithful and prudent. This is revealed in the parable of the talents.

The way to be watchful is through the infilling of the Holy Spirit; it is by having the extra portion of oil. By ourselves we can be neither watchful nor ready. The only way to have the extra portion of oil is by the infilling of the Holy Spirit. This is the way for us to be watchful and ready. Likewise, the way to be faithful and prudent in the Lord's service is through the spiritual gifts. Without the spiritual gifts, we do not have the ability to be faithful or prudent. Our faithfulness and prudence depend upon the gifts we have received of the Lord. Therefore, in chapter twenty-five we have both the infilling of the Spirit and the gifts of the Spirit. The Spirit affords us the infilling for life and also the gifts for service. It all depends upon the Spirit. How can we be watchful? Only by the infilling of the Holy Spirit. And how can we be faithful? Only by the gifts of the Holy Spirit.

One indication that the parables in chapter twenty-five are a completion of 24:32-51 is found in the numbers two and ten. Matthew 25:1 says, "Then shall the kingdom of the heavens be likened to ten virgins." Ten is the major part of twelve (Gen. 42:3-4; 1 Kings 11:30-31; Matt. 20:24). Hence, these ten virgins represent the majority of the believers, who will have died before the Lord's coming. The two men or two women in 24:40-41 represent the remaining believers, who will be alive until the Lord's coming.

The two men in the field or the two women grinding at the mill represent the living believers. However, when the Lord's parousia comes, the majority of the believers will have died. In chapter twenty-four we have the rapture of the living believers, but this chapter says nothing about the dead saints. This is covered by the parable of the virgins in 25:1-13. The fact that the virgins "became drowsy and slept" (v. 5) indicates that they died. In the eyes of the Lord, when a saint dies, he goes to sleep. Therefore, the ten virgins, who all fell asleep, represent the dead saints.

In the Bible God's people are of the number twelve, for this number represents the whole body of God's people. In the Bible one way the number twelve is composed is of ten plus two. Ten denotes the majority of twelve, and two signifies the remainder. For example, two of the twelve apostles asked the Lord to let them sit on His right hand and on His left hand, whereas the other ten were indignant. In the Old Testament ten tribes rebelled against the house of David, whereas only two remained faithful. The principle is the same here in chapters twenty-four and twenty-five. In chapter twenty-four we have the two and in chapter twenty-five we have the ten. When the ten and the two are put together, we have the whole body of believers. At the time of the Lord's coming, the majority of the believers will have died. Only a small number, the remainder represented by the two men in the field or the two women grinding, will be alive. Therefore, 25:1-13 is the completion of 24:40-41.

Another indication that chapter twenty-five is the completion of chapter twenty-four is found in the fact that one of the men and one of the women were taken and the other man and other woman were left. Why was one taken and the other left? The answer is not found in chapter twenty-four, but in chapter twenty-five. The reason one was taken was that he was filled with the Holy Spirit, and the reason the one was left was that he lacked the extra portion of oil. Let us now consider the parable of the virgins, the parable for watchfulness, verse by verse.

C. Parable for Watchfulness

1. Ten Virgins

Matthew 25:1 says, "Then shall the kingdom of the heavens be likened to ten virgins, who took their lamps and went forth to meet the bridegroom." The word "Then" here means "at that time," that is, at the time of the parousia. When the parousia described in chapter twenty-four is taking place, many things will be happening. Then the kingdom of the heavens will be likened to ten virgins.

Virgins signify believers in the aspect of life (2 Cor. 11:2). Believers, who are the kingdom people, are like chaste virgins, bearing the Lord's testimony (the lamp) in the dark age and going out of the world to meet the Lord. For this they need not only the indwelling, but also the fullness of the Spirit of God.

We Christians firstly are virgins. Being a virgin is not a matter of work, service, or activity, but a matter of life. Moreover, we are not only virgins, but chaste, pure virgins. Being a virgin is not a matter of what we do or are able to do; it is absolutely a matter of what we are. Whether we are male or female, we are virgins. Although I am an old man, I conduct myself like a virgin. I would never sell my status as a virgin. Even before the enemy, I am a virgin.

a. Taking Their Lamps

Verse 1 says that the virgins took their lamps and went forth to meet the bridegroom. Lamps signify the spirit of the believers (Prov. 20:27), which contains the Spirit of God as the oil (Rom. 8:16). The believers shine with the light of the Spirit of God from within their spirit. Thus, they become the light of the world, like a lamp shining in the darkness of this age (Matt. 5:14-16; Phil. 2:15-16) to bear the testimony of the Lord for the glorification of God. Thus, as virgins we do not take weapons for fighting or sports equipment for playing, but lamps for testifying, shining, and enlightening. In our hand is a lamp shining for the Lord's testimony.

b. Going Forth

The virgins went forth. This signifies that the believers are going out of the world to meet the coming Christ. The virgins do not linger or settle in any place. Instead, they are going out of the world. In one of his writings, D.M. Panton said that the world was just a pathway to him and at the end of this pathway there would be a grave. If the Lord delays His coming back, the world eventually will afford me only a resting place, a tomb in which to lie as I wait for the Lord's coming. We are not settled in this world. We are going out of the world.

c. To Meet the Bridegroom

The bridegroom signifies Christ as the pleasant and attractive person (John 3:29; Matt. 9:15). How good it is that in this parable the Lord likens Himself not to a victorious general or great commander-in-chief, but to a bridegroom, a most pleasant person. Thus, we are the virgins going, and He is the Bridegroom coming.

2. The Five Foolish Ones Not Taking Oil with Them

Verse 2 says, "And five of them were foolish, and five were prudent." Five is composed of four plus one, signifying that man (signified by four) with God (signified by one) added to him bears responsibility. The fact that five are foolish and five prudent does not indicate that half the believers are foolish and the other half are prudent. It indicates that all believers bear responsibility to be filled with the Spirit of God.

The Old Testament reveals clearly that five is the number of responsibility. For example, the ten commandments were divided into two groups of five. Also, the number five appears frequently with respect to the tabernacle and its furniture. Five is the basic factor of many of its dimensions.

The five fingers on our hand indicate how the number five is composed in the Bible. It is composed of four plus one. As we have pointed out, the number four signifies the creature and the number one the Creator. The creature plus the Creator gives the ability to bear responsibility. If we had just four fingers without a thumb, it would be difficult for us to do anything. This means that by ourselves, as the number four, we cannot bear responsibility. But when God is added to us, we are able to bear responsibility.

Verse 2 says that five of the virgins were foolish and five were prudent. The Lord Jesus mentions the foolish first because in the bearing of responsibility the problem is not with the prudent ones, but with the foolish ones. Being foolish does not make these five virgins false. In nature they are the same as the five prudent ones.

Verse 3 tells us the reason they were foolish: "For the foolish, when they took their lamps, did not take oil with them." Oil signifies the Spirit of God (Isa. 61:1; Heb. 1:9). The foolish ones were foolish because they had oil only in the lamp, but not the extra portion of oil in the vessel. In addition to the regenerating Spirit, they did not have the infilling Spirit, the extra portion of the Holy Spirit.

3. The Five Prudent Ones
Taking Oil in Their Vessels

Verse 4 says, "But the prudent took oil in their vessels with their lamps." Man is a vessel made for God (Rom. 9:21, 23-24), and man's personality is in his soul. Hence, vessels here signify the soul of the believers. The five prudent virgins not only have oil in their lamps, but also take oil in their vessels. Having oil in their lamps signifies that they have the Spirit of God dwelling in their spirit (Rom. 8:9, 16), and taking oil in their vessels signifies that they have the fullness of the Spirit of God saturating their souls.

We need to be very clear about the lamps and the vessels. According to the Hebrew text, Proverbs 20:27 says that the spirit of man is the lamp of the Lord. Within the lamp is the oil, the Holy Spirit. The New Testament reveals that our spirit is the place the Holy Spirit indwells. According to Romans 9, we are vessels made by God. Our being, our personality, is in our soul. Therefore, the vessel in this verse signifies our soul. Through regeneration we have the Spirit of God in our spirit. This causes our lamp to burn. But the question is whether or not we have the extra portion of the Holy Spirit filling our soul. Although we have the oil in our lamp, we need the extra portion of the oil in our soul. This signifies that the Spirit must spread from within our spirit to every part of our soul. Then in our soul we shall have an extra amount of the Holy Spirit. If we have this extra portion, we are prudent. If we do not have it, we are foolish. In other words, if we are indifferent to the infilling of the Holy Spirit, we are foolish. If we are wise, we shall pray, "Lord, have mercy on me. I want to have Your Spirit not only in my spirit, but also in my soul. Lord, I need the infilling of the Spirit. I need the extra portion of the Holy Spirit to fill my entire being." Without this extra portion of the Spirit, we cannot be watchful or ready. In order to be watchful and ready, we need the infilling of the Holy Spirit, the spreading of the Spirit Himself from our spirit to every part of our inward being.

4. The Bridegroom Delaying

Verse 5 says that the Bridegroom delayed His coming. The Lord Jesus truly has delayed His coming again. In Revelation He promised to come quickly, but nearly two thousand years have passed, and still He delays his coming.

5. All the Virgins
Becoming Drowsy and Sleeping

Because the Bridegroom delayed His coming, all the virgins "became drowsy and slept." Becoming drowsy signifies becoming sick (Acts 9:37; 1 Cor. 11:30), and going to sleep signifies dying (1 Thes. 4:13-16; John 11:11-13). While the Lord delays His coming back, the majority of the believers firstly become sick and then die.

6. A Cry at Midnight

Verse 6 says, "But at midnight there is a cry, Behold, the bridegroom! Go forth to meet him!" Midnight signifies the darkest time of this dark age (night). That will be the end of this age, the time of the great tribulation. "Cry" signifies the voice of the archangel (1 Thes. 4:16).

7. All the Virgins Arising

Verse 7 says, "Then all those virgins arose and trimmed their lamps." "Arose" signifies resurrection from the dead (1 Thes. 4:14). This is the resurrection predicted in 1 Thessalonians 4:16 and 1 Corinthians 15:52.

8. Trimming Their Lamps

After the virgins arose, they "trimmed their lamps." This signifies their dealing with their testimony in life. This indicates that after resurrection our life for the Lord's testimony will still need to be dealt with if it is not perfect before we die.

9. The Foolish Wanting to Borrow Oil from the Prudent

Verse 8 says, "And the foolish said to the prudent, Give us some of your oil, for our lamps are going out." This word implies that even after resurrection the foolish believers will still need the fullness of the Spirit of God. "Going out" proves that the lamps of the foolish virgins are lighted, having oil in them, but not having an adequate supply. The foolish virgins represent the believers who have been regenerated by the Spirit of God dwelling in them, but who are not filled with the Spirit of God so that He may saturate their whole being.

10. The Answer of the Prudent

Verse 9 says, "But the prudent answered, saying, Lest there be not enough for us and for you, go rather to those who sell and buy for yourselves." This indicates that no one can have the fullness of the Holy Spirit for others. We may borrow many things, but we cannot borrow the infilling of the Holy Spirit. This is like eating. No one can eat for you.

The prudent virgins told the foolish ones to go to those who sell and buy for themselves. Those who sell oil must be the two witnesses during the great tribulation, the two olive trees and the two sons of oil (Rev. 11:3-4; Zech. 4:11-14). During the great tribulation, the two sons of oil, Moses and Elijah, will come to help God's people.

To buy indicates the need of paying a price. The fullness of the Holy Spirit is obtained at a cost, such as giving up the world, dealing with the self, loving the Lord above all, and counting all things loss for Christ. If we do not pay this price today, we must pay it after resurrection. Those who do not pay the price do not have the extra portion of the Holy Spirit. Eventually, the foolish virgins will realize that they need to love the Lord with all their heart and soul. They will see that they need to give up the world and deal with the self.

11. The Bridegroom Coming and the Ready Ones Going In with Him to the Marriage Feast

Verse 10 says, "And as they were going away to buy, the bridegroom came, and those who were ready went in with him to the marriage feast, and the door was shut." The word "came" refers to the Lord's coming to the air (1 Thes. 4:16), a part of His parousia. Those who are ready must be those who are invited to the marriage dinner of the Lamb (Rev. 19:9). We should be ready (24:44) by always having oil in our vessel, always being filled with the Spirit of God in our whole being. To watch and be ready should be our daily exercise for the Lord's parousia.

To go in with Him refers to the rapture of the resurrected believers to the air (1 Thes. 4:17) during the Lord's parousia. The marriage feast in verse 10 is the marriage dinner of the Lamb (Rev. 19:9), which will be held in the air (1 Thes. 4:17) during the Lord's coming, His parousia. It will occur before the manifestation of the kingdom as a reward of mutual enjoyment with the Lord to the believers who are ready, who have been equipped with the fullness of the Holy Spirit before they die.

After those who are ready go in with the Bridegroom to the marriage feast, the door is shut. This is not the door of salvation, but the door to enter into the enjoyment of the Lord's marriage feast.

12. The Foolish Virgins Coming Later, but the Bridegroom Not Knowing Them

Verses 11 and 12 say, "And later the rest of the virgins came also, saying, Lord, Lord, open to us! But he answered and said, Truly I say to you, I do not know you." The later coming of the foolish virgins refers to the later rapture of the resurrected believers. They paid the price for the extra portion of oil, but they obtained it too late. Time means a great deal here, for when they came, the door was shut.

When they asked the Lord to open to them, He said, "I do not know you." To not know here indicates not to recognize, not to approve, as in Luke 13:25; John 1:26, 31; 8:19. The foolish virgins had their lamps lighted, went forth to meet the Lord, died, and were resurrected and raptured, but were late in paying the price for the fullness of the Holy Spirit. Because of this, the Lord would not recognize or approve of them for participation in His marriage feast. They missed this reward dispensationally, but they do not lose their salvation eternally.

In telling them that He did not know them, the Lord was saying, "I do not appreciate you or recognize you, and I do not approve of the way you lived on the earth. Also, I do not approve of your coming so late." Thus, they are rejected from the enjoyment of the kingdom feast.

13. Watching

Verse 13 concludes, "Watch therefore, for you do not know the day nor the hour." Chapter 24:40-44 refers to the rapture only of the living believers who are ready. Chapter 25:1-13 is needed to cover the rapture of the dead and resurrected ones. When we read this portion of the Word, we see how watchful we need to be. To be watchful and ready is a very serious matter.

No other book warns us as often as the book of Matthew does. I can testify before the Lord that for more than forty years I have been warned by this book. Whenever I have been a little careless, I have remembered the warnings contained in Matthew. Yes, we all are virgins, but are we foolish or prudent? We all need to answer this question for ourselves. Whether we are prudent or not depends on whether or not we have the extra portion of the Holy Spirit in our vessel.

LIFE-STUDY OF MATTHEW

PROPHECY OF THE KINGDOM

(5)

Concerning the Christian life, the New Testament reveals that firstly we need to receive the Spirit of God into our spirit so that we may be regenerated. Following this, we need to grow. To grow is to be transformed, and to be transformed is mainly to be renewed in the spirit of the mind. Transformation and the renewing of the mind issue in the infilling of the Holy Spirit in our soul. Our mind is the leading part of our soul. To be renewed in the spirit of our mind is to have our mind filled and saturated with the Spirit. Then the Spirit that has saturated our mind will renew our whole being. Thus, our being, our soul, will be saturated with the infilling Spirit. This is the way to have the extra portion of oil in the vessel.

As we pointed out in the foregoing message, to be regenerated, to have the new birth, is to have the Spirit in our spirit, that is, to have the oil in our lamp. To have the Spirit in our soul means that we grow in life, are transformed, are renewed in our whole being, and have our soul saturated with the Holy Spirit of God. This is to have the oil in the vessel. This is the way to be watchful and to be ready for the Lord's coming. It is also the way to be prepared to be raptured into the Lord's presence.

D. Parable for Faithfulness

Having covered the parable for watchfulness (25:1-13), we proceed in this message to the parable for faithfulness (25:14-30). The parable of the virgins is for watchfulness, but the parable of the talents is for faithfulness.

When we were on chapter twenty-four, we pointed out

that concerning the believers, there are two aspects: the aspect of watchfulness and readiness and the aspect of faithfulness and prudence. The believers have these two aspects because they have a dual status. The first aspect of this dual status is related to life, and the second aspect is related to service. No Christian should neglect these two aspects; rather, we must pay the proper attention to both, becoming proper in life and in service. Regarding life, we are virgins; regarding service, we are slaves. This means that in watchfulness we are virgins. This relates to what we are. But in faithfulness we are slaves. This relates to what we do.

Although we may like the term "virgins," we may not like hearing that we are slaves. Nevertheless, we are not only virgins, but also slaves. To the virgins, the Lord is the Bridegroom, but to the slaves, He is the Master. Thus, not only we have a dual status, but the Lord also has a dual status. On the one hand, He is our pleasant Bridegroom and, on the other, our strict Master. Sometimes He is very pleasant with us, but at other times He deals with us in a strict way.

The virgins need something inward — the inward filling of the oil in the vessel. The slaves, however, need something outward — the spiritual talent. The infilling of the Holy Spirit is inward, but the talent, the spiritual gift, is outward. As vessels we need the oil inwardly, and as slaves we need the talents outwardly.

The oil that fills the vessel reaches the very bottom of the vessel. It is from within that the renewing of our being takes place, and it is from within that transformation transpires. There is a great lack of this inward working among Christians today. Rather, many Christians are striving to improve their outward appearance in order to make a show. Religion is concerned with outward show, but God's grace in the infilling of the Holy Spirit gets into us and transforms us from within. The inward oil is very different from outward makeup. Makeup changes our complexion immediately. But God's way is that we drink of the Spirit and let the Spirit saturate our being. Then our appearance will change from within. For example, I eat and drink well, and nourishing food saturates my being. This gives me a healthy complexion.

The fact that we need to be renewed from within does not mean that we do not need outward activities. The one who received five talents traded with them diligently and gained another five talents. This indicates that we need both the inward renewing and the outward service, the inward growth and the outward actions. We need to be deeply impressed with this principle. Regarding the aspect of life, we need to be renewed from within, and regarding the aspect of service, we need to be very active outwardly. Sometimes we may be so active outwardly that we neglect the inward renewing. But at other times we may care so much for the inner life that we do not work adequately. To be like this is to be an unturned cake (Hosea 7:8). On one side we are burned to charcoal, and on the other side we are raw. Neither side is good for eating. We need to be a turned cake. If we work too much, the Lord will tell us to rest. But if we rest too much, the Lord will tell us to work.

1. A Man Going into Another Country

Verse 14 says, "For it is as a man who, going into another country, called his own slaves and delivered to them his possessions." The word "it" refers to the kingdom of the heavens, indicating that this parable of the talents, like the parable of the ten virgins, is also concerning the kingdom of the heavens. The man here signifies Christ, who was going into another country, that is, into the heavens.

2. Delivering His Possessions to His Slaves

Verse 14 says that this man delivered his possessions to his slaves. The slaves signify believers in the aspect of service (1 Cor. 7:22-23; 2 Pet. 1:1; James 1:1; Rom. 1:1). As we have seen, the status of the believers in their relationship toward Christ is of two aspects: in life they are the virgins living for Him; in service, in work, they are His purchased slaves serving Him.

I believe that the possessions delivered to the slaves include the gospel, the truth, the believers, and the church. The believers are God's inheritance, God's possession (Eph. 1:18). Matthew 24:45 indicates that the believers are also His household.

3. Giving Five Talents, Two Talents, and One Talent

Verse 15 says, "And to one he gave five talents, to another two, to another one; to each according to his own ability." While oil in the parable of the virgins signifies the Spirit of God, talents in this parable signify spiritual gifts (Eph. 4:8; Rom. 12:6; 1 Cor. 12:4; 1 Pet. 4:10; 2 Tim. 1:6). For life we need oil, the Spirit of God, even His fullness, that we may be enabled to live the virgin life for the Lord's testimony; for service, for work, we need the talent, the spiritual gift, that we may be equipped as a good slave for the accomplishment of the Lord's work. The fullness of the Spirit in life is for us to use the spiritual gift in service, and the spiritual gift in service matches the fullness of the Spirit in life that we may be perfected as members of Christ.

Verse 14 says that the man gave his slaves his possessions, but verse 15 says that he gave them talents. This indicates that the talents in verse 15 are the possessions in verse 14. In other words, the Lord uses His possessions as talents for us. For example, the gospel is the Lord's possession. But when it is given to us, it becomes our talent. Likewise, the truth is the Lord's possession. But when the truth is given to us, it becomes a talent. In the same principle, all the believers are the Lord's possessions. When the believers are given to us, they become our talents. Without all the believers, my talent would not be very big. Furthermore, the church is the Lord's possession. When the church is given to us, it becomes our talent. The more of His possessions the Lord gives to us, the more talents we shall have. In like manner, the more the Lord burdens us, the more talents we shall have.

Many Christians know that in this parable the talents

are gifts. However, they do not know that the source of the gifts is the Lord's possessions. Today the Lord's possessions primarily are the gospel, the truth, the believers, and the church. If you do not care for these things, you will not have any talents. The gospel needs to become our possession. The same is true of the truth, the believers, and the churches. My talents are not natural. Rather, they are the gospel, the truth, the believers, and the church. If you took all these things away from me, I would have nothing left. I have a strong talent because I have not only the gospel and the truth, but also thousands of believers and hundreds of churches. This is the reason this ministry has had impact.

We should not wait in an indifferent way for the Lord to give us something. No, we must diligently seek the gospel and the truth. We should be eager to know the fall of man, redemption, regeneration, salvation, the cleansing of the blood, and the washing of the Spirit. All these are aspects of the full gospel. The more you receive of the gospel, the more talents you will have. We need to pray that the Lord would help us to know the truth and to experience it. We need to experience the truth concerning the church, God's eternal purpose, and God's economy. Eventually, these truths will become our talent. Then we shall be able to minister them to others. In this way, the Lord's possessions become our talent. Furthermore, we need to pray, "Lord, I want to take care of the saints and bear their burdens. My heart is for them." If we have a heart for the saints and are burdened for them, they, the Lord's possession, will be given to us as a talent. How thankful I am that so many saints and churches have become my talent! My ministry is strongly backed up by all the saints and all the churches in the Far East. If the Lord sent me to another place, I would also have the support of the churches in the United States, for the churches here have become an addition to my talent.

If you want to receive more talents, you must have a heart to care for the saints. For example, when someone is unemployed, you need to pray for him and bear his burden.

This will be a proof that the Lord has given that one to you as a talent. However, not to bear the saints or care for them means that you forsake the Lord's possession. Every dear saint is a precious part of the Lord's possession. It is not a small matter to be concerned for the saints, for they are the Lord's possession.

When the Lord's possessions are in His hand, they remain His possessions. But when they are delivered to us, they become our talent. Do not drop any burden that the Lord has given you. No matter how busy I am, I cannot drop any talent, for to do this is to drop the Lord's possession. The Lord has a vast work in His recovery. For this work, He needs thousands of young brothers and sisters to be raised up to bear the responsibility.

The talent is not something of your natural birth; rather, it is altogether related to your burden. If you take up a burden, you will receive a talent. If you take up a burden for one local church, you will receive one talent. But if you take up the burden for five churches, you will have five talents. During the past twenty-eight years, more than two hundred eighty churches have been built up under this ministry. Recently, when I was accused, criticized, and condemned, I asked the Lord whether or not this ministry was wrong. At that time He pointed out to me that the way to know the tree is by its fruit. He told me to look how many churches have been established and built up by this ministry. However, if we are ambitious for ourselves, this ambition will kill the talents.

4. To Each according to His Ability

Although the talents are not our ability, but the Lord's possession, they are delivered to us according to our ability. Our ability is constituted by God's creation and our learning. The capacity of our ability is based upon the willingness of our heart. If we do not have any willingness in our heart, then we shall not have the capacity to receive the talent. The capacity to receive the talent is measured by the willingness of our heart.

5. *Those with Five Talents and Two Talents Trading with Them*

Verses 16 and 17 say, "Immediately, he who received the five talents went and traded with them and gained another five; similarly, he who received the two gained another two." To trade with the talents signifies using the gift the Lord has given us, and to gain other talents signifies that the gift we received from the Lord has been used to the fullest extent, without any loss or waste.

According to chapter twenty-four, the slave is to supply food to those in the household. This refers to the ministering of the nourishing Word with the riches of Christ as the life supply to those in the Lord's house. Here, however, it speaks of trading with the talents to cause the talents to multiply. Therefore, the result of our service has two aspects. The first aspect is that others are fed and given rich nourishment. The second aspect is that the Lord's possessions are multiplied. For example, the more we preach the gospel, the richer the gospel becomes. It is the same with the truths. As we minister the truths to others, the truths multiply. This is also true of the saints and the churches. Both the believers and the churches will multiply. Thus, five talents are multiplied into ten, and two talents are multiplied into four.

6. *The Slave with One Talent Digging in the Earth and Hiding It*

Verse 18 says, "But he who received the one went away and dug in the earth and hid his lord's silver." The main emphasis in this parable is on the one-talented one, the one who received the smallest gift. It is very easy for the least-gifted ones to fail to make the proper use of their gift.

As the earth signifies the world, so to dig in the earth signifies getting into the world. Any association, any involvement with the world, even a little worldly talk, will bury the Lord's gift to us. Hiding the Lord's silver signifies rendering the Lord's gift useless, letting it lie waste under the cloak of certain earthly excuses. Any excuse for not using the Lord's gift is to hide it. This is always the danger with the one-talented ones, those who consider their gift as the smallest.

With the one-talented slave in this parable, there is no multiplication. For instance, in a certain area there may be one church. Ten years later, there is still just one church in that area. Some may think that the one-talented slave did well in not losing his talent and in returning to the Lord what was His. The one-talented slave seemed to say, "Lord, here is what is Yours. You gave me one talent, and I have been faithful to keep, guard, protect, and preserve it. By Your mercy and grace, I have kept it." But the issue of our service must be the multiplication of our talents. It is not the Lord's will for us simply to maintain what He has given us. If you are faithful merely to keep the gospel, the truth, and the church without any multiplication, the Lord will say that you are slothful. Furthermore, He will call you an evil slave. In the eyes of the Lord, it is evil to bury the talent and not to multiply it. The Lord does not care for our argument or excuses. He cares only that the one talent is multiplied into two. This is a serious matter. Our service must issue in the feeding and satisfaction of others and in the multiplication of the talent.

LIFE-STUDY OF MATTHEW

PROPHECY OF THE KINGDOM

(6)

In this message we shall continue our consideration of the parable for faithfulness (25:14-30).

7. The Lord of the Slaves Coming to Settle Accounts with Them

Verse 19 says, "Now after a long time the lord of those slaves comes and settles accounts with them." A long time signifies the entire church age, and the coming signifies the Lord's coming to the air (1 Thes. 4:16) in His parousia. To settle accounts signifies the Lord's judgment at His judgment seat (2 Cor. 5:10; Rom. 14:10) in the air (within His parousia), where the believers' life, conduct, and work will be judged for reward or punishment (1 Cor. 4:5; Matt. 16:27; Rev. 22:12; 1 Cor. 3:13-15).

8. The Five-talented and the Two-talented Ones Both Receiving a Reward

Verse 20 says, "And he who received the five talents came and brought another five talents, saying, Lord, you delivered to me five talents; behold, I have gained another five talents." The coming of the five-talented one refers to the coming to the judgment seat of Christ. Gaining another five talents is the result of the full use of the gift of the five talents.

Verse 21 says, "His lord said to him, Well done, good and faithful slave; you were faithful over a few things, I will set you over many things; enter into the joy of your lord." The "few things" signify the Lord's work in this age,

"over" signifies the ruling authority in the coming kingdom, and the "many things" signify the responsibilities in
the coming kingdom. The joy of the Lord signifies the
enjoyment of the Lord in the coming kingdom. This is the
inward satisfaction, not the outward position. To participate in the Lord's joy is the greatest reward, better than
the glory and position in the kingdom. Here we see two
aspects of the reward given to the faithful slave: authority
and enjoyment. The faithful will enter directly into the
Lord's presence in the manifestation of the kingdom.

The same reward is given to the two-talented one as to
the five-talented one. When the two-talented one came
and said that he had gained another two talents, the Lord
said the same thing to him that He had said to the five-
talented one (vv. 22-23). Although the gift given to the two-
talented one is smaller than that given to the five-talented
one, the Lord's appraisal and reward to both are the same.
This indicates that the Lord's appraisal and reward are not
related to the size and quantity of our work, but to our
faithfulness in using His gift to the fullest extent. The
same appraisal and reward would also have been given to
the one-talented one if he had been as faithful.

9. The One-talented One
Receiving a Rebuke and Being Punished

Verse 24 says, "And he also who received the one talent
came and said, Lord, I knew you, that you are a hard man,
reaping where you did not sow, and gathering where you
did not scatter." The one-talented one, who did not gain
any profit for the Lord, also came to the judgment seat of
Christ in the air. This proves that he is not only saved, but
also raptured to the air. No unsaved person could be raptured and come to the judgment seat of Christ.

The one-talented one said that the Lord was a hard
man, reaping where he did not sow and gathering where he
did not scatter. Apparently the Lord is hard in His strictness, demanding that we use His gift to the fullest extent
for His absolute work. It seems that the Lord's work always

begins from zero. He seemingly demands us to work for Him with nothing. This should not be an excuse for the one talented one to neglect the use of his gift. Rather, this should force him to exercise his faith to use his gift to the uttermost.

Verse 25 says, "And I was afraid, and went away and hid your talent in the earth; behold, you have what is yours." To be afraid is negative. We should rather be positive and aggressive in using the Lord's gift. If we are faithful, we shall not be afraid of anything.

The one-talented slave went away and hid the talent in the earth. In doing this he was too passive. We should be active for the Lord's work. Because he had buried his talent, he could only give it back to the Lord. Merely to keep the Lord's gift and not lose it is not sufficient; we must gain a profit by using it. The one-talented one seemed to be saying, "Behold, Lord, here is what is Yours. I didn't lose anything. I have been faithful to keep what You gave me."

Verse 26 says, "But his lord answered and said to him, Evil and slothful slave, you knew that I reap where I did not sow, and gather where I did not scatter." Here the Lord admits that He is strict in what He demands of His slaves for His work. In a sense, the Lord is such a hard man. He always reaps where He has not sown and gathers where He has not scattered. Consider the fact that the Lord's recovery began from scratch, from nothing.

In a sense the slave's word about the Lord's gathering where He has not scattered and reaping where He has not sown is true. But in another sense it is not true. We should not say that the Lord has not scattered, for He has given each of us at least one talent. His giving the talent to us is the sowing and the scattering. Now the Lord sends us to gather where He has not scattered and to reap where He has not sown. None of us can say that the Lord has given us nothing. At least we have one talent. This talent is the seed for sowing and the possessions for scattering. Therefore, we need to reap where the Lord has not sown and gather where

He has not scattered. What the Lord has given you contains the producing element. Wherever you go with your talent, it will be productive. This productiveness, however, depends upon your practice, your exercise of the talent. If you use the talent, it will produce. But if you hide it, it will not produce anything.

To hide the talent in the earth is to get involved with something earthly, with something other than the Spirit. Gossiping is an example of such an involvement. Some claim to have no time to visit the saints, but they have a great deal of time to gossip. If you look to the Lord for His mercy and grace to stop your gossiping, much time will be saved, and you will be able to use this time to care for the saints.

In the Lord's recovery we do not have pastors to do the work of caring for the saints. This type of pastoring comes from fallen Christianity. In the Lord's recovery every brother and sister must bear the burden to take care of others, especially the young ones and the new ones. After the meeting, many are accustomed to visit only with certain ones. Instead of doing this, they should take this opportunity to contact the new ones, the young ones, and even some backsliding ones for whom they have been praying. If we all did this, all the young ones and weak ones would be taken care of. Although you may be very busy, you can still take care of someone if you have the heart to do so and are willing to exercise your talent. By spending even ten minutes with someone, we can render him a great deal of edification. After someone has been built up in this way, he will feel warmed and know that he has been cared for. Then he will desire to receive more help. If we all practice this, no one will be neglected. There will be no need for the elders to do everything, for everyone will be functioning to take care of others.

Many, however, consider that functioning is just a matter of speaking in the meetings. But the proper function of the members is to minister the life supply to others by taking care of them. The main aspect of the service is not simply to clean the meeting hall or take care of the gardening. We are here for God's possessions.

Not everyone has the ability to speak in the meeting. I would like to say a word of comfort to those who were not born with the ability to speak well. There is no need for you to speak in the meetings. In order to make a show that everyone functions in the meetings, the elders sometimes try to make people function. The elders may say, "If you do not function, you are not in the flow. You are not up-to-date." This kind of word frustrates those who cannot speak well from coming to the meetings. They will be afraid to come to the meetings because the elders might force them to function. An attitude has been created that it is a shame not to speak in the meetings, but that it is glorious to do so. Yes, a number of years ago I did say that we can all prophesy one by one. At that time, I was genuinely burdened to encourage everyone to speak. But since that time a misleading attitude has been created regarding functioning in the meetings. Although I do not wish to stop anyone from speaking, I want to point out that functioning in the church life is not merely a matter of speaking.

We all need to learn to use our talent to multiply the Lord's possessions. The Lord has given each of us part of His possessions as a talent, and our burden, duty, and responsibility are to see that this talent is multiplied. Do not make excuses for yourselves, and do not say that you have no time to take care of others. No matter how busy you are, it is still possible to use your function by taking care of others, even if you are able to come to only one meeting a week. Do not think that you are so weak. Perhaps you are weak; however, others are even weaker, and they need you. Even if you feel that you are the weakest one, there are some who are almost dead, and they need your help. The best way to use your talent is to take care of others, to become interested in others and concerned for them. This does not mean that you should become interested in the affairs of others. The Lord has employed you not for this purpose, but to take care of others.

If you have received one talent, you need to use it. Before you come to a meeting, you need to pray, "Lord, I believe that I have a talent. I don't want to bury my talent by getting involved with earthly things. Rather, I would like to use it to take care of others." Show some love to those whose heart has grown cold. Go to see them or invite them to your home. As you spend time with the Lord and open to Him regarding whom you should take care of, He will burden you. As you contact others and have fellowship with them, you will spontaneously use your talent. Do not say, "Lord, You are a hard man, reaping where You have not sown and gathering where You have not scattered." On the contrary, the Lord has sown and scattered a great deal. But there is much for you to reap and to gather. Oh, the harvest is vast, but the workers are few! There is no need for you to sow — simply go to reap. After every meeting there is time for you to reap and to gather. By doing this, we shall exercise our talent. In this way, the one talent will become two, the two talents will become four, and the five talents will become ten. The talents, God's possessions which have been committed to us, will be multiplied. If we are all faithful to practice this, the Lord's recovery will truly multiply.

Verse 27 says, "You ought therefore to have deposited my silver with the bankers, and when I came I would have recovered what is mine with interest." Depositing the silver with the bankers signifies using the Lord's gift to lead others to salvation and to minister His riches to them. Interest signifies the profitable result we gain for the Lord's work by using His gift.

In a sense, we may say that the bankers are all the new ones, weak ones, young ones, and backsliding ones. We need to deposit the Lord's possession with these bankers. The bankers are not the leading brothers, but the weaker ones, those who have problems. Suppose a certain brother is dissenting and speaks negatively about the church. Those who speak negatively concerning the church will always have something negative to say about the elders.

Such a one must speak like this in order to vindicate himself. If the church is wrong, then he is right; but if the church is right, then he is wrong. If the elders in particular are wrong, then he is truly vindicated. Nevertheless, these dissenting ones are brothers, and they love the Lord. How good it would be for such a dissenting brother to be contacted, not by one of the elders, but by another brother in the church who loves him and cares for him! If a dissenting brother is contacted by a number of others, he will eventually come back to the church and praise the Lord for the church.

If you use your talent in this way to take care of others, you will not only multiply the talent, but you yourself will be in the third heaven and will quickly grow and be transformed. You will be renewed in the spirit of the mind, and among us there will be a marvelous testimony of the Body to the whole universe. The universe will see that we are not a religious gathering, but a living Body. For this, we all need to use our talent, the Lord's possession. The result will be multiplication. I can testify that the more we take care of the saints and the churches, the richer we become.

Verse 28 says, "Take away therefore the talent from him, and give it to him who has the ten talents." Taking away the talent signifies that the Lord's gift will be taken away from slothful believers in the coming kingdom. The giving of the talent to the one with ten talents signifies that the gift of faithful believers will be increased.

Verse 29 continues, "For to everyone who has shall be given, and he shall have abundance; but from him who has not, even that which he has shall be taken away from him." To everyone who gains profit in the church age, more gift shall be given in the coming kingdom age; but from him who has not gained profit in the church age, even the gift he has shall be taken away from him in the coming kingdom age.

Verse 30 says, "And cast out the useless slave into the outer darkness; there shall be the weeping and the gnashing of teeth." This word, the same as in 24:51, indicates that

25:14-30 is a completion to 24:45-51 concerning faithfulness for the Lord's work. Matthew 24:45-51 has dealt with the slave's unfaithfulness in fulfilling the Lord's commission, but 25:14-30 is still needed to deal with the slave's unfaithfulness in using the Lord's talent.

In both chapters twenty-four and twenty-five we see the matters of reward and punishment. According to 24:47, the reward to the faithful and prudent slave is that the Lord will set him over all His possessions. The evil slave, who beats his fellow slaves and eats and drinks with the drunken, will be cut asunder and have his portion with the hypocrites, where there will be weeping and gnashing of teeth (24:49-51). In chapter twenty-five the five-talented one and the two-talented one are rewarded by being put over many things and by entering into the joy of the Lord. The slothful, one-talented slave, however, is punished by being cast into outer darkness. To many Christian teachers, being cast into outer darkness denotes eternal perdition of a false believer. But the context proves that this is not an accurate understanding. This is not the punishment of false believers, but of genuine believers who are not faithful. It does not refer to eternal perdition, but to punishment during the coming kingdom age.

The phrase "weeping and gnashing of teeth" is used six times in the Gospel of Matthew. It is used twice concerning the perdition of the false believers (13:42) and the evil heathen (13:50). Matthew 13:42 concerns the tares, the false believers who will be cast into the furnace of fire. The furnace of fire is not the outer darkness, but the lake of fire. Matthew 13:50 concerns the evil Gentiles, the corrupt fish that are equivalent to the goats in chapter twenty-five. They also will be cast into the furnace of fire. Thus, those who perish in eternal fire will weep and gnash their teeth.

Matthew 8:12 says, "But the sons of the kingdom shall be cast out into the outer darkness; there shall be the weeping and the gnashing of teeth." Because the sons of the kingdom certainly are saved ones, they will not be cast into the furnace of fire. Rather, they will be put into outer darkness. I do not believe that there is darkness in the furnace of fire. Although there will be weeping and gnashing of teeth both for the ones who perish and for the defeated believers, the defeated believers will not be cast into the lake of fire, but into the outer darkness outside the glorious sphere of the Lord's presence.

Matthew 22:13 says, "Then the king said to the servants, Bind his feet and hands, and cast him out into the outer darkness; there shall be the weeping and the gnashing of teeth." This refers to the one who did not have a wedding garment. This, of course, does not refer to an unbeliever, but to a saved one. This saved one will not be cast into the lake of fire, but into outer darkness.

This phrase is used two other times, in 24:51 and in 25:30. According to 24:51, the evil slave will be cut off from the Lord's presence and have his portion with the hypocrites where there will be weeping and gnashing of teeth. The sister verse, 25:30, says that the slothful slave will be cast out into the outer darkness where there is weeping and gnashing of teeth. By reading all these verses, we see that the false believers, the tares, and the evil Gentiles will be cast into the furnace of fire, the lake of fire, where there will be weeping and gnashing of teeth. However, the defeated believers, such as the sons of the kingdom in chapter eight, those without the wedding garment in chapter twenty-two, and the unfaithful slave in chapters twenty-four and twenty-five, will be cast out into the outer darkness. There, in the outer darkness, they will suffer weeping and gnashing of teeth. This does not refer to eternal perdition, but to dispensational punishment. In addition to salvation, there is still the matter of the reward and punishment that will be rendered during the coming kingdom age. If we are faithful to the Lord, we shall be rewarded during the next age. But if we are not faithful to Him, we shall receive punishment. This is very clear in God's holy Word.

In the previous message and in this message we have seen the matters of life and service. For life we need the infilling of the Holy Spirit, and for service we need the gifts of the Holy Spirit. In our life we need to be watchful, and in our service we need to be faithful. Our watchfulness in life is related to the early rapture, and our faithfulness in service is related to the reward. If we are watchful and faithful, then we shall be raptured early and we shall be rewarded when the Lord comes back. To be raptured early is to participate in the enjoyment of the wedding feast, and to be rewarded is to participate in the authority in the coming kingdom age.

LIFE-STUDY OF MATTHEW

PROPHECY OF THE KINGDOM

(7)

In this message we come to 25:31-46, the Lord's word concerning the judgment of the nations.

III. CONCERNING THE NATIONS

In the first two sections of the Lord's prophecy of the kingdom, the Lord covered the Jews and the church. At the end of this age, the people on earth will be in three categories: the Jews, the believers, and the Gentiles. The word "but" at the beginning of verse 31 indicates that what is spoken from verse 31 to verse 46 is another section, the section concerning the Gentiles. When the Lord's prophecy turned from the Jews to the church in 24:32, the word "but" was used to indicate this change. The same is true in 25:31.

If the Lord's prophecy had covered only the Jews and the church, it would not be complete, for there would be nothing about the nations. In order to make His prophecy all-inclusive, the Lord had to say a word about what would happen to the nations at the close of this age. Many Christian teachers have mixed up the Lord's word in the three sections of the prophecy of the kingdom, with some applying the verses concerning the Jews to the church. Both the word to the Jews and the word to the Gentiles have been applied to the believers. Many have taught that the judgment of the nations is the final judgment that the Lord will execute upon us all. In the past I heard certain Christian teachers warn us not to be goats. We were told to love the poor and suffering ones so that when the Lord Jesus came back we might be regarded as the sheep. Otherwise, He will consider us the goats. Thank the Lord that in His prophecy He used the little word "but" in two crucial places, in 24:32 and in 25:31. This word indicates that the prophecy turns from the Jews to the believers in the first case and then from the believers to the Gentiles.

A. Christ on the Throne of Glory

Verse 31 says, "But when the Son of Man comes in His glory, and all the angels with Him, then He shall sit on His throne of glory." The Son of Man is the title of Christ for His kingdom, the Messianic kingdom (13:41). His judgment here in these verses is a preparation for that kingdom.

The coming spoken of in this verse is the open aspect of the Lord's coming. It will be the continuation of His coming mentioned in 24:30. His glory comprises the glory of His divinity (John 17:22-24), the glory of His humanity (Psa. 45:3), the glory of His resurrection (John 7:39; Acts 3:13-15), and the glory of His ascension (Heb. 2:9). The throne on which He will sit is the throne of David (Luke 1:32-33), which will be in Jerusalem (Matt. 19:28; Jer. 3:17).

B. Judgment on All the Nations

1. All the Nations Being Gathered before Christ's Throne of Glory

Verse 32 says, "And all the nations shall be gathered before Him." All the nations are all the Gentiles who will be left at Christ's coming back to the earth after He destroys at Armageddon those Gentiles who follow Antichrist (Rev. 16:14, 16; 19:11-15, 19-21). They will all be gathered and judged at Christ's throne of glory. This will be Christ's judgment on the living before the millennium (Acts 10:42; 2 Tim. 4:1), differing from His judgment on the dead at the great white throne after the millennium (Rev. 20:11-15). This judgment on the living will occur after His judgment on believers at His judgment seat in the air (Matt. 25:19-30).

Verse 32 says that the nations, the Gentiles, will be gathered before Him. When the Lord spoke of the ten virgins, however, He did not say that they would be gathered. Rather, He said that they came. As we have pointed out, coming denotes rapture. In speaking about the slaves who received the talents, the Lord also said that they came. But the nations will not come; they will be gathered. In a parable equivalent to the parable of the sheep and the goats, the seventh parable in Matthew 13, the fish are also gathered out of the sea. All the nations will be gathered to Christ's throne of glory to be judged there.

2. Christ's Separating Them As a Shepherd Separates the Sheep from the Goats

Verses 32 and 33 say, "He shall separate them from one another, as the shepherd separates the sheep from the goats; and He shall set the sheep on His right hand and the goats on the left." This indicates that the Lord is the Shepherd not only of the believers (John 10:11; Heb. 13:20) and the Jews (Psa. 80:1; Jer. 31:10), but also of all the Gentiles (Psa. 100:1-3). The sheep will be gathered to His right hand, the place of honor (1 Kings 2:19; Psa. 45:9).

3. The Sheep Inheriting the Kingdom Prepared for Them from the Foundation of the World

Verse 34 says, "Then the King shall say to those on His right hand, Come, you who are blessed of My Father, inherit the kingdom prepared for you from the foundation of the world." After the judgment at Christ's throne of glory, the sheep will be transferred into the millennium to be the people under the kingly ruling of Christ and the overcoming believers (Rev. 2:26-27; 12:5; 20:4-6) and under the priestly ministry of the saved Jews (Zech. 8:20-23). In this way, they will "inherit the [coming] kingdom." In the millennium there will be three realms: the realm of the earth, where the blessing of God's creation, as mentioned in Genesis 1:28-30, will take place; the realm of the nation of Israel in Canaan, from the Nile to the Euphrates, in which the saved Jews will rule over the whole earth (Isa. 60:10-12; Zech. 14:16-18); and the heavenly and spiritual realm (1 Cor. 15:50-52), where the overcoming believers will enjoy the kingdom reward (5:20; 7:21). The kingdom which the sheep will enter will be the first realm. The blessing of the first realm in the millennium, the blessing of God's creation, was prepared for the sheep from the foundation of the world, whereas the blessing in the third realm, the blessing of the heavenly and spiritual kingdom, was ordained for the believers before the foundation of the world (Eph. 1:3-4).

The whole earth is under God's administration, which is for the carrying out of His economy. God's economy is to recover the earth and to establish His kingdom in a full way on the earth. God is more interested in the earth than in the heavens. According to the Bible, God's intention is to leave the heavens. He desires to come down from the heavens and set up His kingdom on the earth.

In the kingdom of God as the sphere of God's administration, there is the need for three kinds of people: the priests, the kings, and the people or the citizens. The prophecy concerning the kingdom given by the Lord on the Mount of Olives concerns God's economy to bring in His kingdom. This final word tells us the result of God's activity on earth to establish His kingdom. The result is that God will obtain three peoples, the priests, the kings, and the citizens, with whom He will have a complete kingdom. The nation of Israel is like a woman in travail to deliver the remnant of Jews who will be the priests during the millennium. Zechariah 8 reveals that the Jews will be the priests during the coming kingdom. They will teach all the nations to serve God. There will no longer be any idolatrous worship. The believers, covered in the second section of this prophecy, will be the kings, and the citizens will be taken from among the nations. How wise the Lord is, including all of God's economy in a prediction just two chapters long!

Very few Christians have seen that God judges people according to three things. Even the fundamental Christians believe that God judges people only according to two things — the law and the gospel. According to the law, every descendant of Adam is condemned to perish. But according to the gospel, every believer in Christ is saved. Thus, perdition is according to the law, and salvation is according to the gospel. However, there is yet a third thing according to which God will judge people. This is the eternal gospel.

During the persecution under Antichrist, for the care of the believers who will be left on earth, an eternal gospel will be preached to the nations (Rev. 14:6-7), as illustrated by the parable of the net in Matthew 13:47-50. The Lord will then judge the nations, not according to the law of Moses nor according to the gospel of Christ, but according to the eternal gospel. This is a matter of God's dispensation. Those who listen to that gospel and treat the suffering believers well will be blessed and reckoned as righteous (v. 46) to inherit the kingdom (v. 34), but those who do not will be cursed (v. 41) and perish for eternity. The gospel of grace (Acts 20:24) brings eternal life into the believers (John 3:15-16) that they may live by God's life, whereas the eternal gospel brings the sheep into eternal life (v. 46) that they may live in the sphere of God's life.

The eternal gospel will tell people to fear God and to worship Him. It will say nothing about repentance or believing. The gospel we have heard is absolutely different from the eternal gospel, for we were told to repent to God and to believe in the Lord Jesus. The gospel of grace says nothing about fear or worship; rather, it emphasizes repentance and believing. Furthermore, the center of the gospel of grace is Christ.

In addition to the law and the gospel of grace, the eternal gospel is the third thing according to which God will judge people. All those who are perishing are judged according to the law, the saved ones are judged according to the gospel of grace, and the nations gathered before Christ's throne of glory are judged according to the eternal gospel. Matthew 25:31-46 is concerned neither with the law nor with the gospel of grace. Christ will not separate the nations according to the ten commandments or according to their repentance and belief in Him. Rather, He will separate them according to the way they have treated the least of His brothers according to the eternal gospel (v. 40). Those who treat the least of His brothers in a good way will be "sheep" (vv. 34-40), but those who do not treat them well will be "goats" (vv. 41-46).

The treatment of Christ's brothers that will be the subject of the judgment before the throne of His glory will take place during the great tribulation when the believers will suffer the persecution of Antichrist (Rev. 13:6-7; 20:4). All the sufferings in verses 35 through 39 will betide the believers who are left for the trial (Rev. 3:10) during the great tribulation (Matt. 24:21). According to Revelation 14, during the great tribulation Antichrist will force God's people to worship him. At that time an angel will preach the eternal gospel warning the people to fear God and not to mistreat His people. The Christians that will be mistreated by Antichrist will be considered by the Lord His little brothers. The bigger brothers will have been raptured, and the little ones will be left to pass through the tribulation. Antichrist will mistreat them, persecute them, and imprison them. Thus, they will be short of food and clothing, and many will be ill. But a voice from heaven will say something like this: "Fear God and worship Him, and don't do anything to harm God's people. Those who fear Antichrist instead of God will perish."

God deals with the unbelievers according to the law and with the believers according to the gospel of Christ during the age of grace. But at the end of this age, the three and a half years of the great tribulation, God will send an angel to preach a specific gospel, the eternal gospel. This is a dispensational matter. Then, after Christ has judged the believers at the judgment seat in the air, He will come with the overcomers to destroy the armies of Antichrist, save the remnant of the Jews, and set up His throne of glory in Jerusalem. Then all the living Gentiles will be gathered before Him to be judged. By the judgment seat in the air, He will clear up the situation among the believers. By descending to the Mount of Olives He will clear up the situation among the Jews. Finally, at His throne of glory He will clear up the situation among the nations. He will judge them not according to the law or according to the gospel of grace, but according to the eternal gospel, according to how they have treated His little brothers during the great tribulation. Acts 10:42 and 2 Timothy 4:1 both say that Christ will be the Judge of the living and the dead. Christ will judge the dead at the white throne after the millennium. But He will judge the living at the throne of His glory before the millennium. The judgment according to the law for eternal perdition depends upon how one deals with God, the judgment according to the gospel for eternal salvation depends upon how the believer deals with Christ, and the judgment according to the eternal gospel for the "sheep" to inherit the millennial kingdom depends upon how they deal with the Lord's little brothers.

4. The Goats Going into the Eternal Fire Prepared for the Devil and His Angels

Verse 41 says, "Then He shall say also to those on the left, Go from Me, you who are cursed, into the eternal fire prepared for the Devil and his angels." This fire is the fire in the lake of fire (Rev. 20:14-15). The "goats" will perish in the lake of fire after Antichrist and the false prophet (Rev. 19:20) and before the Devil and the resurrected sinners (Rev. 20:10, 15). This is part of the fulfillment of Revelation 14:10. The lake of fire was prepared for the Devil and his angels, not for man. However, if any man follows the Devil to oppose the Lord, he will share the lake of fire with the Devil and the fallen angels.

The sheep will receive the kingdom prepared from the

foundation of the world. But the Christians who will be kings during the millennium will receive what was predestinated from before the foundation of the world. The portion of the sheep will be simply to enjoy what God has created from the foundation of the world. In the millennial kingdom there will be a heavenly part and an earthly part. The heavenly part will be the manifestation of the kingdom, the kingdom of the Father. The Jews will be in the center of the earthly part as the priests, and around the Jews there will be the sheep, the saved nations, as the people. We, the overcoming believers, will share in the spiritual enjoyment of Christ and in all the heavenly blessings. Our enjoyment will be heavenly, spiritual, and divine. But the enjoyment of the "sheep," the restored nations, will not be heavenly or spiritual. Rather, it will be the blessing God gave men when He created the earth, the blessing lost by Adam's fall. I am glad that we are in the best category, the category of the kings. The Jews will be in the earthly part, but we shall be in the heavenly part. Our portion will be to exercise authority over the nations. How I thank the Lord for giving us this clear view of the millennium!

In the prophecy of the kingdom neither the section concerning the Jews nor the section concerning the Gentiles is related to life. But the section concerning the believers, the church, is very much concerned with life. As we have pointed out, we need to be faithful, watchful, and ready, and we need to be wise and prudent. All these are indications that we must be full of life. Life is with us. Hallelujah, we are the life people!

LIFE-STUDY OF MATTHEW

A TEST TO ALL PEOPLE
AND THE ESTABLISHING OF THE TABLE

It is not an easy matter to understand the doctrinal point Matthew conveys in his Gospel. Many of us were taught that the Gospel of Matthew was simply a storybook. However, Matthew is not a storybook, but a book on the doctrine of the kingdom of the heavens. In order to touch the depths of this book, we need to apply this point to every chapter. In chapters twenty-six through twenty-eight we cannot find the term the kingdom of the heavens. However, everything contained in these chapters is related to the kingdom of the heavens. If we spend time in the Lord's presence to see the significance of these chapters in relation to the kingdom of the heavens, He will reveal it to us.

I. LAST UNVEILING OF THE CRUCIFIXION
FOR THE FULFILLMENT OF THE PASSOVER

Matthew 26:1 and 2 say, "And it came to pass when Jesus had finished all these words, He said to His disciples, You know that after two days the Passover is coming, and the Son of Man is being delivered up to be crucified." The word "And" at the beginning of verse 1 joins chapter twenty-six with chapters twenty-four and twenty-five, the prophecy concerning the Jews, the believers, and the Gentiles. Immediately after giving this prophecy of the kingdom, the Lord told His disciples that in two days the Passover was coming and that the Son of Man was being delivered up to be crucified. The significance of the Lord's word here is that His crucifixion is the fulfillment of the Passover. This Passover was to be the last. The Passover had been observed for more than fifteen centuries. But now the Passover was to be terminated and, in a sense, replaced. By putting together the Passover and the crucifixion of the Son of Man, the Lord was implying that His crucifixion was the fulfillment of the Passover and that He Himself was the Passover Lamb.

The Passover was a type of Christ (1 Cor. 5:7). Christ is the Lamb of God that God may pass over us, the sinners, as portrayed in typology by the Passover in Exodus 12. Hence, Christ as the Passover Lamb had to be killed on the day of the Passover for its fulfillment.

According to the type, the Passover Lamb had to be examined for its perfection during the four days preceding the day of the Passover (Exo. 12:3-6). Before His crucifixion, Christ came to Jerusalem the last time, six days before the Passover (John 12:1), and was examined by the Jewish leaders for a few days (Matt. 21:23—22:46). There was no blemish found in Him, and He was proved to be perfect and qualified to be the Passover Lamb for us.

II. A TEST TO ALL THE PEOPLE

As the Passover Lamb, Christ was a test to all the people. Throughout the centuries, Christ has constantly been such a test. We cannot be neutral regarding Him. Rather, whatever we are will be tested by Him. We must do something about Him, and we must react to Him. Our reaction will reveal our attitude toward this Passover Lamb.

A. Hated by the Religionists

Verses 3 through 5 indicate that Christ was hated by the religionists. The chief priests and the elders of the people took counsel together how they might seize Jesus by craftiness and kill Him. Can you believe that religion exercised craftiness in order to kill the Lord Jesus? Verse 5 says, "But they said, Not at the feast, lest there be an uproar among the people." Eventually, under God's sovereignty, they did kill the Lord Jesus at the feast (27:15) for the fulfillment of the type. This indicates that Christ's crucifixion was sovereignly under God's hand to fulfill the Passover. By hating the Lord Jesus, the first class of people, the religionists, were exposed.

B. Loved by the Disciples

Although the religionists hated the Lord Jesus, His disciples loved Him (vv. 6-13). Two of those who loved Him were Simon the leper and Mary, the woman who poured the oil upon His head. A leper signifies a sinner (8:2). Simon, as a leper, must have been healed by the Lord. Being grateful to the Lord and loving Him, he spread a feast (v. 7) in his house for the Lord and His disciples in order to enjoy His presence. A saved sinner would always do this. Simon must have known that the Lord was about to be killed. He probably realized that this was the last opportunity for him to express his love to the Lord. Therefore, he grasped the opportunity for a further intimate, loving contact with the Lord. He opened his home, spread a feast, and invited the Lord and all those who loved Him.

Verses 7 and 8 say, "A woman came to Him, having an alabaster jar of ointment of great value, and she poured it on His head as He reclined at table. But when the disciples saw it, they were indignant, saying, Why this waste?" The disciples considered Mary's love offering to the Lord a waste. Throughout the past twenty centuries, thousands of precious lives, heart treasures, high positions, and golden futures have been wasted upon the Lord Jesus. To such lovers He is altogether lovely and worthy of their offering. What they have poured upon Him is not a waste, but a fragrant testimony of His sweetness.

In verse 11 the Lord said to the indignant disciples, "For the poor you have with you always, but you do not always have Me." This indicates that we must love the Lord and grasp the opportunity to express our love to Him.

Verse 12 says, "For in pouring out this ointment on My body, she has done it for My burial." Mary received the revelation of the Lord's death by the Lord's words in 16:21;

17:22-23; 20:18-19; and 26:2. Hence, she grasped the opportunity to pour the best she had upon the Lord. To love the Lord with our best requires a revelation concerning Him.

Along with Simon, Mary also probably thought that this was her last chance to do something over the Lord's body to anoint Him for burial. In a very real sense, Mary buried the Lord Jesus before He was crucified. What a contrast there is between the religionists who hated the Lord and wanted to kill Him and His lovers who took the opportunity to express their love for Him! I believe that the others like Peter, James, and John did not receive the Lord's prophecy concerning His crucifixion properly. According to the Lord's testimony, Mary certainly received His word regarding this, for the Lord testified that in pouring out the ointment, she had done it for His burial. This was a sign that Mary understood what the Lord had prophesied concerning His crucifixion.

Verse 13 says, "Truly I say to you, wherever this gospel is preached in the whole world, that also which this woman has done shall be spoken of for a memorial of her." In the foregoing verse, the Lord spoke of His burial, implying His death and resurrection for our redemption. Hence, in this verse He called the gospel "this gospel," referring to the gospel of His death, burial, and resurrection (1 Cor. 15:1-4). The story of the gospel is that the Lord loved us, and the story of Mary is that she loved the Lord. We must preach both, the Lord loving us and us loving the Lord. One is for our salvation, and the other is for our consecration. The gospel tells us how the Lord loved us, but the loving story of Mary stirs us up to love the Lord. Thus, there needs to be a mutual love. This must accompany the preaching of the gospel.

C. Betrayed by the False Disciple

In verses 14 through 16 we see that the Lord Jesus was betrayed by the false disciple. The word "Then" at the beginning of verse 14 indicates that while one of the Lord's followers expressed her love to the Lord to the uttermost, another was about to betray Him. One was treasuring the Lord, and at the same time another was delivering Him up. Not even a false believer should have been this evil. The Lord Jesus had never wronged Judas. Judas, however, was filled and possessed with Satan, the Devil. In John 6:70 and 71 the Lord Jesus referred to Judas as a devil. According to John 13:2, the Devil had put it into the heart of Judas to betray Him, and John 13:27 says that Satan entered into him. Thus, Judas became the embodiment of the Devil. The idea of betraying the Lord Jesus did not originate with him, but with the enemy, the Devil.

In these verses we see three categories of people: the religious ones, the loving ones, and the betraying ones. To which category do you belong? Have you opened your home and prepared a feast for the Lord Jesus? Have you broken the alabaster jar and poured ointment upon His body? Surely, we are the lovers of Jesus. Nevertheless, we must learn to love Him to the uttermost.

III. THE ESTABLISHING OF THE TABLE

A. At the Feast of Passover

In verses 17 through 30 we see the keeping of the Passover and the establishing of the table. Verse 17 says, "Now on the first day of the Unleavened Bread the disciples came to Jesus, saying, Where do You want us to prepare for You to eat the Passover?" The Unleavened Bread is a feast of seven days (Lev. 23:5-6). It is also called the Passover (Luke 22:1; Mark 14:1). Actually, the Passover was the first day of the feast of Unleavened Bread (Exo. 12:15-20). The table mentioned in verse 20 refers not to the Lord's table, but to the table of the feast of Passover.

B. At the Time of His Betrayal

Verses 21 through 25 reveal that the Lord established the table at the time of His betrayal. Verse 21 says, "And as they were eating, He said, Truly I say to you, that one of you shall deliver Me up." When the disciples heard this, they were grieved, and each one began to say to Him, "I'm not the one, am I, Lord?" When Judas asked this question, the Lord let Judas' own word condemn him (v. 25). After this, Judas left. He could not bear to stay there any longer. After Judas had gone, the Lord established the table. Thus, Judas participated in the Passover feast, but he did not partake of the Lord's table. After the betrayer, the false believer, was exposed, the Lord established the table with the eleven real believers.

C. To Replace the Feast of Passover

Verse 26 says, "And as they were eating, Jesus took the bread and blessed and broke it and gave it to the disciples, and said, Take, eat; this is My body." Beginning at verse 26, the Lord's table is established. The Lord and the disciples firstly ate the Passover (vv. 20-25; Luke 22:14-18). Then the Lord established His table with the bread and the cup (vv. 26-28; Luke 22:19-20; 1 Cor. 11:23-26) to replace the feast of the Passover, because He was going to fulfill the type and be the real Passover to us (1 Cor. 5:7). Now we are keeping the real feast of Unleavened Bread (v. 17; 1 Cor. 5:8).

In this chapter there are two tables: the table of the Passover and the table of the New Testament. The table of the Passover was the table of the Old Testament economy, but the Lord's table is the table of the New Testament economy.

1. With the Bread

In verse 26 the Lord took bread, blessed it, broke it, and gave it to the disciples, saying, "Take, eat; this is My body." The bread of the Lord's table is a symbol signifying the Lord's physical body broken for us on the cross to release His life that we may participate in it. By participating in this life we become the mystical Body of Christ (1 Cor. 12:27), which is also signified by the bread of the table (1 Cor. 10:17). Hence, by partaking of this bread, we have the fellowship of the Body of Christ (1 Cor. 10:16).

At the Passover the people ate the meat of the Passover lamb. But after the Passover feast, the Lord Jesus did not take the flesh of the lamb, but He took bread and gave it to His disciples to eat. As we have pointed out, this bread signifies the Lord's body to nourish us. However, we all have some kind of religious background that keeps us from comprehending this. Due to our religious background, we have some doctrinal impression regarding the Lord's table. When Christians attend holy communion today, they do not have the realization that they are taking the Lord Jesus into them as their nourishment. Did you have this realization when you were in religion? I did not. Rather, we were told to examine ourselves; we were not told that we were taking the Lord's body as our nourishment. But if someone came to the Lord's table without any doctrinal concept, he would spontaneously realize that to eat the Lord's body is to receive the Lord into us as nourishment.

Many pastors and preachers today charge people to remember Christ's death as they participate in holy communion. Many endeavor to review the Lord's suffering and death on the cross. However, the Lord did not tell us to remember His death, but to remember Him, for He said, "Do this unto the remembrance of Me" (Luke 22:19). He told us to remember Him by eating the bread and drinking the cup. This is not just a remembrance, but also an enjoyment of the Lord. To partake of the Lord's table in this way is to eat and drink of Him.

Luke 22:19 says, "And having taken a loaf, when He had given thanks, He broke it, and gave it to them, saying, This is My body which is given for you; do this unto the remembrance of Me." According to this verse, we are to eat in remembrance of the Lord. Thus, the genuine remembrance is not to review the story of the Lord's life, but to eat Him, to take Him in.

For the symbol of His body, the Lord did not use a grain of wheat, but a loaf. A loaf signifies that many grains have passed through a long process to become bread. Firstly, the seed is sown into the field. Then it grows and produces many grains. After the wheat is harvested, the grains are ground into fine flour that is blended into a lump and baked in an oven to make a loaf of bread. Only then do we have a loaf of bread to eat. As a grain of wheat (John 12:24), the Lord Jesus passed through such a process until He eventually became the bread on the table for us to eat. Every time we come to the Lord's table we should have this realization. We should be able to say, "Lord, today You are our bread because You have been processed for us. Now You are the bread on the table for us to eat."

The bread on the table firstly signifies the Lord's physical body that was crucified on the cross. But after His resurrection, this body became mysterious, for it was enlarged into His mystical Body. According to John chapter two, the Jews killed His physical body, but it was resurrected in a mysterious way to become His mystical Body. The Lord's mystical Body comprises all of us. Therefore, when we see the bread at the Lord's table, we need to realize that it is a symbol both of the Lord's physical body and His mystical Body. For this reason, when we break the bread and eat it, we have the fellowship of the Lord's Body (1 Cor. 10:16). All the members of Christ's mystical Body are represented in the loaf. Therefore, at His table, we enjoy not only the Lord Jesus, but also the believers. In other words, we enjoy Christ and the church. Both Christ and the church are our enjoyment.

2. With the Cup

Verse 27 says, "And taking the cup and giving thanks, He gave it to them, saying, Drink of it, all of you." The bread is mentioned before the cup because God's eternal purpose is not to have redemption. It is to have the Body of Christ. Therefore, the bread as the symbol of the Body of Christ comes first. Nevertheless, we need to be reminded that as sinners we have the problem of sin and that the Lord Jesus shed His blood to cleanse us. His blood has made a complete redemption for us so that all our sins might be forgiven.

The Lord's blood redeemed us from our fallen condition back to God and back to God's full blessing. Concerning the Lord's table (1 Cor. 10:21), the bread signifies our participation in life, and the cup, our enjoyment of God's blessing. Hence, it is called the cup of blessing (1 Cor. 10:16). In this cup are all the blessings of God and even God Himself as our portion (Psa. 16:5). In Adam our portion was the cup of God's wrath (Rev. 14:10). Christ has drunk that cup for us (John 18:11), and His blood has constituted the cup of salvation for us (Psa. 116:13), the cup that runs over (Psa. 23:5). By partaking of this cup we also have the fellowship of the blood of Christ (1 Cor. 10:16).

Verse 28 says, "For this is My blood of the covenant, which is poured out for many for forgiveness of sins." The fruit of the vine (v. 29) within the cup of the Lord's table is also a symbol, signifying the Lord's blood shed on the cross for our sins. His blood was required by God's righteousness for the forgiveness of our sins (Heb. 9:22).

Some manuscripts insert the word "new" before the word "covenant" in verse 28. The Lord's blood, having satisfied God's righteousness, enacted the new covenant. In this new covenant, God gives us forgiveness, life, salvation, and all spiritual, heavenly, and divine blessings. When this new covenant is given to us, it is a cup (Luke 22:20), a portion for us. The Lord shed the blood, God established the covenant, and we enjoy the cup, in which God and all that is of Him are our portion. The blood is the price Christ paid for us, the covenant is the title deed God made to us, and the cup is the portion we receive from God.

3. Until the Kingdom Age

Verse 29 says, "And I say to you, I will by no means drink henceforth of this fruit of the vine until that day when I drink it new with you in the kingdom of My Father." By speaking this word, the Lord made it clear that from the time He established the table He would be physically away from the disciples and not drink the fruit of the vine with them until He drinks it new with them in the Father's kingdom. This is the heavenly part of the millennium, the manifestation of the kingdom of the heavens, in which the Lord will drink with us after His coming back.

D. Praising the Father with a Hymn

Verse 30 says, "And having sung a hymn, they went out to the Mount of Olives." This hymn was a praise to the Father by the Lord with the disciples after the Lord's table. It is based upon this verse that we sing praises to the Father at the end of the Lord's table.

LIFE-STUDY OF MATTHEW

MESSAGE SIXTY-NINE

PRESSED IN GETHSEMANE, ARRESTED BY THE JEWS, JUDGED BY THE SANHEDRIN, AND DENIED BY PETER

In this message we come to 26:31-75, a long section in the Gospel of Matthew that is also related to the kingdom. The verses in this chapter regarding the Lord's table indicate that the Lord's death and resurrection have a great deal to do with the kingdom of the heavens. In these verses, however, we cannot find the resurrection, although we do have a clear reference to the Lord's death in the breaking of the bread, which signifies the breaking of the Lord's body. The Lord's word about the pouring out of His blood (v. 28) is also an obvious reference to His death. Although there is no explicit mention of it, resurrection is implied by the fact that the bread signifies the Lord as our bread for our enjoyment. His death accomplished redemption for us, but He becomes our enjoyment through redemption in resurrection. When we come to the Lord's table, we see on the table a symbol of the Lord's death, but we remember Him, not in death, but in resurrection. In this remembrance we display His death. Both the Lord's crucifixion and resurrection are for the kingdom. Apart from Christ's crucifixion and resurrection, it is impossible for the kingdom to be established.

By our natural life it is not possible for us to be the kingdom people. This fact is made abundantly clear in 26:31-75. Here we have a picture of the arrest and judgment of Christ. This record reveals that no one can follow Christ on the pathway of the cross by the natural life. The King can take this pathway, but we in our natural life cannot. Therefore, the Lord must die for us and enter into resurrection for us. Through His death our negative situation is settled, and by His resurrection He is able to be taken in by us and even become us.

Years ago, I could not understand why in the record of the Lord's arrest and judgment Matthew includes a long story about Peter's denial of the Lord. I used to think that a few verses would have been sufficient to describe how Peter denied the Lord three times. But Matthew presents this in detail. It is important for us to see the significance of Peter's denial. In chapter twenty-six the Lord Jesus and Peter stand in absolute contrast to each other. In every respect Jesus was able to pass through the pathway of the cross. But in every respect Peter was defeated in taking this pathway. All the other disciples, of course, were the same as Peter. If we see this matter clearly, we shall pay careful attention to Peter's denial as well as to Christ's victory.

What was Matthew's main intention in 26:31-75 — to unveil the victory of Christ or to expose the defeat of Peter? I believe that his intention was to present both — each in vivid contrast to the other. When we look at the Lord Jesus, we see complete success, but when we look at Peter, we see total defeat. For the establishment of the kingdom, Christ's victory is necessary. He had to be victorious in every respect. At the same time, we must come to realize that we, as fallen human beings, are not able to be the kingdom people.

Do not have any trust in yourself. Peter is our representative. As far as our natural life is concerned, we are all Peter. For the kingdom of the heavens to be established, there was the need of a man like Jesus. Throughout chapter twenty-six, the Lord Jesus stood in the position of a man, not in the position of the Son of God. In order for the kingdom of the heavens to be established, He stood as a man, a successful man, a victorious man, as a man that could withstand any hardship, defeat, opposition, and attack.

As we consider this picture of the Lord Jesus, we should receive the clear impression that in our human life it is impossible for us to be the kingdom people. The twelve disciples had been under the Lord's teaching and training for three and a half years. During this period of time, they were with the Lord constantly. Peter, a fisherman, was called in chapter four, and he began from that time onward to follow the Lord Jesus. The Lord took special care to train Peter in a particular way. Peter heard the decree of the constitution of the kingdom of the heavens, and he heard all the mysteries concerning the kingdom. He was trained concerning Christ's being the Son of God, concerning the building up of the church, and concerning the pathway of the cross. He was dealt with on the Mount of Transfiguration and corrected regarding the paying of the poll tax. Time and time again, Peter was adjusted. It is difficult to believe that such a qualified and trained person could take the lead in denying the Lord. If Peter could not succeed in following the Lord, then who can? If Peter had denied the Lord in chapter four, I would not have been surprised. But it is hard for me to believe that in chapter twenty-six, after being with the Lord for three and a half years, Peter could deny Him.

Not even Peter himself believed that he would do this. In verse 33 Peter said boldly to the Lord, "If all shall be stumbled in You, I will never be stumbled," and in verse 35 he said, "Even if I must die with You, I will by no means deny You." Peter was confident that he would follow the Lord to the uttermost. But, as this picture makes clear, all he could do was to deny the Lord to the uttermost. This proves that no human being can succeed in living the kingdom life. Perhaps after reading these messages, you have been stirred up for the kingdom and desire to be today's kingdom people. But we must realize that none of us can make it. Therefore, we need to humble ourselves, bow down, and say, "Lord, I simply can't make it. I am a Peter. If Peter could not make it, then who am I to think that I can make it? Lord, I can't do it."

I. WARNING THE DISCIPLES

In the light of the contrast between Christ's victory and Peter's failure, let us now consider verses 31 through 75. Verse 31 says, "Then Jesus says to them, You will all be stumbled in Me this night, for it is written, I will smite the Shepherd, and the sheep of the flock shall be scattered." The Lord was the Shepherd, and the disciples were the sheep who were to be scattered. However, all the disciples said that they would not deny Him. All of them, especially Peter, had the assurance and the confidence that they would follow the Lord to the end, no matter what the pathway might be.

In His warning the Lord promised that He would be raised up and go to meet with them in resurrection in Galilee (v. 32). He also predicted that, on the night of His betrayal, Peter would deny Him three times (v. 34).

II. PRESSED IN GETHSEMANE

After warning the disciples, the Lord went with them to Gethsemane (v. 36). Gethsemane means the place of the oil press. The Lord was pressed there to flow out the oil, the Spirit. After taking Peter, James, and John, the Lord went to pray alone. When He returned from praying the first time, He found the disciples sleeping (v. 40). The Lord Jesus had told them seriously that His soul was "exceeding sorrowful, even unto death," and He had asked them to watch with Him (v. 38). But it seemed to them that nothing was going to happen and that everything was peaceful. Perhaps the disciples fell asleep because they had been tired out by the Lord's presence. According to the other Gospels, Peter and John were the ones sent ahead to prepare the room for the Passover. Perhaps they were tired from all the events of the day. Peter might have said to himself, "I would like to stay away from Jesus for a little while. Since I cannot get away from Him, let me take a little sleep. The Lord may need to pray, but I need to sleep." This was a full exposure of the fact that Peter was unable to make it in following the Lord. It is also a portrait of our situation. We love the Lord, but like Peter we may get tired out from being in His presence. Although it is wonderful to have the Lord's presence, sometimes we may get too weary to care for it.

According to verses 40 and 41, when the Lord came to the disciples and found them sleeping, He said to Peter, "So, you were not able to watch with Me one hour? Watch and pray that you may not enter into temptation; the spirit indeed is ready, but the flesh is weak." In spiritual things our spirit is often ready or willing, but our flesh is weak. Notice that the Lord Jesus spoke this word specifically to Peter, for Peter was the "nose," the one who was the most prominent.

When the Lord came back after praying the third time, the disciples were still sleeping. In verses 36 through 46 we see a contrast between the life that is absolutely able for the kingdom and the life that is completely unable. We do not have the first life by our natural birth. The life we have by our natural birth is completely unable to be for the kingdom.

In the garden of Gethsemane, the Lord was pressed to be sorrowful and distressed, even unto death. After praying to the Father three times, He took the Father's will and was prepared to be crucified for the fulfillment of the Father's will.

III. ARRESTED BY THE JEWS

Verse 47 says, "And while He was still speaking, behold, Judas, one of the twelve, came, and with him a great crowd with swords and clubs, from the chief priests and elders of the people." Judas kissed the Lord Jesus affectionately as a sign that He was the one to be seized. If it had been a stranger who had led the crowd to the Lord, it would not have been so painful to Him. But the one who led the crowd in arresting Him was one who had been so close to Him for three and a half years. Humanly speaking, this hurt the Lord Jesus.

When the Lord was arrested, one of the disciples, Peter, reacted by drawing his sword, striking the slave of the high priest, and cutting off his ear (v. 51). Instead of helping the Lord Jesus, this action merely caused trouble. In his Gospel, John gives Peter's name (John 18:10), and Luke mentions the fact that the Lord had to heal the ear (Luke 22:51). After telling Peter to put his sword into its place, the Lord said, "Do you think that I cannot beseech My Father and He will provide Me at once more than twelve legions of angels? How then shall the Scriptures be fulfilled that it must be so?" (vv. 53-54). The word "so" refers to His death on the cross, which was prophesied in the Scriptures and needed to be fulfilled.

Once again we see here a contrast between two persons in the light of the kingdom. Peter resisted the Lord's arrest, but the Lord was willing to accept it for the fulfillment of the Scriptures. Jesus' life is more than able to be for the kingdom, but this is impossible for our life. Our life simply cannot withstand the events and environment related to the kingdom. We all must come to realize this. If we did not have this record of Peter's failure, defeat, and denial, we might think that our natural life could succeed in being for the kingdom, and we would want to be bold like Peter. However, our natural life is not adequate. Here in chapter twenty-six we see a natural Peter, but in Acts 2, 3, and 4 we see a resurrected Peter. Following the Lord Jesus on the pathway for the kingdom can only be done in the life of resurrection.

IV. JUDGED BY THE SANHEDRIN

In verses 57 through 68 the Lord was judged by the Sanhedrin. He was accused unjustly with false testimonies, but He did not say a word to vindicate Himself (vv. 59-63). The Lord, standing before the Sanhedrin like a sheep before its shearers, would not say a word to vindicate Himself. By remaining silent, He was fulfilling Isaiah 53:7.

Then the high priest said to Him, "I adjure you by the living God that you tell us if you are the Christ, the Son of

God" (v. 63). This was the same question the Devil used in tempting the Lord (4:3, 6). Verse 64 says, "Jesus says to him, You said it! Moreover, I say to you, Henceforth you shall see the Son of Man sitting at the right hand of power and coming on the clouds of heaven." The high priest asked the Lord if He was the Son of God, but He answered with "the Son of Man." He answered the Devil in the same way in His temptation (4:4). The Lord is the Son of Man, not only on the earth before His crucifixion, but also in the heavens on the right hand of God after His resurrection (Acts 7:56), and even at His coming back on the clouds. To accomplish God's purpose and to establish the kingdom of the heavens, the Lord had to be a man. Without man, God's purpose could not be carried out on earth and the kingdom of the heavens could not be constituted on earth.

The Lord seemed to be saying to the high priest, "You asked Me whether or not I am the Son of God. I am the Son of Man. Even after you have crucified Me and I have been resurrected from the dead, I will be in the third heaven as a man. And when I come back on the clouds to take the earth, I will still be the Son of Man."

When the Devil in the wilderness tested the Lord regarding His being the Son of God, the Lord answered by saying, "Man." The Lord seemed to say to the Devil, "I'm not here as the Son of God to be tempted by you. If I were the Son of God, I could not be tempted. I am standing here as a man." The high priest, Caiaphas, was the same as the Devil, and his question was the same as the Devil's temptation in the wilderness. The Lord also answered him in the same way.

When the high priest heard the Lord's answer, he tore his garments and said, "He has blasphemed! What further need do we have of witnesses? Behold, now you have heard the blasphemy" (v. 65). After the others said that the Lord was liable to death, they spit in His face, beat Him with their fists, slapped Him, and mocked Him (vv. 67-68). When the Lord was treated this way, He was victoriously silent. Thus, He was victorious not only before

the Sanhedrin, but also before Peter, who had followed
Him afar off to the courthouse of the high priest and had
sat down with the deputies to see the end (v. 58). Again we
see here that only the life of Jesus is good for the kingdom.
Even the life of a man as strong and as bold as Peter is not
fit for the kingdom.

V. DENIED BY PETER

Verses 69 and 70 say, "Now Peter sat outside in the
courtyard; and a maid came to him, saying, You also were
with Jesus the Galilean. But he denied before all, saying, I
do not know what you are saying!" Peter could not withstand even one fragile little female. Peter's denial of the
Lord was an exposure. It seems to me that this one test was
sufficient to expose Peter. But under God's sovereignty,
the environment would not let Peter go until he was tested
to the uttermost, that he might realize he was absolutely
not trustworthy and should no longer have any confidence
in himself. Thus, verses 71 and 72 say that another maid
came to him and said, "This man was with Jesus the
Nazarene. And again he denied with an oath, I do not know
the man!" Finally, those standing by said, "Surely you also
are one of them, for your speech also makes you known"
(v. 73). Then Peter "began to curse and to swear, I do not
know the man!" (v. 74). In his first denial, Peter said only
the word; in his second denial, he replied with an oath; and
in his third denial, he cursed and swore. After denying the
Lord the third time and hearing the cock crow, Peter
remembered the word of the Lord, and he went out and
wept bitterly (v. 75). As the Lord was suffering an evil and
unjust judgment, Peter denied Him. By denying Him,
Peter was exposed to the uttermost.

We should not read this account merely as a story about
Peter, for it reveals that it is impossible for our natural life
to enter into the kingdom. Because we all are the same as
Peter, we should not try to follow the pathway into the
kingdom by our natural life. No matter what kind of mind
or will we may have, we cannot succeed. The test will come

that will fully expose us. Sooner or later, all of us on the pathway to the kingdom will face the same tests. Praise the Lord that there is still the way of repentance, weeping, and confessing that brings in the Lord's forgiveness and His further visitation. For the kingdom, we must have another life and be another person. Only after we have passed through all the tests and have suffered all the defeats and failures will we realize our need for another life.

Praise the Lord for the strong contrast presented in this chapter! In Peter we see the black, and in the Lord Jesus we see the white. All the way from the garden to the cross, Peter and the other disciples were defeated. Only one man, Jesus, was victorious. Actually, He was not even arrested; He handed Himself over to those who came for Him. Thus, His death was not a matter of compulsion, but a voluntary fulfillment of the prophecies of the Old Testament concerning His crucifixion. Truly, only the life of Jesus is good for the kingdom.

LIFE-STUDY OF MATTHEW

JUDGED, CRUCIFIED, AND BURIED

In this message we come to chapter twenty-seven of Matthew. Apparently, this chapter is not related to the kingdom of the heavens. Actually, it is very much related to it. If we do not read this chapter in the light of the kingdom of the heavens, we shall not be able to understand it adequately.

The first verse of chapter twenty-seven begins with the word "Now." This word indicates that one thing has been completed and that another is about to take place. We may think that chapter twenty-seven is merely a continuation of chapter twenty-six. But in spiritual significance, chapter twenty-seven is much different from chapter twenty-six. The spiritual significance of chapter twenty-six is that it reveals the life that can succeed in being for the kingdom and exposes the life that cannot succeed. The spiritual significance of chapter twenty-seven is that it is related to righteousness. In 27:19 Pilate's wife referred to the Lord Jesus as a righteous man, and in verse 24 Pilate himself called Him a righteous man. In this chapter the Lord Jesus was treated in a very unrighteous manner.

I. JUDGED BY PILATE

A. Jesus Delivered by the Jewish Religious Leaders to Pilate, the Roman Governor

Verses 1 and 2 reveal that it was the Jewish religious leaders who delivered the Lord Jesus to Pilate. Pilate was a Roman procurator, an agent of Caesar Tiberius in Judea (Palestine), A.D. 26-35. Not long after he unjustly delivered the Lord Jesus up to be crucified, his government ended abruptly. He was banished and committed suicide. In their evil conspiracy, the Jewish religionists persuaded the heathen politician to collaborate with them to kill the Lord Jesus.

B. The Destiny of Judas

In verses 3 through 10 we read of the destiny of Judas. When I was young, I was troubled by the fact that this record of Pilate's judgment upon Christ speaks of the destiny of Judas. I could not see the relationship between these two things. Verses 1 and 2 speak of the delivering up of the Lord Jesus to Pilate by the religious leaders. Then verse 3 begins the account of Judas' hanging himself. Verses 3 and 4 say that Judas "repented and returned the thirty pieces of silver to the chief priests and elders," saying that he had "sinned in delivering up innocent blood." Then Judas threw the pieces of silver into the temple, departed, and hanged himself. The chief priests took the pieces of silver and, knowing that it was not lawful to put them into the temple treasury because they were the price of blood, used them to buy a field as a burial place for strangers (vv. 6-7). They would not receive back the price of blood. Actually, what they did to the Lord Jesus was more evil than Judas' deed. After giving us an account of all this, in verse 11 Matthew resumes his record of the judgment of Christ by Pilate.

It is very meaningful that Matthew inserted the record of the destiny of Judas into his account of Pilate's judgment of Christ. The record of Judas testifies of righteousness. Even the betrayer of the Lord Jesus eventually realized that He was a righteous man and that what had been done to Him was altogether unrighteous. In an attempt to be righteous, he threw away the thirty pieces of silver, for his conscience did not allow him to keep them. This is righteousness. When Judas returned the money, the religious leaders seemed to say, "We cannot keep this money, the price of blood, for the service of God. It is better that we use it to buy a parcel of land for burying strangers." This shows that even the religious leaders had a formal righteousness. Thus, the concept here was that of righteousness.

The kingdom of the heavens is built upon righteousness. In 5:10 the Lord said, "Blessed are those who have been persecuted for the sake of righteousness, for theirs is the kingdom of the heavens," and in 5:20 He said, "For I say to you, that unless your righteousness surpass that of the scribes and Pharisees, you shall by no means enter into the kingdom of the heavens." In 6:33 the Lord said to seek first the kingdom and God's righteousness. These verses reveal that righteousness is related to the kingdom and that the kingdom is built upon righteousness. We need to be clear about this if we are to get into the depth of chapter twenty-seven.

At the time Christ was crucified, the Jews had no legal right to judge Him or to sentence Him. Although they could spy on the Lord Jesus regarding certain things, they did not have the governmental position to judge anyone. They were simply a religious group, and government was not under their control. Therefore, the Jewish Sanhedrin had no governmental authority, and it could not pronounce judgment regarding justice or injustice, righteousness or unrighteousness. It could only express religious opinion. Hence, the actual judgment of the Lord Jesus did not take place in chapter twenty-six, but in chapter twenty-seven.

C. Jesus before Pilate

In Jesus' answering Pilate, Jesus admitted that He was the King of the Jews (v. 11). But to the accusation of the Jewish leaders He answered nothing.

Pilate, the Roman governor, had the position to judge Christ. In principle, he should have judged Him according to righteousness. The kingdom of the heavens is based upon righteousness, but chapter twenty-seven reveals that the kingdom of the world is absolutely unrighteous. This chapter affords a contrast between righteousness and unrighteousness. The earthly government, the kingdom of this world, is unrighteous, but the kingdom of the heavens. is righteous. The Lord Jesus stood before Pilate as the uniquely righteous One, yet He was condemned to death by the unrighteous worldly government. Later we shall see that actually Christ was judged and killed by the righteous God. Apparently, He was sentenced to death by the unrighteous worldly government. This sentence was unrighteous. Actually, He was condemned to death by God. This sentence was righteous.

The concept here in chapter twenty-seven is rather deep. In chapter twenty-six we saw a contrast between the life that can make it to be for the kingdom and the life that cannot make it. Now in chapter twenty-seven we have a contrast between righteousness and unrighteousness. The significance of chapter twenty-seven is that it shows the contrast between the kingdom of the world and the kingdom of the heavens. On the side of the kingdom of the world, there is unrighteousness, but on the side of the kingdom of the heavens, there is righteousness. On the one hand, Jesus was sentenced and condemned to die on the cross in unrighteousness; on the other hand, He was sentenced to die in righteousness. Both rightly and wrongly, Jesus was crucified. He was wrongly sentenced by the unrighteous worldly government. He was righteous and innocent, as even His betrayer testified. Pilate also testified that Christ was a righteous man, even washing his hands to show that he did not want to get involved in any unrighteousness. As we shall see, the Lord was sentenced rightly because He was sentenced to die by the righteous God. Thus, chapter twenty-seven is a chapter concerning unrighteousness and righteousness.

This contrast implies that the kingdom of the world cannot stand. The reason it cannot stand is that it is not built upon righteousness. However, the kingdom of the heavens and of God is altogether righteous. God's king-

dom is built upon righteousness. Because of the unrighteousness of the government of the kingdom of this world,
Christ was wrongly condemned to die. Nevertheless, actually He was rightly sentenced to death by the righteousness of God. Thus, this chapter exposes the unrighteousness of the worldly government, and it reveals the righteousness of God's government.

According to Roman law, the Sanhedrin acted illegally
in arresting Christ. If Pilate had been just, he would have
stopped the Sanhedrin from doing this. He would have
said, "You have no right to do this because you are just a
religious party. You cannot arrest people and judge them.
This is illegal." Pilate did not say this because he was unrighteous and fearful. Afraid of the Jewish religious
leaders, Pilate acted against Roman law, which was very
strong. The Roman Empire was famous for its law. But
although the law was strong, the enforcement of the law
was weak. Pilate was not even as righteous as Judas. If the
betrayer of the Lord Jesus was able to say that he had sold
innocent blood, the governor of the kingdom should have
been even more righteous. Nevertheless, Pilate "washed
his hands before the crowd, saying, I am innocent of the
blood of this righteous man" (v. 24). This was a timid and
irresponsible withdrawal. Verse 26 says, "Then he released to them Barabbas; but Jesus he scourged and
delivered Him up that He might be crucified." This was an
utmost exposure of dark, unjust politics. This injustice fulfilled Isaiah 53:5 and 8.

When Jesus was appearing before Pilate, Pilate's wife
"sent to him, saying, Have nothing to do with that righteous man, for I have suffered much today in a dream
because of him" (v. 19). This dream was sovereign of God.
Pilate's wife did not want him to get involved with this unrighteous matter. According to his conscience, Pilate also
knew that Jesus was righteous and that the Jews were unrighteous in arresting Him. He also knew that he should
have released this righteous man, but he was afraid to do
this. Accustomed at the time of the feast to release to the

crowd one prisoner whom they wanted, Pilate asked, "Which of the two do you want me to release to you? And they said, Barabbas" (v. 21). Barabbas was a most sinful criminal. No doubt, Pilate intended to release Jesus and to keep Barabbas. But the people wanted him to release Barabbas and to crucify Jesus. Pilate seemed to be saying, "You ask me to release the most sinful criminal and to crucify the innocent one." Verse 23 says, "But he said, Why, what evil has he done? But they cried out the more, saying, Let him be crucified!" Pilate was subdued by the voices of the crowd. In order to appease his conscience, he "took water and washed his hands before the crowd, saying, I am innocent of the blood of this righteous man; you see to it" (v. 24). Then the people answered and said, "His blood be on us and on our children!" (v. 25). Thus, Pilate released Barabbas, but scourged Jesus and delivered Him up that He might be crucified. What a portrait this is of unrighteousness!

The Jewish death penalty was by stoning (Lev. 20:2, 27; 24:23; Deut. 13:10; 17:5). Crucifixion was a heathen practice (Ezra 6:11), adopted by the Romans for the execution of slaves and heinous criminals only. To crucify the Lord Jesus was not only a fulfillment of the Old Testament (Deut. 21:23; Gal. 3:13; Num. 21:8-9), but also of the Lord's own word concerning the mode of His death (John 3:14; 8:28; 12:32), which could not have been fulfilled by stoning.

II. CRUCIFIED BY MEN

A. Mocked by the Roman Soldiers

Verses 27 through 32 show how the Lord Jesus was mocked by the heathen soldiers. They stripped Him and put on Him a scarlet robe (v. 28). Verse 29 says, "And having woven a crown of thorns, they placed it on His head, and a reed in His right hand; and they kneeled before Him and mocked Him saying, Hail, King of the Jews!" Thorns are a symbol of the curse (Gen. 3:17-18). The Lord Jesus became a curse for us on the cross (Gal. 3:13). After spitting on the Lord, beating Him on His head, and mocking Him, they took the robe off Him, put His garments on Him, and led Him away to be crucified (vv. 30-31). The Lord here, as the Passover Lamb to be sacrificed for our sins, was brought like a lamb to the slaughter, fulfilling Isaiah 53:7-8.

B. Simon the Cyrene Being Compelled to Bear His Cross

Verse 32 says, "And as they were coming out, they found a man of Cyrene, Simon by name; this man they compelled to bear His cross." Cyrene was the Greek colonial city, the capital of Cyrenaica in North Africa. It seems that Simon was a Cyrenian Jew.

C. Brought to Golgotha

Verses 33 through 44 reveal how the Lord was mocked by men and killed. Verse 33 says, "And coming to a place called Golgotha, which is called Place of a Skull." Golgotha is a Hebrew name (John 19:17) which means skull (Mark 15:22). Its equivalent in Latin is *Calvaria,* anglicized into Calvary (Luke 23:33). It does not mean a place of dead men's skulls, but simply skull.

D. Given Wine Mingled with Gall

Verse 34 says, "They gave Him wine to drink mingled with gall; and having tasted it, He would not drink." The wine mingled with gall (and also with myrrh — Mark 15:23) was intended as a stupefying draught. But the Lord would not be stupefied; He would drink the bitter cup to the dregs.

E. Crucified

Verse 35 says, "And when they had crucified Him, they divided His garments among them, casting lots." The Lord suffered the sinners' robbery to the uttermost, fulfilling

Psalm 22:18. This also exposed the darkness of Roman politics.

F. Labeled King of the Jews
as an Accusation

Although the Jewish leaders rejected the Lord Jesus as their King, it was sovereign of God that they set up above His head as a charge "the King of the Jews" (v. 37).

G. Two Robbers at His Side

Verse 38 says, "Then two robbers were crucified with Him, one on the right hand and one on the left." This was for the fulfillment of Isaiah 53:9.

H. Blasphemed and Mocked

Verses 39 and 40 say, "And those who were passing by blasphemed Him, wagging their heads, and saying, You who destroy the temple and build it in three days, save yourself! If you are the Son of God, come down from the cross!" This was a repetition of the Devil's temptation in the wilderness. The chief priests, scribes, and elders also mocked Him by saying, "He saved others; himself he cannot save! He is king of Israel, let him come down now from the cross, and we will believe on him" (v. 42). If He could have saved Himself, He could not have saved us.

I. Reproached by the Robbers
Crucified with Him

When the Lord was crucified, even the robbers crucified with Him reproached Him as the others did. In 27:1-44 we see what unrighteous man did to the righteous One. He was mocked, beaten, and crucified. Pilate and all the mockers and persecutors were unrighteous. Even the soldiers of the Roman Empire were unrighteous. If any of them had been righteous, they would not have done anything to the Lord Jesus. The fact that they did something to this righteous One proves that they were unrighteous.

III. JUDGED BY GOD

A. Forsaken by God

Although man was unrighteous, beginning in verse 45 God came in in a righteous way. This verse says, "Now from the sixth hour darkness came over all the land until the ninth hour." The sixth hour is our 12 noon, and the ninth is our 3 p.m. The Lord was crucified at the third hour, our 9 a.m. (Mark 15:25). He was suffering on the cross for six hours. In the first three hours, He was persecuted by men for doing God's will; in the last three hours, He was judged by God for the accomplishment of our redemption. It was during this time that God counted Him as our suffering substitute for sin (Isa. 53:10). Hence, darkness came over all the land because our sin and sins and all negative things were dealt with there, and God forsook Him (v. 46) because of our sin.

By the time of verse 45, men had exhausted their deeds. They had done everything they could. At that time, God came in to judge this crucified Savior and to forsake Him. Verse 46 says, "And about the ninth hour Jesus cried out with a loud voice, saying, Eli, Eli, lama sabachthani? that is, My God, My God, why have You forsaken Me?" God forsook Christ on the cross because He took the place of sinners (1 Pet. 3:18), bearing our sins (1 Pet. 2:24; Isa. 53:6) and being made sin for us (2 Cor. 5:21).

According to the four Gospels, the Lord Jesus was on the cross exactly six hours. During the first three hours, men did many unrighteous things to Him. They persecuted and mocked Him. Thus, in the first three hours the Lord suffered man's unrighteous treatment. But at the sixth hour, twelve noon, God came in, and there was darkness over all the land until the ninth hour, until three o'clock in the afternoon. This darkness was God's doing. In the midst of this darkness, the Lord cried out the words quoted in verse 46. When the Lord was suffering the persecution of man, God was with Him, and He enjoyed the presence of God. But at the end of the first three hours,

God forsook Him, and darkness came. Unable to tolerate this, the Lord shouted loudly, "My God, My God, why have You forsaken Me?" As we have pointed out, God forsook Him because He was our substitute bearing our sins. Isaiah 53 reveals that this was the time God put our sins on Him. In the three hours from twelve noon to three o'clock in the afternoon the righteous God put all our sins upon this substitute and judged Him righteously for our sins. God forsook Him because during these hours He was a sinner there on the cross; He was even made sin. On the one hand, the Lord bore our sins; on the other hand, He was made sin for us. Therefore, God judged Him. This was altogether a matter of righteousness.

B. Mocked by Being Given Vinegar to Quench His Thirst

Close to the end of His crucifixion, people still mocked Him by giving Him vinegar to quench His thirst (vv. 48-49; John 19:28-30; Luke 23:36).

C. Dismissing the Spirit

Verse 50 says, "And Jesus cried out again with a loud voice and dismissed the spirit." This was to give up His spirit (John 19:30), indicating that the Lord voluntarily yielded up His life (Mark 15:37; Luke 23:46). The Lord Jesus was not killed, but willingly yielded up His life. He gave His life for us, and He died.

IV. THE EFFECT OF HIS DEATH

A. The Veil of the Temple Torn from Top to Bottom

Verses 51 through 56 reveal the effect of Christ's crucifixion. Verse 51 says, "And behold, the veil of the temple was torn in two from the top to the bottom." This signifies that the separation between God and man was abolished, because the flesh (signified by the veil) of sin taken by Christ (Rom. 8:3) had been crucified (Heb. 10:20). The

words "from the top to the bottom" indicate that the rend-
ing of the veil was God's doing from above. Because sin had
been judged and the flesh of sin had been crucified, the
separation between God and man was taken away. Now
the way to enter into the presence of God is open for us.
What a wonderful effect of the Lord's death! His death was
not martyrdom; it was an act of redemption.

B. The Earth Shakes and the Rocks Split

Verse 51 also says that "the earth was shaken and the
rocks were split." The shaking of the earth signifies that
the base of Satan's rebellion has been shaken, and the
splitting of the rocks signifies that the strongholds of
Satan's earthly kingdom have been broken. Hallelujah, the
Lord's death tore the veil, shook the base of Satan's
rebellion, and broke the strongholds of Satan's kingdom!
What a death! Praise the Lord for His death! Because
God's righteousness was fully satisfied, Christ's death
could be so effective.

C. The Tombs Opened and the Bodies of Many Saints Raised

Verses 52 and 53 say, "And the tombs were opened; and
many bodies of the saints who had fallen asleep were
raised; and coming out of the tombs after His rising, they
entered into the holy city and appeared to many." The
opening of the tombs signifies that the power of death and
Hades has been conquered and subdued, and the raising of
the bodies of the saints signifies the releasing power of the
death of Christ. Verse 53 says that they came out of the
tombs after His rising, entered into the holy city, and
appeared to many. In typology, the firstfruits of the harvest were not a single stalk of wheat, but a sheaf of wheat,
typifying not only the resurrected Christ, but also the
saints who were raised from the dead after His resurrection, as revealed here. Where the saints went after they
appeared to many, we have no way to trace. The Roman

centurion and guards testified that Jesus was truly God's Son when they saw what happened at the death of Christ (v. 54). Many women, including Mary the Magdalene, Mary, the mother of the Lord Jesus, the mother of the sons of Zebedee, and others, witnessed these happening.

V. BURIED BY A RICH MAN

Verses 57 through 66 reveal that the Lord Jesus was buried by a rich man. The Lord Jesus was wrapped in a clean linen cloth and laid in a new tomb (vv. 59-60). Mary the Magdalene and the other Mary sat opposite the grave to witness the burial. This kind of burial was for the fulfillment of Isaiah 53:9. This righteous One was surely worthy of such a burial.

After the Lord Jesus was buried, the chief priests and the Pharisees came to Pilate and asked him to secure the grave until the third day (vv. 62-64). Verses 65 and 66 say, "Pilate said to them, You have a guard; go, make it as secure as you know how. And they went and secured the grave with the guard, sealing the stone." This was intended by the opposing Jewish leaders as a negative precaution, but it turned out to be a strong positive testimony of the Lord's resurrection. Without such a sealing, the resurrection of Christ would not have been as significant.

LIFE-STUDY OF MATTHEW

MAN'S UNRIGHTEOUSNESS
AND GOD'S RIGHTEOUSNESS

In Matthew 27 we see a contrast between man's unrighteousness and God's righteousness. In the crucifixion of Christ, man's unrighteousness turns into God's righteousness. We need to see this matter very clearly.

MAN'S UNRIGHTEOUSNESS

As we pointed out in the previous message, the Lord Jesus was on the cross for six hours. During the first three hours, He was dealt with by man, and during the second three hours, He was dealt with by God. Everything man did to the Lord Jesus in chapter twenty-seven was unrighteous. Not only was Pilate unrighteous toward the Lord Jesus, but the Jewish leaders were also unrighteous toward Him. They arrested Christ in an unrighteous way, and they also judged and bound Him in an unrighteous way. Everything the religious leaders did to the Lord was unrighteous. Judas, of course, was also unrighteous in betraying the Lord Jesus. The Roman soldiers also treated Him unrighteously. Their mocking, spitting, and beating were unrighteous. Furthermore, they unrighteously forced Simon of Cyrene to bear the Lord's cross. Thus, on man's side, there was nothing righteous.

MAN'S UNRIGHTEOUSNESS TURNING
INTO GOD'S RIGHTEOUSNESS

Praise God that man's unrighteousness turned into God's righteousness! Man could only go so far. He could mistreat the Lord and put Him on the cross as the Passover Lamb. Everything man did to the Lord Jesus set the stage for God's righteousness to come in. On man's side, everything was black, but on God's side, everything was white. On man's side, everything was unrighteous, but on God's side, everything was righteous. Man's unrighteousness prepared the way for God's righteousness to be fully manifested. In this way, man's unrighteousness turned into God's righteousness. In the crucifixion of Christ, man's unrighteousness was fully exposed; yet it brought in God's righteousness. Thus, the killing of Christ was the first way through which man's unrighteousness brought in God's righteousness.

CHRIST EXPOSING
MAN'S UNRIGHTEOUSNESS

However, this was not the basic way. The basic way in which man's unrighteousness turned into God's righteousness was through Christ. In turning man's unrighteousness into God's righteousness, Christ first exposed man's unrighteousness to the uttermost. In all of human history there has not been a case in which man's unrighteousness has been as totally exposed as in the crucifixion of Christ. As we all know, there is unrighteousness in the judicial branch of any earthly government. But no earthly court has seen as much unrighteousness as was exposed in the case of the trial and crucifixion of the Lord Jesus. The Lord Jesus completely exposed human unrighteousness. We have seen that the Lord's betrayal at the hands of Judas was unrighteous. The elders, the high priests, and the Sanhedrin all were unrighteous. Thus, the case of the crucifixion of Christ was unique in being filled with unrighteousness. Nearly everyone involved with His case was unrighteous. In every way and in every aspect, it was unrighteous. The very presence of Christ in this unrighteous situation was a full exposure of man's unrighteousness.

CHRIST BEARING
MAN'S UNRIGHTEOUSNESS

Secondly, the Christ who exposed man's unrighteousness to the uttermost also bore all the unrighteousness He had exposed. He firstly exposed man's unrighteousness and then He bore it on the cross. This is like housecleaning. If you do not clean, you may not see the dust hidden under the furniture. In cleaning a room the dust is firstly exposed. Then it is swept into the dustpan. Likewise, on the day of the Passover, the Lord Jesus firstly exposed all the "dust," all of man's unrighteousness. Then He cleaned up the "dust" He had exposed. Oh, the very presence of the Lord Jesus exposed every particle of hidden "dust" in the whole universe. Eventually, the Lord Jesus Christ Himself became the "dustpan," and all the "dust" was collected upon Him. During the first three hours He was on the cross, the time of man's dealing with Him, all the sins, all the unrighteousness, all the universal "dust," were put on Him. As He hung there on the cross, He was the universal "dustpan" into which all the "dust" in the universe had been gathered. Thus, after all man's unrighteousness had been exposed, it was borne by Christ on the cross. This made everything ready for the righteous God to come in to judge the unrighteous ones and all their unrighteousness.

Without the black, the white could not be clearly manifest. Because all the "dust," all man's unrighteousness, was put on the cross, the stage was prepared for God's righteousness to be revealed. If there had not been so much unrighteousness, it would not have been possible for so much righteousness to be manifested. The complete unrighteousness of mankind was heaped upon the Lord on the cross so that God's righteousness could be manifested. The righteous God came in to exercise His righteousness by judging all this unrighteousness. This is the reason that through Christ man's unrighteousness eventually turned into God's righteousness. By this we have been saved.

Christ was the turning point. Man's unrighteousness turned into God's righteousness through Christ. Firstly, Christ exposed man's unrighteousness, and then for judgment by God's righteousness He bore upon Himself all of man's unrighteousness that He had exposed. Today are you still in man's unrighteousness, or are you now under God's righteousness? Hallelujah, we, the saved ones, are under God's righteousness!

GOD'S RIGHTEOUSNESS
IN THE GOSPEL

This matter of righteousness is a crucial aspect of the truth of the gospel. This is very basic, for it is our ground and basis for being saved. Our salvation rests upon the solid rock of God's righteousness. Romans 1:16 and 17 say, "For I am not ashamed of the gospel; for it is the power of God unto salvation to every one who believes, both to Jew first and to Greek. For the righteousness of God is revealed in it out of faith to faith." Because of God's righteousness, the gospel is powerful to save everyone who believes in the Lord Jesus. The gospel of Christ is so powerful not because of God's love nor because of God's grace, but because of God's righteousness.

Legally speaking, both love and grace can fluctuate, but righteousness, especially God's righteousness, cannot. Madame Guyon once said that even if God wanted to change His mind regarding her salvation, He could not do it because He had already judged her on the cross. Through Christ our substitute, we have already been judged according to righteousness on the cross. Therefore, God must save us. God is a just God. Because He has already righteously dealt with us judicially, He is now obligated to save us. We can boldly say to Him, "God, I do not speak now of Your love or of Your grace, but of Your righteousness. I appeal to You regarding Your righteousness. According to Your righteousness, You must save me. If You do not save me, it means that You are unrighteous." If we say this to God, He will reply, "I surely must save you."

Nothing binds God as much as His righteousness. Psalm 89:14 says, "Righteousness and justice are the foundation of thy throne" (A.S.V.). If God's righteousness could be taken away, His throne would be cast down. We can say, "Praise the Lord! Even if God wants to change His mind, He cannot do it because He is a just God!" How meaningful this is!

RIGHTEOUSNESS, LOVE, AND GRACE

Righteousness, or justice, is a judicial matter. Love, on the contrary, is a matter of the emotion. If I love you, I may choose to pay attention to you. But if I do not love you, I may simply forget about you. Many Christians like to quote John 3:16, the verse that says that God so loved the world that He gave His only begotten Son. Yes, God has so loved the world, but His love is not as firm as His righteousness. God, of course, will not change in His love. But suppose His love did change. God has the right to change in His love, but He does not have the right to change in His righteousness. Whether God loves us or gives us up, He is not wrong. He also would not be wrong in showing grace to us or in not showing grace to us. Grace is a matter of God's wish. In Matthew 20 the Lord told Peter that He wanted to give the same reward to the last as to the first. This is a matter of the Lord's wish, and there is nothing wrong with it. But righteousness is a matter neither of emotion nor of wish; it is a judicial matter. A judicial matter is related to the execution of the law, to legislation. God's gospel is altogether a judicial matter, a matter of divine legislation. God has saved us judicially. Of course, God's salvation is initiated by His love and accomplished through His grace. Eventually, however, it issues in His righteousness. Therefore, the salvation we have received today is not merely a matter of love or of grace, but also a judicial matter of God's righteousness. Our salvation has been sealed and confirmed by God's righteousness. Now not even God Himself can change our salvation.

THE KINGDOM OF GOD
BUILT UPON RIGHTEOUSNESS

It is upon this righteousness that the kingdom of God is built. Have you seen the contrast between man's unrighteousness and God's righteousness, between man's kingdom and God's kingdom? Man's kingdom is not built upon righteousness. This fact was fully exposed in the way Pilate, the Roman governor, dealt with the Lord Jesus. In chapter twenty-six Matthew fully exposed the weakness of Peter's natural life, and in chapter twenty-seven he exposed man's unrighteousness. Man's unrighteousness is even seen after the burial of Christ. The chief priests and the Pharisees gathered together to Pilate and said to him, "Sir, we remembered that that deceiver said, while he was still living, After three days I will arise. Command therefore that the grave be secured until the third day, lest the disciples come and steal him away and say to the people, He was raised from the dead; and the last deception will be worse than the first" (27:63-64). Pilate replied, "You have a guard; go, make it as secure as you know how" (v. 65). Pilate's answer to the chief priests and Pharisees was unrighteous. Later, in 28:11-15, the chief priests and the elders bribed the soldiers, paying them to lie about the resurrection of Christ. This shows that the Roman soldiers also were unrighteous. Thus, regarding man's government, the record is filled with unrighteousness. This exposes the fact that man's government is built upon unrighteousness. But God's government is built upon righteousness. Righteousness is the solid foundation of God's kingdom. We are saved under God's righteousness. Therefore, the foundation of our salvation is solid.

In chapter twenty-seven we have seen man's unrighteousness and God's righteousness. Praise the Lord that eventually man's unrighteousness turned into God's righteousness! We used to be in man's unrighteousness, but now we are under God's righteousness and in God's kingdom. God's kingdom is the kingdom of righteousness, and we are the righteous people in His kingdom.

LIFE-STUDY OF MATTHEW

MESSAGE SEVENTY-TWO

THE KING'S VICTORY

In this message we come to the King's victory recorded in 28:1-20. Compared to chapters twenty-six and twenty-seven, chapter twenty-eight is short and simple. When we are in resurrection, everything is simple.

I. RESURRECTED

The resurrection of Christ was a matter of God's righteousness. Have you ever considered the resurrection of Christ in this light? God was righteous to come in to judge Christ as our substitute on the cross. This judgment of Christ on the cross was just and righteous. By being judged by God, Christ fulfilled all the requirements of God's righteousness. He bore our sins on the cross to fully meet all the righteous requirements of God. Thus, through Christ's death on the cross, God's righteousness has been wholly satisfied. In other words, the righteous God was judicially satisfied with Christ's death on the cross. Therefore, Christ was buried in a new tomb that belonged to a rich man. This indicates that immediately after Christ's judicial death and immediately after the satisfaction of God's righteous requirements, Christ rested as the fulfillment of the prophecy of the Scriptures.

After Christ was buried, God was held responsible in His righteousness to release Christ from among the dead. Not many Christians realize this. Most think that the resurrection of Christ was only a matter of the divine power of God's life. Few realize that the resurrection of Christ was not only a matter of power, but also a matter of righteousness. If God had not raised Christ up after His death on the

cross to satisfy all the requirements of God's righteousness, God would have not been righteous. It was righteous
for God to release Christ from death. According to His
righteousness, God had to judge Christ on the cross
because Christ was bearing all our unrighteousness. But
after God had judged Christ in full, God's righteousness
held Him responsible to release Christ from death and to
raise Him up from among the dead.

In the Gospel of John there is the concept that Christ
was resurrected by the power of an endless life. But this is
not the concept of Christ's resurrection in the Gospel of
Matthew. The concept in Matthew regarding Christ's
resurrection is that it is related to God's righteousness.
John is a book on life, and life is a matter of power. But
Matthew is a book on the kingdom, and the kingdom is a
matter of righteousness. Therefore, according to Matthew,
for Christ to be raised from the dead meant that God
released Him according to His righteousness. Thus, Christ
was both righteously judged and put to death and righteously raised up from the dead.

Eventually, Christ became not only the powerful King,
but also the righteous King. If you read the prophecies
concerning Christ's kingship, you will see that His kingship is not very much related to power, but that it is closely
related to righteousness and justice. Kingship is not a
matter of power; it is a matter of righteousness. The
heavenly Savior-King was righteously judged by God on
the cross, and He was righteously raised up from the dead
by Him to become the righteous King. He is altogether
righteous. He is the righteous King for God's righteous
kingdom.

We need to have this concept as we read Matthew 28. In
this chapter we cannot find a hint that the resurrection of
Christ is related to power. However, if we read carefully,
we can find that it is related to righteousness. Perhaps you
have wondered why in this chapter, a chapter concerned
with Christ's resurrection, Matthew includes the account
of the bribery of the Roman soldiers (vv. 11-15). This is

mentioned for the purpose of exposing man's unrighteousness. The opposite of unrighteousness is not power, but righteousness. Because of His righteousness, God was held responsible to raise Christ up from the dead. Therefore, Christ's resurrection was according to God's righteousness. This was the reason that Matthew inserted the historical account of the bribery of the soldiers. No other Gospel mentions this. Matthew includes it to show that Christ's resurrection was related to God's righteousness, which is versus man's unrighteousness. Again I say that it is difficult to find in chapter twenty-eight any hint that Christ's resurrection was related to power or to life.

At this point we need to consider Romans 4:25. This verse says, "Who was delivered because of our offenses and was raised because of our justification." This verse links resurrection with righteousness. The Bible makes resurrection not only a matter of power, but also a matter of righteousness. Not only was God's righteousness manifested in raising Christ from the dead, but we were justified because of Christ's resurrection. Therefore, Christ's resurrection is a proof both of God's righteousness and of our justification. Hallelujah, in Christ's resurrection God is the righteous God, and we are the justified people!

We have seen that resurrection is very closely related to God's righteousness. The kingdom of the heavens is built and established upon God's righteousness, which held God responsible to raise up the righteous Redeemer and to make us righteous. Hence, Christ's resurrection is a realm of righteousness. In the sphere of Christ's resurrection, God is the righteous God, and we are the justified people of God. Here we have the kingdom.

Many Christians today know only the kingdom of love or the kingdom of grace. In other words, they are familiar only with the realm of love and grace. They have no understanding of the realm of God's righteousness. But God's righteousness, not His love or grace, is the foundation of God's kingdom. The kingdom of the heavens is built not upon God's love or grace, but upon His righteousness. How

precious, necessary, and vital the righteousness of God is!
It is absolutely necessary for the kingdom life. If we realize
this, the churches in the Lord's recovery will be greatly
strengthened. Hallelujah, our kingly Savior has been resurrected through the righteousness of God!

A. On the First Day of the Week

Let us now consider some of the details of Christ's
resurrection as presented in chapter twenty-eight of
Matthew. Verse 1 says, "Now late on the Sabbath, as it
began to dawn toward the first day of the week, Mary the
Magdalene and the other Mary came to look at the grave."
Christ was resurrected on the first day of the week. This
signifies that His resurrection brought a new start with a
new age for the kingdom of the heavens.

B. Discovered by Mary the Magdalene
and the Other Mary

The resurrection of Christ was firstly discovered by two
sisters, Mary the Magdalene and the other Mary. They discovered it by loving the Lord to the uttermost. Then they
became the first two witnesses of the Lord's resurrection.

C. Pointed Out by the Angel

Christ's resurrection was pointed out by an angel
(vv. 2-7). Verse 2 says, "And behold, there was a great
earthquake; for an angel of the Lord descended out of
heaven and came and rolled away the stone and sat upon
it." The earthquake signifies that the earth, the base of
Satan's rebellion, has been shaken by the Lord's resurrection. The angel came to confirm the Lord's resurrection
by rolling away the stone that was sealed and to explain
the resurrection to His seekers. The coming of the angel,
which terrified the guards, indicates the power of the
heavens. All this implies the authority mentioned in verse
18.

According to verses 5 and 6, the angel said to the women, "Fear not, for I know that you seek Jesus, Who has been crucified. He is not here, for He was raised, as He said." What good news this was! What glad tidings!

Verse 7 says, "And go quickly and tell His disciples that He was raised from the dead, and behold, He goes before you into Galilee; there you shall see Him. Behold, I have told you." As the heavenly King began His ministry from Galilee of the Gentiles (4:12-17), not from Jerusalem, the holy city of the Jewish religion, so after His resurrection, He would still go to Galilee, not to Jerusalem. This strongly indicated that the resurrected King had fully abandoned Judaism and initiated a new era for God's economy of the New Testament.

D. Meeting with Mary the Magdalene and the Other Mary

According to verses 8 through 10, the resurrected Christ met with Mary the Magdalene and the other Mary. Verse 8 says, "And going away quickly from the tomb with fear and great joy, they ran to bring word to His disciples." They went away with fear because of the great earthquake and with great joy because of the Lord's resurrection. Verse 9 says that the Lord Jesus met them and that they "came and took hold of His feet and worshipped Him." This transpired after the Lord's appearing to Mary the Magdalene (John 20:14-18).

E. Rumors of the Jewish Leaders

Verses 11 through 15 indicate that the Jewish leaders with the Roman soldiers spread a false rumor about Christ's resurrection. They gave the soldiers a large sum of money to say that the Lord's disciples came by night and stole Him away while the guards slept. This word from the mouth of the religious leaders was a bare lie, indicating the lowest standard and falsehood of their religion. In verse 14 they said to the soldiers, "And if this be heard by the

governor, we will persuade him and free you from worry."
The evil religionists always persuade the evil politicians to
carry out falsehood. Verse 15 indicates that this false saying "was spread abroad among the Jews until this day." As
the lie concerning the Lord's resurrection was spread
abroad, so were the rumors concerning His followers and
His church after His resurrection (Acts 24:5-9; 25:7).

II. REIGNING

A. The Disciples Going to Galilee
to Meet with Him on the Mountain

Verse 16 says, "But the eleven disciples went into
Galilee, to the mountain where Jesus appointed them."
The constitution of the kingdom was decreed on a mountain, the heavenly King's transfiguration transpired on a
high mountain, and the prophecy concerning this age was
also given on a mountain. Now, for God's economy of the
New Testament, the disciples needed to go to the mountain again. Only on the high level of a mountain can we
realize the New Testament economy.

B. Appearing to the Disciples
and Being Worshipped by Them

Verse 17 continues, "And when they saw Him, they
worshipped Him, but some doubted." When the disciples
saw the resurrected King, they did nothing but worship
Him; yet some among them still doubted, or hesitated,
wavered, in recognizing Him in His resurrection.

C. Declaring that All Authority
Has Been Given to Him
in Heaven and on Earth

Verse 18 says, "And Jesus came and spoke to them,
saying, All authority has been given to Me in heaven and
on earth." In His divinity as the only begotten Son of God,

the Lord had authority over all. However, in His humanity as the Son of Man to be the King of the heavenly kingdom, all authority in heaven and on earth was given to Him after His resurrection.

Matthew's account of the resurrection is very different from John's. According to John's record, after His resurrection the Lord met with His disciples in a room where the doors had been shut (John 20:19). The disciples were frightened, being afraid of the Jews. Because they needed to be strengthened by life, the Lord came to them as life, breathed upon them, and told them to receive the holy breath (John 20:22). How different is Matthew's account! According to Matthew, the Lord charged the disciples to go to a mountain in Galilee. Surely He met with them on that mountain during the day, not during the night. Furthermore, when He met with them on the mountain, He did not breathe upon them and tell them to receive the holy breath. Instead, He said, "All authority has been given to Me in heaven and on earth." In Matthew it is not a matter of breath, but a matter of authority. John's concern was for life, and life requires breath. But Matthew's concern was for the kingdom, and the kingdom requires authority. The Gospel of John reveals that we need life to care for the little lambs and to feed the Lord's flock. But in Matthew 28 there is no word about feeding the lambs. In Matthew the Lord commands the disciples to disciple all the nations (v. 19) to make all the nations part of the kingdom. This requires authority. Therefore, in John resurrection is a matter of life, power, breath, and shepherding. However, in Matthew it is a matter of righteousness, authority, and discipling the nations.

D. Charging the Disciples to Go and Disciple All the Nations

Verse 19 says, "Go therefore and disciple all the nations, baptizing them into the name of the Father and of the Son and of the Holy Spirit." Because all authority had been given to Him, the heavenly King sent His disciples to go and disciple all the nations. They go with His authority. To disciple the nations is to cause the heathen to become the kingdom people for the establishment of His kingdom, which is the church, even today on this earth.

Notice that the Lord did not charge the disciples to preach the gospel, but to disciple the nations. The difference between preaching the gospel and discipling the nations is that to preach the gospel is simply to bring sinners to salvation, but to disciple the nations is to cause the Gentiles to become the kingdom people. We have been sent by the Lord not only to bring people to salvation, but also to disciple the nations. This is a matter of the kingdom.

In verse 19 the Lord speaks of baptizing the nations into the name of the Father and of the Son and of the Holy Spirit. Baptism is to bring the repentant people out of their old state into a new one, by terminating their old life and germinating them with the new life of Christ, that they may become the kingdom people. John the Baptist's recommending ministry began with the preliminary baptism by water only. Now, after the heavenly King accomplished His ministry on earth, passed through the process of death and resurrection, and became the life-giving Spirit, He charged His disciples to baptize the discipled people into the Triune God. This baptism has two aspects: the visible aspect by water and the invisible aspect by the Holy Spirit (Acts 2:38, 41; 10:44-48). The visible aspect is the expression, the testimony, of the invisible aspect; whereas the invisible aspect is the reality of the visible aspect. Without the invisible aspect by the Spirit, the visible aspect by water is vain; and without the visible aspect by water, the invisible aspect by the Spirit is abstract and impractical. Both are needed. Not long after the Lord charged the disciples with this baptism, He baptized them and the entire church in the Holy Spirit (1 Cor. 12:13) on the day of Pentecost (Acts 1:5; 2:4) and in the house of Cornelius (Acts 11:15-17). Then, based upon this, the disciples baptized the new converts (Acts 2:38), not only visibly into water, but also invisibly into the death of Christ (Rom. 6:3-4), into Christ Himself (Gal. 3:27), into the Triune God (Matt. 28:19), and into the Body of Christ (1 Cor. 12:13). The water, signifying the death of Christ with His burial, may be considered as a tomb to terminate the old history of the baptized ones. Since the death of Christ is included in Christ, since Christ is the very embodiment of the Triune God, and since the Triune God is one with the Body of Christ, so to baptize new believers into the death of Christ, into Christ Himself, into the Triune God, and into the Body of Christ is to do just one thing: on the negative side to terminate their old life, and on the positive side to germinate them with a new life, the eternal life of the Triune God, for the Body of Christ. Hence, the baptism ordained by the Lord here is to baptize people out of their life into the Body life for the kingdom of the heavens.

The word "into" in verse 19 indicates union, as in Romans 6:3; Galatians 3:27; and 1 Corinthians 12:13. The same Greek word is used in Acts 8:16; 19:3, 5; and 1 Corinthians 1:13, 15. To baptize people into the name of the Triune God is to bring them into spiritual and mystical union with Him.

There is one name for the Trinity. The name is the sum total of the divine Being, equivalent to His Person. To baptize anyone into the name of the Trinity is to immerse him into all the Triune God is.

Matthew and John are the two books in which the Trinity is more fully revealed, for the participation and enjoyment of God's chosen people, than in all the other books of Scripture. John unveils the mystery of the Godhead in the Father, Son, and Spirit, especially in chapters fourteen through sixteen, for our experience of life; whereas Matthew discloses the reality of the Trinity in the one name for all Three, for the constitution of the kingdom. In the opening chapter of Matthew, the Holy Spirit (v. 18), Christ (the Son — v. 18), and God (the Father — v. 23) are upon the scene for the producing of the man Jesus (v. 21), who, as Jehovah the Savior and God with us, is the very embodiment of the Triune God. In chapter three Matthew presents a picture of the Son standing in the water of baptism under the open heaven, the Spirit as a dove descending upon the Son, and the Father out of the heavens speaking to the Son (vv. 16-17). In chapter twelve, the Son, in the person of man, cast out demons by the Spirit to bring in the kingdom of God the Father (v. 28). In chapter sixteen, the Son is revealed by the Father to the disciples for the building of the church, which is the life-pulse of the kingdom (vv. 16-19). In chapter seventeen, the Son entered into transfiguration (v. 2) and was confirmed by the Father's word of delight (v. 5) for a miniature display of the manifestation of the kingdom (16:28). Eventually, in the closing chapter, after Christ, as the last Adam, had passed through the process of crucifixion, entered into the realm of resurrection, and become the life-giving Spirit, He came back to His disciples, in the atmosphere and reality of His resurrection, to charge them to cause the heathen to become the kingdom people by baptizing them into the name, the Person, the reality, of the Trinity. Later, in the Acts and the Epistles, it is disclosed that to baptize people into the name of the Father, Son, and Spirit is to baptize them into the name of Christ (Acts 8:16; 19:5, Gk.), and that to baptize them into the name of Christ is to baptize them into Christ the Person (Gal. 3:27; Rom. 6:3), for Christ is the embodiment of the Triune God, and He, as the life-giving Spirit, is available any time and any place for people to be baptized into Him. Such a baptism into the reality of the Father, Son, and Spirit, according to Matthew, is for the constitution of the kingdom of the heavens. The heavenly kingdom cannot be organized with human beings of flesh and blood (1 Cor. 15:50) as an earthly society; it can only be constituted with people who are immersed into the union with the Triune God and who are established and built up with the Triune God who is wrought into them.

E. Promising to Be with the Disciples
All the Days
until the Consummation of the Age

In verse 20 the Lord told His disciples, "Behold, I am with you all the days until the consummation of the age." The heavenly King is Emmanuel, God with us (1:23). Here He promised to be with us in His resurrection with all authority all the days until the consummation of the age, that is, until the end of this age. Hence, wherever we are gathered into His name, He is in our midst (18:20).

In the four Gospels, the Lord's ascension is recorded only in Mark (16:19) and Luke (24:51). John testifies that the Lord, as the Son of God, even God Himself, is life to His believers. As such, He can never leave them and would never leave them. Matthew proves that He, as Emmanuel, is the heavenly King who is with His people continually until He comes back. Hence, in both John and Matthew, the Lord's ascension is not mentioned.

As the King in the kingdom with the kingdom people, the Lord is with us all the days until the consummation of the age. Today is included in all the days. The Lord is with us today, and He will be with us tomorrow. Not one day will be an exception. He will be with us until the consummation of the age. This refers to the end of this age, which will be the time of the Lord's parousia, the Lord's coming. The consummation of the age, the end of the age, will be the great tribulation. We do not want to be here during that time. Rather, we prefer to be raptured into the Lord's parousia, into His presence. This is a matter of the kingdom.

In the Lord's resurrection with His righteousness the kingdom is present, and we have the authority, commission, and position, to disciple the nations. In this way the kingdom is spreading.